Torts and Personal Injury Law for the Paralegal

DEVELOPING WORKPLACE SKILLS

Richard N. Jeffries

J.D. with Distinction University of North Dakota

PEARSON

Boston   Columbus   Indianapolis   New York   San Francisco   Upper Saddle River
Amsterdam   Cape Town   Dubai   London   Madrid   Milan   Munich   Paris   Montréal   Toronto
Delhi   Mexico City   São Paulo   Sydney   Hong Kong   Seoul   Singapore   Taipei   Tokyo

Editorial Director: Vernon Anthony
Executive Editor: Gary Bauer
Editorial Project Manager: Linda Cupp
Editorial Assistant: Tanika Henderson
Director of Marketing: David Gesell
Marketing Manager: Stacey Martinez
Marketing Assistant: Les Roberts
Production Project Manager: Susan Hannahs
Manager Central Design: Jayne Conte
Image Permission Coordinator: Mike Lackey
Cover Designer: Bruce Kenselaar
Manager, Rights and Permissions: Beth Wollar
Cover Art: Zwola Fasola/ Shutterstock; BioMedical/ Shutterstock; Andy Dean Photography/Shutterstock
Full-Service Project Management: Sudip Sinha, PreMediaGlobal, Inc.
Composition: PreMediaGlobal, Inc.
Text Printer/Bindery: Edwards Brothers Malloy, Inc.
Cover Printer: Lehigh-Phoenix Color, Inc.
Text Font: 11/13 Minion Pro

Photo Credits: Georgios Kollidas/Shutterstock, p. 1; Cartoonresource/Shutterstock, pp. 26, 95, 123, 149, 177, 202, 222, 249, 276, 299, 351, 377; Andy Dean Photography/Shutterstock, p. 29; RLRRLRLL/Shutterstock, p. 49; prodakszyn/Shutterstock, p. 52; G. Campbell/Shutterstock, p. 73; © Corbis Premium RF/Alamy, p. 76; Deklofenak/Shutterstock, p. 99; imageegami/Shutterstock, p. 126; imageegami/Shutterstock, p. 152; digitalreflections/Shutterstock, p. 181; Tatiana Makotra/Shutterstock, p. 205; Angela Waye/Shutterstock, p. 222; Tischenko Irina/Shutterstock, p. 224; Yuganov Konstantin/Shutterstock, p. 251; AVAVA/Shutterstock, p. 278; StockLite/Shutterstock, p. 301; cla78/Shutterstock, p. 324; mangostock/Shutterstock, p. 353.

Library of Congress Cataloging-in-Publication Data
Jeffries, Richard N.
    Torts and personal injury law for the paralegal : developing workplace skills / Richard N. Jeffries. — 1st ed.
        p. cm.
    Includes index.
    ISBN-13: 978-0-13-291984-5
    ISBN-10: 0-13-291984-2
    1. Torts—United States.   2. Personal injuries—United States.
    3. Legal assistants—United States—Handbooks, manuals, etc.
    I. Title.
    KF1250.Z9J44 2014
    346.7303—dc23

                                                                                2012042687

10 9 8 7 6 5 4 3 2 1

ISBN 10:   0-13-291984-2
ISBN 13: 978-0-13-291984-5

Dedication

This book is dedicated to my small but precious family:

my wife, Linda, my mother, Eleanor,
my mother-in-law, Leona, my son, Paul,
my daughter, Kim, and
my three wonderful grandchildren, Tanner, Chelsea, and Spencer.

BRIEF CONTENTS

CONTENTS

PREFACE

PURPOSE OF THIS BOOK

Sometimes titles of textbooks can be misleading. There are several fine textbooks on the market with titles similar to this book combining the words "torts," and "personal injury." Yet most of these textbooks tend to focus primarily on the black letter law of torts. They tend to provide scant coverage of the practical side of the torts area of law, which is the personal injury side. They tend to focus upon the legal concepts and theories of torts and do not provide coverage of important areas of practical knowledge and skills that a paralegal will need to function in a workplace setting. This textbook seeks to address this situation.

In the first two-thirds of the book, the student is presented with a solid foundation in the traditional law of torts. However, within that traditional torts presentation, practical personal injury concepts are constantly interwoven into theoretical, traditional torts concepts. Then, in the last one-third of the book, a deeper dive is taken into the area of a torts and personal injury practice, including the rudiments of medical and insurance issues. In the torts chapters, the medical chapters, and the insurance chapters, the student will obtain experience working with real cases performing the tasks that a paralegal will actually be performing in a real work environment, whether it is a law firm, a corporate legal department, or a government agency. My goal is to provide a framework for the paralegal graduate to "hit the ground running" after being hired by an employer.

Why concentrate on personal injury practice alongside of torts? The field of personal injury is the natural offshoot of the field of torts. The field of personal injury would not exist without the bedrock of torts supporting it. This textbook will provide special emphasis on those torts that are most prevalent in a modern personal injury practice. Many personal injury cases based on the torts typically handled by a law firm, a corporation's legal department, or a government agency will arise out of negligence as opposed to intentional torts. Few, for example, will arise out of the torts of assault and battery, trespass, or false imprisonment. A recent report was prepared by the U.S. Department of Justice studying various aspects of tort trials in the nation's 75 most populous counties.[1] Interestingly, the report showed that nearly 60% of all the cases concluded by a jury or bench trial were automobile accident cases. This was followed by medical malpractice at 15% and premises liability at 11%. The tort of conversion was approximately 2%, defamation was approximately 1%, and false arrest/false imprisonment was less than 1%.

When I was a young attorney in a litigation firm, one of the quotes of the senior partner, made tongue-in-cheek, was "I never met a lawyer that made a nickel on the Constitution." Obviously, some attorneys certainly do make a very good living and derive great satisfaction from handling legal matters that arise from the Constitution, both in criminal law and civil law. However, after 37 years "in the trenches" of the torts and personal injury field, this tongue-in-cheek comment is perhaps better directed toward the intentional torts, in spite of my own personal

---

[1]Bureau of Justice Statistical Bulletin, November, 2009 NCJ 228129, Thomas H. Cohen, J.D. PhD. http://bjs.ojp.usdoj.gov/content/pub/pdf/tbjtsc05.pdf

fascination with them. My experience and my bias lean toward torts based on negligence and those based on strict liability, especially products liability. My purpose is to try to explore those areas of torts and personal injury that will best prepare the paralegal student for the most likely cases to be encountered when they enter the workforce. This purpose is in line with the above-mentioned Department of Justice study. To be fair, complete, and respect tradition, all of the traditional torts will be covered in this textbook. In fact, this textbook will address all of those areas of "tort law" as recommended by the American Association for Paralegal Education (AAfPE) for a model torts course. They will not necessarily be presented in the same order, and different weight will be given to various torts.

I spent 37 years as a personal injury trial lawyer traveling around the country handling numerous tort-based personal injury cases that were based primarily on negligence and strict liability. A vast majority of my cases were on the defense side, but I also handled numerous personal injury cases for the plaintiff. After retiring from practice, I was extended the privilege of becoming an adjunct professor at Minnesota State University Moorhead located in Moorhead, Minnesota. This required a substantial paradigm shift. That shift was from being a lawyer first to becoming a teacher first and a lawyer second.

Based upon my experience as a trial lawyer, torts is but one building block, among others, in fully preparing the personal injury paralegal for the real world. The other two vital building blocks in the torts/personal injury area are the blocks of medicine and insurance. It is inconceivable for a paralegal to commence employment in a personal injury law firm, plaintiff or defense, in the legal department of a corporation, or in various government agencies without having first received a proper background in medical and insurance issues. To commence employment in any aspect of the personal injury field after receiving a background solely in the black letter law of torts shortchanges both the paralegal graduate and the employer.

ORGANIZATION OF THIS BOOK

All chapters in this book begin with a relevant quotation and Learning Objectives, both of which provide a chapter roadmap of what lies ahead for the student. Each chapter is also liberally sprinkled with practical Workplace Skills Tips. These tips provide practical observations and suggestions to the student based upon my many years of torts/personal injury experience. These tips may also be utilized as a source of class discussion or assignments. Some of the chapter tips may relate specifically to the subject matter of the particular chapter, while others may relate to a more general but important part of the personal injury paralegal field. For example, some may relate to the extremely important topics of English, grammar, legal writing, interviewing, evidence, or civil procedure. While they are included to provide a valuable learning tool, they also serve the purpose of breaking the monotony of reading the written text.

To assist in understanding the material covered in a chapter, numerous examples, hypothetical cases, and exhibits are included. Exhibits consist of actual workplace documents (such as a sample letter, a sample medical authorization, or other document frequently encountered in the workplace) as well as condensed reported judicial decisions. At the conclusion of each chapter, there are a chapter summary, review questions, and a special Hypothetical Case: Developing Workplace Skills. These special hypothetical workplace skills cases provide a real-world case based upon the principles learned in the chapter. These workplace skills cases will not only provoke thought about what was just learned in the chapter, but also promote the development of practical workplace skills. Most of these cases arise out of a law firm setting with the supervising attorney preparing a memo or e-mail to the paralegal requesting the performance of a task essential to the case. The task assigned relates directly to the subject matter of the chapter. The instructor may choose to use some of these hypothetical workplace skills cases as a source of class discussion or as an actual graded assignment. These workplace skills assignments, whether a legal research project or the drafting of a certain document, can be used as sample work product for a prospective employer.

The first portion of the book consists of 11 chapters covering the traditional black letter law of torts. Chapter 1 is an introductory chapter to torts with special emphasis on legal history, ethical considerations, and attributes of a good paralegal. As mentioned, included in the first and major section of the book are all of those traditional torts and tort concepts recommended by AAfPE in their model torts course. Tradition is being respected by doing this. However, the student and instructor should both take note that not all torts share equal weight in the judicial system as demonstrated in the Department of Justice report cited above.

The next portion of the book, utilizing two chapters, covers the medical field and medical issues. Based upon my background and experience, the majority of personal injury cases are won or lost based upon the medical preparation and presentation of the case. The properly educated personal injury paralegal must know how to locate, obtain, review, analyze, and summarize medical records. Using negligence as an example, after having studied the substantive law of torts, the paralegal will understand the significance of medical records as those records demonstrate a proof (or lack of proof) of not only the element of damages, but also the elements of breach of duty and causation. For the legal team on either side of a case, medical records can truly be either a "gold mine" or a "mine field."

To enhance the students' understanding of medical issues, there are included in the text and in the Appendices, various forms, such as HIPAA-compliant medical authorizations, a sample medical summary, and sample medical records (handwritten, typed, and electronic). There are also form letters requesting medical records and forms for keeping track of records requested and received. There are lists of medical abbreviations and medical symbols for medical terms, charts/diagrams demonstrating human anatomy, a list of commonly prescribed medications and their purpose, a list of physician specialties, and other medical-related documents. There is also included a sample set of hospital records beginning with ambulance run reports and ending with physicians' orders. Hypothetical medical chart entries using medical terms are used as examples in the text, and they are also used as a learning tool for chapter-end questions.

The final portion of the book relates to insurance issues, which are covered in two chapters. The properly educated personal injury paralegal must have a background, first, in the general theory of insurance and, second, in both third-party liability insurance and first-party liability insurance. With the large number of automobile accidents comprising much of the personal injury practice today, paralegals must have a basic understanding of those insurance issues. This involves an understanding of general insurance principles, how an insurance policy is constructed, first-party liability issues including automobile uninsured motorist (UM) issues, automobile underinsured motorist (UIM) issues, no-fault issues, and automobile third-party liability issues.

Other vital insurance topics covered in this portion of the book are subrogation, collateral source, duty to defend/indemnify, the tripartite relationship among insurer, insured, and defense counsel, bad faith, insurance coverage issues, significance of reservation of rights letters, declination letters, declaratory judgments, and various other insurance issues that affect settlement and trial. There is a section on the anatomy of a liability insurance policy in which a liability insurance policy and a Declarations Page of a policy are carefully examined from top to bottom. This is so that students learn the significance of the Declarations Page, the insuring agreement, definitions, conditions, exclusions, and how they all relate to one another. The area of insurance was an area in which I was extensively involved for all of the years of my practice. Insurance issues are extremely important and sometimes influence the strategy, evaluation, and final disposition of a particular torts/personal injury case.

SPECIAL FEATURES/PEDAGOGY

This book is unique. Frankly, compared to the traditional textbooks primarily covering the black letter law of torts, it is revolutionary. This is because it makes a significant expansion upon the standard traditional "torts" discussion by providing a more extensive skill development approach. That approach is accomplished by:

- Incorporating chapters with a thorough discussion of medical issues and appropriate medical-related documents.
- Incorporating chapters with a thorough discussion of insurance issues and appropriate insurance-related documents.
- Utilizing Workplace Skills Tips interspersed throughout each chapter based upon my substantial tort/personal injury experience.
- Providing, at the end of each chapter, thought-provoking questions, many of which are based upon real cases in which I was involved.
- Providing, at the end of each chapter, a section entitled "Hypothetical Case: Developing Workplace Skills." This case applies real-world skill development to the tort theories just learned in the chapter. As mentioned, the assignments can be used as the student's work product and shown to a prospective employer.
- Providing to the instructor in the Instructor's Manual, for use at his or her discretion, six practical assignments. These are six practical assignments based upon an actual automobile negligence case that I personally handled. This case was tried to a jury, appealed, tried again, appealed again, and then settled. It is a real case taking many twists and turns from a factual standpoint, a medical standpoint, and a legal standpoint. The suspense builds as the case progresses with each assignment distributed periodically throughout the term of the course. There are three assignments on the plaintiff's side. These are (1) gathering, analyzing, and summarizing plaintiff's initial medical records after the new case has been accepted by the attorney; (2) preparing a settlement demand letter to the liability insurance carrier; and (3) preparing a complaint.

  Then the students shift to the defense side after a new assignment has been received from the defendant's liability insurance carrier on this same case. There are also three assignments on the defense side. These are (1) preparing an answer; (2) gathering, analyzing, and summarizing additional medical records of plaintiff from different medical facilities discovered through interrogatories; and (3) obtaining the highway patrol crash report, deciphering it with the overlay, and analyzing its importance in the case. The medical records and the crash report are provided to the students on the assumption that the proper letter and authorization have been utilized to gather them as demonstrated in the textbook. The exhibits in the textbook and the documents in the appendices provide guidance for all of these assignments. For example, there is a sample settlement demand letter and a sample medical records summary in the appendices.

All of these assignments are in the form of a memo from the supervising attorney to the paralegal. A time sheet is required to be submitted along with the student's work product in response to the memo. The student's work product on these assignments may also be provided to a prospective employer as a sample of their workplace skills. When students come to the realization that they are working on a real case, the enthusiasm and excitement builds. It provides a unique learning experience in which the tort theories presented in the book immediately come alive through the application of paralegal tasks performed in a genuine tort and personal injury case.

- There are extensive appendices to the textbook. The first appendix consists of such items as a client acceptance letter, a client rejection letter, a contingency fee agreement, a settlement demand letter, and time-keeping forms and documents. Appendix 2 includes medical documents containing HIPAA-compliant medical authorizations, letters requesting medical records, medical diagrams, medical symbols, medical abbreviations, sample hospital records, and many other practical medical documents. Appendix 3 contains a sample form automobile insurance policy to which the student will be referring when reading the insurance chapters. An insurance checklist concerning the various insurance issues that may arise in a personal injury case is also contained in Appendix 3.

RESOURCES

For the instructor, there will be a comprehensive Instructor's Manual with answers and analysis to chapter-end questions and to the hypothetical workplace skills assignments. There are also suggested additional hypothetical fact situations for discussion, suggested additional assignments, as well as the above-mentioned six automobile negligence assignments based on an actual case. In addition, a PowerPoint® Lecture Package and a MyTest test generator have been prepared for the instructor.

MISSION

Our mission as teachers is to properly educate the student, but it should also be to educate in a manner that properly prepares the student for the working world ahead after graduation. My hope is that this textbook will accomplish two main goals: (1) enhance the student's learning experience by making theoretical torts come alive through application of real-world personal injury principles, and (2) improve the student's opportunities for obtaining a job after graduation. Job placement after graduation is a top priority now more than ever, so it behooves the learning institution to require both practice and theory in its paralegal courses.

ACKNOWLEDGEMENTS

The brainchild for this book was Deb Kukowski, chair of the excellent Paralegal Studies Department at Minnesota State University Moorhead. She is the one who first suggested, because of my long career in torts/personal injury litigation and interest in teaching, that this textbook should be written. I also want to thank Kiki Swanson, a friend and author, who encouraged me early on to undertake the fulfilling task of writing a book. Thanks go to Denise Hulbert, a former top student of mine who reviewed each chapter and was not bashful about pointing out deficiencies in the text as it was developing. A thank you goes to two physician friends of mine, Dr. John Thomas and Dr. Don Opgrande, for their assistance with various medical issues. For additional assistance in the medical area, I also need to thank a friend and former nurse/paralegal in my office, Judy Kolb, and her daughter, Claudia Laliberte, also a nurse. Thanks also go to Gary Bauer and Linda Cupp at Pearson without whose professional guidance this project could not have come together. A further thank you goes to Martina Gast, an attorney friend of mine, who checked all of my legal citations.

Thanks go to my former paralegal, Terri Smith, who helped me with numerous aspects of the book and the appendices. An extra special thank you also goes to my current paralegal, Joy Hoeffler, whose English background, teaching background, and paralegal background proved absolutely invaluable. Her tough questions, persistence, and thoughtful and detailed critical reviews vastly improved my presentation of this book. I must also thank Dale Haake from Nodak Mutual Insurance Company for his insight into various points included in the insurance chapters. A special thank you goes to a friend and colleague of mine, attorney David Bossart, a nationally recognized plaintiff's attorney. Thanks go as well to his extremely capable legal assistant, Sue McKigney. The two of them provided some most helpful materials for the book from the plaintiff's perspective. Thanks also go to another friend and colleague of mine, attorney Jack Marcil, with whom I had many cases over the years. As a successful and well-recognized mediator, he provided me with some excellent ADR materials for use in this textbook. A thank you goes to my secretary, Ingrid Roehlk, who graciously assisted with some last-minute and much-needed typing. I would be remiss if I did not mention all of the students in my personal injury class. I utilized my draft chapters to teach the class this past year and offered some extra credit if they would critique each chapter after it was assigned. They willingly did so and their comments were invaluable. These students are Scott Born, Heidi Bourasa, Amber Cleveland, Heather Dodd, Marie Friedt, Maggie Johnson, Ivy Keely, Cody Krieg, Danielle Kukuzke, Karissa Rothmeier, April Schlafmann, Jacqueline Stewart, Sheri Vander Wolde, and Megan Zerface. Of course, the book would never have been completed without the ever-present patience and support of Linda, my dear wife of 47 years.

Thanks are also due the following reviewers for their helpful suggestions throughout the development of the manuscript.

- Steven C. Kempisty, Esq., Bryant & Stratton College
- Elizabeth Mann, Greenville Technical College
- Greg Markham, Kapiolani Community College
- James R Hodge, Hodges University
- Heidi Koeneman, Ivy Tech Community College- Northeast
- Elaine S. Lerner, Valencia College and Kaplan University
- Steve Dayton, Fullerton College
- Jane Breslin Jacobs, Esq., Community College of Philadelphia

ABOUT THE AUTHOR

RICHARD N. JEFFRIES is a semi-retired civil litigation personal injury attorney with 37 years of experience. His areas of practice included automobile, asbestos, construction, insurance coverage issues (declaratory judgment (DJ) actions and coverage opinions), premises liability, products liability, medical malpractice, legal malpractice, and other areas of professional negligence.

He is an adjunct professor at Minnesota State University in Moorhead, Minnesota, teaching personal injury law in the paralegal studies program. He was a speaker at numerous bar association continuing legal education (CLE) seminars and produced several publications for his peers. These publications were written on the subjects of legal malpractice, statutes of limitation, and issues concerning an insurance carrier's duty to defend and indemnify. He has been a lecturer for various paralegal organizations. He was given the honor of being appointed by the Center for International Legal Studies to be a Senior Lawyer Visiting Professor to teach in Poland.

For the years 1995 to 2003, he was named a Leading Minnesota Attorney by his peers. His attorney rating in Martindale Hubbell is "av," the highest rating, also given based on recommendations from peers. He is an active member of the bar association of Minnesota and an inactive member in good standing in North Dakota and Florida. He started his own boutique insurance defense law firm in 1986 and was the president, managing shareholder, and chairman of the board of directors. The firm represented national and international clients and insurance companies. Although his litigation work was primarily on the defense side, he also represented plaintiffs in numerous personal injury cases and other types of cases. He has also participated extensively in the alternative dispute resolution process both as an attorney representing clients and as a mediator and an arbitrator.

He keeps busy working at a local law firm in Phoenix, Arizona and travelling to Minnesota State University to teach his night class in personal injury. He is also currently working on a new textbook.

He is a graduate of Moorhead State University with a B.A. in Business Administration and received his Juris Doctorate with distinction from the University of North Dakota.

chapter 1
INTRODUCTION TO PERSONAL INJURY AND TORTS

"Education is a progressive discovery of our ignorance."

Will Durant

Introduction

We are about to embark on a journey into the field of torts and personal injury. This journey will involve a discovery of both legal theory and real-world practice. A blending of the two will result in the student developing authentic workplace skills. The beginning point is legal theory. The subject of legal theory will examine the substantive law of torts. From there we will navigate into some of the most important, practical, and real-world aspects of the field of personal injury: medical issues and insurance issues. The student should keep the following basic principle in mind throughout the journey:

> The goal of the plaintiff's attorney and the legal team is to "build up" the plaintiff's personal injury case. The goal of the defendant's attorney and the legal team is to "tear down" the plaintiff's personal injury case.

A word of caution to the paralegal student is in order at this point. This textbook will discuss the general common law of a particular subject. Also, a particular state's court decision or a particular state's statute may be examined to help the student understand a certain concept. *The personal injury paralegal must know the law of his or her jurisdiction.*

In addition, various "Workplace Skills Tips" are provided to the student based on the author's nearly 40 years of litigation experience in the tort and personal injury fields. However, if a particular task, concept, or methodology directed by the paralegal's employer differs from such tips, obviously, the paralegal should perform the task as directed by his or her employer. These tips will not necessarily always relate to the subject matter of the particular chapter. Some may relate to civil procedure, evidence, investigation, legal research and writing, grammar, or some other unrelated but practical advice. While their main

LEARNING OBJECTIVES

After studying this chapter, you should be able to:

- Identify and reflect upon those qualities that constitute a good personal injury paralegal.

- Define a tort.

- Analyze how the fields of torts and personal injury are interrelated.

- Appreciate Anglo-American legal history.

- Realize that judges may "legislate" from the bench.

- Identify and distinguish the various public policy purposes for tort law.

- Analyze the reasoning behind tort reform.

- Identify and distinguish the various bases of tort law.

1

purpose is to provide a learning tool, they will also fulfill the purpose of breaking the monotony of reading the written text.

Traits of a Good Personal Injury Paralegal

There is a concept in psychology called primacy. It simply means that a person tends to remember those items first presented to the senses. With that concept in mind, the first subject of this textbook is a list of the author's "Top 20" traits of a good paralegal. The hope is that this beginning subject will stick and will be remembered throughout the student's journey here and into the workplace.

1. **Confidentiality is a must.** It is of the utmost importance for the paralegal to have this mandate firmly in mind at all times—both when in the office and out of the office. As an example, when the paralegal reviews the medical records of a plaintiff, as will be discussed in later chapters, the paralegal will become intimately knowledgeable about a very private aspect of a human being's life. Each state has its own rules of professional conduct. While these rules govern attorneys and not paralegals, the paralegal's conduct will affect the attorney. For an example of a confidentiality rule imposed upon an attorney, review Exhibit 1-1, which is Rule 1.6 of the Michigan Rules of Professional Conduct dealing with an attorney's responsibility toward "Confidentiality of Information." Then also review Exhibit 1-2, which is Rule 5.3 of the Michigan Rules of

EXHIBIT 1-1 Michigan Rules of Professional Conduct Rule 1.6 Confidentiality of Information

(a) **"Confidence"** refers to information protected by the client-lawyer privilege under applicable law, and **"secret"** refers to other information gained in the professional relationship that the client has requested be held inviolate or the disclosure of which would be embarrassing or would be likely to be detrimental to the client.

(b) Except when permitted under paragraph (c), a lawyer shall not knowingly:
   1. Reveal a confidence or secret of a client;
   2. Use a confidence or secret of a client to the disadvantage of the client; or
   3. Use a confidence or secret of a client for the advantage of the lawyer or of a third person, unless the client consents after full disclosure.

(c) A lawyer may reveal:
   1. confidences or secrets with the consent of the client or clients affected, but only after full disclosure to them;
   2. confidences or secrets when permitted or required by these rules, or when required by law or by court order;
   3. Confidences and secrets to the extent reasonably necessary to rectify the consequences of a client's illegal or fraudulent act in the furtherance of which the lawyer's services have been used;
   4. The intention of a client to commit a crime and the information necessary to prevent the crime; and
   5. Confidences or secrets necessary to establish or collect a fee, or to defend the lawyer or the lawyer's employees or associates against an accusation of wrongful conduct.

(d) A lawyer shall exercise reasonable care to prevent employees, associates, and others whose services are utilized by the lawyer from disclosing or using confidences or secrets of a client, except that a lawyer may reveal the information allowed by paragraph (c) through an employee.

Source: Michigan Rules of Professional Conduct.

EXHIBIT 1-2 Michigan Rules of Professional Conduct Rule 5.3 Responsibilities Regarding Nonlawyer Assistants

---

With respect to a nonlawyer employed or retained by or associated with a lawyer:

(a) a partner in a law firm shall make reasonable efforts to ensure that the firm has in effect measures giving reasonable assurance that the person's conduct is compatible with the professional obligations of the lawyer;

(b) a lawyer having direct supervisory authority over the nonlawyer shall make reasonable efforts to ensure that the person's conduct is compatible with the professional obligations of the lawyer; and

(c) A lawyer shall be responsible for conduct of such a person that would be a violation of the Rules of Professional Conduct if engaged in by a lawyer if:

    1. The lawyer orders or, with the knowledge of the specific conduct, ratifies the conduct involved; or

    2. The lawyer is a partner in the law firm in which the person is employed, or has direct supervisory authority over the person, and knows of the conduct at a time when its consequences can be avoided or mitigated but fails to take reasonable remedial action.

Source: Michigan Rules of Professional Conduct.

Professional Conduct dealing with the attorney's "Responsibilities Regarding Nonlawyer Assistants." The paralegal student must review the attorney professional rules in his or her jurisdiction. In addition, the student must read the paralegal codes of ethics as outlined by national paralegal organizations such as the National Federation of Paralegal Associations (NFPA) and the National Association of Legal Assistants (NALA).

2. **Deadlines are crucial.** Personal injury attorneys and personal injury paralegals live and die by the clock. Deadlines appear in the state rules of civil procedure. They appear in the federal rules of civil procedure. They appear in court orders and in reported court decisions. They appear in court rules, and they appear in statutes. They appear in a memo or e-mail the paralegal receives from a supervising attorney. A civil **statute of limitation** is a statute that provides the maximum period of time in which a civil lawsuit must be commenced. If it is not commenced within that time period, the claim is forever barred. For example, a civil action in federal court is commenced by filing the complaint. If the paralegal does not timely accomplish that task, this inaction will result in a statute of limitation being missed. This inaction will forever destroy the client's right to pursue his or her personal injury case. In addition, if a deadline is missed, the result can range from a strong reprimand by the supervising attorney to the paralegal's termination on the spot. Also, if a statute of limitation is missed, the attorney may be subject to claims of both ethical violations and legal malpractice.

Statute of Limitation
In civil law and procedure, a statute that prescribes the maximum period of time in which a civil lawsuit must be commenced or it is forever barred.

3. **Be a "nag."** For many, many years, numerous TV sitcoms and movies have developed a negative theme surrounding a nagging spouse. One of the first is *The Honeymooners*, popular back in the 1950s and continuing up to *Modern Family*, a weekly TV sitcom currently popular today. Contrary to that popular negative cultural theme, a trait of a good paralegal is actually to be a "nag." Perhaps a softer and better term is "backup." As a personal injury litigation team member, always remember that your role is to be a true backup to the attorney. If the attorney appears to be on the wrong track or to have missed an important item, have the courage to point it out at every turn—in a respectful, professional manner, of course.

4. **Be alert.** Do not assume everything will proceed on a prim and proper course throughout the preparation and trial of a personal injury case. The author was attending a deposition one time in which he was defending a physician in a medical malpractice case. The defense attorneys were gathered in a conference room in the plaintiff's attorney's office in the downtown of a major U.S. city. As we were conversing among ourselves, one of the defense paralegals, to her credit, happened to notice a small camera on the wall that was moving. We were being secretly videotaped by the other side!

5. **Do not be a "yes" man or woman.** The legal teams who have assembled independent, forthright paralegals who are not afraid to express their honest opinion when asked are truly the most successful.

6. **Develop good habits early on.** The common saying is: "Practice makes perfect." The popular, highly successful, and motivational football coach of the Green Bay Packers, Vince Lombardi, however, put a slightly different twist on that popular saying by declaring: "*Perfect* practice makes perfect." Just as it does no good to practice the fundamentals of blocking or tackling incorrectly, it does no good to continue to perform a task over and over again if the paralegal is performing it incorrectly.

7. **Develop an inquisitive nature.** Ask questions. The paralegal's role is neither to assume nor to march forward with blinders on. Is everything really as it appears?

8. **Avoid the procrastination trap.** "I work best under pressure" is a myth. If the paralegal is aware of the deadline to complete an assignment in an attorney's memo or e-mail, the paralegal should not wait to begin working on it the day of or the day before the deadline. If the paralegal has until midnight to electronically file a document, the paralegal should not wait until 11:00 p.m. to start working on it. Invariably, some event, whether job-related, health-related, or family-related, will inconveniently arise to cause a further delay. It is no sin to have an assignment completed well before the deadline. Indeed, if a statute of limitation is missed, the severe consequences would likely be those discussed in item 2.

9. **Pay attention to detail.** This is not a profession that rewards sloppiness. Read and reread. Proofread again and again and again. Avoid generalities and sloppiness. Pay attention to detail. A detail can and will make the difference between a successful and an unsuccessful outcome in personal injury litigation.

10. **Develop good organizational skills.** It is meaningless for the personal injury paralegal to have performed a superb job on a particular project if the paralegal cannot thereafter locate the particular document(s) when needed at a meeting, conference, deposition, arbitration, or trial.

11. **Be flexible.** Avoid rigidity in your thinking and in your actions. When all seems under control, the judge, the client, the opposing counsel, a member of your litigation team, or some other person or event may throw you a curveball requiring a total refocusing of your efforts toward the case.

12. **Develop good communication skills, both orally and in writing.** This is also a field that does not reward poor English. To the contrary, good communication skills create success in the personal injury field. When the author was in law school, the prominent attorney F. Lee Bailey spoke at a luncheon for law students. One of the students inquired of Mr. Bailey what he believed to be the most favorable background to become a lawyer. The response came back in a confident, booming voice without a moment's hesitation: "*English! Master the King's English!*"

13. **Avoid timidity and inaction.** Be decisive and accomplish promptly and efficiently what you have set out to do. As Robert Half stated, "Acting on a good idea is better than just having a good idea." This is with the caveat that you will also learn when to check with the attorney before embarking on a completely new and unfamiliar activity.

14. **Thorough preparation wins personal injury cases.** The paralegal will participate in trials and will witness attorneys who, for example, have the names of the potential jurors memorized in the *voir dire* selection process or a medical record memorized such that no notes are utilized by that attorney. While extremely impressive and downright jaw-dropping, it is still competent and thorough preparation that will make the difference in the outcome of a personal injury case. Never take shortcuts because it appears a case is likely to settle.

15. **Stick-to-itiveness and determination win out.** As President Calvin Coolidge said, "Nothing in the world can take the place of persistence. Talent will not. Nothing is more common than unsuccessful men with talent. Genius will not. Unrewarded genius is almost a proverb. Education will not; the world is full of educated derelicts. Persistence and determination alone are omnipotent...." Could anyone better state this trait?

16. **Confidence is the key to success.** Note that confidence does not equal success. Confidence does not guarantee success. It simply opens the door to success. The personal injury paralegal will routinely encounter obstacles, including intimidating people, whether judges, opposing counsel, expert witnesses, court administration personnel, or others. With the passage of time and the acquiring of knowledge and experience, confidence will naturally follow. When developing a new skill set, it may take as long as five years before that professional confidence meets up with and matches any personal confidence possessed by the paralegal.

17. **An analytical mind is extremely beneficial.** Try to logically solve problems—of which there will be many—and keep emotion out of an area of law in which it is only natural to become emotionally involved with a particular case or client.

18. **"If clients leave the office feeling worse than they did before they came in, the lawyer hasn't done his job."** This is an actual quote by an "old school lawyer," personally concerned about his clients, and overheard by the young lawyer he was mentoring. The student can probably figure out who the young lawyer was. The same principle applies to the paralegal. Clients typically come into a law office under pressure, pain, stress, and turmoil. The good paralegal will show empathy, calmness, and restraint with those clients.

19. **Good Judgment.** Unfortunately, some possess it … some do not. You cannot teach "get it." Good judgment and common sense are a gift. Contrast the intellectually gifted paralegal that spins his or her wheels researching various sources to answer a perplexing question about an unwritten court procedure versus the paralegal with good judgment who decides to simply pick up the phone and call the proper person in court administration for the answer. The street smart paralegal with good judgment is a true asset in the field of personal injury law. According to Miles Kington, "Knowledge is knowing a tomato is a fruit. Wisdom is not putting it in a fruit salad."

20. **Honesty.** Last but not least, this field is not for the dishonest, unscrupulous, unethical person. Trustworthiness is essential to relationships with the client, the supervising attorney, opposing counsel, witnesses, the court, and the entire judicial system in general.

Workplace Skills Tip

When preparing a memo to the supervising attorney or when assisting with preparing a brief, try to be creative and interesting. For example, avoid legalese, such as "hereinafter," "herein," or "heretofore." Do not use "said" as an adjective or an article, such as "the said product" or "the said motor vehicle." Avoid that commonly used, catchall word "get." Instead, use more descriptive words, such as "obtain" or "acquire." Verizon, when locating an attachment on a cell phone, even uses a more creative word than "get." It uses "fetch."

There is another trait—an implied, unspoken trait not specifically listed above. It is so basic and so fundamental that it should not need to be specifically included in a list. This is the trait of *professionalism*. Be proud of the profession of which you are a part. Show respect for this profession and our judicial system. This can be accomplished by what you speak and how you speak it and how you conduct yourself at all times, even down to a simple detail of how you dress when you are in the office and in the courtroom. Your demeanor, appearance, and dress will reflect upon your professionalism and your pride in and respect for the entire legal system of which you are about to become a vital part.

Anglo-American Legal History

Common Law
"Judge-made" law as established from the English system of law, originating sometime in the 1150s.

Statutory Law
A source of law that is based upon a statute enacted by a legislative body, whether state or federal.

Stare Decisis
Also known as precedent; a concept of judges respecting previous judicial decisions.

Precedent
Also known as "*stare decisis*," it is a concept of a judge following decisions of earlier judges, which provides uniformity and stability to the law.

Reception Statutes
Statutes utilized by British colonies in America after independence was achieved from England that gave full legal effect to the existing body of English common law.

The two primary sources of law in the United States are **common law** and **statutory law**. Common law is "judge-made" law. Statutory law is that law created by the enactment of a statute by a legislative body, whether state or federal. Common law originated with King Henry II of England sometime in the 1150s. This became the law that was "common" throughout the land as established by the King's judges. The judges would be sent from the King's central court to hear cases throughout England. Those judges would return and file their decisions. Eventually the concept of *stare decisis* developed in which judges came to respect and follow decisions of earlier judges. *Stare decisis* is also known as **precedent**. If a case with identical or similar facts to a previous decision is before the court, the court must follow the holding used in the previous decision. This concept provides uniformity and stability to the law. This body of precedent—the common law—has the effect of binding future decisions.

This judge-made law, known as the common law, existed for several hundred years until the English Parliament received authority to create statutory law. From that point forward, the two sources of law began—judge-made law and laws enacted by legislatures. When the British colonies later achieved independence from England, they began to specifically adopt the existing body of English common law. This was done by **reception statutes**. These statutes gave full legal effect to the existing body of English common law.

Isn't it a bit ironic that our country, wanting so desperately to be free and independent from a tyrant, had no difficulty in embracing that same tyrant's common law? Obviously, our forefathers must have strongly appreciated the English common law. Maybe it was the uniformity, logic, and stability that the English common law had so well established. Today, the common law as derived originally from England exists in every legal system in the United States, except for

Workplace Skills Tip

When preparing a memo or e-mail to your supervising attorney, a longer memo is not necessarily a better memo, just as a longer brief is not necessarily a better brief. Omit needless words. Try to use short sentences. Finally, consider numbering your thoughts as an organizing technique. The use of numbers acts as a built-in checklist for the attorney. For example:

We should do the following items ASAP:

1. Arrange a meeting promptly with opposing counsel, Tanner J. Brandt.

2. Inform client, Chelsea Christell, of new judge assigned, Judge Kimberlee Ann Moen, who could be unfavorable to her case.

3. Provide more test samples to engineering expert, Dr. Spencer Richard.

Louisiana, which adopted a code based on the Napoleonic Code of 1804. The current main body of law in the United States consists of the English common law, additional state and federal case law articulated by our judges, and state and federal statutes.

While case law and statutory law are considered to be the two primary sources of law, there are actually three other potential sources of law. First is the law contained in a constitution such as our United States Constitution and the constitutions of our 50 states. A **constitution** is a written document that embodies a set of fundamental principles by which the state or federal government is ruled or governed. Second is a body of law known as **administrative law**. This law arises from rules established by various public agencies, both state and federal. A few examples of well-known federal agencies are the Federal Trade Commission, the National Labor Relations Board, and the Equal Employment Opportunity Commission (EEOC). Examples of such state agencies might be a workers' compensation agency, a state equal employment opportunity commission, and a state securities commission. Finally, there is an additional source of law—a secondary authority—which is that law embodied in the various **Restatements of the Law**. These scholarly treatises, called Restatements, are concerned with analysis of the common law and are published by the **American Law Institute (ALI)**. The ALI is an independent organization formed in 1923, which consists of various attorneys, judges, and law professors. It is mentioned here because these Restatements tend to enjoy the favor and respect of the courts. It is not uncommon to find a particular Restatement section cited in a court opinion.

Legal Theory

In legal theory, the state legislatures and Congress make the law and the state and federal judges interpret the law. But do judges sometimes also "make" the law in the sense that they legislate from the bench? If they do, should they do so? This is a historical debate that has occurred for centuries. The main objection to judges making law is that when they do so they become activists and are infringing upon the function of the legislature—a group of elected officials responsible to their

Constitution
A written document embodying a set of fundamental principles by which a state or federal government is governed. It constitutes a source of law.

Administrative Law
Law that is developed from rules established by various public agencies, both state and federal. Examples of federal agencies are the Federal Trade Commission, the National Labor Relations Board, and the Equal Employment Opportunity Commission (EEOC).

Restatements of the Law
A source of secondary law in the nature of a treatise prepared by ALI, which provides analysis of law in several areas, including torts.

American Law Institute (ALI)
An independent organization formed in 1923 that is made up of various attorneys, judges, and law professors who have compiled various Restatements of the Law over the years in several areas of the law, including torts.

electorate. They become dictators from the bench with little or no accountability. Those in favor of judges making law take the position that when a statute or constitution is enacted, the creators could not have possibly envisioned all of the ramifications in the future. Therefore, judges have a responsibility to clarify those ramifications. In other words, those proponents would argue that this is what the law says, but this is what the law ought to be.

The issue often arises in the interpretation of a statute or a constitution. Should the judge follow the words strictly as written (a strict constructionist approach) or should the interpretation reflect current social, economic, and political circumstances? The judge may likewise be in a position of making law when there is no precedent to guide the judge. This is called a **case of first impression**.

Proponents of the judge making law would argue the judge must use his or her discretion. The other side would argue that there really is no discretion required because if one looks closely, there is always an underlying "legal principle" that will guide the judge. Therefore, the judge is simply discovering and declaring the existing law and not making new law.

This age-old debate surfaces even today at the U.S. Senate confirmation hearings required for the president's choice of a nominee to be a U.S. Supreme Court justice. A federal judge, whether a federal district judge, a judge of the U.S. Court of Appeals, or a U.S. Supreme Court justice, is a lifetime appointment made by the president of the United States. In addition to the obvious legal importance of these appointments, there are also obvious political considerations. A federal judge, appointed in his or her 40s or 50s can continue to influence a president's preferred policy into his or her 80s or 90s (or 100s). Consider the case of the oldest federal judge in our U.S. history, Judge Wesley E. Brown, a federal district court judge in Wichita, Kansas, who was, at the time this book went to press, still hearing cases at age 105. He was born on June 22, 1907. He was appointed to the federal bench in 1962 by President John F. Kennedy!

There is tension created by this fundamental issue of judges interpreting law versus making law, or whether a judge is labeled a "conservative" or a "liberal." Because of that, questioning by some senators of the nominee at these U. S. Senate hearings is typically tough, and sometimes, downright brutal. It is not uncommon to see a senator from the opposite party as that of the president grilling that particular president's nominee.

Consider the recent hearings conducted for Elena Kagan, who was nominated by Democratic President Obama and later confirmed by the U.S. Senate. Republican Senator Tom Coburn remarked to her: "You are dancing a little bit, much to my chagrin. I would rather you not win. Maybe you should be on 'Dancing with the Stars' or something.... I know what a liberal is, and I think you are a liberal. I think you're proud enough to defend that.... I don't know one judge that can 100 percent separate themselves from who they are...." One of her responses at the hearing was: "I am not sure how I would characterize my politics but one thing I do know is that my politics would be, must be, have to be completely separate from my judging. Judging is about considering how the law applies to the case not how your own personal views might suggest anything about the case."[1]

On the other hand, in January 2006, Senate confirmation hearings were held for Republican President George W. Bush's U.S. Supreme Court nominee, Samuel

Case of First Impression
A case that arises for the first time and there is no precedent to guide the judge.

A. Alito, Jr., who was also later confirmed by the U.S. Senate. This exchange occurred between Democratic Senator Arlen Specter and Judge Alito who expressed the view that the law always retains a guiding principle such that no new law need be made:

> **Specter:** Would you agree with Cardozo on *Palco* that it represents the values of a changing society?
>
> **Alito:** ...As times change, new factual situations come up and the principles have to be applied to those situations. The principles don't change. The Constitution itself doesn't change, but the factual situations change, and as new situations come up, the principles and the rights have to be applied to them.[2]

As you, the paralegal student, read various decisions from this point forward, pay attention to the philosophy and reasoning of the court. Try to determine whether the court is really interpreting existing law in which there are always guiding principles or the court is outright making the law conform to what it "ought to be."

Torts

DEFINITION OF A TORT

Exactly what is a **tort**? The famous legal scholar Dean William Prosser defined a tort as "a term applied to a miscellaneous and more or less unconnected group of civil wrongs other than breach of contract for which a court of law will afford a remedy in the form of an action for damages."[3] In its simplest sense, it is a wrong for which money damages becomes the remedy for the person wronged. Dean Prosser purposely mentions an exclusion from his definition of torts—breach of contract. A **contract** is a legally enforceable oral or written agreement between at least two parties with mutual obligations. Breach of contract has its basis in a broken *promise* to another. Tort law has its basis in the breach of a *duty* owed to another.

The actual word "tort" is an old French word derived from the Latin word "*torquere*," which means "something twisted or wrong" or "to twist." The person responsible for committing the tort is labeled the **tortfeasor**. The person injured may be referred to as the "victim" or "the injured party." When suit is commenced, the injured party formally becomes the "plaintiff" and the tortfeasor formally becomes the "defendant."

Conduct on the part of a person committing a tort may also be conduct that can equate to a crime. While the primary purpose of civil tort law is to make the wrongdoer compensate the injured party with money damages, the primary purpose of criminal law is to punish the wrongdoer. For example, a punch thrown in a bar fight might result in the wrongdoer being subject to both a civil suit based on the intentional tort of assault and battery for money damages and a criminal prosecution for the crime of assault and battery. A murder, subjecting a person to criminal prosecution, might also result in that person being subjected to a civil wrongful death suit for money damages. A motor vehicle collision in which the driver is drinking and speeding that results in the

Tort
A wrongful act other than a breach of contract that injures another and for which the law imposes civil liability.

Contract
A legally enforceable oral or written agreement between at least two parties with mutual obligations.

Tortfeasor
The person responsible for committing the tort.

death of a person might subject that driver to both a civil lawsuit in negligence for wrongful death money damages and a criminal prosecution for negligent homicide or manslaughter.

Personal Injury

DEFINITION OF PERSONAL INJURY AND THE INTERRELATIONSHIP BETWEEN TORT LAW AND THE FIELD OF PERSONAL INJURY

Personal Injury
An injury to a person's body, mind, or emotions.

The simplest definition of **personal injury** is that it is an injury to a person's body, mind, or emotions. It should be clarified that personal injury also encompasses the death of a person for which various items of money damages may be recovered. The field of personal injury is much broader than the field of torts. A paralegal working in the field of personal injury must have a general understanding of tort law. However, the paralegal must also have a general understanding of other areas of the law such as civil procedure and evidence. Other important areas are legal research and writing, interviewing clients and witnesses, and investigation techniques. To fully complete a paralegal's background in the field of personal injury, knowledge of medical issues and insurance is vital. The field of personal injury is a very broad field requiring knowledge in many areas of study. These various areas of study will converge as the paralegal assists in the preparation and trial of the personal injury case.

Public Policy Purposes of Tort Law

Compensation
The primary public policy purpose for tort law. A tortfeasor should be responsible for payment of reasonable money damages to the plaintiff the tortfeasor has injured.

Compensatory Damages
Those monetary/money damages that are awarded to compensate the plaintiff and make the plaintiff whole.

The principles of tort law began with the common law in England. The body of law in this country has since grown from this country's adoption of the English common law to include our country's own case law and our own statutory law. The primary purpose of American tort law is to provide reasonable compensation in the form of money damages to one who has been injured by the tortfeasor's tort. Other purposes of tort law are justice, deterrence, distribution of risk, and setting minimum standards of conduct.

Compensation to an injured party in the form of money damages is probably the primary purpose for tort law today. **Compensatory damages**, which will be studied in Chapter 4, are awarded to compensate the plaintiff and to make the

Workplace Skills Tip

Whether the paralegal is on the plaintiff's team attempting to "build up" a case or on the defendant's team attempting to "tear down" a case, the team will (or should) have a basic, underlying, simple "theory of the case." This theory of the case should be developed early on as it will be a roadmap for the paralegal in assisting with the presentation of evidence. It may be a theory as simple as:

"The defendant has told so many different stories about how this accident happened that none of them can be believed." Or "The plaintiff claims Dr. Smith committed malpractice, yet she continues to receive care and treatment from him to this day." Or "This unfortunate incident could have been prevented if this manufacturer had just spent $0.87 for a different component part."

plaintiff whole. The tortfeasor or the tortfeasor's insurer is the one who should be made responsible for the tortfeasor's actions or inactions that caused the loss, damage, and injury. Liability insurance, to be discussed in a later chapter, generally provides the means for that compensation, usually without causing the financial ruin of the tortfeasor/defendant. It certainly makes sense for the tortfeasor or the tortfeasor's liability insurance company to pay for the wrong the tortfeasor inflicted. Why should society and the taxpayer bear that burden?

Justice is a worthy goal of tort law. For the most part, every reasonable citizen has a sense of fairness instilled in him or her. Litigants desire a just and fair result by a judge or jury when litigation ensues. The one basic characteristic that litigants can ask of a judge is that the judge be fair. Whether the judge possesses great intellectual capacity, is ambitious, or is a legal scholar is somewhat secondary. The number-one trait all should ask of our judges is that they be fair and impartial. The same can be said of an arbitrator or a jury. The simple goal is to fairly apply the facts to the correct law. Interestingly, a very famous lawyer from the past, Clarence Darrow, made this cynical comment about justice: "There is no such thing as justice—in or out of court."

Deterrence is present in our tort law system. The threat of knowing that if a tort is committed, the tortfeasor may well be "hauled into court" and made to pay money damages has the effect of deterring that wrongful conduct. This deterrence purpose is obvious in the area of **punitive damages**, which will also be studied in a later chapter. Punitive damages, also called **exemplary damages**, are exceptional money damages over and above compensatory damages. Punitive means "to punish." Exemplary means "to make an example of." These damages, not available in all jurisdictions, are awarded in those unique cases where the act or omission of the defendant was particularly uncivilized, egregious, or done with the willful or reckless disregard for the rights and safety of others. Punitive/exemplary damages have as their purposes to punish the wrongdoer, to make an example of the wrongdoer, and to deter the wrongful conduct.

The **distribution of risk**, sometimes referred to as "loss allocation," is an important purpose behind tort law. This is probably best illustrated in the field of products liability. Between the innocent consumer or user and the manufacturer of the product, who is better prepared to bear the risk of loss? Who is in the best position to avoid loss? The manufacturer, who stands to make a profit, is better prepared to bear the risk of loss. So, too, the manufacturer, who is involved in the testing and research of its own product, is in the best position to attempt to correct a problem, avoid a defective product, and prevent a resulting loss, damage, or injury to a consumer or user.

Setting certain minimum **standards of conduct** is another purpose of tort law. For example, tort law, in the form of a state statute governing the speed, the proper lookout, and the keeping of a motor vehicle under proper control sets standards of minimum conduct for the use and operation of a motor vehicle on public highways. The violation of those statutory duties might establish below standard conduct in the community and subject the tortfeasor to liability and damages. Motorists on the public highways have the right to expect that other motorists will conform to those standards and obey the law in the interest of and respect for public safety.

Justice
A public policy purpose of tort law based upon a basic concept of fairness by a judge or jury.

Deterrence
A public policy of tort law based upon the threat of knowing that if a tort is committed, the tortfeasor may be subject to a civil lawsuit and the imposition of money damages.

Punitive Damages
A type of civil damages, the purpose of which is not to compensate the plaintiff but "to punish" the defendant.

Exemplary Damages
A type of civil damages, the purpose of which is not to compensate the plaintiff but "to make an example of" the defendant.

Distribution of Risk
A public policy of tort law based upon the principle of which party should bear the risk of loss as between a plaintiff and a defendant.

Standards of Conduct
A public policy purpose of tort law in which a person is expected to meet certain minimum standards of conduct.

Tort Reform

Catapulting from the beginning of tort law in England in the 12th century to the United States in the 21st century, one might expect that criticism of our tort law system would eventually arise. In the 1980s a movement began for the reform of our tort system. It was perceived as a crisis situation by those calling for reform. It arose by those primarily concerned with the mushrooming of civil litigation to solve problems as well as perceived and actual excessive jury verdicts and frivolous lawsuits. The approach to **tort reform**, in essence, is to curb the number of civil lawsuits and also to reduce certain tort damages.

While not all-inclusive, some primary avenues of reform have included shortening the statutes of limitation in certain cases and placing a limit or cap on certain types of damages. For example, a common time period for a negligence statute of limitation may be six years. One approach is to reduce that time period from six years to, say, two years. The typical law of damages for a personal injury case is that any damages awarded by a jury must not be speculative but rather must be reasonable. In an effort to ensure that verdicts are not excessive, some states have also placed a dollar cap on certain damages that a jury may award, say $250,000. This is notable in medical malpractice actions, for example. The reasoning here is that because of excessive awards in medical malpractice cases, the cost of health care has risen due to increased health insurance premiums.

Another avenue of reform has included the adoption of the **English Rule** concerning attorneys' fees. The English Rule is a rule that states, in civil litigation, the loser pays the other side's attorney's fees. It applies to both the plaintiff and the defendant. If plaintiff wins, defendant pays the fees. If defendant wins, plaintiff pays the fees. Contrast this with the **American Rule**. Under the American Rule the prevailing party is not entitled to obtain attorney's fees from the losing party. However, a statute or a contract may overcome this rule. A statute may authorize the recovery of attorney's fees in a particular type of case, such as a mortgage foreclosure action. Parties to a contract may agree that attorney's fees that are incurred to enforce their agreement will be awarded to the prevailing party.

There are differences in attorney fee structures that the personal injury paralegal will typically encounter. While there may be hybrids of each fee structure, there are two basic structures. The first type of fee typically encountered in the personal injury field when representing a plaintiff is the **contingency fee**. The fee is paid to the attorney only if there is a favorable result, whether by litigation or by settlement. A typical contingency fee arrangement would be on a one-third basis. If the attorney recovers money damages for the client, by way of settlement or verdict or appeal, the attorney receives one-third of the award as his or her fee. For example, if the plaintiff received a settlement of $100,000, the attorney's fee would be $33,333.33.

A sample contingency fee agreement is shown at Exhibit 1-3. Another sample contingency fee agreement is shown in Appendix 1 at Exhibit 1-4. Also, at Exhibit 1-4A, a lengthier sample contingency fee agreement in a medical malpractice case is shown. The fee may be increased if an appeal is necessary because appeals require additional time-consuming and specialized work. This contingency fee is necessary and serves a real purpose. If such a fee arrangement were not available to the client, those of meager or limited means could not afford to retain an attorney to pursue that personal injury case. Most people could not afford to pay the lawyer's hourly fees that mount quickly in the pursuit of a personal injury case. Because there is a real risk that the attorney may not be paid under a contingency fee arrangement, there is an incentive on the attorney's part to (1) screen carefully all such cases before acceptance of the case and (2) work diligently and efficiently on the case after its acceptance.

The other type of fee that is typical on the defendant's side of the personal injury case is the hourly fee. This fee arrangement is typical whether the client is a self-insured individual or entity or the client is insured and an insurance company

---

Tort Reform
A movement to change the American tort system with a view toward curbing the number of civil lawsuits and reducing certain tort damages.

English Rule
A rule that the loser pays the other side's attorneys' fees. It applies to both the plaintiff and the defendant.

American Rule
A rule that each party pays for his or her own attorneys' fees unless a statute or contract provides otherwise.

Contingency Fee
A fee paid only if there is a favorable result, whether by litigation or by settlement; typically a percentage of the amount recovered such as one-third of the recovery.

EXHIBIT 1-3 Retainer Contract

The undersigned does hereby retain the law firm of Bull & Bear, P.A. to represent (him, her, them) in asserting claims against any and all who may be claimed to be responsible for any injury, loss, or damage sustained by the undersigned, arising out of an occurrence that took place at or near _____ _____on _____.

Payment to Bull & Bear, P.A. shall be contingent upon a recovery of money being made, and if there is no recovery of money, then no fee will be paid or charged.

In the event there is a recovery of money, then the undersigned agree that Bull & Bear, P.A. shall receive for their services one-third of all monies paid or monies in the future payable, by way of settlement or judgment, except that if an appeal is required such fee shall be 40% of all monies paid or payable by way of settlement or judgment. Expenses incurred or advanced on behalf of the aforesaid persons will be repaid to Bull & Bear, P.A. by the undersigned from the undersigned's share of any recovery, and should there be no money recovery, the undersigned shall remain liable to Bull & Bear, P.A. for such sums.

If (I, we) agree to accept a structured settlement that calls for periodic payments in the future, (I, we) agree that Bull & Bear, P.A., at its option, may either be paid its fee based upon the present value of the total structured settlement from any cash sum paid at the time of settlement, or it may be paid the percentage referred to above of the cash sum paid at the time of settlement, plus the percentage referred to above, of all periodic payments.

(I, we) have read this agreement, voluntarily signed it, and received a copy of it.

Dated: _____   _____

                                                  Name of Client(s)

is paying the fee. In this scenario, it makes no economic difference to the attorney whether the case is won or lost. The attorney is paid either way. In the contingency fee arrangement, however, it makes an enormous difference whether the case is won or lost. Winning equals a fee. Losing equals no fee. From the paralegal's standpoint, the pressure to bill hours is greater in an hourly fee firm. In a contingency fee firm, the pressure is to be efficient with your time.

Some advocates of tort reform have proposed that the English Rule be adopted. The theory is that a plaintiff would think twice before commencing a lawsuit because of the economic threat of having to pay the other side's fees if the case is lost. An important point is that the discussion between the American Rule and the English Rule is about attorney's fees and not litigation costs. Generally speaking, those costs are still borne by the losing party. Examples of such costs may be reasonable expert witness fees, filing fees, and other costs specifically allowed by a particular state's statute or court rule. It should also be noted that some states have provided for sanctions if a case is deemed by the court to be a frivolous claim. The sanctions may provide that either the party or the attorney may be responsible for fees and costs in defending a frivolous claim. Some of the tort reform concepts discussed here—as well as other concepts—will be discussed in later chapters. The personal injury paralegal needs to be aware of the concept of tort reform as it continues to influence and affect the personal injury practice.

Workplace Skills Tip

When assisting with the preparation of a legal memo or a brief, recognize that judges are busy. They must read through many, many documents submitted to them each day. Try to capture the judge's attention in your case by using expressive language. Do not be afraid to "spice up" the language. Exercise some professional creativity. Make the brief interesting to the reader. For example, compare the two opening sentences of a sample brief: (1) "This litigation, based on a negligence theory, arises out of an automobile collision that occurred on May 1, 2010, in which the defendant was negligent because he was inattentive, conversing with a new girlfriend, and struck the plaintiff's motor vehicle in the rear end…." and (2) "They say 'Spring is when a young man's fancy turns to love'; unfortunately, in this case, tragic consequences resulted." Which first sentence better captures the judge's attention, curiosity, and interest? Each person has his or her own individual writing style. The important point is to try to capture the interest, curiosity, and attention of the reader. In this case, it is the yawning judge who will read many dull, boring, lengthy briefs that he or she wishes were far more interesting and half the length.

Bases upon Which Tort Law Is Predicated

There are several bases upon which tort theories are predicated. There are essentially three traditional bases of torts—negligence, intentional, and strict liability. We will briefly examine each one at this juncture with more detail and analysis to follow in upcoming chapters.

NEGLIGENCE

Negligence
An act or omission by the tortfeasor that is a failure to use due care under the circumstances and that causes loss, damage, or injury to the injured party.

This is probably the most common basis and the one that will receive the greatest attention in later chapters. **Negligence** is an act or omission by the tortfeasor that is a failure to use due care under the circumstances that causes loss, damage, or injury to the injured party. In its simplest terms, negligence means that the tortfeasor was careless or was at fault. The basis for this tort has nothing to do with an intention or purpose to cause any harm or injury to the injured party. A good example of this would be a driver texting while driving a motor vehicle without keeping a proper lookout, and a collision occurs with another person, vehicle, or object.

INTENTIONAL TORTS

Intentional Torts
A basis of tort law consisting of a tortfeasor's intentional or purposeful action intending and causing loss, damage, harm, or injury to the injured party's person or property.

As one would expect from the title, **intentional torts** are based upon the tortfeasor's intentional or purposeful action intending and causing loss, damage, harm, or injury to the injured party's person or property. A good example of this is the tort of battery, which is the injurious or offensive touching of a person without that person's consent. This may range from a violent punch thrown in a bar fight to a tender but offensive pat on the head in the workplace. The key to the tort of battery is that it is a touching without the other person's consent.

STRICT LIABILITY

Strict Liability
A basis of tort law that applies primarily to those situations involving the tortfeasor's use, handling, or engaging in abnormally dangerous activities, or the ownership or control of a wild or domestic animal. Defendant is liable regardless of fault.

The basis for this tort has nothing to do with either negligence or intention. **Strict liability** applies primarily to those situations involving the tortfeasor's use, handling, or engaging in abnormally dangerous activities, such as explosives or radioactive materials. It also arises in situations involving the ownership or control of an animal, wild or domestic. Liability is imposed regardless of the tortfeasor's intent and regardless of the tortfeasor's negligence, carelessness, or fault. The theory is that the conduct is so egregious or so abnormally dangerous that the law imposes liability as a matter of public policy. As will be examined in future chapters, strict liability may also be a basis for imposing liability on the manufacturer or seller of an unreasonably dangerous product. Courts adopt the reasoning that when harm ensues from such a product, the financial burden should not be borne by the consumer or user. Rather, the burden is best borne by the manufacturer or seller, who is in the best position to guard against defects in its own product and who stands to make a profit from the product.

Alternative Dispute Resolution

Before embarking upon the torts and personal injury journey, the student may have an expectation of assisting with the trials of numerous cases. While the personal injury paralegal will assist with the preparation of many cases for trial, the reality is that few are tried. Typically, 80% to 90% of personal injury cases are settled. There was a time in which it could take five years or more from filing a case until the case was called for trial. This was an intolerable situation, and the public demanded more expedient justice.

The concept of **Alternative Dispute Resolution (ADR)** came about in earnest during the late 1970s and early 1980s. Alternative dispute resolution is a term that encompasses numerous means for resolving a litigant's case without involvement of the court process in which a judge or jury traditionally decides the case. This type of resolution is typically cheaper, more efficient, and speedier than a resolution through the court process. It has the further advantage of the parties' dispute being handled privately and behind closed doors versus open to the public. Even in instances in which a case is being handled through the court process, some jurisdictions mandate some form of ADR before the court or jury trial can proceed.

Alternative Dispute Resolution (ADR)
A term that encompasses numerous means for resolving a litigant's case without involvement of the judicial process in which a judge or jury traditionally decides the case.

ARBITRATION

Arbitration is a form of ADR in which the dispute is submitted to either one arbitrator or a panel of arbitrators who will actually decide the case just as a judge or a jury would do. Arbitrators usually consist of attorneys, retired attorneys, and retired judges. However, unless an agreement or a statute states otherwise, an arbitrator need not be legally trained. For example, a case involving a construction defect in a house may have a contractor or realtor as an arbitrator.

Arbitration may be conducted by one arbitrator or a panel of arbitrators. A panel is typically made up of three arbitrators. There are two primary methods for selecting the panel. In the first method, each side picks an arbitrator. Those two then pick a "neutral" third arbitrator, and thus the panel of three is formed. While the decision may be unanimous, it can be seen that two of the three arbitrators will likely decide the case. The case will tend to go in favor of the side whose arbitrator persuaded the neutral third arbitrator of the merits of that side. Another method frequently used to select the arbitration panel is for the sponsoring arbitration facility, such as the American Arbitration Association, to submit to each side a list of potential arbitrators. Each side has the right to strike potential arbitrators, including every person on that list. However, it may happen that one or more arbitrators on a list not stricken by one side are also not stricken by the other side. With some limitations under the rules, lists are submitted until a total of three mutually

Arbitration
A form of ADR in which the dispute is submitted to either one arbitrator or a panel of arbitrators who will actually decide the case just as a judge or a jury would do.

agreeable arbitrators are left standing after both parties have exercised their right to strike arbitrators.

Arbitration typically comes about in one of three ways: (1) A statute may mandate it. (2) A contract that the parties have signed may mandate it. (3) The parties may agree on their own when a dispute arises initially or during the litigation process that they want to use arbitration to resolve their dispute. A statute in a state that has no-fault automobile insurance, for example, may require that a dispute between the insured and the no-fault carrier be resolved by arbitration. A dispute between a government employee and the governmental agency may be required by statute to be resolved by arbitration. As far as arbitration arising by contract, it is common to find mandated arbitration in some employment agreements, in customer agreements with stock brokerage firms, and in insurance policies in which there is a dispute between the insurer and the insured.

Judicial Arbitration and Mediation Services (JAMS) and American Arbitration Association (AAA) are nationally recognized organizations providing arbitration services. JAMS is the largest private ADR service in the world. AAA does not actually perform ADR but provides a framework of rules for ADR and provides administrative support for ADR. Arbitration that arises by voluntary agreement of the parties with equal bargaining power tends to be the fairest. When two parties come to the conclusion that they both desire the process of arbitration, a certain arbitration procedure and process is not forced on the parties as is the case with arbitration mandated by statute. In that case, both parties are bound by the statutory scheme of the arbitration process set forth in the statute.

Even in arbitration arising from a written contract, the one party may not have equal bargaining power with the other. In the examples used earlier, a customer doing business with a national stock brokerage firm or a national insurance company will, in essence, be forced to take the arbitration process as drafted by the large national entity if the customer chooses to do business with that entity. There is also no equal bargaining power if the employee signs an employment agreement with a large national company that mandates a certain type of arbitration process in the event of an employment dispute. However, because arbitration and the entire ADR process is so favored by the courts, the courts are reluctant to set aside an arbitration agreement based upon unequal bargaining power between the contracting parties.

Binding Arbitration
ADR arbitration in which the decision of the arbitrator is final and neither party may appeal except upon very limited grounds.

Binding arbitration means that the decision of the arbitrator is final and neither party can appeal the decision. In most jurisdictions, however, even where the method is binding arbitration, the arbitration award may be able to be attacked if, for example, the arbitrator exceeded his or her scope of authority, the arbitrator had a conflict that was not disclosed, or there was some other fraud or misconduct on the part of the arbitrator. If a party believed that one of those three grounds occurred, the party would bring an action in court, following the arbitration award, asking the court to vacate the award. Barring that, with binding arbitration the decision is final and the case is at an end. If the losing party does not pay the award or otherwise try to attack it on the above-mentioned three grounds, the prevailing party will make a motion to the local court to confirm the arbitration award. This means that the award will be reduced to a judgment, which can be legally enforced allowing the prevailing party to utilize legal remedies to collect the judgment.

Non-binding arbitration is a decision made by an arbitrator that the parties may choose to disregard. In essence a non-binding arbitration acts merely as an advisory opinion from the arbitrator. Non-binding arbitration from a respected arbitrator may help to bring about a settlement. Binding arbitration is by far more prevalent and more practical as most litigants want some finality to their dispute.

> ## Workplace Skills Tip
>
> A word of caution is in order to the paralegal about arbitration. Just because this procedure is more informal, the case may be heard in an attorney's office instead of a courtroom, and the rules of procedure and evidence are relaxed, do not let down your guard. An important decision affecting your client will be made. Prepare for it diligently. Treat it just as importantly as one would treat a trial by a judge or jury in a formal courtroom setting.

The student should also be aware that there are some specific statutes dealing with the subject of arbitration. In 1925 Congress passed the Federal Arbitration Act (FAA), which applies to arbitration provisions in contracts covering virtually any activity in which interstate commerce is involved. In 1955 the Uniform Arbitration Act (UAA) was approved by the National Conference of Commissioners on Uniform State Laws. The UAA was revised in 2000 by Congress and required states to adopt their own version of it. The Revised Uniform Arbitration Act (RUAA) affirms the prevailing policy in this country that arbitration is encouraged because of its speed, lower cost, and efficiency. The RUAA sets up a default mechanism for a particular issue if the parties did not specifically address that issue in their arbitration agreement, such as the issue of discovery. Under the RUAA the arbitrator must make certain disclosures to the parties. It is beyond the scope of this textbook to provide a detailed analysis of these two statutes, but they are mentioned here for the personal injury paralegal's information. The paralegal will need to ascertain if the state jurisdiction in which he or she is working has adopted some form of the UAA and then become familiar with its provisions.

In line with grounds for attacking an arbitrator's award, the FAA provides that a court may vacate an award for the following reasons:

1. Where the award was procured by corruption, fraud, or undue means;
2. Where there was evident partiality or corruption in the arbitrators, or either of them.
3. Where the arbitrators were guilty of misconduct in refusing to postpone the hearing, upon sufficient cause shown, or in refusing to hear evidence pertinent and material to the controversy; or any other misbehavior by which the rights of any party have been prejudiced; or
4. Where the arbitrators exceeded their powers or so imperfectly executed them that a mutual, final, and definite award upon the subject matter submitted was not made.

MEDIATION

Mediation is another form of ADR. The mediator has no power or authority to decide the case. The mediator acts as a facilitator to try to assist the parties in resolving their dispute. Mediation typically may be imposed by statute, court order, or contract. Some states may have a statute or court rule that before a case is tried, it must be mediated or some other form of ADR must first be utilized. The parties may also voluntarily agree to this form of ADR. A mediator is typically a practicing attorney, a retired attorney, or a retired judge. While somewhat rare, a mediator may be someone with no legal training. In federal court, it is not uncommon to see federal magistrates handling mediations.

Mediation
A form of ADR that is non-binding—the mediator has no power or authority to decide the case and the mediator acts as a "facilitator" to try to help resolve the case.

The personality and style of the mediator can have a large bearing on whether or not a particular case is resolved. Typically, a mediator employs shuttle diplomacy. The mediator segregates the parties in different rooms and goes back and forth presenting ideas and positions, probing and asking questions in an effort to make the parties soften their position. Generally, a mediator who is merely a message carrier will have less success than a mediator who takes an active role and attempts some arm-twisting.

Mediations also tend to have a greater chance of success when three factors are present: (1) a strong-minded, skilled mediator is conducting the mediation; (2) the parties are truly prepared, know their case, and are serious and in good faith about settling the case; and (3) all parties with full authority are present at the mediation session. If any one of the three factors is missing, the chances of a successful mediation tend to go down significantly. In a mediation, what one party tells to the mediator is confidential and not disclosed to the other side unless the mediator is given express authorization to provide such disclosure.

While the mediator has no power or authority to decide a case, the parties can voluntarily agree to any terms of the mediation, just as the parties can voluntarily agree to the terms of any form of ADR. For example, the parties may agree that if the case is not settled, the mediator may then become the arbitrator and actually decide the case at a later arbitration hearing date. This would be atypical since the mediator has just become privy to the most intimate details of the case, including strengths and weaknesses of each side of the case. However, in some instances, the parties may believe that the mediator is so extremely fair and so knowledgeable in the particular area of dispute that they will agree to him or her transforming into being the arbitrator in the event of an unsuccessful mediation. As mentioned, while this procedure would be atypical, it points out the enormous flexibility in utilizing the ADR process. It is limited only by the imagination and creativity of the parties and their attorneys.

Baseball Arbitration
A form of ADR in which each side provides the arbitrator with a final number. The arbitrator picks one or the other.

To expand upon that imagination and creativity, if the case is not settled by the end of the day (or days) at a mediation, it sometimes happens that the parties may agree to allow the mediator to become the arbitrator and quickly resolve the dispute by "baseball arbitration." After a day or more of mediation, the mediator is now extremely knowledgeable about the case. In **baseball arbitration**, each side puts down a realistic number that each side believes is what the arbitrator should award. The arbitrator must choose only one of the two numbers. The arbitrator will pick the award that the arbitrator believes is closer to the proper award in the case. This form of baseball arbitration is actually called "day baseball arbitration." The arbitrator is aware of both of the submitted awards before picking the number that the arbitrator believes is most appropriate and just. The procedure forces the parties to become more realistic in their numbers as each side hopes its number will be closer to the number the arbitrator has in mind. In "night baseball arbitration," each party's award is kept secret from the arbitrator. The arbitrator then issues his or her award number. The party's submitted award number that is mathematically closer to the arbitrator's award becomes the award. While these examples are provided to demonstrate the great flexibility and creativity with ADR, the more typical situation is simply that if the case is not resolved by mediation, the parties will proceed with their case in court or will select a different arbitrator(s) to decide the case.

Exhibit 1-4 is a sample letter from a mediator requesting certain information from the attorneys before a mediation is held. Exhibit 1-5 is a sample agreement the parties would sign before commencing the mediation. In a mediation, the personal injury paralegal will likely assist the attorney in assembling and providing information requested by the mediator. In addition to information required by the mediator, it may be important to provide other information to the mediator that a

EXHIBIT 1-4 Mediator's Letter

January 26, 2012

Re: Adams v. Long

Dear Counsel:

The above-entitled matter has been scheduled for an all-day mediation on February 20, 2012, commencing at 9:00 a.m. at the Smith Law Firm at the above address.

If we are to have a successful mediation, it is important that the following occur:

1. Each side must have a person with <u>authority</u> to settle the case at the mediation. (If one of the parties intends to not have a person with authority attend the mediation, then counsel must contact me.)
2. Each side must set aside the entire day to ensure that the mediation process is given a fair opportunity to work.
3. If there is a subrogation issue involved, I ask that you have that resolved, if possible, before the mediation.

At least three days before the mediation, e-mail to me a brief statement outlining the following:

1. The strengths and weaknesses of your case;
2. The strengths and weaknesses of your opponent's case;
3. Your confidential view of the probable settlement range;
4. Settlement negotiations to date;
5. Venue of the case and trial date, if applicable;
6. Names of the individuals who are going to accompany you to the mediation; and
7. Is the mediation voluntary or court ordered?

All of the information submitted to me will be treated as confidential and will not be shared with the other side. I am enclosing a copy of my qualifications and the Mediation Agreement that will be signed on the date of the mediation.

I look forward to seeing you on February 20, 2012. I sincerely hope that this matter will be settled at the mediation.

Sincerely,

SMITH LAW FIRM

John L. Smith

JLS:ir

EXHIBIT 1-5 Mediation Agreement

This agreement is entered into between John L. Smith (herein called the mediator) and the undersigned parties who have agreed to participate in a settlement procedure to be conducted by the mediator. The purpose of the mediation is to build a mutually agreeable resolution of all claims each may have against the other arising out of the following transaction:

The participants agree to abide by the following rules:

GOOD FAITH	Each party will make a good faith effort to settle this matter. To that end, each promises to be open, candid, and flexible in their efforts to resolve this dispute.
ATTENDANCE	The parties themselves along with the attorney responsible for the case will attend the mediation session. A representative of the insurance carrier that may be interested in the outcome of the mediation will PERSONALLY attend the mediation and will have FULL AUTHORITY to settle on behalf of the insurer.
MEDIATOR'S DUTY	I understand and agree that the mediator does not represent any of us. The mediator has no duty to provide advice or information to me or to ensure that I have an understanding of the problems and/or the consequences of my actions. The mediator's function is to promote and facilitate voluntary resolution of the matter. The mediator shall have no responsibility concerning the fairness or legality of any mediated settlement agreement.
CONFIDENTIALITY	The mediator, parties, and attendees agree that mediation sessions are settlement negotiations and are confidential to the extent required by applicable law. The parties and attendees agree that they will not (1) use any part of the mediation or any statement or disclosure made in the mediation in any future proceedings; (2) subpoena documents or other information relating to the mediation; (3) subpoena or attempt to require John L. Smith to testify or produce documents or information relating to the subject matter of this mediation. Any party or attendee who signs this Agreement who later attempts to compel such testimony or production, shall be liable for and shall indemnify the mediator for his expenses, cost, and time spent (at the hourly rate set forth herein) and all reasonable attorney fees that the mediator incurred in responding to such compulsion.
PAYMENT	It is agreed that John L. Smith's fees will be billed at $400.00 per hour for all mediated conferences, outside preparation time, telephone calls, travel time, and scheduling. Mr. Smith will also be reimbursed for out-of-pocket expenses incurred in the process. Unless otherwise agreed, the fees and expenses will be borne equally by the parties. In the event that the parties do not pay the mediator's fee, the lawyers or law firm that retained the mediator shall be ultimately responsible for and shall pay their respective client's portion of the mediator's fees. If the controversy or dispute is settled or cancelled prior to the scheduled mediation, the mediator will have the option to charge a fee for any time spent in scheduling, telephone calls, and/or reviewing material that may have been submitted.
QUALIFICATIONS	Pursuant to qualification of State Statute, a written statement of the qualification of the mediator is attached hereto.

Dated this _____Day of _____, 2012.

_____
John L. Smith, Mediator

_____
Plaintiff(s)

_____
Attorney for Plaintiff(s)

_____
Defendant(s) _____

_____
Attorney for Defendant(s)

party believes has an important bearing on the case. These could be items such as a physician's medical report, excerpts from medical records, the motor vehicle crash report, a letter, or other documents that have an important bearing in settlement negotiations.

NEUTRAL EVALUATION

Neutral evaluation is an ADR procedure in which the parties agree that they will each submit their case position to a neutral person who will provide a written evaluation concerning the issues in the case. Both sides may hold a particular attorney or retired judge in high esteem believing him or her to be fair and extremely knowledgeable in the area of law or type of case involved. Each side will prepare a written submission to the evaluator outlining each side's case. The neutral evaluator will then prepare a letter or report outlining his or her honest evaluation of the case. The issues may be liability only or damages only or both liability and damages or some other issue. The report or letter from the neutral evaluator is not binding. However, because of the respect each side holds for the evaluator, it can result in one side reconsidering its position if the evaluator's evaluation is closer to the other side's evaluation. Mutual respect for the evaluator can sometimes bring about a reconsideration of a party's position leading to a settlement of the case.

Neutral Evaluation
Non-binding ADR procedure in which the parties agree that they will each submit their side of the case to a neutral person who will provide a written evaluation concerning the issues in the case.

SUMMARY JURY TRIAL

Summary jury trial is another commonly used ADR procedure. Typically, the court will assemble a select number of people, usually six or eight to hear a mock trial. People who have been summoned for jury duty may be given the option of sitting on a real case or participating in a mock summary jury trial, either of which will provide jury service credit. Sometimes, the mock jury panel will not be told it is not a real case and the jury will believe it is deciding a real case. Each side gives an opening statement and a final argument. Typically, no witnesses are called and no exhibits are introduced, but it can also occur with a limited amount of evidence being taken. From this brief sampling of the case the jury then returns a verdict. This likewise is non-binding unless, of course, the parties agree that it is binding, keeping in mind that parties can agree to resolve their case in any way they see fit. While not binding, the decision of the impartial jury, just like the neutral evaluator, may have a softening effect on the side that did not prevail, and it may prompt settlement.

Summary Jury Trial
A non-binding ADR technique in which a select number of people are assembled to hear a mock trial and a jury will render a mock verdict.

FLEXIBILITY OF ADR

As can be seen, voluntary ADR is limited only by the creativity and imagination of the parties and the attorneys. There is no one standard, uniform, rigid way of resolving disputes. The parties are free to engage in one or more forms of ADR or a combination of several. They may, by agreement, come up with a traditional approach or a novel approach to resolving their dispute. In theory, they could agree to resolve a dispute with a flip of a coin. They could agree to resolve a dispute by locking themselves in a room for a minimum of four hours and if the case is not resolved, then they go to trial—or then they go to mediation. ADR is any conceivable method (legal, of course) that resolves a dispute short of involving a court trial or a jury trial.

With an understanding of the role of the personal injury paralegal, the history of tort law, legal theory, the public policy purposes for tort law, tort reform, and the bases for tort law, the first tort will be examined. That first tort is negligence.

THE APPENDICES

As progression is made through the various chapters, the student will need to refer to the appendix. It is a good idea to peruse the appendix at this point in order to have a general familiarity with it. Because many of the forms in the appendix will be used for class assignments and may even be useful when the paralegal enters the workforce, the entire appendix is perforated, allowing pages to be easily removed. Organizationally, the appendix is broken down into three portions and a table of contents for each is provided for easy reference.

Appendix 1 is the general portion of the appendix. It consists of samples of the following: a client acceptance letter, a client rejection letter, a written client settlement authorization, a contingency fee agreement, and a settlement demand letter. Also included are standard time entries and a daily time sheet. The paralegal, whether on the plaintiff's side or the defendant's side, will need to become proficient at recording time spent working on a particular case.

Appendix 2 is a compilation of many important medical documents relating to the medical aspect of a case including, but not limited to, such items as a proper HIPAA medical authorization, a letter requesting medical records, sample medical records, a sample medical summary, and various medical abbreviations, medical symbols, and diagrams.

Appendix 3 is the insurance portion of the appendix. This contains an insurance checklist for the paralegal to make sure that all relevant important insurance issues in a case are addressed. There is also an actual automobile insurance policy contained in Appendix 3, which will prove vital in the later study of the chapters on insurance.

GRAMMAR RESOURCES

Using proper English and developing good grammar skills in writing will be emphasized throughout this textbook. Some helpful websites for the student in this area are the following:

http://grammar.quickanddirtytips.com/
http://owl.english.purdue.edu/
http://www.kentlaw.edu/academics/lrw/grinker/LWTA.htm

CASE 1.1 Hypothetical Case: Developing Workplace Skills

E-mail

To: Paralegal

From: Bruno Whiplashki, Esq.

Re: New file

One of our former personal injury clients, Bill Shaydee, was just in to see me this afternoon. I didn't have much time to meet with him. As you know, I'm getting ready to go on my four-day vacation with my dear wife, as it's our upcoming anniversary this week. I'm in a huge hurry to get to the airport.

Shaydee bought a new condominium here in town as an investment about a year ago. He believes with the good economy in this state, the condo should double in value in five years because of its location. Shortly after moving in, he noticed some problems in the unit. The hot water is lukewarm more often than not and water pressure is weak. Also, he can't regulate the room temperature. It's either way too hot or way too cold. He's had numerous conversations with representatives of the owner/developer of the project, Scoundrel, Inc., incorporated in this state. Scoundrel apparently has made some half-baked efforts to fix things but they haven't fixed anything. Shaydee's patience has worn thin. He told me he hasn't given any "Claim Notice" yet but he doesn't understand the CC&R (Covenants, Conditions, and Restrictions) documents that their manager, Willy Nelson, is supposed to drop off today. He wants to sue Scoundrel here in state court. He thinks a jury would be very sympathetic to him and give a good verdict.

Just as I'm going out the door, the manager of the condo project dropped off three pages from the Condo Association's CC&R's, which I've attached to this e-mail. I just had a brief moment to review the first page and skim the other two. I will be back in the office on Monday at which time I need your response to this done.

In just briefly reviewing the first page all I can tell you is that our client, Bill, would be the "Claimant" and Scoundrel would be the "Respondent." No claim notice given yet. Saw something about mediation. Please give me a brief memo (no more than one page) and answer these questions:

1. Can Bill sue Scoundrel in court like he wants to do? Why or why not? Explain answer.
2. If not, what kind or kinds of ADR are provided in the three pages of documents?
3. I saw something about mediation on page 50. Can we just start out with mediation if we have to do ADR or do we have to do something else before we can even do mediation? Explain.
4. If arbitration is in there, can we appeal? Why or why not?
5. Any serious consequences to our client's claim if we don't meet any ADR deadlines? If so, what are they?

As always, will need your time sheet. See you Monday.

BW

(Continued)

CASE 1.1 *(Continued)*

Mr. Whiplashki –
Bill said to drop
this off for your
review – 3 pages.
Thanks.

Willy

11.5 <u>Mediation</u>. The ~~Claimant and the Respondent~~ shall negotiate in good faith in an attempt to resolve the claim. If the Parties do not resolve the Claim through negotiation within thirty (30) days after the date of the Claim Notice or within such longer period as may be agreed upon by the Parties ("Termination of Negotiations"), Claimant shall have thirty (30) additional days within which to submit the Claim to mediation by the American Arbitration Association ("AAA") or such other independent mediation service selected by mutual agreement of the Claimant and the Respondent. If Claimant does not submit the Claim to mediation within thirty (30) days after Termination of Negotiations, Claimant shall be deemed to have waived the Claim, and Respondent shall be released and discharged from any and all liability to Claimant on account of such Claim. If the Parties do not settle the Claim within thirty (30) days after submission of the matter to the mediation process, or within such time as determined reasonable or appropriate by the mediator, the mediator shall issue a notice of termination of the mediation proceedings ("Termination of Mediation Notice"). The Termination of Mediation Notice shall

(Continued)

CASE 1.1 (*Continued*)

set forth when and where the Parties met, that the Parties are at an impasse, and the date that mediation was terminated.

    11.6   **Binding Arbitration**. In the event a Claim is not resolved by mediation, the Claimant shall have ninety (90) days after the date of the Termination of Mediation Notice to submit the Claim to binding arbitration in accordance with this <u>Section 11.6</u>. If the Claimant fails to timely submit the Claim to arbitration, then the Claim shall be deemed waived and abandoned and the Respondent shall be relieved of any and all liability to Claimant arising out of the Claim. A Claimant may only submit a Claim in arbitration on its own behalf. No Claimant may submit a Claim in arbitration as a representative or member of a class, and no Claim may be arbitrated as a class action. The Association, the Unit Owners and all Declarant Parties agree that all Claims that are not resolved by negotiation or mediation shall be resolved exclusively by arbitration conducted in accordance with this <u>Section 11.6</u>. The Association, the Unit Owners and all Declarant Parties waive their right to have a Claim resolved by a court, including, without limitation, the right to file a legal action as the representative or member of a class or in any other representative capacity. The Claimant and Respondent shall cooperate in good faith to assure that all Declarant Parties who may be liable to the Claimant or Respondent with respect to the Claim are made parties to the arbitration. If the Claimant submits the Claim to binding arbitration in accordance with this <u>Section 11.6</u>, the arbitration shall be conducted in accordance with the following rules:

    (a)   **Initiation of Arbitration**. The arbitration shall be initiated by either party delivering to the other a Notice of Intention to Arbitrate as provided for in the AAA Commercial Arbitration Rules or such other rules as the AAA may determine to be applicable (the "AAA Rules").

    (b)   **Governing Procedures**. The arbitration shall be conducted in accordance with the AAA Rules, ~~[redacted]~~ In the event of a conflict between the AAA Rules and this <u>Section 11.6</u>, the provisions of this <u>Section 11.6</u> shall govern.

    (c)   **Appointment of Arbitrator**. The parties shall appoint a single Arbitrator by mutual agreement. If the parties have not agreed within ten (10) days of the date of the Notice of Intention to Arbitrate on the selection of an arbitrator willing to serve, the AAA shall appoint a qualified Arbitrator to serve. Any arbitrator chosen in accordance with this <u>Subsection (c)</u> is referred to in this <u>Section 11.6</u> as the "Arbitrator".

    (d)   **Qualifications of Arbitrator**. The Arbitrator shall be neutral and impartial. The Arbitrator shall be fully active in such Arbitrator's occupation or profession, knowledgeable as to the subject matter involved in the dispute, and experienced in arbitration proceedings. The foregoing shall not preclude otherwise qualified retired lawyers or judges from acting as the Arbitrator.

    (e)   **Disclosure**. Any candidate for the role of Arbitrator shall promptly disclose to the parties all actual or perceived conflicts of interest

(*Continued*)

CASE 1.1 (*Continued*)

involving the dispute or the parties. No Arbitrator may serve if such person has a conflict of interest involving the subject matter of the dispute or the parties. If an Arbitrator resigns or becomes unwilling to continue to serve as an Arbitrator, a replacement shall be selected in accordance with the procedure set forth in Subsection 11.6.(c).

(f) <u>Compensation</u>. The Arbitrator shall be fully compensated for all time spent in connection with the arbitration proceedings in accordance with the Arbitrator's usual hourly rate unless otherwise agreed to by the parties, for all time spent by the Arbitrator in connection with the arbitration proceeding. Pending the final award, the Arbitrator's compensation and expenses shall be advanced equally by the parties.

(g) <u>Preliminary Hearing</u>. Within thirty (30) days after the Arbitrator has been appointed, a preliminary hearing among the Arbitrator and counsel for the parties shall be held for the purpose of developing a plan for the management of the arbitration, which shall then be memorialized in an appropriate order. The matters which may be addressed include, in addition to those set forth in the AAA Rules, the following: (i) definition of issues; (ii) scope, timing and types of discovery, if any; (iii) schedule and place(s) of hearings; (iv) setting of other timetables; (v) submission of motions and briefs; (vi) whether and to what extent expert testimony will be required, whether the Arbitrator should engage one or more neutral experts, and whether, if this is done, engagement of experts by the parties can be obviated or minimized; (vii) whether and to what extent the direct testimony of witnesses will be received by affidavit or written witness statement; and (viii) any other matters which may promote the efficient, expeditious, and cost-effective conduct of the proceeding.

(h) <u>Management of the Arbitration</u>. The Arbitrator shall actively manage the proceedings as the Arbitrator deems best so as to make the proceedings expeditious, economical and less burdensome than litigation.

(i) <u>Confidentiality</u>. All papers, documents, briefs, written communication, testimony and transcripts as well as any and all arbitration decisions shall be confidential and not disclosed to anyone other than the Arbitrator, the parties or the parties' attorneys and expert witnesses (where applicable to their testimony), except that upon prior written consent of all parties, such information may be divulged to additional third parties. All third parties shall agree in writing to keep such information confidential.

"I'm a paralegal, son, I know what it's like to do things you don't want to do."

CHAPTER **SUMMARY**

The primary purpose of the plaintiff personal injury legal team is to "build up" the plaintiff's personal injury case. The primary purpose of the defense personal injury team is to "tear down" the plaintiff's personal injury case. There are certain traits or characteristics that define a good personal injury paralegal.

There are two basic sources of law in the United States— common law ("judge made") and statutory law (statutes enacted by legislative bodies). Our common law is based upon the English common law. The common law as derived from England forms the basis for common law in all states in the United States except for Louisiana whose law derives

from the Napoleonic Code of 1804. Besides the two primary sources of law—common law and statutory law—law is also based upon a constitution, whether the U.S. Constitution or a state's constitution. There is also a field of law surrounding administrative agencies, state and federal. The various Restatements are published by the American Law Institute. They are not a primary source of law, but they are an important secondary source of law. Restatements are frequently cited by courts in their judicial opinions.

In legal theory, legislatures make the law and judges interpret the law. However, there is a centuries-old debate about whether or not judges themselves also "make the law" and, if so, whether or not they should. One side of the debate takes the position that judges need never make law because there are always certain guiding legal principles. To try to make new law interferes with the function of the legislature. The other side takes the position that a judge needs discretion to make law to reflect current social, economic, and political circumstances. This side argues that the framers of a statute or constitution could not possibly have envisioned all ramifications of that statute or constitution at the time it was enacted. Further, in trying to follow case law, there are certain cases—ones of "first impression" in which there is no precedent, and the judge must make new law.

A tort is a wrongful act or omission other than a breach of contract that injures another person in their person or property, giving rise to civil liability in the form of money damages. The word "tort" is an old French word derived from the Latin word "*torquere*," which means "something twisted or wrong" or "to twist." The person committing a tort is the "tortfeasor." The injured party is the "victim" or "the injured party." When suit is commenced, the tortfeasor becomes the defendant and the injured party becomes the plaintiff.

A personal injury is an injury to one's body, mind, or emotions. The field of personal injury law is broader than the field of tort law. The personal injury field involves a basic understanding of the law of torts as well as the laws of civil procedure and evidence. Other skill areas required of the personal injury paralegal are legal research and writing, interviewing clients and witnesses, as well as an understanding of medical issues and insurance issues.

The primary public policy rationale for tort law is to compensate an injured party with reasonable money damages. Other purposes are justice, deterrence, efficient allocation or distribution of risk, and setting minimum standards of conduct.

Tort reform is a movement concerned with making changes in the tort system in the United States. This has arisen from a concern over the volume of civil cases flooding the court system, the problem of excessive jury awards (actual and perceived), increased costs, and the concern with frivolous lawsuits that have no merit. Avenues of approach to tort reform have included shortening civil statutes of limitation, placing limitations on certain damage awards ("caps"), and adopting the English Rule concerning attorneys' fees. The English Rule means that the losing party pays the other side's attorneys fees. The American Rule means that each side pays their own attorneys fees, regardless of who wins or loses, unless a statute or contract provides otherwise. There are two basic types of attorney's fees—contingency and hourly. The contingency fee is paid only if the attorney wins the case and makes a recovery. The hourly fee is paid regardless of whether the party wins or loses. There is a difference between attorney's fees and costs. Costs include items such as court filing fees, witness fees and mileage reimbursement, and expert witness fees.

Tort law is predicated upon three main bases. These are negligence, intentional torts, and strict liability. Negligence is based upon the tortfeasor's act or omission, which amounts to a failure to use due care under the circumstances. Intentional torts are based upon the tortfeasor's intentional or purposeful action. Strict liability is typically based upon abnormally dangerous activities and animals, wild and domestic, as well as unreasonably dangerous products.

Alternative dispute resolution (ADR) is any method of resolving a civil dispute without the involvement of the court process in which a judge or jury decides the case. It is typically cheaper and quicker than pursuing the traditional legal process. Arbitration is a form of ADR in which the dispute is submitted to either one arbitrator or a panel of arbitrators, typically three. In binding arbitration, the decision of the arbitrator is final and binding with no appeal allowed. Mediation is another form of ADR. The mediator does not have the power to decide the case. The mediator is placed in the role of a facilitator who goes back and forth between the two sides with the goal of bringing about a voluntary settlement. A neutral evaluation is an ADR procedure in which the parties agree that they will each submit their side of the case to a neutral person who will provide a written evaluation concerning the issue(s) in the case. A summary jury trial is a procedure in which a selected group of people acts as a jury. Based on each side's opening statement and closing argument only, the jury renders a decision, which is not binding on the parties.

KEY TERMS

Statute of Limitation	American Law Institute (ALI)	Deterrence
Common Law	Case of First Impression	Punitive Damages
Statutory Law	Tort	Exemplary Damages
Stare Decisis	Contract	Distribution of Risk
Precedent	Tortfeasor	Standards of Conduct
Reception Statutes	Personal Injury	Tort Reform
Constitution	Compensation	English Rule
Administrative Law	Compensatory Damages	American Rule
Restatements of the Law	Justice	Contingency Fee

Negligence   Arbitration   Neutral Evaluation
Intentional Torts   Binding Arbitration   Summary Jury Trial
Strict Liability   Mediation
Alternative Dispute Resolution (ADR)   Baseball Arbitration

REVIEW **QUESTIONS**

1. What is your goal or purpose for taking this class? For becoming a paralegal? For becoming a personal injury paralegal?

2. Certain traits of a good personal injury paralegal are outlined at the beginning of this chapter. Do you possess any of those traits? What other traits do you believe would be valuable to a competent, successful personal injury paralegal?

3. Assume that as a paralegal in a personal injury law firm, you sent an e-mail to your plaintiff client. Intending to copy your firm's expert witness, John Black, you inadvertently sent the e-mail copy to the defense attorney, John Blackman. What do you do now?

4. Before reading this chapter, did you realize that the basic foundation for our common law is based upon the English common law? The United States fought the bitter, bloody Revolutionary War in order to be free from British rule. In spite of that, why do you think this country wanted to retain its enemy's common law?

5. Do judges make law in the sense that they "legislate from the bench"? Should they? Why or why not? From only the brief exchanges quoted in the text concerning Justice Kagan's confirmation hearings and Justice Alito's confirmation hearings, are there any clues about which side of the legal theory debate each might fall?

6. In deciding a case, do you think some judges know what their decision will be and, to that end, they set out to research the law to justify their decision as opposed to being uncertain as to what the law is and then researching the law to reach the correct decision?

7. What are the rationales or goals to be achieved with tort law?

8. How and why does tort reform seek to alter our tort law system of so many years?

9. A jurisdiction currently has no restriction on attorneys' fees other than ethical rules that provide they must be reasonable. The current, typical contingency fee in this jurisdiction ranges from 30% to 50%. What do you think would be the effect on personal injury cases if this jurisdiction enacted a statute stating that attorneys' contingency fees could not exceed 10% through trial and could not exceed 15% if an appeal were required?

10. What is the difference between the English Rule and the American Rule? If the English Rule were adopted in your jurisdiction, what do you think would be its effect on a person with a personal injury case? Would it affect some people more than others? Which ones and why?

11. What is the difference between the contingency fee agreement contained in Exhibit 1-3 above and the contingency fee agreement contained in Appendix 1 at Exhibit 1-4A insofar as the client's responsibility to reimburse file expenses in the event there is no recovery of money?

12. What are the three traditional bases of tort law?

13. Define ADR, provide examples, and explain the difference between mediation and arbitration.

chapter 2

NEGLIGENCE: DUTY AND BREACH OF DUTY

"It takes less time to do a thing right than it does to explain why you did it wrong."

Henry Wadsworth Longfellow

Negligence

Negligence is the failure to use due care or reasonable care under the circumstances that causes loss, damage, or injury to the injured party for which the injured party may seek civil money damages. As discussed in Chapter 1, negligence is synonymous with the words "carelessness" and "fault."

Beginning with the discussion of this first tort and continuing throughout, the student will note that there are always certain unique elements making up a particular tort. For the plaintiff to make out a ***prima facie* case,** the plaintiff must offer proof of each element that makes up that tort. The word "*prima facie*" is derived from Latin and one meaning is "at first sight." Because a tort is defined by certain elements, it means that the plaintiff has the burden of proof of providing facts as to each element. Failure to establish proof of each required element will result in the court dismissing the plaintiff's case as a matter of law at the outset and there will be no trial. Assuming that plaintiff makes out a *prima facie* case, the burden shifts to the defendant. If the defendant then provides proof that is contrary to plaintiff's proof, there is now a "fact issue" for the jury, judge, or arbitrator to decide.

The tort of negligence has four well-defined elements, each of which will be discussed in detail in this and later chapters:

1. Duty
2. Breach of duty
3. Causation
4. Damages

LEARNING OBJECTIVES

After studying this chapter, you should be able to:

- Identify the four basic elements of the tort of negligence.

- Differentiate between the concept of a "reasonably foreseeable plaintiff" and a "reasonably foreseeable injury."

- Recognize that a duty to use reasonable care is measured by the objective "reasonable person" standard.

- Articulate the concept of the "emergency rule" as it bears on the duty to use reasonable care.

- Recite the elements of the concept of "*res ipsa loquitur.*"

- Recognize the concept of "negligence *per se*" as it relates to breach of duty.

Prima Facie Case

This term is derived from Latin and one meaning is "at first sight." Because a tort is defined by certain elements, it means that the plaintiff has the burden of proof of establishing facts as to each element.

Duty—The First Element

Duty
An obligation; in tort law, a legal obligation not a moral obligation. It is the first element of negligence, meaning that a person has a duty to act reasonably or to reasonably refrain from acting in such a way so as to not cause harm or injury to another person.

Act of Commission
An affirmative negligent act. See "misfeasance."

Act of Omission
A negligent failure to act. See "nonfeasance."

Misfeasance
An affirmative negligent act as opposed to a failure to act.

Nonfeasance
A negligent failure to act. See "act of omission."

Another good word for **duty** is obligation. A person has a duty or an obligation to act reasonably or to reasonably refrain from acting in such a way as to not cause harm or injury to another. Negligence may consist of an **act of commission**, which is an affirmative negligent act, or an **act of omission**, which is a negligent failure to act. Also, the technical legal term **misfeasance** is an affirmative negligent act, whereas **nonfeasance** is a negligent failure to act. Operating a motor vehicle in excess of a posted speed limit is an example of an affirmative act. Failing to repair a heavy, loose bracket on a wall that comes loose and falls on a person is an example of an act of omission.

Duty, the first element of negligence, presents a legal question that is to be decided by the court, not the jury. It is conceivable that a court, in certain cases, could also decide as a matter of law one or more of the other elements of negligence, but it is unlikely. When the phrase "as a matter of law" is used, it means that the issue is taken from the jury, and the issue is decided by the judge. Breach of duty, causation, and damages are typical issues for the jury to decide. Duty, however, is a function of the court. Whether or not a duty is owed by the defendant to the plaintiff is a threshold legal question for the court to answer.

The court, in fulfilling this function of determining duty, will *first* determine whether the defendant owed a duty of care to the plaintiff and *second* determine the scope of that duty. If the defendant's unreasonable action creates a risk of injury to the plaintiff, then the defendant owes the plaintiff the duty to exercise due care. Examine this hypothetical case:

> Leonardo is exiting a supermarket pushing a grocery cart full of groceries. As he enters the parking lot area heading for his SUV, he receives a text message on his cell phone, which he is carrying in one hand. His other hand is pushing the grocery cart. He now becomes preoccupied with checking the text message that just arrived. As he is looking down and focusing his attention on his cell phone, he ends up ramming his cart into Reese, an elderly lady who is putting groceries into the trunk of her car. She is knocked down, rendered unconscious, and sustains a personal injury consisting of a broken leg.

Did Leonardo have a duty or obligation to act reasonably and pay attention to where he was pushing his cart in a parking lot with vehicles and people? From what is known of this simple fact scenario, the answer is yes.

SCOPE OF DUTY

The second legal question for the court is to define the scope of the duty. Clearly, Reese was within the scope of Leonardo's duty to use reasonable care. She was in the same parking lot as Leonardo and close enough to him that his actions or inactions would have an impact on her personal safety. Leonardo, however, does not owe this legal duty to all people everywhere. He would not owe a duty to those people in a parking lot of a competing grocery store ten miles away, for example.

What if Leonardo stopped in the parking lot and then used both hands to operate his cell phone in order to return the text message? While focused on the task of his text message, unbeknownst to him, the shopping cart started rolling. This is because the grocery store is located in a hilly area. What if the cart ended up rolling approximately 100 feet—all the way down to the bottom of the hilly incline and into the street striking a pedestrian crossing the street, which caused a personal injury to the pedestrian? This is a more difficult question of duty for the court, is it not? Did Leonardo owe a duty of reasonable care to a person in a street almost 100 feet away? The answer will lie in which tort theory of duty is adopted, as outlined in the famous case of *Palsgraf v. Long Island Railroad Co.*, 248 N.Y. 339 (1928).

THE *PALSGRAF* CASE

A portion of the *Palsgraf* case is reprinted in Exhibit 2-1.

EXHIBIT 2-1 Relevant Case Law

Helen Palsgraf, Respondent, v. The Long Island Railroad Company, Appellant.

Court of Appeals of New York.

Cardozo, Ch. J.

Plaintiff was standing on a platform of defendant's railroad after buying a ticket to go to Rockaway Beach. A train stopped at the station, bound for another place. Two men ran forward to catch it. One of the men reached the platform of the car without mishap, though the train was already moving. The other man, carrying a package, jumped aboard the car, but seemed unsteady as if about to fall. A guard on the car, who had held the door open, reached forward to help him in, and another guard on the platform pushed him from behind. In this act, the package was dislodged, and fell upon the rails. It was a package of small size, about fifteen inches long, and was covered by a newspaper. In fact it contained fireworks, but there was nothing in its appearance to give notice of its contents. The fireworks when they fell exploded. The shock of the explosion threw down some scales at the other end of the platform, many feet away. The scales struck the plaintiff, causing injuries for which she sues.

The conduct of the defendant's guard, if a wrong in its relation to the holder of the package, was not a wrong in its relation to the plaintiff, standing far away. Relatively to her it was not negligence at all. Nothing in the situation gave notice that the falling package had in it the potency of peril to persons thus removed. Negligence is not actionable unless it involves the invasion of a legally protected interest, the violation of a right....

The diversity of interests emphasizes the futility of the effort to build the plaintiff's right upon the basis of a wrong to some one else. The gain is one of emphasis, for a like result would follow if the interests were the same. Even then, the orbit of the danger as disclosed to the eye of reasonable vigilance would be the orbit of the duty. One who jostles one's neighbor in a crowd does not invade the rights of others standing at the outer fringe when the unintended contact casts a bomb upon the ground. The wrongdoer as to them is the man who carries the bomb, not the one who explodes it without suspicion of the danger. Life will have to be made over, and human nature transformed, before prevision so extravagant can be accepted as the norm of conduct, the customary standard to which behavior must conform....

The range of reasonable apprehension is at times a question for the court, and at times, if varying inferences are possible, a question for the jury. Here, by concession, there was nothing in the situation to suggest to the most cautious mind that the parcel wrapped in newspaper would spread wreckage through the station. If the guard had thrown it down knowingly and willfully, he would not have threatened the plaintiff's safety, so far as appearances could warn him. His conduct would not have involved, even then, an unreasonable probability of invasion of her bodily security. Liability can be no greater where the act is inadvertent....

(Continued)

EXHIBIT 2-1 *(Continued)*

The judgment of the Appellate Division and that of the Trial Term should be reversed, and the complaint dismissed, with costs in all courts.

Andrews, J. (dissenting).

Assisting a passenger to board a train, the defendant's servant negligently knocked a package from his arms. It fell between the platform and the cars. Of its contents the servant knew and could know nothing. A violent explosion followed. The concussion broke some scales standing a considerable distance away. In falling they injured the plaintiff, an intending passenger.

Upon these facts may she recover the damages she has suffered in an action brought against the master? The result we shall reach depends upon our theory as to the nature of negligence. Is it a relative concept—the breach of some duty owing to a particular person or to particular persons? Or where there is an act which unreasonably threatens the safety of others, is the doer liable for all its proximate consequences, even where they result in injury to one who would generally be thought to be outside the radius of danger? This is not a mere dispute as to words. We might not believe that to the average mind the dropping of the bundle would seem to involve the probability of harm to the plaintiff standing many feet away whatever might be the case as to the owner or to one so near as to be likely to be struck by its fall. If, however, we adopt the second hypothesis we have to inquire only as to the relation between cause and effect. We deal in terms of proximate cause, not of negligence....

The proposition is this. Every one owes to the world at large the duty of refraining from those acts that may unreasonably threaten the safety of others. Such an act occurs. Not only is he wronged to whom harm might reasonably be expected to result, but he also who is in fact injured, even if he be outside what would generally be thought the danger zone. There needs be duty due the one complaining but this is not a duty to a particular individual because as to him harm might be expected. Harm to some one being the natural result of the act, not only that one alone, but all those in fact injured may complain. We have never, I think, held otherwise. Indeed in the *Di Caprio* case we said that a breach of a general ordinance defining the degree of care to be exercised in one's calling is evidence of negligence as to every one. We did not limit this statement to those who might be expected to be exposed to danger. Unreasonable risk being taken, its consequences are not confined to those who might probably be hurt....

Under these circumstances I cannot say as a matter of law that the plaintiff's injuries were not the proximate result of the negligence. That is all we have before us. The court refused to so charge. No request was made to submit the matter to the jury as a question of fact, even would that have been proper upon the record before us.

The judgment appealed from should be affirmed, with costs.

Source: Palsgraf v. Long Island Railroad Co., 248 N.Y. 339 (1928).

This is the landmark negligence case on breach of duty. It is hard to imagine any law school textbook on torts after 1928 not including it. If a paralegal is familiar with *Palsgraf,* his or her employer will definitely be impressed!

The facts are a bit bizarre. A potential passenger carrying a package wrapped in newspaper, jumped aboard the Long Island Railroad Company train that had proceeded to move forward. He seemed unsteady after the jump so a railroad guard on the train car reached forward to assist him, and a guard on the platform pushed him from behind. In the process, the package became dislodged from the passenger's grip and fell on the rails. As it turned out, the package contained fireworks. There was nothing, however, about the appearance of the package that would give any indication that it contained fireworks. These fireworks exploded so violently that the shock waves knocked over heavy scales located approximately 30 feet away at the other end of the train platform. These scales tipped over on Helen Palsgraf and injured her. She commenced a personal injury lawsuit against the railroad company.

The prominent jurist and Chief Justice of the New York Court of Appeals, Benjamin Cardozo, authored the majority opinion. A strong dissent was issued by Justice Andrews. Justice Cardozo, while noting that tort law must involve a wrong, also noted that the wrong must be directed to the person injured. Mrs. Palsgraf, standing approximately 30 feet away, was outside the radius of danger, often referred to as the **zone of danger**.

Justice Cardozo's reasoning was that there was a clear risk of harm to the passenger carrying the fireworks or to others near him. However, a reasonable person would not foresee any risk to the plaintiff who was 30 feet away. It was also an important fact that there was nothing about the package to put the railroad on notice of its contents. Accordingly, Justice Cardozo found that no duty was owed to her by the railroad company.

The student must read and study the eloquent dissent by Justice Andrews. He takes the position that a duty to use reasonable care to prevent a wrong is owed to virtually everyone, even those outside the zone of danger. The essence of *Palsgraf* is this: According to the Cardozo view, duty is a function of the court, and the court may only impose a duty of care upon a defendant after it is determined that a reasonable person would have foreseen a risk of harm to the plaintiff. In other words, under this narrower view, a duty is owed by a defendant only to a reasonably foreseeable plaintiff who is in the zone of danger. The broader view, advocated by Justice Andrews, is that if a duty is owed to one person, it is owed to everyone who suffers injury as a result of the defendant's breach of duty. Justice Cardozo believed that judges should determine as a matter of law who is a reasonably foreseeable plaintiff to whom a duty is owed. Justice Andrews believed that if it was foreseeable that any plaintiff could be harmed, then this becomes an issue of causation that should be decided by the jury, not the judge. Justice Cardozo focused on the **reasonably foreseeable plaintiff** with a duty owed only to those plaintiffs in the foreseeable zone of danger. Justice Andrews focused on the **reasonably foreseeable injury** with a duty owed to anyone whose personal injury was caused by a negligent tortfeasor.

To analyze the runaway grocery cart example above, under the Cardozo view, there would be no duty to the pedestrian at the bottom of the hill as that pedestrian is clearly out of the zone of danger and is an unforeseeable plaintiff. Under the Andrews view, there would be such a duty. This is because Leonardo committed a wrong and it caused a foreseeable injury to someone whether they were in the zone of danger or not.

Zone of Danger
A test formulated by Justice Cardozo in the *Palsgraf* case states that a defendant owes a duty only to a plaintiff who is in an area the defendant might expect that a plaintiff would be injured.

Reasonably Foreseeable Plaintiff
A plaintiff who is owed a duty of care because the plaintiff is in the foreseeable "zone of danger" (Justice Cardozo view in *Palsgraf*).

Reasonably Foreseeable Injury
A plaintiff who is owed a duty of care that is owed to anyone whose personal injury was caused by a negligent tortfeasor (Justice Andrews view in *Palsgraf*).

DUTY IN FAILING TO ACT

A tortfeasor/defendant may be held liable on a negligence theory based upon a duty of failing to act. Leonardo's act in pushing the grocery cart into Reese was clearly an affirmative act. Difficult duty questions arise when it is alleged that the defendant failed to act. Consider this factual scenario:

> A city police officer was on duty patrolling city streets. He stopped a very intoxicated motorist for speeding. The officer knew or should have known that the operator was intoxicated to the extent that his normal

faculties were impaired and that his continued operation of the vehicle would injure persons upon the public highways. Notwithstanding this, the officer allowed the drunk driver to leave and continue driving on the public highway. Shortly thereafter, the drunk driver collided with an automobile driven by the plaintiff's husband, fatally injuring him. Did the police officer owe a duty to the plaintiff who lost her husband for his failure to apprehend and arrest the drunk driver, thus preventing this deadly collision? The answer is no.

This factual scenario is the actual scenario from the case of *Evett v. City of Inverness*, 224 So.2d 365 (Fla. Dist. Ct. App. 1969). The court in *Evett* stated the issue as "whether the City's police officer owed any duty to the plaintiff's deceased husband, *as an individual,* which would support a cause of action...." (Emphasis added.) The court noted the "well recognized principle of tort law that a fundamental element of actionable negligence is the existence of a duty owed by the person charged with negligence to the person injured." The court held that there was no duty owed to the plaintiff because there must be a duty owed to the individual, which is more than what a public officer owes to the general public. "We hold that the city's police officer ... cannot be held personally liable for damages resulting from his negligence, if any, in the performance of his duties. *If he did negligently permit the intoxicated driver to continue operating his vehicle on the public highway, he still owed no duty to plaintiff's deceased husband in any way different from that owed to any member of the public.*" (Emphasis added.) This is also referred to as the **public duty doctrine**.[1]

> **Public Duty Doctrine**
>
> For a public officer to be liable, a separate duty must be owed to an individual and not a duty owed to the public as a whole.

Returning to the supermarket cart incident with Leonardo, assume that before the collision with the cart, a nearby bystander, Brad, walking in the parking lot with his girlfriend, Angelina, witnessed the cart coming toward Reese. The collision could have been prevented if Brad had yelled out and warned Reese of the impending collision. Instead, in a hurry to buy groceries and head to the beach, he decided to continue on walking and conversing with Angelina. If Reese sued both Leonardo for his affirmative alleged act of negligence and Brad for his alleged negligence in failing to act, would the court likely find a duty on the part of Brad? Probably not. Generally, there is no duty to control the conduct of a third person so as to prevent that third person from causing harm to another. While Brad may have had a moral obligation to take action, he had no legal obligation or duty to act and did not owe Reese a duty to use reasonable care.

Assume that while loading her groceries into her trunk, instead of being struck by Leonardo's cart, Reese suffered a stroke or heart attack. Brad, a trained medic, does nothing to help her. Is there a legal duty on the part of Brad to render aid and assistance to Reese? Brad may have had a moral duty to act—either help Reese himself or call 911—but he had no legal duty to act and did not owe Reese a duty to use reasonable care. A person who did not cause the injury to the injured person has no legal duty to rescue or come to the aid of the injured person. In the first hypothetical, Leonardo would have a duty to come to the aid of Reese after ramming into her with his grocery cart. However, Brad, who had nothing to do with Reese's injury, had no duty to come to her aid. There is a caveat to this general rule, however. If a person decides, as a volunteer (a "Good Samaritan") to come to the aid, assistance, or rescue of a person, then that person owes a duty of reasonable care in performing the aid, assistance, or rescue.

GOOD SAMARITAN LAW

Unless there is a certain relationship, such as physician/patient or parent/child, as examples prior to the illness or injury, no person is under any *legal duty* to provide aid or assistance to any ill or injured person. One's personal or religious beliefs and values, however, may compel a *moral duty* to voluntarily provide such aid or assistance. While there is no legal duty to render aid or assistance to a person, one who voluntarily undertakes such aid or assistance is subject to civil tort liability with money damages. This is because if a person undertakes such aid or assistance, it must be done reasonably.

Because of this potential civil liability on the part of a volunteer, some jurisdictions have enacted "Good Samaritan" statutes. The term is derived from Jesus' parable of the Good Samaritan in Luke 10:30:37. It tells the story of a traveler from Samaria who gives assistance to another traveler of a different religious and ethnic background who had been beaten and robbed by bandits. A **Good Samaritan law** is a statute that provides immunity from suit to those who voluntarily choose, on a moral basis, to tend to others who are ill or injured. The purpose of such law is to encourage a bystander to assist another person in need. Without the benefit of the law, the Good Samaritan might otherwise fear the threat of being sued for causing an aggravated injury or death to the person in need. A Good Samaritan statute reflects the public policy of encouraging humanitarian efforts toward a person in need without the fear of a later lawsuit from that person.

Good Samaritan Law
Statutes enacted to provide immunity from suit to those who voluntarily choose, on a moral basis, to tend to others who are ill or injured.

An interesting twist is provided by the Vermont Good Samaritan law, Title 12, V.S.A. Section 519. This statute provides immunity from civil liability in damages for a person without compensation rendering reasonable assistance to one in grave physical harm unless he or she acted with gross negligence. This is the twist:

> (a) A person who knows that another is exposed to grave physical harm shall, to the extent that the same can be rendered without danger or peril to himself or without interference with important duties owed to others, give reasonable assistance to the exposed person unless that assistance or care is being provided by others....
> (c) A person who willfully violates subsection (a) of this section shall be fined not more than $100.00.

With some qualifications, the statute mandates an affirmative duty to provide reasonable assistance to one exposed to grave physical harm.

In our grocery parking lot example above, Brad and Angelina could be in violation of this statute for *failing* to provide assistance to Reese who would appear to be in danger of grave physical harm. This statute provides an extremely rare exception to the general common law rule that a Good Samaritan has no legal duty to come to the aid or assistance of an ill or injured person. This particular statute is also an example of tort liability based upon a statute.

Breach of Duty—The Second Element

Once it has been established that a duty of reasonable care is owed to the plaintiff, the next element that needs to be established is a breach of that duty. **Breach of duty** is a showing by the plaintiff that the defendant's act or omission exposed the plaintiff to an unreasonable risk of injury or harm. If there is an act or omission, a duty owed to the plaintiff, and a breach of that duty, a negligent act or

Breach of Duty
The second element of negligence. Defendant's act or omission exposed the plaintiff to an unreasonable risk of injury or harm.

omission has been established. A negligent act or omission, from this point forward, will simply be referred to as "negligent conduct." Establishing breach of duty requires (1) proof of the facts and circumstances of the alleged negligent conduct, and (2) proof that the defendant acted unreasonably under the facts and circumstances.

While the first element of negligence—duty—is a function of the court, whether or not that duty has been breached is typically a function of the jury. However, if the facts are undisputed and no reasonable jury could find for the party against whom the motion is made, the court may rule as a matter of law in favor of a defendant who makes the appropriate motion. Such cases are rare. Most courts are reluctant to take this issue of breach of duty from the jury unless it is extremely clear-cut. The case of *Charlton v. Toys R Us*, 246 P.3d 199 (Wash. App. 2010), reprinted in part in Exhibit 2-2, is illustrative of this point.

EXHIBIT 2-2 Relevant Case Law

Pamela Charlton, Appellant, v. Toys "R" Us—Delaware, Inc., a Foreign Corporation, Respondent.

Court of Appeals of Washington, Division 3.

FACTS AND PROCEDURAL BACKGROUND

In January 2008, Ms. Charlton slipped and fell within several feet of the front door to a Toys R Us store and injured her knee. It had snowed earlier that day and the night before. Ms. Charlton testified, "I ... walked through the parking lot, which was extremely wet to the point where I believe my pants were wet." Clerk's Papers (CP) at 72–73. After entering the store, Ms. Charlton crossed two floor mats and then slipped and fell when she stepped off the second mat onto the floor.

Ms. Charlton did not allege that there was anything on the floor besides water. She did not see the water before her fall and could not describe the amount of water; she explained, "as I was going down, right at that second I saw it, you know, and then I was in it." *Id.* at 31. She also testified, "I know there was water there because my feet, you know, my feet wouldn't have slipped out from underneath me." *Id.* Ms. Charlton did not know how the water got onto the floor or how long it had been there before she entered the store. She did not know if the floor had been recently mopped or cleaned.

In April 2009, Ms. Charlton filed suit against Toys R Us. She alleged it was negligent for failing to keep its floors in a reasonably safe condition and failing to warn of the slippery condition of its floors, claimed she was injured as a result of the store's negligence, and sought compensation.

Following Ms. Charlton's deposition and other discovery, Toys R Us moved for summary judgment, arguing Ms. Charlton could demonstrate no facts suggesting it had breached its duty of care, and specifically, no evidence that an unsafe condition existed or that Toys R Us had actual or constructive notice of the unsafe condition.

The court granted the motion and dismissed Ms. Charlton's claims. She appeals.

ANALYSIS

At issue is whether Ms. Charlton presented sufficient evidence to survive the motion for summary judgment....We engage in de novo review of an order of summary judgment, performing the same inquiry as the trial court....When considering a summary judgment motion, the court must construe all facts and reasonable inferences in the light most favorable to the nonmoving party....

EXHIBIT 2-2 *(Continued)*

Ms. Charlton argues that she demonstrated a genuine issue of fact that the floor of the Toys R Us entryway presented an unreasonable risk of harm to invitees. She points to her own testimony that the floor was either linoleum or tile, was wet, and she fell " 'because there was no traction.' " Br. of Appellant at 3. She argues nothing more was required to demonstrate an issue of fact, because "everyone knows that a floor of vinyl or tile is slippery when wet." *Id.* at 9.

Washington cases make it clear that the mere presence of water on a floor where the plaintiff slipped is not enough to prove negligence on the part of the owner or occupier of the building. To prove negligence, the plaintiff must prove that water makes the floor dangerously slippery and that the owner knew or should have known both that water would make the floor slippery and that there was water on the floor at the time the plaintiff slipped.

Ms. Charlton complains that in dismissing her claim, the trial court erroneously held that a wet floor is never a dangerous condition, as a matter of law, and contends that this position is "absurd." Br. of Appellant at 7, 9. But Ms. Charlton has it backwards—the trial court did not hold that water on a floor is *never* a dangerous condition; it rejected her position that a wet floor is *always* a dangerous condition, and that she was therefore excused from presenting evidence of an unreasonable risk created by this particular wet floor. She failed to present any evidence that the floor in the entryway of the Toys R Us store presented an unreasonable risk of harm when wet. For that reason alone, summary judgment was proper.

We affirm.

Source: Charlton v. Toys R Us, 246 P.3d 199 (Wash App. 2010).

Reasonable Person Standard

Part of the definition of negligence is that a person must use reasonable care to avoid injuring others. That sounds good in theory, but what does it really mean and how is reasonable care or reasonableness determined? One must use that care that a reasonable person would use. Whether or not one acted as a reasonable person would act is an *objective test*. It does not matter that the defendant honestly believed that he or she was acting reasonably. That would be a *subjective test*. The question is how would a reasonable person of ordinary prudence act? Every person owes a duty to act as a reasonable person would act under the same or similar circumstances.[2]

The objective **reasonable person standard** requires an examination not of what the defendant actually did or failed to do, but what the defendant *ought to have done* under the circumstances with which the defendant was faced. Unfortunately, with the advent of the cell phone, texting and driving has become a common practice. However, just because texting and driving may be a common practice now or because a juror may do the same thing, the test is not what might be usual or common practice. In a case before a jury, this practice may have constituted an unreasonable risk of injury to the plaintiff. This is particularly so if the facts and circumstances were that the defendant was texting while driving in heavy traffic going 70 miles per hour resulting in inattention and a resulting collision.

Note the language in the definition of the reasonable person standard, "under the same or similar circumstances." The standard itself of acting reasonably does

Reasonable Person Standard
The test for determining duty in a negligence action. To avoid civil tort liability, a person must act as a reasonable person of ordinary prudence would act under the same or similar circumstances. It is an objective test.

not vary. The standard is always the same. The standard is that which the reasonable person would have exercised under the surrounding circumstances at the time. What may vary are the surrounding circumstances. A motorist may be driving reasonably at 60 miles per hour on a flat, level public highway, with light traffic conditions, excellent weather conditions, and a posted speed limit of 65 miles per hour. However, if the surrounding circumstances drastically change, such as heavy traffic, hilly, curvy roads, a dust storm, or a winter blizzard, it may then be unreasonable to be driving at 60 miles per hour. The amount of care and the type of conduct a reasonable person would use will differ with the surrounding circumstances.

Exceptions to the General Standard of Due Care/Reasonable Care

MINORS

If the tortfeasor is a minor, then the standard is still the same, but the minor's age, intelligence, and experience now become part of the surrounding circumstances. The question becomes: How would a reasonable person with this person's age, education, intelligence, and experience have acted?

Some states have declared that children below a particular age cannot legally be capable of negligence.[3] The opposing view is that stating a predetermined age at which negligence can occur on the part of a child has little basis in logic. One day's difference in age should not serve as the dividing line as to whether or not a child is capable of negligence.[4]

COMMON CARRIERS

While a common carrier such as an airline, train, cab, or bus may be held to the same reasonable person standard, such carriers have traditionally been held to a higher standard of care than other defendants.

PERSONS WITH DISABILITIES

Persons with disabilities are still judged as a reasonable person, but with their disability or impairment as part of the surrounding circumstances. How would a reasonable person with this person's disability of deafness, blindness, or diabetes have acted?

PERSONS WITH SPECIAL KNOWLEDGE, EDUCATION, TRAINING, OR SKILLS

If a defendant possesses certain knowledge, education, training, or skills, such as an attorney, medical doctor, contractor, electrician, accountant, engineer, or architect, the defendant must meet the standard of care exercised by that particular skilled profession or trade. This is true even if the defendant does not actually possess that skilled training.

Workplace Skills Tip

Some state court jurisdictions may have a rule identical or similar to Federal Rule 38 providing that if a party does not timely demand a jury trial, then the case is required to be decided by a judge—a bench trial. The paralegal may be working on a case in which the last thing in the world the attorney wants is a court trial. Assist with making sure that does not happen. While the attorney should know the rules, the paralegal should know the rules also. Be looking over the attorney's shoulder. Be a nag!

Generally, those individuals who are involved in a specialized trade or profession are held to a "national standard" and not a "local standard." Knowledge obtained from national sources, whether publications or organizations, are utilized to resolve local problems faced by the person with special knowledge, education, training, or skills. A contractor would typically be aware of and utilize the International Building Code (IBC). The same is true for an electrician's use of and reliance on the National Electrical Safety Code (NESC) and a plumber's use of and reliance on the Uniform Plumbing Code (UPC).

Medical Malpractice

Physicians used to be held to a standard of care that existed in their local community. However, with national medical certifications, such as a Family Practice certification or a General Surgery certification, the small town doctor is held to the same standard as his big city counterpart. The plaintiff's proof in a medical negligence or medical malpractice case is to establish the standard of medical care and then show a departure from that standard. Unless the conduct of the physician is so obvious or egregious, such as leaving a surgical sponge inside the body or performing a procedure on the wrong body part, expert medical testimony is required to establish the standard and the departure.

Gross Negligence

There is also a concept in negligence called **gross negligence**. Gross negligence means severe or extreme carelessness, bordering on reckless conduct. The standard of reasonable care is used for ordinary negligence. If one is negligent, he or she has fallen below the standard. One who is grossly negligent has plummeted far below the standard.

Gross Negligence
Severe or extreme carelessness bordering on reckless conduct.

The Trier of Fact

Who decides whether the defendant acted as a reasonable person and whether the defendant was negligent or not? The person who decides that issue and all of the other contested issues in a case is called the **trier of fact**. The trier of fact in a personal injury case is typically the jury. The trier of fact could be a judge. The trier of fact could be an arbitrator. Even if a jury trial were permissible, the parties could voluntarily stipulate and agree to have a judge or arbitrator decide a particular case. Oversight on the part of the attorney, however, may

Trier of Fact
The person who decides all of the contested issues in a case, including a personal injury case. The trier of fact may be a jury, a judge, or an arbitrator.

Workplace Skills Tip

When the trier of fact is a jury, the jury's decision is rendered by a "verdict." When the trier of fact is a trial judge, the judge's decision is not a verdict. The judge's decision is typically required to be contained in "Findings of Fact" and "Conclusions of Law." The judge will issue an "Order for Judgment" from which judgment will be entered for the prevailing party. An arbitrator makes an "award." That award will later be reduced to a judgment by a process of bringing a proceeding in court to confirm the judgment.

require a trial by a judge when the attorney was expecting a jury trial. Rule 38 of the Federal Rules of Civil Procedure specifically requires that a timely written demand for a jury trial be made and filed. Further, that rule provides: "*A party waives a jury trial unless its demand is properly served and filed.*" (Emphasis added.)

Typically, it will be up to the jury to determine whether the defendant acted reasonably under the circumstances. The jury has seen and heard all of the witnesses and the documentary evidence, and the judge will instruct the jury on the law. In the final analysis, the jurors will use as a basis for their decision, their own experiences in life and their own collective common sense. It would not be uncommon for a judge, in a jury instruction, to provide guidance to the jury in how to evaluate the testimony of a witness, such as: Will a witness gain or lose if this case is decided a certain way? What is the witness's relationship to the parties? How did a witness learn the facts? What was his or her manner or demeanor? What was his or her age and experience? Did the witness appear to be honest and sincere? Is the witness's testimony reasonable compared with other evidence? It is also typical for the judge to tell the jury that in evaluating testimony they should rely upon their own *experience, good judgment, and common sense.*

Jury Instructions

Learning the substantive law of negligence and the elements that make it up is not merely an academic exercise. The substantive law of negligence will become a part of the development of the personal injury paralegal's workplace skills. This is because the paralegal may be involved in assisting the attorney with the proposed jury instructions that the court will eventually provide to the jury. Most states have their own set of official jury instructions covering virtually every type of case that may be tried before a jury. There are also federal jury instructions. Both state and federal jury instructions may be accessed on either Westlaw or Lexis. These jury instructions may be referred to as "pattern," "model," "approved," or "guide." To be consistent, a jury instruction referenced in the text from this point forward will be referred to as a **Jury Instruction Guide** or JIG. These JIGS are typically prepared by a panel or committee made up of judges, attorneys, and law professors. At the close of the case, the judge will "instruct" or "charge" the jury on the applicable law in the case they have just seen and heard. In addition to the standard JIGs, the judge may utilize a more specialized, tailored jury instruction that either party has submitted or that the judge creates on his or her own.

Jury Instruction Guide (JIG)
A compilation of jury instructions that state the applicable law in a particular jurisdiction; it may be called by other names such as a pattern jury instruction.

EXHIBIT 2-3 Jury Instruction Guide

Negligence and Reasonable Care—Basic Definition

Reasonable care is the care that a reasonable person would use under the same or similar circumstances.

Negligence is the failure to use reasonable care. You should ask yourself what a reasonable person would have done under these same or similar circumstances. Negligence occurs when a person:

1. Does something a reasonable person would not do; or
2. Fails or omits to do something a reasonable person would do.

The duty to use care is based upon the knowledge of danger. The care that a person must exercise in a particular situation is in direct proportion to the degree of danger of injury to himself or to others in the act to be performed. The care necessary to constitute the ordinary care required of a person upon any particular occasion is measured by reference to the circumstances of danger known to him at the time or which he reasonably should have foreseen. The greater the danger, the greater is the care required.

Before the trial commences, in a pretrial order, the trial judge will typically require each party to submit its proposed jury instructions. After receiving proposed jury instructions from each side, the court will determine which particular instructions the court will be utilizing to charge the jury. Jury instructions must correctly and adequately inform the jury of the applicable law and must not mislead or confuse the jury. Submitting proper proposed jury instructions is a crucial task in which the personal injury paralegal may be involved. A case may be won or lost at trial depending upon the giving or failure to give a particular jury instruction on a given point of law. By the same token, the giving or failure to give a particular jury instruction may cause a case to be won or lost on appeal. It is important for the personal injury paralegal to have some background knowledge of various legal theories and principles. This knowledge will be invaluable in assisting the attorney with the law presentation of the client's personal injury case, whether on the building up side or the tearing down side. Having just discussed the issues of negligence and duty of care, a sample JIG on that subject is contained in Exhibit 2-3.

As various principles of tort law are being discussed in this textbook, a sample JIG may be provided to the paralegal student as a further development of workplace skills.

Workplace Skills Tip

Locate the Jury Instruction Guides in your jurisdiction. It is likely they can be accessed online. The authors of these guides, typically attorneys, judges, and law professors, generally do an excellent job of compiling the applicable law in a particular jurisdiction. They tend to reflect the current law in a jurisdiction. They can also be utilized as an additional legal research tool. The JIGs will typically recite the correct law with citations to court decisions and statutes being provided after the language of the instruction. If you are spinning your wheels on a research project, examine the JIGs of your jurisdiction as an aid in your legal research.

Emergency Rule

Certain action or conduct that is unreasonable may be justified in an emergency. The **emergency rule** means that if the defendant is confronted with an emergency, *not of the defendant's own making,* and the defendant does not choose the safest or best course of action, the defendant is not negligent. Assume that motorist Linda Rae is traveling on a public highway keeping a reasonable lookout and traveling at a reasonable speed. Jonathan, her hairdresser, is riding as a passenger in the front seat. Suddenly, seemingly out of nowhere and without warning, a large adult deer bolts in front of Linda Rae's vehicle. She has only enough time to react by sharply swerving to the right to successfully avoid a collision with the deer. However, this maneuver causes the car to go too far to the right and into the ditch. The vehicle strikes a pole and injures her passenger, Jonathan.

The application of the emergency rule depends upon the source or cause of the emergency. If it is a true emergency, and it was not brought about by the defendant's own negligence, it allows for a lesser standard of care. In this example, assume Linda Rae was driving prudently to begin with, it does not matter that she should have, in hindsight, tried to swerve in the other direction, brake, or honk the horn, or done something differently to avoid hitting the deer or the pole. The defendant is now judged by what would be reasonable under the circumstances. The circumstances in this case now happen to be an emergency situation. A sample JIG on the emergency rule is contained in Exhibit 2-4.

Review the decision of *Lawson v. Walker*, 206 S.E.2d 325 (N.C. 1974) contained in Exhibit 2-5 for a good explanation of the emergency rule doctrine.

EXHIBIT 2-4 Jury Instruction Guide

Emergency Rule

One who is suddenly and without warning, confronted by a peril, through no fault of his own, who, in the attempt to escape the peril, does not choose the best or safest way, should not be held negligent because of that choice, unless it was so hazardous that the ordinary, prudent person would not have made it under similar conditions.

EXHIBIT 2-5 Relevant Case Law

Patricia Weaver Lawson v. Vickie Paulette Walker and Roger Dale Walker.

Court of Appeals of North Carolina.

This is an action for damages for personal injuries sustained in an automobile accident allegedly caused by the negligence of defendants. The plaintiff, Patricia Weaver Lawson, was operating her automobile on Seitz Drive just outside Forest City, North Carolina, on 25 February 1972. She was traveling at approximately 20—25 miles per hour. As she came down a hill, she met an automobile operated by defendant Vickie Paulette Walker and owned by defendant Roger Dale Walker. The defendants' automobile swerved across the center line and collided with plaintiff's car causing the injuries complained of. The defendant testified that her fourteen-month-old baby fell from the car seat to the floor and that when she reached to grab her baby the automobile veered to the left and collided with plaintiff's automobile. From a jury verdict in favor of defendant, plaintiff appealed.

Campbell, Judge.

The plaintiff assigns as error the following portion of the charge by the trial court:

EXHIBIT 2-5 *(Continued)*

'Now, in this case, the defendant contends that she was confronted with a sudden emergency. Now, I instruct you that if a person through no negligence on her part is suddenly or unexpectedly confronted with peril arising from either the actual presence or the appearance of imminent danger to herself, danger to herself or to others is not required to use the same judgment that is required when there is more time to decide what to do. Her duty is to exercise only that care which a reasonably, careful and prudent person would exercise in the same situation. If at that moment her course and manner of action might have been followed by such a person under the same conditions, then she does all the law requires of her. Although in the light of after events it appears that some different action would have been better and safer. So the plaintiff's contention in this case which the defendant denies is that even though she might have not kept which would be ordinarily a reasonable lookout or kept her car under proper control or done her best to keep her car on the right-hand side of the road that she was confronted with sudden emergency and that her infant son caused some disturbance in the car. You will recall exactly the details of it, and that was sudden emergency. So that she could not be held quite as high a standard so far as staying on the right-hand side of the road and keeping her car under control or keeping a proper lookout. But I do want to instruct you there's no change in the law of negligence. The law as far as negligence is concerned says that a person is negligent if they do something that a reasonably, careful and prudent person would not have done or failed to do something which a reasonably, careful and prudent person would have done. And the 'Sudden Emergency Doctrine' just means what a reasonably, careful and prudent person would have done when confronted with a sudden emergency, as the defendant contends she was in this case. So I *instruct you if you are satisfied by the greater weight of the evidence that the defendant was* confronted with a sudden emergency, then, you would consider that as to whether she conducted herself as a reasonably, careful and prudent person would have done.'

The plaintiff contends that under Rule 51 of North Carolina Rules of Civil Procedure the above charge is generally an insufficient explanation of the doctrine of sudden emergency and particularly an insufficient explanation of the requirement that defendant must not cause the alleged emergency by his own negligence. Rule 51 requires that the trial court in its charge explain the law as it applies to the evidence of the case. The source or cause of the alleged sudden emergency is a vital issue in any consideration of the doctrine of sudden emergency. The trial court made only one reference, and that reference was parenthetical, to the requirement that the defendant, to be able to take advantage of the sudden emergency doctrine, must not bring on the emergency by his own negligence. The clear inference from the charge is that the trial court felt that the fall of the baby did in fact cause a sudden emergency and that said emergency was not brought on by the negligence of the defendants. It is the duty of the trial court in a case allegedly involving a sudden emergency to not only instruct that a lesser standard of care is applied in an emergency situation, but also the trial court must instruct that the jury must find that in fact a sudden emergency did exist and that the jury must further find that the emergency was in fact not brought on by the negligence of the defendants. The charge by the trial court was insufficient and we grant a new trial.

Source: Lawson v. Walker, 206 S.E.2d 325 (N.C. 1974).

The Learned Hand Approach vs. "Reasonable Care under the Circumstances"

In the case of *United States v. Carroll Towing Co.*, 159 F.2d 169 (2d Cir. 1947), reprinted in part in Exhibit 2-6, Judge Learned Hand actually arrived at an algebraic formula to determine reasonable care by analyzing whether the perceived magnitude of the risk outweighs its utility.

EXHIBIT 2-6 Relevant Case Law

United States, et al. v. Carroll Towing Co., Inc., et al.

Circuit Court of Appeals, Second Circuit.

L. Hand, Circuit Judge.

These appeals concern the sinking of the barge, 'Anna C,' on January 4, 1944, off Pier 51, North River. The Conners Marine Co., Inc., was the owner of the barge, which the Pennsylvania Railroad Company had chartered; the Grace Line, Inc., was the charterer of the tug, 'Carroll,' of which the Carroll Towing Co., Inc., was the owner. The decree in the limitation proceeding held the Carroll Company liable to the United States for the loss of the barge's cargo of flour, and to the Pennsylvania Railroad Company, for expenses in salving the cargo and barge; and it held the Carroll Company also liable to the Conners Company for one half the damage to the barge; these liabilities being all subject to limitation. The decree in the libel suit held the Grace Line primarily liable for the other half of the damage to the barge, and for any part of the first half, not recovered against the Carroll Company because of limitation of liability; it also held the Pennsylvania Railroad secondarily liable for the same amount that the Grace Line was liable. The Carroll Company and the Pennsylvania Railroad Company have filed assignments of error.

It appears from the foregoing review that there is no general rule to determine when the absence of a bargee or other attendant will make the owner of the barge liable for injuries to other vessels if she breaks away from her moorings. However, in any cases where he would be so liable for injuries to others obviously he must reduce his damages proportionately, if the injury is to his own barge. It becomes apparent why there can be no such general rule, when we consider the grounds for such a liability. Since there are occasions when every vessel will break from her moorings, and since, if she does, she becomes a menace to those about her; the owner's duty, as in other similar situations, to provide against resulting injuries is a function of three variables: (1) The probability that she will break away; (2) the gravity of the resulting injury, if she does; (3) the burden of adequate precautions. Possibly it serves to bring this notion into relief to state it in algebraic terms: if the probability be called P; the injury, L; and the burden, B; liability depends upon whether B is less than L multiplied by P: i.e., whether B less than PL. Applied to the situation at bar, the likelihood that a barge will break from her fasts and the damage she will do, vary with the place and time; for example, if a storm threatens, the danger is greater; so it is, if she is in a crowded harbor where moored barges are constantly being shifted about. On the other hand, the barge must not be the bargee's prison, even though he lives aboard; he must go ashore at times. We need not say whether, even in such crowded waters as New York Harbor a bargee must be aboard at night at all; it may be that the custom is otherwise, as Ward, J., supposed in 'The Kathryn B. Guinan,' supra; and that, if so, the situation is one where custom should control. We leave that question open; but we hold that it is not in all cases a sufficient answer to a bargee's absence without excuse, during working hours, that he has properly made fast his barge to a pier, when he leaves her. In the case at bar the bargee left at five o'clock in the afternoon of January 3rd, and the flotilla broke away at about two o'clock in the afternoon of the following day, twenty-one hours afterwards. The bargee had been away all the time, and we hold that his fabricated story was affirmative evidence that he had no excuse for his absence. At the locus in quo—especially during the short January days and in the full tide of war activity—barges were being constantly 'drilled' in and out. Certainly it was not beyond reasonable expectation that, with the inevitable haste and bustle, the work might not be done with adequate care. In such circumstances we hold—and it is all that we do hold—that it was a fair requirement that the Conners Company should have a bargee aboard (unless he had some excuse for his absence), during the working hours of daylight.

Source: United States v. Carroll Towing Co., 159 F.2d 169 (2d Cir. 1947).

The case involved a barge that had broken away from its moorings and caused damage to other vessels because an attendant (a "bargee") of the defendant company was not on duty 24 hours a day, 7 days a week. Judge Hand's formula was this: The probability of loss = P. The resulting loss, damage, or injury = L. The burden of defendant taking adequate precautions to prevent the loss = B. Therefore the formula for a breach of duty is the following: There is a breach of duty if the probability (P) times the amount of loss (L) is greater than the burden on the defendant to prevent the loss. The shortened formula is Breach = $P \times L > B$.

This is a risk-benefit analysis. It may work better in certain circumstances such as products liability in which economics is a factor. In other words, if the risk of injury or harm is slight but the cost to the manufacturer of making the product safer is high, it may be that the defendant's conduct is reasonable, and there has been no breach of duty. On the other hand, if the risk of injury or harm is high and the cost to the manufacturer of making the product safer is slight, it may be that the defendant's conduct is unreasonable and there has been a breach of duty.

In real life, most negligence situations do not lend themselves to the arithmetic formula utilized in *Carroll Towing*. The trial court is more likely to instruct the jury that the standard is "reasonable care under the circumstances." Review the sample JIG on negligence/reasonable care in Exhibit 2-3.

Res Ipsa Loquitur ("The Thing Speaks for Itself")

In some cases, the mere fact that a certain event caused an injury to occur may tend to establish the defendant was negligent. Under the doctrine of ***res ipsa loquitur***, which means "the thing speaks for itself," the law allows an inference that the defendant breached a duty and was negligent. The defendant is in a better position than plaintiff to prove what occurred so the burden is placed upon the defendant if certain requirements are met. Those requirements are:

Res Ipsa Loquitur
Literally, "the thing speaks for itself." A legal doctrine aiding the plaintiff's proof. It applies in those instances in which defendant is in a better position than plaintiff to prove what occurred. The evidentiary burden is placed on defendant if certain requirements are met.

1. The occurrence must be one that does not normally occur without negligence.
2. The negligence can be attributed to the defendant because the occurrence is of a type that the defendant had a duty to guard against/prevent.
3. Neither the plaintiff nor any third person caused or contributed to the plaintiff's harm or injury.

THE OCCURRENCE IS ONE THAT DOES NOT NORMALLY OCCUR WITHOUT NEGLIGENCE

To analyze this legal principle of *res ipsa loquitur*, sometimes referred to by judges and lawyers as "*res ipsa*," examples may be instructive. If the occurrence is one that normally does not occur in the absence of negligence, the occurrence—the happening itself—permits the conclusion that someone was negligent. The following are examples of such happenings: In a retail lighting store with many light fixtures hanging from the ceiling, a chandelier falls on the head of a customer. A person receives an injury after eating cereal that contained a small metal screw in the box. A surgical piece of gauze is left in the body of a patient following surgery.

THE NEGLIGENCE CAN BE ATTRIBUTED TO THE DEFENDANT BECAUSE THE OCCURRENCE IS OF A TYPE THAT THE DEFENDANT HAD A DUTY TO GUARD AGAINST/PREVENT

The question is now whether it is more likely than not that the occurrence or happening can be focused upon the defendant. This usually involves a discussion of defendant's control over the source of the occurrence or happening. Some courts impose a requirement that the defendant had exclusive control over the instrumentality causing the harm or injury. Using the example above of the customer in a retail lighting store, the defendant store owner would probably be deemed to be in exclusive control of the chandelier. But consider the case of a Saks shopper who was injured when an escalator she was riding suddenly stopped. Why the escalator stopped was unknown. There were emergency stop buttons at both the top and bottom landings that could be pushed by anyone. Since Saks was not in exclusive control of the escalator, the principle of *res ipsa loquitur* did not apply.[5]

In addition to the exclusive control factor, some courts utilize the factor of whether or not the plaintiff's injury was one that the defendant owed a duty to guard against or prevent. A brake manufacturer may be liable for injury to a driver when the brakes failed one week after purchase of a new vehicle. While the brake manufacturer was no longer in exclusive control of the brake system, an occurrence of failed brakes from a manufacturing error or a design error was the type of occurrence the manufacturer had a duty to guard against or prevent.

NEITHER THE PLAINTIFF NOR ANY THIRD PERSON CAUSED OR CONTRIBUTED TO THE PLAINTIFF'S HARM OR INJURY

In the example above concerning the failure of the new brakes manufactured by the brake manufacturer, the application of *res ipsa loquitur,* as discussed above, also assumes there is no evidence that plaintiff, the dealer, or anyone else had worked on the brakes since purchase of the vehicle. It must be shown that neither plaintiff nor any other third party contributed to or caused plaintiff's harm or injury.

Plaintiff may attempt to prove how a certain event occurred, such as the falling chandelier example above. The plaintiff may try to prove that the injury resulted from the weight of the chandelier and the weak support holding it. However, even if plaintiff tried to specifically establish how the event occurred, this still does not prevent application of *res ipsa loquitur* since chandeliers do not ordinarily fall from ceilings in the absence of someone's negligence.

EFFECT OF ESTABLISHING *RES IPSA LOQUITUR*— INFERENCE VS. PRESUMPTION

Inference
Evidence in a case that creates a conclusion that the trier of fact may or may not choose to accept.

An **inference** creates a conclusion that the trier of fact, usually a jury, may or may not choose to accept based on the facts of the case. There may be facts, however, that are so strong that an inference must be drawn, such as the falling chandelier. Some courts take the approach that *res ipsa loquitur* merely creates a permissible inference of negligence (breach of duty) if the jury so chooses. On the other hand, some courts take the approach that *res ipsa loquitur* creates a rebuttable presumption of negligence. A **presumption** is a principle of evidence establishing that once plaintiff offers some evidence or proof of a fact, the burden of proof shifts to the defendant. Under that approach to *res ipsa loquitur*, the burden shifts to defendant to now come forward with evidence to explain and rebut how the incident occurred.

Presumption
An evidentiary principle providing that once plaintiff offers some evidence or proof of a fact, the burden of proof shifts to the defendant.

Evidence of Custom and Statutes in Establishing Breach of Duty

Courts will typically allow evidence of safety-related customs in a community or safety-related statutes. The evidence is allowed to show defendant's compliance with or departure from such customs or statutes as they pertain to the reasonable person standard. Such evidence is allowed, but it is not conclusive on the issue of breach of duty. Whether the defendant violated or complied with the custom is simply another factor in determining whether the defendant acted as a reasonable person under the circumstances. For example, if it was customary in a community for residents to jump from a bridge into a pond below, the facts and circumstances of the particular case may show that such custom should not have been practiced that day because of bad weather and floodwaters flowing into the otherwise tranquil pond.

The fact that the defendant complied with an applicable safety-related statute or code is admissible evidence but not conclusive on the issue of breach of duty. The reasonable person standard still applies. For example, a fire safety statute or code may require that windows in a basement of a dwelling that is rented must be of a certain minimum size. However, depending upon the actual facts and circumstances, a jury may believe that reasonable conduct would dictate making the basement window larger than the minimum.

Negligence *Per Se*

A criminal statute may exist that prohibits conduct identical to the conduct in the civil negligence action. A violation of the criminal statute may establish breach of duty as a matter of law in the civil negligence action. The violation of the statute is **negligence** *per se*. However, the Restatement (Third) of Torts §15 (2010) provides for certain legally acceptable excuses for a violation of a safety statute:

Negligence *Per Se*
An act is considered negligent (breach of duty) because of the violation of a statute.

- Where the violation is reasonable in light of the defendant's childhood, physical disability, or physical incapacitation;
- Where the defendant exercised reasonable care in attempting to comply with the statute;
- Where the defendant neither knows nor should know of the factual circumstances that render the statute applicable;
- Where the defendant's violation of the statute is due to the confusing way in which the statute's requirements are presented to the public; or
- Where the defendant's compliance with the statute would involve a greater risk of physical harm to the actor or to others than noncompliance.

Imagine, in a civil action, a motor vehicle collision in which the defendant was driving in the left-hand lane of a two-lane public highway. This is contrary to state statute mandating that motor vehicles must drive on the right side of the roadway at all times except when necessary to safely pass another vehicle. If defendant provides evidence that the highway in the right lane was blocked because a semi had tipped over with spilled cargo upon the highway in the right lane, the jury may find that it was reasonable under the circumstances for the defendant driver to be in the left lane at the time of the collision. Even though the statute was violated, it did not amount to a breach of the duty of reasonable care under the circumstances. The court and jury must hear the reason or excuse for a violation of a statute; otherwise, the case no longer becomes one of negligence but one of absolute liability regardless of fault.

Three Approaches to a Violation of Statute

The first approach taken by the courts is that if a statute has been violated, it is "negligence *per se*." Using this first approach, a violation of a statute means that the defendant has breached a duty as a matter of law. The second approach is that if a statute has been violated, it creates a rebuttable presumption of negligence. The statutory violation does not rise to the level of being negligence *per se*. Defendant can offer a reason or excuse for the violation to rebut the presumption. The third approach is that if a statute has been violated, it is "evidence" of a breach of duty. It is conceivable that a statute was violated, but under the facts and circumstances the jury may believe the defendant acted as a reasonable person.

Unavoidable Accident

Unavoidable Accident
In the personal injury field, an occurrence or happening without any fault or negligence on a person; typically a cause is an "act of God."

Not all personal injuries arise from negligence. It may be that a personal injury did not arise from any breach of duty on the part of the alleged tortfeasor. It may have been a pure **unavoidable accident** in which no one was negligent or at fault. Such accidents may be directly related to acts of God, such as a fire, flood, or earthquake. For example, a ship's captain may be piloting a boat on the sea in a reasonable manner, but if a freak storm comes out of nowhere that was not predicted and passengers are injured or killed, this constitutes a pure unavoidable accident. A driver of a motor vehicle with passengers may be using the utmost of care when a freak, flash flood suddenly comes across the road and washes the vehicle into deep water causing the deaths of all occupants. Someone may have been using the utmost of reasonable care, but a pure, unavoidable accident may still occur. Negligence simply plays no part in the occurrence resulting in harm or injury. Has the paralegal student ever overheard a statement identical or similar to this? "It wasn't my fault … it was an accident."

Workplace Skills Tip

In developing workplace skills, when representing a plaintiff, a good habit for the plaintiff paralegal to develop is to avoid use of the word "accident," a word that technically means it was no one's fault or that negligence was involved in causing the plaintiff's injury. As an example, if the personal injury case arises out of a motor vehicle factual scenario, instead of using the term "motor vehicle accident," develop the habit of using the term "motor vehicle crash" or "motor vehicle collision." On the other hand, when representing a defendant, the defendant paralegal should develop the habit of using the precise term "accident" or "motor vehicle accident." Likewise, when on some plaintiff's teams in a medical malpractice case, the doctor's conduct may be described as "simple negligence." When on some defendant's teams, conduct may be described as "accused of being guilty of malpractice." Perfect practice makes perfect!

CASE **2.1** Hypothetical Case: Developing Workplace Skills

You are employed as a paralegal in a newly formed insurance defense firm started by two attorneys who broke off from a large, prestigious defense firm in town. You have been assigned to work on a new case just assigned by Double Indemnity Insurance Company whose insured is Harry "Lucky" Luciano. The case has the following facts: Your client, the defendant, was involved in a motor vehicle accident in which the plaintiff received rather serious personal injuries. Lucky was the owner of a parrot named "Max." At the time of the accident, Lucky had Max in his cage in the back seat. He was on his way to the veterinarian because, for some reason, Max had not said a word nor eaten for two days. Roads were dry. Weather was beautiful. Lucky was driving down an extra wide, flat, level city street with three lanes in each direction.

The plaintiff's vehicle was traveling ahead of Lucky and Lucky was maintaining a safe and reasonable distance behind. All of a sudden, Max started screaming at the top of his parrot lungs. Lucky, startled and surprised at this sudden distracting outburst, turned around to see what was happening. Apparently, Lucky had not completely latched the cage door at the beginning of the journey to the vet. Max was out of his cage on the back seat, flopping around, screeching and screaming. Lucky then looked back ahead, but the plaintiff's vehicle was now very close. A collision was imminent. Lucky, in the brief time after realizing an impact was imminent, chose to hit the brake rather than swerve into the right lane, which was wide open. However, by then it was too late, and he forcefully crashed into the rear of the plaintiff's vehicle. Had he swerved to the right in the open lane there, he probably would have avoided the collision.

The two attorneys are discussing the case at the firm's weekly "roundtable" meeting in which all paralegals are invited to offer their input. Someone mentions that if they can convince the judge to give the jury the "emergency rule" instruction, they should flat out win the case. Since you are very familiar with the facts of the case and have assisted in assembling some of the JIGS to submit to the judge, someone asks you if you think the emergency rule applies here. What do you think?

CHAPTER **SUMMARY**

Negligence is the failure to use due care or reasonable care under the circumstances that causes loss, damage, or injury for which money damages may be sought. There are four basic elements of negligence: (1) duty, (2) breach of duty, (3) causation, and (4) damages.

Duty is an obligation. In negligence law, a person has a duty to act reasonably or to reasonably refrain from acting in such a way as to not cause harm to another. Negligence may consist of an affirmative act, which is an act of commission or "misfeasance." Negligence may also consist of a failure to act, which is an act of omission or "nonfeasance." The element of duty is an issue for the court to decide as a matter of law. The court will consider if a duty is even owed, and then consider the scope of that duty.

The famous *Palsgraf* case stands for the proposition that a defendant owes a duty of reasonable care only to those reasonably foreseeable plaintiffs who are in the zone of danger.

The dissent in the *Palsgraf* case by Justice Andrews stands for the proposition that a defendant owes a duty of reasonable care to those who receive a reasonably foreseeable injury whether or not they are in the zone of danger.

Under the "public duty doctrine," a law enforcement officer generally owes no duty to an individual plaintiff, only to the general public. A person who did not cause injury to another person has no legal duty to voluntarily render aid or assistance to that injured person and is not subject to civil tort liability. However, if one volunteers to come to the aid or rescue of an injured person, such aid or rescue must be performed reasonably. There are "Good Samaritan" laws that give some protection to those who voluntarily come to the aid or rescue of an injured person.

Under a negligence theory, the first element is a duty to use reasonable care under the circumstances so as to avoid injuring others. However, the determination of whether or not one acted as a reasonable person is an objective test. The amount of care a reasonable person should use will differ with the facts and surrounding circumstances. A minor is judged as a reasonable person, but with the minor's age, intelligence, and experience becoming part of the surrounding circumstances. Common carriers may be held to a higher standard of care. Persons with disabilities are judged as a reasonable person, but with their disability considered as part of the surrounding circumstance. If a defendant possesses certain knowledge, education, training, or skills the defendant must meet the standard of care exercised by that particular skilled profession or trade. Generally, such persons are held to a national standard of care and not a local standard of care.

The emergency rule doctrine states that if the defendant is confronted with an emergency not of the defendant's own making, and the defendant does not choose the safest or best course of action, the defendant is not negligent. The reasonable person standard still applies. However, the facts and circumstances to be considered in judging the defendant's conduct consist of the facts and circumstances of the emergency situation confronting the defendant at the time.

The trier of fact is the person(s) who decides the contested issues in a case, including whether or not a defendant is negligent. Typically, this will be a jury, but the court or an arbitrator may be the trier of fact in certain cases. In deciding whether or not a defendant has breached a duty, a jury is likely to use the collective common sense and past experiences of each juror. Not all personal injuries arise from negligence. Sometimes pure, unavoidable accidents occur in which no one was negligent, and frequently those occur from acts of God.

Once duty has been established, the next element of negligence is breach of duty. This is established by showing that the defendant's act or omission exposed the plaintiff to an unreasonable risk of injury or harm. Breach of duty requires proof of the facts of the alleged negligent act or omission and proof that the defendant acted unreasonably under those facts and surrounding circumstances.

In the case of *United States v. Carroll Towing Co.*, Judge Learned Hand utilized an algebraic formula to determine reasonable care by analyzing whether the perceived magnitude of the risk outweighed its utility. There is a breach of duty if the probability of loss (P) times the expected loss, damage, or injury (L) is greater than (>) the burden of taking precautions to avert the loss (B). This is expressed as follows: Breach = $P \times L > B$. Other courts simply instruct the jury that in considering whether or not there has been a breach of duty, they should simply consider whether the defendant exercised reasonable care under the circumstances.

Res ipsa loquitur is a legal doctrine using Latin words that mean "the thing speaks for itself." This doctrine has to do with proof of breach of duty. The defendant in some cases is in a better position than the plaintiff to prove what occurred. There are three elements that must be present for the doctrine to apply. First, the occurrence must be one that does not normally occur without negligence. Second, the negligence can be attributed to the defendant because the occurrence is of a type that the defendant had a duty to guard against or protect. Third, neither the plaintiff nor any third person caused or contributed to the plaintiff's harm or injury. If the three elements are established, some courts take the position that there is an inference of negligence, and others take the position that a rebuttable presumption arises.

In establishing breach of duty, evidence of safety-related customs and statutes may be considered. In some cases, violation of a statute may be "negligence *per se*." The defendant is allowed to offer excuses for a violation of statute. It may be that the defendant's excuse for violating the statute is proper. Even though the statute was technically violated, it may not amount to a breach of the duty of reasonable care under the circumstances. It will depend upon the defendant's excuse having to do with the defendant's claim that he or she was acting as a reasonable person under the circumstances.

KEY **TERMS**

Prima Facie Case	Reasonably Foreseeable Injury	Emergency Rule
Duty	Public Duty Doctrine	*Res Ipsa Loquitur*
Act of Commission	Good Samaritan Law	Inference
Act of Omission	Breach of Duty	Presumption
Misfeasance	Reasonable Person Standard	Negligence *Per Se*
Nonfeasance	Gross Negligence	Unavoidable Accident
Zone of Danger	Trier of Fact	
Reasonably Foreseeable Plaintiff	Jury Instruction Guide (JIG)	

REVIEW **QUESTIONS**

1. What are the four basic elements of the tort of negligence?

2. In the context of duty, give an example of an affirmative act and a failure to act.

3. Explain the difference in approach/reasoning in *Palsgraf* between the majority opinion and the dissent. Which approach/reasoning do you think is better? Why? Which approach better furthers the objectives of tort law as described in Chapter 1? Which approach would a plaintiff prefer? Which approach would a defendant prefer?

4. What does the "reasonable person standard" mean? Is a reasonable person under the negligence standard: Average? Above average? Perfect? Is this a better standard than a subjective standard? Why or why not?

5. Provide an example of a pure, unavoidable accident.

6. Explain the Learned Hand approach and contrast it with simply judging conduct by whether or not a defendant used reasonable care under the circumstances. Which approach is better? Easier to apply? More practical and realistic?

7. Literally, what does the Latin phrase *res ipsa loquitur* mean? Think of an example and consider whether all elements apply.

8. Explain and provide an example of "negligence *per se.*"

9. Two city police officers were on duty and allowed automobile drag racing to occur in their presence for a substantial period of time on a street adjacent to the sidewalk on which plaintiff stood. They knew or should have known, in the exercise of due care, that such activity could cause injury. They failed to stop the drag racing knowing that it was a violation of ordinance and statute. They also failed to disperse the people congregating on the public sidewalk. They failed to arrest the participants of the drag races. The plaintiff was seriously injured after being struck by one of the drag racing automobiles while standing on the adjacent sidewalk.

   Did the police officers owe a duty to the plaintiff, who was seriously injured by their failure to stop the drag racing and arrest the participants, thus preventing this serious personal injury? Why or why not?

chapter 3

NEGLIGENCE: CAUSATION

LEARNING OBJECTIVES

After studying this chapter, you should be able to:

- Describe the concept of actual cause and the significance of the "but for" test.

- Determine and identify concurrent liability.

- Determine and identify the "substantial factor" rule and alternative liability.

- Recite the rationale of "a case within a case" in a legal malpractice case.

- Analyze and differentiate proximate cause from actual cause.

- Recognize the concepts of foreseeability, dependent intervening forces, independent intervening forces, and how they affect causation.

- Differentiate between several liability and joint and several liability.

- Differentiate between the concepts of contribution and indemnity.

Actual Cause

The third element of negligence; defendant's negligent conduct must have been the cause in fact of the plaintiff's injury. If plaintiff would not have been injured but for the defendant's negligent conduct, the negligent conduct is an actual cause of plaintiff's injury.

"But for" Test

A test to determine actual cause. "But for" the defendant's negligent act or omission, plaintiff would not have been injured.

"What we anticipate seldom occurs, what we least expect generally happens."

Benjamin Disraeli

Thus far, we have discussed the first two elements of the tort of negligence—duty and breach of duty. The third element is causation. Before the defendant's negligent conduct can impose liability on the defendant, that conduct must be the cause of the plaintiff's injury.

Actual Cause ("Cause in Fact")

While causation is presented in this textbook as the third element of negligence, there are actually two distinct concepts of causation, both of which will be examined in greater detail in this chapter. The first concept is **actual cause**, also sometimes referred to as "cause in fact." Actual cause means that the defendant's negligent conduct must have been the cause in fact of the plaintiff's injury. If the plaintiff would not have been injured but for the defendant's negligent conduct, the negligent conduct is an actual cause of the plaintiff's injury. From the definition of actual cause, it can be seen that there is a rule or a test to determine whether the defendant's negligent conduct was the actual cause of the plaintiff's injury. That test is called the **"but for" test**. This test of causation means that but for the defendant's negligent conduct, plaintiff would not have been injured.

The second concept of causation is **proximate cause**. Proximate cause is the primary cause of an injury. It is the natural, direct, and uninterrupted consequence of negligent conduct without which the injury would not have occurred. Proximate cause requires an analysis of whether or not the consequences—the end result—of the defendant's negligent conduct were too far removed or too remote from the risk such that defendant should not be held liable. When the issue of causation is reached, it can be assumed that duty and breach of duty have been established. In other words, the defendant's negligent conduct has occurred. The question now is whether or not that negligent conduct caused the plaintiff's injury.

Proximate Cause
The primary cause of an injury; the natural, direct, and uninterrupted consequence of negligent conduct without which the injury would not have occurred.

EXAMPLES OF ACTUAL CAUSE

Defendant approaches an intersection in his motor vehicle. The plaintiff is walking in the crosswalk with the green light. However, defendant runs the red light, strikes plaintiff, and causes a personal injury. Defendant's affirmative negligent act of running the red light (breach of duty) causing a collision with plaintiff's person was clearly the actual cause of plaintiff's injury. "But for" defendant's negligent act of running the red light, the collision and resulting injury would not have occurred.

A physician is treating a patient who has an allergy to sulfa. The allergy is clearly noted in several places in the patient's chart. The physician negligently prescribes a sulfa-based drug to treat the patient. The patient suffers an allergic reaction and becomes violently ill. The physician's negligent act of prescribing sulfa caused the obviously expected allergic reaction along with the resulting injury. "But for" the physician prescribing sulfa, the allergic reaction and illness would not have occurred.

EXAMPLES OF NO ACTUAL CAUSE

Defendant driver is speeding, traveling 60 miles per hour in a posted 45-mile-per-hour speed limit zone. There is a statutory duty to drive at or below the posted speed limit. That statute establishes a duty. Defendant has clearly breached that duty. Plaintiff, an intoxicated driver, is traveling behind defendant at a speed of 85 miles per hour and smashes into the rear of defendant's vehicle. The plaintiff driver is injured and brings suit against the defendant driver alleging negligence. While defendant was technically negligent for exceeding the speed limit, defendant's speed was not the actual cause of the plaintiff's injury. Using the "but for" test, did defendant's speed really have anything to do with the causation of this collision?

Dr. J. Sooper, a physician specializing in infectious diseases, clearly misdiagnoses a serious disease of the plaintiff. However, the plaintiff immediately obtains a second opinion from another physician, Dr. J. L. Hicks. Dr. Hicks makes a proper diagnosis and begins proper medication and treatment within the crucial five-day period. This care and treatment prevents any serious complications from this disease. Dr. Sooper's departure from the standard of care in her misdiagnosis of the plaintiff's condition was negligent conduct. However, such negligent conduct was not the actual cause of any further serious complications from the disease because of the appropriate actions on the part of Dr. Hicks. In a later medical malpractice (professional negligence) case, Dr. Sooper would argue that there was not only no element of actual causation established, but also no element of damages established. The real personal injury damages to the plaintiff would have been severe complications from the disease, and those were prevented by Dr. Hicks. The patient had already contracted the disease at the time the patient first saw Dr. Sooper. Her misdiagnosis had nothing to do with causing the disease itself.

Assume a patient contracted a terminal disease and had but a year to live. The patient's physician, during the course of treatment for the illness, was clearly and admittedly negligent. The patient died approximately a year later from complications of the disease. In a later wrongful death suit, the defendant physician would establish that there was no actual cause. Regardless of the physician's negligent act, the patient would have died anyway.

Concurrent Liability

Thus far, the discussion has centered around one negligent defendant. Many personal injuries occur as the result of the negligence of two or more defendants. **Concurrent liability** refers to an incident in which separate negligent acts of two or more defendants concur and combine to cause a single personal injury to the plaintiff. If plaintiff would not have been injured but for the concurrence of the negligence of two tortfeasors, then both tortfeasors have produced the actual causes for plaintiff's injury. Assume Al, the plaintiff, is a passenger in Bart's motor vehicle. Bart is texting and not keeping his eyes on the road. A collision occurs with a motor vehicle driven by Craig who has consumed an excessive amount of alcohol, is speeding, and is not paying attention to the road. Bart's negligence consists of texting and not paying attention to the road. Craig's negligence consists of having consumed excessive alcoholic beverages, excessive speed, and not paying attention. "But for" the negligence of both of them, this motor vehicle collision would not have occurred.

Multiple Causes
THE "SUBSTANTIAL FACTOR" RULE

The **"substantial factor" rule** means that a tortfeasor is liable to the plaintiff if the tortfeasor's negligent act or omission was a "substantial factor" in producing the injury. If the plaintiff's injury results from the negligence of two tortfeasors but the conduct of either one of them would have been sufficient to cause plaintiff's injury, both are liable if each of their negligent acts was a "substantial factor" in causing plaintiff's injury. If two motorists are drag racing and suddenly come over a hill near the plaintiff with a weak heart who is literally frightened to death, each driver is a "substantial factor" in causing plaintiff's death. It can be seen that it is not the concurrence of the negligence of the two drivers that causes the damage (the death) because either driver's negligence alone would have produced the same

Workplace Skills Tip

In the course of handling a personal injury case, you may be asked by the supervising attorney to assist with the preparation of an upcoming deposition (sometimes referred to by lawyers as "depo prep"). Unless the attorney states otherwise, do not try to set forth questions but rather areas for possible questions the attorney might ask. For example, if preparing for the deposition of an expert retained by the other side, you may point out a weakness in the expert's C.V., such as a lack of certification in a certain specialty, a previous deposition the expert gave in another case that could provide possible impeachment, or areas in the expert's report in which there are discrepancies. Focus on areas and ideas, not questions, unless the attorney specifically requests your suggested questions. Hopefully, the lawyer knows how to ask the questions. Also, another good backup practice before the deposition is to assemble important documents in the case that the attorney might want to review or even use as an exhibit at the deposition.

fright with the same result. The "but for" rule does not work in this case, because both negligent drivers would technically be absolved of liability.

ALTERNATIVE LIABILITY

The landmark case establishing **alternative liability** is the case of *Summers v. Tice*, 33 Cal. 2d 80, 199 P.2d 1 (1948). In that case, three companions were out quail hunting. Two of the defendant hunters each fired their shotguns after a bird was flushed. One of the pellets from one of the shotguns struck the plaintiff causing personal injuries. Both defendants were using 12-gauge shotguns with 7 ½ size shot pellets, so it was impossible to establish which defendant's shot pellet actually hit the plaintiff's eye. The court held that each defendant was liable for the plaintiff's injury even though it was unknown which actual shot pellet from which shotgun did damage to the plaintiff's eye. The court commented that to hold otherwise would be to exonerate both defendants from liability, even though each was negligent.

> **Alternative Liability**
> Plaintiff is injured by the negligent conduct of only one of two or more defendants but it is unknown which defendant actually caused the injury.

Note that application of the "but for" rule does not work in this case either. This is because it cannot be demonstrated which defendant's negligent act caused the plaintiff's injury. It is, therefore, impossible to ascertain if the injury would have occurred but for that particular defendant's negligent act. Also, since the plaintiff is unable to prove which defendant's negligent act was the actual cause of plaintiff's injuries, the burden of going forward with the evidence shifts to the defendant. In *Summers*, each defendant was required to show that his negligence was not the actual cause of the injury. "They are both wrongdoers—both negligent toward plaintiff. They brought about a situation where the negligence of one of them injured the plaintiff, hence it should rest with them each to absolve himself if he can."[1] The student should recognize the technical difference between *Summers* and the previous example of the two drivers who caused the plaintiff's heart attack. In the two drivers' example, each defendant was a cause of the damage. In *Summers*, even though both were negligent, only one of them actually caused the damage. These rules of substantial factor and alternative liability promote the primary purpose of tort liability, which is to compensate innocent tort victims.

Review of Tests/Rules for Actual Cause

"But For" Test	But for defendant's negligent conduct, plaintiff would not have been injured.
Concurrent Cause	But for the concurrence (combination) of two or more defendants' negligent conduct, plaintiff would not have been injured.
"Substantial Factor" Rule	Several causes produced the injury to plaintiff, any one of which would have been sufficient to cause the injury, and defendant's negligent conduct was a substantial factor in causing the plaintiff's injury.
Alternative Liability	Plaintiff is injured by the negligent conduct of only one of two or more defendants, but it is unknown which defendant actually caused the injury. The burden of proof shifts to the defendants to prove their negligent conduct was not the actual cause of the plaintiff's injury.

Legal Malpractice Cases ("A Case Within a Case")

A special word needs to be mentioned about attorney legal malpractice while on the subject of causation. A frequent source of legal malpractice is an attorney missing a statute of limitation. A statute of limitation was first discussed in Chapter 1. A statute of limitation is a statute that provides the maximum period of time in which a civil action may be commenced. For example, assume a client has retained an attorney to pursue a personal injury action received in a slip and fall in a place of business. For some reason, however, the attorney misses the applicable statute of limitation against the business owner. The elements of a professional negligence claim against an attorney are the following: (1) The existence of an attorney-client relationship; (2) the defendant attorney was negligent; (3) the attorney's negligent act or omission was the cause of the plaintiff's damages; and (4) damages were incurred by the plaintiff. There is, however, in this type of case, another element that relates to the causation issue. The element is that but for defendant attorney's negligent conduct the plaintiff would have been successful in his or her slip-and-fall case against the business owner. It is not enough to merely prove that the attorney missed the statute of limitation. The plaintiff's burden of proof in a legal malpractice action is a fairly heavy one. Some misguided plaintiff's attorneys may believe they have a slam dunk because it is undisputed that the attorney missed the statute of limitation.

Assume an attorney-client relationship exists. If so, there is a duty owing from the attorney to the client. Assume the attorney missed the applicable statute of limitation. If so, plaintiff will likely prove the element of breach of duty. However, in this type of case, the plaintiff must also prove that he or she would have prevailed in the underlying action. In the hypothetical case, the plaintiff must prove that the defendant business owner was causally negligent for the slip and fall and resulting damages. Assume, however, that the plaintiff's underlying case involves these facts: The plaintiff had been drinking, was not watching where he or she was going, and missed a well-marked, well-lit step with a handrail. Plaintiff fell down and was injured while exiting the store. The plaintiff entered at the same place 10 minutes earlier.

A legal malpractice case requires proving "a case within a case." Plaintiff, as part of the legal malpractice case, must present facts and evidence of the underlying case itself that was allegedly lost by the attorney's negligence. How good was that case? Did the attorney's negligence by missing the statute really cause any damages? In a 50-50 comparative fault state, assume a jury decided that the plaintiff was 65% at fault and the business owner was 35% at fault. It can be seen that the defendant attorney's negligence in missing the statute of limitation did not cause any loss to the plaintiff. As it turned out, the plaintiff had a poor negligence case against the business owner and would not have recovered anything anyway. Therefore, it does not matter that the attorney missed the statute of limitation. Or, consider a different underlying case in which liability is not contested. The potential defendant in the underlying case was 100% at fault, and the only issue was damages. The plaintiff in the attorney malpractice case may believe that the underlying case, if it could have been pursued but for the attorney's negligence in missing the statute, is worth $750,000. However, after hearing evidence of the plaintiff's injury, the jury in the legal malpractice case may decide that the damages to the plaintiff are $100,000. This is what is meant by the causation concept of "a case within a case" when referring to legal malpractice actions.

Proximate Cause

The courts have adopted a second part of causation called "proximate cause." Proximate cause is the primary cause of an injury. It is the natural, direct, and uninterrupted consequence of a negligent act or omission without which the injury would not have occurred. Proximate cause focuses on the issue of whether or not the consequences of defendant's negligent conduct are too far removed, too remote, or just plain too bizarre that defendant should not be held legally liable. The analysis of proximate cause asks this question: Just how far does defendant's legal liability extend for consequences set in motion by the defendant's negligent conduct?

Foreseeability Test for Proximate Cause

There are several approaches or tests that courts utilize to analyze proximate cause, depending upon the jurisdiction. The **foreseeability test** focuses on the foreseeability of the manner in which the resulting injury comes about, the foreseeability of the result itself, and whether or not the plaintiff was a foreseeable plaintiff. The primary approach discussed in this text will focus on the foreseeability test, because it is more commonly utilized by the courts to limit the scope of the defendant's liability. In analyzing foreseeability for proximate cause, the focus is very specific. Is it foreseeable that this particular injury to this particular plaintiff would occur in this particular manner? To impose liability on a defendant, his or her negligent conduct must not have produced a remote, unusual, or bizarre result. Using this foreseeability approach, there is no proximate cause and no liability on defendant's part:

Foreseeability Test
A test of proximate cause that limits the scope of defendant's liability. Foreseeability requires that in order to impose liability on a defendant his or her negligent conduct must not have produced a remote, unusual, or bizarre result.

- If the result was unforeseeable.
- If the result was foreseeable, but it arose in an unforeseeable manner.
- If the plaintiff was unforeseeable. (The plaintiff was not a member of a group that might be expected to be at risk.)

FORESEEABLE RESULT, MANNER, AND PLAINTIFF

Assume a scenario in which all three of the above are present. The driver of a motor vehicle is not paying attention and strikes a pedestrian in the crosswalk. The impact causes a broken arm and a broken pelvis. This is a case in which there was a foreseeable result that occurred in a foreseeable manner to a foreseeable plaintiff.

The result is foreseeable. The driver operating a vehicle on a public roadway that intersects a crosswalk knows or reasonably should know that a person on foot is likely to be at that location. A driver also knows or reasonably should know that if an automobile strikes that person in that crosswalk, a personal injury will likely result to that pedestrian.

The manner of the injury is foreseeable. It is foreseeable that a plaintiff in a crosswalk intersecting a public roadway would be struck and injured by an automobile. There is nothing unusual or bizarre about a pedestrian being injured from being struck by a motor vehicle in a place both would precisely be expected to converge or cross paths at the same time.

The plaintiff is foreseeable. A driver in a motor vehicle on a public roadway knows or reasonably should know that pedestrians cross roadways at crosswalks. Pedestrians are expected to be in this location where vehicles travel. A driver should reasonably anticipate or foresee a pedestrian being in a crosswalk that intersects the very same roadway upon which the driver is traveling.

UNFORESEEABLE RESULT, MANNER, AND PLAINTIFF

Now, assume this scenario: Defendant negligently struck a parked motor vehicle causing it to roll down a hill. At the bottom of the hill the unoccupied vehicle struck a truck carrying gasoline, which caused a gasoline spill. At the same time, a pedestrian happened to flick a cigarette butt into the spilled gasoline on the street causing an explosion and fire. This caused a burn injury to a person on a motorcycle who happened to be driving by. A court or jury may well find that because a burn injury to the motorcycle driver was so remote and so bizarre it was an unforeseeable result, thus exonerating the defendant from civil liability. Defendant may also be exonerated from liability on the ground that the injured motorcycle driver was an unforeseeable plaintiff who was down the hill, a great distance away. The manner of the occurrence itself was also unusual, bizarre, and arguably unforeseeable.

EXCEPTION: THE "EGGSHELL PLAINTIFF" RULE

There is a rather common situation involving an unforeseeable result in which liability is universally imposed on a defendant. This creates an exception to the principle of there being no liability on a defendant when the result is unforeseeable. This common situation arises when a defendant's negligent conduct causes an unforeseeable result because the nature of the plaintiff's injuries is unexpected. This occurs when there is an injury to a plaintiff with a preexisting condition. The rule, sometimes referred to as the **"eggshell plaintiff" rule**, requires "the defendant to take the plaintiff as the defendant finds him."[2] (See Exhibit 3-1.)

"Eggshell Plaintiff" Rule
The causation principle that makes the negligent defendant liable for an unforeseeable result because of a preexisting condition of the plaintiff.

It makes no difference that a plaintiff has a more severe reaction or severe result than a normal person would have to the same injury. In *Benn*, plaintiff received a bruised chest and a fractured ankle in an automobile accident. Plaintiff had a history of heart disease and died from a heart attack shortly after the automobile accident. The trial court refused to give a jury instruction based on the "eggshell plaintiff" rule, which requires defendant to compensate the plaintiff for harm or injury an ordinary person would not have suffered. The Supreme Court of Iowa ruled that a new trial was warranted and that the jury should be given the "eggshell plaintiff" jury instruction. In other words, the jury should know that if plaintiff's death was the result of the automobile accident, the defendant can be liable despite plaintiff's remote, unusual susceptibility to heart attacks.

FORESEEABLE RESULT ARISING IN AN UNFORSEEABLE MANNER

Assume a motor vehicle driver is approaching a crosswalk and a pedestrian is crossing there. Instead of striking the plaintiff in the crosswalk, defendant swerves to the right and strikes a parked car. The defendant's vehicle is then spun around and thrown back into the pedestrian crossing in the crosswalk. An injury to the plaintiff is foreseeable if defendant's vehicle struck the plaintiff in the crosswalk. However, because of the extremely bizarre manner in which plaintiff was injured, a court may find no immediate, proximate cause from the defendant's negligent act. The result (striking a pedestrian in the crosswalk) is foreseeable but it arose in an unforeseeable manner (striking another vehicle first and being thrown back into plaintiff).

EXHIBIT 3-1 Relevant Case Law

Carol A. Benn, As Executor of the Estate of Loras J. Benn, Deceased, Appellant, v. Leland R. Thomus, k-g, Ltd., and Heartland Express, Inc., of Iowa, Appellees.

Supreme Court of Iowa.

Motorist's estate brought action for injuries and death allegedly caused by motor vehicle accident. The District Court, Johnson County, August F. Honsell, J., entered judgment on jury verdict for estate, and estate appealed. The Court of Appeals reversed, and appeal was taken. The Supreme Court, McGiverin, C.J., held that estate was entitled to have jury instructed on "eggshell plaintiff" rule....

McGiverin, Chief Justice.

The main question here is whether the trial court erred in refusing to instruct the jury on the "eggshell plaintiff" rule in view of the fact that plaintiff's decedent, who had a history of coronary disease, died of a heart attack six days after suffering a bruised chest and fractured ankle in a motor vehicle accident caused by defendant's negligence. The court of appeals concluded that the trial court's refusal constituted reversible error. We agree with the court of appeals and reverse the judgment of the trial court and remand for a new trial.

I. *Background facts and proceedings.* On February 15, 1989, on an icy road in Missouri, a semi-tractor and trailer rear-ended a van in which Loras J. Benn was a passenger. In the accident, Loras suffered a bruised chest and a fractured ankle. Six days later he died of a heart attack.

Subsequently, Carol A. Benn, as executor of Loras's estate, filed suit against defendants Leland R. Thomas, the driver of the semi-tractor, K-G Ltd., the owner of the semi-tractor and trailer, and Heartland Express, the permanent lessee of the semi-tractor and trailer. The plaintiff estate sought damages for Loras's injuries and death. For the purposes of simplicity, we will refer to all defendants in the singular.

At trial, the estate's medical expert, Dr. James E. Davia, testified that Loras had a history of coronary disease and insulin-dependent diabetes. Loras had a heart attack in 1985 and was at risk of having another. Dr. Davia testified that he viewed "the accident that [Loras] was in and the attendant problems that it cause[d] in the body as the straw that broke the camel's back" and the cause of Loras's death. Other medical evidence indicated the accident did not cause his death.

Based on Dr. Davia's testimony, the estate requested an instruction to the jury based on the "eggshell plaintiff" rule, which requires the defendant to take his plaintiff as he finds him, even if that means that the defendant must compensate the plaintiff for harm an ordinary person would not have suffered.... The district court denied this request.

The jury returned a verdict for the estate in the amount of $17,000 for Loras's injuries but nothing for his death. In the special verdict, the jury determined the defendant's negligence in connection with the accident did not proximately cause Loras's death.

II. *Jury instructions and the "eggshell plaintiff" rule.* The estate claims that the court erred in failing to include, in addition to its proximate cause instruction to the jury, a requested instruction on the eggshell plaintiff rule. Such an instruction would advise the jury that it could find that the accident aggravated Loras's heart condition and caused his fatal heart attack. The trial court denied this request, submitting instead a general instruction on proximate cause. The court of appeals reversed, concluding that the trial court erred in refusing to specifically instruct on the eggshell plaintiff doctrine....

A tortfeasor whose act, superimposed upon a prior latent condition, results in an injury may be liable in damages for the full disability.... This rule deems the injury, and not the dormant condition, the

(Continued)

EXHIBIT 3-1 *(Continued)*

proximate cause of the plaintiff's harm. *Id.* This precept is often referred to as the "eggshell plaintiff" rule, which has its roots in cases such as *Dulieu v. White & Sons,* [1901] 2 K.B. 669, 679, where the court observed:

If a man is negligently run over or otherwise negligently injured in his body, it is no answer to the sufferer's claim for damages that he would have suffered less injury, or no injury at all, if he had not had an unusually thin skull or an unusually weak heart....

The proposed instruction here stated:

If Loras Benn had a prior heart condition making him more susceptible to injury than a person in normal health, then the Defendant is responsible for all injuries and damages which are experienced by Loras Benn, proximately caused by the Defendant's actions, even though the injuries claimed produced a greater injury than those which might have been experienced by a normal person under the same circumstances....

Defendant contends that plaintiff's proposed instruction was inappropriate because it concerned damages, not proximate cause. Although the eggshell plaintiff rule has been incorporated into the Damages section of the Iowa Uniform Civil Jury Instructions, we believe it is equally a rule of proximate cause.

The proximate cause instruction in this case provided:

The conduct of a party is a proximate cause of damage when it is a substantial factor in producing damage and when the damage would not have happened except for the conduct.

"Substantial" means the party's conduct has such an effect in producing damage as to lead a reasonable person to regard it as a cause.

See Iowa Uniform Jury Instruction 700.3. Special Verdict Number 4 asked the jury: "Was the negligence of Leland Thomas a proximate cause of Loras Benn's death?" The jury answered this question, "No."

We agree that the jury might have found the defendant liable for Loras's death as well as his injuries under the instructions as given. But the proximate cause instruction failed to adequately convey the existing law that the jury should have applied to this case. The eggshell plaintiff rule rejects the limit of foreseeability that courts ordinarily require in the determination of proximate cause. *Prosser & Keeton* § 43, at 291 ("The defendant is held liable for unusual results of personal injuries which are regarded as unforeseeable...."). Once the plaintiff establishes that the defendant caused some injury to the plaintiff, the rule imposes liability for the full extent of those injuries, not merely those that were foreseeable to the defendant. Restatement (Second) of Torts § 461 (1965) ("The negligent actor is subject to liability for harm to another although a physical condition of the other ... makes the injury greater than that which the actor as a reasonable man should have foreseen as a probable result of his conduct.").

The instruction given by the court was appropriate as to the question of whether defendant caused Loras's initial personal injuries, namely, the fractured ankle and the bruised chest. This instruction alone, however, failed to adequately convey to the jury the eggshell plaintiff rule, which the jury reasonably could have applied to the cause of Loras's death.

Defendant maintains "[t]he fact there was extensive heart disease and that Loras Benn was at risk any time is not sufficient" for an instruction on the eggshell plaintiff rule. Yet the plaintiff introduced substantial medical testimony that the stresses of the accident and subsequent treatment were responsible for his heart attack and death. Although the evidence was conflicting, we believe that it was sufficient for the jury to determine whether Loras's heart attack and death were the direct result of the injury fairly chargeable to defendant Thomas's negligence.

Source: Benn v. Thomas, 512 N.W.2d 537 (Iowa 1994).

UNFORESEEABLE PLAINTIFF

Recall from the discussion of the *Palsgraf* case in the previous chapter that under the Cardozo view, whether or not one is a foreseeable plaintiff is analyzed as a breach of duty and decided by the court. If the court finds that plaintiff is not a foreseeable plaintiff in the zone of danger, such as Mrs. Palsgraf, the issue of proximate cause is not even reached. If the plaintiff is a foreseeable plaintiff with a duty owed, then the remaining issues of causation are considered: Was the manner of the occurrence foreseeable and was the result foreseeable? Jurisdictions following the Justice Andrews dissent in *Palsgraf* let the jury decide if the plaintiff was a foreseeable plaintiff or not.

There may be other examples of an unforeseeable plaintiff. Assume the pedestrian in the crosswalk is struck by a motor vehicle and thrown into the air striking a plaintiff on the sidewalk. A person on the sidewalk would be assumed to be in a place of safety. A court or a jury could find no liability on the ground of no proximate cause because the plaintiff is an unforeseeable plaintiff. Defendant negligently manufactured a dangerous drug that produced a brain disorder in a person. That person, five years later, because of the brain disorder, randomly picked an unknown victim, and shot and wounded the plaintiff. A court or a jury could find no liability on the ground of no proximate cause because the plaintiff was not a foreseeable plaintiff coupled with the remoteness from the negligent act because of the passage of time.

Indirect Causation and Superseding, Intervening Forces

Certain acts or forces may occur that cut off the chain of causation begun by the defendant's original negligent conduct. **Indirect causation** refers to a situation in which some force intervenes between the defendant's negligent conduct and the occurrence of plaintiff's harm or injury. There are two basic types of intervening forces—dependent intervening forces and independent intervening forces. A **dependent intervening force** is an act of a third person or an animal that is a natural, normal, or usual response to the occurrence caused by defendant's negligent conduct. These forces are normal responses that arise because of defendant's negligent conduct. They are foreseeable and do not relieve defendant of liability if they lead to a foreseeable result. An **independent intervening force** is a force that arises after the defendant's negligent conduct, but it is not a response or a reaction to the defendant's negligent conduct. It may be an act of God, such as a fire, flood, or storm, an act of an animal or an act of a third person—not the plaintiff. With an independent intervening force, the defendant will remain liable for the result of his negligent conduct unless the force is an unforeseeable intentionally tortious or criminal act. Whether it is a dependent intervening force or an independent intervening force, the primary factor to analyze is whether or not, when defendant acted negligently, the *result* was reasonably foreseeable.

A force set into motion by the defendant is typically not an intervening force cutting off the chain of causation. For example, if a negligent defendant strikes a trailer carrying a snowmobile causing the snowmobile to tip, fall off the trailer, and strike the plaintiff, that is still a force set into motion by the defendant. The issue boils down to whether, when the defendant's negligent conduct occurred, it was reasonably foreseeable that the result that occurred would occur.

Indirect Causation
Some force intervenes between the defendant's negligent conduct and the occurrence of plaintiff's harm or injury; typically an act of God, an animal, or the act of a third person, not the plaintiff.

Dependent Intervening Force
An act of a third person or an animal that is a natural, normal, or usual response to the occurrence caused by defendant's negligent conduct.

Independent Intervening Force
A force that is an unnatural, abnormal, or unusual response to the occurrence caused by the defendant's negligent conduct.

Assume plaintiff is riding as a passenger in defendant's motor vehicle. Defendant falls asleep at the wheel and strikes a bridge abutment injuring both plaintiff and defendant and pinning them in the vehicle. Before help arrives, an escaped convict from another state in a stolen car stops, robs, shoots, and kills both plaintiff and defendant. The criminal act of the escaped convict will cut off the causation of the defendant's original negligent conduct, because this intervening criminal act was unforeseeable and the result was unforeseeable. There is nothing the defendant did that caused or enhanced the risk of this unnatural, unusual, and abnormal result. The criminal conduct is an independent intervening force cutting off causation.

Contrast that with a different factual situation involving the same motor vehicle collision. Plaintiff is injured. Help arrives and plaintiff is taken to the hospital. Unfortunately, plaintiff is negligently treated at the hospital and dies. Such medical malpractice is foreseeable. The chain of causation would not be broken. The defendant would be liable for his original negligence. Being treated at a hospital after an injury is a natural, normal, and usual response to an injury caused by defendant's negligence. It is reasonably foreseeable that an injured person would need to go to the hospital as a result of injuries. It is also reasonably foreseeable that unsuccessful medical treatment would occur, whether or not because of medical malpractice. The medical malpractice at the hospital is a dependent intervening force. The negligence of the hospital is considered a normal risk or a normal response to the defendant's original act.

The general rule is that a defendant remains liable for his or her original negligent conduct unless the force is an unforeseeable tortious or criminal act. The focus is still on the result, however, and whether or not the result was foreseeable. In that regard, compare the *Kush* case in Exhibit 3-2.[3] In that case, the intentional acts of 15-year-old students did not break the chain of causation. The school board was causally negligent for a minor child's injuries from exploding chemicals. The court held that it was reasonably foreseeable that dangerous chemicals would be stolen by students when the school failed to secure the dangerous chemicals.

Assume plaintiff's brakes fail on a newly purchased vehicle. Such brakes were negligently designed. As plaintiff is coasting down a hill to safety, a large boulder releases from a nearby bluff and rolls down striking the plaintiff's vehicle and injuring him. This would likely be considered an act of God, an independent intervening force, cutting off the chain of causation begun by the manufacturer's original negligence.

Assume a highway contractor incorrectly and negligently blocks a road, causing plaintiff to take a detour. Plaintiff's vehicle stalls while it is on the detoured road. Plaintiff decides to walk to a nearby service station but decides to take a shortcut through the woods, rather than walking on the road. While doing so, he is attacked by a bear and seriously injured. Likely, the action of the wild animal would cut off the chain of causation begun by the highway contractor's original negligence. The independent intervening force (the bear) and the result (injury by a bear) are unforeseeable. The important point is that this result was unforeseeable. A court could find there was an independent intervening force, but if the end result is foreseeable, defendant is still liable, as in the *Kush* case in Exhibit 3-2. For example, assume the highway contractor blocked the road, forcing plaintiff to drive on a detour. That detour took the plaintiff into areas where there were known falling rocks. If a falling rock struck the plaintiff's car and injured the plaintiff, defendant could still be liable. The risk and danger of one being injured from the independent intervening force of falling rocks could be found to have produced a foreseeable result.

EXHIBIT 3-2 Relevant Case Law

David Kush, an Infant, By Sally Marszalek, His Mother and Natural Guardian, et al., Respondents, v. City of Buffalo et al., Appellants.

Court of Appeals of New York.

A school that negligently fails to secure dangerous chemicals from unsupervised access by children will not be relieved of liability when an injury occurs and it is reasonably foreseeable that the chemicals might be stolen by children.

During 1972, as part of a summer youth program sponsored by the Buffalo Board of Education, two 15-year-old students were hired to assist the custodial staff at Kensington High School. On July 11, while the adult employees were on their coffee break, the two, unsupervised student employees went to the school's chemistry laboratory. Neither the laboratory nor its adjacent storeroom were locked. The employees took some magnesium powder and potassium nitrate from glass jars, placed the chemicals into plastic sandwich bags, and dropped the bags from a fourth story window into the bushes below. They intended to retrieve the chemicals after work that day.

The infant plaintiff, then eight years old, lived near the school and regularly played on its grounds. On the day of the accident, as he had done previously, the child walked along a trodden path behind the bushes where the chemicals had been dropped. He found the chemicals and, believing them to be sand, began playing with the chemicals and with matches he had earlier found. The chemicals exploded and the boy sustained second degree burns to his hands, arms and face.

Plaintiffs brought this negligence action and the jury found the board of education liable for the infant plaintiff's injuries. This appeal presents issues concerning the scope of defendant's duty to secure dangerous chemicals stored on school premises, whether defendant breached this duty, and, if so, whether defendant's breach proximately caused plaintiff's injury....

First deciding to whom a duty, if any, was owed, plaintiff's presence on the school grounds could be found to be foreseeable. By their very nature, a school and its playgrounds attract children. In addition, Kensington High School is located in a residential neighborhood. It is true that the boy's accident occurred when school was out of session, a factor germane to the issue of the foreseeability of his presence on the grounds. This, however, does not vitiate defendant's duty to the infant plaintiff because there was proof that school authorities were aware that children played on the school property during the summer months.

Consideration now turns to what constituted reasonable care under the circumstances and whether defendant exercised that care. Defendant maintained on the school premises a store of dangerous chemicals for use in science classes. Defendant recognized that unsupervised access to these chemicals by children created a grave risk of harm to all present on the school grounds. The dangers inherent in many of the chemicals stored at the school included flammability and toxicity....

The severity of potential injuries from the misuse of chemicals is manifest. Accounts of children being maimed, blinded, or killed by playing with dangerous substances are legion. This danger could be averted with great ease and at little cost merely by storing the chemicals in a locked, fireproof cabinet—a remedy recognized in defendant's own regulations.

Thus, defendant purposely maintained a store of chemicals, some of which were inherently dangerous, and recognized that, in the environs of a school, a serious hazard would arise if deliberate safeguards were not in place. Reasonable care under the circumstances required the securing of the dangerous chemicals in such a way that their unsupervised access could not be readily obtained by children.... In light of the foreseeability of the risk and potential severity of harm to others engendered by a breach of this duty and the ease with which this duty could be satisfied, the jury acted

(Continued)

EXHIBIT 3-2 *(Continued)*

rationally in finding that defendant failed to exercise reasonable care under the circumstances by failing to secure the dangerous chemicals from unsupervised access by school children....

There remains the issue whether defendant's breach proximately caused plaintiff's injury. To establish a prima facie case, plaintiff must show that "defendant's negligence was a substantial cause of the events which produced the injury"...An interruption of the nexus between defendant's negligence and plaintiff's injury by the act of a third party may affect defendant's liability. An intervening act will be deemed a superseding cause and will serve to relieve defendant of liability when the act is of such an extraordinary nature or so attenuates defendant's negligence from the ultimate injury that responsibility for the injury may not be reasonably attributed to the defendant....When, however, the intervening act is a natural and foreseeable consequence of a circumstance created by defendant, liability will subsist....

Defendant argues that the student employees' stealing of the chemicals was an intentional act and, hence, a superseding cause of plaintiff's injury, relieving it of liability. Defendant is correct that an intervening intentional or criminal act will generally sever the liability of the original tort-feasor (see *Perry v. Rochester Lime Co., supra;* Prosser, Torts [4th ed.], § 44, p. 287), but, on the facts here, it may not rely on this doctrine.

That doctrine has no application when the intentional or criminal intervention of a third party or parties is reasonably foreseeable....Defendant's duty was to take reasonable steps to secure the dangerous chemicals from unsupervised access by children. By its very definition, any breach of this duty that leads to injury will involve an intentional, unauthorized taking of chemicals by a child. When the intervening, intentional act of another is itself the foreseeable harm that shapes the duty imposed, the defendant who fails to guard against such conduct will not be relieved of liability when that act occurs.

Source: Kush, by Marszalek v. City of Buffalo, 59 N.Y.2d 26, 462 N.Y.S.2d 831, 449 N.E.2d 725 (1983).

By way of summary on the issue of causation, the student should recognize that the key to the analysis of causation boils down to whether or not the result is foreseeable. As can be seen in the examples on intervening forces, such forces can be extremely unusual, bordering on the bizarre. It is those bizarre results that a defendant could not reasonably expect. A bizarre result works in favor of the defendant. It is those highly unusual, bizarre results that will likely cause a court or jury to find that the chain of causation has been broken. The more unusual and bizarre the result, the more likely the result will be held to be unforeseeable and the element of causation not established.

Joint and Several Liability

In the example discussed above in concurrent liability, Al was a passenger in Bart's vehicle. There was a collision with Craig's vehicle. Bart was found to be 30% at fault and Craig was found to be 70% at fault. The jury awarded $100,000. Accordingly, Bart is responsible for 30% of the $100,000 award and Craig is responsible for 70% of the $100,000 award. But what if one of the two defendants in our example is unable to pay his proportionate share as apportioned by the jury? One of the defendants has no insurance and is insolvent. This question brings up the important issue between the difference in the legal principles of "joint liability," "several liability," and "joint and several liability." **Joint liability** simply means that two

Joint Liability
Two or more defendants are legally responsible for the monetary award.

or more defendants are legally responsible for the entire money damages award. This principle of joint liability only takes on meaning, however, when two other principles are recognized. First, **several liability** means that where two or more defendants are found jointly liable for damages, a defendant is liable only for his or her separate, proportionate part of the award. Second, **joint and several liability** means that where two or more defendants are found jointly liable for damages, the plaintiff may collect the entire award either proportionately if each is able to pay his or her proportionate share *or* from any one of the defendants *or* from any and all of the defendants in various amounts until the legal obligation is fully satisfied.

It may be helpful to apply these principles using actual numbers from the case example involving the motor vehicle collision between Bart and Craig. Utilizing the principle of "several liability," each defendant is responsible only for his or her portion of the harm caused. In our example, with a jury verdict of $100,000, under several liability, Defendant Bart would be responsible for $30,000 (30% of $100,000). Defendant Craig would be responsible for $70,000 (70% of $100,000). Assume that Defendant Bart is a wealthy individual. He has significant assets and is able to cover the entire verdict amount. Or, more likely in today's world, Bart is a defendant with large enough liability insurance limits to cover this entire verdict amount. Assume that Defendant Craig is not only bankrupt but also has no liability insurance on the vehicle. Al has a right to receive $100,000. As a practical matter, however, Al will likely only collect a total of $30,000 and it will be from defendant Bart. This is because of Defendant Craig's bankruptcy, lack of insurance, and inability to pay his $70,000 share under the several liability principle.

Under the principle of joint and several liability, however, the plaintiff will be able to make a full recovery of the jury award of $100,000 because Defendant Bart is legally liable for the entire $100,000 jury award. Defendant Bart's remedy is then to try to obtain his $70,000 overpayment back from insolvent, uninsured Defendant Craig. Under the concept of joint and several liability, as long as a defendant has been found legally responsible—even as little as 1%—that defendant is legally responsible for the *entire* jury award. In fact, that exact scenario occurred in the case of *Walt Disney World v. Wood*, 515 So.2d 198 (Fla. 1987). (See Exhibit 3-3.)

The case arose out of the plaintiff's injury on the "Grand Prix" bumper-car ride at Walt Disney World in Orlando, Florida. With total negligence consisting of 100%,

Several Liability
A defendant is liable only for his or her separate, proportionate part of a monetary award.

Joint and Several Liability
In a situation in which two or more defendants are found liable for damages, the plaintiff may collect the entire award either proportionately if each is able to pay his or her proportionate share or from any one of the defendants or from any and all of the defendants in various amounts until the legal obligation is fully satisfied.

EXHIBIT 3-3 Relevant Case Law

Walt Disney World Co., et al., Petitioners, v. Aloysia Wood, et al., Respondents.

Supreme Court of Florida.

Aloysia Wood was injured in November 1971 at the grand prix attraction at Walt Disney World (Disney), when her fiance,[FN1] Daniel Wood, rammed from the rear the vehicle which she was driving. Aloysia Wood filed suit against Disney, and Disney sought contribution from Daniel Wood. After trial, the jury returned a verdict finding Aloysia Wood 14% at fault, Daniel Wood 85% at fault, and Disney 1% at fault. The jury assessed Wood's damages at $75,000. The court entered judgment against Disney for 86% of the damages. Disney subsequently moved to alter the judgment to reflect the jury's finding that Disney was only 1% at fault. The court denied the motion. On appeal, the fourth district affirmed the judgment on the basis of this Court's decision in *Lincenberg v. Issen*, 318 So.2d 386 (Fla.1975). Wood married her fiancé prior to this action....

(Continued)

EXHIBIT 3-3 *(Continued)*

> While arising in the context of a faultless plaintiff, it cannot reasonably be said that the Court in *Lincenberg* did not pass on the question now before us. Understandably, courts addressing the issue in subsequent decisions, including this Court, have interpreted *Lincenberg* as upholding the doctrine of joint and several liability....Therefore, the certified question, as worded, must be answered in the affirmative.
>
> The real issue before us is whether we should now replace the doctrine of joint and several liability with one in which the liability of codefendants to the plaintiff is apportioned according to each defendant's respective fault. According to Disney, this Court in *Hoffman* set for itself the goal of creating a tort system that fairly and equitably allocated damages according to the degrees of fault. Therefore, a defendant should only be held responsible to the extent of his fault in the same way as a plaintiff under comparative negligence.
>
> Joint and several liability is a judicially created doctrine. *Louisville & N.R.R. v. Allen,* 67 Fla. 257, 65 So. 8 (1914). This Court may alter a rule of law where great social upheaval dictates its necessity. *Hoffman,* 280 So.2d 435. The "social upheaval" which is said to have occurred here is the fundamental alteration of Florida tort law encompassed by the adoption of comparative negligence. Following the adoption of comparative negligence, some states have passed laws eliminating joint and several liability, and the courts of several others have judicially abolished the doctrine....
>
> There is nothing inherently fair about a defendant who is 10% at fault paying 100% of the loss, and there is no social policy that should compel defendants to pay more than their fair share of the loss. Plaintiffs now take the parties as they find them. If one of the parties at fault happens to be a spouse or a governmental agency and if by reason of some competing social policy the plaintiff cannot receive payment for his injuries from the spouse or agency, there is no compelling social policy which requires the codefendant to pay more than his fair share of the loss. The same is true if one of the defendants is wealthy and the other is not....
>
> On the other hand, the majority of courts which have faced the issue in jurisdictions with comparative negligence have ruled that joint and several liability should be retained....
>
> While recognizing the logic in Disney's position, we cannot say with certainty that joint and several liability is an unjust doctrine or that it should necessarily be eliminated upon the adoption of comparative negligence. In view of the public policy considerations bearing on the issue, this Court believes that the viability of the doctrine is a matter which should best be decided by the legislature. Consequently, we approve the decision of the district court of appeal.
>
> It is so ordered.

Source: Walt Disney World v. Wood, 515 So.2d 198 (Fla. 1987).

the jury found the plaintiff 14% at fault for her own injury and her fiancé to be 85% at fault for ramming his bumper car into the back of hers. (Comparative negligence/fault will be discussed in Chapter 6.) The Disney Corporation was found to be 1% at fault. However, under the principle of joint and several liability, Disney was ordered to pay 86% of the damages—its 1% portion plus the fiancé's 85% portion, because the fiancé was financially unable to pay his proportionate share.

As discussed in Chapter 1, one of the main purposes of our tort system is to compensate the injured plaintiff. The joint and several rule strongly affirms and promotes that purpose. Under the concept of joint and several liability, the courts place the risk and the burden of any loss on the defendant and not the plaintiff. This concept attempts to ensure that the innocent plaintiff will be compensated in full for the plaintiff's injuries. It protects innocent plaintiffs from being undercompensated in the event that one of the defendants cannot pay his or her proportionate share. The idea is that once liability and damages have been established, the defendants can battle it out among themselves to work out any overpayments. However, in examining

> ### Workplace Skills Tip
>
> The personal injury paralegal should understand the technical difference between the words "recovery" or "recover" and "collect" in terms of a plaintiff's claim. They are often confused and misused. When a plaintiff institutes suit in a personal injury action, plaintiff is attempting to "recover" money damages from a defendant.
>
> Once the jury, judge, or arbitrator renders a decision in favor of the plaintiff, the plaintiff has made a "recovery." Now, the plaintiff is in a position to "collect" the recovery, which may be done by obtaining a defendant's assets or income or by obtaining proceeds from a defendant's insurance policy.

our motor vehicle example and the *Walt Disney World* case, it can be seen that the battle by the solvent defendants Bart and Disney to recover money back from the insolvent defendants Craig and the fiancé will probably be difficult, if not futile.

FINAL COMMENTS ON SEVERAL LIABILITY VS. JOINT AND SEVERAL LIABILITY

Students sometimes inquire as to who decides whether there is to be a doctrine of several liability or joint and several liability. The answer is that the legislatures of the states will make that determination in the vast majority of cases. In some states, the courts have judicially created the doctrine involving several liability or joint and several liability.

In addition, some states will adopt, for example, a doctrine of several liability, but there may be exceptions. Section 12-2506 of Arizona Revised Statutes provides in pertinent part:

A. In an action for personal injury, property damage or wrongful death, the liability of each defendant for damages is several only and is not joint, except as otherwise provided in this section....

B. The liability of each defendant is several only and is not joint, except that a party is responsible for the fault of another person, or for payment of the proportionate share of another person, if any of the following applies:

1. Both the party and the other person were acting in concert.
2. The other person was acting as an agent or servant of the party.

An example of "acting in concert" might be two or more drivers drag racing and a person suffers a personal injury or death. In that instance several liability will not apply and one driver will be responsible for more than the driver's proportionate share of the total fault. In Paragraph D.2 of the statute, an employer will be responsible for the negligence or fault of the employer's employee.

Finally, the question is often asked how a plaintiff must or might go about choosing which defendant or defendants from whom to collect an award. Assume plaintiff has obtained a $500,000 jury verdict against four different defendants, each of whom is jointly and severally liable. Defendant A has a $1 million dollar liability policy. Defendant B has a $100,000 liability policy. Defendant C has a $250,000 policy. Defendant D has a $200,000 policy. The plaintiff could commence an action against B, C, and D to garnish those policies, because it will take all three to cover the $500,000 award. However, plaintiff will likely take the path of least resistance and just proceed against A, the defendant with the $1 million dollar policy. Barring a particular state's statutes, there is no requirement that plaintiff must attempt to collect from a certain defendant in any particular order.

Workplace Skills Tip

If the personal injury paralegal is in a firm representing a plaintiff, that client's cause needs to be vigorously pursued so that the client will be fully and reasonably compensated for his or her injury. If joint and several liability is the law in your jurisdiction, it is your responsibility to be on the alert for a defendant with "deep pockets." Your concern is not whether joint and several liability is fair or not. You may personally believe that it is not fair that a defendant who is only 1% at fault should shoulder the entire responsibility for a plaintiff's damages. It is your responsibility to assist in the development of facts that will establish liability on that defendant, even if only 1% because that will make your client whole. Remember your responsibility as a plaintiff personal injury paralegal. You are there to "build up" your client's case regardless of whether you agree with the law or believe the law should be something different.

Opponents of joint and several liability argue that a person with a slight portion of the legal responsibility unfairly shoulders the entire burden of the full damages award. It leads to plaintiff attorneys seeking a defendant with "deep pockets" to add to the list of defendants. It is probably no secret that if a large corporation or an extremely wealthy individual can be joined as a defendant, a plaintiff probably has a better chance of obtaining a favorable jury verdict as opposed to having joined defendants with limited economic means. Further, in terms of settlement, a defendant with deep pockets may consider participating in settlement negotiations precisely because of a concern over being held only 1% at fault but having to pay the full amount of an award. Chapter 1 discussed tort reform. The area of joint and several liability is also an area that has been the subject of tort reform. Some states have abolished the joint and several legal principle altogether, and some states have enacted legislation placing limitations on joint and several liability. Interestingly, following *Walt Disney World Co. v. Wood*, the Florida legislature enacted legislation limiting the joint and several rule.[4]

Contribution and Indemnity

Contribution
The right of one tortfeasor to recover from the other joint tortfeasor(s) when that tortfeasor has paid or may be liable to pay more than his or her proportionate share to the injured party.

Indemnity
An equitable remedy allowing one party to recover the entire amount from the other party.

When two or more defendants are involved in a negligence action, it is important to recognize and differentiate between the legal principles of contribution and indemnity. Contribution is a legal principle that may arise from time to time when multiple tortfeasors are involved. **Contribution** is the right of one tortfeasor to recover from the other joint tortfeasor(s) when that tortfeasor has paid or may be liable to pay more than his or her *proportionate share* to the injured party. **Indemnity**, however, is an equitable remedy allowing one party to recover the *entire amount* from the other party because it would be unfair and unjust for that party to shoulder the entire burden.

The application of the contribution principle can be demonstrated in that same example involving parties Al, Bart, and Craig under the joint and several liability discussion. Under the principle of joint and several liability, solvent Defendant Bart paid to the plaintiff Al the entire amount owing of $100,000. Defendant Bart paid his 30% proportional share of liability to the plaintiff, plus the 70% proportional share owed by insolvent Defendant Craig. Defendant Bart would have a right of contribution against Defendant Craig to seek and recover back the disproportionate share that Defendant Bart paid—the 70%. As pointed out in the Workplace Skills Tip, there is a vast difference between the right to "recover" and the ability to "collect."

Using our same example, contribution may also arise in a situation in which passenger plaintiff Al sues only defendant Bart for Bart's negligence in causing the plaintiff's personal injuries. Under the applicable rules of civil procedure, defendant

Bart, as a third-party plaintiff, may bring an action against Craig as a third-party defendant. This is pursuant to Federal Rule 14 and its state counterparts. Rule 14 is a rule that provides for the remedy of both contribution and indemnity. "A defending party may, as third-party plaintiff, serve a summons and complaint on a nonparty who is or may be liable to it for *all or part* of the claim against it." Rule 14, Federal Rules of Civil Procedure. (Emphasis added.) "All," of course, refers to the remedy of indemnity, and "or part" refers to the remedy of contribution. See the diagram in Exhibit 3-4 illustrating third-party practice. The principle of contribution applies to one defendant seeking contribution from a co-defendant, such as where Al sued both Bart and Craig. It also applies to a factual situation in which one defendant brings in a new third-party defendant for contribution, such as where Al sued Bart, and Bart, as a third-party plaintiff, impleaded Craig as a third-party defendant. Indemnity, likewise, applies to one defendant seeking indemnity from a co-defendant or that defendant, as a third-party plaintiff, seeking indemnity from a third-party defendant.

The principle of indemnity may arise by statute or by a contract. It may also arise by the court ordering indemnity in a particular case involving two or more parties. A classic example of indemnity is in the employment area, which will be discussed in Chapter 5. If an employee is negligent in the operation of an employer's motor vehicle while on the job, the employer is responsible in full to the injured plaintiff. The employer may seek indemnity from the employee to recover back all that the employer has paid to the plaintiff.

Also, it is not uncommon to find an indemnity clause in certain contracts, such as a lease agreement or a construction agreement. As an example, an indemnity clause in a construction agreement involving a contractor and a subcontractor may be similar to the following:

> Subcontractor shall protect and defend Contractor against and indemnify and save it harmless from all liability, claims, demands, and causes of action arising out of the execution and performance of work under this agreement. Subcontractor further agrees to procure a liability insurance policy with liability limits of $10,000,000 (Ten Million and no/100 Dollars) naming Contractor as an additional insured under such policy.

The important point for the student to remember is that contribution is a remedy in which the first party requests that *proportionate share* back from the second party that has been paid or may have to be paid by the first party. Indemnity, however, is a remedy in which the first party seeks the *entire amount* back from the second party.

EXHIBIT 3-4 Suit for Indemnity and Contribution

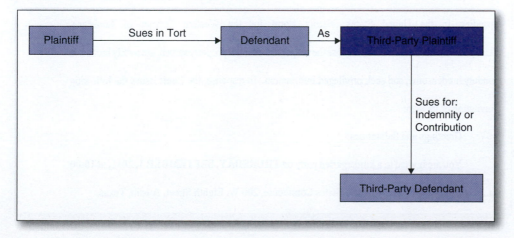

Workplace Skills Tip

The personal injury paralegal, plaintiff or defendant, will assist with cases in both state court and federal court. *Generally speaking*, state courts are less strict and perhaps a bit more forgiving on both procedure and law. State courts tend to be more "courts of equity." *But do not bank on that*! Generally, federal courts follow law and procedure strictly and precisely. Besides the Federal Rules of Civil Procedure, be aware of a federal court's local rules. The federal judges and the staff take those rules seriously. Finally, hope that the attorneys on your team do not ever have to face the wrath of a displeased federal judge. (See Exhibit 3-5.)

EXHIBIT 3-5 Federal Court Order

IN THE UNITED STATES DISTRICT COURT
FOR THE WESTERN DISTRICT OF TEXAS
AUSTIN DIVISION

FILED
2011 AUG 26 PM 1:58
CLERK US DISTRICT COURT
WESTERN DISTRICT OF TEXAS
BY_____
DEPUTY

THERESA MORRIS, WIFE OF
BOB MORRIS,

        Plaintiff,

-vs-

        Case Nos. A-11-MC-712-SS
                      A-11-MC-713-SS
                      A-11-MC-714-SS
                      A-11-MC-715-SS

JOHN COKER, ALLIS-CHALMERS
CORPORATION AND/OR STRATE
DIRECTIONAL DRILLING, INC.,
        Defendants.

_____

ORDER

BE IT REMEMBERED on this day the Court reviewed the files in the above-styled causes, and now enters the following opinion and orders.

Non-parties Lance Langford, Erik Hoover, and Brigham Oil & Gas, L.P. invite the Court to quash subpoenas issued to them on behalf of Jonathan L. Woods, in relation to a matter currently pending in the United States District Court for the Western District of Louisiana, Lafayette-Opelousas Division, because the subpoenas were not properly served, are overly broad and unduly burdensome, and seek privileged information. In response, the Court issues the following invitation of its own:

Greetings and Salutations!

You are invited to a kindergarten party on **THURSDAY, SEPTEMBER 1, 2011, at 10:00 a.m.** in Courtroom 2 of the United States Courthouse, 200 W. Eighth Street, Austin, Texas.

(Continued)

EXHIBIT 3-5 *(Continued)*

The party will feature many exciting and informative lessons, including:

- How to telephone and communicate with a lawyer

- How to enter into reasonable agreements about deposition dates

- How to limit depositions to reasonable subject matter

- Why it is neither cute nor clever to attempt to quash a subpoena for technical failures of service when notice is reasonably given; and

- An advanced seminar on not wasting the time of a busy federal judge and his staff because you are unable to practice law at the level of a first year law student.

Invitation to this exclusive event is not RSVP. Please remember to bring a sack lunch! The United States Marshals have beds available if necessary, so you may wish to bring a toothbrush in case the party runs late.

Accordingly,

IT IS ORDERED that defense counsel Jonathan L. Woods, and movants' attorney Travis Barton, shall appear in Courtroom 2 of the United States Courthouse, 200 W. Eighth Street, Austin, Texas, on **THURSDAY, SEPTEMBER 1, 2011, at 10:00 a.m.**, for a memorable and exciting event;

IT IS FINALLY ORDERED that Mr. Barton is responsible for notifying Mr. Woods of this order by providing him with a copy by mail or fax on this date.

SIGNED this the _2b_ day of August 2011.

SAM SPARKS
UNITED STATES DISTRICT JUDGE

CASE **3.1** Hypothetical Case: Developing Workplace Skills

You are a paralegal working in a plaintiff's personal injury law firm doing primarily insurance defense work. Your firm represents a defendant, Abbot, in a serious personal injury case. Benny, the plaintiff, suffered a traumatic brain injury in a most unfortunate automobile collision. Benny is a successful farmer, married with four minor children. He was operating his vehicle in a rural area going south on State Highway 23, a well-maintained two-way asphalt road. Your client, Abbott, was at a dead stop on the highway facing north in the opposite direction from Benny. Abbott intended to turn left onto a gravel road that intersected Highway 23 from the west. As he was waiting for the Benny vehicle to pass by, Abbott did not have his left turn signal depressed because it did not work. Abbott also had his foot on the brake as he was waiting to make his turn, but his brake lights did not work, either. He knew they did not illuminate but, thus far, he just hadn't found the time to have the lights repaired. The temperature was 75 degrees. It was approximately 3:00 p.m. There was no traffic. It was sunny with excellent visibility. The roadway, for miles both north and south, was flat and level. There was no traffic other than the vehicles involved.

Defendant Costello, also traveling north behind Abbott, was traveling 80 miles per hour. The posted speed limit on this highway was 55 miles per hour. Costello, not paying attention, was not aware of Abbot's vehicle until it was too late. When he first saw the Abbott vehicle up ahead, he knew he would have to swerve to avoid hitting it. He braked and swerved to the left and missed the Abbott vehicle but struck Benny's vehicle head-on in the opposite lane. The collision was severe and resulted in the brain injury to Benny, rendering him unable to continue in his farming operation.

The case is in suit in state court in your jurisdiction. The Rules of Civil Procedure there require that insurance information is discoverable. This jurisdiction also follows the joint and several liability rule. You know Abbott has a $5 million liability insurance policy on his vehicle because Abbott's liability insurance company has hired your firm to represent Abbott. You have also determined, through interrogatories, that defendant Costello has a $100,000 liability insurance policy on his vehicle.

You have just received this email from the lead attorney:

I note that you just received interrogatory answers from co-defendant Costello indicating that he has a $100,000 liability policy. As you know, our client, Mr. Abbott, has a $5 million policy with Rural Heartland Mutual Insurance Company. You are very familiar with these types of cases. Please excuse my hand-drawn diagram, but I thought it might help you understand what occurred. I'd be interested in your thoughts:

1. The insurance company, Rural Heartland insuring our client, is taking a hard-line position that there is no fault on their insured, Mr. Abbott, and it is 100% on Costello for speeding at 80 miles per hour, not keeping a proper lookout and not having his vehicle under control. The company believes that our client was perhaps negligent for having defective lights but that those lights did not cause the accident in question. Our client Costello was legally stopped on the highway, waiting to make a left-hand turn. Do you think a jury could find our client was negligent for having defective lights but that those defective lights did not cause the accident? Or is there some way that the lack of lights caused or contributed to causing this accident?

2. As you know, we have joint and several liability in our state. Do we need to tell the insurance company that they should consider offering some money instead of taking the position that this accident was all Costello's fault and making no offers to settle? Why?

Please enter your time on the Abbott 001 file.

EXHIBIT 3-6 Diagram of Accident

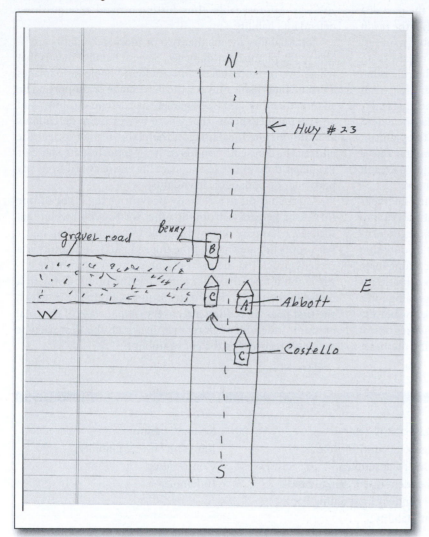

CHAPTER **SUMMARY**

Causation is the third element of the tort of negligence. There are two parts to causation. One part is actual cause. The other part is proximate cause. The test to determine actual cause is the "but for" test. That test means that but for the defendant's negligent conduct, the plaintiff would not have been injured. Proximate cause is the primary cause of an injury. Analyzing proximate cause involves an analysis of whether or not consequences of the defendant's negligent conduct were too remote or too removed from the risk the defendant created such that defendant should not be held liable.

Concurrent liability is the liability created when the separate negligent acts of two or more defendants combine or concur to cause a single injury to the plaintiff.

The "substantial factor" rule is a rule of causation that makes a tortfeasor liable to the plaintiff if the tortfeasor's negligent conduct was a "substantial factor" in producing the injury. It has been adopted by the courts because the "but for" rule does not work well in all situations.

Alternative liability occurs when plaintiff is injured by the negligent conduct of only one of two or more defendants but it is unknown which defendant caused the injury. The burden of proof shifts to the defendants to prove that their negligent conduct was not the actual cause of the plaintiff's injury. Legal malpractice cases present a unique element of proof for causation. This is called proof of "a case within a case." The plaintiff must prove that but for the attorney's negligence the plaintiff would have been successful in his or her case.

Proximate cause is the second part of causation to be examined after actual cause. Proximate cause is the primary cause of an injury. It is the natural, direct, and uninterrupted consequence of a negligent act or omission without which the injury would not have occurred. The primary test to determine proximate cause is foreseeability. Under this test, there is no proximate cause and no liability on the part of a defendant: (1) if the result was unforeseeable; (2) if the result was foreseeable, but it arose in an unforeseeable manner; or (3) if the plaintiff was unforeseeable. With regard to an unforeseeable result, there is an exception to the rule of no proximate cause if the result was unforeseeable. This arises in what are sometimes referred to as the "eggshell plaintiff" cases. The "eggshell plaintiff" rule mandates that the defendant takes the plaintiff as the defendant finds the plaintiff, and the defendant will be liable. It does not matter that a plaintiff has a far more severe or serious reaction or result than what a normal person would have experienced.

Indirect causation brings into play superseding intervening forces that cut off the chain of causation that was set into motion by the defendant's negligent conduct. Some force intervenes between the defendant's negligent act or omission and the occurrence of plaintiff's injury. An intervening force may be a dependent intervening force in which causation is not broken. It may also be an independent intervening force in which causation is typically broken. Whether or not the defendant remains liable will depend upon whether or not the intervening force was foreseeable. Typically, the more

unusual and more bizarre the result, the more likely the result was unforeseeable, thus cutting off and extinguishing defendant's liability.

Joint liability means that two or more defendants are liable to the plaintiff for damages. Several liability means that where two or more defendants are found liable for damages a defendant is liable only for the percentage or proportionate share of liability assessed against that defendant. Joint and several liability means that where two or more defendants are found liable for damages, the plaintiff may collect the entire award based upon his or her proportionate share or the plaintiff may choose to collect the entire award from any particular defendant or defendants.

Contribution is a remedy providing the right of one tortfeasor to recover from the other tortfeasor(s) when that tortfeasor has paid or may be liable to pay more than his or her proportionate share to the injured party. Indemnity is a remedy providing the right of one party to recover the entire amount from the other party. The important distinction between the two is that contribution is a remedy in which the first party is seeking a recovery of *a portion* of the total amount. Indemnity is a remedy in which the first party is seeking a recovery of the *entire* amount.

KEY TERMS

Actual Cause
"But for" Test
Proximate Cause
Concurrent Liability
"Substantial Factor" Rule
Alternative Liability

Foreseeability Test
"Eggshell Plaintiff" Rule
Indirect Causation
Dependent Intervening Force
Independent Intervening Force
Joint Liability

Several Liability
Joint and Several Liability
Contribution
Indemnity

REVIEW QUESTIONS

1. What is actual cause, also referred to as cause in fact? Provide an example.
2. Defendant manufacturer did not do a proper job of quality control at its processing plant in which it processes and cans salmon. A toxic chemical found its way into some cans of salmon during a several day period of time in the canning process. It was not discovered until consumers began complaining of becoming ill after eating the salmon. Plaintiff purchased a can of the contaminated salmon from a local grocery store. Plaintiff ate it the same day and became seriously ill after consuming the contents of the can. Was the defendant manufacturer's negligent conduct in not discovering the toxic chemical in the salmon the actual cause of plaintiff's injury? Should you apply the "but for" test and, if so, what result do you reach? Was the

manufacturer's negligent conduct a negligent act or a negligent omission?

3. Chelsea is riding in a speedboat on Pelican Lake with her boyfriend, Joe. Joe is not paying attention as he is trying to impress Chelsea with his juggling while trying to steer the boat with his knees. Gunner, driving his new jet ski at its top speed of 60 miles per hour can't believe it can travel that fast. His eyes are fixated on the instrument panel. With both Joe and Gunner not paying attention, there is a collision between Joe's boat and Gunner's jet ski. Chelsea receives serious injuries to both knees and can no longer be a professional swimmer. She sues both Joe and Gunner in negligence for her personal injuries. In this example, concerning causation, are there two separate negligent acts? Apply the "but for" test. Would the collision have occurred

without the negligent acts of both Joe and Gunner? What kind of liability arises if both are negligent?

4. Explain the holding and rationale for the holding in *Summers v. Tice* cited in the text.

5. What is the difference between actual cause and proximate cause?

6. A wealthy grandfather made a gift of a new Maserati automobile to his young but responsible 21-year-old grandson. The next day, the grandson was in a serious motor vehicle collision in which the plaintiff, his girlfriend, was seriously injured. The grandson was driving too fast for conditions, lost control of the car, and the car went into the ditch rolling several times. The grandson, with limited assets and temporarily unemployed, only carried the jurisdiction's minimum statutory liability insurance limits of $25,000. You are working as a personal injury paralegal in a new law firm just formed by an attorney fresh out of law school. Your firm represents the grandson's girlfriend. The inexperienced attorney, eager to find a way to obtain more compensation for the client, comes up with the idea of suing the grandfather. Knowing that you have studied torts and possibly testing you, the attorney tells you, "After all, 'but for' Gramps giving the car to the grandson, this tragic incident would not have happened!" The attorney asks your opinion. What is your response?

7. Defendant homeowner failed to fix a weak, rotting board on some steps leading up to a highly elevated deck attached to the home. Plaintiff stepped on the board. It gave way and plaintiff fell approximately 15 feet to the ground. Plaintiff was rendered unconscious for several minutes. While unconscious, a poisonous Brown Recluse spider bit him in the arm causing permanent skin damage, nerve damage, and partial paralysis in his arm. Is defendant homeowner liable in money damages in a lawsuit brought by plaintiff for his personal injury?

8. Explain the difference between joint and several liability and several liability only.

9. What is the difference between contribution and indemnity?

chapter 4

NEGLIGENCE: DAMAGES

LEARNING OBJECTIVES

After studying this chapter, you should be able to:

- Differentiate between general damages and special damages.

- Differentiate between past damages and future damages.

- Recognize the importance of medical testimony in proving damages.

- Determine the concept of "mitigation of damages."

- State and differentiate between the "collateral source rule" and "subrogation."

- Describe "nominal damages."

- Recognize the distinction between "survival" and "wrongful death" causes of action and damages awarded for each.

Preponderance of Evidence
The greater weight of the evidence so that proof of a fact is "more likely than not" true.

"Revenge is an act of passion; vengeance of justice. Injuries are revenged. Crimes are avenged."

Samuel Johnson

Compensatory Damages

The last of the four elements of negligence is damages. The elements of duty, breach of duty, and causation have been established. Now, the plaintiff must establish the fourth and final element—his or her damages that have resulted from the defendant's negligent conduct. The burden of proof of damages is on the plaintiff. The plaintiff must furnish this evidence by a **preponderance of the evidence**. Preponderance of the evidence is the greater weight of the evidence so that proof of a fact is "more likely than not" true. See Exhibit 4-1 for a sample JIG on the burden of proving damages.

The main public policy purpose for tort law is compensation. Compensatory damages are money damages awarded to compensate the plaintiff and make the plaintiff whole. The system is not perfect. Life, limb, and freedom from pain cannot be restored. However, compensatory damages are a means of attempting to place the plaintiff in the same relative position that he or she was in before the loss by way of monetary compensation.

EXHIBIT 4-1 Jury Instruction Guide

BURDEN OF PROVING DAMAGES

Ladies and gentlemen of the jury, you cannot assess damages against the defendant unless the plaintiff has satisfied the burden of proof with respect to her damages, if any. That is to say, the burden rests upon the plaintiff to prove the elements of her damages in this case, if any, by the greater weight of the evidence. If a breach of duty has caused no appreciable detriment to the plaintiff, she is entitled to recover nominal damages.

EXHIBIT 4-2 Jury Instruction Guide

FAIR AND ADEQUATE DAMAGES

Each person who suffers an injury or a detriment from a wrongful act or omission of another person may recover from that person money compensation, which is called damages. Damages, should you award them, should be adequate to fairly compensate the plaintiff for all detriment proximately caused by the acts or omissions of those you find to be at fault, whether or not the injury or detriment could have been anticipated.

In all cases, any damages must be reasonable.

Damages may be awarded for injury or detriment into the future. It is not necessary that the evidence show conclusively or without a shadow of a doubt that future injury or detriment will be incurred. While absolute certainty is not required, mere conjecture or mere possibility does not warrant an award of damages for future injury or detriment that is not likely to exist or occur.

Compensatory damages must be reasonable. Compensatory damages must be adequate. Compensatory damages must be fair. Stated another way, compensatory damages must fairly, reasonably, and adequately compensate the plaintiff. As a reminder, just as in studying the law of the elements of duty, breach of duty, and causation, studying the law of the element of damages is not something that is being learned in the abstract or in a vacuum. This study has a genuine workplace skills application to the personal injury paralegal. This is because of the personal injury paralegal's anticipated workplace involvement with both JIGs and medical records. Proof of the damages element of negligence is not possible without the use of medical testimony and medical records. Exhibit 4-2 provides a sample JIG on damages in general.

TYPES OF COMPENSATORY DAMAGES

Compensatory damages are categorized as either **general damages** or **special damages**. General damages are "non-economic" losses, such as pain and suffering, disfigurement, or mental anguish, all of which have no specific, itemized value. Special damages are "economic" losses, such as medical expenses, lost wages, or the cost of hiring household help, all of which do have a specific itemized value and can be more easily determined or calculated on a simple mathematical basis. General damages and **non-economic damages** are sometimes used interchangeably. Similarly, special damages and **economic damages** are sometimes used interchangeably. Concerning those damages, the terms "general" and "special" will be used in this textbook.

Compensatory damages, whether general damages or special damages, may be categorized as **past damages** or **future damages**. Past damages are those damages that have been suffered or incurred from the date of the loss caused by defendant's negligent conduct to the date of the trial. Future damages are those damages that are reasonably certain to occur from the date of the trial until a reasonable time into the future. For special damages, the plaintiff may have incurred past medical bills from the date of defendant's negligent conduct up to the date of the trial. Therefore, the plaintiff will present a claim for past special damages representing medical bills incurred from the date of the negligent conduct up to the date of the trial. The plaintiff's injury may be more serious so that medical bills are reasonably certain to continue into the future. The plaintiff will then present an additional claim for future special damages representing future medical bills to

General Damages
These damages are synonymous with "non-economic damages," which include losses such as pain and suffering, disfigurement, or mental anguish, all of which have no specific, itemized value.

Special Damages
These damages are synonymous with "economic damages," which include losses such as medical expenses, lost wages, or the cost of hiring household help, all of which do have a specific itemized value and can be more easily determined or calculated on a simple mathematical basis.

Non-Economic Damages
These damages are synonymous with "general damages," which include losses such as pain and suffering, disfigurement, or mental anguish, all of which have no specific, itemized value.

Economic Damages
These damages are synonymous with "special damages," which include losses such as medical expenses, lost wages, or the cost of hiring household help, all of which do have a specific itemized value and can be more easily determined or calculated on a simple mathematical basis.

Past Damages
Those damages that have been suffered or incurred from the date of the loss caused by defendant's negligent conduct to the date of the trial.

Future Damages
Those damages that are reasonably certain to occur from the date of the trial until a reasonable time into the future.

be incurred from the date of the trial and continuing into a reasonable time in the future.

As to general damages, for example, the plaintiff may have suffered with past pain and suffering from the date of defendant's negligent conduct up to the date of the trial. Therefore, the plaintiff will present a claim for past general damages, which represents pain and suffering suffered from the date of the negligent conduct up to the date of the trial. The plaintiff's injury may be more serious because it is a permanent injury. The plaintiff will then present an additional claim for future general damages. These future damages will represent future pain and suffering to be incurred from the date of the trial forward and continuing into a reasonable time in the future.

One point about future damages is that the amount of time future damages may reasonably last into the future will depend upon the type of damages claim, the age of the plaintiff, and the evidence presented. A claim for a permanent injury involving future pain and suffering will use a person's life expectancy as a reasonable guide for a length of time into the future such pain and suffering will likely last. An injury to a child could involve a period of time of 50 years, 60 years, or more depending upon the child's age and life expectancy. An injury to an elderly person may only be for 5 or 10 years or several years, again, depending upon the person's actual age and life expectancy. See the sample life expectancy JIG in Exhibit 4-3, which discusses the concept of mortality tables.

A claim of damages for future medical expenses will depend primarily upon the physician's testimony. For example, the physician may state that plaintiff will require physical therapy and will incur expenses for physical therapy for the rest of his or her life. Life expectancy is then the measure of time into the future that those damages will reasonably last. Life expectancy will then become relevant in assessing money damages for those future damages. On the other hand, assume the physician testifies that a plaintiff needs physical therapy for three more years. In this case, the amount of time such future damages will last is reasonably measured by the finite time period of three years instead of by an assumed life expectancy.

Finally, if a plaintiff were suffering an economic/financial loss of not being able to work in the future, medical testimony will again provide reasonable guidance to the jury. The doctor may testify that the plaintiff will not be able to work

EXHIBIT 4-3 Jury Instruction Guide

LIFE EXPECTANCY

The plaintiff _____, was _____ years of age at the time of this accident. According to the American Table of Mortality published by the American Insurance Institute, the life expectancy of an individual _____ years of age is _____ years. This fact, of which the court takes judicial notice, is now in evidence to be considered by you in arriving at the amount of damages, if any, you may choose to award.

The restricted significance of this evidence should be noted. Life expectancy, as shown by a mortality table, is merely an estimate of the average remaining length of life of all individuals in our country of a given age, based upon a limited record of experience. Therefore, the inference that may be drawn from the life expectancy shown by the table applies only to the one who has the average health, habits, and exposure to danger of people that age. Therefore, in considering the life expectancy of any individual, including the plaintiff _____, you should consider, in addition to the table of mortality, all other facts and circumstances in evidence bearing on his life expectancy, including his occupation, activities, habits, and state of health at the time of the mishap.

Workplace Skills Tip

If the paralegal is assisting with a more serious plaintiff's personal injury case, future damages of some type will likely be introduced into evidence for the jury's consideration. If a permanent injury is involved, some damages, whether general or special, may reasonably be expected to last for the rest of a person's life. One method of determining how long those damages might last will depend upon how long the plaintiff might reasonably live. The jury will typically receive evidence of a plaintiff's life expectancy from mortality tables published by various sources. It is the job of the plaintiff's attorney, at the close of the evidence, to ask the court to take judicial notice of the mortality tables. Be a good backup and make sure the attorney does just that.

for one more year. Guidance to the jury is thus provided. If the plaintiff's annual salary is $50,000 a year, the task is fairly easy. On the other hand, the doctor may testify that a plaintiff with a debilitating injury who is say, 40 years old, cannot ever work again in his or her lifetime. To determine those damages it would then be the jury's task to consider a reasonable retirement age in determining how long such future income loss would last. If a jury determines that age 65 is a reasonable retirement age for this person, there would be 25 years of future economic loss to be calculated.

SPECIAL DAMAGES

Following are some examples of special damages ("economic loss"):

- Medical and medical care expenses
- Rehabilitation services
- Custodial care
- Loss of earnings
- Loss of earning capacity
- Loss of income
- Loss of support
- Cost of substitute domestic services

A sample JIG concerning special damages is found in Exhibit 4-4.

EXHIBIT 4-4 Jury Instruction Guide

SPECIAL DAMAGES

The term "special damages" includes those types of damages arising from medical expenses and medical care, physical therapy, rehabilitation services, custodial care, loss of earnings, loss of earning capacity, loss of income, loss of support, cost of substitute domestic services, loss of employment, loss of business, and loss of employment opportunities.

Compensation for special damages such as medical expenses and medical care, custodial care, substitute domestic services, and rehabilitation services is measured by the reasonable value, but not to exceed the actual cost of the goods or services reasonably required and actually furnished to the injured party or that are reasonably certain to be required in the future.

Compensation for special damages such as loss of earnings, loss of earning capacity, loss of income, loss of support, loss of employment, loss of business, and loss of business opportunities is measured by the reasonable value of those losses the injured party is reasonably certain to sustain in the future.

From reviewing the list of examples of special damages, you can see that special damages are usually capable of being calculated and proved with some simple math. Special damages are economic losses in the form of actual expenses that the plaintiff has already incurred, (past damages), or is reasonably likely to incur in the future, (future damages). They are sometimes referred to by lawyers and judges as "out-of-pocket costs" or "specials." The list is fairly self-explanatory, but comment on a few of the potentially problematic special damages may be instructive.

PROBLEMATIC SPECIAL DAMAGES ISSUES: A HYPOTHETICAL CASE

Assume, because of defendant's negligent conduct, a plaintiff has incurred medical bills for treatment from several physicians at a medical clinic. Plaintiff has incurred total clinic medical bills of $5,435.21. In addition, because plaintiff had to be hospitalized, plaintiff has incurred hospital bills from a hospital totaling $9,109.43. Following release from the hospital, physical therapy was prescribed that lasted several months. Rehabilitation bills from a physical therapist total $2,358.30. Further, assume the plaintiff was earning $7,000 per month at the time of the incident caused by defendant's negligent conduct. Plaintiff missed three months of work. Total lost earnings are easily calculated with simple math at $21,000 ($7,000 a month $\times$ 3 months = $21,000). Special damages consisting of actual economic loss are the following:

Medical Expenses	Rehabilitation Expenses	Lost Earnings
$5,435.21 Doctor/Clinic bills	$2,358.30 Therapy bills	$21,000.00
$9,109.43 Hospital bills		
$14,544.64 Total Medical		

Total Special Damages (Total Economic Loss or "Total Specials")

$14,544.64 Medical
$2,358.30 Rehabilitation
$21,000.00 Lost Earnings
$37,902.94 Total

Compiling and analyzing special damages is primarily a mathematical task for the personal injury paralegal. Admittedly, a past wage loss is easier to mathematically calculate when the plaintiff was being paid a salary by the month or by the hour as opposed to being paid by commission. But even in the case of lost commission income, historical past commission earnings can be obtained, and that historical data may be used to reasonably estimate a loss.

Just because the numbers add up to the penny, however, does not mean there cannot be issues with plaintiff's proof of this element of damages. Assume the paralegal has checked the numbers several times. The numbers add up. What could possibly go wrong as the plaintiff's personal injury paralegal is assisting with building up the plaintiff's case with the special damages? First, the medical bills may reflect a pattern of overtreatment. Is the plaintiff sincerely attempting to become well or is the plaintiff needlessly seeking attention from a physician or a chiropractor or a physical therapist? Overtreatment with a chiropractor is not an uncommon occurrence with some plaintiffs.

The jury will be scrutinizing the plaintiff's medical treatment. Medical expenses must be both reasonable and necessary. If medical, chiropractic, physical therapy, or any type of medical treatment is overdone, there will be an issue as to whether or not such treatment was even necessary. In that situation, a jury may not award all of the plaintiff's claimed special damages for medical bills. Typically, the plaintiff and defendant will stipulate at trial that "if the proper person from Clinic X or Hospital Y were called to testify, such person would testify that the necessary and reasonable medical/hospital expenses incurred by plaintiff in this case are $_____." That is not always the case because there are cases in which such expenses are legitimately disputed.

Assume the main injury to the plaintiff is to the left shoulder. The clinic bills total $5,435.21. Intermixed with all of the medical bills representing treatment by plaintiff's various treating physicians at the clinic are some bills for office visits for shingles, the flu, the right shoulder, or some other part of the body other than the left shoulder. The paralegal, whether on a team representing a plaintiff or defendant, must scrutinize medical bills. This is to make certain that those bills relate to the incident caused by the defendant's negligence. Scrutiny is required to determine whether the treatment reflected in the bills supports or contradicts the plaintiff's claimed personal injury. Paying attention to detail in all aspects of a personal injury case, including medical bills, is extremely important.

Review the plaintiff's lost wages in the example. This is an item of special damages that also appears to be clear-cut. The plaintiff earned $7,000 per month and was off work for exactly three months. The astute plaintiff's paralegal has verified those facts from the plaintiff's employer. So, what could possibly go wrong? As the personal injury paralegal learns to obtain, review, and analyze medical records, the paralegal will experience an awakening. These records are documents that truly support or contradict the plaintiff's proof of the element of damages.

In the example, assume the defendant paralegal finds a note in the records of the plaintiff's treating physician dated six weeks after the accident: "After my exam today, full strength and range of motion has returned to patient's left shoulder. There is no more muscle spasm. X-rays are normal. It's my opinion patient is clearly able to return to work as of today." The contradiction between the plaintiff's claim of special damages for lost earnings over a three-month period and the plaintiff's own treating physician's remarks about a lesser period of time is obvious. This contradiction presents a serious difficulty of proof for the plaintiff concerning this particular element of special damages.

The astute personal injury paralegal, whether on the plaintiff's or the defendant's side, should always be scrutinizing claimed special or general damages of the plaintiff in relationship to the plaintiff's own medical records. It is a guarantee that the jury will do so. This is an important topic that will be discussed in greater detail in later chapters dealing with obtaining and analyzing medical records.

SPECIAL DAMAGES: LOSS OF EARNINGS VS. LOSS OF EARNING CAPACITY

As discussed at the beginning of this chapter, special damages and general damages may consist of either past damages that have already been incurred by the plaintiff or future damages that will likely be incurred in the future. In the special damages hypothetical case just discussed, past special damages are those actual expenses that the plaintiff has already incurred up to the time of the trial totaling $37,902.94. Future special damages are those same items of special damages or expenses representing economic losses that are reasonably likely to occur in the future. In the hypothetical example above, only *past* special damages were illustrated. Plaintiff may incur, in the *future,* additional medical expenses, rehabilitation expenses, loss of earnings, or other special damages besides those past special damages as illustrated. This is true if plaintiff received a more serious injury that will leave some lasting and permanent side effects.

To demonstrate this point, focus attention on those items of special damages for plaintiff's "loss of earnings" and "loss of earning capacity." There is a significant difference between loss of earnings and loss of earning capacity, even though they sound similar. Assume the plaintiff, Leo, is injured in a motor vehicle accident while on vacation. Leo is employed by a large construction company as a construction supervisor earning $30.00 an hour. His back is injured by the defendant's negligent conduct. He knows the business forward and backward and has done office work in the past, having worked his way up the ranks. He is unable to do the physical work he was previously doing, but the company wants to keep him on as an office worker making $20.00 an hour. This is $10.00 an hour less than he was previously earning, but he needs a job, and he loves working for this company so he agrees to take the lesser paying job. Damages for past **loss of earnings** represent past damages for an actual loss of income—salary, wages, or commissions from the date of the accident and continuing up to the date of trial. Damages for **loss of earning capacity** are those money damages that will result in the future from the plaintiff not being able to earn the same amount of money earned before the accident.

In the example, if Leo did not work for six months because of his back injury, he would present a past loss of earnings claim of $30 an hour × 40 hours a week, which equals $1,200 a week. Taking that amount times the 26 weeks he was off work, his past loss of earnings claim to the date of the trial would be $31,200 ($1,200 × 26). He may also have additional past loss of earnings based upon the time he started work at the reduced salary of $20 an hour up until the time of the trial based on the $10 per hour loss. Going forward into the future, Leo's earning capacity has been impaired or diminished. He will continue to earn a salary for the rest of his working life, but he will earn less of a salary because of the injury caused by defendant's negligence. Leo will also present a claim for future damages for loss of earning capacity based upon the $10 an hour loss. He had earnings of $30 an hour before the accident, and he now has earnings of $20 an hour. This loss will continue into the future reaching a point when he would likely retire. A reasonable retirement age that a jury may consider is age 65, however, that age is not carved in stone.

For example, Leo may testify that other than his back he is in excellent health, the company is "his life," he is an admitted workaholic, and he actually planned to work until age 70. The jury can reasonably determine a loss of earning capacity based on age 70 instead of the traditional age 65. On the other hand, the company may have a mandatory retirement age of 62 for employees. If so, the age of 62 would establish a reasonable date for computation of future damages. Damages for loss of impairment of earning capacity will require testimony from the plaintiff's treating physician that plaintiff has suffered a permanent injury. Further, testimony may be required from an expert witness economist who can calculate the future loss.

Loss of Earnings

Past damages for an actual loss of income—salary, wages, commissions, and so forth—from the date of the incident caused by defendant's negligent conduct and continuing up to the date of trial.

Loss of Earning Capacity

Those money damages that will result in the future from the plaintiff not being able to earn the same amount of money that he or she earned before the incident in question.

Students sometimes question the difference between "loss of earnings" and "loss of income." Typically, loss of earnings refers to lost wages, lost salary, or lost commissions. This loss typically represents a loss by an employee earning a wage or salary, whether paid by the hour, week, or month. Loss of income typically refers to a loss by one who may be self-employed. This could be someone other than an employee, such as a sole proprietor of a small business, who loses income from his or her business because of a personal injury.

General Damages

Following are some examples of general damages ("non-economic loss"):

- Pain and suffering
- Inconvenience
- Physical impairment
- Disfigurement
- Mental anguish/emotional distress (mental, psychological suffering, which includes fright, distress, anxiety, depression, grief)
- Fear of injury
- Fear of illness
- Loss of society and companionship
- Loss of consortium
- Injury to reputation, humiliation

From reviewing the list of sample general damages, it can be seen that these types of damages are not determined by simple mathematical means, as are special damages. General damages are not precise and are not easily quantifiable. While special damages represent out-of-pocket losses, general damages represent quality-of-life losses. A sample JIG concerning general damages is contained in Exhibit 4-5.

GENERAL DAMAGES: PAIN AND SUFFERING

While most of the elements of general damages are self-explanatory, some elements merit further discussion. Perhaps one of the most significant items of general damages is pain and suffering. Obviously, pain and suffering is not something that is mathematically quantifiable. There is no objective formula or yardstick for a jury to measure human suffering. As discussed in Chapter 1, it is a matter left to the experience, common sense, and good judgment of the jury. Each individual plaintiff's case will be judged by the individual facts and circumstances bearing on the plaintiff's injury.

EXHIBIT 4-5 Jury Instruction Guide

GENERAL DAMAGES

The term "general damages" includes damages arising from pain, suffering, inconvenience, physical impairment, disfigurement, mental anguish, emotional distress, fear of injury, fear of loss, fear of illness, injury to reputation, humiliation, and inconvenience. General damages must be measured by the reasonableness of an award in the light of all of the circumstances of the case. In considering the reasonableness of the award, you may consider whether the element of damages is temporary or permanent and whether or not, in the future, those damages will reasonably be averted or relieved.

The student may be wondering how the jury determines the amount of claimed non-economic damages such as pain and suffering. The plaintiff's attorney guides the jury in calculating those non-mathematical, imprecise, non-economic/general damages such as pain and suffering. As an example, consider a hypothetical final argument from a plaintiff's attorney in a personal injury case:

Ladies and gentlemen of the jury, I have just completed all I have to say concerning the defendant's fault in this case, which has been conclusively established. I have told you how to answer the questions concerning the defendant's negligence in the special verdict form you must complete. It's time to turn to the question of money damages and for you to figure out an amount of money that will fairly, adequately, and reasonably compensate my client for this horrific injury in which he lost most of his right arm.

Let's start with one of the first items of damages on your special verdict form. One of the items of damages that I expect her honor, Judge Kolbe, to instruct you that you may consider is an item called "pain and suffering." Judge Kolbe will tell you there is simply no yardstick to measure pain and suffering. She will tell you that, in the final analysis, it comes down to your own experience, good common sense, and good judgment.

So how might you go about doing this? Let me call upon your experience, good common sense, and good judgment. Let me suggest to you one way you might consider approaching it. I'm not telling you this is the way to do it—only that it is an example of how you might do it. You do it the way you see fit after hearing all of the evidence and after receiving her honor, Judge Kolbe's, instructions to you.

Believe it or not, though, we make assessments of pain and suffering all the time by valuing the opposite of pain and suffering. We put a value on those things in life that give us pleasure and enjoyment. If you were to purchase a ticket for a good seat at a concert by a popular entertainer today, you would probably pay approximately $100 for that ticket. If the concert lasted four hours, you have paid $25 an hour for an experience that is rewarding and provides much pleasure and enjoyment in life. If you would pay $25 an hour for something enjoyable, would you also not pay $25 an hour so as to not experience something unpleasant or painful?

In this case, we know my client, Will, has lost his right arm at the elbow, and he has constant pain and difficulty in his upper arm and shoulder during his entire waking hours each and every day—that's approximately 16 hours of every day. If we multiply $25 an hour times 16 hours we arrive at $400 a day. That $400 a day times 365 days a year equals $146,000 a year. Since it has been two years since this horrific explosion caused this disabling arm injury, simple math tells us that $146,000 × 2 equals $292,000 up to the time of this trial. In the space on the special verdict form where it asks how much money will reasonably compensate my client, Will, for past pain and suffering, and while this is totally up to you, I would suggest that you insert the figure of $292,000 for that particular element of damages for past pain and suffering.

The next item of damages I want to discuss with you is future pain and suffering. Judge Kolbe is also expected to instruct you that you may consider my client's life expectancy in considering future damages. Based on Will's current age and the mortality tables now in evidence, his life expectancy is for another 20 years, approximately. Accordingly, using our same example, $146,000 a year times 20 years is $2,920,000. I would respectfully suggest that you insert the figure of $2.9 million in the space for the damages for "future pain and suffering" on your special verdict form.

The above example represents what is called the per diem (per day) argument permitted in many jurisdictions but with the caveat that it can be mentioned only as an example of how a jury may compute damages. It can be seen that while simple math is reserved primarily for determining special damages, simple math can be utilized by a clever plaintiff's attorney in determining otherwise non-precise, subjective general damages.

GENERAL DAMAGES: IMPAIRMENT VS. DISABILITY

One of the items of general damages is "physical impairment." There is a standard manual entitled *AMA Guides to the Evaluation of Permanent Impairment,* which has been published by the American Medical Association since 1971. This manual is utilized by many physicians, particularly orthopedic surgeons, in assessing a patient's permanent impairment from an injury. The example given above in the hypothetical final argument involving the loss of an arm at the elbow level can be used to analyze this element of general damages. Under the current *AMA Guides to the Evaluation of Permanent Impairment,* 6th edition, a loss of the arm at the elbow would receive a 95% partial permanent impairment rating of the upper extremity (the arm) and a 57% partial permanent impairment rating of the whole body—a substantial permanent impairment rating.

In evaluating damages in a personal injury case, all things being somewhat equal, a higher percentage of partial permanent impairment will generally mean higher compensatory damages than a case with a lower percentage of partial permanent impairment. Attorneys and liability insurance carriers will typically use an impairment rating as an important factor in evaluating a personal injury case for settlement and for trial. For example, if a plaintiff received a permanent injury to the lumbar area (lower part) of the back, a physician's report may state that because of this injury, plaintiff will have limited range of motion and loss of strength in his lower back "for the rest of his life." (In other words, a permanent injury.) Another physician's report may state that because of this permanent injury, based on the limited range of motion and other factors, plaintiff has a 20% partial permanent impairment of the entire back. Regardless of the particular percentage assigned, the fact that an injury is somewhat quantified by the percentage of impairment makes the injury one that is easier to evaluate.

There are organizations that track jury damages awards and settlements based on various types of injuries, various percentages of partial permanent ratings to various parts of the body, and other factors. One such organization is Jury Verdict Research found at *http://www.juryverdictresearch.com.* If a law firm is primarily a firm representing plaintiffs, it may belong to a national plaintiff lawyers' organization called American Association for Justice. If a law firm is primarily a firm representing defendants or insurance companies, it may belong to an organization called the Defense Research Institute. Those organizations typically have valuable resources consisting of recent case analyses, brief banks, and expert witness information. They may also have information on jury verdicts and settlements.

While there may be others, there is a computer software program called **Colossus** which some insurance companies utilize. Information such as the age, sex, type of injury, medical expenses, permanent impairment rating, and other factors and data are imputed into the system. The system then performs a calculation of points to assess a dollar range of the value of the case. Plaintiff attorneys complain that some insurance companies then become stuck on the Colossus value and do not take into account such items as a plaintiff's emotional distress, pain and suffering, loss of enjoyment of life, or the personality and quality of the anticipated testimony of the plaintiff and other witnesses.

While each case is different, a plaintiff with a 20% partial permanent impairment rating to the back may provide a range of settlement or verdict based on other settlements and verdicts with that same 20% impairment rating to the back. Of course, a partial permanent impairment rating is only one factor in evaluating a case. The most important factor is still the likeability and believability of the plaintiff, and how the injury has affected that individual person's life, socially and financially.

There is a distinct difference between **impairment** and **disability**. Under the current *AMA Guides*, an impairment is "an alteration of an individual's health status; a deviation from normal in a body part or organ system and its functioning." Under that same *AMA Guides*, a disability is "an alteration of an individual's capacity to meet personal, social or occupational demands because of an impairment."[1] The plaintiff's impairment needs to be viewed from the standpoint of how that impairment affects daily living and the impact on the performance of one's vocation.

One may have an "impairment" to a limb but not suffer a "disability" from performing the usual and regular duties of a particular occupation or profession. For example, if a person lost the use of a finger causing a permanent impairment, it is still necessary to consider the impact of that finger's loss on the plaintiff's daily living and occupation or profession. If the person were a professional concert violinist, the loss of a finger with perhaps a minor partial permanent impairment rating, would be a ruinous disability. The problem could range from not being able to play music at all to no longer being able to precisely and perfectly hit the notes as required of a professional musician. Either way, the musician's life vocation would likely be seriously affected—even to the point of career termination with obvious serious financial consequences.

On the other hand, if the person with the injured finger were a lawyer, the lawyer would have an impairment but not a disability. The lawyer could still perform all of the usual and regular duties of his or her profession. The injury would likely not affect this professional's ability to earn a living. There would be no financial consequences to the lawyer. There would be dire financial consequences to the concert violinist. It can be seen that the item of general damages for physical impairment cannot be viewed in a vacuum. The effect on the individual's life must be considered.

Colossus
Software program utilized by some insurance companies to evaluate a personal injury case.

Impairment
"An alteration of an individual's health status; a deviation from normal in a body part or organ system and its functioning." *AMA Guides to the Evaluation of Permanent Impairment*

Disability
"An alteration of an individual's capacity to meet personal, social, or occupational demands because of an impairment." *AMA Guides to the Evaluation of Permanent Impairment*

Workplace Skills Tip

In assisting the litigation team with a personal injury case, whether plaintiff or defendant, the paralegal must always consider the effect of the personal injury on the plaintiff's ability to earn a living. A case in which a person's ability to earn a living has been adversely affected will have greater monetary value than one in which there may be a technical permanent impairment, but the individual is still able to earn a living.

GENERAL DAMAGES: FEAR OF INJURY, LOSS OF CONSORTIUM, DISFIGUREMENT

One of the elements of general damages is fear of injury. Consider a plaintiff who has received a serious orthopedic injury, such as a fractured leg or fractured hip. A person may have a legitimate fear of reinjuring that leg or hip. Another person could have a legitimate fear of arthritis developing at the injury site. That fear is an element of compensable general damages. Likewise, there is no yardstick to measure that fear in general damages. It will still be up to the sound discretion of the jury. Factors might include the plaintiff's age, general health, how reasonable the fear is in relationship to what the treating physician has opined, and of course the general likeability and believability of the plaintiff. As in the final argument example above, a creative plaintiff's attorney will try to create a damages number for the jury.

Some further discussion is required concerning the element of general damages entitled loss of consortium. The typical understanding of these damages is that they represent only a loss of the sexual relationship between one spouse and the other. However, a claim for damages for loss of consortium has a broader meaning. **Loss of consortium** damages compensate for the loss of *any services* one spouse provides to another. Besides those sexual in nature, such services may consist of cooking, cleaning, household chores, household repairs, and the like. How are those general damages calculated? Again, there is no objective yardstick. Refer to the factors provided in the example concerning fear of injury. In addition to those factors, a creative plaintiff's attorney may establish that the going rate in the community for household help is $25.00 an hour. The injured husband probably spent, on average, 10 hours a week helping with cleaning the house, washing windows, taking out garbage, and doing needed simple household repairs. If the husband were unable to perform these duties for say 12 weeks, a jury might reasonably conclude there has been loss of consortium damages of $3,000 ($25 an hour $\times$ 10 hours = $250 a week $\times$ 12 weeks = $3,000). If a loss of a sexual service is also being pursued, one can only imagine the final argument of the bold, creative plaintiff's attorney who presents a case for loss of consortium damages based on the dollar value an upper echelon Las Vegas prostitute might charge for the same services. Finally, some states may allow loss of consortium damages in a parent-child relationship. A parent may claim the loss of services of a child or a child may claim the loss of services of a parent.

Loss of Consortium
A loss of the services between one spouse and another or between a parent and a child.

There is also an important point to make about the general damages of disfigurement. Disfigurement may consist of any scarring on the body or the loss of a body part. The personal injury paralegal needs to understand that the disfigurement in question need not arise directly from the defendant's negligently caused trauma. For example, in an automobile collision, a person may have no scarring from the automobile collision itself. However, assume surgery is needed for the injury, which leaves scarring on the plaintiff's body. Such scarring from the surgery is compensable under this item of general damages. The same is true for the loss of a body part that may come about because of surgery required after the trauma itself. In the example above, if the plaintiff did not lose his arm directly in the accident itself but lost it from a later surgical amputation, there would still be damages allowed for disfigurement for loss of body part.

Workplace Skills Tip

In any personal injury case in which a plaintiff is alleging general damages, plaintiff bears the burden of proof. Plaintiff will testify to facts supporting a particular item of general damages whether it is pain and suffering, fear of injury, loss of consortium, or any other item of general damages. That proof is significantly aided if complaints/concerns about a particular claim for general damages are actually documented in the medical records. The personal injury paralegal should be reviewing medical records with that in mind. Do the plaintiff's medical records substantiate or contradict the plaintiff's claims for damages? The personal injury paralegal will need to become skilled in the acquiring, assembling, reviewing, and summarizing of medical records. Be aware of this concept now. It will be explored in great detail in later chapters.

Medical Testimony

In establishing damages, medical testimony is essential to establish a causal relationship between the injury and the injury-producing incident caused by defendant's negligence. The treating physician will testify that the injuries suffered by the plaintiff were caused by the particular accident in question, whether an automobile collision, an airplane crash, or a defective product. The element of causation may also be supported or contradicted in the plaintiff's own medical records, a topic that will be dealt with in later chapters dealing with the analysis of medical records by the personal injury paralegal.

In addition, medical testimony is essential to establish whether or not a plaintiff has suffered a permanent injury, as that bears on future damages likely to last a lifetime. In reviewing a sample jury instruction on damages in Exhibit 4-2, note that future damages cannot be based on "possibility." Neither do they need to be based on "absolute certainty." The test is reasonable medical certainty. The physician's opinions concerning the plaintiff's permanent injury and outlook for the future must be based on reasonable medical certainty.[2] However, depending upon the jurisdiction, those exact words may not need to be used. Such opinions may be expressed in terms of "more likely than not, "honestly held," or "at least 51%."

In an example of a plaintiff who received a fractured hip, if the issue was whether or not arthritis would develop at that injury site in the future, medical testimony that "it could" or "it might" or that "it's certainly possible" would not be permitted. Any testimony from the physician would need to be expressed in the form of language that a development of future arthritis is "likely" or "probable." The same is true if the issue was whether or not plaintiff could reasonably be expected to have future medical expenses, future pain and suffering, or any type of future special damages or future general damages. Any and all such future special damages and future general damages must be to a reasonable medical certainty or reasonably certain to occur. The following are examples of descriptive words or phrases that would likely be proper, leading to an admissible opinion: "reasonable medical certainty," "reasonably certain," "likely," "probable," "more likely than not," or "a 51% chance." The following are examples of descriptive words or expressions by the physician that would likely be improper, leading to an inadmissible opinion: "possible," "maybe," "there's a chance," "it might," "it could," or "a 30% chance."

Workplace Skills Tip

In assisting the litigation team with a plaintiff's personal injury case, the plaintiff's paralegal will soon discover a vast difference in the philosophy and approach of a plaintiff's treating physician. Some physicians will be outright advocates for the patient, your firm's client. That physician may even volunteer information about the personal injury that will be beneficial to your client's case. Other physicians will simply tolerate the litigation process. For those physicians, any beneficial information for the client may have to be slowly and painfully extracted from them.

EXHIBIT 4-6 Jury Instruction Guide

DAMAGES—AGGRAVATION OF A PREEXISTING CONDITION

A plaintiff's preexisting condition does not bar an award of damages. The defendant is responsible for the defendant's fault that aggravates the plaintiff's condition even if that fault would not have caused as serious of an injury to a normal, healthy person.

If a defendant's fault aggravates a preexisting condition, then the defendant is responsible for the worsening effect caused by the aggravation, but not for the preexisting condition itself. Any damages for aggravation are limited to the additional injury or worsening of the condition.

Damages for Aggravation of an Injury

The "eggshell plaintiff" rule was discussed in Chapter 3 dealing with causation. This is the causation principle that makes the negligent defendant liable for an unforeseeable result because of a preexisting condition of the plaintiff. This rule carries over to the element of damages. If the paralegal's firm is representing a plaintiff with a preexisting injury, the paralegal may be called to assist with assembling jury instructions, as previously mentioned. A sample JIG dealing with damages to a plaintiff with a preexisting condition is shown in Exhibit 4-6.

As discussed in the causation section, the tortfeasor or defendant takes the victim as he or she finds him or her. If the defendant's negligent conduct aggravated and made worse a condition the plaintiff suffered from at the time, the defendant is liable for those aggravated, additional injuries and damages. It sometimes happens that a plaintiff received an injury from a previous trauma and shortly thereafter received an aggravation of that injury from a second trauma. Plaintiff may have received an injury to his or her back in automobile collision number one. Plaintiff may have then aggravated that injury in automobile collision number two six months later. The general rule is that the burden of proof is upon the defendant to establish apportionment and the extent of harm attributable to each distinct cause. However, if the defendant is not able to apportion the harm, the defendant will be responsible for the entire harm.

Future Damages Reduced to Present Value

It is important to note the general rule that future damages must be reduced to their present value. The general rule applies to future economic damages and not future non-economic damages, such as pain and suffering.[3] (See sample JIG in Exhibit 4-7.)

EXHIBIT 4-7 Jury Instruction Guide

> **DAMAGES FOR FUTURE DETRIMENT REDUCED TO PRESENT WORTH**
>
> In computing any economic damages that the plaintiff will suffer in the future, you should take into account the present value of those future damages and reduce the damages to the present worth. The present worth of damages for future damages is the sum that, with interest at rates that may be reasonably expected, will equal the amount of the future damages.

This means that the present worth of economic damages for future loss is the present sum of money that, when added with interest at rates that may reasonably be expected on that sum of money, will equal the amount of the future loss.

For example, based upon the evidence presented, assume a jury determined that a sum of $100,000 represented a plaintiff's total future damages for a claim of loss of earning capacity based on a reduction of earnings for 10 more years. Assume that this loss of earning capacity is one in which plaintiff's injury has caused him or her to earn $10,000 a year less for 10 more years. Assume current interest rates were at 5%. Following the court's instruction, the jury should try to arrive at a sum of money that when invested presently at 5% for 10 years would equal $100,000. If $66,000 were the amount awarded by the jury for the element of future damages, that amount invested today at a simple interest rate of 5% a year, would earn $3,300 a year times 10 years equals $33,000. The $33,000 of interest that would be earned is added to the present sum of $66,000 and that equals $99,000. Rather than trying to be mathematically precise, a jury may simply award anywhere between $65,000 and $70,000 as the present sum of money that will produce an amount of future damages of $100,000.

This is the rationale for the rule of damages that states all future economic damages must be discounted to present value. The plaintiff is receiving all of the future money damages now in a lump sum and will be able to invest it and earn more money. To award the plaintiff the full $100,000 in the above example and then allow the plaintiff to invest that sum and earn another $5,000 a year or $50,000 over 10 years would overcompensate the plaintiff. Accordingly, the total future damage amount needs to be reduced to a lump sum of money. That money received today can be invested at an assumed current interest rate. The lump sum will continue to grow and earn interest over the period of time in the future that the damages are expected to last. Accordingly, the interest, when added to the current lump sum, will approximately equal the total amount of the jury's award for future damages. This general rule of discounting to present value applies only to future economic damages such as a loss of earning capacity as discussed above or damages for future medical or therapy expense. Typically, the rule does not apply to future non-economic damages such as pain and suffering. For a good discussion of the differences between future economic damages and future non-economic damages, see *Miller v. Pacific Trawlers, Inc.*, 131 P.3d 821 (Or. Ct. App. 2006) and *Brant v. Bockholt*, 532 N.W.2d 801 (Iowa 1995).

Hedonic Damages

Hedonic Damages
Damages awarded for the loss of the enjoyment of life or the quality of life.

Hedonic damages are a special category of general/non-economic damages that are awarded for the loss of the enjoyment or quality of life. This type of damages category would allow compensation for a plaintiff's inability to perform activities

Workplace Skills Tip

Proof of the element of damages is a vital factor in completing proof of all four elements of negligence. This consists primarily of assembling and calculating dollar numbers to place in front of a jury. Besides examining hard, cold tangible numbers, there is a crucial intangible factor at work that will ultimately affect the jury's decision on the final dollar award of damages. That factor is the personality and demeanor of the plaintiff. If you are on the plaintiff's side, you may have a grumpy, unpleasant, unlikeable, whining, or unbelievable plaintiff. On the other hand, you may be fortunate and have a plaintiff who is charming, likeable, sympathetic, believable, or who actually tends to minimize, rather than exaggerate, his or her own injuries. Expect a greater damages award or a greater settlement with the latter plaintiff. Obviously, neither the lawyer nor the paralegal has the power to change a plaintiff's personality. However, the paralegal can assist, before the plaintiff's deposition or before trial, in providing the plaintiff with ideas for proper and positive responses to questions.

that had given pleasure to a particular plaintiff. They are distinguished from losses of a purely mechanical bodily function such as walking or lifting or throwing a football. Examples would be the loss of the enjoyment of going out on a first date, the loss of the enjoyment of a first kiss, or the loss of the enjoyment of the plaintiff's love for debating politics. It is a controversial subject in damages law with some jurisdictions taking the position that it is impossible to define or value an enjoyment of life. Some jurisdictions do not allow evidence of damages of this kind.

Mitigation of Damages

There is a doctrine in the law of damages called **mitigation of damages**. This means that a plaintiff has a duty to mitigate his or her damages so as to minimize the plaintiff's injury. It is sometimes referred to as the "avoidable consequences rule." This doctrine means that once a person has been injured by the defendant's negligence, the plaintiff must take reasonable steps to avoid further injury or damages. The defendant will not be responsible for those injuries or damages that could have been reasonably avoided by the plaintiff. The plaintiff always has the burden of proof of damages. However, the defendant has the burden of proof to show that plaintiff unreasonably failed to mitigate plaintiff's damages.

> **Mitigation of Damages**
> A plaintiff has a duty to take steps to avoid further injury; sometimes referred to as the "avoidable consequences rule."

For example, assume a plaintiff received a type of injury for which surgery would likely make the plaintiff better. Surgery may improve range of motion, lessen pain, alleviate numbness, or something similar. If the plaintiff refuses to submit to surgery, the defendant will argue the mitigation of damages rule. The defendant's position will be that defendant is not responsible for any damages such surgery would have prevented or lessened. However, whether or not plaintiff was acting reasonably in refusing surgery will depend upon factors such as the risk to the patient, the probability of success, further pain and suffering to be incurred, and inconvenience and cost in mitigating the damages.

Collateral Source Rule and Subrogation

The **collateral source rule** of damages provides that plaintiff may recover all of plaintiff's damages, and the damages do not need to be reduced by any payments plaintiff received from another source. An example of such payments might be

> **Collateral Source Rule**
> The plaintiff may recover all of plaintiff's damages and the damages do not need to be reduced by any payments plaintiff received from another source.

Workplace Skills Tip

Medical testimony from a physician is a vital element in a personal injury case, whether plaintiff or defendant. However, as part of the legal team in assisting with the preparation of a personal injury case, do not underestimate the power and impact of testimony from a lay medical witness. These are friends, acquaintances, neighbors, co-workers, and the like who have firsthand observations about any changes in a plaintiff's lifestyle after the accident compared with before the accident. For example, if a plaintiff claims that he or she cannot do daily jogging any longer and one of these lay witnesses verifies that fact (*or not*), this can be compelling testimony before a jury. In a typical personal injury case, the paralegal will become involved in interviewing these important witnesses.

medical bills that are paid by the plaintiff's health insurance carrier or lost wages that are paid or partially paid by workers' compensation. This rule has the potential of allowing plaintiff a "double recovery." However, in most instances those collateral sources paying benefits to a plaintiff such as health insurance, workers' compensation, or Social Security typically have what is called a subrogation right that prevents a double recovery.

Subrogation is an insurance legal principle meaning that if one party has paid a person's benefits or damages, that party may recover the amount paid from the negligent defendant. Such party has a subrogation right—the right to proceed against the defendant for any sums it has paid to the plaintiff. For example, the health insurance carrier, Social Security Administration, workers' compensation entity, or other person or entity making payments to a plaintiff is subrogated to the claims the plaintiff may have against the defendant. They step into the shoes of the plaintiff. Assume that a plaintiff was injured on the job by a negligent defendant and workers' compensation benefits were paid to the plaintiff employee. Typically, the workers' compensation entity would have a right of subrogation to recover from the defendant the amounts it paid to the plaintiff. Also, a health insurance carrier that paid medical bills incurred by a plaintiff would typically have a right of subrogation against the at-fault defendant for the amount paid. That subrogation right would be expressed in the insurance policy. Subrogation rights are contained in various insurance policies and other agreements and will be discussed further in the chapters dealing with insurance.

Subrogation
A legal principle meaning that if one party, typically an insurer, has paid money and benefits to a plaintiff, that party may recover the amount paid from the negligent defendant.

Punitive/Exemplary Damages

These damages were briefly covered in Chapter 1 in connection with the discussion on tort reform. Punitive damages and exemplary damages are one and the same. The terms are used interchangeably. Punitive damages have a purpose to punish and deter bad conduct. Exemplary damages are awarded to make an example of a person or entity who has engaged in bad conduct. It can be seen that the purpose of punitive/exemplary damages is clearly not to compensate an injured plaintiff but to punish the defendant. The purpose of achieving compensation to a plaintiff is left to compensatory damages discussed above.

Punitive/exemplary damages are typically awarded in a case in which there is egregious conduct on the part of the defendant. All states vary in their approach toward the standard for these types of damages. The standard may be language such as "willful and wanton," "reckless disregard for the rights and safety of others," "extreme and outrageous conduct," and other forms of language conveying extreme, outrageous, or egregious behavior on the part of the defendant.

Some states have caps on punitive damages awards. Some states require a more stringent form of proof, such as "clear and convincing evidence" as opposed to a "preponderance of the evidence." While the subject of punitive/exemplary damages is being discussed here, the student must realize that these types of damages would not be allowed in a simple negligence case. They are mentioned here because they were first mentioned in Chapter 1 and because the general subject of damages is being discussed at this point.

Nominal Damages

Finally, there is a category of damages entitled **nominal damages**. Nominal damages are those damages awarded to a plaintiff that validate a plaintiff's claim but by their small amount, establish plaintiff has suffered no significant loss. These are relatively small damages, which send a message that the loss suffered was more of a technical nature than an actual nature. Review again the sample JIG at Exhibit 4-1. That JIG describes an award of nominal damages in those instances in which there is "no appreciable detriment."

As an example, in 1986 there was an antitrust lawsuit brought by the United States Football League against the National Football League (NFL). The verdict was for one dollar ($1.00). Pursuant to federal antitrust law, the award was required to be tripled, which increased the award to a whopping three dollars ($3.00). Obviously, from a monetary standpoint, this was a significant verdict for the NFL. However, if one talked to a representative of the United States Football League, it is possible to hear that age-old argument: "It was not about the money; it was about principle, we proved our point, and so we actually won." At best, nominal damages prove a point.

Tripling of damages as mentioned in the NFL case occurs when a statute provides for treble damages. **Treble damages** are typically awarded by statute to punish the wrongdoer for willful, intentional actions. Treble damages are in the nature of punitive/exemplary damages discussed in Chapter 1. Examples of treble damages that may be typically awarded by statute are cases involving patent infringement, writing bad checks, not paying rent to a landlord, and even cutting down trees. However, they can arise even in a personal injury case by statute in some states. Connecticut General Statutes Title 14 § 14-295 provides:

> In any civil action to recover damages resulting from personal injury, wrongful death or damage to property, the trier of fact may award double or treble damages if the injured party has specifically pleaded that another party has deliberately or with reckless disregard operated a motor vehicle in violation of ... [various moving motor vehicle violations] and that such violation was a substantial factor in causing such injury, death or damage to property.

The Connecticut statute cites various motor vehicle violations such as traveling unreasonably fast, speeding, reckless driving, driving under the influence, and driving in the wrong lane. If those violations occurred deliberately or with reckless disregard, the jury is entitled to award double or treble damages. It is important for the personal injury paralegal to know whether the law of his or her jurisdiction has a similar statute. However, as will be discussed in Chapter 14, such damages will

Nominal Damages
Those damages awarded to a plaintiff that validate a plaintiff's claim but by their small amount, establish plaintiff has suffered no significant loss.

Treble Damages
A form of damages in the nature of punitive/exemplary damages imposed by statute; purpose is to punish or make an example of a wrongdoer who commits an intentional, willful, or reckless act.

likely not be covered under a driver's liability insurance policy. Unless the defendant has deep pockets in the form of personal assets, it may be merely a theoretical claim without a practical remedy.

Actions for Death—Survival vs. Wrongful Death Actions

DIFFERENCE BETWEEN A WRONGFUL DEATH STATUTE AND A SURVIVAL STATUTE

At common law, when either a plaintiff or a defendant died, that was the end of the tort action. The action was said to not survive the deceased plaintiff or defendant. This was a harsh rule, particularly considering the primary purpose of tort law, which is to compensate innocent victims. At common law, a widow and children were out of luck if either the defendant or the husband/father died. Many jurisdictions have enacted either "survival statutes" or "wrongful death statutes" or both.

Survival Statute
Allows the decedent's claim to survive and damages can be awarded to the decedent's estate for those damages the decedent could have pursued.

A **survival statute** allows the decedent's claim to survive and damages can be awarded to the decedent's estate for those damages the decedent could have pursued. For example, assume that the decedent was seriously injured in a fire caused by the defendant's negligence. The plaintiff suffered extensive pain and suffering from the burn injury for six months before the plaintiff died. Under a survival statute, the estate could recover damages for those six months of pain and suffering as well as any other general and special damages, such as lost wages and medical bills incurred by the decedent during those six months.

Wrongful Death Statute
Creates a new cause of action for the surviving next of kin in which they may recover their pecuniary loss from the death of the decedent.

A true **wrongful death statute** creates a new cause of action for the surviving next of kin in which they may recover their pecuniary loss from the death of the decedent. For example, the action may be maintained by a surviving spouse and children of the decedent for their pecuniary loss arising from the decedent's death. A **pecuniary loss** is the money loss of the value of the companionship, support, services, and contributions they would have received from the decedent had he lived.

Pecuniary Loss
In a death action, the money loss of the value of the companionship, support, services, and contributions a survivor(s) would have received from the decedent had he or she lived.

A particular jurisdiction may have both a survival statute and a wrongful death statute. If so, damages for items such as pain and suffering, medical bills, and lost wages of the decedent would be recovered by the decedent's estate under the survival statute. Damages for items such as the value of the loss of the decedent's income to support the surviving family and the value of the loss of the decedent's companionship, services, and contributions would be recovered by the family members under the wrongful death statute. As a practical matter, the surviving beneficiaries are the same. Technically, in a survival statute, the damages are based on the decedent's loss, and in a wrongful death statute, the damages are based on the survivors' loss. While not entirely logical, the general rule is that punitive/exemplary damages cannot be recovered against the estate of a deceased tortfeasor.

DEFENSES IN SURVIVAL/WRONGFUL DEATH CASES

Any defenses that could have been asserted against the decedent had he or she lived can still be asserted by the defendant. For example, in a negligence case defendant may allege plaintiff's claim should be barred or reduced by the decedent's own contributory negligence, assumption of the risk, or comparative fault. The defense of the statute of limitation also applies. Some states start the statute running from the date of the accident and some from the date of death, which can, in some cases, be different if the decedent was not killed instantly.

Workplace Skills Tip

Many jurisdictions do not allow as damages in a wrongful death action a recovery by the survivors for their grief, sorrow, emotional pain, and emotional distress arising out of the death of the decedent. But make no mistake. A trial involving the death of a person is emotional. In most cases, the jury will consciously or unconsciously include these sympathy factors into the damages award.

CASE **4.1** Hypothetical Case: Developing Workplace Skills

You are employed as a paralegal in the corporate legal department of Roadrunner Express Railway Company. You are on the legal team defending against a serious crossing accident in which the claim is that the vehicle entered onto the tracks because the required whistles had not been sounded as the train approached the crossing. The plaintiff driver, Wiley, testified in his deposition that he was alert and awake when this accident occurred at approximately 9:00 p.m., and he had not consumed any alcohol immediately before the accident. He said that no whistles were sounded, and because of that, there was no reason to think a train was even near, so he proceeded ahead to cross the tracks. The suit has been commenced by Wiley against the railroad company in state court in your jurisdiction.

Wiley received a minor injury to his lower back, which has resolved, and his right leg was broken. He was off work for four months but has returned to full-time employment. He has brought suit for past medical expenses, past wage loss, past pain and suffering, and future pain and suffering for a claimed permanent injury to his right leg involving a loss of movement in his leg and what he describes as "significant daily pain."

In the course of working on this case, you have obtained Wiley's medical records. The first are excerpts of hospital records from where Wiley was taken to the emergency room by the ambulance immediately after the railroad accident. In reviewing the ER records, you note this entry:

Pt admitted at approximately 2200. He is alert and oriented, c/o severe pain in R lower extremity and pain in his lumbar area. Very strong odor of alcohol on pt's breath. Pt states he "got in a fight with a train and lost." He also states "I heard the whistle and saw the train coming but I thought for sure I could beat it. I guess I was wrong."

Kay Kollitz, R.N.

In addition, you have also obtained the medical records of Wiley's treating doctor. In reviewing those physician records, you find this entry approximately one year after the accident:

Pt returns for his final visit for R leg injury from his train crossing accident a little over a year ago. Strength testing is normal. ROM is normal. Pt states the pain has completely gone away, he's been back to work for some time now, and his leg "feels even better than it did before the accident." Based on the pt's history and my exam, his leg is completely healed with no further pain or difficulties. I do not believe that he has received any permanent injury to his leg.

Jill Moses, M.D.

Based on the medical records you have obtained and reviewed, tell your supervising attorney of any potential problems Wiley may have with proof of any of the four elements of negligence in his case against the railroad. Write an email to the supervising attorney listing each problematic element of negligence for Wiley. You may need to refer to the medical portion of the appendix to fully understand the medical chart entries.

"See that dark spot? That's potential litigation."

CHAPTER **SUMMARY**

The fourth and last element of the tort of negligence is damages. The burden of proof of this fourth element is upon the plaintiff who must prove damages by a preponderance of the evidence. A preponderance of the evidence means the greater weight of the evidence so that proof of a fact is more likely than not true. Compensatory damages are for the purpose of compensating the plaintiff and making the plaintiff whole. Compensatory damages must be fair, reasonable, and adequate.

Compensatory damages may be categorized as either general damages or special damages. General damages are non-economic losses such as pain and suffering, disfigurement, or mental anguish, all of which have no special itemized value. Special damages are economic losses such as medical expenses, lost wages, or the actual cost of hiring household help, which do have a specific itemized value. Special damages are more susceptible to being calculated by simple mathematical means. Special damages represent out-of-pocket losses. General damages represent quality-of-life losses.

Compensatory damages are also categorized as past damages and future damages. Both general damages and special damages may be in the categories of both past damages and future damages. Past damages represent those damages that have been suffered or incurred from the date of the loss caused by defendant's negligent conduct to the date of the trial. Future damages are those damages from the date of the trial that are reasonably certain to occur until a reasonable time into the future.

Physical impairment is an item of general damages. "Impairment" and "disability" are not synonymous. The standard manual for rating permanent impairments is the *AMA Guides to the Evaluation of Permanent Impairment*. It has been published by the American Medical Association since 1971. The *AMA Guides* defines an "impairment" as "an alteration of an individual's health status; a deviation from normal in a body part or organ system and its functioning." A "disability" is defined as "an alteration of an individual's capacity to meet personal, social, or occupational demands because of an impairment." An impairment must be viewed from the standpoint of how it affects daily living and the impact on performance of one's occupation or profession. A slight impairment to the body that may not be a disability to one person may amount to a complete disability to the body of another person.

The "eggshell plaintiff" rule discussed in Chapter 3 is the principle that makes a defendant liable for an unforeseeable result that is the preexisting condition of the plaintiff. This rule states that the defendant must take the plaintiff as he or she finds him or her. If there are two different injuries from two different sources, the burden of proof is upon the defendant to establish the apportionment between the two. If the defendant cannot do so, the defendant will be responsible for the entire harm.

Future economic damages must be reduced to present value. The present value or worth of damages for future loss is a present sum of money that, when added with interest at a reasonable interest rate, will equal the amount of future loss.

Mitigation of damages is also called the doctrine of avoidable consequences. It means that the plaintiff has a duty to mitigate or minimize the plaintiff's injury. Once a plaintiff has been injured by the defendant, the plaintiff must take reasonable steps to avoid further loss, damage, or injury. Plaintiff bears the burden of proof for plaintiff's damages, but defendant bears the burden of proof to show that plaintiff unreasonably failed to mitigate or minimize plaintiff's injuries and damages.

The collateral source rule of damages is that the plaintiff may recover all damages, and those damages do not need to be reduced by payments plaintiff received from another source—a source collateral to the defendant. The rule will allow for a double recovery. However, double recovery will not occur if the person or party paying benefits to the plaintiff has a subrogation right. Subrogation is a legal principle that if one party has paid all or part of the plaintiff's damages, the party may recover the amount paid from the negligent defendant.

Nominal damages are damages awarded to a plaintiff that validate the plaintiff's claim but are a small amount indicating that plaintiff has suffered no serious or significant loss. They "send a message" that the loss suffered was more technical than actual.

At common law, when either a plaintiff or a defendant died, the tort action was extinguished. A survival statute allows the decedent's claim to survive. Damages can be awarded to the decedent's estate for those damages the decedent could have pursued if living—pain and suffering, medical bills, and wage loss, as examples. A wrongful death statute creates a cause of action for damages suffered by the survivors. Damages can be awarded for pecuniary losses for the value of the companionship, support, services, and contributions they would have reasonably received from the decedent had he or she lived. Any defenses that could have been asserted against the decedent had he or she lived can be asserted by the defendant.

KEY **TERMS**

Preponderance of the Evidence	Loss of Earning Capacity	Subrogation
General Damages	Colossus	Nominal Damages
Special Damages	Impairment	Treble Damages
Non-Economic Damages	Disability	Survival Statute
Economic Damages	Loss of Consortium	Wrongful Death Statute
Past Damages	Hedonic Damages	Pecuniary Loss
Future Damages	Mitigation of Damages	
Loss of Earnings	Collateral Source Rule	

REVIEW **QUESTIONS**

1. Explain "preponderance of the evidence" and compare it to the criminal standard of evidentiary proof, which is "beyond a reasonable doubt."

2. What is the difference between general damages and special damages? Provide an example of each. Which type is easier for the jury to calculate?

3. Past damages cover what period of time? Are the beginning and the end of this time period always the same in each personal injury case? Future damages cover what period of time? Is the actual amount of time that future damages cover always the same in each case?

4. Leona Ruth, a single, retired elderly lady, was injured in a slip and fall accident at a supermarket. She slipped on some liquid from a bottle of liquid soap that had spilled. The liquid was left on the floor of a grocery aisle for an unreasonable length of time. When she is released from the hospital, she will need to be confined to her home with a back brace for three months. She will be unable to clean her apartment or do any of the household chores that she did before the supermarket accident. As she contemplates her personal injury lawsuit against the supermarket, she wonders whether she could receive any compensation if she hires some people to assist with these household duties. If so, under what general heading of damages would these duties fall—general or special damages? What is the specific name of the item of damages for which she would seek to be compensated?

5. Thor, a CPA, was injured in a serious multi-vehicle accident on a freeway and was rendered a paraplegic. Lars, a skilled neurosurgeon, cut off his thumb in an accident at his second vacation home while cutting down a tree. This was due to the negligent design of a chain saw. Did both men suffer a permanent impairment? Which one has the worst impairment? Which one will suffer the most financially? Which one has the greater future pain and suffering claim? Which one has the greater loss of earnings/future loss of earning capacity claim? Is either man disabled? Which one and why?

6. What is the rationale for reducing future economic damages to present value? Assume future damages have been calculated to be a total of $240,000 from the date of trial and into the future to last seven more years. Assume a current reasonable simple interest rate of 3%. What is the present value of the award for these future damages?

7. Rolf, an extremely successful farmer and rancher, has brought suit against a local implement dealer for personal injuries. He received a severe injury to his lower back when a tractor fell over on him and the dealer as a demonstration was being performed by the dealer. The dealer was demonstrating to Rolf how easily the new model tractor could climb a steep hill at full throttle. The dealer was killed. Several of the lower vertebrae in Rolf's back were crushed with severe, irreversible nerve damage. The injury has caused excruciating pain in his lower back and numbness radiating down both legs. Rolf is not able to return to work. However, Rolf could have a special new robotic surgery just developed in Mexico. This involves removing bone chips, reconstructing the nerves, reversing the nerve damage, fusing the lower back, and taking some special "nerve enhancement" medication also developed in Mexico. The Mexican surgeon, Giraldo, believes the surgery will likely relieve most if not all of the pain, remove the leg numbness, and repair all the nerves to virtually normal such that Rolf likely could return to work in his farming and ranching operation. The problem with this new surgery technique is that it has not been extensively tested. Giraldo, the surgeon from Mexico, has only done five of these—three were successful, one patient died during surgery, and one was not able to walk again. Because of this extremely delicate nerve operation, a risk of the surgery is that additional permanent nerve damage can result. The special medication

has also been known to cause schizophrenia. The cost of the surgery is approximately $200,000, not counting the expense to travel to Mexico. The city in which the surgery would be performed has recently been the target of Mexican drug lords. The drug lords just blew up a police station located a block from the doctor's office. Defendant claims plaintiff must have the surgery. On what ground or legal theory is defendant making this claim? Should plaintiff be required to submit to this surgery? Why or why not?

8. Explain the collateral source rule and how the doctrine of subrogation affects it.
9. Define and provide an example of nominal damages.
10. Explain the difference between a survival statute and a wrongful death statute.

chapter 5

SPECIAL DUTIES AND OTHER NEGLIGENCE ISSUES

"You can't legislate intelligence and common sense into people."

Will Rogers

To this point, the focus has been on the tort of negligence. This chapter will discuss some variations of negligence and some statutory changes to some well-established torts based on negligence. These are important issues and ones that will arise frequently for the personal injury paralegal. To illustrate the importance of the issues, when the subject of agency is discussed, the student will realize that in a personal injury suit the plaintiff may be looking for "deep pockets." As a result, it may be necessary to sue the employer to achieve that goal. In the motor vehicle context, a great deal of driving involves driving after consuming alcoholic beverages. In the quest again for deep pockets, a bar may be joined as a defendant in addition to the driver and owner.

Agency

EMPLOYER/EMPLOYEE RELATIONSHIP

The traditional law of employment has its origins in agency law. In agency law the party for whom another person acts and from whom that person obtains authority to act is a **principal**. The one receiving the power and authority from the principal to accomplish actions on behalf of the principal is an **agent**. The agent stands in the shoes of the principal and acts as a substitute or a proxy for the principal. The acts of the agent will bind the principal under a theory called **vicarious liability**. Vicarious liability is a fundamental rule of agency law meaning that the principal is liable for the actions of the agent who was acting on the principal's behalf. The actions of the agent are said to be "imputed" to the principal. The principal becomes liable only through the actions of the agent.

If Ronnie, the principal, gives Ralph, the agent, authority to sell Ronnie's diamond ring for $100,000, and Ralph agrees to sell the ring

LEARNING OBJECTIVES

After studying this chapter, you should be able to:

- Recognize the employment relationship, the doctrine of *respondeat superior,* and distinguish between an employee and an independent contractor.

- Differentiate between vicarious liability in a motor vehicle permissive use statute and a family purpose doctrine.

- Appreciate the purpose of workers' compensation and recognize when a personal injury arises out of and in the course of employment.

- Analyze dram shop liability and identify its strict statutory liability requirements for recovery.

- Differentiate between land occupier liability related to trespasser, licensee, and invitee and the modern view of an entrant.

- Describe the tort of negligent infliction of emotional distress and the differences in approach for a recovery based on this tort.

Principal
In agency law the party for whom another person acts and from whom that person obtains authority to act.

Agent
One receiving the power and authority from the principal to accomplish actions on behalf of the principal.

Vicarious Liability
A fundamental rule of agency law that means that the principal is liable for the actions of the agent who was acting on the principal's behalf.

to Carolee, Ronnie is liable to Carolee even if Ronnie changes his mind. Ralph, as an agent of Ronnie, has the power to bind Ronnie to this transaction. It is as if Ronnie dealt directly with Carolee. Therefore, Ronnie will be legally obligated to sell the ring to Carolee. The theory of vicarious liability is broader than just tort liability, because the example provided involves a contract to sell a piece of property, namely, a ring.

While the purpose here is not to become engaged in a full discussion of agency law, one other point needs to be made. In the diamond ring example, the authority given by Ronnie to Ralph was to sell the ring for $100,000. However, if Ralph sold the ring to Karen for only $70,000, Ralph's actions still bind Ronnie. This means that Ronnie would have to sell the ring to Karen for $70,000. However, Ronnie as the principal now has the right to pursue Ralph as the agent for the $30,000 loss from circumventing Ronnie's authority.

In the employment context, an employee is the agent of the employer who is the principal. The employee is the employer's representative. The employee stands in the shoes of the employer and acts as a substitute or proxy for the employer. The acts of the employee/agent bind the employer/principal under this same theory of vicarious liability. The older court decisions often used the terms "master" and "servant" instead of "employer" and "employee," respectively.

RESPONDEAT SUPERIOR

Respondeat Superior
The Latin phrase means literally, "let the master answer." The employer is liable or responsible for a tort that is committed by the employee while the employee is acting within the scope of the employment relationship.

Only in the employment context of agency does the doctrine of ***respondeat superior*** apply. The Latin phrase means literally, "let the master answer." In other words, let the master answer for the torts of the servant. In modern language it might be phrased as "let the employer answer for the torts of the employee." This is a fundamental doctrine of agency law in the employment relationship. It means that the employer is liable or responsible for a tort that is committed by the employee while the employee is acting within the scope of the employment relationship. The scope of the employment relationship consists of those duties that are required by the employer to be performed by the employee. The scope of the employment relationship requires an analysis of whether or not the employee was engaged in the furtherance of the employer's interest. The doctrine does not apply to tortious conduct committed by an employee that is outside the scope of the employment relationship. The reasoning behind the doctrine of *respondeat superior* is that if an employee is furthering the interest of the employer, it is fair to make the employer liable for damage caused by the employee. On the other hand, if the employee is not furthering the interest of the employer, it is unfair to make the employer liable for damage caused by the employee. Some examples will clarify this important doctrine.

Assume a store clerk is hired by an auto parts store to wait on customers and sell auto parts. In the course of waiting on a customer, a fight breaks out and the employee punches the customer in the nose. This intentional action by the employee may be considered beyond or outside the scope of the employment relationship. The employer would argue that punching a customer in the nose is not a duty required to be performed, and it does not further the employer's interest; indeed, it is bad for business. The employer would probably not be liable for the employee clerk's actions under the doctrine of *respondeat superior*.

However, assume a bouncer is hired by a bar. An unruly bar patron attacks another patron. To defend the other patron, the bouncer punches the unruly patron in the nose. The bouncer's action of punching an unruly customer in the nose

> ## Workplace Skills Tip
>
> Note the spelling of the word "principal" in the agency discussion of "principal" and "agent." The words "principal" and "principle" are probably the most confused and misused in the English language. The personal injury paralegal will be drafting memos and briefs. Learn the difference between these words so you know their proper use. The word "principal" is usually an adjective meaning "main" or "key." For example: "This is the principal reason for the discussion." It can, however, be a noun meaning a "head" or "chief," such as "He is a high school principal." The word "principle" is a noun. It usually refers to certain rules, theories, or beliefs, such as "We will be discussing a basic legal principle" or "Try applying the Watson principle of physics."

would probably be considered within the scope of the employment relationship. Physical contact with unruly patrons to protect other patrons in the bar is a duty required to be performed, and it furthers the bar owner/employer's interest. The bar owner/employer would probably be liable for the employee/bouncer's actions under the doctrine of *respondeat superior*.

One basic principle to keep in mind is that an employer's liability under *respondeat superior* is purely vicarious. The employer's liability *only* comes about if it is first shown that the employee was negligent or committed some other tort. If, for example, the employee is not found negligent or is found negligent but not a cause of the injury, then there can be no legal liability against the employer because there was no legal liability first established against the employee.

Is the employer vicariously liable if the employee violates an internal company rule? For example, an employer may have a rule in its company employee manual expressly prohibiting the use of alcohol and illegal drugs while on the job. The employee violates that rule and uses an illegal drug on the job, which interferes with the employee's ability to drive. The employee is then involved in a motor vehicle collision while driving the employer's delivery truck to a job site with a resulting personal injury. When sued by the plaintiff on a theory of *respondeat superior*, the employer will likely argue that the violation of an internal company rule means that the employee is acting outside the scope of employment. However, this argument will likely be unsuccessful.

If the employee is furthering both the employee's interest and the employer's interest at the time of the accident, the employer will be liable under *respondeat superior*. Review the decision of *Rahman v. State of Washington*, 246 P.3d 182 (Wash. 2011) in Exhibit 5-1.

In *Rahman*, the court analyzes Restatement (Second) of Agency § 242 *(1958)* in reaching its decision. As discussed in Chapter 1, courts typically give a great deal of deference to the Restatements. The student should also note the blistering dissent in which the majority is accused of ignoring precedent and "making law," or "legislating," a subject discussed in Chapter 1. Justice Johnson states at the outset in his dissenting opinion why he dissents: "…[B]ecause the majority's ruling *legislates* new policy to extravagantly expand state liability, I dissent." (Emphasis added.) *Rahman* at 189.

COMING AND GOING RULE

There are two well-developed exceptions carved out by the courts to an employee being in the scope of employment. One is the "coming and going rule," and the other is the "frolic and detour rule," referenced in the *Rahman* decision. The

EXHIBIT 5-1 Relevant Case Law

Rizwana Rahman, Respondent, v. State of Washington, Petitioner.

Supreme Court of Washington.

In this case, we must decide if the State is liable under the doctrine of respondeat superior for injuries to an unauthorized passenger in a state vehicle. Rizwana Rahman was injured in an automobile accident while riding with her husband, Mohammad Shahidur Rahman, from Olympia to Spokane on state business. The trial court dismissed her suit against the State on the ground that Mohammad was not authorized to allow his wife to ride with him in a state car and was thus acting outside the scope of his employment at the time of the accident. The Court of Appeals reversed, holding that as a matter of law the State is vicariously liable for Mohammad's negligence. We affirm the Court of Appeals.

FACTS

Mohammad was employed as an intern with the Washington State Department of Ecology during the summer of 2005. He worked in the dam safety office where, among other duties, he accompanied senior engineers on inspections and helped to write reports. On July 26, 2005, Mohammad drove from Olympia to Spokane in a state-owned vehicle to meet a department hydrologist with whom he would inspect a construction site; unbeknownst to his employer, he brought his wife, Rizwana, along. At the time, department policy 11–10 provided: "Ecology vehicles are not to be used for personal trips unrelated to the state business for which they were assigned, nor to transport passengers that are not on official state business." Clerk's Papers at 155.

While driving near Tiger Mountain Summit on State Route 18, Mohammad failed to negotiate a curve. The car left the roadway, struck a tree and rolled several times. Rizwana was badly injured. She brought this action for negligence against both Mohammad and the State. The complaint was later amended to name the State as the sole defendant. Rizwana moved for partial summary judgment, seeking an order determining that the State was vicariously liable under the doctrine of respondeat superior for her husband's negligence in causing the accident. The State filed a crossmotion for summary judgment, seeking dismissal on the ground that its employee's use of a state vehicle to transport an unauthorized passenger fell outside the scope of his employment....

Rizwana argues that Mohammad was acting within the course of his employment at the time of the automobile accident because he was driving from Olympia to Spokane in a state vehicle at his employer's direction. The State counters that Mohammad's unauthorized act of allowing his wife to ride along took his conduct outside the scope of his employment, as it was done for his own purposes and was contrary to department policy. In a sense, both parties are correct. Mohammad was indisputably engaged in the duties his employment required, not having departed on a "frolic or detour," but he was also serving his own interests (and his wife's) by having Rizwana along on the drive. His conduct at the time reflected a mixture of both benefit to his employer and to himself....

[T]he Court of Appeals correctly concluded that Mohammad was acting within the scope of his employment at the time of the automobile accident that injured Rizwana. Though he combined his own business with the State's by allowing Rizwana to ride along as a passenger, the trip and the route taken were dictated by official state business, and there is no evidence that Rizwana's presence in any way contributed to the accident.

The State objects that applying the doctrine of respondeat superior in this manner ignores the important fact that Mohammad violated department policy by inviting his wife to ride with him in a state vehicle, leaving the State no meaningful way to limit its liability exposure. This argument

(Continued)

EXHIBIT 5-1 *(Continued)*

deserves careful scrutiny, as we should be sensitive to the increased risk employers may face when employees disregard workplace rules. Nonetheless, both precedent and sound policy weigh in favor of recognizing vicarious liability....

These cases underscore the sound policy supporting respondeat superior. The doctrine rests upon the relationship between an employer and employee, which is characterized by a right of control. The very fact that the employer is in a position to impose workplace rules and standards justifies vicarious liability, even where the employee acts in a forbidden way....

Under that analysis, the fact that Mohammad acted against department policy by inviting Rizwana to ride with him in a state car does not defeat vicarious liability. At the time of the accident, Mohammad was driving from Olympia to Spokane on official state business. Though bringing Rizwana along certainly served Mohammad and his wife's interests, Mohammad's conduct at the time was also in the service of the State's business. Based on the undisputed facts, vicarious liability must be recognized as a matter of law.

J.M. Johnson, J. (dissenting).

The majority holds the State of Washington liable for injury to Mohammad Shahidur Rahman's wife (Rizwana Rahman), even though he was prohibited from taking her in the state vehicle and he negligently drove off the road, causing the injury. Faithful application of this court's precedent, ... however, requires the conclusion that Mr. Rahman was outside the scope of state employment. The question under Washington State law should turn on the issue of whether Mr. Rahman was authorized to transport his wife in this state-owned vehicle. Because Mr. Rahman was not so authorized, and indeed was specifically prohibited from doing so, and because the majority's ruling legislates new policy to extravagantly expand state liability, I dissent.

Source: Rahman v. State of Washington, 246 P.3d 182 (Wash. 2011).

coming and going rule is a legal principle in employment law that means that an employer is not legally liable for the negligence of an employee who is either coming to work or going from work. These cases typically involve motor vehicle accidents. For example, a factory worker leaves his home and while on his 20-minute commute to work, he negligently operates his motor vehicle injuring another person. If that person brought suit against the employer on the theory of *respondeat superior*, the employer will raise the defense (probably successfully) of the coming and going rule. The employer will argue that the employee was not yet on the job performing his job duties, was not furthering the employer's interest, and could not be acting in the scope of his employment. The result is the same if the accident had occurred while the factory worker had left the plant and was returning home.[1]

However, the coming and going rule is not that hard and fast. An employee can still be in the scope of employment if the employee is conducting employer business while coming to work or going home from work. For example, consider this scenario: A sales representative for a company is returning home from a business appointment. On her way home, she stops to drop off company supplies at a company-provided self-storage unit. On the way to that storage unit, the employee is involved in a motor vehicle accident. Even though the employee was going home from work, the employee was involved in an act of furthering the employer's business at the time of the accident.

Another example is an employee, while on the way to the employer's office, decides to be efficient and call on a client who is on the way to the office. Even

Coming and Going Rule
A legal principle in employment law that means that an employer is not vicariously liable for the negligence of an employee who is either coming to work or going from work.

though the employee was coming to work at the time, the employee was involved in an act of furthering the employer's business. These examples demonstrate activities on the part of the employee that are in furtherance of the employer's business. Even though the employee is technically on the way to the job or on the way home from the job, the coming and going rule will not apply if the employee is performing work-related activities that further the employer's interest in whole or in part. In that event, the employer will be liable for the employee's negligence under the doctrine of *respondeat superior.*[2]

FROLIC AND DETOUR RULE

Frolic and Detour Rule
A legal principle in employment law that means that an employer is not vicariously liable for the negligence of an employee who deviates or departs from the business of the employer to serve the employee's own personal purpose.

This rule is another exception to *respondeat superior.* The **frolic and detour rule** is a legal principle in employment law that means that an employer will not be vicariously liable for the negligence of an employee who deviates or departs from the business of the employer to serve the employee's own personal purpose.[3] The *Pontillo* decision, in one of the longest sentences imaginable, describes the frolic and detour rule this way:

> If an employee who is delegated to perform certain work for his employer steps or turns aside from his master's work or business to serve some purpose of his own, not connected with the employer's business, or, as is often expressed, deviates or departs from his work to accomplish some purpose of his own not connected with his employment—goes on a 'frolic of his own'—the relation of master and servant is thereby temporarily suspended, and the master is not liable for his acts during the period of such suspension; he is then acting upon his own volition, obeying his own will, not as a servant, but as an independent person, even though he intends to and does return to his employer's business after he has accomplished the purpose of his detour from duty.[4]

For example, consider a case in which a salesman with a regular route to call on customers deviates from that route. He is furnished a company vehicle. His set hours are 8:00 a.m. to 5:30 p.m. He decides to visit a strip joint at 3:00 p.m. and have a few drinks. He becomes intoxicated, leaves the strip joint at 5:00 p.m., and decides to head home early. A few minutes after leaving, and while on a public highway, he is involved in a motor vehicle collision that injures the plaintiff. If the plaintiff brings suit against the employer, the employer will likely successfully raise the "frolic and detour rule" defense. The employer will argue that this was a true frolic and detour on the part of the employee. The employee was furthering his own personal interest and was not furthering any business interest of the employer at the time of the accident. This is true even though the accident happened with a company car and during the employee's regular working hours. However, if the salesman left at 5:00 to call on a customer, there might be a different result.

Some courts have made a distinction in those cases in which the deviation was "slight."[5] In *Karangelen,* a policeman, operating a Cushman scooter, deviated from his duties of checking parking meters. He drove toward a friend who had motioned the policeman over to talk. Being unfamiliar with the Cushman scooter, he misjudged his distance and struck the friend who later became the plaintiff. The court discussed the frolic and detour rule but held it did not apply because of the officer's slight deviation from duty. "This deviation was so slight that ... it may be held as a matter of law to be insufficient to constitute a 'frolic' which would take the appellee outside the scope of his employment as a police officer."[6]

INDEPENDENT CONTRACTOR

The discussion so far has centered around the employment relationship and the principle that an employer may be held liable for an employee's negligence if the employee is in a work-related activity at the time. Difficulties may arise in an effort to draw a distinction between an "employee" and an "independent contractor." An **independent contractor** is a person who contracts with a principal to perform a task according to that person's own methods and who is not under the principal's control regarding the method and the manner of the work. In an employment relationship, the employer has the right to control the terms, conditions, method, and manner of an employee's work. As to the employee, the employer sets the hours of work, provides the tools and equipment for performing the work, and directs how, by when, and in what order the work must be accomplished. In some cases, the right of control may be shown from the requirement that a certain uniform be worn on the job. In short, there is an element of "control" exerted by the employer over the employee. Such control or right to control is missing when dealing with an independent contractor.

Assume Foghorn finds it necessary to hire someone to trim dead branches from some large trees at his home. By word of mouth, he hears about a young man named Henry who occasionally does this kind of work. He hires Henry to do the work. Foghorn provides the ladder and the saw to Henry. He instructs Henry to start trimming the oak trees first and then trim the spruce trees next. He requires that Henry come no later than 10:00 a.m. and leave by 4:00 p.m. each day. The work must be completed no later than one week. Foghorn agrees to pay Henry $20 an hour for the job. Henry agrees to do the work on those terms. While Henry is on the job and up on the ladder, the saw slips from his hand, falls, and strikes Sam, a neighbor of Foghorn's who has stopped by to talk to Foghorn about the tree-trimming operation. Sam is injured and sues Foghorn on a theory of *respondeat superior*.

Assume a slightly different scenario. Assume Foghorn checks the Internet and finds a business website called "Henry's Tree Trimming Service" with a phone number. He calls and Henry says he would be interested in doing the work after looking at the trees and providing a "bid." Henry inspects the proposed job and gives Foghorn a total price of $750 to do the complete trimming job. Henry has his own truck, his own ladder, and his own set of specialized saws. Henry is busy with other jobs and says he won't be able to start for a couple of weeks. He also tells Foghorn, because he is busy with other jobs, he may have to come early in the morning and leave for a while and come back later in the evening to finish work for a given day. Foghorn agrees to hire Henry for the tree-trimming project. Again, while Henry is up on his ladder trimming a tree, his saw slips from his hand, and falls on Sam's head, injuring him. Sam sues Foghorn on a theory of *respondeat superior*.

The results in the two cases will be markedly different. In the first scenario, Henry is likely an employee because Foghorn has the right to control the hours, terms, and conditions of employment. Henry's negligence in dropping the saw and injuring Sam will result in Foghorn being vicariously liable for Henry's negligence. On the other hand, in the second scenario, Henry is likely an independent contractor. He is advertising his own business on the Internet. He is using his own tools and equipment to perform the job, setting his own hours of work, and working for a set sum of compensation. Foghorn has no right to control the hours, terms, and conditions of employment. Because Henry is an independent contractor and not an employee, Foghorn cannot be vicariously liable under *respondeat superior* for

Independent Contractor
A person who contracts with a principal to perform a task according to that person's own methods and who is not under the principal's control regarding the method and the manner of the work.

Henry's negligence in dropping the saw on neighbor Sam's head. Sam will need to bring his negligence suit only against Henry. The test for determining whether one is an employee or an independent contractor is the right of control the hiring party has over the person hired. If the hiring party has the right to control (whether exercised or not) the terms, conditions, method, and manner of the work, the person hired will be considered an employee. If the right to control those elements of work are lacking, the person hired will be considered an independent contractor.

Motor Vehicle/Vicarious Liability

PERMISSIVE USE

Permissive Use Statute
A statute that makes the owner of a motor vehicle liable for damages caused by one to whom the owner has given permission, express or implied, to drive the motor vehicle.

The subject of vicarious liability has been discussed in the employment context. There is another important area of vicarious liability that the personal injury paralegal will likely encounter which is a **permissive use statute**. A permissive use statute is a statute that makes the owner of a motor vehicle liable for damages caused by one to whom the owner has given permission to drive the motor vehicle. For example, a father allows his son to take the father's car on a Saturday evening for a homecoming dance. If the son is involved in a motor vehicle collision in which a plaintiff sustains injury, the father will be vicariously liable for the son's negligence, just as the employer would be vicariously liable for the employee's negligence in the scope of employment.

Interestingly, in a family relationship, some states have carried permissive use even further than the initial permission given to the first driver. In the example used, if the son, while at the homecoming dance, gave permission to his friend to use his father's car, the father would still be vicariously liable for the friend's negligence.[7] A permissive use statute reflects public policy that innocent injured persons will be compensated by the negligent operation of a motor vehicle upon the public highways.

While one jurisdiction may make it easier for a plaintiff to recover against an owner by imputing a driver's negligence to an owner when there has been permissive use, another jurisdiction may not be quite so lenient. Some states may not recognize imputing liability to an owner based on permission alone. Liability will not be imputed to an owner unless one of the following factors is present in addition to permission: (1) the operator was acting as the owner's agent or employee; (2) the owner was actually present in the vehicle; or (3) the owner and driver were engaged in a joint enterprise.[8] In a tort and personal injury practice, the paralegal may encounter the theory of joint enterprise in the motor vehicle arena.

Joint Enterprise
An arrangement in which each person has authority, express or implied, to act for all in the group concerning the control or means employed to execute the common purpose the group intends to carry out.

Joint enterprise is sometimes referred to as a "common enterprise" or a "joint venture." In a joint enterprise, each person has authority, express or implied, to act for all in the group concerning the control or means employed to execute the common purpose that the group intends to carry out. This concept sometimes arises in the motor vehicle context in which liability may be imputed to an owner on the theory that an owner and driver were engaged in a joint enterprise at the time of the accident.[9]

FAMILY PURPOSE DOCTRINE

Some states, by statute or case law, have adopted the **family purpose doctrine**. This legal doctrine renders the owner of a motor vehicle legally responsible for damages caused by the driver's negligent operation of the vehicle if the driver is a member of the owner's immediate family or household and is driving the vehicle with the express or implied permission of the owner. Exhibit 5-2 is a sample JIG concerning the family purpose doctrine.

The family purpose doctrine is more restrictive than a permissive use statute. A permissive use statute makes the owner liable for any person, family member or not, who is using the vehicle with permission. The family purpose doctrine specifies that the family member/owner will be vicariously liable only for the negligence of one who is another specified family member who received permission from the owner. For example, assume a father gave permission to his 16-year-old son, living at home, to drive the father's vehicle to the grocery store for groceries. The father would be liable for the son's negligence. If the father gave permission to operate this same vehicle to his 22-year-old son living down the street in his own home, the father would not be liable if the state's doctrine required the child to be a resident of the owner's household.

Family Purpose Doctrine
A legal doctrine rendering the owner of a motor vehicle legally responsible for damages caused by the driver's negligent operation of the vehicle if the driver is a member of the owner's immediate family or household and is driving the vehicle with the express or implied permission of the owner.

EXHIBIT 5-2 Jury Instruction Guide

Family Purpose Doctrine

If a member of a family provides an automobile for the use of other members of the family, and they use the automobile with the provider's permission, they become the agents of the provider for the purpose of that use, which includes their own personal pleasure. If a member of the family uses the automobile and wrongfully causes injury to another, the provider of the automobile is liable for the resulting damages sustained. Applying this doctrine it must be established:

1. That the [plaintiff] [defendant] provided for members of the [plaintiff's] [defendant's] family the motor vehicle involved in the accident;

2. That the driver of the motor vehicle was a member of the provider's family; and

3. That the driver was using the vehicle for the purpose for which the [plaintiff] [defendant] provided it, with the [plaintiff's] [defendant's] express or implied permission.

Although a member of a family may provide an automobile for general use by the family members, the automobile's use can rightfully be denied to any other member at any time. A provider who does so cannot be held liable for the fault of a member whose right of use has been denied.
It is for you to determine, from all of the evidence and under these instructions, whether the automobile provided by the [plaintiff] [defendant] and driven by _____, the [plaintiff's] [defendant's] _____, was maintained for the use of the members of the family and whether the [plaintiff] [defendant] _____, at the time of the accident, was using the automobile as a member of the [plaintiff's] [defendant's] family, with express or implied permission of the [plaintiff] [defendant].

Workers' Compensation

Workers' Compensation
A type of insurance or special fund that provides an employee with certain wage loss benefits, medical benefits, and other statutory benefits for an injury (or death) that arises out of and in the course of employment.

Workers' compensation provides an employee with certain wage loss benefits, medical benefits, and other statutory benefits for an injury or death that arises out of and in the course of employment. It is sometimes referred to by attorneys and judges as "workers' comp" or just "comp." With some exceptions, such as an intentional injury by the employer, this is the exclusive remedy for an employee injured on the job. The employee cannot sue his or her employer or a co-employee for the tort of negligence. These statutes began to be enacted originally by various states in the early 1900s. Each state administers its own program with some states providing more liberal benefits than others.

Before enactment of workers' compensation statutes, if an employee was injured or killed on the job, the task of recovering against the employer was nearly impossible. When the employee sued the employer for negligence, the employer could throw up in the employee's face some extremely tough defenses. These defenses included contributory negligence (the accident at work was caused by the employee's own fault), assumption of the risk (the employee voluntarily assumed the risk or danger of the work), or the fellow servant rule (the employer is not liable if the injury was caused by a fellow employee). The defenses were harsh and difficult to overcome, and employees rarely prevailed in their suits against the employer.

With workers' compensation, all the employee is required to show is that his or her injury is "work related," that is, the injury arose out of *and* in the course of his employment. Both elements are necessary for the employee to prove in order to be eligible for workers' compensation benefits. It is commonly stated that the employee need only show that he or she was "hurt on the job." The requirement of "arising out of" means that there must be some causal connection between the job duties and the resulting injury. An injury arising "in the course of" the employment requires the injury to occur within the period of employment at a location where the employee would be expected to be while fulfilling duties of employment.

Once the employee satisfies these two requirements along with his or her demonstrated injury, the employee will then be entitled to receive certain fixed, limited statutory compensation amounts for the involved injury. These amounts are quickly paid as opposed to lengthy litigation. Each state's statute is different, but typically, the employee will be entitled to recover medical expenses, wage loss or a percentage of wage loss, a lump sum for a certain type of injury, and benefits such as retraining benefits. There is no recovery for general damages such as pain and suffering. Lump sum benefits for a certain type of injury are specifically enumerated by statute. There may be a specific schedule for various types of injuries. For example, the loss of a finger is worth X dollars, and a certain partial permanent impairment to the back is worth Y dollars.

There is no question that the amounts paid under workers' compensation are less than what might be recovered in a common law tort action based on negligence. However, this is the trade-off for workers' compensation being the employee's exclusive remedy: The employer assumes all liability for a work-related accident resulting in injury or death without regard to fault in exchange for monetary limitations on the amount of that liability. The employee is given prompt and certain fixed payment of benefits without having to prove fault, but in exchange, relinquishes the broader scope of damages that would be available in a tort recovery.

As might be expected, under this workers' compensation exclusivity rule, the employee is relinquishing a right to sue not only the employer for negligence, but also a fellow employee. Otherwise, an injured employee would be able to circumvent the workers' compensation concept by suing a negligent employee in tort with the idea that the employee's negligence would then be imputed to the employer under *respondeat superior*. Under workers' compensation, depending on the state's statute, both the employer and the fellow employees are immune from a negligence suit. To better understand the concept and rationale of workers' compensation, review the *Varela* decision in Exhibit 5-3.[10]

EXHIBIT 5-3 Relevant Case Law

Catalino Varela, Appellee and Cross-Appellant, v. Fisher Roofing Co., Inc., and Union Insurance Company, Appellants and Cross-Appellees.

Court of Appeals of Nebraska.

Sievers, Judge.

FACTUAL BACKGROUND

A roofing crew from Fisher was working at the Banner County School in Harrisburg, Nebraska, on September 28, 1994. This crew included a number of Hispanic workers, including Varela, who worked as an "assistant" because, in his words, "I would help the others … that knew the job, I didn't know very much." Another worker present was Gonzalez, who has been working for Fisher in excess of 12 years. On the day in question, the crew was preparing to do roofing work on the school. The preparations included moving their equipment onto the roof and sweeping the roof's surface. Although Varela, testifying through an interpreter, denies any horseplay, there is substantial evidence that the men were mocking Varela's work efforts for carrying a half-full bucket of material when others were carrying heavier buckets. In response, Varela issued a challenge to Gonzalez to arm-wrestle. The record is unclear as to exactly how the participants were physically positioned, except that Varela had one foot on the edge of a raised skylight and that both men fell, at which time Varela's ankle was severely fractured. Fisher's employee handbook, written in English, prohibits "[b]oisterous or disruptive activity in the workplace" and fighting. Varela does not read English….

ANALYSIS

There is no question that Varela was injured while on the roof of the Banner County School in Harrisburg. Workers' compensation benefits are payable when personal injury is caused to an employee by an accident arising out of and in the course of his or her employment. Neb.Rev.Stat. § 48-101 (Reissue 1993). This statutory language is conjunctive, requiring a claimant to establish both conditions by a preponderance of the evidence…. The phrase "arising out of" describes the accident and its origin, cause, and character, i.e., whether it resulted from a risk arising within the scope of the employee's job, whereas the phrase "in the course of" refers to the time, place, and circumstances of the accident. *Id.*

The evidence shows, and the Workers' Compensation Court trial judge found, that Varela's injury had its genesis in some on-the-job activity which can fairly be called horseplay. The issue is whether an injury sustained in the course of horseplay is not compensable because it either does not arise out of the employment or does not occur in the course of the employment.

The "in the course of" requirement has been defined as testing the work connection as to time, place, and activity, or in other words, it demands that the injury be shown to have arisen within the time and space boundaries of the employment and in the course of an activity whose purpose is related to the employment…. The "arising out of" requirement is concerned with causation….

Having used 1A Larson & Larson, *supra*, § 23.50 et seq., in our analysis, we observe that the treatise contains 56 pages of text devoted to the subject of "horseplay," with numerous cases summarized therein. From our review of the treatise, it is apparent that workers can conjure up an endless

(Continued)

EXHIBIT 5-3 *(Continued)*

> variety of creative foolish, and dangerous ways to "goof off" while on the job often with disastrous consequences....
>
> We believe that Larson and Larson's proposed test for compensability is appropriate and that certain incidents of horseplay, resulting in injury, may be within the scope of employment and arise out of it. We look to whether the deviation was substantial because, obviously, Varela and Gonzalez were not directly working when the injury occurred. We find that the work stoppage was of momentary duration, the injury happened at the very outset of the horseplay, this was not the sort of incident which carried a significant risk of serious injury, and the incident was a trifling matter, at least in its intention by the two employees. These factors lead to the conclusion that the arm-wrestling was an insubstantial deviation and did not measurably detract from the work (but for the injury).

Source: *Varela v. Fisher Roofing Co., Inc.*, 567 N.W.2d 569 (Neb. 1997).

There is another caveat to workers' compensation and its exclusivity rule. This, too, relates to the language of the particular workers' compensation statute in a given state. While, generally, there is immunity from a tort lawsuit, there may be statutory exceptions to co-employee immunity and employer immunity if there is an intentional act involved. A state's statute may create exceptions to the employee and employer immunity from suit. If an employee injures another employee in an incident that is well beyond horseplay, the injured employee may be able to sue the employee and the employer, depending upon the particular language of the statute. Under a California statute, if an employee proximately causes another employee's injury or death by a "willful and unprovoked physical act of aggression" with an "intent to injure," the employee and employer may be liable in tort, albeit this would be a tort based on an intentional act, not a negligent act.[11]

A final point needs to be made concerning workers' compensation so that there is no confusion about an employee's remedy when injured on the job. While the employee is prevented from making a negligence claim against his or her fellow employee and employer for a work-related accident, that does not mean that the employee may not be able to make such a claim against a third party. For example, assume that an employee is on the job and is working for a general contractor. The employee is high above the ground on some newly purchased scaffolding. The scaffolding is defective, it fails, and the employee falls to the ground and is injured. The employee cannot sue the employer since his or her exclusive remedy is workers' compensation. However, if there is evidence that the new scaffolding is defective, there is nothing to prevent the injured employee from also making a claim for pain and suffering and other special and general damages against the scaffolding manufacturer. Likewise, if an employee is on the job driving a company vehicle

Workplace Skills Tip

In a personal injury case that is "work related," there will likely be workers' compensation involved that paid benefits to the plaintiff. Workers' compensation will likely have a subrogation interest. Subrogation was discussed in Chapter 4. The plaintiff's paralegal will need to know the particular workers' compensation statute and the "formula" that will define the subrogation interest and how it is computed. This must be determined because a plaintiff will want to know what net amount he or she will receive after attorneys' fees and a workers' compensation subrogation amount are deducted from any recovery.

and is in an accident with another negligent motorist, the employee, besides receiving workers' compensation benefits, can still bring a tort claim for damages against the negligent motorist.

Dram Shop Liability

Historically, a "dram shop" was a local bar or tavern where intoxicating beverages were sold by the "dram." A dram was a unit of measurement of a small drink of spirits. **Dram shop liability** is imposed on those business establishments (and in some cases, those "social hosts") who sell or furnish alcoholic beverages to minors and to those who have noticeably had too much to drink. This illegal sale must then cause or contribute to causing an injury to a person. While the basis for liability here smacks of a blend of negligence and strict liability, the basis for tort liability here is usually statutory.

The dram shop statute of the paralegal's particular jurisdiction must be carefully studied in order to understand what must be proven by the plaintiff to establish liability and what kinds of damages are recoverable. Court decisions from the particular jurisdiction will also have interpreted various portions of that jurisdiction's dram shop statute. Each state's dram shop statute, along with court decisions interpreting the statute, varies significantly. As mentioned in the first chapter, to be an effective team player, the personal injury paralegal must know the law concerning a particular personal injury issue.

For example, depending upon the particular state's dram shop statute, it may not matter how carefully and how reasonably the bartender or other wait staff acted. If the bartender or other wait staff served a visibly intoxicated person, one of the statutory elements for liability has been established. Period. These statutes are not predicated on the negligent conduct of the liquor establishment. Liability is predicated on the liability strictly imposed by the statute. Some statutes will not allow the alleged intoxicated person (sometimes referred to as the "AIP") to recover for his or her own injuries. Some statutes do not allow "social host" liability. Some statutes do not allow social host liability unless the illegal sale or furnishing of alcoholic beverages was to a minor. Some statutes place limits or caps on damages that can be recovered in a dram shop action. Some statutes require that a written notice be given to the liquor establishment prior to suit.

Also, each state utilizes its own specific language to define who is considered to be an alleged intoxicated person. Examples of such language defining an AIP, a sale to whom will impose liability on the bar, are the following: "obviously intoxicated person," Minnesota (Minn. Stat. Ann. § 340A.502.801); "habitually addicted to the use of any or all alcoholic beverages," Florida (Fla. Stat. § 768-125); "visibly intoxicated," Montana (Mont. Code. Ann. § 27-1-710); "any habitual or common drunkard or any obviously intoxicated person," California (Cal. Bus. Prof. Code § 25602); "any person visibly or noticeably intoxicated or ... any habitual drunkard," Mississippi (Miss. Code Ann. § 67-3-33).

The most effective way for the paralegal student to learn this area of the law is to review and analyze a hypothetical dram shop statute and then present a hypothetical fact situation. With that purpose in mind, review this hypothetical dram shop statute:

1. No licensed commercial vendor or municipality may sell, give, furnish, or in any way procure for another natural person any alcoholic beverages for the use of a person under the age of 21 or an obviously intoxicated person.

Dram Shop Liability
Statutory liability imposed on those business establishments (and in some cases, those "social hosts") who sell or furnish alcoholic beverages to minors and to those who have noticeably had too much to drink.

2. It is a defense for a defendant to prove by a preponderance of the evidence that the defendant reasonably, and in good faith, relied upon the representation of proof of age furnished by a minor.

3. A spouse, child, parent, guardian, employer, or other person injured in person, property, or means of support, or who incurs other pecuniary loss by an intoxicated person or by the intoxication of another person, has a right of action in the person's own name for all damages sustained against a person who caused the intoxication of that person by illegally selling alcoholic beverages.

4. Any person commencing an action must give a written notice to the licensee or municipality, which must be served by the claimant's attorney within 90 days of the date of entering an attorney-client relationship with the person in regard to the claim.

To simplify, and break down a claim under this statute, there are certain basic elements that must be proved:

- An illegal selling, giving, furnishing, or procuring of alcohol to either a minor or an obviously intoxicated person. (For simplicity, from this point forward, instead of repeating all four words, "selling" or "sale" will be used to also refer to giving, furnishing, or procuring.)
- The illegal sale causes or contributes to the intoxication of the minor or the obviously intoxicated person, which causes injury to the plaintiff.
- A proper plaintiff sustained damages allowed under the statute.
- Proper notice was provided.

ILLEGAL SALE TO AN OBVIOUSLY INTOXICATED PERSON OR TO ONE UNDER AGE 21

The first element of proof is that there must be an illegal sale of alcoholic beverages. An illegal sale is an illegal sale by a "licensed commercial liquor vendor or a municipality" (no statutory social host liability) to either (1) a minor—someone under age 21 or (2) an "obviously intoxicated person." Sales to minors are fairly clear-cut. Someone is either 21 years of age or older or not. The hypothetical statute above, however, does provide a defense to a liquor establishment that reasonably and in good faith relies upon proof of age provided by the minor. In general, if a liquor establishment asks the minor for identification, a false driver's license is shown, and the bar employee takes some time and effort to review the ID, which appears genuine, the liquor establishment will have a defense for the jury to consider.

Litigation frequently tends to center around sales to individuals who have had too much to drink. This hypothetical statute defines such a person as an "obviously intoxicated person." Assume Justin, a 55-year-old single man stops in after work to a local bar, Lynyrd's Office. He is accompanied by his girlfriend, Britney. They arrive at approximately 5:30 p.m. He has approximately five vodka sours in the course of an hour and a half. Britney nurses two Miller Lite beers during the hour and a half. Justin pays for all the drinks. They are served by Christina, the bar waitress on duty, and Josh, the bartender on duty. Justin and Britney leave Lynyrd's at approximately 7:00 p.m. to go home. Justin is driving his car with Britney as a passenger. Justin crosses the center line and collides with a vehicle driven by Katy. Following an investigation by the highway patrol, Justin's blood alcohol level is .19. Katy is injured and commences a dram shop action against Lynyrd's. She may also sue Justin for negligence, of course. Katy alleges an illegal sale of alcohol to Justin at a time when he was "obviously intoxicated." Katy's legal team retains a toxicologist who will testify that someone with a blood alcohol level of .19 would be showing severe outward, obvious signs of intoxication, such as slurred speech, bloodshot eyes, and difficulty with motor coordination, and that such person would be obviously intoxicated to a reasonable observer.

Assume the facts presented in the following two different scenarios and assume that these facts were observed or known by both servers in the bar, Christina and Josh:

1. Justin, a naturally outgoing, happy person was that way when he entered Lynyrd's. He continued that pattern throughout his time there, laughing and joking with both Christina and Josh. Justin and Britney each ordered a hamburger and fries while there at about 6:00 p.m. or so and both completely finished their meals. Christina and Josh saw no difference in Justin's behavior, speech, or outward appearance from the time he entered the bar until he exited the bar. No incidents occurred involving Justin during the entire time he and Britney were there. Justin was a complete gentleman and was fun to converse with. Their only recollection is that perhaps his voice became a bit louder and some of his jokes became a bit more vulgar as the evening progressed.

2. Justin, after the fourth drink at approximately 6:15, started slurring his words. Shortly after that, Justin knocked over Britney's beer bottle. In an effort to avoid the spilled beer, he fell off his chair. He then started to pick himself up but fell back again and sat on the floor for a few moments, seemingly confused. He then, slowly and unsteadily, regained his balance with the help of Christina and Britney. Justin started walking unsteadily to the men's bathroom but started to enter the women's bathroom. At that point, he bumped into another patron with whom he had an argument over whether or not he was about to enter the proper bathroom. Both Christina and Josh broke up the argument. Justin continued to the men's bathroom and came back to the table. At that point, Christina asked him if he would like to order something to eat, and he replied, "I'm drinkin' my dinner tonight, baby." Before leaving, he hollered to Christina in extremely slurred speech: "Hey Honey, I got just 'nuf time for 'nother round so bring me 'nother one!" Christina brought him this final drink, wished him a "Happy Birthday," and he chugged it down. He and Britney then promptly exited the bar.

Scenario number 1 will present a difficult proof case for Katy against Lynyrd's. It is true that Justin had consumed several drinks in the course of an approximate hour and a half and had a blood alcohol reading of .19. A qualified toxicologist will likely be permitted to express opinions about the effects of alcohol on a person's demeanor, appearance, and physical performance at various blood alcohol levels or concentrations. Generally, the higher the level the more obvious or visible is the intoxication. However, there is really no firsthand evidence that he was obviously intoxicated; indeed, there is no firsthand evidence that he was even intoxicated by observing his speech, physical actions, and demeanor. The proof of this first statutory element of serving an obviously intoxicated person will rest solely on a high blood alcohol reading and only two very weak indices of obvious intoxication—Justin's increasingly louder voice and increasingly vulgar jokes.

Scenario number 2 presents a much easier proof case for Katy on this issue. The high blood alcohol test is verified by firsthand eyewitness testimony of Justin's "obvious intoxication"—falling off his chair, being disoriented after the fall,

Workplace Skills Tip

When assisting with the investigation of a dram shop case, whether plaintiff or defendant, it is extremely important for the paralegal to determine various items: Besides determining the AIP's height and weight, health, drug use, and alcohol consumed before entering the bar in question, determine whether the AIP is an "experienced drinker" or not. The plaintiff will typically retain a toxicologist to try to prove, through a high blood alcohol reading, that symptoms of intoxication must have been obvious to the bar personnel. However, people who have been drinking for an extended period of time do develop a tolerance for alcohol—they "can hold their liquor." It probably explains scenario number 1 in the Lynyrd's Office example.

Determine the extent of the AIP's eating of food before and during the drinking. Ingesting food slows the rate of absorption of alcohol into the blood stream. Food was eaten in scenario number 1 but not in scenario number 2.

Determine whether the AIP was a "newcomer" or a "regular." It can make a difference concerning this issue of obvious intoxication if the bar personnel are very familiar with the drinking habits and traits of the AIP as opposed to a person they have never dealt with before.

The AIP may have consumed a great deal of alcohol, but unless he or she is exhibiting some outward symptoms or signs of intoxication, proof of this type of illegal sale will be lacking. For obvious reasons, the bar personnel will typically testify no outward or visible intoxication symptoms were present in spite of the number of drinks served. Other bar patrons can help decide a close case. A jury will be very interested to hear what other disinterested witnesses in the bar (assuming they were sober) have observed about the AIP showing any obvious signs of intoxication. Bar patrons are important witnesses for the paralegal to interview in any investigation with which the paralegal is assisting.

having Britney assist him in arising, mixing up the men's and women's bathrooms, an altercation with another patron, unsteady on his feet (staggering), and slurred speech. All of these actions of Justin were witnessed by either Josh or Christina or both of them.

CAUSES OR CONTRIBUTES TO INTOXICATION THAT CAUSES INJURY TO THE PLAINTIFF

The second element of proof under the hypothetical statute is that the illegal sale must have caused or contributed to intoxication that caused the injury complained of. While not contained in the example above, if Justin were "bar hopping," each drink at each bar is causing or contributing to his intoxication. In the Lynyrd's Office example, the alleged intoxication was caused completely by Lynyrd's Office.

Causation for the statutory tort of dram shop liability is the same as causation for the tort of negligence. Assume in the example above, after leaving Lynyrd's Office, Justin is proceeding down the highway in his own lane of travel and driving at an appropriate speed. Instead of crossing the center line, assume that the other driver, Katy, suddenly and without any warning, crossed the center line into Justin's lane of travel and caused a collision with his vehicle. It may be true that Justin was intoxicated. However, Justin's intoxication did not cause the collision. The collision was proximately caused by the overwhelming negligence of the other driver, Katy. Even if the plaintiff, Katy, proved the first element of an illegal sale, the second element of causation is lacking.

PROPER PLAINTIFF AND PLAINTIFF'S DAMAGES

The purpose of this statute is to protect innocent third parties from the mischief of the illegal furnishing of liquor that causes a person's intoxication. The hypothetical statute quoted above states that certain people or entities may be plaintiffs in a dram shop case: "A spouse, child, parent, guardian, employer, or *other person* injured in person, property, or means of support…." Damages may be recovered for an injury to (1) one's person, (2) one's property, or (3) one's means of support. Katy, the other driver with whom Justin collided in the first example, would be able to sue Lynyrd's Office for her personal injuries. She is an innocent person—an "other person" who is entitled to sue under the dram shop act in question. If Justin were injured in the collision, the question would be whether or not he was an innocent "other person." He may have no right to sue for his injuries under this hypothetical dram shop statute. If Justin's passenger, Britney, sustained a personal injury, she could, like Katy, make a claim for her damages against the bar. She is an "other person" as stated in the statute.

Consider damages for the element of loss of means of support. Assume Britney, Justin's girlfriend, did not receive any personal injury, but assume Justin was injured or killed. If Britney happened to be dependent upon Justin for support, would she have a claim under this statute for a loss of means of support based on Justin's injury or death? It would depend if Britney were considered to be an "other person" who was injured in her means of support. Clearly, for example, a "spouse" or a "child" and others in the definition of a proper plaintiff could do so.

WRITTEN NOTICE

As noted above, this hypothetical state's dram shop statute does require that written notice be given by the claimant's attorney to the business licensee or municipality within 90 days of the claimant's entering into an attorney-client relationship. The paralegal will need to determine whether the jurisdiction where he or she is employed has any notice requirement in that state's dram shop law. Providing a good backup to the attorney will mean helping to ensure that such notice is timely provided pursuant to the statute. This raises the same point made in the first chapter. Missing the notice requirement could result in the plaintiff's case being forever barred, the paralegal being terminated on the spot, and the attorney facing ethical violations and a malpractice lawsuit.

DEFENSES

The basic elements of a hypothetical dram shop statute have just been discussed. As mentioned at the outset of this textbook, it is vital that the paralegal is familiar with the law of the paralegal's jurisdiction. Each state's dram shop statute will be different, and there will also be court decisions interpreting the statute. Analysis of the above statute should provide a flavor of this type of tort liability.

As noted above, with regard to the illegal sale to a minor, the hypothetical statute does provide a defense to the bar for its good faith effort to determine a minor's age. In the obviously intoxicated illegal sale scenario, the bar may have a defense of **complicity**. In the dram shop context, complicity is the act of affirmatively assisting with an illegal sale of alcoholic beverages. Assume in the Lynyrd's Office example that Britney bought a round or rounds of drinks for Justin. If Britney brings a dram shop suit for her injuries from the collision, the bar may be able to allege the defense of complicity. Assume it is proven that Britney bought a round or two for Justin and complicity is a defense. The particular state's statute will need to be reviewed. It may operate as a complete bar to plaintiff's claim or it may reduce the claim under comparative fault principles.

Complicity
A defense to a dram shop action that is the act of affirmatively assisting with an illegal sale of alcoholic beverages.

Duties of Land Occupier

The next general area involving a special duty concerning the tort of negligence is the area of land occupier liability. When the term "land occupier" is used, it refers to the person who is in possession of the land. This is not necessarily the owner. For example, it could be the owner or it could be a tenant or a lessee under a lease. What is the occupier's duty to a person coming onto the land? Statutes have significantly changed the common law rules of land occupier liability. Those basic common law rules will first be discussed, and then some important statutory changes will be discussed.

There are three areas upon land that may create liability: (1) natural conditions, (2) artificial conditions, and (3) activities occurring on the land. Natural conditions consist of such conditions as rocks, trees, cliffs, bluffs, ponds, and natural lakes and rivers. Artificial conditions consist of conditions such as buildings, fences, poles, and towers. Activities may include either personal or business activities being conducted upon the land. The common law approach examines the status of the person coming onto the land in order to determine the duty owed. The three categories of status are *trespasser*, *licensee*, and *invitee*.

TRESPASSER

Trespasser
A person who comes upon the land without the permission of the land occupier.

A **trespasser** is a person who comes upon the land without the permission of the land occupier. The general rule is that there is no duty of reasonable care owed to one in the category of a trespasser whose presence is unknown. Further, there is no duty to discover trespassers. The basic caveat to the trespasser duty is that there is a duty not to intentionally or maliciously injure a trespasser.

CTULA
This literally means a constant trespasser upon a limited area.

There are certain categories of trespassers that are afforded a higher duty of care. One category is referred to as the **CTULA**. This literally means a "constant trespasser upon a limited area." A constant trespasser is one who is constantly or habitually trespassing on a certain portion of the land. For example, a public road may end at the owner's land. Fifty feet away is another public road. Accordingly, people may typically and constantly cut across that 50-foot stretch as a shortcut. Someone who is a CTULA will receive a higher duty of care than the ordinary trespasser. This is because when someone is habitually and constantly trespassing on one's land and nothing is done about it, the land occupier is apparently tolerating the trespasser and allowing the land's use. At common law, the duty owed to a CTULA is the duty to reasonably warn a CTULA or make safe any artificial conditions or activities that involve a risk of death or serious bodily harm.

ATTRACTIVE NUISANCE DOCTRINE

Attractive Nuisance Doctrine
This doctrine imposes on a land occupier a higher duty of care with respect to conditions and activities on the land that involve a risk of harm to children who are unable to recognize the danger.

Another category of trespasser that will be afforded a higher duty of care is a child trespasser under the **attractive nuisance doctrine**. This doctrine will impose on a land occupier a higher duty of care with respect to conditions and activities on the land that involve a risk of harm to children who are unable to recognize the danger. The child must be so immature that he or she cannot recognize the particular danger involved. As the child becomes older and even into the teens, the doctrine may not apply. Some classic examples of attractive nuisances are items such as a swimming pool, a construction site, unattended equipment or machinery, and a gravel pit. The basic rule is that if a land occupier discovers children trespassing or should know of the trespassing, the duty owed is one of due care to warn or protect the child from dangerous conditions that involve a risk of death or serious bodily harm. Section 339 Restatement (Second) Torts outlines four basic elements of the doctrine:

1. Children are known to trespass or likely to trespass at the place where the condition exists.
2. The land occupier knows or should know of the condition on the land and knows or should know that it involves an unreasonable risk of death or serious bodily harm.
3. The risk of maintaining the condition outweighs the utility of retaining it.
4. The condition on the land is one that a child, because of his or her youth, will not discover the condition or will not realize the danger involved to the child.

Element number 4 probably provides the most fruit for litigation. The issue becomes: Is the child capable of realizing the danger involved? The younger the child, the more likely the condition will be found to be an attractive nuisance. The older the child, the less likely the condition will be found to be an attractive nuisance. A five-year-old child who climbs up on an unattended road grader may not realize the danger involved, whereas a reasonable child of 10 years old will probably realize the danger. A toddler may not realize the danger of a swimming pool whereas a reasonable 10-year-old probably would realize the danger. This issue is the fact issue that will usually be the most hotly contested.

LICENSEE

The second common law category of a person coming onto land is a **licensee**. A licensee is one who comes onto the land with the land occupier's permission—express or implied—for the primary purpose or benefit of the licensee. Examples are a door-to-door salesperson, a process server, or a person involved in a charitable cause for contributions. A licensee relationship may be found when, for example, a church, hospital, or other business allows a charitable organization such as AA, Girl Scouts, or Make-A-Wish Foundation to use a room in its facility for weekly or monthly meetings. The common law duty owed to a licensee is to use reasonable care to warn licensees of, or make safe, natural or artificial conditions. If activities are carried on, such warning must be provided by the land occupier to the licensee of any risk of harm that is known to the land occupier. The land occupier is under no duty to inspect the property to try to discover any dangers to the licensee. Implied permission is usually liberally construed. For example, if a neighbor came to the door of a homeowner to borrow the proverbial cup of sugar or to bring a misdelivered U.S. Post Office letter to the homeowner, the court would probably imply permission to enter.

Licensee
One who comes onto the land with the land occupier's permission—express or implied—for the primary purpose or benefit of the licensee.

INVITEE

The third common law category is an **invitee**. An invitee is one who comes onto the land with the land occupier's permission—express or implied—for a purpose related to an interest of the land occupier. Typically these invitees are either a "public invitee" or a "business invitee." Obviously, these two categories may overlap. A **public invitee** is a person coming onto the land who is invited as a member of the public for a purpose that is open to the public. This does not mean that a formal, personal, written invitation is necessary. If property is open to the public that is considered to be an "invitation." Examples abound: a shopping mall, a hospital, a clinic, a retail store, a movie theater, a federal building, or a county courthouse. In these examples it can be seen that the particular premises may be publicly owned or privately owned. One

Invitee
One who comes onto the land with the land occupier's permission—express or implied—for a purpose related to an interest of the land occupier.

Public Invitee
A person coming onto the land who is invited as a member of the public for a purpose that is open to the public.

Business Invitee
One who enters upon the land occupier's premises for a purpose that
is related to the business conducted
on the premises.

injured entering the county courthouse to use the restroom is just as much a public invitee as one who purchases a ticket at a movie theater to see a movie.

A **business invitee** is one who enters upon the land occupier's premises for a purpose that is related to the business conducted on the premises. Usually the entrance upon the land is to confer a benefit to the occupier of the land. Again, examples abound. Besides the ones mentioned in the preceding paragraph, additional examples might include a motel, an amusement park, a train station, or a shopping mall. While the courts distinguish between a public invitee and a business invitee, it can be seen that they will often overlap, and the duty is the same.

An important point is that once a person enters as an invitee, his or her status may change depending upon the original invitee's location at the time of the injury. For example, if one entered a grocery store to buy groceries, at that point, the person is an invitee. However, assume the customer opened a door upon which was a sign that read: "Danger Keep Out" or "No Admittance — Employees Only." If the person were injured in that room, the person's status could change to that of a trespasser. The person exceeded the scope of the permission, which was only the store aisles and store area where groceries are located.

An invitee is owed a duty on the part of the land occupier to use reasonable care to inspect and discover the presence of any natural or artificial conditions or activities that are dangerous and to use due care to warn of dangers and to also actually make the premises safe for the invitee. At common law, this is the category of entrant that is owed the greatest and highest duty of care by the land occupier. Even a warning may not suffice. For example, in a small downtown restaurant with steps, assume a sign stated: "Caution! Step Down!" If there were a dangerous entryway either inside or outside the restaurant, a court may well take the position that even though a sign was posted, and the step down was obvious, the store should have simply redesigned and reconfigured the steps to make them safe for the patron/business invitee.

MODERN VIEW

Entrant
A person who enters or stays upon
the land of another.

Many courts have modified or abolished the traditional three common law categories of trespasser, licensee, and invitee. The person coming upon the land is simply termed an "entrant." An **entrant** is a person who enters or stays upon the land of another. The person coming upon the land may be described as a "lawful entrant" (in other words, not a trespasser). The land occupant has a duty to an entrant to use reasonable care to protect the entrant from an unreasonable risk of harm caused by the condition of the premises or the activities on the premises. The standard for determining whether a land occupier owes a duty to entrants on the land is that of "reasonable care under the circumstances." Rather than trying to ascertain the status of the person coming onto the land to determine a degree of duty owed, this modern trend simply takes the approach that an entrant or lawful entrant is owed a duty of reasonable care under the circumstances. Some of the circumstances will be the purpose for which the entrant entered the land, the foreseeability of harm, the reasonableness of any inspection or repair, and the opportunity and ease of any repair or correction.

RECREATIONAL USE STATUTES

Recreational Use Statute
Statutes that protect and provide
immunity to owners of land from
personal injury suits commenced by
a person who was using the land for
"recreational purposes."

Many states have enacted special statutes that protect landowners. They provide immunity to landowners from personal injury suits commenced by a person who was using the land for recreational purposes. They are called **recreational use statutes**.

These recreational purposes will be defined in the statute and will consist of such activities as hunting, trapping, fishing, swimming, boating, camping, hiking, bicycling, and horseback riding. Many injuries or deaths occur when a plaintiff is using someone else's land for some type of recreational purpose. A typical exception for landowner immunity is if the landowner has engaged in "willful or wanton conduct" or "willful and malicious conduct." Another exception for immunity may be if the landowner required a charge or fee that was paid to the landowner by the injured person. Otherwise, if there has been no egregious conduct such as willful and malicious conduct and if no charge or fee has been made to use the land, the landowner has complete immunity from suit. The purpose of these statutes is to encourage landowners to allow the public to use their land for recreational purposes in exchange for which they receive immunity from suit.

Read the decision of *Cudworth v. Midcontinent Communications*, 380 F. 3d 375 (8th Cir. 2004) in Exhibit 5-4 for a better understanding of the purpose and application of a recreational use statute.

EXHIBIT 5-4 Relevant Case Law

Irene Cudwortg; Randy Cudworth, Appellants, v. Midcontinent Communications; Midcontinent Communications Investor, LLC; Midco Communications, Inc.; Midcontinent Media, Inc.; Midco of South Dakota, Inc., Appellees.

Steven A. Storslee, argued, Bismarck, North Dakota (Larry B. Leventhal, Minneapolis, Minnesota on the brief), for appellant.

Richard N. Jeffries, argued, Fargo, North Dakota, for appellee.

United States Court of Appeals, Eighth Circuit.

Wollman, Circuit Judge.

Randy Cudworth was pulled from his snowmobile and rendered a quadriplegic when he collided with a rope barrier strung across property owned by the appellees, whom we will refer to collectively as "Midcontinent." In the ensuing lawsuit by Cudworth and his wife, the district court granted summary judgment in Midcontinent's favor, concluding that North Dakota's recreational use immunity statute absolved Midcontinent of liability and that the Cudworths' remaining claims failed as a matter of law. The Cudworths appeal. We affirm. . . .

I.

The Midcontinent property where Cudworth was injured is a largely open, six-acre field located directly north of Langdon, North Dakota, and south of a state-groomed snowmobile trail. Two residential streets, 15th and 16th, run north from Langdon toward the property. 15th Street borders the property to the west and 16th street terminates at its southern boundary. A dirt path (the "prairie road") connects the end of 16th street with 15th street. Although the prairie road is located on Midcontinent's land, Langdon residents and the City itself have used it for many years. In addition, residents have used Midcontinent's field as a site on which to operate their all-terrain vehicles during the summer months and as an access route to established snowmobile trails during the winter months. . . .

In the summer of 2000, Midcontinent became upset because garbage was being dumped on the prairie road and because traffic across the road, including that by City-owned vehicles, was causing ruts. To remedy the situation, the City hauled in dirt, graded the ruts, and seeded portions of the area with grass. Midcontinent employee Jerry Reiser then erected barriers at each end of the prairie road. The eastern barrier, the point at which Cudworth was injured, consisted of 200 feet of quarter-inch diameter yellow nylon rope tied between metal stakes and wooden cable spools, each of which was affixed with a "keep out," "private property," or "no trespassing" sign. The rope originated on the

(Continued)

EXHIBIT 5-4 *(Continued)*

southwest corner of 16th street, ran northeast across the end of the prairie road, and east beyond the end of 16th street into Midcontinent's field. Reiser, who knew that snowmobilers used the property during winter, erected the barrier to prevent damage to the newly seeded grass, but the barrier remained even after snow had started falling.

On February 23, 2001, Cudworth drove up 16th street on his snowmobile towards Midcontinent's field, destined for the trails to the north. He had not used a snowmobile in the area before and was unaware of the barrier, which was by now partially obscured in a bank of plowed snow at the end of 16th street. Although the other persons in Cudworth's snowmobiling party observed the barrier and avoided it, Cudworth did not see the rope and collided with it as he rounded the east side of the snowbank....

A. Applicability of the Recreational Use Immunity Statute

The relevant portions of North Dakota's Recreational Use Immunity statute, N.D. Cent.Code § 53-08-01 et seq., are as follows:

53-08-02. Duty of care of landowner. Subject to the provisions of section 53-08-05, an owner of land owes no duty of care to keep the premises safe for entry or use by others for recreational purposes or to give any warning of a dangerous condition, use, structure, or activity on such premises to persons entering for such purposes.

53-08-03. Not invitee or licensee of landowner. Subject to the provisions of section 53-08-05, an owner of land who either directly or indirectly invites or permits without charge any person to use such property for recreational purposes does not thereby:

1. Extend any assurance that the premises are safe for any purpose;

2. Confer upon such persons the legal status of an invitee or licensee to whom a duty of care is owed; or

3. Assume responsibility for or incur liability for any injury to person or property caused by an act or omission of such persons....

53-08-05. Failure to warn against dangerous conditions-Charge to enter. Nothing in this chapter limits in any way any liability which otherwise exists for:

1. Willful and malicious failure to guard or warn against a dangerous condition, use, structure, or activity; or

2. Injury suffered in any case when the owner of land charges the person or persons who enter or go on the land other than the amount, if any, paid to the owner of the land by the state.

The Cudworths first argue that the recreational use immunity statute does not apply because a prerequisite to statutory immunity is the landowner's "opening" of property for public recreational use, something which the Cudworths contend Midcontinent did not do when it roped off and posted the prairie road. State courts interpreting similar legislation are divided over this question, but the district court ultimately rejected "permissive use" as a statutory prerequisite to immunity in North Dakota....

As in other states, the acknowledged purpose of North Dakota's recreational use immunity statute is to encourage landowners to open land for recreational use by the public.... The statute does not, however, explicitly require that landowners open property to public use before receiving immunity, nor does it specify that immunity applies only where entrants are invitees or licensees. At common law, the status of the entrant as invitee, licensee, or trespasser was often crucial to determinations of landowner duties.... North Dakota has abolished the common law distinction between licensee and invitee and the elaborate permutations of each, but still recognizes that lesser duties are owed to trespassers. *Id.*...

B. Exception for Willful and Malicious Failure to Warn

Although the statute applies regardless of permissive use, it does not protect landowners who engage in a "willful and malicious failure to guard or warn against a dangerous condition, use, structure,

(Continued)

EXHIBIT 5-4 *(Continued)*

---

or activity" on premises. N.D. Cent.Code. § 53-08-05. The parties contest the application of this exception and, more specifically, the meaning of "malicious," a term which the statute does not define. The district court concluded that "malicious" conduct requires proof of "actual malice" or "evil intent," and it found such evidence lacking....

We further agree with the district court that summary judgment was appropriate. There is no evidence from which a reasonable jury could find that Midcontinent's barrier was constructed or left in place to injure snowmobilers. The barrier was constructed months before the winter season for an unrelated purpose, and Midcontinent had no notice that snowmobilers were having difficulty observing it. Moreover, the nature of the barrier itself is not sufficient for a jury to infer "willful and malicious" conduct, as such a reading would include every landowner who uses a rope, wire, or other fencing material to restrict access to portions of private property adjacent to snowmobiling trails, thereby allowing the exception to entirely swallow the general rule....

The judgment is affirmed.

Source: Cudworth v. Midcontinent Communications, 380 F.3d 375 (8th Cir. 2004).

As an aside, the author handled the *Cudworth* case for Midcontinent. This is precisely the type of case that will strike fear in the heart of any tort lawyer defending against such a case. It is a classic "skinny liability ... catastrophic injury" case with a potential for enormous money damages. In spite of the vast investigation and discovery in this case, the resolution of the case came down to a few undisputed material facts succinctly stated by the court in three short paragraphs. Note the procedural history of the case. Summary judgment was granted at the trial court level, and the summary judgment was affirmed on appeal. Mr. Cudworth received nothing. If there had been a disputed fact issue such that this case had gone to a jury, do you think it likely that Mr. Cudworth would still have received nothing?

Negligent Infliction of Emotional Distress

As discussed in Chapter 4, in a negligence case, there may be alleged damages for "emotional distress" caused by a physical personal injury. Emotional distress may be a natural result of a broken bone or an amputation or a scar. Damages for the emotional distress are recoverable as an incident to the personal injury involved. Here, the discussion centers around a specific tort, which is a **negligent infliction of emotional distress**. Emotional distress is the only resulting damage. The student will recall the definition of a personal injury in Chapter 1, which is an injury to a person's body, mind, or *emotions*.

Negligent Infliction of Emotional Distress
A type of non-economic/general damages caused by negligence.

Workplace Skills Tip

In a jury case in which there is a catastrophic injury such as a brain injury or paraplegia or quadriplegia, but defendant's liability is thin to nonexistent, the extremely serious injury will often override the liability aspect of a case. When instructing a jury, the court will typically instruct the jury that the case is to be decided on the evidence presented. The court will also typically instruct the jury that "sympathy" is to play no part in their decision. But it does.

PHYSICAL IMPACT

The traditional view of this tort is that the tortfeasor owes a duty to exercise due care not to subject a person to a risk of physical injury through a physical impact that might foreseeably result in emotional distress. This rule requires that before damages for emotional distress may be recovered, there must be some type of physical impact to the plaintiff. This need not be a forceful blow. It could include a mere touching of the person. The rationale for this rule is to protect against fraudulent claims generated by a pure emotional distress claim without some injury or contact to the plaintiff's body.

ZONE OF DANGER

The physical impact rule has been modified to include a duty to exercise due care not to subject a person to *the threat of a physical impact* that might foreseeably result in emotional distress provided that the plaintiff is in the "zone of danger." For example, if a defendant lost control of his or her motor vehicle, ran up the curb and onto the sidewalk, missing a pedestrian but scaring the daylights out of the pedestrian, the pedestrian would have a claim for negligent infliction of emotional distress. Even though there was no impact in this example—only a threat—the pedestrian who was nearly struck by a motor vehicle on a sidewalk was clearly within the zone of danger.

PHYSICAL MANIFESTATION

Another modification to the physical impact rule is a rule that in addition to emotional distress without a physical impact or touching, there must be some type of physical manifestation. In the preceding example, the pedestrian plaintiff would need to demonstrate that some physical symptoms arose from the event. Besides proof of emotional distress the plaintiff would need to show a physical manifestation of the emotional distress such as an ulcer, weight gain, weight loss, or high blood pressure. The requirement of a physical manifestation is the concern about a fraudulent claim involving only a purely subjective, invisible claim of emotional distress.

GENUINE EMOTIONAL DISTRESS

Some jurisdictions will allow a claim for purely emotional distress without physical impact, without a threat of physical impact, without physical manifestations, or without being in the zone of danger. These cases involve facts in which there is a great likelihood that the mental distress is genuine. Examples might include a false death report of a relative or the mishandling of a relative's corpse. For example, if a hospital erroneously notified the plaintiff that a close relative had died, the plaintiff would likely be allowed to pursue a claim for pure emotional distress. If a funeral home mixed up the cremated remains of a close relative, the plaintiff would likely be allowed to pursue a claim for pure emotional distress.

BYSTANDER EMOTIONAL DISTRESS

There is a final point concerning this tort and that is the approach utilized by the courts when the plaintiff is a bystander and not the actual victim. This refers to a factual scenario in which the plaintiff is not personally at risk but witnesses an injury to someone else and suffers emotional distress. The traditional rule is that the plaintiff must be in the zone of danger and must suffer some physical manifestation of the distress although some courts have not required the latter. For example, assume a mother is standing on a street corner with her young child, and the young child suddenly decides to run out into the street and is struck by a car a few feet away. The mother, close by, witnesses the collision of the car with the child. She would be in the zone of danger, but the case may still turn on whether or not a particular court required some physical manifestation.

The more modern view allows the plaintiff to recover for emotional distress with or without physical manifestation in cases where the defendant's negligence physically injures or threatens to physically injure a member of the plaintiff's family. The landmark decision is *Dillon v. Legg*, 441 P.2d 912 (Cal. 1968). *Dillon* eliminated any requirement of zone of danger and focused upon whether or not this emotional distress injury was reasonably foreseeable. The modern view requires three basic elements:

1. The plaintiff and the victim were closely related.
2. The plaintiff must be physically present at the accident scene and must be aware of the victim's suffering.
3. The plaintiff must suffer extreme or extraordinary emotional distress—beyond that of an unrelated bystander.

CASE **5.1** Hypothetical Case: Developing Workplace Skills

You are employed as a paralegal in a firm that does workers' compensation work and employment law. You have received the following e-mail from the senior partner one day at 1:00 p.m.:

We have a case in the office with which you may be familiar, but I don't believe you have worked on it. The name of the case is *Samuel Yosemite v. F. C. "Foghorn" Leghorn*. The case arises out of an accident that occurred last year in which our client, Mr. Leghorn, had a young man by the name of H. C. "Henry" Hawke do some tree trimming for him. When Mr. Hawke was up on the ladder, the saw fell out of Mr. Hawke's hand and landed on Mr. Yosemite, a neighbor, as he and our client were visiting. The saw hit him in the face causing an injury to his nose and some facial scarring. I won't go into all of the facts at this point because I'm in a hurry. I have a meeting with Mr. Leghorn at 3:00 this afternoon. I want to provide him with some type of initial evaluation of this case. Our defense is basically that Mr. Hawke was an independent contractor and not Mr. Leghorn's employee so that Mr. Leghorn cannot be liable under *respondeat superior* for this unfortunate accident. Somewhere in the back of my mind I recall the IRS had a Revenue Ruling or some other document listing "20 factors" as to whether one is an employee or an independent contractor. I remember reading it one time, and it is very good. Look on the Internet ASAP and see if you can find it, print out a hard copy, and bring it in to my office. Keep track of your time and bill to WB1950.

"Give me another... and don't worry, I'm not litigious."

CHAPTER **SUMMARY**

Under the law of agency, a principal provides authority to an agent to act on behalf of the principal. The agent's actions bind the principal and make the principal liable to a third party. The principal is said to be vicariously liable for the actions of the agent. The actions of the agent are also said to be imputed to the principal.

The employee is the agent of the employer, and the employee's actions bind the employer when the employee is acting within the scope of his or her employment. The scope of employment consists of duties that are required by the employer to be performed by the employee. In the employment context, the employer is liable under the doctrine of *respondeat superior.* The Latin term means "let the master answer." In other words, let the employer answer for the torts of the employee.

The employer will ordinarily be liable under *respondeat superior* unless it is shown that the employee was not serving his or her employer in any way at the time of the incident causing the plaintiff's injury. The coming and going rule is a legal principle that states an employer is not legally liable for the negligence of an employee who is either coming to work or going from work. The frolic and detour rule is a legal principle that states an employer is not legally liable for the negligence of an employee who deviates or departs from the employer's business to serve the employee's own personal purposes.

Because an employer may be held responsible for the negligence of the employer's employees, it is sometimes necessary to determine whether the person hired is an employee or an independent contractor. If the person is an employee, the employer will be responsible for the employee's negligence. However, if the person is an independent contractor, the employer will not be responsible for the independent contractor's negligence. The independent contractor controls the method and the manner of the work. In an employment relationship, the employer has the right to control the terms, conditions, and method and manner of an employee's work. The key to differentiating between an employee and an independent contractor is the right of control that can be exercised over the worker concerning the work result and the means for accomplishing the work.

In addition to the employment relationship, vicarious liability is found in motor vehicle cases. A permissive use statute is one that makes the owner of a motor vehicle liable for damages caused by one to whom the owner has given permission to drive the motor vehicle. The family purpose doctrine also makes the owner of a motor vehicle legally responsible for damages caused by the driver. However, the doctrine is stricter than permissive use. To hold the owner liable under family purpose, the driver must be a member of the owner's immediate family or household and must be driving the vehicle with the express or implied permission of the owner.

Workers' compensation provides an employee with certain statutory benefits. These are typically benefits for wage loss, medical expenses, lump sum benefits for a particular injury, and other benefits such as retraining benefits. There is no recovery permitted for general damages such as pain and suffering. This is the exclusive remedy for an employee who is injured on the job. The employee would be required to show that the injury arose out of and in the course of the employment. The trade-off is that the employer assumes all responsibility for a work-related accident without regard to fault in exchange for monetary limitations on the amount of that liability.

Dram shop liability is based on liability created by statute. A dram shop was a local bar or tavern in which alcoholic beverages were sold by the "dram"—a unit of measurement that was a small drink. Liability is imposed on business establishments and possibly social hosts who sell or furnish alcoholic beverages to two groups: an underage drinker—a minor under 21 years of age, and someone who is noticeably or visibly intoxicated. Both are considered "illegal sales."

At common law, the liability of a land occupier is based upon the category or status of the person entering the land. The three categories are trespasser, licensee, and invitee. Further, there are three areas upon the land that may create liability: natural conditions, artificial conditions, and activities occurring on the land. A trespasser is one who comes upon the land without permission of the land occupier. A child trespasser is afforded a higher duty of care based upon the attractive nuisance doctrine. This imposes liability on a land occupier with respect to conditions and activities on the land that involve a risk of harm to children who are unable to recognize the danger.

Recreational use statutes protect owners of land from personal injury suits brought by a person who was using the land for recreational purposes. There are exceptions in some statutes for an owner's willful or wanton conduct or willful and malicious conduct. There also may be an exception if the landowner makes a charge or a fee to enter to use the land.

Negligent infliction of emotional distress is a separate tort in itself. In a negligence case, as discussed in Chapter 4, damages for emotional distress may be a natural result of some personal, physical injury. For this specific tort, the only damage that occurs is the emotional distress itself. So as to prevent fraudulent claims, the traditional view has been that before damages for emotional distress can be recovered, there must be some type of physical impact to the plaintiff. The traditional view has been modified if the plaintiff is in the zone of danger, the plaintiff developed some physical manifestations resulting from the claimed emotional distress, or in cases of egregious conduct by defendant.

Bystanders to traumatic events who experience emotional distress must be in the zone of danger according to the traditional rule. Some courts even require some physical manifestation besides being in the zone of danger. A modern view first articulated by *Dillon v. Legg*, 441 P.2d 912 (Cal. 1968) is to eliminate the zone of danger rule and focus upon whether or not the emotional distress was reasonably foreseeable. The modern view requires that the plaintiff and the victim be closely related, the plaintiff must be physically present at the accident scene and be aware of the victims' suffering, and the plaintiff must suffer extreme or extraordinary emotional distress.

KEY TERMS

Principal
Agent
Vicarious Liability
Respondeat Superior
Coming and Going Rule
Frolic and Detour Rule
Independent Contractor
Permissive Use Statute

Joint Enterprise
Family Purpose Doctrine
Workers' Compensation
Dram Shop Liability
Complicity
Trespasser
CTULA
Attractive Nuisance Doctrine

Licensee
Invitee
Public Invitee
Business Invitee
Entrant
Recreational Use Statute
Negligent Infliction of Emotional
   Distress

REVIEW QUESTIONS

1. Define *respondeat superior*. Provide its literal meaning, and apply that literal meaning to its legal meaning. Provide an example.

2. Petal Pusher Flower Shop, Inc. just purchased a new delivery truck for its flower business. Petunia, an employee of Petal Pusher, is involved in a collision with the truck while en route to deliver flowers to a residence. She collides with another vehicle driven by Rose, and Rose sustains a personal injury. Under what theory or theories might Petal Pusher be vicariously liable to Rose if she brings suit for her personal injuries?

3. Laura, a workaholic attorney with the Manhattan law firm of Bull and Bear, Ltd., is on a commuter train at 6:30 A.M. on her way to work. All attorneys at Bull and Bear are expected to be at their desks promptly at 8:00 a.m. Laura is working on an important brief for the firm during the commute to work. She has just poured herself an extra hot cup of coffee from her thermos. In trying to work with her pen and legal pad and drink coffee, she carelessly spills some hot coffee on a nearby passenger who happens to have a condition of extra sensitive skin. The spilled coffee causes a burn and a disfigurement to the passenger's arm and hand. The passenger sues Bull and Bear. Are they liable for Laura's negligence? Why or why not?

4. Bluto is employed by a spinach processing and canning factory. His job is to go to the various factory sites within a 100-mile radius from the home office and inspect the premises for both cleanliness and efficiency. He is ahead of schedule and notes he has a good hour and a half before he needs to be at the next factory site 20 miles away. His route naturally takes him close to where his mistress, Olive, lives. With time to spare, Bluto turns off the main highway to take the county road to Olive's house. In his excitement to see Olive, he is speeding and not paying attention. He negligently causes a collision with another vehicle at a crossing in which he runs a stop sign. The other driver is injured and sues Bluto's employer on a theory of *respondeat superior*. What defenses will the employer likely raise

and will the employer likely be successful in raising those defenses? Why or why not?

5. What is the difference between a permissive use statute and the family purpose doctrine?

6. Brian is a mechanic who works at a large tank manufacturing plant. While on the job, he is in the process of grinding a piece of metal. He is wearing his newly issued company goggles. Unfortunately, the strap is defective. It breaks, which causes the goggles to fall off Brian's face. At the same time a piece of metal is thrown into his eye, and he receives a serious eye injury. What are his remedies?

7. What is a dram shop statute, and what is its purpose? Is it a tort? If so, on what basis of liability is it based—negligence, intentional, or strict liability?

8. Explain the difference among the terms "trespasser," "licensee," and "invitee."

9. Joey, a six-year-old boy is with his parents at a public restaurant sitting outside on the patio. Approximately 30 feet away there is another restaurant immediately adjacent called The Trojan Horse. That restaurant has a large horse in front of the restaurant. Joey sees it, and while his parents are engaged in a serious conversation, Joey, intrigued by the horse, wanders over to the horse, climbs up part way, loses his grip, falls, and is injured. Is The Trojan Horse restaurant liable? What might be their defense?

10. Plaintiff was treated by a psychologist for approximately a year and a half. Defendant psychologist engaged in sexual intercourse with her under the guise of "therapy." Following the termination of her "treatment," she experienced emotional distress in the form of fear, shame, humiliation, and guilt. She sued on a theory of negligent infliction of emotional distress. She had no physical symptoms, only the emotional distress mentioned. Defendant psychologist's position is that there was no physical injury. Indeed, he argues there was no pain, suffering, inconvenience, or injury of any kind—only an experience that she willingly participated in and thoroughly enjoyed. Would plaintiff prevail on her claims and Why or why not?

chapter 6
DEFENSES TO NEGLIGENCE

LEARNING OBJECTIVES

After studying this chapter, you should be able to:

- Articulate the defense of contributory negligence.

- Explain the last clear chance doctrine.

- Recognize and appreciate the rationale for comparative negligence.

- Identify and analyze the defense of assumption of the risk.

- Distinguish between a statute of limitation and a statute of repose.

- Step into the shoes of the defendant and appreciate the defense perspective.

Affirmative Defense
A defense interposed in the defendant's answer that will have the legal effect of defeating a plaintiff's claim even if the facts supporting the plaintiff's claim are true.

Contributory Negligence
Conduct that falls below the standard to which the plaintiff must conform for the plaintiff's own safety or protection and that contributes to the causing of the plaintiff's own personal injury.

"The best defense in the world is no money!"

James E. Garrity, Esq.

Affirmative Defenses

When a plaintiff brings a case against the defendant, the plaintiff is on the offense. The defendant is on the defense. Several affirmative defenses to a plaintiff's negligence claim will be discussed in this chapter. An **affirmative defense** is a defense interposed in the defendant's answer that will have the legal effect of defeating a plaintiff's claim even if the facts supporting the plaintiff's claim are true. A defense will ordinarily be waived unless it is alleged in the defendant's responsive pleading, the answer. Rule 15 of the Federal Rules of Civil Procedure and state counterparts do allow for the amendment of pleadings. Amendments to pleadings, whether on behalf of plaintiff or defendant, are to be liberally allowed or "freely given."

Contributory Negligence

The first affirmative defense is contributory negligence. **Contributory negligence** is conduct that falls below the standard to which the plaintiff must conform for the plaintiff's own safety or protection and that contributes to the causing of the plaintiff's own personal injury. There are similarities between the tort of negligence alleged against the defendant and the defendant's defense of contributory negligence alleged against the plaintiff. The plaintiff has the burden of proof of negligence against the defendant. Likewise, the defendant has the burden of proof of contributory negligence against the plaintiff. When plaintiff brings a claim of negligence against the defendant, the defendant's conduct is measured by the reasonable person standard. Likewise, when the defendant asserts the defense of contributory negligence on the part of the plaintiff, the plaintiff's conduct is measured by the same reasonable person standard.

The emergency rule was discussed in Chapter 2 as it relates to the defendant's negligence. The same rule applies in the plaintiff's case when contributory negligence has been alleged by the defendant. If the plaintiff is confronted with an emergency, not of the plaintiff's own making, and plaintiff does not choose the safest or best course of action, the plaintiff is not negligent. For example, assume a two-vehicle collision at an intersection. Defendant is alleged to be negligent for operating defendant's vehicle with excessive speed. Defendant alleges contributory negligence on the part of plaintiff because plaintiff did not keep a proper lookout and did not attempt to brake sooner. However, assume that plaintiff produces evidence that as plaintiff was approaching the intersection, the brakes on plaintiff's new vehicle suddenly failed. That fact or circumstance would likely qualify as an emergency so that plaintiff would not be contributorily negligent.

Assume there is no emergency in the example. Assume plaintiff was conversing with a passenger and listening to the radio. Even though the defendant may have been extremely negligent by being drunk, speeding, and running a "yield" sign, a jury may find the plaintiff was contributorily negligent for not keeping a proper lookout even though it was but a moment's inattention.

EFFECT OF CONTRIBUTORY NEGLIGENCE

What is the effect of contributory negligence? Its effect is extremely harsh. Any slight bit of negligence on plaintiff's part *bars* plaintiff's recovery. This is true even if defendant is mostly negligent and plaintiff is just slightly negligent. Assume the facts of our automobile collision above in which defendant was drunk, speeding, and ran a yield sign compared to plaintiff's momentary inattention. Listen to the defense attorney, in final argument, dramatically demonstrating for the jury the effect of contributory negligence in this example:

> Ladies and gentlemen of the jury, you all took an oath to apply the law as given to you by Judge Kasdan. In this case his honor, Judge Kasdan, will instruct you on the effect of the plaintiff's contributory negligence. Judge Kasdan will tell you, I believe, that if you find the plaintiff negligent—in any degree—the plaintiff must recover nothing. The evidence has clearly shown two things. First, my client, Mike White, the defendant, acknowledges he was speeding, had been drinking, and ran the yield sign. Second, the plaintiff, Steve Weber, acknowledges that he was momentarily distracted by the radio and the conversation with his passenger, Ms. Ochoa.
>
> You must follow that law I expect to be given by Judge Kasdan, even if you do not agree with it or you think the law should be something different. The law is simply this: Any tiny bit of negligence on Mr. Weber's part means that he cannot recover anything. Let me demonstrate. In my left hand, I'm holding a glass of clear, pure water. In my right hand I'm holding an eyedropper filled with black ink. Watch carefully as I squeeze the dropper … There … What happened? You can see that only one little drop of black ink meeting up with the pure water taints the water completely and turns it black. The same thing is true here. Any tiny, little bit of negligence on plaintiff's part—his momentary inattention—taints Mr. Weber's case. He cannot recover. That is the law, and I know you will follow that law as given to you by his honor, Judge Kasdan.

Last Clear Chance

Last Clear Chance
This doctrine states that plaintiff's contributory negligence does not bar plaintiff's recovery if the defendant, immediately before the accident, had the "last clear chance" to avoid the accident but did not do so.

To somewhat soften the blow of contributory negligence, courts developed the doctrine of **last clear chance**. This doctrine states that plaintiff's contributory negligence does not bar plaintiff's recovery if the defendant, immediately before the accident, had the "last clear chance" to avoid the accident, but did not do so. For example, assume Jim, the plaintiff, is jaywalking across a public street with two lanes of traffic going north and two lanes of traffic going south. Jim intends to walk from the west side of the street where he is standing to the east side. This will require walking across four lanes of traffic. He starts jaywalking from the far west side and walks across the two southbound lanes of traffic. He then walks across the left lane of northbound traffic. As he enters the right lane of northbound traffic he is struck by a motor vehicle driven by Scott. Jim receives personal injuries. Jim brings suit against Scott in negligence for damages.

Jim, the jaywalker, claims that Scott, the driver, is negligent for speeding and for failure to keep a proper lookout. Scott argues contributory negligence on the part of Jim for jaywalking and not watching out for Jim's own safety. Jim counters with the last clear chance doctrine. Jim argues that even if he were negligent for jaywalking, Scott had ample time to avoid the collision. Jim will argue that he walked for a great distance in plain view of Scott. After all, Jim walked across both lanes of the southbound lane of traffic. Jim then walked across the left-hand lane of the northbound lane of traffic. Scott, traveling in the right-hand northbound lane, should have seen Jim walking across three entire lanes in front of him. Therefore, Scott had the last clear chance to avoid striking Jim by the time the accident occurred at the fourth lane of traffic.

Comparative Negligence

Comparative Negligence
The trier of fact determines the percentage of negligence of each party and the plaintiff's recovery will then be reduced or barred—depending upon the percentage assessed against the plaintiff.

It can be seen that contributory negligence is a harsh defense. Accordingly, by both statute and case law, the doctrine of comparative negligence was developed. **Comparative negligence** means that the trier of fact determines the percentage of negligence of each party, and the plaintiff's recovery will then be reduced or barred—depending upon the percentage assessed against the plaintiff. There are various approaches to comparative negligence taken by the various states.

PURE COMPARATIVE NEGLIGENCE APPROACH

Under the "pure" approach, the plaintiff recovers a percentage of the money recovery based solely on the percentages as determined by the trier of fact. Assume a jury awards the sum of $100,000. Also assume the jury finds that the defendant is 20% at fault, and the plaintiff is 80% at fault. With this approach, even though the plaintiff's negligence far exceeds that of the defendant, the plaintiff will recover 20% of plaintiff's damages or the sum of $20,000. If plaintiff were found 95% at fault, plaintiff would still recover $5,000. If plaintiff were found 55% at fault, plaintiff would recover $45,000.

Obviously, the only way that the plaintiff would recover nothing is if plaintiff is found to be 100% negligent. Review the landmark California decision of *Li v. Yellow Cab Company of California*, 532 P.2d 1226 (Cal. 1975) shown in Exhibit 6-1. The Supreme Court of California, after over a century of operating under the doctrine of contributory negligence, judicially adopted the doctrine of pure comparative negligence. Note the dissent by Justice Clark, who states: "By abolishing this century old doctrine today, the majority seriously erodes our constitutional function. *We are again guilty of judicial chauvinism.*" (Emphasis added.) His complaint is that these justices are "making law," not "interpreting the law," the same concept as discussed in Chapter 1.

EXHIBIT 6-1 Relevant Case Law

Nga Li, Plaintiff and Appellant, v. Yellow Cab Company of California et al., Defendants and Respondents.

Supreme Court of California.

SUMMARY

In an automobile accident case, the court, sitting without a jury, found that when defendant entered an intersection, the traffic light was yellow and he was travelling at an unsafe speed. It was also found that plaintiff's left turn across adjacent lanes just before her vehicle was struck by defendant's automobile was made when a vehicle was approaching from the opposite direction so close as to constitute an immediate hazard. On the basis of conclusions that plaintiff had been negligent, that her negligence had been a proximate cause of the collision, and that she was barred from recovery by reason of her contributory negligence, the court entered judgment for defendants.

The Supreme Court reversed in a decision in which it declared no longer applicable in California courts the doctrine of contributory negligence, and held it must give way to a system of comparative negligence, which assesses liability in direct proportion to fault. Preliminarily, in rejecting the contention that the 1872 enactment of Civ. Code, § 1714, expressing the doctrine of contributory negligence, codified the common law and rendered the doctrine invulnerable to attack in the courts except on constitutional grounds, the court held that the Legislature had not intended to, and did not, preclude present judicial action in furtherance of the statute's purposes. Although recognizing the existence of practical difficulties in application of the comparative negligence system, the court held they were not of sufficient substantiality to dissuade against the charting of a new course.

In summary, the court held that the "all-or-nothing" rule of contributory negligence as it presently exists in this state is superseded by a system of "pure" comparative negligence, the fundamental purpose of which shall be to assign responsibility and liability for damage in direct proportion to the amount of negligence of each of the parties. In all actions for negligence resulting in injury to person or property, the contributory negligence of the person injured in person or property shall not bar recovery, but the damages awarded shall be diminished in proportion to the amount of negligence attributable to the person recovering. The doctrine of last clear chance is abolished, and the defense of assumption of risk is also abolished to the extent that it is merely a variant of the former doctrine of contributory negligence. Both last clear chance and assumption of risk are to be subsumed under the general process of assessing liability in proportion to negligence. Pending future judicial or legislative developments, trial courts are to use broad discretion in seeking to assure that the principle stated is applied in the interest of justice and in furtherance of the purposes and objectives set forth in the opinion....

(Continued)

EXHIBIT 6-1 *(Continued)*

> Clark, J.
> I dissent.
>
> For over a century this court has consistently and unanimously held that Civil Code section 1714 codifies the defense of contributory negligence. Suddenly—after 103 years—the court declares section 1714 shall provide for comparative negligence instead. In my view, this action constitutes a gross departure from established judicial rules and role....
>
> By abolishing this century old doctrine today, the majority seriously erodes our constitutional function. We are again guilty of judicial chauvinism.

Source: Li v. Yellow Cab Company of California, 532 P.2d 1226 (Cal. 1975).

50–50 APPROACH TO COMPARATIVE FAULT

With a 50–50 approach to comparative fault, the plaintiff will recover his or her portion of damages reduced by plaintiff's negligence up to 50%. If plaintiff is found to be *50% or more* at fault, plaintiff's recovery is *barred*. Using our above example, if plaintiff were found to be 20% at fault and defendant 80%, plaintiff would recover $80,000 of the $100,000 award. The award is reduced by the 20% of negligence assessed against plaintiff. If plaintiff were found to be 45% at fault and defendant 55% at fault, plaintiff would recover $55,000. However, if plaintiff were found to be 50% or more at fault, plaintiff would receive nothing. Using this approach, if plaintiff's negligence equals the defendant's negligence, plaintiff cannot recover anything. There is no bar to a plaintiff's recovery unless the plaintiff's fault was *as great as* the fault of the defendant. Review the North Dakota comparative fault statute in Exhibit 6-2.

EXHIBIT 6-2 North Dakota Comparative Fault Statute

> North Dakota
>
> N.D.C.C. § 32-03.2-02
>
> Contributory fault does not bar recovery in an action by any person to recover damages for death or injury to person or property unless the fault was *as great as* the combined fault of all other persons who contribute to the injury, but any damages allowed must be diminished in proportion to the amount of contributing fault attributable to the person recovering. The court may, and when requested by any party, shall direct the jury to find separate special verdicts determining the amount of damages and the percentage of fault attributable to each person, whether or not a party, who contributed to the injury. The court shall then reduce the amount of such damages in proportion to the amount of fault attributable to the person recovering. When two or more parties are found to have contributed to the injury, the liability of each party is several only, and is not joint, and each party is liable only for the amount of damages attributable to the percentage of fault of that party, except that any persons who act in concert in committing a tortious act or aid or encourage the act, or ratifies or adopts the act for their benefit, are jointly liable for all damages attributable to their combined percentage of fault. Under this section, fault includes negligence, malpractice, absolute liability, dram shop liability, failure to warn, reckless or willful conduct, assumption of risk, misuse of product, failure to avoid injury, and product liability, including product liability involving negligence or strict liability or breach of warranty for product defect. (Emphasis added.)

Source: North Dakota Century Code § 32-03.2-02.

Workplace Skills Tip

Good communication is essential in a law firm. As mentioned in Chapter 1, the legal profession lives and dies by the clock. Besides a file diary/calendaring system many firms will meet once a week to make sure that all deadlines will be met, whether serving a complaint on the plaintiff's side, serving an answer on the defendant's side, or calendaring a date when a brief is due. The paralegal needs to assist the attorney in watching deadlines.

51–49 APPROACH TO COMPARATIVE FAULT

Under this approach, the plaintiff's recovery is barred if the plaintiff is found to be *51% or more* at fault. Here, the plaintiff could recover if plaintiff were 50% at fault but not if the plaintiff's fault were 51%. The plaintiff's fault must *exceed* the defendant's fault in order to bar a recovery. Using our same example as above, if plaintiff were found to be 40% at fault and defendant 60%, plaintiff would recover $60,000 of the $100,000 damages awarded. If plaintiff were 50% at fault and defendant 50% at fault, the plaintiff would still recover $50,000 even though plaintiff's fault *equals* the defendant's fault. If, however, plaintiff were found to be 60% at fault, plaintiff's recovery is barred because it is more than 51%. The plaintiff will recover his or her portion of damages reduced by plaintiff's negligence up to as much as 50%. However, once plaintiff is found 51% or more at fault, the plaintiff's recovery is barred. Plaintiff cannot recover if plaintiff's negligence "exceeds" the defendant's negligence, but plaintiff can recover even if it is "equal" to the defendant's negligence. There is no bar to a plaintiff's recovery if the plaintiff's fault was "not greater than" the fault of the defendant. Review the Minnesota comparative fault statute in Exhibit 6-3.

EXHIBIT 6-3 Minnesota Comparative Fault Satute

Minnesota

M.S.A. § 604.01

Subdivision 1. Scope of application. Contributory fault does not bar recovery in an action by any person or the person's legal representative to recover damages for fault resulting in death, in injury to person or property, or in economic loss, if the contributory fault was not *greater than* the fault of the person against whom recovery is sought, but any damages allowed must be diminished in proportion to the amount of fault attributable to the person recovering. The court may, and when requested by any party shall, direct the jury to find separate special verdicts determining the amount of damages and the percentage of fault attributable to each party and the court shall then reduce the amount of damages in proportion to the amount of fault attributable to the person recovering. (Emphasis added.)

Subd. 1a Fault. "Fault" includes acts or omissions that are in any measure negligent or reckless toward the person or property of the actor or others, or that subject a person to strict tort liability. The term also includes breach of warranty, unreasonable assumption of risk not constituting an express consent or primary assumption of risk, misuse of a product and unreasonable failure to avoid an injury or to mitigate damages, and the defense of complicity under section 340A.801. Legal requirements of casual relation apply both to fault as the basis for liability and to contributory fault. The doctrine of last clear chance is abolished.

Source: Minnesota Statutes Annotated § 604.01.

COMPARATIVE FAULT WITH MULTIPLE DEFENDANTS

Up to this point, the discussion of comparative fault has assumed a case with one plaintiff and one defendant. However, how is the plaintiff's fault compared when there is more than one defendant? Is the plaintiff's fault compared against the total combined fault of all defendants or is it compared with each defendant? It depends upon a particular state's comparative fault scheme. Each jurisdiction is different in that regard. For example, utilizing the same comparative fault laws of the states of California, Minnesota, and North Dakota, examine the differing results based on a given fact situation.

Assume the plaintiff's jury award for personal injury damages was $100,000. Assume that the jury apportioned fault as follows:

Plaintiff: 20%		
	Defendant 1: 20%	
	Defendant 2: 50%	
	Defendant 3: 10%	
		100%

California

Under the California pure comparative fault statute, since the plaintiff was 20% at fault, the damages are reduced by 20% or to $80,000. Each defendant simply pays his percentage of fault in this pure comparative fault jurisdiction. Therefore, defendant 1 would pay $20,000; defendant 2 would pay $50,000; and defendant 3 would pay $10,000. The applicable California statute, which follows the *Li* decision, states that the liability of each defendant for non-economic damages is "several only."

North Dakota

Using our same example and applying the outcome based on the North Dakota comparative fault statute, that statute does not bar a plaintiff's recovery unless the plaintiff's fault was "as great as the *combined fault of all other persons who contribute to the injury.*" (Emphasis added). What is the combined fault of defendants 1, 2, and 3? It is 80%. Plaintiff's fault of 20% is clearly not as great as that *combined fault.* Note that the North Dakota statute, as the California statute did, specifically addresses the several liability issue. With certain exceptions listed in the statute, the liability of each defendant is *several*: "[T]he liability of each party is several only...."

In this case, the plaintiff's recovery of $100,000 would be reduced by the plaintiff's percentage of fault. That percentage is 20% so it is reduced by $20,000—down to $80,000. Assume that none of the exceptions to several liability apply, such as "acting in concert," defendant 1 will pay 20% of $100,000 or $20,000; defendant 2 will pay 50% of $100,000 or $50,000; and defendant 3 will pay 10% of $100,000 or $10,000. Also, note the last section of the statute indicating all of the various causes of action that are included under the concept of "fault."

Minnesota

Under the Minnesota statute, damages are to be diminished in proportion to the amount of fault on the plaintiff, in this case, 20%. Therefore, potential recoverable damages are $80,000 ($100,000 reduced by $20,000). As to each defendant's liability, however, this comparative fault statute states that recovery is not barred if the contributory fault of the plaintiff "was *not greater than* the fault *of the person against whom recovery is sought....*" Plaintiff's 20% fault is not "greater than" defendant 1's 20% fault, so plaintiff may recover against defendant 1. Plaintiff's 20% fault is certainly not greater than defendant 2's 70% fault. However, when the plaintiff's 20% fault is compared with defendant 3's 10% fault, plaintiff's fault is clearly "greater than" defendant 3's fault. Thus, any recovery of money damages against defendant 3 is barred. It appears that defendant 1 would pay $20,000 (20% of $100,000) and defendant 2 would pay $50,000 (50% of $100,000).

However, those two amounts to be paid by defendant 1 and defendant 2 do not add up to $80,000, do they? That is why the word "appear" was used in concluding what these two defendants would pay. Plaintiff's recovery is supposed to be $80,000 ($100,000 reduced by the plaintiff's 20% or $20,000 amount). If we add up the $20,000 and the $50,000, that is $70,000 not $80,000. We are missing the $10,000 that defendant 3 would have paid. Review the discussion in Chapter 3 regarding "several" liability and "joint and several" liability. If liability is several/separate, each defendant will pay only his percentage of the $100,000 award. Defendant 1 will pay his 20% or $20,000, and defendant 2 will pay his 50% or $50,000 as it would outwardly appear. Plaintiff would recover $70,000. However, if liability is joint and several, the plaintiff may have a recovery against either or both of defendants 1 and 2 for the full $80,000. Note, also, that the Minnesota statute defines all of the various causes of action that are included in the concept of "fault" and that the concept of last clear chance is specifically abolished.

This discussion illustrates the importance of knowing the statutory law and the case law in the paralegal's own jurisdiction. It also illustrates how various principles of law are interrelated. The discussion here is focused primarily on comparative fault. However, the principles of several liability and joint and several liability, previously studied, must necessarily enter into the discussion.

Workplace Skills Tip

As a personal injury paralegal, you will attend meetings with the other side in attendance, depositions, hearings, trials, mediations, and arbitrations. Put on your "poker face." Do not display emotion. Do not smile, frown, grimace, nod your head, shake your head, put your face in your hands, or give the lawyer an elbow. This is important. There is no reason to give something away to the other side by your body language. Also, in jury trials, jurors will be watching carefully the reactions of both sides to a witness' testimony and other developments at trial.

Assumption of the Risk

Assumption of the risk is another defense to negligence. **Assumption of the risk** is the plaintiff's giving consent, expressly or impliedly, to confronting the harm or danger from a risk caused by the defendant. If the fact finder finds that the plaintiff assumed the risk, then that is a complete bar to the plaintiff's recovery. There are, however, two basic requirements of this defense. First, the plaintiff must have *recognized and understood* the risk. Second, the plaintiff must have *voluntarily* chosen to confront it.

THE FIREFIGHTER'S RULE

A classic example of the application of the assumption of the risk defense involves actions of a first responder—law enforcement personnel, ambulance personnel, and firefighters. Due to the nature of their occupations, they must necessarily be involved in clearly recognized risks, dangers, and emergencies. They would not be able to sue the person who created the risk, danger, or emergency. This is sometimes referred to as the **firefighter's rule**.

ASSUMPTION OF THE RISK BY CONTRACT/EXCULPATORY PROVISIONS

Another classic example of assumption of the risk arises in situations of **exculpatory provisions**. An exculpatory provision is a provision placed in writing by the defendant to try to limit or exclude liability in advance. Exculpatory language arises out of some form of a contract. It is the exculpatory language in the contract that the defendant asks the court to enforce. When one parks their motor vehicle in a parking lot or ramp, it is customary to take a ticket. The ticket may contain language similar to the following: "Urban Parking is not liable for any damage to person or property occurring on these premises." The same type of language may be printed on a ticket upon entering such facilities as a go-cart track, a public swimming pool, or an amusement park.

As a general rule, these exculpatory provisions are not favored by the courts. Whether or not these exculpatory provisions are enforceable may depend on several factors. First, how likely is it that the person was even aware of the exculpatory language? Such language is less likely to be enforced if it is on the back of a ticket or a document, and it is in very small print.

Second, the language will be very strictly construed against the drafter of the language. What is the scope of the exculpatory language? For example, a hot air balloon company taking customers up in its hot air balloons may have language in its document stating: "Lofty Cloud Balloon Company expressly denies any liability for injuries or deaths sustained in its hot air balloon rides." Assume a customer trips and is injured on a defect in the company's parking lot where customers meet before being driven to the open field. Or, assume that on the way out of town to the field where the balloons will be launched, the company driver's negligence causes a motor vehicle accident injuring a customer passenger. A court will construe the exculpatory language narrowly and strictly. It is likely the court would reason that injuries from these two accidents did not occur during a balloon ride. They occurred before the ride even began. Therefore, the language does not bar the plaintiff's recovery.

Third, are the parties in an equal bargaining position? If a plumbing company orders plumbing parts from a plumbing manufacturer, and the manufacturer limits its liability, such a provision may well be upheld. Both companies are involved in the business world in which other suppliers and manufacturers are available. A person selling a motorcycle on his own from his home posts a note on the machine: "Not responsible for injuries/deaths during test drive." In these examples, there is more of an equal bargaining position. There is no real public policy against striking down the provision in these examples involving two private individuals or entities with seemingly equal bargaining power.

However, there are many instances in which there is an unequal bargaining position. A **contract of adhesion** is a contract in which one party, in superior bargaining position, sets the terms of the agreement and the other party has no negotiating or bargaining power. Consider the purchase of an airline ticket. Try calling the airline company and telling them: "I see your flight from Los Angeles to Denver is $129.00. I'll give you $100 for the flight." Students usually laugh when that example is used. It is laughable because everyone knows the purchaser of an airline ticket has zero bargaining power when it comes to negotiating the price of airfare. Try making a lower offer to the price plan offered by the company that provides your cell phone service. Other examples of contracts of adhesion are those contracts with utility companies, and cable TV companies, The same is true of tickets purchased to attend a movie, an amusement park, such as Disney World, a ski lift, or a tour of the Empire State Building. Exculpatory language in these unequal bargaining position cases has the potential of being held invalid as against public policy depending on the jurisdiction.

> **Contract of Adhesion**
> A contract in which one party, in superior bargaining position, sets the terms of the agreement and the other party has no negotiating power.

ASSUMPTION OF THE RISK BY THE PLAINTIFF'S CONDUCT

The recent discussion involved assumption of risk in a contract setting. Assumption of the risk can also arise when the plaintiff voluntarily assumes the risk by the plaintiff's own conduct. In the discussion of negligence in Chapter 2, the standard of negligence is based upon the reasonable person standard, an objective standard. Likewise, the contributory negligence of the plaintiff is judged by the reasonable person standard. However, assumption of the risk on the part of the plaintiff is treated somewhat differently by the courts. The plaintiff's knowledge of the particular danger or risk and plaintiff's voluntary exposure to the danger or risk are judged on a *subjective* basis. The test is what the plaintiff actually knew. It is not what the plaintiff should have known.

If one attends a baseball game and is struck by a foul ball, a person would know that being hit by a foul ball is an inherent risk of the game. Likewise, there is the same risk of being hit by a puck at a hockey game. If one is standing too close on the sidelines of a football game, there is the risk of being hit by a player running off the field. Courts would likely hold that when one seeks admission to sporting events, one must have voluntarily chosen to encounter such risks. However, one attending the same baseball game who assumes the risk of being hit by a foul ball does not assume the risk that a part of the upper deck lighting would fall on his or her head. Also, since the subjective test is being applied, a person's age and experience would be taken into account. A very young child, for example, cannot voluntarily assume the risk of being hit by the same foul ball at a baseball game.

The players themselves assume the risk of injury when actually participating in the sport. Courts may consider whether or not the conduct of the sports participant is within the range of ordinary behavior of a participant. See, for example, *Pfenning v. Lineman*, 947 N.E.2d 392 (Ind. 2011) in Exhibit 6-4. However, a player does not assume the risk of an intentional violation of the rules of the game that results in a player's injury. See, for example, *Nabozny v. Barnhill*, 334 N.E.2d 258 (Ill. 1975) in Exhibit 6-5. Compare the decision of *Pfenning*, which involved the plaintiff being struck in the head by a golf ball, and the decision of *Nabozny*, which resulted in a soccer goal tender being kicked in the head.

EXHIBIT 6-4 Relevant Case Law

Cassie E. Pfenning, Appellant (Plaintiff below), v. Joseph E. Lineman, Whitey's 31 Club, Inc., Marion Elks Country Club Lodge # 195, and The Estate of Jerry A. Jones, Appellees.

Supreme Court of Indiana.

Dickson, Justice.

The relevant facts presented in the designated evidence are mostly undisputed. On August 19, 2006, a golf outing, the annual Whitey's 31 Club Scramble, was held at the Elks and attended by customers and friends of Whitey's and its proprietor. Persons wishing to participate signed up on a poster board that had been hung on a wall at Whitey's. Each golfer paid a charge of $45.00 per person to the Elks, which provided the golf carts and the beverages that were made available to the golfers. Whitey's provided the sign-up list to the Elks, which then made cart signs, team sheets, score cards, and starting hole assignments. The plaintiff, Cassie Pfenning, then sixteen years old, attended the outing at the invitation of her grandfather and with the permission of her mother. The grandfather previously had signed up at Whitey's as a volunteer to drive a beverage cart at the event. He brought the plaintiff with him for company. Shortly after the plaintiff and her grandfather arrived at the event, he retrieved a gasoline motor powered beverage cart for their use. It had a large cooler on the back containing water, soda pop, and beer. This beverage cart had no windshield, and the evidence is in conflict regarding whether it was equipped with a roof. Shortly after providing the plaintiff with the beverage cart, the grandfather joined a shorthanded group of golfers and left the plaintiff at the beverage cart with Lottie Kendall, sister of the grandfather and a great aunt of the plaintiff. But within about ten minutes, the great aunt also joined another group of golfers, and an employee of Whitey's, Christie Edwards, joined the plaintiff and was present with her on the beverage cart during the event. The plaintiff drove the cart, and Christie served the beverages to groups of golfers on the golf course for about three and a half hours. After making several trips around the 18–hole golf course, the plaintiff was suddenly struck in the mouth by a golf ball while driving the beverage cart on the cart path approaching the eighteenth hole's tee pad from its green. The ball was a low drive from the sixteenth tee approximately eighty yards away. The golfer's drive traveled straight for approximately sixty to seventy yards and then severely hooked to the left. He noticed the roof of another cart in the direction of the shot and shouted "fore." But neither the plaintiff nor her beverage-serving companion heard anyone shout "fore." After hearing a faint yelp, the golfer ran in the direction of the errant ball and discovered the plaintiff with her injuries. She suffered injuries to her mouth, jaw, and teeth....

We hold that, in negligence claims against a participant in a sports activity, if the conduct of such participant is within the range of ordinary behavior of participants in the sport, the conduct is reasonable as a matter of law and does not constitute a breach of duty....

In any sporting activity, however, a participant's particular conduct may exceed the gambit of such reasonableness as a matter of law if the "participant either intentionally caused injury or engaged in

(Continued)

EXHIBIT 6-4 *(Continued)*

[reckless] conduct."… Such intentional or reckless infliction of injury may be found to be a breach of duty.

As to the golfer's hitting an errant drive which resulted in the plaintiff's injury, such conduct is clearly within the range of ordinary behavior of golfers and thus is reasonable as a matter of law and does not establish the element of breach required for a negligence action.…

Summary judgment was properly granted in favor of the golfer.

Source: Pfenning v. Lineman, 947 N.E.2d 392 (Ind. 2011).

EXHIBIT 6-5 Relevant Case Law

Julian Claudio Nabozny, a minor by Edward J. Nabozny, his father, Plaintiff-Appellant, v. David Barnhill, Defendant-Appellee.

Appellate Court of Illinois, First District, Fourth Division.

Adesko, Justice.

Plaintiff, Julian Claudio Nabozny, a minor, by Edward J. Nabozny, his father, commenced this action to recover damages for personal injuries allegedly caused by the negligence of defendant, David Barnhill. Trial was before a jury. At the close of plaintiff's case on motion of defendant, the trial court directed a verdict in favor of the defendant. Plaintiff appeals from the order granting the motion.

Plaintiff contends on appeal that the trial judge erred in granting defendant's motion for a directed verdict and that plaintiff's actions as a participant do not prohibit the establishment of a prima facie case of negligence. Defendant argues in support of the trial court's ruling that defendant was free from negligence as a matter of law (lacking a duty to plaintiff) and that defendant was contributorily negligent as a matter of law.…

A soccer match began between two amateur teams at Duke Child's Field in Winnetka, Illinois. Plaintiff was playing the position of goalkeeper for the Hansa team. Defendant was playing the position of forward for the Winnetka team. Members of both teams were of high-school age. Approximately twenty minutes after play had begun, a Winnetka player kicked the ball over the midfield line. Two players, Jim Gallos (for Hansa) and the defendant (for Winnetka) chased the free ball. Gallos reached the ball first. Since he was closely pursued by the defendant, Gallos passed the ball to the plaintiff, the Hansa goalkeeper. Gallos then turned away and prepared to receive a pass from the plaintiff. The plaintiff, in the meantime, went down on his left knee, received the pass, and pulled the ball to his chest. The defendant did not turn away when Gallos did, but continued to run in the direction of the plaintiff and kicked the left side of plaintiff's head causing plaintiff severe injuries.

All of the occurrence witnesses agreed that the defendant had time to avoid contact with plaintiff and that the plaintiff remained at all times within the 'penalty area,' a rectangular area between the eighteenth yard line and the goal. Four witnesses testified that they saw plaintiff in a crouched position on his left knee inside the penalty zone. Plaintiff testified that he actually had possession of the ball when he was struck by defendant. One witness, Marie Shekem, stated that plaintiff had the ball when he was kicked. All other occurrence witnesses stated that they thought plaintiff was in possession of the ball.

Plaintiff called three expert witnesses. Julius Roth, coach of the Hansa team, testified that the game in question was being played under 'F.I.F.A.' rules. The three experts agreed that those rules prohibited all players from making contact with the goalkeeper when he is in possession of the ball in the penalty area. Possession is defined in the Chicago area as referring to the goalkeeper having his hands on the ball. Under 'F.I.F.A.' rules, any contact with a goalkeeper in possession in the penalty area is an

(Continued)

EXHIBIT 6-5 *(Continued)*

infraction of the rules, even if such contact is unintentional. The goalkeeper is the only member of a team who is allowed to touch a ball in play so long as he remains in the penalty area. The only legal contact permitted in soccer is shoulder to shoulder contact between players going for a ball within playing distance. The three experts agreed that the contact in question in this case should not have occurred. Additionally, goalkeeper head injuries are extremely rare in soccer. As a result of being struck, plaintiff suffered permanent damage to his skull and brain....

This court believes that the law should not place unreasonable burdens on the free and vigorous participation in sports by our youth. However, we also believe that organized, athletic competition does not exist in a vacuum. Rather, some of the restraints of civilization must accompany every athlete onto the playing field. One of the educational benefits of organized athletic competition to our youth is the development of discipline and self control.

Individual sports are advanced and competition enhanced by a comprehensive set of rules. Some rules secure the better playing of the game as a test of skill. Other rules are primarily designed to protect participants from serious injury. (Restatement (Second) of Torts, Sec. 50, comment B.)

For these reasons, this court believes that when athletes are engaged in an athletic competition; all teams involved are trained and coached by knowledgeable personnel; a recognized set of rules governs the conduct of the competition; and a safety rule is contained therein which is primarily designed to protect players from serious injury, a player is then charged with a legal duty to every other player on the field to refrain from conduct proscribed by a safety rule. A reckless disregard for the safety of other players cannot be excused. To engage in such conduct is to create an intolerable and unreasonable risk of serious injury to other participants. We have carefully drawn the rule announced herein in order to control a new field of personal injury litigation. Under the facts presented in the case at bar, we find such a duty clearly arose. Plaintiff was entitled to legal protection at the hands of the defendant. The defendant contends he is immune from tort action for any injury to another player that happens during the course of a game, to which theory we do not subscribe.

It is our opinion that a player is liable for injury in a tort action if his conduct is such that it is either deliberate, wilful or with a reckless disregard for the safety of the other player so as to cause injury to that player, the same being a question of fact to be decided by a jury.

Defendant also asserts that plaintiff was contributorily negligent as a matter of law, and, therefore, the trial court's direction of a verdict in defendant's favor was correct. We do not agree. The evidence presented tended to show that plaintiff was in the exercise of ordinary care for his own safety. While playing his position, he remained in the penalty area and took possession of the ball in a proper manner. Plaintiff had no reason to know of the danger created by defendant.

Source: Nabozny v. Barnhill, 334 N.E.2d 258 (Ill. 1975).

Statutes of Limitation/Repose

A statute of limitation was first discussed in Chapter 1. The point was made there that deadlines are crucial in the legal profession. A statute of limitation in a civil case is a statute that provides the maximum period of time in which a civil lawsuit must be commenced or it is forever barred. The purpose of a statute of limitation is to prevent an injured party from delaying the commencement of an action. Delay brings about the undesired result of evidence becoming lost, fading memories with crucial facts now forgotten, or witnesses having died. Statutes of limitation rest on the basic premise that if one person has a claim against another person, he or she should not be able to assert such a claim after an unreasonable length of time during which the defendant has been lulled into the security that no such claim even exists.

The commencement time may vary depending upon whether the case is in state court or federal court. For example, in federal court an action is commenced by filing the complaint with the court. Depending upon the particular state jurisdiction, an action may be considered commenced only when the defendant has been personally served with the appropriate papers. Another state's statute may provide that the action is commenced on the date when the sheriff receives the papers for service even though they are not actually served upon the defendant until a later date, which might be after the statute of limitation would technically run.

Failure to timely commence the lawsuit will result in the plaintiff's claim being barred. Concepts of equity and fairness or excuses for the delay will afford no relief by the courts. The case will be over. There will be no remedy to cure it. Judges and attorneys will sometimes refer to a claim as being "time barred." If the paralegal is researching a particular statute in a particular jurisdiction, it can sometimes be located under "limitation of actions." Depending upon the type of claim, statutes of limitation for a personal injury will typically be as short as one year and as long as six years. The consequences of missing a statute of limitation were first mentioned in Chapter 1. Those consequences may result in not only a legal action against the attorney for legal malpractice, but also charges of ethics violations by the particular bar licensing authority. For an example of both of those unpleasant ramifications being thrust upon the attorney who missed a statute of limitation in a personal injury case, read the decision of *Kentucky Bar Association v. Griffith*, 186 S.W.3d 739 (Ky. 2006) in Exhibit 6-6.

EXHIBIT 6-6 Relevant Case Law

Kentucky Bar Association, Movant, v. Caroline Laurie Griffith, Respondent.

Supreme Court of Kentucky.

Background: Attorney disciplinary proceeding was instituted.
Holdings: The Supreme Court held that:

(1) attorney's conduct in failing to pursue personal injury claim and respond to disciplinary investigation violated professional rules mandating competent and prompt representation and cooperation with disciplinary authority, and

(2) attorney's conduct warranted one-year suspension.
 Suspension ordered.

OPINION AND ORDER

The Kentucky Bar Association has recommended that this Court issue an order against the Respondent, Caroline Laurie Griffith, whose Bar Roster Address is 3125 Randolph Avenue, # 2, Louisville, KY, 40206 and whose KBA Member Number is 86217, suspending her from the practice of law for one-year and that this suspension be served consecutively with Respondent's current five-year suspension, which was imposed in *Kentucky Bar Association v. Griffith*, 136 S.W.3d 429 (Ky.2004). As with the prior disciplinary case, Respondent has once again failed to respond to any of the charges alleged against her. As such, we see no reason to deviate from the disciplinary measures recommended by the majority of the KBA's Board of Governors and order Respondent to be suspended from the practice of law for one year, with said suspension to be served consecutive to the five year suspension set forth in our earlier Opinion and Order.

(Continued)

EXHIBIT 6-6 *(Continued)*

The charges giving rise to this recommendation arose from Respondent's representation of James R. Brown. Brown was injured in November 1999 and incurred medical expenses and lost wages as a result of his injury. He hired Respondent shortly thereafter to represent him in a suit against United Parcel Service (hereafter UPS), the alleged tortfeasor. Although Respondent notified Liberty Mutual, the insurance carrier for UPS, of her representation of Brown, she did nothing further to pursue his claim.

In March 2002, Brown retained another attorney, Robert A. Donald, III, to pursue his claim against UPS. Although Donald advised Brown that the statute of limitations had likely passed on his claim against UPS, Liberty Mutual was nevertheless informed of the change of counsel. Liberty Mutual responded that Brown's claim was denied based upon the expiration of the statute of limitations. Thereafter, Donald advised Respondent that Brown would be seeking a legal malpractice claim against her. Eventually, Brown settled his claim against Respondent for $3,000 and Respondent provided six post-dated checks to satisfy the agreed settlement. Although the first two of these six checks were returned for insufficient funds, Respondent ultimately complied with the terms of the settlement.

On March 4, 2003, Donald filed a bar complaint with the KBA against Respondent. The complaint was mailed by certified mail to Respondent's bar roster address on March 7, 2003, but was returned "Unclaimed." On April 17, 2003, the complaint was served on Respondent by the Jefferson County Sheriff's office and a reminder letter was also served on Respondent by the Sheriff on May 15, 2003. Respondent did not respond to either communication from the KBA.

On July 8, 2004, the KBA Inquiry Commission issued a four-count Charge against Respondent alleging violations of the following rules: (1) SCR 3.130–1.1 ("A lawyer shall provide competent representation to a client."); (2) SCR 3.130–1.3 ("A lawyer shall act with reasonable diligence and promptness in representing a client."); (3) SCR 3.130–1.4(a) (requiring a lawyer to "keep a client reasonably informed about the status of a matter and promptly comply with reasonable requests for information."); and (4) SCR 3.130–8.1(b) (stating, in pertinent part, that "[a] lawyer … in connection with a disciplinary matter, shall not … knowingly fail to respond to a lawful demand for information from an admissions or disciplinary authority…."). The Charge was mailed by certified mail to Respondent's bar roster address and to an alternate address. The copy sent to Respondent's roster address was returned, again marked "Unclaimed." The copy that had been mailed to Respondent's alternate address was signed for, and presumably received, by an individual other than Respondent. Subsequently, the Charge was served on Respondent by the Jefferson County Sheriff's office on August 17, 2004. Having failed to receive an Answer from Respondent, the KBA sent a reminder letter on September 17, 2004, but did not receive any response. In fact, Respondent has failed to answer any correspondence from the KBA concerning this case.

After hearing a report by a board member, discussing the facts contained in the record, and considering Respondent's failure to answer the allegations against her, the Board of Governors unanimously found Respondent guilty of each of the four counts listed in the Charge. Sixteen members of the Board voted to recommend that Respondent be suspended for one year, to be served consecutively with Respondent's previous five-year suspension. Two members of the Board voted to recommend that Respondent be suspended for two years, to be served consecutively with Respondent's previous five-year suspension.

Respondent has not filed notice for this Court to review the Board's decision, and we do not elect to do so pursuant to SCR 3.370(9). As such, the decision of the Board of Governors is hereby adopted as to all matters, pursuant to SCR 3.370(10).

ACCORDINGLY, IT IS HEREBY ORDERED:

(1) That Respondent is suspended from the practice of law in Kentucky for a period of one year pursuant to SCR 3.380. This suspension is to be served consecutive to Respondent's current five-year suspension and shall commence on the expiration of that period. Said suspension shall continue until Respondent is reinstated to the practice of law by Order of this Court pursuant to SCR 3.510.

(Continued)

EXHIBIT 6-6 *(Continued)*

> (2) That, in accordance with SCR 3.450, Respondent is directed to pay the costs of this action in the amount of $162.70, for which execution may issue from this Court upon finality of this Opinion and Order.
>
> All concur.
> ENTERED: March 23, 2006.
> /s/Joseph E. Lambert
> CHIEF JUSTICE

Source: Kentucky Bar Association v. Griffith, 186 S.W.3d 739 (Ky 2006)

ACCRUAL VS. DISCOVERY RULE

A statute of limitation begins to run when the plaintiff's claim **accrues**. A claim accrues when a plaintiff had reason to know of harm or injury caused by defendant's wrongful act or omission. For example, if a plaintiff is in a motor vehicle collision on a certain date and receives an injury, the claim accrues and the statute begins to run on that date. However, assume that a physician performed a negligent act or omission on a certain date, but the effects or symptoms of that negligent conduct did not manifest themselves until after the statute had run. Assume that a jurisdiction had a two-year statute of limitation for medical malpractice actions. Plaintiff had surgery on February 10, 2005. The statute would run on February 10, 2007. However, assume the physician did some negligent act during surgery that caused symptoms to be produced that did not start until sometime in April 2007. Many states have adopted a **discovery rule**. In other words, the statute of limitation does not begin to run until the plaintiff *discovers* the injury and the defendant's likely connection to the injury or when the plaintiff should have reasonably known of the injury and defendant's likely connection to it.

Accrues
A claim accrues when a plaintiff had reason to know of harm or injury caused by defendant's wrongful act or omission or should have reasonably known.

Discovery Rule
Statute of limitation does not begin to run until the plaintiff discovers the injury and the defendant's likely connection to the injury.

TOLLING OF STATUTE OF LIMITATION

If it appears that a statute of limitation has been missed, there may be a saving grace in some instances. It is typical to see provisions in statutes of limitation that provide the statute may be "tolled." A statute is **tolled** if the time period is suspended until a certain circumstance or condition occurs or while a certain circumstance or condition is occurring.

For example, assume the applicable negligence statute was four years in a particular jurisdiction. A minor child, age 10, was injured by the negligence of a defendant on an attractive nuisance theory. Assume the state's statute of limitation provides that an action for negligence does not begin to accrue until a child reaches the age of 18. In this case the statute is tolled from running for eight more years from

Tolled (Statute of Limitation)
The time period for a statute of limitation is suspended until a certain circumstance or condition occurs or while a certain circumstance or condition is occurring.

Workplace Skills Tip

In a plaintiff's personal injury firm, it will occasionally happen that a potential client will come in to see an attorney shortly before a statute of limitation or repose is about to run. It could be months, weeks, or even days before the statute is about to run. A competent plaintiff's personal injury firm will have the ability to screen the bad cases from the good—those with merit and those without merit. A decision will need to be made quickly if the case is to be accepted or not. If the case is not accepted, in some jurisdictions, further action may be required. It may be a requirement to provide the person with written documentation that the case is not being taken, the reason why it is not being taken, informing the person of the applicable statute of limitation and urging prompt action. See the letter to the client declining representation from Attorney Stefans in Appendix 1, Exhibit 1–3.

the date of the accident—until the child reaches age 18. At that point, the statute will start running, and there will be four more years in which to timely commence the personal injury action. There are other examples. A statute may be tolled while a person is going through bankruptcy. A statute may be tolled if the defendant resides outside the state or is away from the state in which the defendant could be sued.

Tolling Agreement
An agreement between the parties that alter the statute of limitation for an agreed upon period of time so that it does not continue to run for that period of time.

The paralegal may become involved in assisting with a **tolling agreement**. A tolling agreement is an agreement between the parties that alter the statute of limitation for an agreed upon period of time so that it does not continue to run during that time period. In a pending case, the attorneys for the plaintiff and the defendant may agree that the appropriate statute of limitation will be suspended from running for a certain length of time. This may be because there is some event that makes the tolling potentially desirable for both sides. For example, there may be results of some test, inspection, or other event that both sides wish to know before proceeding further and incurring more time and expense. It may be that the parties will agree to toll the statute pending settlement negotiations or a scheduled mediation. Such a tolling agreement may range from a formal written agreement to a simple exchange of e-mails confirming the agreement.

STATUTE OF REPOSE

Statute of Repose
A statute that determines the maximum period of time that an action may be brought, regardless of when the claim may have accrued.

The discussion thus far has centered on the statute of limitation as a defense to negligence. There is, however, another statute that is somewhat similar to a statute of limitation, but also quite different. It may, likewise, provide a defense to a negligence action. A **statute of repose** is a statute that determines the maximum period of time that an action may be brought, regardless of when the claim may have accrued. For example, such a statute may state that no action may be brought any later than 15 years after the manufacture of a product. Another such statute may state that no action may be brought more than 10 years after the substantial completion of an improvement to real property.

Assume this 10-year statute of repose for real property is applicable. Assume a concrete driveway was added to a home and substantially completed on March 15, 2001. Because of a defect in the concrete, a visitor to the defendant's home tripped, fell, and was injured on June 15, 2011. The plaintiff's fall, injury, and date of accrual of plaintiff's claim is clearly June 15, 2011. However, the statute of repose ran 10 years from the date of the substantial completion—on March 15, 2011. This date was three months before the plaintiff's injury even occurred and the claim even accrued. Statutes of repose may bar a party from bringing suit *before* the party is even injured. For an example of a combined statute of limitation and repose, review the Massachusetts statute in Exhibit 6-7. The Massachusetts statute

EXHIBIT 6-7 Combined Statute of Limitation and Repose

Massachusetts General Laws Annotated Title V. Chapter 260 § 2B Tort actions arising from improvements to real property

Actions of tort for damages arising out of any deficiency or neglect in the design, planning, construction or general administration of an improvement to real property ... shall be commenced only within three years next after the cause of action accrues; provided, however, that in no event shall such actions be commenced more than six years after the earlier of the dates of: (1) the opening of the improvement to use; or (2) substantial completion of the improvement and the taking of possession for occupancy by the owner.

Source: Massachusetts General Laws Annotated Title V. Chapter 260 § 2B.

of limitation is for three years and the statute of repose is for six years in an action involving an improvement to real property.

Tort Immunity

Immunity or protection from tort liability will be discussed here under the topic of defenses to negligence. However, the student must realize that certain immunities about to be examined are applicable to all torts whether based on negligence, intention, or strict liability.

SOVEREIGN IMMUNITY

Beginning with the old English common law, government entities such as the King and branches of the official monarchy could not be sued for any torts that were committed by the King and his official court. The doctrine came to be phrased, "The King can do no wrong." Official government individuals were completely immune from any tort liability. The doctrine of **sovereign immunity** carried over to this country with government bodies and government employees (federal, state, county, and city) being protected for any torts committed by such government employees. Gradually, this doctrine has been eroded by the courts and by the state legislatures.

Much litigation has surrounded the liability of cities and counties. These entities, particularly the cities, perform numerous functions for the benefit of their citizens. The traditional approach to liability has been for the courts to decide whether the city was performing a "governmental" function or a "proprietary" function. Governmental functions are immune. Proprietary functions are not immune. **Governmental functions** tend to be those functions performed solely by the government such as police, fire, and the court system. **Proprietary functions** are functions that the government entity may perform but they could also be performed just as well by private entities. Examples are utilities such as water, electricity, gas, and ambulance services. Various courts and legislatures have abolished the sovereign immunity doctrine or placed limitations upon it. For example, a state statute may provide that a state, county, or city may be sued but only up to a certain amount such as $500,000, and the municipality may be required to carry liability insurance in at least that amount.

With regard to the liability of the federal government and its employees, the Federal Tort Claims Act enacted in 1946 allows the federal government to be liable for negligent or wrongful acts of government employees as well as many intentional torts committed by federal law enforcement personnel. There are still limitations and immunity is reserved in some instances, such as certain intentional torts and strict liability torts. The student should also be aware of the Eleventh Amendment to the U.S. Constitution, which deals with each state's sovereign immunity.

Similar to sovereign immunity, certain government officers may also be immune. Judges, prosecutors, legislators, and higher-ranking members of the executive branch are immune for acts done within the scope of their official duties. However, some states grant immunity to lower-level governmental employees only when they are performing "discretionary" functions as opposed to "ministerial" functions. A **discretionary function** is a function in which the governmental employee has some discretion or choice in his or her decision. For example, a state or county engineer decides to locate a certain bridge or highway in a certain location. There is a requirement that the employee must act in good faith. A **ministerial function** is a function in which the governmental employee has no

Sovereign Immunity
Beginning with the old English common law, government entities could not be sued for any torts that were committed by the King and his official court. "The King can do no wrong." Official government individuals were completely immune from any tort liability.

Governmental Function
A function performed solely by the government such as police, fire, and the court system.

Proprietary Function
A function that the government entity may perform but that could also be performed just as well by private entities. Examples are the providing of utilities such as water, electricity, gas, and ambulance services.

Discretionary Function
A function in which the governmental employee has some discretion or choice in his or her decision.

Ministerial Function
A function in which the governmental employee has no discretion or choice; the employee is carrying out orders or complying with certain established duties.

discretion or choice; the employee is carrying out orders or complying with certain established duties. For example, a state codes administrator allows a building to be built in violation of clear established code setback requirements.

The post–civil war Civil Rights Act of 1871 subjects liability for damages on a person who acts "under color of state law" to deprive anyone of a federal constitutional right. The enforcement statute is 42 U.S.C. Section 1983. It is sometimes referred to by attorneys and judges as a **Section 1983 action**. It is frequently brought by individuals who have been arrested or have been incarcerated in a jail or prison. For example, a city police officer makes an arrest of a Native American individual for driving under the influence (DUI). In the process of the arrest, there is a scuffle, and the individual is injured and later brings a Section 1983 action against the officer and the local police department alleging a deprivation of his civil rights.

The case may boil down to why the officer stopped the individual. Was it because the officer and the department had a biased policy toward Native Americans and so the officer just decided to stop the individual because the officer knew a Native American was driving the vehicle? That is likely a violation. Or was it just a case of some individual swerving all over the road before the arrest? That is probably not a violation. Irrespective of the fact it turned out to be a Native American operating the vehicle, the vehicle was swerving, thus, giving the officer probable cause to stop the vehicle. Did the officer use excessive force because of the department's policy concerning the color/national origin of the individual? If the department had a policy of using excessive force on, for example, Hispanics or Native Americans, this would likely be a violation of civil rights. On the other hand, if the officer was making a proper, lawful arrest or reasonably acting in self-defense, which resulted in an injury to the individual, this is not a violation.

CHARITABLE IMMUNITY

At common law, under the doctrine of **charitable immunity**, tort immunity was granted for non-governmental charitable organizations. The idea was that the money on hand in these organizations came from donated funds that were to be used for the common good. Thus, schools, hospitals, and nonprofit organizations, such as the Boy Scouts and the Red Cross, were immune from tort liability. Just like sovereign immunity, this immunity doctrine has been abolished or eroded by the courts and the legislatures. For example, just as in governmental immunity, some states place restrictions or caps limiting the size of money damages that can be awarded in a tort action against charitable organizations. Recalling the discussion in Chapter 1 concerning the purposes of tort law, courts and legislatures tend to create a policy that compensates innocent tort victims over a policy of protecting charitable organizations.

FAMILY IMMUNITY

At common law, under **family immunity**, the husband could not sue the wife, and the wife could not sue the husband. Neither could sue the other for a tort committed against the other regardless of whether the tort occurred before the marriage or during the marriage. As with other immunities discussed here, this immunity has, likewise, gone the road of abolition of the doctrine or a severe limitation on the doctrine. Again, the goal of compensating innocent victims of torts outweighs the concept that a husband and wife are a single legal entity.

A similar immunity is that between parent and child. A body of early law developed that a parent could not sue a child in tort nor could a child sue a parent

Section 1983 Action
Refers to an action brought under 42 U.S.C. 1983 imposing liability for damages if one acts under "color of state law" to deprive another of a federal constitutional right.

Charitable Immunity
At common law, under the doctrine of charitable immunity, tort immunity was granted for non-governmental charitable organizations. The theory is that the money on hand in these organizations came from donated funds that were to be used for the common good.

Family Immunity
Tort immunity given to husband-wife and parent-child relationships.

Workplace Skills Tip

It is somewhat common for a defendant to ask for more time to interpose an answer to the plaintiff's complaint. The request may range from a week to several weeks or to an indefinite extension. This may be directed by the insurance carrier for the defendant who perhaps wants to try to settle a case early on and wants to forgo additional expense. The defense paralegal and the defense team should recognize some potential pitfalls in agreeing to extend the time to interpose an answer. By doing so, other important deadlines may be missed. First, the venue of a case may not be proper. A jurisdiction's law may be that a demand for a change of venue will be granted as a matter of right if done so within 20 days from service of the summons and complaint. Furthermore, if the case is improperly in state court and one wishes to remove it to federal court, 28 U.S.C. Section 1446 (b) requires that a notice of removal "shall be filed within thirty days...." Finally, requesting an extension of time to answer may result in a defendant giving up his or her right to challenge personal jurisdiction. When on the defense side, be careful what you ask for.

in tort. The rationale for the immunity was to protect family relationships and the authority and control of a parent over a child. This doctrine has also gone the road of either abolition or restriction. Even if a jurisdiction still recognizes a spousal immunity or a parent and child immunity, the line is drawn in the sand as to those family relationships. There is typically no such immunity, for example, concerning siblings, grandparents, or other family members.

Special Verdict vs. General Verdict

DIFFERENCE BETWEEN A SPECIAL VERDICT AND A GENERAL VERDICT

The student has now completed the study of negligence—all of the elements making up the tort and the defenses to the tort. This study has been leading to one final outcome. This outcome is the jury's decision in a negligence case. That decision may be rendered either by a special verdict or by a general verdict. A special verdict form is one that the jury will typically complete in a personal injury case. A **special verdict** is a written form verdict in which specific questions formulated by the court are answered by the jury, which will determine the outcome of the case.

A sample special verdict form is found in Exhibit 6-8. The special verdict form represents a hypothetical case in which the defendant is alleged to be negligent. Defendant's defense is that plaintiff was also negligent. This special verdict has numerous specific questions to be answered by the jury. This approach is quite opposite to a **general verdict**. A general verdict is an abbreviated decision by the jury stating which party won or lost. A general verdict has no detailed questions and would simply state words to the effect of: "We the jury find for the plaintiff in the sum of $100,000" (plaintiff receives $100,000) or "We the jury find for the defendant" (plaintiff receives nothing).

Special Verdict
A written form verdict in which several specific questions formulated by the court are answered by the jury, which will determine the outcome of the case.

General Verdict
A decision by the jury briefly stating which party won or lost.

EFFECT OF JURY'S ANSWERS TO QUESTIONS IN SPECIAL VERDICT FORM

A special verdict form has become more prevalent with the advent of comparative fault, multiple parties, and more complex issues. One important issue to be resolved after reviewing the sample special verdict form in the exhibit is whether or not the

EXHIBIT 6-8 Special Verdict Form

STATE OF DESPAIR	IN DISTRICT COURT
COUNTY OF NOHOPE	7th JUDICIAL DISTRICT

Ann Berg

        Plaintiff,   )

)

vs.   )   Case No.: 011-4211

)

)

)

        Lee Weiss   )   The Honorable Edward N. Ellenson

)

)

)   SPECIAL VERDICT FORM

)

        Defendant.)

_____

1. Was plaintiff Ann Berg negligent?

Yes _____   No _____

2. If your answer to question 1 was "yes," then answer this question:

Was the negligence of plaintiff Ann Berg a direct cause of the accident?

Yes_____   No _____

3. Was defendant Lee Weiss negligent?

Yes _____   No _____

4. If your answer to question 3 was "yes," then answer this question:

Was the negligence of defendant Lee Weiss a direct cause of the accident?

Yes _____   No _____

5. Taking all of the negligence that contributed as a direct cause of the accident as 100 percent, what percentage of negligence do you attribute to:

If you answered "yes" to question 2,

Plaintiff, Ann Berg   _____percent

If you answered "yes" to question 4,

Defendant, Lee Weiss   _____percent

TOTAL: 100 PERCENT

6. What amount of money for past damages and future damages will fairly and adequately compensate plaintiff?

$_____

YOU MUST ANSWER QUESTION 6 IRRESPECTIVE OF YOUR ANSWERS TO QUESTIONS 1 THROUGH 5.

_____

Jury Foreperson

jury can be told by the judge or the attorneys what the effect of their answers will be. For example, in the case of the North Dakota statute cited earlier in this chapter, unless the jury is so informed, they will not know that if the plaintiff is 50% at fault the plaintiff will recover nothing. The jury may think that if the parties were equally at fault then plaintiff will simply receive 50% of the damages. Similarly, if the jury, under California law, placed 75% of fault on the plaintiff thinking that plaintiff will not receive any money, they will not know that plaintiff will still receive 25% of plaintiff's damages. Obviously, if the jury knows the effect of their answers, it can affect how they provide their answers in certain cases. In a given case, one side or both may want very much to be able to tell the jury of the effect of their answers. Some states allow the jury to be informed of the effect of their answers and some do not.

To illustrate this point, assume that you are a member of the jury in the hypothetical case above in Exhibit 6-8, *Berg v. Weiss*. Comparative negligence, utilizing the 50–50 approach, is the law in the jurisdiction. This is a case in which there is fault on both the plaintiff, Ann Berg, and the defendant, Lee Weiss. The negligence between Ms. Berg and Mr. Weiss is somewhat equal, but there is perhaps slightly more negligence on Ms. Berg. The jury likes Ann Berg and believes that she did sustain a serious injury. The jurisdiction allows counsel to explain the effect of the jury's answers to the questions. You have the special verdict form, Exhibit 6-8, in your hands. Follow along with what the attorney for the plaintiff, Ann Berg, knowing the importance of explaining the effect of your answers, is about to tell you in the final argument.

> Ladies and gentlemen of the jury, you have all been provided with the Special Verdict Form prepared by his honor, Judge Ellenson. You each have a copy of the form in front of you. Now, I'm going to tell you how I think you should answer these questions. There are only six of them, as you can see.
>
> This is a case in which we acknowledged to you, right up front in our opening statement, there was definitely some fault on my client, Ann Berg. In this motor vehicle collision case, it is undisputed that she probably could have seen the defendant, Lee Weiss, sooner than she did. Mr. Weiss ran the red light, but Ann admits that she was speeding and texting on her cell phone at the time. Mr. Lanning, counsel for Mr. Weiss, admits that his client, Mr. Weiss was negligent for running the red light. Both sides seem to agree that both parties were negligent and both parties' negligence caused this serious collision.
>
> Therefore, question number one asking if plaintiff was negligent should be answered "yes." Question number two asking if plaintiff's negligence was a cause of the accident should be answered "yes." Question number 3 asking if defendant Lee Weiss was negligent should be answered "yes" and question number 4 asking if his negligence was a cause of the accident should also be answered "yes."
>
> It boils down to the fact that this is really a case about splitting up the percentages of fault between my client, Ann Berg, and the defendant, Lee Weiss, and then determining the appropriate amount of money that will fairly and adequately compensate my client for her serious injuries. The real point here, which is obvious, is that my client was seriously injured. She needs to be fully compensated for her serious and disabling injuries, and my hope is that you feel the same. What you need to know is this: You could write "ten million dollars" in answer to question number 6 regarding money damages, but if you don't answer question number 5 correctly, she won't receive one penny of it!

This is simply because the law that I expect his honor, Judge Ellenson, to instruct you on is that the plaintiff's money damages award will be reduced by the percentage of negligence you place on her. For example, if, in question number 5, you found her 20% at fault, she would receive 80% of her damages. If you found her 40% at fault she would receive 60% of her damages. HOWEVER, if you found her to be at fault by 50% OR MORE, she will not receive anything! She will receive *zero*, if you find her 50% or more at fault! That is just the way the law in our state works. Under our rules, I am allowed to inform you of this.

I explained the seriousness of her injuries to you earlier. Therefore, I would respectfully suggest that you fill in that damages question—question number 6—with the sum of $650,000. As far as her percentage of fault in question number 5, I would suggest that maybe you put 40% or 45% on her, but remember that if you make it as high as 50%, she won't receive anything. If you really think she is pretty close to equal in causing this collision, but believe that she is entitled to her money damages, then you could go as high as 49% on her, and she would still receive 51% of that damages figure you put in at number 6. But remember, if you put 50% or more on her, she will receive nothing for this serious injury. I have confidence that you will do the right thing and that you will answer these questions correctly. Thank you.

This chapter has presented the tort of negligence from the side of the defendant. The student has now explored the basic elements of the tort of negligence as well as the defenses to negligence. Intentional torts—having no basis in carelessness, negligence, or fault—will next be explored.

CASE 6.1 Hypothetical Case: Developing Workplace Skills

You are a paralegal working in the prestigious insurance defense firm of Bullee & Nastee, LPC. The senior partner, Bart Bullee, has an assignment for you in an upcoming trial in a case with which you have been involved from day one. He needs you to draft a proposed special verdict form for the upcoming pretrial conference, which is set in two weeks. The judge requires the parties to prepare proposed jury instructions and a proposed special verdict form. The proposed instructions are completed, but the proposed special verdict form needs to be prepared for Mr. Bullee's review.

THE FACTS ARE AS FOLLOWS:

This is a two-vehicle collision involving our client, William "Bill" Treble. The date of the accident was Thursday, June 17, 2010, and it occurred at approximately 4:00 p.m. Treble was driving his 2007 Ford F-150 south on State Highway 75. Treble is 69 years old, retired, and was on his way home. He was returning from the local hardware store where he had purchased some merchandise for a project he was working on in his shop. Treble was in good health and had nothing to drink of an alcoholic nature. He has always been a fast driver, however. On the day in question, as he was proceeding down the highway, the posted speed limit was 55 miles per hour. Bill admits he was probably going 75 to 80 as he was in a "little hurry" to return home to finish the project he was working on.

He maintained that speed all the way down the highway. He was still going 75 to 80 as he approached the junction with County Highway 20, which runs east and west in a perpendicular fashion to Highway 75. There is a stop sign on both the east

(Continued)

CASE 6.1 *(Continued)*

side of the highway and the west side of the highway to protect north/south traffic traveling on Highway 75. Weather was good. Roads were dry. Visibility was good. The contour of the two intersecting highways for several miles is flat and level. There was no traffic ahead of Bill or behind him.

As Bill approached the intersection, another vehicle was coming from the west—to Bill's right—traveling east toward the stop sign. The owner of the vehicle was Blowhard Bagpipe Company ("Blowhard"). This company supplies bagpipes, accordions, and other specialized musical instruments to retail music stores. The vehicle was a 2003 Mercedes ML 350 SUV. The driver of the vehicle was Henry Bass. Bass was an employee of Blowhard. Bass had, as a passenger in the vehicle, another employee, Salma Notes. Bass and Notes were out calling on customers and had been paired up for the last six months. Their regular work hours were from 8:00 a.m. to 5:00 p.m. Monday through Friday.

In the course of working together, they developed a romantic relationship, which they had been successful in hiding from the supervisors and other employees. At the time of the accident, they were supposed to be going the opposite direction to call on their final customer for the day. However, they decided to have a little fling and go east on Highway 20 to a motel on the highway that was located approximately five miles east of the junction of Highway 20 and Highway 75. This was not the first time they had done this so they were familiar with the route. Bass stopped at the stop sign and saw Bill's vehicle "quite a ways away" with plenty of time to cross. The problem is that Bass didn't realize Bill was traveling as fast as he was. At 80 miles per hour, Bill would have been covering approximately 120 feet per second. Bill slammed into the rear driver side area of the Blowhard SUV. Bill said he saw Bass stop and never saw him again until "he was right in front of me."

To complicate matters, Bass was wearing a seat belt but Salma was not. In fact, at the time they had approached the intersection, stopped at the stop sign and took off again, Salma had been kissing Bass on the neck and massaging his knee. After the collision, Salma was thrown from the car and was permanently and seriously injured. She brought suit on a negligence theory against Defendant William Treble, Defendant Blowhard Bagpipe Company—the employer, and Defendant Henry Bass.

In her complaint, Notes alleged negligence against Bass and Treble. She alleged that Henry Bass was an employee and that he was in the scope of his employment at the time of the accident. She alleged that Blowhard is, therefore, vicariously liable under the doctrine of *respondeat superior* for the negligence of Bass. Our client Treble alleged negligence on the part of the plaintiff and negligence on the part of the other defendants, Bass and Blowhard. Bass alleged negligence on the part of the plaintiff and negligence on our part. Our client admitted that Bass was an employee of Blowhard and in the scope of his employment at the time of the accident. Bass admitted that he was an employee and in the scope of his employment at the time of the accident. Blowhard alleged, first, that Bass was not negligent. Next, Blowhard alleged if Bass were negligent, Blowhard was not liable for his negligence as he was outside the scope of his employment on a "frolic and detour" at the time, for which Blowhard could not be vicariously liable. Blowhard also alleged negligence on the part of Plaintiff Notes and our client.

Using the special verdict form in the chapter exhibit, including the case caption, as a model and assuming there is some type of comparative negligence in your jurisdiction, prepare "Defendant William Treble's Proposed Special Verdict Form." You may assume that the court will want the jury to answer the damages questions regardless of the liability questions. Even though Salma, Bill, and Henry are adverse to each other—claiming the other was at fault—on what issue in this case would they likely sing in harmony?

"Don't do what we tell you to do because we're your parents. Do what we tell you to do because we're both attorneys and won't hesitate to sue you."

CHAPTER **SUMMARY**

Contributory negligence is an affirmative defense to the tort of negligence. Contributory negligence is conduct on the part of the plaintiff that falls below the standard to which the plaintiff must conform for plaintiff's safety or protection and that contributes to causing plaintiff's personal injury and damages. The defendant has the burden of proving the defense of contributory negligence, and the conduct of the plaintiff is judged by the reasonable person standard.

The effect of contributory negligence is harsh. It bars a plaintiff's recovery completely. This is true even when the negligence of the defendant is great and the negligence of the plaintiff is slight. To offset the harshness of the contributory negligence rule, the doctrine of "last clear chance" was developed. This means that plaintiff's contributory negligence will not bar a recovery if the defendant, immediately before the accident, had the last clear chance to avoid it, but failed to do so.

Comparative negligence is a doctrine that has been developed by both case law and statutory law to offset the harshness of contributory negligence. There are essentially three types of comparative negligence. The first type is pure comparative negligence. Even if plaintiff's negligence far exceeds the defendant's negligence, the plaintiff will still recover an amount reduced by plaintiff's fault. If the plaintiff was awarded $100,000, and plaintiff was 95% at fault and defendant 5% at fault, plaintiff would still recover $5,000. Under pure comparative negligence, plaintiff would recover nothing only if plaintiff was 100% at fault.

Under the 51–49 approach, the plaintiff can recover only if the plaintiff's negligence/fault was not greater than the defendant's negligence/fault. For example, if the verdict were $100,000, the plaintiff could recover an amount reduced by plaintiff's fault unless the plaintiff was 51% at fault, in which case the plaintiff would receive nothing. If plaintiff was 50% at fault and defendant was 50% at fault, plaintiff would recover 50% of plaintiff's damages.

Under the 50-50 approach, the plaintiff can still recover so long as the plaintiff's fault is not equal to the defendant's fault. If plaintiff was 40% at fault, plaintiff would recover 60% of the awarded damages. However, if plaintiff was 50% at fault or more, plaintiff would recover nothing.

With multiple defendants, the issue is whether the negligence of the plaintiff is compared to each defendant or if it is compared to all defendants as a group. The law of the particular jurisdiction needs to be ascertained.

Assumption of the risk is another affirmative defense to negligence. Assumption of the risk is the plaintiff's giving consent, expressly or impliedly, to confronting the harm or danger from a risk caused by the defendant. If assumption of the risk is proved by the defendant, it is a complete bar to

plaintiff's recovery. The plaintiff, however, must have recognized and understood the risk for the defense to apply, and the plaintiff must have voluntarily chosen to confront it. The plaintiff's conduct in assumption of the risk is not judged by the reasonable person standard. It is judged by what the plaintiff subjectively knew about the risk.

Assumption of the risk may arise by contract in what are called "exculpatory provisions" or clauses. These are typically found on a ticket received from facilities such as parking ramps, public swimming pools, and amusement parks. These provisions generally are not favored by the courts. Determining factors of their validity will be (1) the person's knowledge of the provision, (2) the actual language defining its scope, and (3) whether or not the parties are in an equal bargaining position.

A statute of limitation may provide an affirmative defense to the tort of negligence. A statute of limitation in a civil case is a statute that provides the maximum period of time in which a civil lawsuit must be commenced or it will be barred. The statute begins to run when the plaintiff's claim accrues. A claim accrues when the plaintiff knew or had reason to know of injury caused by the defendant's wrongful conduct. A statute of limitation may be "tolled." A statute is tolled if the time period is suspended until a certain circumstance or condition occurs or while a certain circumstance or condition is occurring. A statute of repose is similar to but different from a statute of limitation. A statute of repose determines the absolute maximum period of time that an action may be commenced, regardless of when the claim accrued.

There are several immunities from tort liability. These immunities do not relate solely to torts based on negligence. They apply to all torts—those based on negligence, intentional torts, and strict liability torts. The first is sovereign immunity. This doctrine means that certain government employees may be immune from liability for torts committed by them while performing their official functions or duties. Charitable immunity is a form of immunity from tort liability given to charitable organizations. Family immunity means that certain family members, such as a husband and wife or a parent and child, cannot sue each other in tort.

A special verdict form is a form written verdict in which specific questions formulated by the court are answered by the jury, and the answers will determine the outcome of the case. A general verdict simply makes a statement to the effect that "we the jury find for the defendant" or "we the jury find for the plaintiff in the sum of $100,000." Special verdict forms are more prevalent with the advent of comparative fault, multiple parties, and more complex issues.

KEY **TERMS**

Affirmative Defense
Contributory Negligence
Last Clear Chance
Comparative Negligence
Assumption of the Risk
Firefighter's Rule
Exculpatory Provisions
Contract of Adhesion

Accrues
Discovery Rule
Tolled (Statue of Limitation)
Tolling Agreement
Statute of Repose
Sovereign Immunity
Governmental Function
Proprietary Function

Discretionary Function
Ministerial Function
Section 1983 Action
Charitable Immunity
Family Immunity
Special Verdict
General Verdict

REVIEW **QUESTIONS**

1. What is contributory negligence, and what is its effect on the case, if proven?
2. Differentiate and explain the difference between contributory negligence and comparative negligence. Which do you believe is a fairer doctrine and why?
3. Byron's motor vehicle became stalled on the railroad tracks out in the country. As the train was approaching, the conductor was conversing with the brakeman and not paying particular attention to the tracks ahead. Byron stayed on the tracks as long as he could, trying to move his vehicle off the tracks, to no avail. The train struck the vehicle. Luckily, Byron jumped out of the way in the nick of time, but part of the vehicle flew into Byron and injured him. Byron sues the railroad alleging negligence. Assume this is a jurisdiction that still retains common law defenses and concepts. What will the railroad likely raise as a defense? What should Byron's response be?
4. This chapter discusses whether or not a particular jurisdiction will allow the court or counsel to comment on the effect of comparative negligence. Which rule do you think is a better rule? Why?
5. Assume you were on the plaintiff's team representing a plaintiff with a catastrophic personal injury, such as quadriplegia, but your client did a very stupid thing that contributed to the accident, such that there is likely to be a great deal of negligence/fault placed on him. If you had your choice of a comparative fault statute that was 50–50, 51–49, or pure comparative fault, which would you choose? Why?
6. Read the quotation at the beginning of the chapter. It was uttered with tongue in cheek, but is there a ring of truth to it? Why or why not?
7. In the special verdict form shown in Exhibit 6-8, note that the court requires the jury to answer the damages questions, irrespective of the previous questions on fault. If the jurisdiction involved were a 50-50 jurisdiction, and the jury found the plaintiff 55% at fault and the defendant 45% at fault, plaintiff would recover nothing. So, why do you think the court still wants answers to the damages questions?
8. Explain the difference between a statute of limitation and a statute of repose. What is the purpose/rationale for both of them?

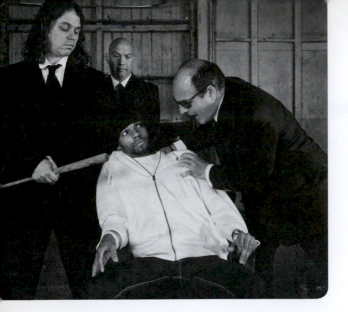

chapter 7
INTENTIONAL TORTS TO THE PERSON

LEARNING OBJECTIVES

After studying this chapter, you should be able to:

- Identify the elements of the tort of battery.
- Identify the elements of the tort of assault.
- Identify the elements of the tort of false imprisonment.
- Identify the elements of the tort of intentional infliction of emotional distress.
- Recognize and analyze the defenses to intentional torts to the person.

"Civilized society is perpetually menaced with disintegration through this primary hostility of men towards one another."

Sigmund Freud

Up to this point, all of the various torts that have been discussed have been based on negligence—a failure to exercise due care. The analysis has been based upon the reasonable person standard. The second basis for tort liability is one that is based upon conduct that the defendant intends. It is not measured by the reasonable person standard. A negligent tortfeasor does a sloppy or careless act and means no harm. An intentional tortfeasor acts with purpose and intent, desiring a certain result from the intentional act or believing a certain result is substantially certain to occur from the intentional act. Quite frankly, the personal injury paralegal will find that a very small portion of personal injury cases will be based on intentional torts. This is a point made by the author in the Preface to this book. The greatest number of cases will likely be based on negligence, products liability and tort-based statutory liability. To be complete, however, intentional torts to both the person and to a person's property must be discussed. As mentioned in Chapter 1, some torts may also be crimes. That is the case with many of the torts about to be considered in this chapter. Intentional torts to the person will be discussed first.

Battery

Battery
An intentional tort consisting of an act by the defendant who intends and accomplishes a harmful or offensive touching on the plaintiff.

The first intentional tort to the person to be discussed is the tort of **battery**. The elements of the tort of battery are:

1. An act by the defendant
2. Intent
3. A harmful or offensive touching
4. Causation

AN ACT BY THE DEFENDANT

When the word "act" is used in reference to an intentional tort, it means that there has been some external or outward manifestation of the defendant's will, that is, some actual *voluntary* movement of a part of the defendant's body. If a person is asleep and makes an involuntary movement while asleep, this does not qualify as an external manifestation of the defendant's will. Similarly, if one who was having an epileptic seizure or a stroke struck another person, the act is involuntary not voluntary. Furthermore, if the act is a reflexive act, it is not an act that is voluntary. The student has no doubt been involved in a physical examination by a physician in which the physician taps the knee. This tap causes the leg to involuntarily fly forward. This reflexive action is not an act, because it is not an external manifestation of the person's will. It is not voluntary. The essential element of the tort of battery—an act—is missing in these examples.

INTENT

The intent required of the defendant is that he or she performed the act with the intent to inflict a harmful or offensive touching on the plaintiff. The intent required for this element of proof is that either the defendant had the actual desire to inflict the touching or defendant believed that such a touching was *reasonably certain* to occur. If defendant pushed a pedestrian out of the way of an oncoming car causing the person to strike the pavement and be injured, certainly the defendant did not desire or want the touching to occur. However, the defendant would realize that a harmful or offensive touching was reasonably certain to occur by physically reaching out and doing the pushing. As mentioned at the beginning of this chapter, unlike negligence, which rests upon the reasonable person standard, an intentional tort is judged by what was subjectively occurring in the defendant's mind.

Keep in mind that other objective evidence or objective facts may contradict what a defendant says was actually in his or her mind concerning the person's intent. For example, a defendant may testify that he did not intend to harm the plaintiff by shooting an arrow in the direction of the plaintiff, which struck the plaintiff in the leg. However, that testimony may be contradicted by other evidence that there had been an earlier disagreement between plaintiff and defendant. It may also be contradicted by evidence that two other arrows were later found at the scene.

TRANSFERRED INTENT

Transferred intent means that if the defendant does an act intending to cause harm to a person, the defendant will be liable for battery if the harm occurs to some other unintended and unexpected person. For example, assume that Alphonse threw a rock intending to hit and harm Barry. Barry was standing near Charles having a conversation with him. Alphonse's aim was not good. He missed Barry but hit Charles. Even though Alphonse did not intend to harm Charles, his intent to harm Barry is transferred to Charles. Alphonse has committed a battery as to Charles. The doctrine of transferred intent is not limited to the intentional tort of battery. The theory or doctrine of transferred intent also applies to other intentional torts, as will be discussed later.

Transferred Intent
An intentional tort doctrine meaning that if the defendant does an act intending to cause harm to a person, the defendant will be liable if the harm occurs to some other unintended and unexpected person.

HARMFUL OR OFFENSIVE TOUCHING

The touching of the plaintiff by the defendant may be either harmful or offensive. Further, battery may occur if the touching is to the plaintiff's person *or* even something "closely associated" with the plaintiff. Assume that plaintiff is sitting on a chair, and defendant walks by and kicks the chair. This actual intentional physical contact with the chair is considered to be the same as kicking the plaintiff's person in terms of the element of touching. A **harmful touching** is any touching that causes, for example, pain, suffering, anguish, impairment, disfigurement, or disability to the plaintiff.

An **offensive touching**, however, does bring back into play the reasonable person standard. To be offensive, the plaintiff must show that the touching would offend the sense of personal dignity of a *reasonable person*. For example, if the defendant simply pats a stranger on the back, this touching may not have been wanted or welcomed by the plaintiff. However, the defendant's conduct will be judged by whether or not a reasonable person would really take offense to such a touching. The result may be different, however, if the defendant had actual knowledge that the plaintiff is overly sensitive to such a touching. A slap or pat on the back may ordinarily be reasonable. However, if the defendant knew that plaintiff had just had upper back surgery or knew of a sensitive skin condition on plaintiff's back, the intentional slap or pat on the back may amount to a battery.

Harmful Touching
A touching in the tort of battery that causes, for example, pain, suffering, anguish, impairment, disfigurement, or disability to the plaintiff.

Offensive Touching
A touching in the tort of battery that would offend the sense of personal dignity of a reasonable person.

CAUSATION

Just as in cases based on negligence, the intentional tort of battery must be caused by the defendant's intentional act. The Restatement (Second) of Torts § 13 (1965) states that there is sufficient causation shown if the defendant's intentional act or conduct "directly or indirectly" results in the injury to the plaintiff. Besides the defendant's direct intentional act, it is also sufficient to prove the tort of battery if the injury to the plaintiff was indirectly caused by some force that the defendant "sets into motion" with the intentional act.

For example, assume that defendant, operating a motor vehicle, intentionally tried to run down a pedestrian in the street. As the defendant is speeding toward the plaintiff, the defendant loses control of the vehicle. The vehicle strikes a light pole causing it to fall on the plaintiff and injure the plaintiff. Defendant's intentional act in this case indirectly brought about the injury by knocking down the light pole. If defendant had succeeded in striking plaintiff with the motor vehicle, the intentional act would have directly brought about the injury.

There is a difference in the causation element between negligence and intentional torts. An intentional tortfeasor is liable for all consequences of the intentional

Workplace Skills Tip

Knowing the difference between a tort based on an intentional act and a tort based on a negligent act will have extremely important practical ramifications for the personal injury team. In later chapters, discussion will focus on insurance issues. In a liability policy, typically, there is no liability coverage for an insured defendant if the act was done intentionally, but there is coverage if the act was done negligently. It is typical to find an "intentional acts" exclusion in most liability insurance policies.

act that were *set in motion* by the tortfeasor. In the negligence discussion, it was pointed out that the resulting loss, damage, or injury had to be reasonably foreseeable. Concerning battery and other intentional torts, it does not matter whether or not the resulting injury was foreseeable. In the above example, if the light pole fell on a box of explosives that exploded, which in turn caused a store awning to fall on the plaintiff, battery has been established. If the same driver were negligent in striking the light pole ending up with the explosion and falling awning, there would likely be no proximate cause established as discussed in Chapter 3.

DAMAGES

Damages need not be proved. Nominal damages will be awarded at a minimum. Other damages may be awarded. The damages awarded may also include all of those as discussed in Chapter 4. These are compensatory damages consisting of general damages and special damages. As discussed in Chapter 4, intentional torts may give rise to a claim for punitive or exemplary damages.

EXHIBIT 7-1 Relevant Case Law

QBE Insurance Corporation, Plaintiffs, v. Jorda Enterprises, Inc., Defendant.

United States District Court, S.D. Florida, Miami Division.

Jonathan Goodman, United States Magistrate Judge.

ORDER DENYING DEFENDANT'S MOTION TO EXCLUDE EXPERT OPINION

The Honorable Alan S. Gold referred (ECF 109) to me Defendant's Motion to Exclude Expert Opinion (ECF 107). For the reasons outlined below, the Court denies the motion.

Plaintiff QBE filed this lawsuit against Jorda for equitable subrogation after paying its insured, a condominium, approximately $3.03 million for damage resulting from water which poured out of a PVC pipe in the building's air conditioning system during Hurricane Wilma. Defendant Jorda installed the air conditioning system nearly two years before the hurricane, and QBE alleges that Jorda did so negligently and is therefore obligated to pay QBE for the money it paid out on the insurance claim.

On July 25, 2011, QBE served Jorda with a letter which it describes as a summary of the opinions of its expert witness, Sherri Hankal, an engineer. On September 30, 2011, Jorda took Ms. Hankal's deposition, which generated a 190-page transcript. More than four months later, on February 6, 2012, Jorda filed a motion to exclude Ms. Hankal's expert opinion testimony. Jorda's primary argument is that the written summary provided the previous July was inadequate and that Ms. Hankal, in her deposition, added new opinions.

Jorda's motion violates Local Rule 7.1, which requires a movant to confer about the relief sought before filing a motion and to include a written certification about the results of, and circumstances surrounding, the rule-required conference.

The local rule also provides the consequences for failure to comply: "to grant or deny the motion and impose on counsel an appropriate sanction, which may include an order to pay the amount of the reasonable expenses incurred because of the violation, including a reasonable attorney's fee."

(Continued)

EXHIBIT 7-1 *(Continued)*

Because Jorda violated the local rule, the Court will deny the motion.

In connection with the denial, the Court makes several observations:

First, the local rule is clear, straightforward and unequivocal.

Second, at the risk of stating the obvious, parties are required to follow the local rules.

Third, there is no "but-the-opposing-party-would-never-have-agreed-to-the-motion-had-I-both-ered-to-confer" exception to the local rule. If there were such an exception carved out, then it would swallow the rule, as movants would routinely invoke the exception as a rationale for not bothering to follow the pre-filing conference requirement.

Fourth, Jorda is familiar with the local rule. It has in this case filed several motions complying with the local rule. Those motions range from routine ones, such as a motion for enlargement of time (ECF 116) and motions to compel (ECF 47 and 58), to more-atypical, case-specific ones, such as a motion for sanctions for failure to comply with Rule 30(b)(6) (ECF 70).

Fifth, Jorda routinely sought to persuade this Court to invoke negative consequences against QBE for its purported failure to follow rules, such as the Federal Rules of Civil Procedure, the Local Rules and the orders entered by the Court. Jorda has, in fact, obtained significant relief in this case because of QBE's failure to comply with applicable rules. For example, the Court entered an Order (before Jorda failed to follow the local rule in connection with the instant motion) granting, in part, Jorda's motion for sanctions because of QBE's failure to follow Federal Rule of Civil Procedure 30(b)(6) (ECF 70).

Sixth, it would be inequitable for Jorda to seek significant relief against QBE for its failure to follow the rules but also expect to obtain relief when it commits a clear-cut violation of the local rules.

Because of the local rule violation, Jorda's motion to exclude Ms. Hankal's testimony is denied.

Source: Miami Division. QBE Insurance Corporation, v. Jorda Enterprises, Inc., No. 10–21107–CIV. March 16, 2012.

Workplace Skills Tip

The personal injury paralegal will witness, from time to time, various discovery disputes in a case. Examples are: A party has not fully answered an interrogatory; a party has not produced certain discoverable documents in response to a request for production of documents; a party has not complied with a particular court order or court rule. The natural tendency for the attorney is to immediately react and file a discovery motion. Know all of the rules of your jurisdiction in order to be a good backup to the attorney. Most jurisdictions will have a rule requiring the attorneys to first "meet and confer" in order to try to resolve the dispute before filing the discovery motion. First, as a general statement, most judges do not like what they consider refereeing discovery disputes. They are to be avoided whenever possible. Second, it will be embarrassing to have filed a motion without showing the court that your side tried to first voluntarily resolve the dispute under the applicable rule. Your side may have the winning hand on the merits of the dispute so don't lose it on a technicality. Review the *QBE* case in Exhibit 7-1.

Assault

The elements of the tort of **assault** are:

1. An act by the defendant
2. Intent
3. Apprehension
4. Causation

AN ACT BY THE DEFENDANT

For the tort of battery, as discussed above, there must be some external manifestation of the defendant's will—a voluntary act. The requirement of an act by the defendant for assault is the same as it is for battery. This is a tort in which an "apprehension" of an immediate touching to the plaintiff must be shown (element 3). Therefore, words are generally not enough to constitute an act. There must be some type of voluntary movement of some part of the body of the defendant. For example, if defendant said, "I'm going to slit your throat," regardless of the menacing tone, that would not constitute an act. However, if defendant pulled out a switchblade, that voluntary movement of the defendant's body would be a sufficient act. Also, even if defendant started to reach for a nearby switchblade or other knife, that voluntary movement of the defendant's body would, likewise, be a sufficient act. The tort of intentional infliction of emotional distress will be discussed later in this chapter. Words alone, by themselves, can be sufficient for establishment of the tort of intentional infliction of emotional distress.

INTENT

The element of intent for assault means that defendant intended to perform a harmful or offensive touching to the plaintiff or to put the plaintiff in apprehension of an imminent harmful or offensive touching. Just as in battery, the defendant must act with an actual desire to inflict the touching or believe that it is reasonably certain to occur. The concept of transferred intent also applies to assault.

APPREHENSION

The intentional act of the defendant must have put the plaintiff in apprehension of a harmful or offensive touching of plaintiff's person that would be "imminent." The requirement of apprehension simply means that plaintiff must be aware of the assault at the time it was committed. In the example above, if the defendant made the same comment about slitting the plaintiff's throat and reached for a switchblade, but plaintiff, for some reason, did not see the defendant reach for the switchblade, the element of apprehension is missing. Recall that for the tort of battery, no apprehension is even required, and the plaintiff does not need to have knowledge of the touching at the time it occurs. Finally, the plaintiff's apprehension must be about a touching only to the plaintiff's body. The element is not satisfied if the apprehension arises from a threat to plaintiff's property or to another person.

An important part of the definition of apprehension is that the apprehension must be that the harmful or offensive touching will be *imminent*. Using our same example, if the defendant said to the plaintiff, "I'm going to slit your throat *one of these days*," the use of the words "one of these days" removes the requirement of apprehension of an immediate, imminent touching. The general rule, as in battery, is that the plaintiff's apprehension must be reasonable and will be judged by the reasonable person standard, not by what the plaintiff was subjectively thinking. There is a further distinction to be made about this particular tort. Note that fear is not an element, only apprehension. It may well be that plaintiff is not afraid of the defendant making the slitting of the throat threat because plaintiff is carrying a loaded gun. However, the plaintiff may still experience apprehension.

CAUSATION

The element of causation is the same as was discussed for the intentional tort of battery.

DAMAGES

The element of damages is the same as was discussed for the intentional tort of battery.

False Imprisonment

False Imprisonment
An intentional act of the defendant that results in the confinement of the plaintiff.

The elements of the tort of **false imprisonment** are:

1. An act by the defendant
2. Intent
3. Confinement
4. Causation

An Act by the Defendant

False imprisonment, just like battery and assault, requires some affirmative voluntary act on the part of the defendant that results in the confinement of the plaintiff. However, a difference is that words alone, standing by themselves, without an act may be sufficient. For example, as if out of a Mafia movie, a six-feet-tall, 250-pound goon stands menacingly before a person sitting in a corner restaurant booth pointing a gun at the person and snarls: "Stay where you are for the next 10 minutes and don't move or you're dead!" The act of pointing the gun will certainly suffice as an act. However, even if the Mafia figure had no gun in his hand and made the same statement, the words alone will suffice for the first element of this tort.

Workplace Skills Tip

As a member of a plaintiff's or defendant's personal injury team, you will be given numerous assignments by the supervising attorney to perform various tasks. If you are not successful in completing the assignment, document that fact and the reason(s) why a particular assignment could not be completed. As examples: (1) witness X has died; (2) witness Y has moved to Spain; (3) the information thought to be readily obtained by another attorney with a similar case could not be disclosed by that attorney because of a confidentiality agreement; (4) the records of Company Z have been destroyed. The litigation team should know that you have diligently tried to accomplish the task and why it was impossible to accomplish.

INTENT

The act or words by the defendant must be done or said with the intent to confine the plaintiff. The definition of intent and the concept of transferred intent are the same as battery and assault.

CONFINEMENT

The confinement of the plaintiff must be within boundaries fixed by the defendant for some period of time. In the above example, the words of the Mafia goon do just that. The person in the booth is confined to fixed boundaries (the corner booth) for some period of time (10 minutes). Note that the amount of time need not be lengthy. Confinement also requires that the plaintiff is restricted to a limited area in which the plaintiff has no knowledge of a reasonable means of escape. The element of confinement is missing if there are reasonable means of escape that are known to the plaintiff.

The confinement may come about because of physical force or threats of physical force against the plaintiff or the plaintiff's immediate family. It may also come about because of threats to the plaintiff's property. "Stay where you are—right at your desk in this study—or my buddy will spray paint all of these valuable paintings on the wall!"

The confinement may be in the form of physical barriers—walls, rooms, even a corner booth in a restaurant as in our Mafia goon example, or seated at the desk in a person's study in the threatened spray painting example. Those examples involved physical threats—one to person and one to property. Other more subtle means of confinement may arise such as depriving the plaintiff of the ability to escape or leave a certain area. Assume that an injured patient is due to be released from a hospital or a person who has been in a psychiatric ward is due to be released after cure is complete. The hospital, for whatever reason or motive, intentionally decides not to allow the lawful, scheduled release. Assume the plaintiff is on the roof of a house doing some work and defendant intentionally removes the ladder. The hospital patients and the person on the roof are confined and the element of confinement is satisfied.

All of us have likely traveled by air, train, or bus at some time. If a passenger decides that he or she wants to exit at any time, is it confinement amounting to false imprisonment if the exit is not allowed by the common carrier? Probably not. When one boards a commercial transportation company there is, at least, an implied agreement that the only exit points are at scheduled stops. A confinement could also occur by an arrest such as a citizen's arrest or one posing as a legitimate law enforcement officer or even an arrest by a proper law enforcement officer if there was no basis for the arrest. The legitimate law enforcement officer may be immune from civil suit, which is a topic to be covered under defenses to intentional torts.

CAUSATION

The defendant must have caused the confinement by defendant's intentional act.

DAMAGES

The element of damages is the same as it is for battery and for assault. Once confinement has occurred, which defendant caused by his or her intentional act, then plaintiff is entitled to nominal damages at least. In addition, plaintiff is entitled to any of the broad categories of damages that can also be proved—compensatory (special and general) and punitive/exemplary.

The decision of *Clarke v. Kmart Corporation*, 495 N.W.2d 820 (Mich. Ct. App. 1992), illustrates a factual situation involving false imprisonment (see Exhibit

7-2). Note that the facts there also gave rise to claims for assault and battery. Also note whether the alleged battery to the plaintiff was to herself or to an instrumentality closely associated with her as discussed in the section on battery above. In the intentional tort arena, it is not uncommon to find a fact scenario that supports several of the intentional torts.

EXHIBIT 7-2 Relevant Case Law

Dorothy Clarke, Plaintiff-Appellant, Cross-Appellee, v. Kmart Corporation, Defendant-Appellee, Cross-Appellant.

Court of Appeals of Michigan.

Plaintiff, Dorothy Clarke, appeals from the trial court's grant of summary disposition for defendant, Kmart Corporation, under MCR 2.116(C)(8) and (10) with respect to her claims of discrimination, false imprisonment, and intentional infliction of emotional distress.... Defendant cross appeals from the denial of its motion for summary disposition of plaintiff's claim of assault and battery. We affirm in part, reverse in part, and remand....

Plaintiff, her two small children, and her sister had shopped at defendant's store and purchased many items, including a set of bed sheets. While the items were being rung up, the cashier, an African-American like the plaintiff, accidentally rang up the sheets twice. She set them aside while the overring was voided, then placed the sheets directly in plaintiff's bag.

Defendant's cashier supervisor saw only the last portion of this transaction, i.e., the sheets being placed in the bag without being rung up. She waited until plaintiff was about to leave and approached her with another supervisor.

According to plaintiff, the second supervisor snatched the bag out of her hand. According to defendant, the supervisor took the bag out of plaintiff's shopping cart, not out of her hand. Plaintiff was told that this was a routine package check, and she was detained for about ten or fifteen minutes while the items were matched with her receipt. Plaintiff was given $10 for her inconvenience.

Defendant denied that the stop was racially motivated. According to defendant, it suspected the cashier, not plaintiff, of wrongdoing. This suspicion allegedly was due to the fact that the cashier, who was new, asked during her training a lot of questions regarding overrings, voids, and scanning versus manually ringing up items. From these questions, defendant's employees deduced that the cashier was trying to give away or underring merchandise. Additionally, two African-American women had been seen earlier that day trying to go through the cashier's checkout lane while the cashier was on break, wandering around the store with the cashier, and then leaving without buying anything....

We next examine plaintiff's claim of false imprisonment. In this regard, the trial court found that there was "no indication that there was a restriction in the plaintiff's freedom of movement" and that she "was not arrested nor detained in an office, [that] she was free to roam through the store and, in fact was free to leave if she wished to" do so. Although these observations may be technically accurate, we believe that the court's holding rests on an unduly narrow view of this tort.

"False imprisonment is the unlawful restraint of an individual's personal liberty or freedom of locomotion."..."There can be no such thing as an action for false imprisonment where the plaintiff has not been arrested; and while...manual seizure is not necessary, there must be that or its equivalent in some form of personal coercion."...On the other hand, there is no false arrest if the plaintiff voluntarily agrees to stay with the defendant....

Defendant argues that it had no intent to detain plaintiff, only her merchandise. Given that defendant was detaining property worth about $250, we believe that the question of defendant's intent

(Continued)

EXHIBIT 7-2 *(Continued)*

involves the credibility of its employees and is not appropriate for summary disposition.... We note first that defendant has argued previously that it did not suspect plaintiff of any wrongdoing and had no intention to detain her. On the other hand, defendant has stated that it believed that plaintiff's bag contained merchandise for which she had not paid. Again, given these facts, we believe that whether defendant suspected plaintiff is a question of credibility not appropriate for summary disposition....

Plaintiff next argues that her claim of intentional infliction of emotional distress should be reinstated. We disagree.

Although the trial court correctly noted that our Supreme Court has not recognized this cause of action, panels of this Court have recognized it.... However, we agree with defendant that, although unquestionably offensive, the conduct charged in this case is not "so outrageous in character, and so extreme in degree, as to go beyond all possible bounds of decency, and to be regarded as atrocious, and utterly intolerable in a civilized community." ...

Lastly, we address defendant's cross appeal from the trial court's refusal to grant summary disposition of the assault and battery claim.

Clearly, there is a factual dispute concerning whether defendant's employees snatched the bag out of plaintiff's hands or took it out of her shopping cart. A battery occurs when there is a willful, harmful, or offensive touching of the plaintiff or of an object that is "attached to [the plaintiff] and practically identified with" the plaintiff's body. Espinoza v. Thomas, 189 Mich.App. 110, 119, 472 N.W.2d 16 (1991) (contact with a car occupied by the plaintiff was sufficient). Thus, if the facts are as plaintiff argues, there would be a prima facie case of assault and battery established.

Source: Clarke v. KMart Corporation, 495 N.W.2d 820 (Mich. Ct. App. 1992).

Intentional Infliction of Emotional Distress

The elements of the tort of **intentional infliction of emotional distress** are:

1. An act (includes words) by the defendant that amounts to extreme and outrageous conduct
2. Intent
3. Causation
4. Severe emotional distress
5. Damages

Intentional Infliction of Emotional Distress
An intentional tort consisting of an act consisting of extreme or outrageous conduct (or words) by the defendant who intends to cause severe emotional distress to the plaintiff.

Workplace Skills Tip

As a personal injury team member on either plaintiff's or defendant's side, you will be asked by the supervising attorney to locate certain information that will be helpful in presenting your client's case. This may come to you verbally, by e-mail, or by a more formal memo. Examples may be to try to obtain previous deposition testimony or trial testimony of the other side's expert witness or law enforcement records establishing evidence of defendant's previous wrongful conduct or crimes, or some specific medical records. If the assignment comes verbally, confirm the assignment and its scope by e-mail with the supervising attorney. Furthermore, always know which assignments are "front burner" and which are "back burner." Know the deadline for any assignment. If you are not sure, ask!

AN ACT (INCLUDES WORDS) BY THE DEFENDANT THAT AMOUNTS TO EXTREME AND OUTRAGEOUS CONDUCT

For this intentional tort, either words or actions by the defendant will support the first element. However, the words or acts must exceed all bounds of decent behavior. The words or acts must be "extreme and outrageous" (see Restatement (Second) of Torts § 46 (1965)). The Restatement goes on to state that the conduct must be "so outrageous in character, and so extreme in degree, as to go beyond all possible bounds of decency, and to be regarded as atrocious and utterly intolerable in a civilized society." The real world requires people to be accustomed to a certain amount of rough and tough language and to some acts that are definitely unkind, inconsiderate, and downright rude. The law simply will not step in every time there are some hurt feelings. The Restatement test is whether or not recitation of the facts to an average member of the community would arouse the member's resentment so as to lead him or her to shout "Outrageous!"

Some outrageous examples may be helpful: Harassing behavior by bill collectors, such as calling at all hours of the day and night or threatening physical harm to the debtor or his or her family; a "Peeping Tom" who watches women shower through a small hidden peephole; an insurance company's intentional refusal to pay a claim that it knows is valid and legitimate. The words or actions must be truly extreme and outrageous. It may be difficult to draw the line but common insults or petty acts or words such as giving someone "the finger" or saying "you bitch!" probably would not suffice. It should also be noted that the concept of transferred intent does not apply to this particular intentional tort.

INTENT

The defendant must have actually intended to cause the emotional distress to the plaintiff. There is a point to be made here that compares this tort with the intentional tort of assault. In the discussion of the tort of assault, the defendant must have the intent to touch the plaintiff in a harmful or offensive manner. The plaintiff must have been placed in "apprehension" of the defendant's contemplated touching. The tort of assault is complete once the element of apprehension is proved. The more severe result of emotional distress is not an element of assault. However, if the act of assault by the defendant was truly extreme and outrageous, the plaintiff may also suffer emotional distress as well as apprehension. As mentioned previously, intentional torts frequently overlap as demonstrated in the *Kmart* case in Exhibit 7-2.

CAUSATION

The traditional view of this tort is that physical injuries must result in addition to the emotional distress. The rationale of this rule is that to require otherwise would mean that a particular plaintiff could simply state they had suffered emotional distress with no real proof. The rule was put into place primarily to prevent fraudulent claims. The more modern view is that a recovery can be made without a showing of actual physical injuries. The idea is that the egregious nature of the words or conduct may speak for themselves. The trier of fact will still need to digest all of the evidence to determine whether the plaintiff likely suffered severe emotional distress. The conduct may be so severe and so extreme that it is more likely than not that a person would suffer severe emotional distress.

SEVERE EMOTIONAL DISTRESS

It is not enough that the plaintiff suffered anger, fright, or humiliation (or apprehension). There must be true emotional distress that is severe, extreme, egregious, or far out of the ordinary.

DAMAGES

Severe emotional distress in the form of actual damages , not nominal damages, are required. Nominal damages are not enough as they are for the other three intentional torts just discussed. The same compensatory damages consisting of special damages and general damages are recoverable. It is also possible that punitive/exemplary damages may be recoverable in some jurisdictions.

SEXUAL HARASSMENT

The subject of sexual harassment is not typically included in the study of torts. However, because of its similarity to the intentional torts to the person, it is prudent for the student to be provided with some exposure to the subject. The starting point is Title VII of the Civil Rights Act of 1964. Most would probably agree that this act was enacted primarily in response to this country's long and negative history concerning the issue of race. However, in the act there are other "protected classes." Section 2000e-2 (a)(1) provides that "It shall be an unlawful employment practice for an employer (1) to fail or refuse to hire or to discharge any individual or otherwise to discriminate against any individual with respect to his compensation, terms, condition, or privileges of employment because of such individual's race, color, religion, sex, or national origin."

Frankly, it is doubtful that the term "sexual harassment" was even envisioned or coined at the time of the passage of the Civil Rights Act of 1964. The term refers to two basic forms of sexual harassment in the workplace. First, it can consist of an unwelcome promise of employment rewards in exchange for sexual favors. ("If you sleep with me, you'll definitely have that promotion you want.") Second, it can consist of creating a hostile work environment. This may be, for example, the frequent, obvious, and severe conduct of posting pornographic pictures on an office billboard.

Both the victim and the harasser can be either women or men, and they can also be the same sex. There are two excellent movies portraying sexual harassment. One is *Disclosure* (1994) starring Demi Moore as the harassing supervisor and Michael Douglas as the victim. The other is *North Country* (2005), based on a true story, starring Charlize Theron who plays Lois Jenson. The movie vividly portrays

Workplace Skills Tip

In a claim of intentional infliction of emotional distress the acts or words of the defendant may be so extreme and so severe that it just "hits you in the gut" and you do want to shout "outrageous!" However, if the paralegal is involved in such a case, it is always helpful to examine the evidence and proof of the emotional distress. Lay medical witnesses can be extremely important. Assume co-workers testify that, after the outrageous incident by the defendant, the plaintiff's hands would visibly shake, the plaintiff would vomit nearly every day at work, and would take daily doses of aspirin. This would be powerful testimony, particularly if plaintiff did none of these things before the incident in question. Furthermore, treatment by a psychologist or a psychiatrist with documented symptoms in the chart would dramatically bolster such a case.

Jenson's brutal harassment from men when she went to work on the traditionally all male iron range at Eveleth Taconite Company in Eveleth, Minnesota. When sexual harassment occurs, the torts of assault, battery, false imprisonment, and intentional infliction of emotional distress may also occur.

Defenses to Intentional Torts to Person

Assuming the plaintiff brings suit for damages for assault, battery, false imprisonment, or intentional infliction of emotional distress, what defenses are available to the defendant?

CONSENT

Consent
A recognized defense to certain intentional torts to the person.

Plaintiff's **consent** to defendant's intentional tort is a defense. Plaintiff may consent expressly either orally or in writing. For example, contemplating some arm wrestling, one participant says, "Bet I can take you!" and the other person says, "Bet you can't! Let's go!" A person participating in a dangerous activity such as a boxing match or a wrestling match sponsored by a company may be required to sign a written consent relieving the company and the other participants from liability for injuries from the obvious upcoming intentional acts about to be encountered. Consent may further be implied by one's conduct. If one attends the boxing match or wrestling match as a spectator, that person is impliedly giving consent to a certain amount of touching and jostling by joining a crowd of people. When one goes to a hair stylist, there is an implied consent to the obvious touching of the hair and head.

There is no valid consent, however, if the touching goes beyond the scope of the consent given. If, for example, in the hair stylist example above, while consent is given for the parts of the body reasonably needed to be touched to complete the haircut or hairstyling, if the stylist made some sort of a sexual touching, that touching is not a touching to which consent was given. Also, consent would not be valid if given under fraud or duress. Touching a person after telling them to "Freeze!" and taking the person's wallet in a robbery with a gun pointed at the person does not amount to valid consent given to the robber. Consent will also not be valid if given by someone who is incapable of giving consent such as a minor child or a mentally incompetent person.

No doubt some students have experienced a surgical procedure. Before the surgery begins, a written consent form consenting to the contemplated surgery was likely signed. The physician and the hospital require this because it will be a defense to any later suit claiming the tort of battery. See Exhibit 7-3 for a sample medical/hospital consent form.

PRIVILEGE TO ARREST

This defense is typically raised by a law enforcement officer who has made an arrest of an individual. However, the defense may be raised by a non–law enforcement person who is making a "citizen's arrest." Law enforcement personnel typically arrest persons suspected of committing a crime. More serious crimes are called felonies. Less serious crimes are called misdemeanors. Generally, law enforcement officers are privileged to arrest individuals for a felony whether with a warrant or without a warrant. While the purpose here is not to extensively explore the subject of criminal law, our United States Supreme Court has held that if an arrest is made without a warrant, there must be reasonable grounds for the arrest.[1]

EXHIBIT 7-3 We R Surgery Institute Authorization and Consent

Surgical Procedure Consent

1. I authorize Doctor _____ and/or such assistants he/she may designate to perform on _____ the following surgical operations or
procedures _____
_____ and if any unforeseen condi-
tions or complications arise in the course of the operation calling for, in their judgment,
procedure(s) in addition to or different from those now contemplated and explained to
me, I further request and authorize them to do whatever is deemed advisable in their best
judgment.
2. I authorize the administration of such anesthesia as the physician or his/her associates
may judge necessary or desirable.
3. I authorize the transfusion of blood or blood products as the physician may judge necessary in the interest of my proper medical care.
4. I consent to the disposal by authorities of We R Surgery Institute any tissue or parts which
may be necessary to remove during such operations/procedures.
5. I authorize We R Surgery Institute to photograph, film, or videotape the operating procedure and reproduce the media as deemed necessary by the operating physician for medical, educational, and legal purposes.
6. For the purpose of advancing medical education, I consent to the participation of medical
students and/or medical residents or other health care professional students during my
stay at We R Surgery Institute.
7. I understand that I am free to cross out any paragraph to which I do not consent and that I
am free to revoke my consent.

I hereby certify that I have read and fully understand the above, why the surgery/procedure is necessary, and its advantages and possible complications. I also certify that no guarantee can be made
as to the results of this operation/procedure. I desire no further explanations for the purposes of this
consent.

Signature: _____
(patient/legal guardian)

Witness:_____

Date:_____

Time:_____

Also, as pointed out in Chapter 6, law enforcement officers are subject to liability under 42 U.S.C. Section 1983 based on depriving an individual of his or her civil rights—a Section 1983 action. It is not uncommon in such arrest cases to see other state causes of action such as gross negligence, assault, battery, false imprisonment, and intentional infliction of emotional distress alleged in addition to an alleged violation of this federal statute.[2] (See Exhibit 7-4.)

SELF-DEFENSE

Self-defense is a defense based upon a privilege. The defendant is privileged to use such physical force that is not likely to cause serious bodily injury or death. There are some limitations to the defense. The defendant must reasonably believe that he or she was about to experience an imminent harmful or offensive

Self-Defense
A privileged defense in which the defendant may use means of self-defense that are reasonably necessary to prevent or defend against the plaintiff's threatened harm to the defendant.

EXHIBIT 7-4 Relevant Case Law

Daryl J. Bennett, Plaintiff–Appellee, v. Jeremy Krakowski; Jeffrey Garrison; Alan Leveille; Joshua Urbiel; City Dearborn; James Issacs, Defendants–Appellants.

United States Court of Appeals, Sixth Circuit.

B. Factual History

On October 22, 2008, Officer Urbiel, of the Dearborn Police Department, was dispatched to 7928 Kentucky in Dearborn to respond to a possible car theft in progress. The complainant, Hassan Abdallah ("Abdallah"), reported that he had observed a 20 year-old black male with a medium build, five feet and ten inches tall, wearing a black leather hooded coat and light colored pants, attempting to enter two vehicles in the area. Abdallah reported that he observed the suspect walk south on Kentucky from Tireman and attempt to enter two vehicles, one of which was broken into the night before. Abdallah's mother also observed the suspect through the windows of her home. At one point, she pounded on her window, causing the suspect to run north on Kentucky back toward Tireman, where he met with another individual.

Officer Urbiel drove in a squad car marked "Dearborn Police Department," to the corner of Kentucky and Tireman to try to locate the suspect that Abdallah described. Officer Urbiel testified that he saw a male wearing a black-hooded coat, walking north on Tireman, with another male, Plaintiff, wearing a dark sweatshirt and dark jeans. Officer Urbiel observed the pair cross Dearborn's north border and enter Detroit. Officer Urbiel then drove around the neighborhood to try and get a better look at them. He noticed them standing in front of a house.

Officer Urbiel radioed the location of the pair to other officers, who came into the area and set up a perimeter. Corporal Garrison, Corporal Gordon Morse ("Corporal Morse"), and Officer Isaacs responded to the scene. Corporal Leveille positioned his car on the corner of Indiana and Belton to assist Officer Urbiel. Corporal Garrison, Corporal Morse, and Officer Isaacs walked down the west side of Belton and approached the house where the pair had been seen. Corporal Garrison testified that once Plaintiff and the suspect saw them, they took off running. Officer Isaacs testified that Plaintiff ignored the Officers' commands and kept running.

Defendants assert that Plaintiff led them on a foot chase for several blocks before Corporal Leveille was able to tackle him using a "bear-hold." Once Plaintiff was brought to the ground, Officer Krakowski and Officer Kostiuk attempted to help Corporal Leveille subdue him. However, they contend that Plaintiff "curled up on the ground, refusing to put his hands up." They maintain that Plaintiff then got on his hands and knees and started crawling, or attempting to crawl away. They state that Plaintiff was moving around so much and keeping his hands underneath his body, that they were prevented from handcuffing him. Officer Kostiuk asserts that he warned Plaintiff, "Dearborn Police–Stop resisting," but Plaintiff did not heed his warning.

Officer Krakowski, Officer Kostiuk, and Corporal Leveille contend that they attempted to get Plaintiff's arms out from underneath him, but could not do so. They assert that he kept trying to crawl away as they struggled to gain control of his hands. They maintain that they repeatedly told Plaintiff to stop resisting, with Officer Krakowski specifically warning Plaintiff twice, that if he did not stop resisting, he would be tasered. When he continued to resist, Officer Krakowski proceeded to taser Plaintiff in the back. Officer Krakowski, Officer Kostiuk, and Corporal Leveille assert that they still could not pull Plaintiff's arms out from underneath him at this point, and it was not until Officer Isaacs and Corporal Garrison arrived that they were able to handcuff him.

Plaintiff's version of what happened is drastically different in several respects. He states that he was "chilling outside around the porch" of a friend's house for about an hour and a half when he noticed

(Continued)

EXHIBIT 7-4 *(Continued)*

the Dearborn police car going up and down the street. At some point, he went into the backyard of the house to retrieve his iPod. He was back there about a minute before returning, at which point he saw and heard a police dog attacking his friend, Jordan Graham ("Graham"). When questioned by Defendants' counsel as to why he ran and what happened when he encountered the Officers, Plaintiff stated the following in his deposition:

Q: Why did you run?

A: Because I was scared of the dog.

Q: Was the dog loose or on a leash?

A: I don't know. I think he was on a leash or loose, I really couldn't tell.

Q: Did any police officer order you to stop running?

A: Yeah, that's when I stopped.

Q: So you started running through the Backyard to Indiana to Belton and as soon as a police officer said "stop," you stopped?

A: Yeah. I stopped and I lay down on the grass.

Q: You stopped and laid down?

A: On the ground.

Q: Did he tell you to lay down or did you just lay down?

A: I just laid down.

Q: Why did you do that?

A: I figured the police is chasing me, so I just gave up and laid down.

Q: And then what happened?

A: Then the police came and they started like kneeing me like my back and like punching me. They slammed my face to the ground and they tasered me.

Plaintiff states that he never attempted to strike, nor did he strike any of the Officers. Plaintiff further states that he did not take any aggressive actions toward them, did not have a weapon, and the Officers punched him in the back of the head. Plaintiff also states that, while he was being beaten, he heard an officer say, "we should have let the K–9 bite his ass." Plaintiff maintains that, while he was lying face down on the ground, Officer Krakowski "jumped from his vehicle" and tasered him in the back.

Plaintiff was arrested for resisting and opposing a police officer and failing to obey the lawful commands of a police officer. He was taken to the Dearborn Police Station, where he stayed overnight. He was released on bond the next day. After his release, he sought and received medical treatment. Ultimately, the charges against Plaintiff were dropped....

Defendants argue that they are entitled to summary judgment because no reasonable jury could conclude that they used excessive force against Plaintiff. Defendants contend that Plaintiff "physically prevented [them] from arresting him" and "physically prevented officers from searching him,"

(Continued)

EXHIBIT 7-4 *(Continued)*

while also "[making] repeated furtive movements with his hands ... actively resist [ing] through the entire encounter." Defendants maintain that, based on Plaintiff's behavior, they "used only the amount of force necessary to subdue and handcuff him." They assert that "until Plaintiff was handcuffed and stopped resisting, they clearly had a reason to be fearful." They further argue that the use of the taser was not excessive under the circumstances. Defendants state "[i]n direct response to Plaintiff's physical resistance and his complete refusal to comply with officers' orders and demands, Officer Krakowski resorted to a higher degree of force."

Though both Plaintiff and Defendants acknowledge that Plaintiff initially ran, Defendants fail to take into account the rest of the facts as stated by Plaintiff, such as his non-resistance, and his acquiescence to the Officers' commands that he stop. For purposes of the motion, the Officers do not credit Plaintiff's statement that he surrendered and voluntarily lay on the ground with his arms extended. In arguing that their conduct was reasonable and their use of force was not excessive, they take little, if any, account of the evidence offered by Plaintiff....

a. Assault and Battery

Defendants contend that they are entitled to summary judgment on Plaintiff's assault and battery claims for the same reasons they were entitled to summary judgment on his excessive force claim, and because of the deference they are entitled to under Michigan law. If a police officer lawfully arrests an individual, he may use reasonable force if that individual resists arrest.... However, an officer who uses excessive force may be held liable for assault and battery.... Under Michigan law, a police officer may be subject to tort liability "if the officer has utilized wanton or malicious conduct or demonstrated a reckless indifference to the common dictates of humanity."....

Plaintiff, therefore, must make a showing that the Officers' use of force was objectively unreasonable. The Officers argue that their conduct did not amount to excessive force under the deferential standard of Graham. The district court held that Plaintiff made a sufficient showing to create a genuine issue of fact, preventing the granting of summary judgment in favor of Defendants.

Plaintiff maintains that he did run initially, out of fear of the dog, but came to a stop after hearing the Officers' commands for him to do so. He testified that he then lay on the ground, with his arms extended. As indicated previously, he stated that the Officers proceeded to punch him in the head, knee him in the back, push his face into the ground, and use a taser on him while he lay on the ground. Based on this account, Plaintiff was not resisting arrest and no force was required to restrain him. Furthermore, while the Officers indicate that Plaintiff resisted, they do not maintain that Plaintiff assaulted them or took any aggressive action against their person. Further, no weapon was found on him....

Although Plaintiff's account was disputed by Defendants, it was not "blatantly contradicted" and "utterly discredited by the record," such that "no reasonable jury could believe it." ... Therefore, the district court properly concluded that there was a genuine issue of material fact with regard to whether Defendants' actions were objectively reasonable under the circumstances of the case. Thus, summary judgment was properly denied. Accordingly, this court affirms the district court's denial of summary judgment on Defendants' governmental immunity claim in regard to Plaintiff's assault and battery claims....

Source: Bennett v. Krakowski, 671 F.3d 553 (6th Cir. 2011).

touching. Defendant must utilize only those means of self-defense that were reasonably necessary to prevent or defend against the threatened harm. For example, assume plaintiff pointed a slingshot with a rock in it at the defendant. The defendant pulled a knife and stabbed the plaintiff. Arguably, defendant went beyond a reasonable means of self-defense.

There is a caveat to the rule that defendant's force must not be likely to cause serious bodily injury or death. The defendant is privileged to use such deadly force only if defendant reasonably believes that plaintiff was about to inflict serious bodily injury or death upon the defendant. If plaintiff lunges toward defendant's throat with a knife, defendant would be justified/privileged in stabbing plaintiff with defendant's own knife. If plaintiff holds a peashooter at defendant and threatens to use it, defendant would not be justified/privileged in pulling a 45 Magnum and shooting the plaintiff. With regard to the use of deadly force, there is a split of authority as to whether or not the defendant has a duty to retreat before resorting to the use of deadly force.

As has been mentioned, an intentional tort committed under the civil law system may also consist of an identical act that would be considered a crime under the criminal law system. As an aside, some states do have what are loosely referred to as "stand your ground" laws. These laws have come into the forefront with the recent shooting of Trayvon Martin, an unarmed 17-year-old, by George Zimmerman, a neighborhood watch volunteer. Zimmerman claims that he acted in self-defense when he shot Martin. The case happened in Florida, which has such a "stand your ground" law. The theory of these laws is that one has no duty to retreat from a location in which the defender has a legal right to be, such as a public place or one's own home. There is a current movement under foot now to change Florida's law to tighten it by adding a requirement that one must be in "imminent danger" before resorting to the use of deadly force.

The issue of self-defense in the intentional tort arena is judged by the reasonable person, objective standard. Assume plaintiff started out by threatening defendant with an iron pipe. Defendant disarmed plaintiff, and plaintiff then started running away. Defendant would likely lose the privilege of self-defense if defendant chased plaintiff down, tackled him, and continued to beat plaintiff with the iron pipe. In considering defendant's defense of self-defense, the jury or other fact finder will be asked to determine whether his conduct was reasonable under the circumstances. Using an objective test, under these facts, the defendant probably used excessive force and not the force needed to stop the plaintiff's pipe attack. This is particularly true when the plaintiff himself retreated after being disarmed. A jury may believe that defendant should have simply walked away as the danger was over at that point.

DEFENSE OF OTHERS

The defendant, defending against an intentional tort to the person, clearly has the defense of self-defense as discussed above. What if the defendant's defense to the plaintiff's claim is that defendant was defending a third party other than defendant? The defendant does have this privileged defense if defendant uses force to defend another person. Defendant steps into the shoes of the person the defendant was trying to protect, however. Thus, the defendant is entitled to use only the same force that the person being defended would have been able to use. Defendant cannot use greater force just because defendant is trying to protect or defend a person familiar to defendant or is nobly attempting to defend a complete stranger.

DEFENSE OF PROPERTY

As discussed above, a defendant may be privileged under the defense of self-defense to use deadly force in certain isolated, limited circumstances involving an intentional tort to one's person. However, a defendant who is defending only his real property or his personal property is not entitled to use deadly force. The privilege is to use any force that is not likely to cause serious bodily injury or death provided that (1) plaintiff's intrusion on defendant's land or use of defendant's personal property is without permission, (2) defendant reasonably believes that he or she must use force to defend against the plaintiff's unwanted intrusion, and (3) before using any force, defendant must ask the plaintiff to stop the activity or simply leave and plaintiff ignores the request. This request may not be required if such request would be obviously futile.

There are instances in which a landowner uses certain mechanical means or other means to protect his real and personal property. Examples include an electric fence a farmer may have installed to prevent individuals from stealing cattle or the use of a vicious "watch dog." There is a privilege to use such mechanical means provided the use is reasonable and necessary and an adequate warning of the means is provided or posted. The means employed by the owner cannot unleash deadly force unless the intruder is, in fact, entering to inflict serious bodily injury or death upon the owner or his or her family. Trying to prevent, for example, someone from stealing hubcaps on a car or from stealing chickens in a chicken coop does not justify means calling for serious bodily injury or death. A classic case illustrating this issue is *Katko v. Briney*, 183 N.W.2d 657 (Ia. 1971) reprinted in part in Exhibit 7-5. There, a trespassing thief convicted of larceny was allowed to recover money damages after breaking and entering an unoccupied boarded-up farmhouse for the purpose of stealing personal property in the house. A loaded spring gun was triggered causing a severe injury to his leg.

DEFENSE OF USING FORCE TO RECAPTURE CHATTELS

Chattels
Another word for personal property as opposed to real property.

This defense typically relates to the situation in which the defendant is attempting to recover **chattels** (personal property) that have been wrongfully taken or withheld. The defendant is privileged to use reasonable, nondeadly force. For the defense to be successful, defendant must establish that he or she was entitled to the property taken, a demand was made for its return, and the attempt to recapture the property was done quickly after defendant's discovery of the loss. There must also be a "hot pursuit" or a "fresh pursuit."

EXHIBIT 7-5 Relevant Case Law

Marvin Katko, Appellee, v. Edward Briney and Bertha L. Briney, Appellants.

Supreme Court of Iowa.

Action for damages resulting from injury suffered by trespassing plaintiff when he triggered a spring gun placed in uninhabited house by defendants. The Mahaska District Court, Harold Fleck, J., gave judgment for plaintiff for both actual and punitive damages, and defendants appealed. The Supreme Court, Moore, C.J., held that instructions properly stated that one may use reasonable force for protection of property but that such right is subject to qualification that one may not use such means of force as will take human life or inflict great bodily injury, that fact that trespasser may be acting in violation of law would not change the rule, and that only time when setting of a spring gun is justified would be if trespasser was committing a felony of violence or a felony punishable by death, or where trespasser was endangering human life by his act…

Affirmed.

Moore, Chief Justice.

The primary issue presented here is whether an owner may protect personal property in an unoccupied boarded-up farm house against trespassers and thieves by a spring gun capable of inflicting death or serious injury.

We are not here concerned with a man's right to protect his home and members of his family. Defendants' home was several miles from the scene of the incident to which we refer infra.

Plaintiff's action is for damages resulting from serious injury caused by a shot from a 20-gauge spring shotgun set by defendants in a bedroom of an old farm house which had been uninhabited for several years. Plaintiff and his companion, Marvin McDonough, had broken and entered the house to find and steal old bottles and dated fruit jars which they considered antiques. The jury returned a verdict for plaintiff and against defendants for $20,000 actual and $10,000 punitive damages…

II. Most of the facts are not disputed. In 1957 defendant Bertha L. Briney inherited her parents' farm land in Mahaska and Monroe Counties. Included was an 80-acre tract in southwest Mahaska County where her grandparents and parents had lived. No one occupied the house thereafter. Her husband, Edward, attempted to care for the land. He kept no farm machinery thereon. The outbuildings became dilapidated.

For about 10 years, 1957 to 1967, there occurred a series of trespassing and housebreaking events with loss of some household items, the breaking of windows and 'messing up of the property in general'. The latest occurred June 8, 1967, prior to the event on July 16, 1967 herein involved.

Defendants through the years boarded up the windows and doors in an attempt to stop the intrusions. They had posted 'no trespass' signs on the land several years before 1967. The nearest one was 35 feet from the house. On June 11, 1967 defendants set 'a shotgun trap' in the north bedroom. After Mr. Briney cleaned and oiled his 20-gauge shotgun, the power of which he was well aware, defendants took it to the old house where they secured it to an iron bed with the barrel pointed at the bedroom door. It was rigged with wire from the doorknob to the gun's trigger so it would fire when the door was opened. Briney first pointed the gun so an intruder would be hit in the stomach but at Mrs Briney's suggestion it was lowered to hit the legs. He admitted he did so 'because I was mad and tired of being tormented' but 'he did not intend to injure anyone'. He gave to explanation of why he used a loaded shell and set it to hit a person already in the house. Tin was

(Continued)

EXHIBIT 7-5 *(Continued)*

nailed over the bedroom window. The spring gun could not be seen from the outside. No warning of its presence was posted.

Plaintiff lived with his wife and worked regularly as a gasoline station attendant in Eddyville, seven miles from the old house. He had observed it for several years while hunting in the area and considered it as being abandoned. He knew it had long been uninhabited. In 1967 the area around the house was covered with high weeds. Prior to July 16, 1967 plaintiff and McDonough had been to the premises and found several old bottles and fruit jars which they took and added to their collection of antiques. On the latter date about 9:30 p.m. they made a second trip to the Briney property. They entered the old house by removing a board from a porch window which was without glass. While McDonough was looking around the kitchen area plaintiff went to another part of the house. As he started to open the north bedroom door the shotgun went off striking him in the right leg above the ankle bone. Much of his leg, including part of the tibia, was blown away. Only by McDonough's assistance was plaintiff able to get out of the house and after crawling some distance was put in his vehicle and rushed to a doctor and then to a hospital. He remained in the hospital 40 days.

Plaintiff's doctor testified he seriously considered amputation but eventually the healing process was successful. Some weeks after his release from the hospital plaintiff returned to work on crutches. He was required to keep the injured leg in a cast for approximately a year and wear a special brace for another year. He continued to suffer pain during this period.

There was undenied medical testimony plaintiff had a permanent deformity, a loss of tissue, and a shortening of the leg.

The record discloses plaintiff to trial time had incurred $710 medical expense, $2056.85 for hospital service, $61.80 for orthopedic service and $750 as loss of earnings. In addition thereto the trial court submitted to the jury the question of damages for pain and suffering and for future disability.

III. Plaintiff testified he knew he had no right to break and enter the house with intent to steal bottles and fruit jars therefrom. He further testified he had entered a plea of guilty to larceny in the nighttime of property of less than $20 value from a private building. He stated he had been fined $50 and costs and paroled during good behavior from a 60-day jail sentence. Other than minor traffic charges this was plaintiff's first brush with the law. On this civil case appeal it is not our prerogative to review the disposition made of the criminal charge against him.

IV. The main thrust of defendants' defense in the trial court and on this appeal is that 'the law permits use of a spring gun in a dwelling or warehouse for the purpose of preventing the unlawful entry of a burglar or thief'. They repeated this contention in their exceptions to the trial court's instructions 2, 5 and 6. They took no exception to the trial court's statement of the issues or to other instructions.

In the statement of issues the trial court stated plaintiff and his companion committed a felony when they broke and entered defendants' house. In instruction 2 the court referred to the early case history of the use of spring guns and stated under the law their use was prohibited except to prevent the commission of felonies of violence and where human life is in danger. The instruction included a statement breaking and entering is not a felony of violence.

Instruction 5 stated: 'You are hereby instructed that one may use reasonable force in the protection of his property, but such right is subject to the qualification that one may not use such means of

(Continued)

EXHIBIT 7-5 *(Continued)*

force as will take human life or inflict great bodily injury. Such is the rule even though the injured party is a trespasser and is in violation of the law himself.'

Instruction 6 state:'An owner of premises is prohibited from willfully or intentionally injuring a trespasser by means of force that either takes life or inflicts great bodily injury; and therefore a person owning a premise is prohibited from setting out 'spring guns' and like dangerous devices which will likely take life or inflict great bodily injury, for the purpose of harming trespassers. The fact that the trespasser may be acting in violation of the law does not change the rule. The only time when such conduct of setting a 'spring gun' or a like dangerous device is justified would be when the trespasser was committing a felony of violence or a felony punishable by death, or where the trespasser was endangering human life by his act.'

Instruction 7, to which defendants made no objection or exception, stated:'To entitle the plaintiff to recover for compensatory damages, the burden of proof is upon him to establish by a preponderance of the evidence each and all of the following propositions:

(1.)   That defendants erected a shotgun trap in a vacant house on land owned by defendant, Bertha L. Briney, on or about June 11, 1967, which fact was known only by them, to protect household goods from trespassers and thieves.
(2.)   That the force used by defendants was in excess of that force reasonably necessary and which persons are entitled to use in the protection of their property.
(3.)   That plaintiff was injured and damaged and the amount thereof.
(4.)   That plaintiff's injuries and damages resulted directly from the discharge of the shotgun trap which was set and used by defendants.'

The overwhelming weight of authority, both textbook and case law, supports the trial court's statement of the applicable principles of law.

Prosser on Torts, Third Edition, pages 116–118, states:

'…the law has always placed a higher value upon human safety than upon mere rights in property, it is the accepted rule that there is no privilege to use any force calculated to cause death or serious bodily injury to repel the threat to land or chattels, unless there is also such a threat to the defendant's personal safety as to justify a self-defense. …spring guns and other mankilling devices are not justifiable against a mere trespasser, or even a petty thief. They are privileged only against those upon whom the landowner, if he were present in person would be free to inflict injury of the same kind.' …

The legal principles stated by the trial court in instructions 2, 5 and 6 are well established and supported by the authorities cited and quoted supra. There is no merit in defendants' objections and exceptions thereto. Defendants' various motions based on the same reasons stated in exceptions to instructions were properly overruled…

Study and careful consideration of defendants' contentions on appeal reveal no reversible error.

Affirmed.

Source: Katko v. Briney, 183 N.W.2d 657 (Ia. 1971).

For example, while at the racetrack, defendant feels a person brush up against his back. He then reaches into his back pocket for his wallet. It is missing, and he sees a person running away from him with what appears to be his wallet in his hand. Defendant will have the privilege of using reasonable and nondeadly force to try to retake his wallet from the pickpocket. Assume defendant catches up with the thief, overpowers him, holds him down, and after a minute or so retakes possession of his wallet. In a later suit by the pickpocket plaintiff who claims intentional torts of assault, battery, and false imprisonment, defendant's defense of using force to reclaim his personal property will likely be successful. If, however, the defendant, after reclaiming his wallet, proceeded to beat the plaintiff or proceeded to use some type of deadly force, the privileged defense is lost.

This defense is typically raised when a suspected shoplifter sues a business for false imprisonment. A privilege commonly recognized today is what is termed the **shopkeepers' privilege**. It is a limited privilege belonging to business owners, large and small—from mom-and-pop stores to the largest chains. These shopkeepers are allowed to temporarily stop and detain people they reasonably suspect of shoplifting.

The shopkeepers' privilege does have certain requirements. First, the detention of the suspected shoplifter must be made on the store premises or in the immediate vicinity, such as in the store parking lot or on the adjacent sidewalk. Second, the shopkeeper must have a reasonable suspicion. Third, the shopkeeper may not use deadly force, only reasonable nondeadly force. Finally, the shopkeeper is allowed to detain the suspect for a short reasonable detention, and the investigation/interrogation must be accomplished in a reasonable manner. Even if the suspect turns out to be totally innocent of any wrongdoing, and there was no shoplifting, if the shopkeeper establishes these four elements, the shopkeeper will be immune from liability. As with other intentional torts, besides the tort of false imprisonment in the shoplifting scenario, it would not be uncommon for other torts to be alleged, such as assault, battery, and intentional infliction of emotional distress.

Shopkeepers' Privilege
A limited privilege belonging to business owners who are allowed to temporarily stop and detain people whom they reasonably suspect of shoplifting.

DISCIPLINE PRIVILEGE

Restatement (Second) of Torts § 147 (1965) discusses the common law **discipline privilege** granted to teachers and parents to use reasonable force for the proper discipline, control, and education of minor children. That privilege has been eroded. For an excellent discussion on corporal punishment involving a school bus driver mildly slapping a child, the student must read *Rodriguez v. Johnson*, 504 N.Y.S.2d 379 N.Y. Civ. Ct. in Exhibit 7-6. Even the slightest amount of discipline as occurred in *Rodriguez* can result in the tort of battery against a child. The student will note that this case was decided in the city civil small claims court of the state of New York. Note also that there were no attorneys involved. The plaintiff mother and the defendant bus matron appeared "*pro se*," representing themselves. Only the sum of $250 was awarded but this lowest of courts in New York produced an extremely scholarly opinion on the subject of corporal punishment.

Discipline Privilege
A privilege granted to teachers and parents to use reasonable force for the proper discipline, control, and education of minor children.

STATUTES OF LIMITATION

Just as in negligence, it is important to know the appropriate statute of limitation in the jurisdiction involved for a particular intentional tort to a person. Generally speaking, such statutes tend to be on the shorter side and can be as short as two years or even one year.

EXHIBIT 7-6 Relevant Case Law

Rodriguez v. Johnson.

Civil Court of the City of New York, New York County.

APPEARANCES OF COUNSEL

Elba Rodriguez, plaintiff *pro se.*
Janet Johnson, defendant *pro se.*

Margaret Taylor, J.

In this small claims action, plaintiff, Elba Rodriguez, as guardian of Eric Rodriguez, alleges physical abuse of her child by defendant, Janet Johnson, a school bus matron. Eric Rodriguez's demeanor established his upset and humiliation as a result of being struck, both at the time of, and subsequent to, the incident. Eric's mother testified that prior to the episode her son had looked forward to going to school and to riding the bus with Ms. Johnson. Since the incident, Eric has been apprehensive and agitated about going to school and he is afraid to ride the bus.

It appears from the testimony at trial that the children on the bus Eric was riding were being generally noisy and troublesome. Eric himself was talking loudly and moving about in his seat. The court therefore concludes that defendant acted with some provocation and did not slap Eric because of maliciousness, but rather as a result of frustration and anger. Further, the court does not find that the slap itself was an excessive use of force.

THE HISTORY OF CORPORAL PUNISHMENT

The court finds, however, that the physical assault of children, regardless of the degree, cannot be legally countenanced. Presently the common-law tort of battery protects all adults from unauthorized physical contact. Historically, however, only men moved about freely without fear of physical intimidation, harassment or reprisal. Women and children, on the other hand, were viewed as the property of husbands and fathers. As chattel, they were not entitled to freedom from bodily harm. Under early common law husbands could chastise their wives providing they did not do so in an unusually cruel or violent manner. Such punishment was considered necessary to control a wife's behavior. Indeed, only during the past 15 years have there been significant changes in both the public perception of, and the legal system's response to, abuse of wives by husbands. Notably, the written law which once condoned the batterer's actions now condemns them…

Children have also historically been the victims of approved violence. "Stubborn child laws", which prescribed the death penalty for disobedient children, were at one time contained in the statutes of Massachusetts and Connecticut. Severe beatings were often justified by the need to teach children obedience. Similarly, men justified the sexual harassment of children with references to their inherently provocative nature. To quote one noted historian, " '[t]he history of childhood is a nightmare from which we have only recently begun to awaken. The further back in history one goes, the lower the level of child care, and the more likely children are to be killed, abandoned, beaten, terrorized, and sexually abused'."…

Under the common law, teachers stood in loco parentis to their students. This doctrine authorized the teacher to use whatever force the parent could use to restrain and correct a child.

Thus, the right to physically assault a child extended beyond the child's natural parents; a teacher could use corporal punishment to discipline a child and such punishment did not give rise to a cause of action for damages. Only in the most extreme cases could the teacher be held at all liable…

(Continued)

EXHIBIT 7-6 *(Continued)*

Today, since public education is mandatory, the doctrine of in loco parentis is declining both in importance and acceptance. Nonetheless corporal punishment continues as States begin to propose that they themselves may inflict such punishment as is reasonably necessary for educating and disciplining children. Therefore, the court finds it unnecessary to consider the issues raised by corporal punishment inflicted by parents…

Clearly, society's views of violence against women and children have shifted dramatically. Child abuse is a problem of growing concern. As recognition of children's vulnerability has heightened, penalties for abusive parents have harshened. Corporal punishment by educators, however, has remained an exception to this general trend and this must change…

THE PSYCHOLOGICAL AND PHYSICAL RISKS

Physical violence should never be invoked, least of all against children who are so seriously harmed by it. Studies have consistently shown that not only do children themselves suffer when they are physically violated, but they often respond by being physically abusive to those weaker than themselves. Children justifiably sense a great deal of unfairness in the allocation of corporal punishment. As in this case, it is most often the weaker, misbehaving child who is struck, not the stronger, more powerful and equally ill-behaved one.

Sanctioning *any* degree of corporal punishment can also heighten the risk of serious child abuse by those in positions of authority. Children's emotional dependence on adults makes them especially vulnerable to such abuse, particularly if they are unable to determine when "permissible" physical punishment becomes impermissibly excessive…

While some States today have adopted the common-law approach and have permitted the use of such force as a teacher or administrator reasonably believes to be necessary for the child's proper control and education. The inherent dangers in even the most seemingly reasonable corporal punishment have caused a number of States to prohibit it in all forms. The Legislature of this State has remained silent by neither expressly privileging nor prohibiting the physical assault of children by school personnel. Dicta to the contrary aside, this court finds no value in continuing the practice of corporal punishment out of deference to its historical acceptance. Indeed, only by abandoning past attitudes regarding women, children and minorities has our society been able to progress and become more civilized. Abolishing corporal punishment is another step on this road to a more humane Nation…

It is time for the civil law to recognize that children are entitled to equal protection. The tort of battery, which once protected only the bodily integrity of men, must now protect all persons, be they adults or children, from unauthorized physical contact. Physical abuse in even the slightest degree seriously harms children. It is not only immoral and unethical, but also unfair and unjust and therefore intrinsically illegal. It is most appropriate to consider such abuse as the tort of battery. Any person who physically assaults a child for any reason other than self-defense or the defense of others is liable to that child for monetary damages.

Accordingly, judgment is awarded in the amount of $250 to the mother, Elba Rodriguez, on behalf of the claimant child plus costs and disbursements.

Source: Rodriguez v. Johnson, 132 Misc.2d 555 (Civ. Ct. N.Y. 1986).

TORT IMMUNITY

As pointed out in Chapter 6, the same immunities discussed there apply to all torts, including intentional torts discussed in this chapter. These immunities are sovereign immunity, charitable immunity, and family immunity.

CASE **7.1** Hypothetical Case: Developing Workplace Skills

You are a new paralegal in a plaintiff's personal injury firm. You just received an e-mail assignment from one of the junior shareholders in the firm:

We represent Abagail Jones, a 21-year-old recent college graduate. Her father is a golfing buddy of mine. Our firm is contemplating suing Barney's Discount Jewelry, Inc. and the owner Barney Olson. The suit is for damages for false imprisonment arising out of an incident that occurred exactly two months ago. Abagail tells me she had been shopping at Barney's for a gift for her boyfriend. She was in the store for approximately 15 minutes looking around but didn't find anything. She left the store, and that's when things became interesting. The owner of the store, Barney, stopped her and accused her of taking a bracelet that was in her purse. As it turned out, I have learned that some unknown teenage kid was in the store at the same time she was. He grabbed the bracelet and, as a prank, put it in Abagail's purse, which she had placed on the floor beside her as she was looking at some jewelry. Apparently Barney saw this happen and thought Abagail and the kid were in cahoots with each other.

As she was outside on the sidewalk in front of the store, she heard a voice loudly and firmly state, "Excuse me young lady, please stop right where you are!" She then turned around, and it was the store owner, Barney. She said he politely grabbed her by her arm and grabbed her purse. He then looked into her purse, saw the bracelet, and said, "Where did you get this?" as he reached in to retrieve the bracelet. She said he was very upset and kept going on and on for approximately twenty minutes about the evils of shoplifting, how much money he had lost over the years, how he had four kids and a wife to support, and how hard he had worked to build up his business. Abagail said that Barney was not abusive to her, but he just seemed genuinely upset.

You have handled these cases before and you know our jurisdiction has adopted the shopkeeper's privilege by statute which provides in pertinent part:

(a) A merchant, or his agent or employee, with reasonable cause, may detain **on the premises** in a reasonable manner and for a reasonable time any person suspected of shoplifting. (Emphasis added.)

I have not taken Barney's deposition yet, but we know he will be relying on the shopkeeper's privilege as his main defense. He may well have had reasonable cause to detain Abagail. There will likely be a fact issue as to whether or not his detention of her was done in a reasonable manner and for a reasonable length of time. My experience is that he will likely have a different story as to what he said and did and how long it took, all of which will try to place him in a good light in front of the jury. For me, the main issue is the language in the statute that requires the detention to be "**on the premises**." If the detention was not done on the premises, this statute will not apply, and Barney cannot avail himself of the shopkeeper's privilege. I checked the statute, and there is no definition of "premises." We know this happened outside the store on the sidewalk. Did he detain Abagail on the premises? I am not aware of any case law in our state that has interpreted this language. Please do some research in our jurisdiction as well as any other jurisdiction to see if we have a good argument that outside on the sidewalk is not a detention "on the premises." Bill your time to the above file, RNJ2247-12.

"You wouldn't understand, Judge, it's a Mafia thing."

CHAPTER **SUMMARY**

Tort liability in this chapter is based on torts that are intentional. Battery is an intentional tort to the person in which the defendant commits an act toward the plaintiff with the intent of producing a harmful or offensive touching to the plaintiff's person. The act must be some voluntary, volitional movement of the defendant's body. The intent required is that the defendant either had the actual desire to inflict the harmful or offensive touching or believed that such a touching was reasonably certain to occur.

In the tort of battery, the defendant's intent may be transferred. For example, if A intended to strike B with his fist but missed and struck C, a bystander, then A will be liable for the battery to C. The touching in battery may either be harmful or offensive. A harmful touching is, as the name implies, any touching that causes, as examples, pain, suffering, anguish, impairment, disfigurement, or disability to the plaintiff. The touching may be to the plaintiff's person or to an instrumentality closely associated with the plaintiff. Kicking a chair upon which the plaintiff is sitting is still a battery to the plaintiff.

For the tort of battery and any other tort, plaintiff must also prove causation and damages. Causation in the intentional tort setting is not a causation in which the result must be reasonably foreseeable. The defendant is simply responsible for all consequences of the intentional act that are set in motion by the defendant.

The intentional tort of assault requires an act by the defendant with the intent to cause apprehension on the part of the plaintiff. Words alone are not legally sufficient to create this tort. There must be some type of voluntary movement of some part of the defendant's body—besides the words—that would indicate the act is about to be carried out. The key element for this tort is the element of "apprehension." Plaintiff must be aware of the assault, and it must be an apprehension about an "imminent" touching to the plaintiff's body—not to some other person.

False imprisonment is an intentional act of the defendant that results in the confinement of the plaintiff. Words alone may be sufficient. It is a requirement that the plaintiff is confined within boundaries fixed by the defendant for a certain period of time, even if it is a brief amount of time. It is also a requirement that the plaintiff has no knowledge of a reasonable means of escape.

Intentional infliction of emotional distress is an intentional tort in which the defendant uses extreme and outrageous words or conduct with the intent of causing severe emotional distress in the plaintiff. The words or acts must exceed all bounds or limits of decent behavior. Insulting or petty rudeness will not suffice. The common law rule is that there must be some accompanying physical injuries along with the emotional distress. The rule was put into place to prevent fraudulent claims. Some courts have abandoned that principle in favor of a more modern rule that emotional distress alone is sufficient. The burden is still upon the plaintiff to show that the conduct was so severe and so outrageous that it is likely emotional distress would result. The emotional distress must be caused by the defendant's words or actions.

There are certain defenses to the intentional torts to the person. The first defense is consent. Consent may be given expressly either orally or in writing. Consent may be given by implied conduct. Consent is not valid, however, if the scope of the consent is exceeded. Consent is not valid if given by fraud or under duress. Consent is also not valid if given by someone legally incapable of giving consent, such as a minor child or a mentally incompetent person.

There are defenses based upon privilege or immunity. For example, a law enforcement officer has certain privileges and immunities from a civil tort action if the officer is performing actions within the scope of his or her law enforcement duties, such as making a lawful arrest. Even a private citizen may be afforded immunity in making a citizen's arrest.

Self-defense is a defense in which the defendant is privileged to use such physical force that is not likely to cause serious bodily injury or death. Defendant must utilize only those means of self-defense that are reasonably necessary to prevent or defend against the threatened harm. If, however, defendant reasonably believes that he or she is in danger of serious bodily injury or death, defendant may use deadly force. The issue of self-defense is judged by the reasonable person standard. Was the defendant's conduct reasonable under the circumstances or did defendant exceed his or her privilege of self-defense and become the aggressor?

A defense available to the defendant is that he or she was defending some other person. The defendant may use reasonable force to defend another person, either one the defendant knows or a complete stranger. However, defendant steps into the shoes of the person being defended. The defendant is entitled to use only that same force the person being defended would have been able to use.

A defendant may use force to defend his or her property. However, defendant is not entitled to use deadly force to protect his or her property. Defendant may use reasonable force not likely to cause death or serious bodily injury if certain conditions are met: (1) plaintiff's intrusion on the property is without permission; (2) defendant reasonably believes he or she must use force to defend the property; and (3) defendant must ask the plaintiff to cease the activity and plaintiff ignores the request. Sometimes mechanical means are used by a landowner to protect property. This may be in the nature of a spring gun, dynamite, or an electric fence. The means employed cannot unleash deadly force unless the intruder is, in fact, entering to inflict serious bodily injury or death to the owner or his family.

A defense is available to a defendant to use force to recover or recapture chattels (personal property). The defendant may use reasonable, nondeadly force. The defendant must establish that he or she was entitled to the property wrongfully taken, a demand was made for its return, and the attempted recovery was made in "fresh pursuit." This defense is typically utilized by a business owner who detains a customer suspected of shoplifting. In that situation, there is a privilege that is termed the "shopkeepers' privilege."

There is a privileged defense to discipline that is given to teachers and parents. This is a privilege to use reasonable force for the proper discipline, control, and education of minor children. The privilege is being eroded in the schools where corporal punishment has become frowned upon. Even the slightest amount of discipline to a school child may result in a battery to the child.

Finally, just as in the tort of negligence, the defense of a statute of limitation is available to the defendant. In these types of intentional torts, the statutes of limitation are typically short such as two years or even one year. The same immunities apply for intentional torts that apply to all other torts, namely, sovereign immunity, charitable immunity, and family immunity.

KEY **TERMS**

Battery	Assault	Self-Defense
Transferred Intent	False Imprisonment	Chattels
Harmful Touching	Intentional Infliction of Emotional Distress	Shopkeepers' Privilege
Offensive Touching	Consent	Discipline Privilege

REVIEW **QUESTIONS**

1. In the tort of battery, the doctrine of "transferred intent" was discussed. In reviewing the purposes of tort law from Chapter 1, what purpose or purposes does this doctrine accomplish?

2. Larry is slowly driving down the street in his convertible with the top down. Behind a bush nearby is Slim who throws a rock the size of a baseball intending to hit Larry. Slim is a former semi-pro baseball pitcher who could easily throw a baseball 100 miles per hour. Larry doesn't see Slim but hears a thunderous noise as the rock hits the windshield and cracks and breaks it. Larry later learns it was Slim who threw the rock and broke the windshield. Larry sues Slim for (1) assault and (2) battery. Will Larry prevail on his claims? Why or why not?

3. Slim's rock bounces off the windshield, hits a tree, bounces off the tree, and falls, breaking a glass coffee cup held by Monica who is standing underneath the tree. The breakage of the cup causes a cut to her hand. Monica sues Slim for battery. Slim's defense is "I intended to hit Larry not you. You don't have a case." Does she? Why or why not? Does Slim have any other potential defense? What might it be?

4. Matilda is a spry, alert, little old lady who is 91 years old and an avid pro football fan. She spots a pro football player known, affectionately, as "The Crusher" sitting in a local restaurant where she is having lunch. This is the same 6' 2", 300-pound lineman who tackled the quarterback of her favorite pro team resulting in the sidelining of the quarterback. Matilda leaves her seat and marches up to The Crusher who is eating his meal. Startled, he looks up as she raises her umbrella as if to strike him and says, "I'll show you what happens to players who play dirty." The Crusher winces at first when the umbrella is raised, but then starts to rise from his chair. Matilda then turns around and returns to her seat. The Crusher later sues Matilda for assault. Matilda laughs and says, "That's ridiculous. He's 300 pounds and a professional football player. I'm a 91-year-old woman who weighs barely 100 pounds. He wasn't afraid of me, and he could have easily overpowered me even if I did only threaten to hit him, which I wish to Hell now I would have." Is she right in her assessment of the case? Why or why not? Does The Crusher have a case against Matilda for assault? Why or why not? What is the key element of assault that you would expect to be most hotly contested?

5. Suspecting a theft from the cash register in Roderick's Bar and Grille, Roderick Galarzak, a nasty, burly man who is the owner, calls the two bartenders, Lisa and Ingrid, up to his office. His office is two flights up some stairs and is a small room 12' × 12' with one window looking down onto the street. The building is an old seven-story building built in the 1920s with a dilapidated outside fire escape alongside the building from the top floor to the ground floor. In his office are Roderick's desk, and his chair, and two other chairs. He tells the two women, "Alright ladies, I've been missing about a hundred bucks each day for the last two weeks. You two are the only two who could have taken it. I want to know which one of you did it." Both deny taking the money. "OK, if that's the way you want it," Roderick says, "you're both staying in this office until one of you decides to come clean!" With that he leaves the room and locks the door. Both women are locked

in the office for approximately 15 minutes, after which Roderick comes back to let them out, thinking this probably wasn't such a great idea. Neither confesses, and he apologizes and lets both of them leave. The two women, Lisa and Ingrid, later bring a suit against Roderick for false imprisonment. Will they win? Why or why not? What's Roderick's defense?

6. Oliver, a handyman who likes to tinker with model airplanes, has been expecting a part for one of his planes from Aviation Hobby Sports, Inc. He has called several times and no one seems to know what is going on. In frustration, and after waiting several weeks beyond when the part should have arrived, he calls the company again. He spends the first five minutes trying to figure out their new voice menu and which extension he should even dial. After three mistaken transfers to the wrong people, he finally reaches Waldo in the parts department. Waldo is new and is not familiar with the system for locating an account or an order. Oliver is steaming by now. Finally Waldo says, "I'm sorry, sir, but I just can't seem to find your order. Would you mind calling back tomorrow?" Oliver, now red-faced and boiling over, screams into the phone, "You stupid sonofabitch! You don't know Jack Shit! You loser! You moron! I'm done with this company right now, and I'm going to see that you are fired!" Oliver hangs up. Waldo, a high-strung, sensitive individual is devastated by the comments and sues Oliver for intentional infliction of emotional distress. Does he have a case? Why or why not?

chapter 8
TORTS TO PROPERTY

"Property is the fruit of labor; property is desirable; it is a positive good in the world."

Abraham Lincoln

Introduction

There are two main torts involving land/real property—trespass and nuisance. Both will be discussed in this chapter. At common law, trespass is predicated on an intentional tort theory. Nuisance may actually be predicated on mixed theories of negligence, intention, or strict liability. However, because both torts involve a tort to one's real property, they will be discussed together. The student will soon realize that while they are two separate legal theories, the lines between the two torts sometimes blur and the two torts tend to overlap.

Trespass to Land

The elements of a **trespass to land** are the following:

1. An act by the defendant
2. Intent on the part of the defendant
3. An intrusion/entry upon the land
4. The plaintiff is in possession of the land or has the right to immediate possession
5. Causation

AN ACT BY THE DEFENDANT

Trespass is an intentional tort. Just as in the intentional tort of battery there must be an external manifestation of the defendant's will. There must be some volitional movement that results in an intrusion upon the land of another. The act may not be done while unconscious and

LEARNING OBJECTIVES

After studying this chapter, you should be able to:

- Identify and analyze the tort of trespass to real property.

- Identify and analyze the tort of nuisance and differentiate it from trespass.

- Identify and analyze the tort of trespass to chattels.

- Identify and analyze the tort of conversion and differentiate it from trespass to chattels.

- Recognize the defenses to trespass to real property, nuisance, trespass to chattels, and conversion.

Trespass to Land
An intentional tort consisting of an intrusion upon the land of another without consent or privilege to do so.

the act may not be reflexive. If a person committed an act while having a seizure or suffering a stroke, such act is not a volitional act manifesting the defendant's will. Assume defendant, while driving an automobile, suffers a heart attack, loses momentary consciousness, and the automobile swerves onto plaintiff's land. There is no trespass because the first element of a volitional act has not been established.

INTENT ON THE PART OF THE DEFENDANT

The defendant must have intended to commit the act resulting in the intrusion upon the plaintiff's land. The defendant must have intended to do the act that causes the intrusion onto the land, or defendant must have known with substantial certainty that his or her act would produce the intrusion onto the land. The intent is simply to enter the land. The intent is not that defendant knows or should have known that he or she was not entitled to enter. Even if the defendant may have even entered mistakenly, thinking that he or she is the owner of the land, the defendant has still committed a trespass. If defendant fires a rifle in the direction of the plaintiff's land, though not aiming at any particular target there, he or she knows with substantial certainty that the bullet will intrude upon the plaintiff's land. The doctrine of transferred intent also applies to the intentional tort of trespass.

AN INTRUSION UPON THE LAND

The defendant's entry or intrusion upon the plaintiff's land may be by the defendant making a personal entry upon the land. The entry or intrusion may also occur by defendant causing some other person, animal, or object to intrude upon the land. For example, defendant erects a roadblock on a pedestrian path with a sign stating "Keep Right." This intentional act causes another person or persons to intrude upon plaintiff's land. Defendant chops down a large tree, which falls on plaintiff's land. Defendant blasts with dynamite causing rocks and boulders to fall upon plaintiff's land. These two intentional acts have caused objects to intrude upon plaintiff's land. The blasting with dynamite example may also provide an additional cause of action for trespass based upon strict liability, which will be discussed in the next chapter.

Workplace Skills Tip

Develop the habit of using proper legal terminology. Unless a particular statute, rule, or court decision in a jurisdiction states otherwise, generally, one "files" documents such as a pleading, a motion, a brief, or other legal document with the appropriate court official. In federal court it is the "Clerk of Court." Depending upon the state jurisdiction, this official may be referred to with titles such as "Clerk of Court" or "Court Administrator." On the other hand, one "records" documents such as a deed, a mortgage, or a satisfaction of a mortgage with the appropriate official. Depending upon the state jurisdiction, this official may be referred to with titles such as "Register of Deeds," "Recorder," or "Registrar."

THE PLAINTIFF IS IN POSSESSION OF THE LAND OR HAS THE RIGHT TO IMMEDIATE POSSESSION

Plaintiff must be in possession of the land or have the right to immediate possession. An owner of land who is occupying the land is currently in possession of the land. However, the plaintiff may be someone other than the owner. A tenant or lessee of a property who is renting or leasing the owner's land may have a right to bring suit on the theory of trespass. Dick, the owner of a farm, rents his farm to Jan. Jan plants a crop of soybeans. Ted and Pat, neighbors of Dick, start a bonfire on their land near the property line in order to burn some garbage and even hazardous waste. Some of the material explodes and lands on Dick's land. In addition, the wind carries some of the visible, tangible toxic pieces of waste onto Dick's land. The deposit of these tangible materials causes crop loss to Jan. Jan, as the tenant, has a right of trespass against Ted and Pat. In this example, however, if tangible particles settled in a small lake on Dick's land and polluted the lake, Dick would also have a right of trespass for damage to the lake in addition to Jan's trespass claim for damage to her crops.

Another issue concerning this element of trespass relates to how far the right to possession extends. How high above the land (airspace), for example, does the right to be protected from a trespass extend? How much of the airspace above the land is protected? A landowner does have a right to have his or her airspace protected to some reasonable level. The U.S. Supreme Court has held that the rights of a landowner to the airspace above the land are violated when flights into the "immediate reaches" of the airspace substantially interfere with the landowner's use of the land.[1] "Immediate reaches" was not defined. The Federal Aviation Administration has regulations stating that "except when necessary for takeoff or landing," flights are prohibited below 500 feet of a person or structure.[2]

Any student who has ever flown in or out of John Wayne Airport (perhaps for a trip to Anaheim to Disneyland) knows that there are significant restrictions on commercial flights in order to decrease the noise level to the local community surrounding the airport. After takeoff in certain directions, there will be an abrupt and noticeable power reduction for a short time as the plane passes over the residential area. This airport is not typical. It is very small. It has the shortest main runway of any major airport in the United States, and it is sandwiched between highways and densely packed neighborhoods. There are noise-monitoring stations on the airfield with fines and penalties for violations. The important point is that for the tort of trespass to occur, it is not just an intrusion upon the land itself that is entitled to protection. Some airspace above the land is also entitled to protection.

CAUSATION

This element was discussed under causation for the intentional tort of battery. The causation required is not proximate causation as discussed in the tort of negligence. Rather the intrusion to the land must be caused by defendant's intentional act or by some force set in motion by defendant's act. The defendant's intentional act does not need to be the proximate cause of the damage. For example, a deer hunter is trespassing on plaintiff's land. The hunter intentionally fires a shot at a deer and misses. The shell hits a steel wall on the land, ricochets off, and strikes a propane tank some distance away causing an explosion and fire to a nearby building. Causation is established for the intentional tort of trespass even though this resulting fire is probably remote and unforeseeable for a negligent act. Foreseeable or not, defendant's intentional act set forces in motion that caused ultimate damage. If the hunter were on his or her own land, and negligently fired a shell onto the plaintiff's land causing the same unforeseeable fire, the defendant would likely be excused from liability for negligence under a proximate cause requirement.

DAMAGES

The student should note that this was not an element listed above for the tort of trespass. This is because it does not matter whether or not any actual damages were caused by the defendant's trespass.[3] Courts are generally protective of real property rights. The general rule is that once a trespass has occurred, defendant is liable, period. Defendant must pay nominal damages at a bare minimum. (See Chapter 4.) The student must read the case of *Bradley v. American Smelting and Refining Company*, 709 P.2d 782 (Wash. 1985) in Exhibit 8-1. The court in *Bradley* held that plaintiff was still required to prove actual damages in an environmental case based upon both trespass and nuisance. This case also illustrates the author's point at the beginning of the chapter that the lines between trespass and nuisance tend to blur.

To illustrate again the courts' favorable policy toward an owner's property rights, besides compensatory damages, depending upon the jurisdiction, punitive damages may be allowed. Further, with the tort of trespass the plaintiff may seek equitable relief in the form of an **injunction**. An injunction is a form of equitable relief in which the court is asked to put a halt to the defendant's wrongful act, in this case, the act of trespassing.

The student may legitimately wonder why courts are so protective of land/real property rights. It is because a trespasser's adverse intrusions can, with time, create actual ownership rights to the land or rights to use the land. Real property law is beyond the scope of this textbook. However, there is a doctrine in property law called "adverse possession" and "prescription" in which the defendant's adverse use and actual trespass of land, if continuous for a set period of time, can result in defendant becoming the owner of the land or acquiring certain rights to use that land. **Adverse possession** is a method of acquiring title to real property by the actual, open, adverse, and continuous possession of it to the exclusion of the owner for the period of time prescribed by state law. An easement is the right to use another's property. One way to acquire an easement is by prescription. An easement by **prescription** is created by the adverse, open, obvious, and continuous use of another's property for a prescribed period of time after which it ripens into a permanent right to use the property.

That set period of time typically created by state statute is, in essence, a statute of limitation. This means that a trespass action must be brought by the owner or the one in possession within that time period or the trespasser will acquire the land or rights in the land. For example, assume that A owned some land that was close to a park. Assume the general public became accustomed to walking across the end portion of A's land as it provided a shortcut to a public park. Assume that the general public continued to walk across that end portion even after A erected "no trespassing" signs. The jurisdiction's statute may state that adverse, open, continuous use of another's real property for a period of 15 years will create an easement (a lawful right to use a portion of another's property) by prescription (adverse use for a certain length of time). Therefore, an owner of property with precious property rights must not sit on his or her hands but must act within the prescribed time period or that owner runs the risk of losing the property itself or the right to use certain portions of it solely as his or her own.

Injunction
A form of equitable relief in which the court is asked to put a halt to the defendant's wrongful act.

Adverse Possession
A method of acquiring title to real property by the actual, open, adverse, and continuous possession of it to the exclusion of the owner for the prescribed period of time prescribed by state law.

Prescription
A way of acquiring an easement by the adverse, open, obvious, and continuous use of another's property for a prescribed period of time after which it ripens into a permanent right to use the property.

EXHIBIT 8-1 Relevant Case Law

A. Bradley, husband and wife, Plaintiffs, v. American Smelting and Refining Company, a New Jersey corporation doing business in Washington, Defendant.

Supreme Court of Washington, En Banc.

Landowner sued for damages in trespass and nuisance from deposit of microscopic airborne particles from copper smelter in King County Superior Court, and case was removed to United States District Court. Upon plaintiff's motion for summary judgment on issue of liability for trespass, issues were certified to Supreme Court....

Callow, Justice.

The parties have stipulated to the facts as follows: Plaintiffs Michael O. Bradley and Marie A. Bradley, husband and wife, are owners and occupiers of real property on the southern end of Vashon Island in King County, Washington. The Bradleys purchased their property in 1978. Defendant ASARCO, a New Jersey corporation doing business in Washington, operates a primary copper smelter on real property it owns in Rushton, which is an incorporated municipality surrounded by the city of Tacoma, Washington.

On October 3, 1983, plaintiffs brought this action against defendant alleging a cause of action for intentional trespass and for nuisance.

Plaintiffs' property is located some 4 miles north of defendant's smelter. Defendant's primary copper smelter (also referred to as the Tacoma smelter), has operated in its present location since 1890. It has operated as a copper smelter since 1902, and in 1905 it was purchased and operated by a corporate entity which is now ASARCO. As a part of the industrial process of smelting copper at the Tacoma smelter, various gases such as sulfur dioxide and particulate matter, including arsenic, cadmium and other metals, are emitted. Particulate matter is composed of distinct particles of matter other than water, which cannot be detected by the human senses....

As a part of defendant's smelting process, the Tacoma smelter emits into the atmosphere gases and particulate matter. For the purposes of resolving the certified questions, the parties stipulate that some particulate emissions of both cadmium and arsenic from the Tacoma smelter have been and are continuing to be deposited on plaintiffs' land. Defendant ASARCO has been aware since it took over operation of the Tacoma smelter in 1905 that the wind does, on occasion, cause smelter particulate emissions to blow over Vashon Island where plaintiffs' land is located....

The issues present the conflict in an industrial society between the need of all for the production of goods and the desire of the landowner near the manufacturing plant producing those goods that his use and enjoyment of his land not be diminished by the unpleasant side effects of the manufacturing process. A reconciliation must be found between the interest of the many who are unaffected by the possible poisoning and the few who may be affected.

1. Did the defendant have the requisite intent to commit intentional trespass as a matter of law?

The parties stipulated that as a part of the smelting process, particulate matter including arsenic and cadmium was emitted, that some of the emissions had been deposited on the plaintiffs' land and that the defendant has been aware since 1905 that the wind, on occasion, caused these emissions to be blown over the plaintiffs' land. The defendant cannot and does not deny that whenever the smelter was in operation the whim of the winds could bring these deleterious substances to the plaintiffs' premises. We are asked if the defendant, knowing what it had to know from the facts it admits, had the legal intent to commit trespass.

(Continued)

EXHIBIT 8-1 *(Continued)*

The Restatement (Second) of Torts § 158 (1965) states:

One is subject to liability to another for trespass, irrespective of whether he thereby causes harm to any legally protected interest of the other, if he intentionally

(a) enters land in the possession of the other, or causes a thing or a third person to do so, or
(b) remains on the land, or
(c) fails to remove from the land a thing which he is under a duty to remove.

In the comment on Clause (a) of § 158 at 278 it is stated in part:

i. *Causing entry of a thing.* The actor, without himself entering the land, may invade another's interest in its exclusive possession by throwing, propelling, or placing a thing, either on or beneath the surface of the land or in the air space above it. Thus, in the absence of the possessor's consent or other privilege to do so, it is an actionable trespass to throw rubbish on another's land … In order that there may be a trespass under the rule stated in this Section, it is not necessary that the foreign matter should be thrown directly and immediately upon the other's land. It is enough that an act is done with knowledge that it will to a substantial certainty result in the entry of the foreign matter.

Addressing the definition, scope and meaning of "intent", section 8A of the Restatement (Second) of Torts says:

The word "intent" is used … to denote that the actor desires to cause consequences of his act, or that he believes that the consequences are substantially certain to result from it . . . .

The defendant has known for decades that sulfur dioxide and particulates of arsenic, cadmium and other metals were being emitted from the tall smokestack. It had to know that the solids propelled into the air by the warm gases would settle back to earth somewhere. It had to know that a purpose of the tall stack was to disperse the gas, smoke and minute solids over as large an area as possible and as far away as possible, but that while any resulting contamination would be diminished as to any one area or landowner, that nonetheless contamination, though slight, would follow . . . .

We find that the defendant had the requisite intent to commit intentional trespass as a matter of law.

2. Does an intentional deposit of microscopic particulates, undetectable by the human senses, upon a person's property give rise to a cause of action for trespassory invasion of the person's right to exclusive possession of property as well as a claim of nuisance?

The courts have been groping for a reconciliation of the doctrines of trespass and nuisance over a long period of time and, to a great extent, have concluded that little of substance remains to any distinction between the two when air pollution is involved . . . .

It is also true that in the environmental arena both nuisance and trespass cases typically involve intentional conduct by the defendant who knows that his activities are substantially certain to result in an invasion of plaintiff's interests. The principal difference in theories is that the tort of trespass is complete upon a tangible invasion of plaintiff's property, however slight, whereas a nuisance requires proof that the interference with use and enjoyment is "substantial and unreasonable." This burden of proof advantage in a trespass case is accompanied by a slight remedial advantage as well. Upon proof of a technical trespass plaintiff always is entitled to nominal damages. It is possible also that a plaintiff could get injunctive relief against a technical trespass—for example, the deposit of particles of air pollutant on his property causing no known adverse effects. The protection of the integrity of his

(Continued)

EXHIBIT 8-1 *(Continued)*

possessory interests might justify the injunction even without proof of the substantial injury necessary to establish a nuisance. Of course absent proof of injury, or at least a reasonable suspicion of it, courts are unlikely to invoke their equitable powers to require expensive control efforts.....

Just as there may be proof advantages in a trespass theory, there may be disadvantages also. Potential problems lurk in the ancient requirements that a trespassory invasion be "direct or immediate" and that an "object" or "something tangible" be deposited upon plaintiff's land. Some courts hold that if an intervening force, such as wind or water, carries the pollutants onto the plaintiff's land, then the entry is not "direct." Others define "object" as requiring something larger or more substantial than smoke, dust, gas, or fumes.

Both of these concepts are nonsensical barriers, although the courts are slow to admit it. The requirement that the invasion be "direct" is a holdover from the forms of action, and is repudiated by contemporary science of causation. Atmospheric or hydrologic systems assure that pollutants deposited in one place will end up somewhere else, with no less assurance of causation than the blaster who watches the debris rise from his property and settle on his neighbor's land. Trespassory consequences today may be no less "direct" even if the mechanism of delivery is viewed as more complex....

The view recognizing a trespassory invasion where there is no 'thing' which can be seen with the naked eye undoubtedly runs counter to the definition of trespass expressed in some quarters. [Citing the Restatement (First), Torts and Prosser]. It is quite possible that in an earlier day when science had not yet peered into the molecular and atomic world of small particles, the courts could not fit an invasion through unseen physical instrumentalities into the requirement that a trespass can result only from a direct invasion. But in this atomic age even the uneducated know the great and awful force contained in the atom and what it can do to a man's property if it is released. In fact, the now famous equation $E = MC^2$ has taught us that mass and energy are equivalents and that our concept of 'things' must be reframed. If these observations on science in relation to the law of trespass should appear theoretical and unreal in the abstract, they become very practical and real to the possessor of land when the unseen force cracks the foundation of his house. The force is just as real if it is chemical in nature and must be awakened by the intervention of another agency before it does harm....

The same conduct on the part of a defendant may and often does result in the actionable invasion of both of these interests, in which case the choice between the two remedies is, in most cases, a matter of little consequence. Where the action is brought on the theory of nuisance alone the court ordinarily is not called upon to determine whether the conduct would also result in a trespassory invasion. In such cases the courts' treatment of the invasion solely in terms of the law of nuisance does not mean that the same conduct could not also be regarded as a trespass. Some of the cases relied upon by the defendant are of this type; cases in which the court holds that the interference with the plaintiff's possession through soot, dirt, smoke, cinders, ashes and similar substances constitute a nuisance, but where the court does not discuss the applicability of the law of trespass to the same set of facts.

However, there are cases which have held that the defendant's interference with plaintiff's possession resulting from the settling upon his land of effluents emanating from defendant's operations is exclusively nontrespassory. Although in such cases the separate particles which collectively cause the invasion are minute, the deposit of each of the particles constitutes a physical intrusion and, but for the size of the particle, would clearly give rise to an action of trespass. The defendant asks us to take account of the difference in size of the physical agency through which the intrusion occurs and relegate entirely to the field of nuisance law certain invasions which do not meet the dimensional test, whatever that is. In pressing this argument upon us the defendant must admit that there are

(Continued)

EXHIBIT 8-1 *(Continued)*

cases which have held that a trespass results from the movement or deposit of rather small objects over or upon the surface of the possessor's land.

We hold that the defendant's conduct in causing chemical substances to be deposited upon the plaintiffs' land fulfilled all of the requirements under the law of trespass....

The two actions, trespass and private nuisance, are thus not entirely exclusive or inconsistent, and in a proper case in which the elements of both actions are fully present, the plaintiff may have his choice of one or the other, or may proceed upon both.

Source: Bradley v. American Smelting and Refining Company, 709 P. 2d 782 (Wash. 1985).

Nuisance

The elements of nuisance are the following:

1. An act by the defendant
2. The act may be intentional, negligent, or based upon strict liability
3. An invasion of plaintiff's interest in land that is not a trespass
4. There must be "substantial and unreasonable" harm
5. Causation
6. Damages

AN ACT BY THE DEFENDANT

Public Nuisance and Private Nuisance

Private Nuisance
An interference with the plaintiff's interest in the use or enjoyment of plaintiff's property and the interference is not one of trespass.

Public Nuisance
An act by the defendant that causes inconvenience or damage to the public.

Nuisances are categorized as either a private nuisance or a public nuisance. A **private nuisance** is an interference with the plaintiff's interest in the use or enjoyment of plaintiff's property, and the interference is not one of trespass. A **public nuisance** is an act by the defendant that causes inconvenience or damage to the public that affects rights common to the general public. For example, if a factory was dumping waste into a nearby river that polluted not only plaintiff's well water but also the water of the entire city, which used the river as its source of water, it is a public nuisance affecting the entire public. It is also a private nuisance affecting only the plaintiff's nearby well water. Typically the state would bring an action for a public nuisance, and a private individual would bring an action for a private nuisance as

Workplace Skills Tip

The paralegal will be asked, from time to time, to do legal research on a case. At the outset, if there is an applicable statute, be sure to check the "definitions" section of a particular statute, state or federal. Often the answer to an apparent complex legal issue may be as simple as finding the definition of a key word that involves the central issue. For example, if an issue arose over the protection afforded to a guest of an owner or a tenant involving residential real estate, finding the word "guest" and its definition may solve the problem.

in the polluted well water example. If a private person wants to bring an action for a public nuisance, that person must show an injury that is unique or peculiar in kind from the common injury to the public.

Nuisance vs. Trespass

The student may be wondering, rightly so, what is the technical difference between a trespass and a nuisance? The question is answered by the *Bradley* case in Exhibit 8-1. The technical difference is this: The tort of trespass to land has occurred once there has been a *tangible invasion* of the plaintiff's land that interferes with the plaintiff's right to possession. That invasion may be ever so minor or slight. It is an interference with plaintiff's possession of the land but not necessarily the use and enjoyment of the land, although that may occur too, depending upon the severity of the tangible invasion. The tort of nuisance requires an act by the defendant that interferes with the plaintiff's "use and enjoyment" of plaintiff's land but not necessarily with its possession. With nuisance, nothing tangible is coming onto plaintiff's land, but defendant's use of the land is somehow interfering with plaintiff's use and enjoyment of the land. Also, the interference in nuisance must be substantial and unreasonable in order to prevail under this tort theory.

Note from the analysis in *Bradley*, however, that conduct may be both a nuisance and a trespass. The two legal theories are not mutually exclusive. For example, the conduct of a neighbor in doing some blasting with dynamite may be a nuisance because of the loud noise involved. It would also be a trespass if rocks and other debris were physically deposited on the neighbor's land.

Additional examples explaining the differences in the two theories may be in order. Throwing a rock onto plaintiff's land or shooting a bullet onto plaintiff's land is a technical trespass because it is an actual invasion by a tangible object and interferes with the plaintiff's right of possession. The invasion is slight. No damage may be done. Defendant, out walking her miniature poodle, chooses to briefly walk across a small portion of plaintiff's land. This too is an actual invasion or intrusion by a tangible object—a person and an animal—that interferes with the plaintiff's right of possession. No damage may be done by briefly walking across a small portion of plaintiff's land with a small dog. This invasion or intrusion is slight. The procedural advantage to trespass is that once it has been proven a trespass has occurred, as discussed in the Trespass section, the plaintiff is entitled to damages. The plaintiff is guaranteed to receive at least nominal damages, although the rule may be different in pollution/environment cases, as in the *Bradley* case where damages were required to be proven. Remember why courts are so protective of invasions to land that constitute a trespass. Those trespasses may ripen into ownership rights or rights to use that land or portions of it.

The tort of nuisance arises when the use of defendant's land interferes substantially and unreasonably with the plaintiff's use and enjoyment of plaintiff's land. For example, defendant may be operating a hog farm from which a powerful, unpleasant odor emanates. This use of defendant's land may interfere with plaintiff's use and enjoyment of plaintiff's land. The offensive odor is a temporary fume in the air that leaves no tangible deposit of anything upon the plaintiff's land. The defendant may be operating a popular downtown bar near a residential area. A band plays loud music outside the bar's patio every weekend. This use of defendant's land may cause extremely loud noise that substantially and unreasonably interferes with plaintiff's use and enjoyment of plaintiff's land. This noise coming through sound waves may be an interference with plaintiff's use and enjoyment of plaintiff's land. Like the unpleasant odor, it is transient. No physical, tangible object is being physically deposited on plaintiff's land from the sound. Noise, odors, dust, and the like, are traditionally dealt with as nuisance. (Although dust would appear to be a physical tangible object deposited upon the land, would it not?)

THE ACT MAY BE INTENTIONAL, NEGLIGENT, OR BASED UPON STRICT LIABILITY

The tort of nuisance is slightly different from the tort of trespass to land because it can be based upon alternative theories of negligence, intention, or strict liability. Most nuisance cases are based upon intention because defendant intends the act or defendant is substantially certain some damage will occur with plaintiff's use and enjoyment of plaintiff's land. Also, plaintiff may have complained of the activity, and the complaints have been ignored by the defendant. It can be seen that nuisance could be based on negligence. If plaintiff complained to defendant, and defendant took steps that defendant claimed were reasonable to try to lessen or abate the nuisance, negligence would be the proper basis for the nuisance claim by the plaintiff neighbor. Strict liability will be discussed in a later chapter. Liability is imposed under strict liability in certain cases in which the activity is so ultra hazardous or abnormally dangerous that the law imposes liability without any fault or intention. Examples are blasting with dynamite, using explosives, using fireworks, and possessing wild animals.

AN INVASION OF PLAINTIFF'S INTEREST IN LAND THAT IS NOT BASED UPON TRESPASS

This element states that the act by the defendant is not a trespass-related interference with the plaintiff's interest in the use and enjoyment of land. In other words, there is no physical, tangible deposit of an object on the land. The plaintiff will be the one in possession or the one with the right to possession. This may be the owner or a tenant or lessee.

THERE MUST BE SUBSTANTIAL AND UNREASONABLE HARM

For trespass, the invasion or intrusion upon the land may be slight such as shooting a bullet onto the land or walking a dog across a portion of the land, but defendant is entitled to damage for trespass, even if there are only nominal damages. For nuisance, however, the harm must be *substantial and unreasonable*. The interference cannot be a minor annoyance such as a neighbor's occasional barking dog or a neighbor's occasional running of a car with a loud muffler. It must be an interference judged by the reasonable person standard. The unreasonableness requirement involves a balancing test. Does the damage done to plaintiff outweigh defendant's continuation of the conduct or activity? Are property values being affected? How suitable is the defendant's conduct considering the surrounding neighborhood? Are there any social benefits in allowing the conduct or activity to occur? For example, is the factory that emits noise and smoke employing many people in the community? What is the cost to the defendant to reduce or eliminate the harm? Courts struggle to balance these interests.

Workplace Skills Tip

Using proper English cannot be emphasized enough. It was first mentioned in Chapter 1. It was mentioned again in Chapter 5 in reference to the common misuse of the words "principal" and "principle." Another commonly misused word is the simple word "its." Examples: "The captured bear was released back into *its* natural habitat."

"The corporation's tax documents were returned to *its* CEO." "*Its* history is noteworthy." There is no need for an apostrophe. The word "its" is serving as a possessory word. The word "it's" is a contraction of "it is." Just remember, the only time "it's" should ever be used is if you are using it as a substitute for "it is."

CAUSATION

For nuisance, the test of causation will depend upon the basis of the nuisance theory, whether negligence, intention, or strict liability. If the nuisance is based on intention, defendant must have done an intentional act or set some force in motion that caused the harm. If the nuisance is based on negligence or strict liability, causation principles are the same as for negligence. Proximate cause is required.

DAMAGES

Just as in trespass, besides compensatory and punitive damages, equitable relief in the form of a temporary or permanent injunction may be sought. However, the general rule is different from trespass in that damages must be proven even if a nuisance has been established.

Trespass to Chattels (Personal Property)

The elements of a **trespass to chattels** are the following:

1. An act by the defendant
2. Intent on the part of the defendant
3. Invasion of the chattel interest
4. The plaintiff is in possession of the chattel or has the right to immediate possession
5. Causation
6. Damages

Trespass to Chattels
An intentional tort consisting of an intrusion upon the chattels (personal property) of another without consent or privilege to do so. The intrusion may be a dispossession or an intermeddling.

First, a "chattel" is personal property. As opposed to land, which is fixed, a chattel is moveable. Chattel comes from the word "cattle," which is an old Norman word that was synonymous with any general moveable personal property. For this particular tort, a chattel is any *tangible* property that is not real property. Examples are an automobile, a pet, or an item of clothing or furniture. It does not apply to "intangible" chattels or personal property such as a promissory note or an account receivable.

AN ACT BY THE DEFENDANT

Just as in trespass to land, there must be some volitional movement on the part of the defendant—an external manifestation of the defendant's will that results in either a *dispossession* of chattels or *intermeddling* with another's chattels. Those two concepts will be discussed in the section concerning the invasion of the chattel interest.

INTENT ON THE PART OF THE DEFENDANT

The intent required is that the defendant must have intended to deal with the particular chattel in the way that he or she did so. It does not matter that the defendant made a mistake. For example, defendant, in searching for his newly purchased black cocker spaniel, spots another cocker spaniel two blocks away, picks it up, and takes it home. The next day defendant is informed that the cocker spaniel in his possession actually belongs to a neighbor. The requisite intent for this tort has been established in spite of the defendant's mistake.

INVASION OF THE CHATTEL INTEREST

Dispossession
Conduct in which the defendant attempts to assert dominion, control, or even ownership rights over those of the lawful owner.

Two subcategories of this element come into play. First, the defendant's intentional act must have resulted in either a dispossession of the chattel or an intermeddling with the chattel. **Dispossession** is conduct in which the defendant attempts to assert dominion, control, or even ownership rights over those of the lawful owner. Dispossession is more serious than intermeddling. Dispossession in its most extreme forms may be a theft or destruction of the chattel. If defendant, in the above example, could not find his cocker spaniel, came across one virtually identical to the lost one, and decided to steal it from another person's yard and keep it for his own, this is a serious dispossession. A serious dispossession such as an outright theft of the cocker spaniel will provide a remedy under conversion, which will be discussed next.

Intermeddling
Intentionally interfering with the chattel in some manner but without the intent to challenge the plaintiff's ownership interest in the chattel.

Intermeddling is intentionally interfering with the chattel in some manner but without the intent to challenge the plaintiff's ownership interest in the chattel. Some courts require there to be some actual damage caused to the chattel by the intermeddling or, if no damage, the time of the intermeddling must be so substantial that it is possible to calculate damages for a loss. An example of intermeddling would be striking a neighbor's dog or "keying" an automobile, which causes paint damage. Assume defendant, in search of a parking place, noticed another car against the curb with the engine running. Defendant decided to enter the vehicle and move it forward five feet to make room for a parking space immediately behind the moved vehicle. This intentional act is clearly a trespass to chattels, but it is likely an intermeddling not a dispossession because defendant did not intend to exercise dominion, control, or ownership over the other vehicle. It would also be difficult to prove any damages for the few minutes involved in moving the vehicle.[4]

Trespass to chattels contemplates (1) a lesser/minor dispossession to a chattel or (2) intermeddling with a chattel. For example, a woman takes an expensive mink coat from a coat check room (a dispossession). The expensive one resembles her own, which is made from rabbit, not mink. After an hour or so, she realizes her mistake and returns the coat. This hour-long dispossession did not seriously interfere with the owner's right of dominion, control, or ownership of the coat. It is a minor dispossession, however, amounting to a trespass to chattels. If the woman decided to retain the expensive coat as her own and not return it, this is a serious dispossession giving the owner a right to sue her in conversion for the full value of the coat.

THE PLAINTIFF IS IN POSSESSION OF THE CHATTEL OR HAS THE RIGHT TO IMMEDIATE POSSESSION

As in trespass to land, this is the same element. The person in possession of the chattel may be the owner or may be leasing, renting, or using the chattel with permission from the owner.

Workplace Skills Tip

The paralegal will eventually work on a complex case, whether products liability, medical malpractice, or construction defect, as examples. The client may have retained several experts. Each expert may have a slightly different expertise, but it is important to maintain a common theme in the presentation of the case. It is not uncommon for the experts to be arriving from different cities and then deposed for a full day or more. Because of the importance of a common theme, the later expert(s) to be deposed may want to know what his or her predecessor(s) has said. Tell the court reporter to send a "draft" deposition transcript by e-mail to the paralegal's office for forwarding on to the expert(s) scheduled for the next day or so. Before testifying, each expert will then have some knowledge of what his or her predecessor(s) has said and will be even better prepared.

CAUSATION

As in trespass to land, the invasion must be caused by defendant's intentional act or some force set in motion by the defendant. Proximate cause is not the test.

DAMAGES

As discussed, the two types of invasions of the chattel interest are dispossession and intermeddling. If there is a dispossession, the plaintiff can recover for the loss of possession even if the chattel has not been harmed or damaged. If there is an intermeddling, there must be some actual damage shown to the chattel or an interference with the possessor's interest for a substantial length of time for which damages may be reasonably calculated. In the mink coat dispossession example, the woman intentionally took plaintiff's coat but eventually returned it after an hour. Plaintiff could recover damages for the loss for a trespass to chattels based upon a reasonable rental value of the coat if that could be established on an hourly basis. In the "keyed car" intermeddling example, which caused paint damage, actual damage can be shown. Evidence can be produced to show the reasonable value of services to repair the car.

Conversion

The elements of **conversion** are the following:

1. An act by the defendant
2. Intent on the part of the defendant
3. A substantial invasion of the chattel interest
4. The plaintiff is in possession of the chattel or has the right to immediate possession
5. Causation
6. Damages

Conversion
An intentional tort consisting of a substantial invasion of another's chattel interest.

AN ACT BY THE DEFENDANT

As in trespass to land, there must be a volitional movement on the part of the defendant—an external manifestation of the defendant's will—that results in a substantial invasion of the plaintiff's chattel interest.

INTENT ON THE PART OF THE DEFENDANT

As in a trespass to chattels, the defendant must have intended to deal with the chattel in the way that he or she did so.

A SUBSTANTIAL INVASION OF THE CHATTEL INTEREST

This is a primary distinction between conversion and trespass to chattels. This element generally requires an invasion of the chattel interest that is a substantial invasion. It is something far more than mistakenly taking a mink coat for an hour as in the example for a trespass to chattels. This invasion may involve taking the chattel from the rightful owner or the person in rightful possession with the intent of retaining it as the defendant's own (an outright theft). Or it may amount to a destruction or substantial alteration of the chattel without plaintiff's consent.

For example, A spots B's car in the driveway with the keys in it and drives off with the vehicle intending to keep the car as A's own. Conversion may also arise by not allowing the rightful owner or possessor to reclaim the chattel. A allows B to use A's car for a week. When the week has expired, B refuses to return the vehicle. Conversion may also arise by the obtaining of a chattel by the use of fraud. Defendant purchases a horse from plaintiff with counterfeit money or some other form of fraud and obtains possession of the horse with the intent of becoming its new owner. More serious conduct is required for conversion. In essence, a substantial invasion of a chattel interest of another person amounting to conversion would likely amount to theft under the criminal law.

The issue will turn on whether or not there was a less serious dispossession required for trespass to a chattel versus a substantial dispossession required for conversion. Admittedly, there is a fine line between the dispossession required under trespass to chattels and the substantial dispossession required under conversion. The word "substantial" does not necessarily provide a great deal of guidance. An example may help shed some light. Defendant notices the keys in the plaintiff's car. Defendant intentionally drives off with plaintiff's car. This is a dispossession. Defendant, however, has no intent to retain it as the defendant's own. The car is recovered either because defendant returns it or the car is found abandoned after the joy ride has ended. The proper cause of action is trespass to chattels. Plaintiff could sue defendant on a theory of trespass to chattels for the reasonable rental value of the car during the time of the temporary dispossession.

On the other hand, if defendant took the same car with the intention of permanently retaining it or selling it and keeping the money, this would amount to conversion—a more serious and substantial dispossession. Other examples of substantial dispossessions amounting to conversion would be destroying a chattel or materially

Workplace Skills Tip

In addition to being generally familiar with the organization of the federal court system, be familiar with the organization of the state court system in your jurisdiction. Is the trial court referred to as a "district court," a "superior court," a "circuit court," or is there a different name used? Does your jurisdiction have an intermediate court of appeals? What is the name of the highest court of appeals in your jurisdiction? In New York, for example, the intermediate state court is known as the "supreme court" and the highest court in the judicial system is known as the "court of appeals." Know the difference between a "judge" and a "justice" in your jurisdiction.

altering it. If the defendant took plaintiff's car and crashed it and destroyed it or changed the paint color and put in a new engine, those actions would also amount to conversion allowing plaintiff to sue defendant for the full value of the car.

THE PLAINTIFF IS IN POSSESSION OF THE CHATTEL OR HAS THE RIGHT TO IMMEDIATE POSSESSION

As in trespass to land, plaintiff must be in actual possession of the chattel or have the right to immediate possession of the chattel.

CAUSATION

Causation is the same as it is for trespass to land and trespass to chattels.

DAMAGES

Damages for conversion can be recovered for the duration of time the chattel was in the defendant's possession as well as for the cost of the recovery of the chattel. Plaintiff may elect not to attempt to have the chattel returned but, rather, sue for the value of the chattel plus any damages for the dispossession. The damages alleged would be for the fair market value of the chattel during the defendant's possession of the chattel, as well as the reasonable rental value during that time. If plaintiff is successful in recovering and collecting the judgment, this amounts to a forced sale of the chattel to the defendant. If there has been some kind of serious dispossession such as a theft or refusal to return the chattel and the plaintiff does not care about a return of the chattel itself, only its value, the proper action is conversion for a forced sale. If the plaintiff cares about the chattel and wants to retain ownership, plaintiff will likely sue on a theory of trespass to chattels for any damages, which will be less than the full value of the chattel. The plaintiff may also sue to have the chattel returned in actions, which may be called by various names, such as replevin, detinue, or claim and delivery. A forced sale for the full fair market value of the chattel at the time of the conversion is a remedy for conversion only, not trespass to chattels. For an interesting decision on conversion, review the decision of *Pearson v. Dodd*, 410 F.2d 701 (D.C. CIR. 1969) in Exhibit 8-2.

EXHIBIT 8-2 Relevant Case Law

Drew Pearson and Jack Anderson, Appellants, v. Thomas J. Dodd, Appellee.

United States Court of Appeals District of Columbia Circuit.

Proceeding on interlocutory appeal from an order of the United States District Court for the District of Columbia, Alexander Holtzoff, J., 279 F.Supp. 101, in suit arising out of exposure of alleged misdeeds of United States senator by newspaper columnists. The Court of Appeals, J. Skelly Wright, Circuit Judge, held that newspaper columns giving columnists' version of United States senator's relationship with certain lobbyists for foreign interests and giving interpretative biographical sketch of senator's public career bore on senator's qualifications and as such amounted to published speech not subject to suit for invasion of privacy. The court further held that newspaper columnists who received copies of documents which were removed by others from office of senator

(Continued)

EXHIBIT 8-2 *(Continued)*

and which were photocopied at night and returned to files undamaged before office operations resumed in the morning were not liable for conversion of physical documents taken from senator's files.

Affirmed in part; reversed in part.

J. Skellywright, Circuit Judge.

This case arises out of the exposure of the alleged misdeeds of Senator Thomas Dodd of Connecticut by newspaper columnists Drew Pearson and Jack Anderson. The District Court has granted partial summary judgment to Senator Dodd, appellee here, finding liability on a theory of conversion. At the same time, the court denied partial summary judgment on the theory of invasion of privacy. Both branches of the court's judgment are before us on interlocutory appeal. We affirm the District Court's denial of summary judgment for invasion of privacy and reverse its grant of summary judgment for conversion....

The undisputed facts in the case were stated by the District Court as follows:

'*** On several occasions in June and July, 1965, two former employees of the plaintiff, at times with the assistance of two members of the plaintiff's staff, entered the plaintiff's office without authority and unbeknownst to him, removed numerous documents from his files, made copies of them, replaced the originals, and turned over the copies to the defendant Anderson, who was aware of the manner in which the copies had been obtained. The defendants Pearson and Anderson thereafter published articles containing information gleaned from these documents....

The District Court ruled that appellants' receipt and subsequent use of photocopies of documents which appellants knew had been removed from appellee's files without authorization established appellants' liability for conversion. We conclude that appellants are not guilty of conversion on the facts shown.

Dean Prosser has remarked that 'conversion is the forgotten tort.' That it is not entirely forgotten is attested by the case before us. History has largely defined its contours, contours which we should now follow except where they derive from clearly obsolete practices or abandoned theories....

Conversion is the substantive tort theory which underlay the ancient common law form of action for trover. A plaintiff in trover alleged that he had lost a chattel which he rightfully possessed, FN23 and that the defendant had found it and converted it to his own use. With time, the allegations of losing and finding became fictional, leaving the question of whether the defendant had 'converted' the property the only operative one.

> FN23. A threshold question, not briefed by either party and hence not decided by us, is the nature of the property right held by appellee in the contents of the files in his Senate office. Those files, themselves paid for by the United States, are maintained in an office owned by the United States, by employees of the United States. They are meant to contribute to the work of appellee as an officer of the United States. The question thus is not entirely free from doubt whether appellee has title to the contents of the files or has a right of exclusive possession of those contents, or is a bailee, or even a mere custodian of those contents....

The most distinctive feature of conversion is its measure of damages, which is the value of the goods converted. The theory is that the 'converting' defendant has in some way treated the goods as if they

(Continued)

EXHIBIT 8-2 *(Continued)*

were his own, so that the plaintiff can properly ask the court to decree a forced sale of the property from the rightful possessor to the converter....

Because of this stringent measure of damages, it has long been recognized that not every wrongful interference with the personal property of another is a conversion. Where the intermeddling falls short of the complete or very substantial deprivation of possessory rights in the property, the tort committed is not conversion, but the lesser wrong of trespass to chattels.

The Second Restatement of Torts has marked the distinction by defining conversion as:

'* * * An intentional exercise of dominion or control over a chattel which so seriously interferes with the right of another to control it that the actor may justly be required to pay the other the full value of the chattel.'

Less serious interferences fall under the Restatement's definition of trespass.[FN30]

> FN30. Id., § 217: 'A trespass to a chattel may be committed by intentionally
> (a) dispossessing another of the chattel, or (b) using or intermeddling with a chattel in the possession of another.'

The difference is more than a semantic one. The measure of damages in trespass is not the whole value of the property interfered with, but rather the actual diminution in its value caused by the interference. More important for this case, a judgment for conversion can be obtained with only nominal damages, whereas liability for trespass to chattels exists only on a showing of actual damage to the property interfered with. Here the District Court granted partial summary judgment on the issue of liability alone, while conceding that possibly no more than nominal damages might be awarded on subsequent trial. Partial summary judgment for liability could not have been granted on a theory of trespass to chattels without an undisputed showing of actual damages to the property in question....

It is clear that on the agreed facts appellants committed no conversion of the physical documents taken from appellee's files. Those documents were removed from the files at night, photocopied, and returned to the files undamaged before office operations resumed in the morning. Insofar as the documents' value to appellee resided in their usefulness as records of the business of his office, appellee was clearly not substantially deprived of his use of them.

This of course is not an end of the matter. It has long been recognized that documents often have value above and beyond that springing from their physical possession. They may embody information or ideas whose economic value depends in part or in whole upon being kept secret. The question then arises whether the information taken by means of copying appellee's office files is of the type which the law of conversion protects. The general rule has been that ideas or information are not subject to legal protection, but the law has developed exceptions to this rule. Where information is gathered and arranged at some cost and sold as a commodity on the market, it is properly protected as property. Where ideas are formulated with labor and inventive genius, as in the case of literary works or scientific researches, they are protected. Where they constitute instruments of fair and effective commercial competition, those who develop them may gather their fruits under the protection of the law....

The question here is not whether appellee had a right to keep his files from prying eyes, but whether the information taken from those files falls under the protection of the law of property, enforceable by a suit for conversion. In our view, it does not. The information included the contents of letters to appellee from.... supplicants, and office records of other kinds, the nature of which is not fully revealed by the record. Insofar as we can tell, none of it amounts to literary property, to scientific invention, or to secret plans formulated by appellee for the conduct of commerce. Nor does it appear to be information held in any way for sale by appellee, analogous to the fresh news copy produced by a wire service.

(Continued)

EXHIBIT 8-2   *(Continued)*

Because no conversion of the physical contents of appellee's files took place, and because the information copied from the documents in those files has not been shown to be property subject to protection by suit for conversion, the District Court's ruling that appellants are guilty of conversion must be reversed.

Source: Pearson v. Dodd, 410 F. 2d 701 (U.S. App. D.C. 1969).

Defenses and Privileges to Trespass to Land, Nuisance, Trespass to Chattels, and Conversion

There are various defenses and privileges for the four tort theories just discussed.

CONSENT

Plaintiff may have given consent expressly or impliedly to use land or chattels or to create the nuisance. For example, what would otherwise be a trespass to land by a hunter on another's land is not a trespass if the owner gave consent to be on the land. However, the scope of the consent may be an issue. Was consent given to be on the entire 160 acres or only the east 80 acres? A trespass may still occur if defendant exceeds the scope of the consent given or the one giving consent had no authority to give such consent.

What would otherwise be a trespass to chattels or a conversion by one taking another's motorcycle and riding it may not be the case if consent is shown by conduct. This is so, for example, if defendant can show that plaintiff, in the past, on certain days and times, allowed defendant to take the motorcycle when it was parked in a certain place with the keys in it. Likewise, if plaintiff consents to selling or leasing nearby land to defendant knowing defendant plans to conduct the precise activity amounting to the later nuisance, this is a valid defense to nuisance.

PRIVILEGE TO EXCLUDE TRESPASSING CHATTELS OF ANOTHER PERSON

Defendant is privileged to use reasonable force to exclude another person's chattels when defendant believes that it is reasonably necessary to protect defendant's land or chattels. A's two chickens are habitually trespassing on B's land. These trespasses are destroying B's valuable garden and flowers. After repeated unheeded requests to A to stop the trespassing chickens, B poisons the chickens. B is not liable to A.[5]

PRIVILEGE TO INVADE CHATTELS OR LAND FOR A PUBLIC NECESSITY

The privilege is given to the defendant for the sole protection of the public against some impending public disaster. It must be reasonable conduct and cannot be for the private benefit of the defendant. (The privilege of private necessity will be

Workplace Skills Tip

In most cases, the paralegal will perform the task requested by the attorney, whether given verbally, in a formal memo, or by an e-mail. However, do not always assume that because the attorney directs you to do something, it is the correct task to be performed. Attorneys can become extremely preoccupied with cases. Attorneys can make mistakes. You may have information from your previous research or from a document review that the attorney does not possess. Think before you act. If you suspect there is a mistake in the assignment, direct a polite e-mail to the attorney immediately. Call the attorney's attention to the issue and explain why you are questioning it. Save the e-mail. If the attorney insists that you do the task, you will have the e-mail in the event the attorney or some other attorney working on the case questions why you did what you did.

discussed next.) For example, to stop a spreading flood in a community, the defendant enters upon plaintiff's land and sets off explosives to divert the water. The *Steele* case in Exhibit 8-3 provides an excellent discussion of this privilege.[6]

EXHIBIT 8-3 Relevant Case Law

Waltraud H. Steele et al., Petitioner, v. City of Houston, Respondent.

Supreme Court of Texas.

Pope, Justice.

Waltraud Steele, Jutta Mozingo, and Robert Ingram sued the City of Houston for damages which they say they sustained when officers of the Houston Police Department caused the destruction of their home and belongings while attempting to recapture three escaped convicts who had taken refuge in the house. Mozingo and Ingram were married at the time of the events upon which this action is based. The trial court rendered a summary judgment against the plaintiffs, and the court of civil appeals has affirmed. 577 S.W.2d 373. We reverse the judgments of the courts below and remand the cause for trial....

We accordingly reverse the judgments of the courts below. Plaintiffs, upon remand, will be entitled to make proof that the City of Houston, acting through its officers with authority or color of authority, intentionally set the house on fire or that the City prevented the fire's extinguishment after it was set. They must also prove that the destruction was done "for or applied to public use."...That is the factor which distinguishes a negligence action from one under the constitution for destruction. That the destruction was done for the public use is or can be established by proof that the City ordered the destruction of the property because of real or supposed public emergency to apprehend armed and dangerous men who had taken refuge in the house.

The defendant City of Houston may defend its actions by proof of a great public necessity. Mere convenience will not suffice. Uncompensated destruction of property has been occasionally justified by reason of war, riot, pestilence or other great public calamity. Destruction has been permitted in instances in which the building is adjacent to a burning building or in the line of fire and destined to destruction anyway....

Where the danger affects the entire community, or so many people that the public interest is involved, that interest serves as a complete justification to the defendant who acts to avert the peril

(Continued)

EXHIBIT 8-3 *(Continued)*

to all. Thus one who dynamites a house to stop the spread of a conflagration that threatens a town, or shoots a mad dog in the street, or burns clothing infected with smallpox germs, or, in time of war, destroys property which should not be allowed to fall into the hands of the enemy, is not liable to the owner, so long as the emergency is great enough, and he has acted reasonably under the circumstances. The "champion of the public" is not required to pay out of his own pocket for the general salvation. The number of persons who must be endangered in order to create a public necessity has not been determined by the courts. It would seem that the moral obligation upon the group affected to make compensation in such a case should be recognized by the law, but recovery usually has been denied.

Prosser, The Law of Torts s 24 (4th ed. 1971).

The scant proof made by the City of Houston in this case does not establish as a matter of law that it is excused from making compensation for the destruction of plaintiffs' dwelling and personal property.

The City argues that the destruction of the property as a means to apprehend escapees is a classic instance of police power exercised for the safety of the public. We do not hold that the police officers wrongfully ordered the destruction of the dwelling; we hold that the innocent third parties are entitled by the Constitution to compensation for their property.

The judgments of the courts below are reversed and the cause is remanded for trial.

Source: Steele v. City of Houston, 603 S.W. 2d 786 (Tex. 1980).

PRIVILEGE BASED UPON A PRIVATE NECESSITY

In addition to the privilege to invade or intrude upon another person's land or chattels based on a public necessity, there is a similar privilege for a private necessity. The privilege applies only if the invasion or intrusion is necessary to protect any person (including the defendant) from *death or serious bodily harm* or to protect any land or chattels from injury or destruction. As in the privilege of public necessity, the invasion or intrusion must be reasonable and the defendant would be liable for any damage caused to the land or chattels. For example, if a person is in a rural area riding a bicycle and is chased by a large vicious dog, the person would have a privilege to enter another's land to try to escape the ferocious animal.

PRIVILEGE TO INVADE LAND OR CHATTELS TO ABATE A NUISANCE

As discussed under the nuisance section, a nuisance is an unreasonable interference with the use or enjoyment of a person's property. The defendant may intrude upon the land or chattels of another person for the purpose of abating a private nuisance. There is no privilege of abatement for a public nuisance unless it is causing the defendant some peculiar injury. The defendant must be an owner or possessor of land or chattels that would be affected by the nuisance and any entry or invasion must be reasonable—at a reasonable time—and any force used must be reasonable. Most courts hold that the person entering the land must first make a request or demand to abate the nuisance. If the owner resists, the entrant should retreat and seek relief from the court.

ADDITIONAL DEFENSES RELATED TO NUISANCE

As discussed previously, in addition to the basis of intention, nuisance may also be based upon strict liability or negligence. If the nuisance is based on negligence, defendant has the defenses of contributory negligence or comparative negligence or fault. Assumption of the risk may be a defense if the nuisance is based on negligence, intention, or strict liability. Also, in nuisance cases, there is a defense entitled "coming to the nuisance." In other words, the defendant who is allegedly committing the nuisance says, "I was here first. You knew what you would expect when you moved in." This is a consideration for the courts, but it may be that the conduct or activity only became unreasonable after plaintiff and others moved in.

CASE **8.1** Hypothetical Case: Developing Workplace Skills

MEMO

To: Paralegal

From: Attorney

RE: New file David and Karen Lee v. Farmers & Ranchers Rural Cooperative Company

File: LRJ1943CH

I just finished meeting with David ("Dave") and Karen ("Karrie") Lee, some friends of mine who are successful organic farmers. I was able to obtain a good verdict for them in a car/train accident some years ago. They farm a family farm originally owned by Karrie's great-grandparents. About five years ago, they started the process of converting their conventional family farm to a certified-organic farm. This was done to realize higher prices for organic crops. They raise primarily corn, soybeans, and alfalfa.

Dave and Karrie posted numerous signs along the farm's perimeter stating "Organic Farm Chemical Free" to maintain a buffer zone between their organic fields and their chemical-using neighbors' farms. Photographs of those signs are attached. The Lees, primarily by e-mail and letter, notified Farmers & Ranchers Rural Cooperative Company ("Farmers & Ranchers") of the transition. The e-mails and letters are also attached to this memo. Note that Karrie's one e-mail early-on, which I have highlighted for you, specifically advises Farmers & Ranchers: "As you know, we have converted our farming operation to a certified organic farm, and we will be raising corn, soybeans, and alfalfa. **Therefore, I would caution you to be especially careful to avoid over-spraying pesticide onto our fields when you are treating other fields near ours.**"

Despite Dave and Karrie's requests, Farmers & Ranchers sprayed pesticide and herbicide on fields next to theirs in 2009, 2010, and 2011. The Lees tell me that they violated our state laws by applying pesticides when it was too windy causing these chemicals to drift onto their organic farm. The Lees also tell me there are federal regulations that require a farmer to take a field out of production for three full years after an organic field has been sprayed with a herbicide or pesticide.

Their crop and other related losses for the three years approximate $1.4 million according to a "statement of loss" they prepared, which is also attached to this memo. These losses consist of losses in 2009 and 2010 for past crop losses for the three-year period when the crops had to be destroyed and the fields had to be taken out of production, enhanced weed growth, hiring of extra farm labor to assist with

(Continued)

"Did we do something to upset
the neighbors?"

CASE 8.1 (Continued)

the damaged land, and other losses. They are showing an anticipated future loss for the 2011 incident for those fields currently out of production.

As you know, the bulk of our practice is PI work, and this type of case is somewhat new for our firm. From an ethical standpoint, my obligation is to do research and become competent in this area or even associate with an attorney who may specialize in these types of cases or both. I have indicated to the Lees that we may associate with another attorney, and the case will likely be expensive to pursue with many depositions to be taken and experts to be retained. They still want to sue Farmers & Ranchers for these three overspraying incidents in 2009, 2010, and 2011.

I need you to do some preliminary legal research to determine if this type of overspray of pesticides and herbicides drifting onto an organic farm carried by wind is a nuisance, a trespass, or both.

Your time should be entered on the above file, LRJ1943CH.

CHAPTER **SUMMARY**

The two main torts to land or real property are trespass and nuisance. Trespass is an intentional tort. It requires a volitional act, intent, and an intrusion or entry upon land of which plaintiff has possession or the right to immediate possession and causation. The entry or intrusion upon the land may be by the defendant personally or by causing some other person or object to intrude upon the land. The plaintiff will not necessarily be the owner of the land. The right to bring the claim also belongs to one with the right to immediate possession, which may be a tenant or lessee under a lease. The element of causation is the same for the intentional tort of battery. The causation required is that the defendant's act set forces in motion that caused the intrusion to the land. Proximate cause is not the test. If a trespass has been established, plaintiff is entitled to at least nominal damages regardless of whether or not any actual damages were sustained. In trespass cases, depending upon the jurisdiction, punitive damages may be awarded. Equitable relief in the form of an injunction is a remedy.

Nuisance requires a volitional act by the defendant just as in trespass. While trespass is based solely on an intentional act by the defendant, nuisance may also be based on negligence or strict liability. Nuisance requires that there be an intrusion or invasion of plaintiff's land that substantially and unreasonably interferes with plaintiff's use and enjoyment of the land. A minor inconvenience such as a neighbor's occasionally barking dog will not suffice. Causation is the same as it is for trespass—an act that sets forces in motion causing the nuisance. Proximate cause is not the test.

The courts sometimes have difficulty drawing exact lines between a nuisance and a trespass. Technically, a trespass is a tangible invasion, however slight, of the plaintiff's land (a rock is thrown onto land or a bullet is fired and drops onto land)

that interferes with the plaintiff's right to possession. A nuisance is created when the defendant's use of his or her land interferes substantially and unreasonably with the plaintiff's use and enjoyment of plaintiff's land. Examples of a nuisance may be excessive noise or an offensive odor. It is not always possible to draw distinct lines between these two torts, and a defendant's action may end up being both a trespass and a nuisance. Environmental cases cause particular problems in drawing the distinction between the two. For example, is the deposit of soot, dust, or chemicals on plaintiff's land from an adjoining factory a nuisance or a trespass? Certain conduct may be both a trespass and a nuisance. The case of *Bradley v. American Smelting and Refining Company,* 709 P. 2d 782 (Wash. 1985), cited in the text is important in discussing the historical differences between the two torts and why the differences are not so logical in today's world. Damages for nuisance, like trespass, may consist of compensatory damages, punitive damages, and equitable relief in the form of an injunction.

Trespass to chattels or personal property requires an intentional act that invades the chattel interest of one in possession of the chattel or the right to immediate possession of the chattel. However, the invasion is done with no intent to exercise dominion, control, or ownership over plaintiff's chattel. The intent required is simply that the defendant intended to deal with plaintiff's chattel in the way that he or she did so. Mistake is not a defense.

The invasion of the chattel interest may be in two forms: (1) dispossession and (2) intermeddling. Dispossession is more serious than intermeddling. It is conduct in which defendant attempts to assert some sort of dominion, control, or actual ownership over the chattel. Intermeddling is an intentional act that makes contact or interferes with the chattel but not necessarily with any intent to exercise dominion, control, or ownership of it. Examples of intermeddling would be throwing a rock at a neighbor's pet dog and hitting it or moving another's bicycle a few feet to make room for defendant's bicycle. In these two examples there is no intent on the part of the defendant to exercise any dominion, control, or ownership of the dog or the bicycle.

The element of causation is the same as for trespass to land and for nuisance. There must be an intentional act or some force set in motion by defendant. Damages for trespass to chattels may result in recovering the reasonable rental value of the chattel during the time of the temporary dispossession. If the chattel was damaged, damages may be recovered based upon reasonable amount to repair the chattel.

Conversion, unlike trespass to chattels, requires an intentional act that brings about a substantial invasion of the chattel interest. If there is intermeddling or a minor dispossession, the plaintiff's remedy is trespass to chattels. Conversion requires the same volitional act with the same intent to deal with the chattel in the way defendant did as required under trespass to chattels. The element of causation is the same as trespass to chattels.

One of the main distinctions between conversion and trespass to chattels is that the invasion of the chattel interest for conversion must be a substantial invasion. If it is a substantial invasion, the plaintiff could sue the defendant for the full fair market value of the chattel at the time of conversion thus causing a "forced sale" to the defendant.

Defenses and privileges to the four torts to property are available to the defendant. Examples are consent, privilege to exclude trespassing chattels of another, privilege to invade chattels or land for a public necessity, and privilege to invade chattels or land for a private necessity.

KEY **TERMS**

Trespass to Land	Private Nuisance	Intermeddling
Injunction	Public Nuisance	Conversion
Adverse Possession	Trespass to Chattels	
Prescription	Dispossession	

REVIEW **QUESTIONS**

1. Jessica just purchased a four-wheel off-road vehicle. Joy, an acquaintance of Jessica's, is the owner of 80 acres of grazing land outside of town. Joy gives Jessica permission to ride on a 40-acre parcel of Joy's landv. Jessica is told by Joy that this part of her ranch's boundaries where she will be riding consists of the barb wired fence around the entire 40 acres except for the south boundary line of her property, which is bounded by a small river or creek with a neighbor owning the land to the south of the creek. As Jessica is out riding, she encounters a bull. The bull chases her through an open fence into the other 40 acres. When she is out of danger, she returns to the 40 acres where she was supposed to ride, she spots some of Joy's cattle by the south end of the land. She decides to have some fun and she chases the cattle with her vehicle toward the creek. Some of the cattle do not cross the creek and stay on Joy's land. Some of the panicked cattle, however, run across the shallow creek to the other side ending up on Joy's neighbor's land. None are injured. Jessica always remains on Joy's land while doing the chasing. What are the potential claims against Jessica and by whom? What defenses might Jessica allege?

2. Tanner intends to drive upon land owned by Nick to gain access to a private fishing pond on Nick's land. He has no permission to drive on Nick's land and is fully aware he is trespassing. While doing so, he takes a wrong turn in the woods and actually cuts across land owned by Spencer thinking he is still on Nick's land as he reaches the pond. If Spencer sues him for trespass, can Tanner defend himself by saying "I only intended to trespass on Nick's land, not yours"?

3. It is the Fourth of July, and Gary and his wife, Nancy, have accumulated some heavy-duty fireworks to explode at their home on the lake. Knowing their neighbors, Deb and Paul, are not home, they are less than careful about where the fireworks land. Many of the rockets come onto Deb and Paul's land. One especially powerful one actually lodges in a tree with a dead branch and dead leaves and starts a fire. The burning tree then falls on an electrical line breaking it, and the sparks from the line cause a fire to the home of Deb and Paul's neighbor, John. Who has what claims against Gary and Nancy? What defenses, if any?

4. Brian is an avid bird watcher. He has placed numerous bird feeders in his backyard. Brian's neighbor Fred has a pet cat. The cat is fond of coming over to Brian's yard and on occasion, catching and eating a bird. Brian's patience reaches its limit. He buys a BB gun. One day the cat is sitting in Fred's backyard close to the property line looking at the bird feeders. Brian has a clear shot. He decides to shoot and hits the cat in the foot. The limping cat races off. The cat is fine, but the shot to the foot requires a visit to the veterinarian. Fred sues Brian

for the $150.00 vet bill. What tort theories and what result?

5. Do some research on the noise/height restrictions at the John Wayne Airport. How did these restrictions come about and why? What is the height limit at John Wayne? What are the penalties for violations? Any exceptions, such as emergencies?

6. Your client Shontel has been sued for trespass to the land of Mary Catherine for driving over it and damaging some crops and personal property on Mary Catherine's land. While there is no dispute Shontel drove where she drove, as evidenced by the tire tracks and the crop damage, Shontel claims she was on her land and not Mary Catherine's. What expert witness will your firm likely need to properly defend this case and why?

7. The Fargo North Upper Tundra Nuclear Power Plant located near the outskirts of a major city has temporarily been closed for further investigation by local, state, and federal governmental agencies. There have been public reports that the plant is not safe, some nuclear radiation may have already escaped, and there is a substantial danger of further radioactive release. The public reports have made it clear that the danger of this release can cause cancer, birth defects, and genetic deformities. Your clients, Ginny, Judy, and Carolyn, ignored the "No Trespassing" signs at the closed plant and organized a protest to have the plant permanently closed. Your three clients were sued for damages by the power plant for trespass to property. What is their defense?

8. In the classic teen-age comedy, *Ferris Bueller's Day Off*, the father of Ferris's best friend, Cameron, owned a 1961 Red 250 GT Ferrari convertible. Ferris conned Cameron into Ferris taking the vehicle. Ferris drove it that day with his girlfriend and Cameron and returned it to Cameron's home that day. Was Ferris's intentional act of taking the father's convertible a trespass to chattels? If so, was it a dispossession or an intermeddling? Or was it a conversion? What might Ferris, a clever young man, come up with as a defense to the father's alternative claims of trespass to chattels and conversion and how valid would the defense be?

chapter 9
STRICT LIABILITY

"I like pigs. Dogs look up to us. Cats look down on us. Pigs treat us as equals."

Winston Churchill

Strict Liability

THEORY BEHIND STRICT LIABILITY

In Chapter 1, it was first pointed out that there are three bases for tort liability: torts based upon negligence, torts based upon intentional conduct, and torts based upon strict liability. At this point, the first two have been examined. In this chapter we will examine tort liability based upon strict liability. **Strict liability** is imposed upon a defendant based upon defendant's ownership or possession of animals, wild or domestic, or by engaging in abnormally dangerous activities, regardless of defendant's negligence or intention.

The theory behind strict liability is that some activities are so dangerous that courts will impose liability on the defendant without proof of negligence or proof of intention. If a person or entity engages in these activities, the law is going to make that person or entity assume the financial liability. It is immaterial for the defendant to try to prove how careful he or she acted. Frankly, it is a harsh tort theory. Accordingly, it is restricted to certain limited situations, which will be examined in further detail in this chapter.

ELEMENTS OF STRICT LIABILITY

The elements of strict liability are:

1. An act or omission by defendant
2. A duty to avoid harm (Note this is somewhat different from the negligence duty, which is a duty to use reasonable care under the circumstances.)

LEARNING OBJECTIVES

After studying this chapter, you should be able to:

- Recognize and analyze tort liability that is based upon strict liability.

- Explain strict liability for injury caused by a wild animal.

- Explain strict liability for injury caused by a domestic animal.

- Explain strict liability for injury caused by abnormally dangerous activities.

- Provide and differentiate between the defenses to strict liability.

Strict Liability
Liability imposed upon a defendant based upon defendant's ownership or possession of animals, wild or domestic, or by engaging in abnormally dangerous activities; liability without fault.

3. A breach of that duty
4. Actual cause
5. Proximate cause
6. Damages

Three General Areas Imposing Strict Liability

There are three general areas that will cause strict liability to be imposed upon a defendant: (1) animals, (2) abnormally dangerous activities, and (3) products liability. Products liability will be discussed in Chapter 10.

WILD ANIMALS

First, liability based upon strict liability for the conduct of animals will depend on whether the animal is wild or domesticated. At common law, wild animals were referred to in two categories. Wild animals were referred to as ***ferae naturae*** (wild nature), and domestic animals were referred to as ***domitae naturae*** (domesticated nature). The owner or possessor of a wild animal is strictly liable for all loss, damage, and injury resulting from the particular animal's normally dangerous propensities. For simplicity, from this point forward, both an owner and a possessor will be referred to as "owner." Technically, "animals" are defined as mammals, birds, fish, reptiles, and insects.[1]

If there is a dispute over whether the animal is truly a wild animal, the court makes that determination just as the court makes the determination of duty in negligence. This issue may arise because there are many wild animals that live in nature and are also inherently dangerous, such as a lion or tiger. However, there are many others that live in nature and are not inherently dangerous. Some are even capable of being domesticated such as a pigeon, an iguana, a wild horse, and a parrot. For an illustration of how the court approached the issue of whether a pet ferret fell into the category of a wild animal, review the *Gallick* case in Exhibit 9-1.[2]

Assume a defendant owns a pet wolf. If the wolf bites the plaintiff, strict liability will be imposed. The injury resulted from a wolf's normal vicious propensity to bite. Now, assume the same wolf simply swished its large, strong tail, knocking down and injuring a nearby small child. The injury did not arise from any particular dangerous propensity of this particular wild animal, and there would be no liability based upon strict liability.

Do not make the mistake of assuming that even if strict liability does not apply in a wild animal situation that there is no potential cause of action. There

---

Ferae Naturae
Common law reference to wild animals; literally "wild nature."

Domitae Naturae
Common law reference to domestic animals; literally "domesticated nature."

Workplace Skills Tip

As a member of the legal team, whether it is documenting an important event or conversation concerning the client, opposing counsel, the court, or some other person, it is extremely important to acquire the habit or practice of documenting the event or conversation in writing by either a formal memo or an informal e-mail.

Perfect practice makes perfect. There are three rules in this regard. Rule number one: Document what you do. Rule number two: Document what you do. Rule number three: Don't forget rule number one and rule number two! You will thank yourself later.

EXHIBIT 9-1 Relevant Case Law

Leonard Gallick and Sonina Gallick, his wife, Individually and as Parents and Natural Guardians of Brittany Gallick, a Minor, Plaintiffs, v. Bruce Barto and Betty Barto, his wife, Defendants and Third-Party Plaintiffs, v. Leonard Gallick and Sonina Gallick, his wife, Individually and as Parents and Natural Guardians of Brittany Gallick, a Minor, Third-Party Defendants, and Shawnee Miller and Todd Long, Third-Party Defendants.

United States District Court, M.D. Pennsylvania.

McClure, District Judge.

Parents of child bitten by ferret sued landlords of tenants who owned ferret. On motion for summary judgment, the District Court, McClure, J., held that landlords could be liable under Pennsylvania law for injuries caused by ferret....

MEMORANDUM

BACKGROUND:

Before the court is a motion for summary judgment filed by Bruce and Betty Barto. The resolution of that motion will be determined by the answers to two primary questions: Is a ferret a wild animal? If so, can a landlord not in possession be held liable for injuries caused by a wild animal when the landlord may not have had actual knowledge of the animal's wildness? ....

STATEMENT OF FACTS:

The material facts are undisputed. Leonard and Sonina Gallick are the natural parents of Brittany Gallick, a minor who was seven months old on March 8, 1991. Bruce and Betty Barto are the owners of a rental property located at R.D. # 1, Box 355, Hughesville, Pennsylvania. On July 28, 1990, Todd R. Long signed a lease for the house in Hughesville. Sharon Miller signed the same lease on July 30, 1990. Long and Miller resided in the house on March 8, 1991. The lease indicated that a violation of the lease rules could be enforced with a 30-day notice of eviction. Paragraph 8 of the lease stated, "No Pets."

Approximately one week after Miller and Long moved into the Hughesville property, they informed Betty Barto that they had a ferret. Approximately two weeks after the signing of the lease, Betty Barto visited the premises and there observed one ferret. Betty Barto did not know what a ferret was; in fact, she thought that the ferret was a mink.

Neither Bruce Barto nor Betty Barto issued a 30-day eviction notice after having seen the ferrets. They claim that they had no actual knowledge of any violent propensities on the part of ferrets in general or the ferrets owned by Miller and Long in particular. Bruce and Betty Barto had no right to evict the ferrets or the tenants without legal process.

Three ferrets were purchased by Miller from the pet shop in which she worked and were kept as pets by Miller and Long. They were allowed to roam freely about the rental property and slept on the couch. Although there was a cage, it was used for keeping the ferrets' food and water bowls. The ferrets generally were playful, though some aggressive behavior may have occurred.

On March 8, 1991, Leonard Gallick and Sonina Gallick went to the house rented by Miller and Long at approximately 7:00 p.m. for social purposes. Brittany was left on the floor of the bedroom to sleep, and the door was closed and secured by a chair. Sometime later, Sonina Gallick entered the bedroom to check on Brittany, and found that she had been bitten by one of the ferrets.

(Continued)

EXHIBIT 9-1   *(Continued)*

DISCUSSION:

I. IS A FERRET A WILD ANIMAL?

In Pennsylvania, a person who keeps a wild animal, or a domestic animal with known vicious propensities, may be liable for injuries caused by the dangerous nature of the animal....

If a ferret is a wild animal, then, its owner, and perhaps the owner's landlord, may be liable for injuries caused by the ferret. We conclude that, under the applicable principles of Pennsylvania law, a ferret is a wild animal.

A. GENERAL FACTS ABOUT FERRETS

According to Webster's *New World Dictionary of the American Language* (College Ed.1968), a ferret is "a kind of weasel, easily tamed and used for hunting or killing of rabbits, rats, etc. ..." Generally, two types of ferrets are found in the United States: the black-footed ferret (*Mustela nigripes*) and the domestic or common ferret (*Mustela putorius* or *Mustela putorius furo*) ....

We turn now to the question of whether ferrets are wild animals. Hereinafter, the term "ferret" shall refer to common or domestic ferrets.

B. PENNSYLVANIA LAW ON WILD ANIMALS

As noted above, under Pennsylvania law, one who brings onto his land and keeps a wild animal is liable for any injuries caused by the dangerous nature of the animal....

Under the Game and Wildlife Code, a wild animal is any animal that is not a domestic animal under the general definitions provision, § 1991. Under that section, a ferret is not a domestic animal. Therefore, a ferret must be a wild animal.

C. GENERAL CONSIDERATIONS

In addition to the case law set forth above, we believe that there are general considerations which lead to the conclusion that a ferret is a wild animal.

First, ferrets have been kept by humans for some time basically because of their propensity to attack small animals. According to one article, they were first brought to this country from Europe in 1875 to hunt for rabbits.... The obvious conclusion from this fact is that, while people have kept ferrets, they have done so for the limited purpose of hunting, and ferrets serve that purpose only because of their ferocity.

For this reason, many authorities have warned against keeping ferrets as pets. "Some animals should never be pets. Turtles, poisonous snakes, chimpanzees, skunks, *ferrets*, and other *wild animals* bite and carry diseases. Furthermore, as this type of animal matures, it can become aggressive....

A. Ferrets have been known to attack humans, particularly children, for no reason and without warning.

B. There is no proven vaccine for rabies in ferrets nor is there an accepted procedure for judging a rabid ferret without sacrificing the ferret. A ferret which bites a person may be immediately seized and put to death by the State in order to obtain necessary test samples....

A ferret, on the other hand, is a wild animal which people may, to a point, be successful in keeping in their home. Therefore, a ferret is a wild animal with domestic propensities. However, those propensities do not change its essential character as a wild animal. We hold that a ferret is a wild animal.

Source: Gallick v. Barto, 828 F. Supp. 1168 (U.S. Dist. Ct. Penn. 1993).

may be a cause of action based upon negligence. First, in the pet wolf example, a small child may be attracted to an animal such as this; in other words, an "attractive nuisance." For a negligence theory, plaintiff may argue that defendant knows the wolf has a large, powerful tail, knows it is natural for a wolf to swish his tail around from time to time, knows a young child is present, and knows if the wolf moves its tail suddenly, the child could be hit, knocked down, and injured.

There have been cases in the news recently involving wild animals. One involved a pet boa constrictor that escaped from its cage and suffocated a small child. Another involved a trainer at SeaWorld in Orlando, Florida, who was dragged underwater to her death by one of the trained killer whales. In 2009, a Connecticut woman had her face literally ripped off by her friend and employer's 200-pound pet chimpanzee. The chimp had apparently gotten out of its cage, and the owner called the woman to come over to her home to help corral the chimp. The chimp became irate and literally ripped off the woman's face and most of both of her hands. Both eyes had to be removed. She also has no nose and no lips. She had extensive plastic surgery.

The chimpanzee case is a classic fact pattern supporting suit on a theory of strict liability. It certainly demonstrates the rationale for making a person strictly liable and assuming the financial burden if that person chooses to think that he or she can domesticate a wild animal such as this and make it a pet.

Exception to Wild Animal Liability

There are some exceptions to strict liability based upon an injury caused by a wild animal. The rule of strict liability does not apply to persons or entities who, as part of their public duties, are required to take possession of the animals or to accept them for transportation. One exception is for animals housed under a public duty such as a public zoo or a public park. Another exception is for animals that are required to be taken for transport by a common carrier. Again, even if strict liability is not a viable tort theory against a zoo or a common carrier, both of these entities would have a duty to exercise reasonable care, and negligence may still be a viable tort theory.

DOMESTIC ANIMALS

The Restatement (Second) of Torts § 509 (1977) states this rule: "A possessor of a domestic animal that he knows or has reason to know has dangerous propensities abnormal to its class, is subject to liability for harm done by the animal to another, although he has exercised the utmost care to prevent it from doing the harm. This liability is limited to harm that results from the abnormally dangerous propensity of which the possessor knows or has reason to know." A **dangerous propensity** is a trait or characteristic of a domestic animal that is abnormal to its class that presents a danger such that strict liability will be imposed. The court in *Barto* in Exhibit 9-1 noted: "For example, dogs may be domestic, but there are dogs, such as pit bulls, doberman pinschers, and rottweilers, the hazard of keeping which cannot be denied."[3] Because most dogs are harmless, attacking and biting a person would be considered abnormal so that the dog owner would not be liable under strict liability. However, if the owner knew of an otherwise friendly dog's vicious propensity, the owner will be strictly liable.

The dangerous propensity does not necessarily have to be a vicious propensity. The owner of a large friendly dog that the owner knows has a habit of running and jumping up on people and knocking them down, such as children or the

Dangerous Propensity
A trait or characteristic of a domestic animal that is abnormal to its class that presents a danger such that strict liability will be imposed.

Workplace Skills Tip

If you are working in a firm doing investigative work on a dog bite case, how might one prove the owner had knowledge of the dog's dangerous propensity? One's knowledge of a fact may be proved by circumstantial evidence. This evidence may be the abnormal precautions taken to enclose the dog such as the type of fencing used, walking the dog with a muzzle, using the dog as a watchdog, or having a sign in the yard that says "Beware of Dog." These are possibilities to explore when investigating as well as any statements made by the owner to others, such as "Be careful of my dog!"

elderly, could be liable under strict liability. However, if this same large friendly dog unexpectedly became vicious and bit a person, under the Restatement rule, there would be no liability under strict liability. The harm must result from the abnormally dangerous propensity of which the owner has knowledge. Here, the owner has knowledge of the danger of the dog's abnormally dangerous propensity of jumping up on people but no knowledge of the dog attacking and biting people. For an excellent discussion of whether a horse had a certain dangerous propensity, the student must read the decision of *Kaplan v. C Lazy U Ranch*, 615 F.Supp.234 (D. Colo. 1985) in Exhibit 9-2. This was one smart horse.

To reiterate, even if the facts do not fit a case of strict liability, the theory of negligence must be considered. Consider the case of a vicious Doberman trained to attack on command, which injures a person. Besides strict liability, the owner could be liable on a theory of battery, an intentional tort discussed in Chapter 7. This is because battery requires an intentional, volitional act such as giving a command that sets a chain of events in motion that causes harm to a person.

There is somewhat of a contradiction in the law of strict liability in one certain domestic animal scenario. This involves domestic animals with known dangerous propensities, but the courts tend not to impose strict liability. It is common knowledge that a bull is more dangerous than a cow, a stallion is more dangerous than a mare, and a ram is more dangerous than a ewe.

Courts have generally not imposed strict liability when injury results from those types of domestic animals. So why is there no strict liability imposed when injury is caused by a bull, a stallion, or a ram? Perhaps it is simply the social policy of the law that these agrarian animals are a part of our culture in the United States. They have been here for hundreds of years. The male of those species provides an inherent usefulness because of the needed breeding of livestock. Courts are constantly balancing policy interests. Courts apparently take the public policy position that these particular dangerous animals' utility for breeding purposes outweighs the danger they may impose to society such that strict liability will not be imposed. Negligence is still an available basis to consider, however.

"Every Dog Is Entitled to One Bite"

The general rule is that domestic animals that have not shown dangerous propensities in the past cannot subject their owner to liability, thus, the saying, "every dog is entitled to one bite." The saying probably comes from a case in Scotland over a hundred years ago in which the court stated: "The dog has the privilege of one worry."[4] After that first bite, the owner now has knowledge of the dangerous propensity. Strict liability only applies when the owner of a domestic animal knows or has reason to know (not "should have known" as that is a negligence standard) of the animal's dangerous propensities. In the case of a dog, it may be such traits

EXHIBIT 9-2 Relevant Case Law

Ann K. Kaplan and Robert Z. Kaplan, Plaintiffs, v. C Lazy U Ranch, et al., Defendants.

United States District Court, D. Colorado.

Kane, District Judge.

MEMORANDUM OPINION AND ORDER

This diversity action is based on personal injuries sustained by plaintiff when she fell from a horse owned and allegedly saddled in a negligent manner by defendants, who own and operate the C Lazy U Ranch.

Defendants have moved for partial summary judgment as to plaintiffs' claims based upon res ipsa loquitur, strict liability for a dangerous animal, strict products liability and strict liability for failure to warn and/or instruct as to a dangerous product. Plaintiffs have responded with a brief opposing defendants' motion for partial summary judgment....

II. Strict Liability for Dangerous Animals

Plaintiffs claim that defendants are liable under the theory of strict liability for dangerous animals. The complaint alleges that the horse "posed an unreasonable risk of injury to persons riding her because of her unusual conformation and/or her habit of expanding her chest when saddled, resulting in a propensity for Defendants' saddles to slip or tip to the side." Complaint, p. 6. Defendants have moved for summary judgment claiming that horses are not wild or naturally dangerous animals to which strict liability is applicable, and that any finding of liability must be based upon proof of negligence.

Colorado courts have applied strict liability to owners of wild animals which by their nature are vicious and unpredictable, and have done so without proof of the owners' knowledge of such propensities.... Strict liability also has been applied to owners of a domestic animal proven to be vicious where the owners were aware of their animal's dangerous propensities.... Horses, however, "are regarded as domestic animals virtually everywhere, and as to these, therefore, strict liability requires a showing that the defendant knew, or had reason to know, of an abnormal propensity." W. Prosser and W. Keeton, The *Law of Torts* § 76 (5th ed. 1984); see also Restatement (Second) of Torts § 509 (1977).

Plaintiff's claim that the horse had a "dangerous propensity" is untenable. A horse which is known to kick or bite persons without provocation may have a dangerous propensity. A tendency, however, to expand its chest while being saddled, while it might be classified as fractious, is not a "dangerous propensity" within the scope of this doctrine of liability. Further, that habit alone could never be the proximate cause of plaintiff's injury. Defendant's motion for summary judgment on this claim is granted.

Source: Kaplan v. C Lazy U Ranch, 615 F. Supp. 234 (U.S. Dist. Ct. Colo. 1985).

of biting, scratching, or jumping up on people. If a pet horse, tame and docile, had a known propensity to kick people who are too close, strict liability would be the proper theory.

Some jurisdictions, in order to do away with the "one bite rule," have enacted **dog bite statutes**. These statutes, dealing with dogs only, impose strict liability on the owner for injuries caused by the dog, even though the owner knew of no previous dangerous propensities. For a dog bite case that illustrates these principles, see the *Young* case in Exhibit 9-3.[5]

Dog Bite Statute
Imposes strict liability on the owner for injuries caused by the dog, even though the owner knew of no previous dangerous propensities.

EXHIBIT 9-3 Relevant Case Law

Howard Young et al. v. Gloria Proctor.

Supreme Judicial Court of Maine.

Roberts, Justice.

Howard and Rachel Young appeal from a judgment entered in the Superior Court, York County, upon a jury finding that Gloria Proctor was not liable for injuries caused to their son, Tony Young, by Proctor's dog, Tyler. The Youngs contend that the trial court erred (1) in instructing the jury that the owner's knowledge of the dog's injurious propensities was a prerequisite to common law strict liability and (2) in refusing to admit evidence of a District Court finding against Proctor under 7 M.R.S.A. § 3605 (1979) (Complaints by Persons Assaulted by Dogs). Because we find no error in the Superior Court's actions, we affirm the judgment.

On the morning of June 11, 1982, the eight-year-old Tony walked from his parents' property to the adjoining property of Gloria Proctor to meet Proctor's daughter, Helen Staeth, age twelve, to walk to the school bus stop. At this time, Tony, with Helen's permission, patted the dog, Tyler. It appears that Helen then proceeded to the school bus stop while Tony remained behind. Tyler bit Tony on the shoulder, shaking him and running along his runner with Tony in his mouth. Shortly thereafter Rachel Young, hearing the screams of Helen and Tony, ran to Proctor's property and witnessed her son held by the dog. She was able to free Tony by sitting on the dog's back and forcibly opening his jaws. Tony was then taken to Webber Hospital in Biddeford where he was hospitalized. A number of witnesses testified at trial that Tony had repeatedly teased Tyler before the dog bite incident.

On June 14, 1982, a complaint was filed against Gloria Proctor in Biddeford District Court under section 3605 alleging that she was the keeper of a "dangerous and vicious" dog. Although the complaint indicated that she was being charged with a Class E crime, the proceeding is civil in nature. The District Court records are not clear as to whether she pleaded guilty to the charge or *nolo contendere.* She was convicted of the charge and an order was entered requiring the "dog to be restrained inside a five foot wire fence and a one-quarter inch wire cable secured with padlock." The plea was changed by motion on December 20, 1983 to *nolo contendere.*

FN1. 7 M.R.S.A. § 3605 states in pertinent part:

Whoever is assaulted by a dog when peaceably walking or riding or finds a dog strolling outside the premises of its keeper and the said dog is not safety [sic] muzzled, may, within 4 days thereafter, make written complaint before the District Court having jurisdiction, that he really believes and has reason to believe that said dog is dangerous and vicious. Whereupon said court shall order said owner or keeper to appear and answer to said complaint by serving said owner or keeper of said dog with a copy of said complaint and order a reasonable time before the day set for the hearing thereon. If, upon hearing, the court is satisfied that the complaint is true, he shall order the dog to be killed or order said owner or keeper of said dog to muzzle the same, restrain the same, or confine said dog to the premises of said owner or keeper and the owner or keeper shall pay the costs.

The complaint in this case was filed on December 29, 1982 in Superior Court by Howard Young, individually and as next friend of Tony Young, and Rachel Young for damages resulting from the dog bite incident. The complaint alleged strict liability under the common law and absolute liability under 7 M.R.S.A. § 3651 (1979) FN2 against Proctor. Proctor filed a counterclaim against the Youngs but that claim was voluntarily dismissed.

FN2. 7 M.R.S.A. § 3651 (1979) states:

When a dog does damage to a person or his property, his owner or keeper, and the parent, guardian, master or mistress of any minor who owns such dog, forfeits to the person injured the amount of the

(Continued)

EXHIBIT 9-3 *(Continued)*

damage done, provided said damage was not occasioned through the fault of the person injured, to be recovered by civil action.

At trial the court instructed the jury over plaintiffs' objection that in order to be found strictly liable, Proctor must have had knowledge of Tyler's vicious propensities and that notice meant the same as knowledge. A special verdict form setting forth the two causes of action was submitted to the jury. The jury found in favor of Proctor on both causes of action. They also found specially that Proctor did not have notice of Tyler's injurious propensities and that Tony provoked Tyler. The Youngs seasonably appealed.

The Youngs contend that the trial court erred in instructing the jury that under the common law an owner of a dog is strictly liable for injuries caused by the animal only if the owner had knowledge of the animal's injurious propensities. Young argues that the Maine cases which have discussed this issue have said that mere notice of the dog's injurious propensities is sufficient for liability. Although the Youngs now cite section 509 of the Restatement (Second) of Torts (1977), the proposed jury instruction they submitted to the presiding justice is not supported by that authority. In the Superior Court they cited two Maine cases neither of which support the proposition that mere notice is sufficient or that strict liability attaches when the owner should have known of the animal's injurious propensity.

After a careful review of our cases, we conclude that the trial judge correctly refused the Youngs' requested instruction. Moreover, at the conclusion of the charge, plaintiffs' counsel again focused upon *notice* as opposed to *knowledge*. To clarify any confusion resulting from our use of the terms notice and knowledge interchangeably in our past opinions, we now specifically adopt the Restatement view that

(1) A possessor of a domestic animal that he knows or has reason to know has dangerous propensities abnormal to his class, is subject to liability for harm done by the animal to another, although he has exercised the utmost care to prevent it from doing so.

(2) This liability is limited to harm that results from the abnormally dangerous propensity of which the possessor knows or has reason to know.

Restatement (Second) of Torts § 509 (1977). The Restatement § 12 makes clear the distinction between "reason to know," which implies no duty to know, and "should know." We have never imposed strict liability because the owner should have known of the animal's dangerous propensities; we have always required knowledge. Additionally, in previous cases we have refused to find this requirement too arduous…In this case, the judge correctly instructed the jury that knowledge of the dog's injurious propensities was required to impose strict liability under the common law.

Young also argues that the court erred in refusing to admit the District Court's finding against Proctor under section 3605. Because the violation of that section is civil rather than criminal, and the issues in the two proceedings are different, we find no error in the trial court's ruling….

Judgment affirmed.

Source: Young v. Proctor, 495 A.2d 828 (Me. 1985).

Status of Injured Person

Many injuries caused by animals occur on the plaintiff's premises or on public premises. What if the injury from an animal occurs on the animal owner's land? Strict liability clearly applies to a person who enters with the express or implied permission of the land occupier. (See Chapter 5.) Strict liability does not apply to trespassers whose presence the owner did not know or the owner had no reason to know or anticipate. However, if the landowner had a vicious dog on the premises as a "watchdog," strict liability can still be imposed on the owner.

ABNORMALLY DANGEROUS CONDITIONS AND ACTIVITIES

In addition to liability for wild and domestic animals, a person's engaging in *abnormally dangerous* conditions or activities may subject that person to strict liability. This is so even if the person has utilized the utmost of care to try to prevent the loss, damage, or injury. The concept originates from an English case decided in 1868, *Rylands v. Fletcher*, 159 Eng. Rep. 737 (1868). The case itself involved water bursting from the bottom of a reservoir being constructed on defendant's land. The water damaged adjacent property of the plaintiff. Justice Blackburn stated: "The person who for his own purposes brings on his lands and collects and keeps there anything likely to do mischief if it escapes, must keep it in at his peril." On appeal, affirming the decision for the plaintiff, one of the justices stated that defendant will be strictly liable for harm caused by "a non-natural use" of defendant's land. But as the Restatement (Third) of Torts, PEH § 20 points out: "The 'non-natural use' phrase is itself ambiguous, yielding at least three possible meanings. A 'non-natural use' might be one that departs from a state of nature; it might be one that is uncommon or unusual; or it might be one that is unreasonable or inappropriate in light of the local circumstances."

Courts in this area have struggled over the years with the meaning of activities that impose strict liability. The best way of presenting this struggle may be to examine the various Restatements. Restatement of Torts used the term "ultra hazardous activities." Activities, such as blasting with explosives and the use of fireworks, were typical examples of ultra hazardous activities. The Restatement (Second) of Torts § 520 first used the term "abnormally dangerous activities" instead of the word "ultra hazardous" with six factors to be balanced:

1. The existence of a high degree of risk of some harm to the person, land, or chattels of others.
2. The likelihood that the resulting harm will be great.
3. An inability to eliminate the risk by the use of reasonable care.
4. The extent to which the activity is not a matter of common usage.
5. The inappropriateness of the activity to the location where it takes place.
6. The extent to which its value to the community is outweighed by its dangerous attributes.

The Existence of a High Degree of Risk of Some Harm to the Person, Land, or Chattels of Others

This is a fairly self-explanatory factor. See the discussion under the second factor.

The Likelihood that the Resulting Harm Will Be Great

The Second Restatement comment noted that in examining the first two factors, some activities such as atomic energy involve major risks of harm no matter how, when, or where they are done. Storing explosives creates major risks unless conducted in a remote location. Others, such as hauling ammonia by a common carrier, create a risk to the locations where the carrier passes through.

An Inability to Eliminate the Risk by the Use of Reasonable Care

In commenting on factor 3, the Restatement notes that the manufacture of explosives in a city may involve a risk of detonation no matter how careful the manufacturer is. The manufacturer is not negligent simply for manufacturing the explosives, but the manufacturer would be liable under strict liability if an explosion occurred causing harm.

The Extent to Which the Activity Is Not a Matter of Common Usage

The explanation for factor 4 is that common usage means that an activity is simply conducted by the public in general. Automobiles, for example, may be dangerous, but they are commonly used and thus not an abnormally dangerous activity. Driving a military tank, however, is not a common usage and would be considered abnormally dangerous. Even flying an airplane may be considered abnormally dangerous, but it too has reached such a stage of safety and common usage and acceptance by the public that the proper tort theory may be negligence.

The Inappropriateness of the Activity to the Location Where It Takes Place

Factor 5 means that if the location is one inappropriate to the particular activity, there may be an abnormal danger created. Blasting does not necessarily create an abnormal danger if it is done in a remote location. Storing gasoline, ammonia, propane, or other such materials does not create an abnormal danger if, again, located in a remote area. As the Restatement comment also points out, "Coal mining must be done where there is coal; oil wells can be located only where there is oil; and a dam impounding water in a stream can be situated only in the bed of the stream. If the activities are of sufficient value to the community, they may not be regarded as abnormally dangerous when they are so located, since the only place where the activity can be carried on must necessarily be regarded as an appropriate one."

The Extent to Which Its Value to the Community Is Outweighed by Its Dangerous Attributes

Factor 6 asks the court to consider the value to the community, even though there is unquestionably a serious risk of harm. The comment to that factor points out: "Thus, in Texas and Oklahoma, a properly conducted oil or gas well, at least in a rural area, is not regarded as abnormally dangerous, while a different conclusion has been reached in Kansas and Indiana. California, whose oil industry is far from insignificant, has concluded that an oil well drilled in a thickly settled residential area in the city of Los Angeles is a matter of strict liability."

The current Restatement (Third) of Torts now states: "(a) An actor who carries on an abnormally dangerous activity is subject to strict liability for physical harm resulting from the activity. (b) An activity is abnormally dangerous if: (1) the activity creates a foreseeable and highly significant risk of physical harm even when reasonable care is exercised by all actors; and (2) the activity is not one of common usage."[6] This recent Restatement still utilizes the "abnormally dangerous activity" but adds two other requirements—"foreseeability of harm" and an activity not of "common usage."

Use of the word "foreseeable" means that a defendant may be liable under strict liability if defendant has reason to know or *should know* of the risk involved in the activity. "Common usage" refers to the example above concerning the common usage of automobiles but not military tanks. A utility company that distributes gas or electricity is providing a service that is common to the community, even though it is engaged in by only one or two companies in the community. Dispensing of utilities is one of common usage, and strict liability would not apply under the latest Restatement on Strict Liability. The determination of whether or not an activity is an abnormally dangerous activity, like duty in negligence, is for the court, not the jury, to decide.

Two basic concepts need to be reinforced at this point. If strict liability does not apply in a given fact scenario, the student must always be considering whether or not liability might be established on the other two bases of tort theory, namely, intention or negligence. Second, in analyzing strict liability—whether a wild animal, a domestic animal, or abnormally dangerous conditions or activities—liability is really being imposed for harm that is caused from *abnormal* dangers. Is it not abnormal to have a chimpanzee for a pet? Is it not abnormal for the family black lab to have a propensity to be vicious? Is it not abnormal to be engaging in certain conditions or activities such as blasting with dynamite as compared to other activities?

Other Considerations Concerning Establishment of Strict Liability

It was noted on the first page of this chapter addressing the element of duty that the duty in strict liability is one of avoiding harm. It is not the duty to use reasonable care. Liability under strict liability is being imposed regardless of fault. The duty is typically owed only to foreseeable plaintiffs (discussed in the *Palsgraf* case in Chapter 2). The harm must be the kind of harm foreseeable from the dangerous animal or activity. Refer to the example used in the text concerning the wolf that did not bite the child but knocked the child down with its tail. Actual cause and proximate cause are utilized in strict liability as they are in negligence.

Workplace Skills Tip

As a personal injury paralegal working on the team of a plaintiff's personal injury case, it may seem as if a perfect case has come along. Good facts. Good law. Good client. Good judge. Good venue. Invariably, there will be some little item wrong with every seemingly perfect case. Even though the particular plaintiff's case has every appearance of being a "clear winner," approach it with this conservative philosophy: Presenting and trying this case will be like going out on a church drive or other charitable organization drive. The folks from whom you are asking for money don't have to give you a penny.

Finally, damages must be proved with a preponderance of the evidence. The case of *Yukon Equipment, Inc. v. Fireman's Fund Insurance Company*, 585 P.2d 1206 (Alaska 1978) in Exhibit 9-4 presents a good discussion of the differences between the views in the First Restatement and in the Second Restatement on strict liability as well as causation as it relates to strict liability. Note in *Yukon Equipment* that even the activity of thieves who set off the explosion did not cut off the claim of causation.

EXHIBIT 9-4 Relevant Case Law

Yukon Equipment, Inc., an Alaska Corporation, and E. I. du Pont de Nemours Company, a Delaware Corporation, Petitioners, v. Fireman's Fund Insurance Company et al., Respondents.

Supreme Court of Alaska.

Matthews, Justice.

OPINION

A large explosion occurred at 2:47 a.m. on December 7, 1973, in the suburbs north of the city of Anchorage. The explosion originated at a storage magazine for explosives under lease from the federal government to petitioner E. I. du Pont de Nemours and Company, which was operated by petitioner Yukon Equipment, Inc. The storage magazine is located on a 1,870 acre tract of federal land which had been withdrawn by the Department of the Interior for the use of the Alaska Railroad for explosive storage purposes by separate orders in 1950 and 1961. The magazine which exploded was located 3,820 feet from the nearest building not used to store explosives and 4,330 feet from the nearest public highway. At the time of the explosion it contained approximately 80,000 pounds of explosives. The blast damaged dwellings and other buildings within a two mile radius of the magazine and, in some instances, beyond a two mile radius. The ground concussion it caused registered 1.8 on the Richter scale at the earthquake observation station in Palmer, some 30 miles away.

The explosion was caused by thieves. Four young men had driven onto the tract where the magazine was located, broken into the storage magazine, set a prepared charge, and fled. They apparently did so in an effort to conceal the fact that they had stolen explosives from the site a day or two earlier.

This consolidated lawsuit was brought to recover for property damage caused by the explosion. Cross-motions for partial summary judgment were filed, and summary judgment on the issue of liability was granted in favor of the respondents. Respondents presented alternative theories of liability based on negligence, nuisance, absolute liability, and trespass. The court's order granting partial summary judgment did not specify the theory on which liability was based.

Petitioners contend that none of the theories may be utilized to fix liability on them by summary judgment and further that the intentional detonation of the magazine is a superseding cause relieving them of liability under any theory. Respondents argue that the summary judgment is sustainable under the theory of absolute liability and that the intentional nature of the explosion is not a defense. We agree with respondents and affirm.

I

The leading case on liability for the storage of explosives is *Exner v. Sherman Power Const. Co.*, 54 F.2d 510 (2d Cir. 1931). There dynamite stored by the defendant exploded causing personal injury and property damage to the plaintiffs who resided some 935 feet away from the storage site. A

(Continued)

EXHIBIT 9-4 *(Continued)*

distinguished panel of the Circuit Court of Appeals for the Second Circuit held the defendant liable regardless of fault:

Dynamite is of the class of elements which one who stores or uses in such a locality, or under such circumstances as to cause likelihood of risk to others, stores or uses at his peril. He is an insurer, and is absolutely liable if damage results to third persons, either from the direct impact of rocks thrown out by the explosion (which would be a common law trespass) or from concussion....

As Exner reflects, the particular rule of absolute liability for blasting damage received earlier and more general acceptance in the United States than the generalized rule of absolute liability for unusually dangerous activity which has its antecedents in *Rylands v. Fletcher.* The generalized rule gained added currency in the United States following its adoption by the American Law Institute as sections 519-524 of the Restatement of Torts (1938). Under the Restatement s 519, a rule of absolute liability for "ultra-hazardous" activity was imposed. Section 520 defined an activity as ultra-hazardous if it

(a) necessarily involves a risk of serious harm to the person, land or chattels of others which cannot be eliminated by the exercise of the utmost care, and

(b) is not a matter of common usage.

Comments (c) and (e) to that section make it clear that the storage of explosives is Per se ultra-hazardous....

The storage and transportation of explosive substances are ultra-hazardous activities because no precautions and care can make it reasonably certain that they will not explode and because the harm resulting from their explosion is almost certain to be serious.

Comment (e) addresses the question of common usage, stating:

While blasting is recognized as a proper means of clearing woodlands for cultivating and of excavating for building purposes, the conditions which require its use are usually of brief duration. It is generally required because of the peculiar character of the land and it is not a part of the customary processes of farming or of building operations. Likewise, the manufacture, storage, transportation and use of high explosives, although necessary to the construction of many public and private works, are carried on by a comparatively small number of persons and, therefore, are not matters of common usage.

Thus the particular rule of *Exner*, absolute liability for damage caused by the storage of explosives, was preserved by the Restatement and a general rule, inferred from *Exner* and the authorities on which it was based, and from *Rylands v. Fletcher* and its antecedents, was stated which imposed absolute liability on any other activity which met the definition of ultra-hazardous.

The Restatement (Second) of Torts (1977), adopted by the ALI after the explosion in this case, does not reflect a Per se rule of liability for the storage of explosives. Instead it lists six factors to be considered in determining whether an activity is "abnormally dangerous" and therefore subject to the rule of absolute liability. The factors are:

(a) existence of a high degree of risk of some harm to the person, land or chattels of others;

(b) likelihood that the harm that results from it will be great;

(c) inability to eliminate the risk by the exercise of reasonable care;

(d) extent to which the activity is not a matter of common usage;

(e) inappropriateness of the activity to the place where it is carried on; and

(f) extent to which its value to the community is outweighed by its dangerous attributes.

(Continued)

EXHIBIT 9-4 *(Continued)*

Id. s 520.

Based in large part on the Restatement (Second), petitioners argue that their use was not abnormally dangerous. Specifically they contend that their use of the magazine for the storage of explosives was a normal and appropriate use of the area in question since the storage magazine was situated on lands set aside by the United States for such purposes and was apparently located in compliance with applicable federal regulations. They point out that the storage served a legitimate community need for an accessible source of explosives for various purposes. They contend that before absolute liability can be imposed in any circumstance a preliminary finding must be made as to whether or not the defendant's activity is abnormally dangerous, that such a determination involves the weighing of the six factors set out in section 520 of the Restatement (Second) of Torts, and that an evaluation of those factors in this case could not appropriately be done on motion for summary judgment....

The factors specified by section 520 of the Restatement (Second) of Torts are for consideration of the court, not the jury. Here the petitioners assume, as they must with the case in its present posture, that the superior court found that their activity was abnormally dangerous. They contend that this court in reviewing the superior court's assumed conclusion should not apply the "clearly erroneous" standard of Civil Rule 52(a) but is free to reach an independent conclusion based on the same non-testimonial record of undisputed facts presented below. We agree that this is the appropriate standard of review....

If we were to apply the Restatement (Second)'s six factor test to the storage of explosives in this case we would be inclined to conclude that the use involved here was an abnormally dangerous one. Comment (f) to section 520 makes it clear that all of the factors need not be present for an activity to be considered abnormally dangerous:

In determining whether the danger is abnormal, the factors listed in clauses (a) to (f) of this Section are all to be considered, and are all of importance. Any one of them is not necessarily sufficient to itself in a particular case, and ordinarily several of them will be required for strict liability. On the other hand it is not necessary that each of them be present, especially if others weigh heavily.

The first three factors, involving the degree of risk, harm, and difficulty of eliminating the risk, are obviously present in the storage of 80,000 pounds of explosives in a suburban area. The fourth factor, that the activity not be a matter of common usage, is also met. Comment (i) states:

Likewise the manufacture, storage, transportation and use of high explosives, although necessary to the construction of many public and private works, are carried on by only a comparatively small number of persons and therefore are not matters of common usage.

The fifth factor, inappropriateness of the activity, is arguably not present, for the storage did take place on land designated by the United States government for that purpose. However, the designation took place at a time when the area was less densely populated than it was at the time of the explosion. Likewise, the storage reserve was not entirely appropriate to the quantity of explosives stored because the explosion caused damage well beyond the boundaries of the reserve. The sixth factor, value to the community relates primarily to situations where the dangerous activity is the primary economic activity of the community in question. Thus comment (k) states that such factor applies particularly when the community is largely devoted to the dangerous enterprise and its prosperity largely depends upon it. Thus the interests of a particular town whose livelihood depends upon such an activity as manufacturing cement may be such that cement plants will be regarded as a normal activity for that community notwithstanding the risk of serious harm from the emission of cement dust....

Since five of the six factors required by section 520 of the Restatement (Second) are met and the sixth is debatable, we would impose absolute liability here if we were to use that approach....

(Continued)

EXHIBIT 9-4 *(Continued)*

However, we do not believe that the Restatement (Second) approach should be used in cases involving the use or storage of explosives. Instead, we adhere to the rule of *Exner v. Sherman Power Constr. Co.* and its progeny imposing absolute liability in such cases. The Restatement (Second) approach requires an analysis of degrees of risk and harm, difficulty of eliminating risk, and appropriateness of place, before absolute liability may be imposed. Such factors suggest a negligence standard. The six factor analysis may well be necessary where damage is caused by unique hazards and the question is whether the general rule of absolute liability applies, but in cases involving the storage and use of explosives we take that question to have been resolved by more than a century of judicial decisions....

The reasons for imposing absolute liability on those who have created a grave risk of harm to others by storing or using explosives are largely independent of considerations of locational appropriateness. We see no reason for making a distinction between the right of a homesteader to recover when his property has been damaged by a blast set off in a remote corner of the state, and the right to compensation of an urban resident whose home is destroyed by an explosion originating in a settled area. In each case, the loss is properly to be regarded as a cost of the business of storing or using explosives. Every incentive remains to conduct such activities in locations which are as safe as possible, because there the damages resulting from an accident will be kept to a minimum.

II

The next question is whether the intentional detonation of the storage magazine was a superseding cause relieving petitioners from liability....

The considerations which impel cutting off liability where there is a superseding cause in negligence cases also apply to cases of absolute liability....

Prior to the explosion in question the petitioners' magazines had been illegally broken into at least six times. Most of these entries involved the theft of explosives. Petitioners had knowledge of all of this.

Applying the standards set forth in *Sharp, supra,* to these facts we find there to have been no superseding cause. The incendiary destruction of premises by thieves to cover evidence of theft is not so uncommon an occurrence that it can be regarded as highly extraordinary. Moreover, the particular kind of result threatened by the defendant's conduct, the storage of explosives, was an explosion at the storage site. Since the threatened result occurred it would not be consistent with the principles stated in *Sharp, supra,* to hold there to have been a superseding cause. Absolute liability is imposed on those who store or use explosives because they have created an unusual risk to others. As between those who have created the risk for the benefit of their own enterprise and those whose only connection with the enterprise is to have suffered damage because of it, the law places the risk of loss on the former. When the risk created causes damage in fact, insistence that the precise details of the intervening cause be foreseeable would subvert the purpose of that rule of law.

Source: Yukon Equipment ,Inc. v. Fireman's Fund Insurance Company, 585 P.2d 1206 (Ak. 1978).

Defenses to Strict Liability

Virtually the same defenses available to the defendant in a negligence action are available in a strict liability action. However, contributory negligence is traditionally not a defense to strict liability unless the plaintiff knew of the danger and the plaintiff's own negligence was the exact cause of the activity's end result. Comparative fault statutes such as the ones examined in Chapter 6 may provide a defense. Voluntary assumption of the known risk is traditionally a defense to strict liability.

CASE 9.1 Hypothetical Case: Developing Workplace Skills

You are a paralegal working in a plaintiff's personal injury firm that specializes in plaintiff's auto accident cases and plaintiff's medical malpractice cases. A client of the firm has come in to see the senior partner concerning a dog bite incident. You have received the following memo:

MEMO

To: Paralegal

From: Attorney

RE: New file/client Jake Johnson

File: RNJ 1586

I just finished an office conference with Jake Johnson this morning. His 17-year-old grandson, Reuben, was recently injured from a dog bite, and he wants our firm to represent him.

This is what Jake tells me: First, you may have heard of his grandson, Reuben Black. Reuben is the young man from our community who is one of the finalists on *American Idol*. He is a very handsome kid with a great voice and a promising future in the entertainment industry. Reuben was staying at Jake's house for the weekend. Jake lives next door to Bill Smith, a "ne'er do well" who filed for bankruptcy a year or so ago. Bill was apparently out of town for a few days so he asked a high school buddy and longtime friend John Brown to "house sit" and "dog sit" for the days he was out of town. You've maybe also heard of Mr. Brown. He is the opposite of Bill Smith and has been a highly successful businessman.

At the time of the incident, on Saturday, September 15th of this year around 10:00 a.m., Reuben was going out for a jog. Before doing so, he decided to walk across a little path between an open spot in the bushes of the two back yards and go into Mr. Smith's yard to grab an apple from his apple tree. Reuben said he saw Mr. Brown working in the garage who smiled and waved to him as he went into the back yard. As he grabbed a couple of apples, he saw Smith's pet German Shepherd Sadie, chained and sitting on the ground outside her doghouse growling at him. Reuben decided before he left to simply throw an apple at Sadie, which he did, although he didn't hit either Sadie or the doghouse. The next thing he knew, the dog had him down by the throat and viciously bit him on the face and throat before Mr. Brown could arrive and pull the dog off Reuben. Mr. Brown called the ambulance, and Reuben was taken to the hospital. He eventually had to have surgery for some damage to his vocal cords and plastic surgery on his face. He currently has some pretty bad scars on his face running from the forehead down to the right cheek. The doctors say it is "iffy" if he will still be able to sing as he has done in the past.

For your immediate assistance, the statute in our jurisdiction is short, and this is what it states:

"If a dog, without provocation, attacks or injures any person who is acting peaceably in any place where the person may lawfully be, the owner of the dog is liable in damages to the person so attacked or injured to the full amount of the injury sustained. The term "owner" includes any person harboring or keeping a dog, but the owner shall be primarily liable. The term "dog" includes both male and female of the canine species."

(Continued)

CASE 9.1 (*Continued*)

Let's plan to meet at 3:00 p.m. tomorrow following our other meeting. I'd like to talk with you about this case. After you review this dog bite statute, I want your ideas on the following:

1. Can we sue John Brown? He is the one with the assets, and he probably has a large liability insurance policy.
2. Do we have any problems with our case because Reuben went over to grab an apple and also threw it at the dog, Sadie?

Bill your time to the above file.

CHAPTER SUMMARY

Strict liability is imposed upon a defendant without any fault because the defendant is engaging in certain conduct that courts consider so dangerous or so hazardous that the defendant will be held to be financially responsible. No proof of negligence or intention is required. Defendant will not be allowed to show how careful he or she was nor the precautions taken.

There are three basic areas upon which strict liability arises: (1) animals, (2) abnormally dangerous activities, and (3) products liability. Liability for animals will depend upon whether the animal is wild or domestic. A wild animal's owner will be strictly liable for harm resulting from the particular animal's normally dangerous propensity. The court, not the jury, makes the determination as to whether an animal is wild or domestic. Some wild animals that live in nature are inherently dangerous, such as a lion or tiger. However, some that live in nature can be domesticated, such as a pigeon, wild horse, or parrot. For the owner of the wild animal to be strictly liable, the harm must arise from the animal's natural propensity.

Exceptions for liability on the basis of strict liability are made for persons or entities who, as part of their public duties, are required to take possession of wild animals or accept them for transportation. An exception is made for a public zoo or a common carrier such as a railroad carrying wild animals.

The owner of domestic animals may also be liable on a theory of strict liability. Liability is based upon the dangerous propensity of the animal, and harm must result from the abnormally dangerous propensity of which the owner knows or has reason to know. Because most dogs are harmless, a sudden attack and biting of a person that is out of character for the dog would not impose strict liability. Note that it is not necessarily a "vicious" propensity, only a "dangerous" one. If a case does not fall under strict liability, there may still be a claim to be made on the other two bases of tort liability, which are negligence and intention.

There is a contradiction in the law concerning certain livestock. Courts have not imposed strict liability for harm caused by animals such as bulls, stallions, or rams because they are a part of our culture, and the male of those species are needed for breeding purposes. Courts typically balance the scales in favor of the animals' utility for breeding as that factor outweighs any danger they may impose.

There is a doctrine called "Every dog is entitled to one bite." What this means is that the owner of the animal must know or have reason to know of the dangerous propensity of the dog to be vicious and bite. Once the vicious nature has manifested itself, the next time it happens the owner can be liable without fault under strict liability. Some jurisdictions have enacted dog bite statutes. These statutes, which deal only with dogs, impose strict liability, even though the owner had no previous knowledge of the dog's dangerous propensity.

Strict liability applies to an injury to one to whom the owner has given express or implied permission to enter upon the owner's land. It does not apply to a trespasser whose presence was unknown to the owner. If the owner had a vicious dog on the premises as a watchdog, even the trespasser could bring suit on a theory of strict liability.

The other basis for strict liability besides animals is abnormally dangerous conditions and activities. Courts struggle in this area, and the decisions are not consistent concerning the meaning of activities that impose strict liability. Courts do tend to follow the Restatements. The Restatement of Torts on strict liability required "ultra hazardous activities." Typical examples are blasting and fireworks. The Restatement (Second) of Torts provided six factors to be balanced by the courts. Those factors included the extent to which the activity is not a matter of "common usage," the inappropriateness of the activity in the location where carried out and its value to the community.

The Restatement (Third) of Torts provides that one who carries on an abnormally dangerous activity is strictly liable if the activity creates a foreseeable and highly significant risk of harm even when reasonable care is exercised, and the activity is not one of "common usage." The determination of whether or not an activity is an abnormally dangerous activity is for the court, not the jury, to decide.

Finally, the element of duty in strict liability is that of avoiding harm. It is not the duty to use reasonable care as it is for negligence. The duty is owed to foreseeable plaintiffs. The harm must be the kind of harm foreseeable from the dangerous animal or activity. Actual cause and proximate cause are required for strict liability and, of course, damages must be proven. Defenses may include contributory negligence, comparative fault, and assumption of a known risk.

KEY **TERMS**

Strict Liability	*Domitae Naturae*	Dog Bite Statutes
Ferae Naturae	Dangerous Propensity	

REVIEW **QUESTIONS**

1. What is the reason for imposing strict liability against someone who was not at fault and tried ever so hard to be careful?

2. Charles visited the home of Bennie, a family friend. Bennie lives out in the country. Bennie has a wild boar that he has raised since it was a piglet with tusks removed, and he keeps it as a pet in a corral. As Bennie is showing Charles, who is sitting inside the corral on the ground up against the fence, how fast the boar can run, the boar, while running by Charles, trips, falls, and lands on Charles breaking his leg. Is Bennie liable to Charles for his personal injury under any tort theories? What defense(s) does Bennie have?

3. Bruce, who lives on the outskirts of town, owned a wolfdog as a pet. Bruce's animal is a cross between a wolf and a German Shepherd. The wolfdog was enclosed with a strong, well-maintained chain link fence. Wire was buried under the surface of the pen to prevent the wolfdog from digging out. Approximately 3 feet of wire was placed all around the top of the pen to prevent it from jumping out. One day, Brenda, a 5-year-old girl, wandered into Bruce's yard and came up to the pen, grabbed ahold of it, and peered in at the wolfdog. At the time, the animal was chained with an expensive, heavy-duty chain from its collar to a pipe in the ground. When the animal saw the little girl, it bolted up and broke the chain, which was defective, and before Brenda could move, it bit her hand. What tort theories are available to Brenda's parents? Is it a defense for Bruce that he took all the precautions he did with caging the wolfdog? Is it a defense that this unfortunate incident would not have happened if the chain would not have been defective?

4. George went to Ron and Judy's house for a weekly game of cards. When he arrived, he was greeted, as usual, by Polo, Ron and Judy's miniature poodle. An hour later as George walked into the kitchen and approached the area where Polo was eating his food out of his dish, Polo growled, showed his teeth, and then lunged toward George and bit him in the leg. George sues Ron and Judy. Their defense is that the dog has never bitten anyone before. However, they admitted that he has seen Polo growl and show his teeth when people approach as he is eating. Is this enough to show Ron and Judy's knowledge of a vicious propensity on the part of Polo?

5. At the end of the planting season Lee needs to dispose of dry straw that is spread over much of his 160-acre tract. He begins a controlled burn fire to destroy the straw. For fires of this type there are appropriate precautions, including placing various types of obstacles at the property's boundary line. Even when that is done, these fires escape the farmer's property approximately 10 percent of the time. Because of the size of such fires, when there is such an escape, the damage done to neighboring property is likely to be substantial. When Lee's fire is in progress, the wind unexpectedly picks up. The fire spreads to neighbor Greg's property causing damage. Does Lee's activity in conducting the fire satisfy the requirement of subsection (b) (1) of Restatement (Third) of Torts § 20 as quoted and cited in the text?

chapter 10
PRODUCTS LIABILITY

LEARNING OBJECTIVES

After studying this chapter, you should be able to:

- Analyze the elements of a products liability case based upon strict liability.

- Analyze the elements of a products liability case based upon negligence.

- Analyze the elements of a products liability case based upon warranties, express and implied.

- Recognize and differentiate among the defenses available in products liability cases whether based upon strict liability, negligence, or breach of warranties.

Privity of Contract
Legal rights and obligations are created by parties to a contract; a defense in products liability cases.

"A person buying ordinary products in a supermarket is in touch with his deepest emotions."

John Kenneth Galbraith

Introduction and History of Products Liability

Products liability concerns the liability of a seller/supplier of a product for harm and damage to person or property caused by defects in the product. When a defective product causes a personal injury, there may be various legal theories upon which to recover against the manufacturer, distributor, wholesaler, and retailer of the product. Some recoveries may be based in tort such as the three tort bases for liability already discussed—negligence, intent, and strict liability. Some recoveries may be based in contract such as breach of warranties.

Early product liability cases were resolved under contract law. Furthermore, there could be no recovery by a plaintiff unless the plaintiff was in **privity of contract** with the seller. Privity of contract simply means that legal rights and obligations are created by parties to a contract. If the injured plaintiff had not entered into a contract directly with the seller, there could be no recovery for an injury caused by the plaintiff's use or consumption of the product. Assume the plaintiff bought a hay wagon from a local dealer, and there was a defect in the yoke of the wagon that caused it to overturn and cause a personal injury. The plaintiff could not sue the manufacturer of the wagon because the purchaser had no contract with the manufacturer. The plaintiff's contract was with the dealer.

Eventually, courts rejected the harsh contract privity rule and began to analyze these types of cases under a tort negligence theory. Liability could be established against a negligent seller who was not in privity of contract with the injured user or consumer. The landmark case that first established products liability based on negligence is the case of *MacPherson v. Buick Motor Co.*, 111 N.E. 1050 (N.Y. 1916).

Justice Cardozo, the same justice who authored the famous *Palsgraf* opinion from Chapter 2, wrote the majority opinion in *MacPherson*. Buick Motor Company ("Buick") sold an automobile to a dealer, and the dealer resold it to the plaintiff. While the plaintiff was in the car, it suddenly collapsed, and he was thrown from the vehicle and injured. One of the wheels was made of defective *wood*, and the spokes crumbled. The wheel was bought by Buick from another manufacturer. There was evidence that the defect in the wheel could have been discovered by a reasonable inspection, which was not done.

Buick argued that it could not be liable because there was no privity between it and the plaintiff. Buick argued that its only contract was with the dealer to whom it sold the vehicle. The court held privity did not apply and a manufacturer could be held liable in negligence. The court proceeded to point out how illogical the privity rule is. The manufacturer would know that the dealer was one who would not be using the car. The manufacturer would also know that the plaintiff was precisely the one who would be using the car. Yet Buick wanted to be responsible only to the person to whom it sold the vehicle knowing that person would not be using it. *MacPherson* held that the manufacturer is under a duty to make the car carefully and to inspect its component parts because it is foreseeable that there is a risk of injury if the car is not properly manufactured and inspected. The manufacturer's duty of care was extended to the ultimate consumer.

Some of the early decisions that attempted to make it easier for consumers to prevail against manufacturers or suppliers under a theory of strict liability were in the area of food consumption. This was one of the first areas to adopt a theory of recovery based upon strict liability. It was expanded to products such as cosmetics that were used on the body rather than consumed internally such as food. Eventually, the strict liability theory was expanded beyond products involving a consumer's use with the body. *Spence v. Three Rivers Builders & Masonry Supply, Inc.,* 90 N.W.2d 873 (Mich. 1958) extended products liability to cinder building blocks. Shortly thereafter, the landmark case of *Henningsen v. Bloomfield Motors,* 161 A.2d 69 (N.J. 1960) extended the strict liability theory to automobiles. With some exceptions, eventually the strict liability theory encompassed virtually any defective product that caused harm to the user or consumer or to his property.[1]

Products Liability Based upon Strict Liability: The Restatement View

There are various bases of liability for products-related cases. These bases are strict liability, negligence, breach of warranty, and possibly even intentional acts. The student should note that strict liability, negligence, and intentional acts are tort theories. A breach-of-warranty theory is a contract theory. To better understand the theory of strict liability, various pertinent portions of the Products Liability Restatement Rules will be broken down piece by piece. Before proceeding to examine the law of products liability as outlined in the Restatement, some principles discussed in Chapter 1 should be reviewed.

Chapter 1 discussed public policy purposes of tort law. Distribution of risk, sometimes referred to as loss allocation, is a public policy purpose of tort law that applies to sellers who place products in the stream of commerce. Between the innocent consumer or user of the product and a manufacturer, the manufacturer should bear the risk of loss. The manufacturer stands to make a profit from a sale of the product. The general public expects products to perform properly. The manufacturer can obtain insurance to protect itself from harm caused by its defective products. The manufacturer as a seller is involved in the testing, inspection, research, and development of its own product. It is, therefore, in the superior position of avoiding a defective product being placed into the stream of commerce. Another public policy purpose discussed in Chapter 1 was deterrence. The public policy purpose of deterrence is that if liability against a seller is made easier, the seller, particularly the manufacturer, may have some incentive to make those products safer for the public's use or consumption. Finally, as a practical matter, a rationale for strict liability in tort is that negligence is often an extremely difficult theory to prove in a products liability case.

The beginning point for products liability will be the tort theory of strict liability. An excellent approach to an understanding of products liability based on a theory of strict liability is to examine Restatement (Second) of Torts § 402A (1965). This Restatement will provide an excellent outline for the basic principles of products liability based upon strict liability. There is a newer Restatement dealing with some aspects of products liability based upon strict liability, which is Restatement (Third) of Torts-PL (Products Liability). Some of those aspects will be mentioned where appropriate. The primary roadmap will be Restatement (Second) of Torts § 402A (1965), which states as follows:

1. One who sells any product in a defective condition unreasonably dangerous to the user or consumer or to his property is subject to liability for physical harm thereby caused to the ultimate user or consumer, or to his property, if
   (a) The seller is engaged in the business of selling such a product, and
   (b) It is expected to and does reach the user or consumer without substantial change in the condition in which it is sold.
2. The rule stated in Subsection (1) applies although
   (a) The seller has exercised all possible care in the preparation and sale of his product, and
   (b) The user or consumer has not bought the product from or entered into any contractual relation with the seller.

"One Who Sells"

This rule applies to any seller who is engaged in the business of selling a particular product. It applies to the manufacturer, wholesaler, distributor, supplier, and retailer, all of whom are referred to as a "seller." "One who sells" refers to any person or entity who causes the product to be originally placed into the stream of commerce or who assists in passing it along the stream of commerce. Basically, anyone who participates in the marketing process of the product into the stream of commerce may become strictly liable. This obviously includes the manufacturer. It also includes the middleman or middlemen who participate in the process of the delivery of the product to the dealer as well as the dealer. These middlemen are sometimes referred to as the supplier, the wholesaler, or the distributor. The dealer may also be called the retailer.

"Any Product"

Obviously, for strict liability to be applicable to the field of products liability, there must be a "product." A product is defined by the Restatement (Third) of Torts-PL § 19 (1997), which states:

(a) A product is tangible personal property distributed commercially for use or consumption. Other items, such as real property and electricity, are products when the context of their distribution and use is sufficiently analogous to the distribution and use of tangible personal property that it is appropriate to apply the rules stated in this Restatement.
(b) Services, even when provided commercially, are not products.
(c) Human blood and human tissue, even when provided commercially, are not subject to the rules of this Restatement. The question of what is a product is a question of law for the court.

Examples of products include an automobile, a tire, an airplane, a grinding wheel, a water heater, a gas stove, a power tool, a riveting machine, a chair, and an insecticide.[2] Courts are divided over whether or not pets and livestock are to be considered "products."[3] Note that services are not considered a product. This means, for example, that strict liability would not apply to professional advice given by a physician, attorney, architect, engineer, or accountant. Furthermore, most courts have held that electricity actually becomes a product only when it passes through the customer's meter and enters the customer's premises. Until then, high voltage is a service.[4] Note, too, that the court determines as a matter of law whether an item is to be considered a product.

"In a Defective Condition"

In continuing to break down Section 402A, the next important part is the phrase "a defective condition." What is a defect or a **defective condition** in a product? A defective condition means that the defect renders the product "unreasonably dangerous" for its use or consumption. If the product is safe when it leaves the seller's control, but the user or consumer misuses it or alters it, then the product is not considered defective. It must be in that defective condition when it leaves the hands of the seller. There are three basic types of unreasonably dangerous defects: (1) defects in manufacturing, (2) defects in design, and (3) defects in lack of warnings or insufficiency of warnings.

Defective Condition
The defect renders the product "unreasonably dangerous" for its use or consumption.

DEFECTS IN MANUFACTURING ("MANUFACTURING DEFECTS")

Manufacturing defects are those that do not meet the manufacturer's own manufacturing standards or guidelines. The product is not in the condition the manufacturer intended it to be in when it left the manufacturer's hands (control). For example, assume that, during manufacture on the assembly line, a glass bottle containing a carbonated beverage was subjected to extreme heat or extreme pressure. After the consumer purchased the product, the bottle exploded causing personal injury to the person. This is a manufacturing defect. Likewise, assume that a foreign object such as a screw, a piece of glass, or some other foreign object was found inside the bottle after it left the manufacturer's plant causing illness or injury after drinking the contents. These, too, would be considered manufacturing defects. In this case, it does not matter whether the injury occurred from the container or the liquid inside the container. Both are sold together in combination to form the product.

Manufacturing Defects
Those defects that do not meet the manufacturer's own manufacturing standards or guidelines.

Workplace Skills Tip

In a products liability case, use online resources to research a product involved in a case. Whether you are on the plaintiff's team or the defendant's team, there is typically a wealth of information about the defendant's product online. In fact, product literature, whether promotional or technical, may bolster the manufacturer's defenses in the case or such literature may contradict the manufacturer's defenses. It is a source never to be overlooked. However, do not take anything you see or read online at face value. All sources, including online sources, have an agenda and vary in the degree to which you can rely on their information.

You must make sure your online source is trustworthy. Consider the ending of the web address: ".com" indicates a commercial site, which means the website is trying to make money from its content; ".org" may sometimes indicate a non-profit organization, although now anyone is permitted to purchase a web address ending in ".org"; ".gov" indicates a government website; and ".edu" indicates a website run by an educational institution. Typically, websites ending in ".gov" or ".edu" are more reliable, but not always. If you are researching product information, make sure the website you are on is the actual official website of that product manufacturer and not just a website selling the product. Whenever possible, attempt to verify the information you obtain online. Check multiple sources, and see whether they are consistent in the information they relay. Online resources are similar to fire—extremely useful but potentially dangerous.

DEFECTS IN DESIGN ("DESIGN DEFECTS")

Design Defects
Those defects in which the product was manufactured properly, but its design created an undue risk of harm to the user or consumer in a normal use of the product.

Design defects are those in which the product was manufactured properly, but its design created an undue risk of harm to the user or consumer in a normal use of the product. The product was actually in a condition that was intended by the manufacturer. A machine used in industrial production may be manufactured with stringent requirements so that it is extremely efficient and productive. However, its design does not allow proper safety features such as an easily designed guard preventing hand injuries. An example of a design defect related to a motor vehicle may be the design of a transmission that allows the vehicle to slip out of park. The transmission is manufactured correctly and according to all proper standards and specifications. The problem lies in its placement within the vehicle or other dimensions formulated in the design of it that are creating the defect. Assume a rocking chair is made of the finest wood and assembled absolutely properly. However, its design is such that if one rocks back a bit too far in normal rocking, it will tip over.

In another example, assume that the manufacturer of a motor vehicle designed its car in such a way that the position of the gas tank would cause it to burst into flames when struck in the rear by another vehicle. The gas tank itself and the vehicle itself were manufactured properly and to all standards and specifications. However, the defect is in the design of the vehicle by placing its gas tank in a location in which an undue risk of harm would be caused to the car occupants in the event of a rear-end collision. In the first motor vehicle example involving the transmission design that caused it to slip out of park, the manufacturer is held responsible for a design defect that would actually cause a collision. In this second example involving the gas tank, the manufacturer is held responsible for a design defect that would not actually cause a collision, but rather would exacerbate or enhance any injuries from a collision to the rear end of the vehicle. For a case involving an exploding gas tank, the *Turcotte* case in Exhibit 10-1 provides an excellent analysis of strict liability under § 402A.[5]

EXHIBIT 10-1 Relevant Case Law

Robert L. Turcotte, Administrator of the Estate of Gerard P. Turcotte, Plaintiff-Appellee, v. Ford Motor Company, Defendant-Appellant.

United States Court of Appeals, First Circuit.

McEntee, Circuit Judge.

Plaintiff, a Rhode Island citizen, filed this diversity suit in the United States District Court for Rhode Island, seeking to recover for the alleged wrongful death of his son. The decedent was a passenger in a 1970 Maverick, manufactured by defendant Ford Motor Company, when the car was struck by another car on the Massachusetts Turnpike near Millbury, Massachusetts and burst into flames. Decedent died in the fire. The owner of the Maverick was William J. Sullivan of Woonsocket, Rhode Island, who purchased it from Menard Ford Sales, Inc., of South Bellingham, Massachusetts. The driver was Sullivan's son Michael. The operator of the other vehicle was a Massachusetts citizen.

At trial, plaintiff contended that Ford's positioning of the gas tank in the 1970 Maverick in manner that the tank's top also served as the floor of the trunk constituted a defect in design which caused his son's death by fire. Plaintiff did not argue that the alleged defect caused the collision. Instead, he contended that, upon collision, a properly-designed Maverick would not have burst into flames and that his son would otherwise have survived the initial impact. The case went to the jury on the theory of strict liability, and a verdict was returned for plaintiff in the amount of $500,000. The trial court entered judgment for that amount plus $61,315.08 in interest. Ford's motions for new trial and for alteration or amendment of the judgment were both denied....

II. Strict Liability

We now review the trial court's holding that under Rhode Island law automobile manufacturers can be held strictly liable for defects in design which do not cause highway collisions but instead exacerbate injuries therefrom. This precise question had never been considered by the Rhode Island courts....

Ford argues that since no automobile manufacturer or consumer would rationally intend his car to be involved in a highway collision, the defect in design alleged in the instant case falls outside the scope of the strict liability doctrine as construed in Ritter. This pinpoints the crucial issue before us, namely, whether under Rhode Island law the tort concept of 'intended use' encompasses foreseeable consequences of normal automobile use, such as collisions, even though such consequences are not literally intended or desired.

Among other jurisdictions there has developed a split in authority on this question, symbolized by the conflicting cases of Evans v. General Motors Corp., 359 F.2d 822 (7th Cir. 1966), cert. denied, 385 U.S. 836, 87 S.Ct. 83, 17 L.Ed.2d 70 (1967), and Larsen v. General Motors Corp., 391 F.2d 495 (8th Cir. 1968) ....

We agree with the trial court that Rhode Island would adopt the Larsen interpretation of 'intended use' in construing the doctrine of strict products liability. A literal Evans-type interpretation of 'intended use' fails to recognize that the phrase was first employed in early products-liability cases such as Greenman, supra, merely to illustrate the broader central doctrine of foreseeability. The phrase was not meant to preclude manufacturer responsibility for the probable ancillary consequences of normal use....

Ford has suggested that adoption of the Larsen concept of 'intended use' in automobile cases will result in its having to produce expensive armored tanks so as to avoid liability for defective design. But this need not be the result. First, plaintiff must still prove that the particular car's design constituted a 'defective condition unreasonably dangerous' to the user, and that such defect was the actual and proximate cause of injuries beyond those caused by the collision itself. Ford claims that sympathetic juries will shirk their responsibilities in cases of serious injury and impose liability on

(Continued)

EXHIBIT 10-1 *(Continued)*

the manufacturer no matter what the state of the design or the ferocity of the particular collision. But our review of cases to date shows that juries continue to confound the cynical....

Second, the defense of assumption of risk remains viable in products liability cases. See Restatement (Second) of Torts § 402A, Comment n (1965). Thus, where a design defect is apparent or made known to the automobile purchaser, an action alleging such defect as the cause of injury cannot lie...Automobile manufacturers might often relieve themselves of design liability, at least when the purchaser is plaintiff, if they fully informed such purchaser in advance of the relative safety merits and demerits of their cars as compared to other models....

Source: Turcotte v. Ford Motor Company, 494 F.2d 173 (2d. Cir. 1974).

Tests to Determine Design Defects

There are three tests used to determine when there is a defect in design.

Risk/Utility Test
A test to determine whether a design defect exists that considers whether the product's risks outweigh its benefits or utility. Plaintiff must prove the defendant could have removed the danger caused by the defect without otherwise seriously affecting its utility and price.

1. **Risk/Utility Test.** The first test to determine whether or not a design defect exists is to consider whether the product's risks outweigh its benefits or utility. The question is: Could the defendant have removed the danger caused by the defect without otherwise seriously affecting its utility and price? Assume an injured driver of an automobile involved in a rollover collision claimed that the injury could have been prevented if the car manufacturer had constructed a heavier, more crush-proof type of roof. Assume the car manufacturer presents evidence that to build such a roof would add another $500 to the cost of the car plus make the car look rather unsightly with the odd shape of the roof design. The risk of a rollover injury may not outweigh the considerable increase in price and the effect on the appearance of the design of the vehicle. Some factors to be considered in applying this test are the usefulness of the product, the attractiveness of the product, the actual number of injuries and severity of injuries, the cost of the design change, and its impact on the price to the consumer.

Consumer Expectation Test
A test to determine whether a design defect exists. Plaintiff must prove the product did not perform up to the standard of safety that an ordinary consumer would have expected.

2. **Consumer Expectation Test.** The second test to determine whether a design defect exists is the consumer expectation text, whereby the plaintiff must prove that the product did not perform up to the standard of safety that an ordinary consumer would have expected. Assume a customer buys some peanut brittle from a local candy store manufactured by a national candy company. The customer bites down and chips a tooth. Even if this particular brand of peanut brittle were harder than usual, this type of candy would probably meet the reasonable expectation of the ordinary consumer of peanut brittle. It is typically a hard candy. This test is discussed in the *Perkins* case in Exhibit 10-2 under the "unreasonably dangerous" language of the Restatement involving a pistol. A firearm, whether a pistol, rifle, or shotgun, that fires when the trigger is pulled is functioning precisely as an ordinary consumer would expect. The same could perhaps be said of fireworks.

State of the Art/Alternative Reasonable Design Test
This test means that a product is defective if the risk of harm could have been reduced by a reasonably different design that is state of the art.

3. **State of the Art/Alternative Reasonable Design Test.** The state of the art/ alternative reasonable design test basically means that a product is defective if the risk of harm could have been reduced by a reasonably different design that is state of the art. Assume a car manufacturer is utilizing an air bag designed several years ago. When an air bag opens in a collision, it can produce flying debris that can lodge in the eye. Assume competitors are

utilizing a newer type of air bag of a different design that costs a bit more but significantly reduces flying debris on impact when the bag opens. The manufacturer's current air bag would be defective under this test because the risk of harm could have been reduced by utilizing the differently designed air bag. Greater safety is provided by this newer type of design, which outweighs the disadvantage that it costs a bit more.

DEFECTS DUE TO INSUFFICIENCY/INADEQUACY OF WARNINGS

In addition to defects involving the product itself due to its manufacturing or design, the packaging, warnings, instructions, or labels associated with the product may give rise to a product defect. Lack of warnings or insufficient warnings will make a product defective if the danger is not readily apparent to the user or consumer. The harm or danger must be of the type that a reasonable user or consumer would have no reason to expect from using or consuming the product. If a noisy, slightly visible moving chain is moving behind a metal guard, such as in a grain auger, and the grain auger becomes clogged, the manufacturer does not have a duty to warn of not putting one's hand into moving machinery, as that is a danger that is patently obvious. A manufacturer of a chain saw does not have a duty to warn of the risk of being cut by using the chain saw, as that is also a danger that is patently obvious.

The claim may be that there was no warning provided by the manufacturer or the claim may be that even if a warning was provided, it was insufficient to adequately warn of the danger. For example, there may be no warning on a conveyor belt machine. The worker who injured his hand when it was caught in the moving belt would bring a strict liability claim against the manufacturer on the theory that no warning was provided. The manufacturer would likely argue, through their experts, that the danger was so patent and obvious no warning was required.

In the same scenario, there may be a warning somewhere on the machine: "Be careful! Moving Parts!" If the injured worker brought a claim under this scenario, it would be on a theory that the warning was insufficient or inadequate. An expert in human factors engineering may testify for the plaintiff that for a warning to be meaningful to a busy worker who becomes preoccupied with his or her

---

Workplace Skills Tips

Sooner or later you will probably work on a case in which there is an extraordinary amount of documents. It may be in some type of commercial case involving voluminous corporate documents or it may even be a products liability case against a manufacturer involving the manufacturer's voluminous documents. Do not be intimidated by the size of the project. Among those thousands or even hundreds of thousands of documents you must carefully review, you may come across that one jewel or golden nugget that tips the case in your favor.

Nowadays, there are many software programs available to assist with e-discovery and document review, and optical character recognition (OCR) can be extremely useful. However, not all firms have the money or the desire to invest in expensive e-discovery software. Also, OCR will not work with texts where the scan quality is poor or the text is unclear. You may find yourself forced to do things the old-fashioned way. If time is of the essence, and you need to find a specific type of document, try this method: (1) Find an example of the type of document for which you are looking; (2) fix the shape of it (not the words on it) in your mind; and (3) visually scan the pages of the documents to find that shape. This saves time, as you will not be reading the contents of each page. Later, when there may be more time, go back and actually read through the documents.

work, the warning label needs to state different language such as "Warning!" or "Danger!" This expert may also testify that "Serious Injury May Occur!" should also be on the appropriate warnings. Furthermore, such expert may state that several warnings need to be placed at strategic locations on the machine, and the lettering needs to be of a certain large size and of a certain color to constantly remind the busy worker of the danger. A warning may be inadequate if it does not specifically state the reason for the warning. For example, "Daily use of this product may cause nausea."

The Gerry Spence/Ford Motor Company Story

A true story is in order at this point. Gerry Spence is a prominent national plaintiff's personal injury attorney from Wyoming. In his prime, it was not uncommon to see him on TV talk shows discussing some of his cases. One case is particularly interesting. The Spence Law Firm represented a family that was involved in a serious automobile collision that occurred in 2003. The father and husband ("Dad") was driving the family car, a 1999 Ford Expedition. His wife and several of the children were in the vehicle as passengers. Another driver fell asleep, but when he woke up, he overcorrected, lost control, and slid into the plaintiff's vehicle. This caused the family's vehicle to roll several times. The Dad was killed, and the wife and the minor children all received serious personal injuries.

The plaintiffs' team was bothered by the fact that everyone had walked away from the accident except for the Dad who was also wearing his seat belt. Someone noticed from a picture of the 1999 Ford, taken after the accident, that the driver's door appeared to have opened, hit the ground, and was bent backward. Expert investigation revealed that the door had come open during the numerous rollovers, and the Dad's head would have come out of the car and hit the ground in the process. There are federal regulations requiring car manufacturers to make cars with doors that stay latched and closed during a collision.

In the course of the litigation, there were discovery requests from plaintiffs' attorneys for documents from Ford Motor Company. Ford willingly complied by producing staggering, overwhelming amounts of documents described as "50 to 75 boxes" and "millions of pages" of documents. The Spence team surmised that Ford was doing a "document dump." This refers to the practice of providing so many documents in the hopes that all of them will not be reviewed or they will not be reviewed that carefully, and so likely nothing adverse will be found. Someone on the plaintiff's team, however, (perhaps it was a paralegal) through persistence and diligence, found a video of a test crash done by Ford before the accident in question. The video proved that the door latch was defective and would cause the door to open in a collision. They found that one "jewel" or "golden nugget" referred to in the Workplace Skills Tip. The case was eventually settled by Ford for an undisclosed amount under a confidentiality agreement. For a fascinating video about this case, go to www.legalshowtime.com/video/75/Fords-Deadly-Truck-Defects.

"Unreasonably Dangerous"

The next portion of the Restatement requires that the defective product must be "unreasonably dangerous." The defect in the product must produce a result that is beyond what a reasonable person would expect in the normal use of the product. Consider, however, the situation presented concerning a handgun, a shotgun, or a rifle. All three weapons, when functioning as intended, are without doubt dangerous products. However, the courts have typically held that a firearm that is functioning as intended but is dangerous in its ordinary and expected use is not defective, and there is no basis of liability based on strict liability. Another example would be fireworks. It is always possible that such a weapon could have a defective safety latch or a defective trigger, which would subject the product to liability under strict liability. Assuming the product is functioning as intended, there is no liability based on strict liability as held by the *Perkins* court in Exhibit 10-2.[6]

EXHIBIT 10-2 Relevant Case Law

Joseph Perkins, Plaintiff-Appellant, v. F.I.E. Corporation, Defendant-Appellee. Judie Richman, Individually and as Personal Representative of the Estate of Kathy Newman, Deceased, Plaintiff-Appellee, v. Charter Arms Corporation, Defendant-Appellant.

United States Court of Appeals, Fifth Circuit.

Wisdom, Circuit Judge.

Separate suits were brought seeking damages from the manufacturers of small caliber handguns that caused severe injury during perpetration of one crime and the death of the victim in another crime.... After the Louisiana court declined to accept certification, 460 So.2d 1039, the Court of Appeals, Wisdom, Circuit Judge, held that: (1) marketing of handguns did not constitute an ultrahazardous activity giving rise to absolute or strict liability of manufacturer under Louisiana law, and (2) since the handguns functioned precisely as they were designed and since the dangers of handguns were obvious and well-known to all members of the consuming public, plaintiffs could not recover under Louisiana products liability law, either under consumer expectation test or under risk/utility test....

I. FACTS

A.

This consolidated appeal presents two cases in each of which a criminal using a small caliber handgun shot an innocent victim. On September 18, 1981, Claude Nichols shot Joseph Perkins at the Cut Rate Lounge in Tangipahoa Parish, Louisiana. Nichols entered the lounge after participating in a fight in the barroom's parking lot. He began senselessly firing a .25 caliber automatic pistol at the individual with whom he had been fighting. The barroom was crowded, and two innocent patrons, including Perkins, were wounded. Perkins was struck in the spine and is now permanently paralyzed from the waist down. Nichols pleaded guilty to the crime of aggravated battery and was sentenced to five years of hard labor.

F.I.E. Corporation allegedly manufactured and distributed the handgun used by Nichols. Perkins filed suit against the defendant manufacturer in the 21st Judicial District Court for the Parish of Tangipahoa. The defendant removed the suit to federal court under diversity jurisdiction. The plaintiff alleged that the pistol manufactured by the defendant "is defective in that it is unreasonably dangerous in normal use, that the hazard of injury to human beings exceeds the utility of the pistol and this defect constitutes a proximate cause" of the injury. The plaintiff invoked as a basis for liability La.Civ. Code art. 2315, which provides, in essential part, "Every act whatever of man that causes damage to another obliges him by whose fault it happened to repair it." The plaintiff admitted in answers to interrogatories that there was no defect in the design of the gun, no defect in the manufacture or assembly of the component parts of the gun, no statutory prohibition to the manufacture or

(Continued)

EXHIBIT 10-2 *(Continued)*

distribution of the gun, and that Claude Nichols was not at the time of the shooting an agent, employee, or servant of F.I.E. Corp. The district court granted the defendant's motion for summary judgment without a written opinion, and the plaintiff appealed.

B.

On April 4, 1981, Willie Watson kidnapped Kathy Newman, a third-year medical student at Tulane University, from the parking lot of her apartment in the uptown university section of New Orleans. Watson was armed with a .38 caliber handgun allegedly designed, manufactured, and marketed by Charter Arms Corp. He forced Newman to drive to an isolated area in St. Charles Parish where he robbed her of her jewelry and raped her. Watson then instructed Newman to dress herself, and as she did so he shot her in the back of the head, killing her. Watson later confessed to the murder and stated that he shot Newman because he feared that she could identify him. The jury found Watson guilty of first degree murder, and he was sentenced to death.

Judie Richman, Newman's mother, brought suit against Charter Arms in three federal district courts for the wrongful death of her daughter. The cases were consolidated in the Eastern District of Louisiana. The complaints alleged that the murder weapon was designed, manufactured, and marketed by Defendant in a defective condition unreasonably dangerous to consumers, bystanders, and the general public, because the risk of [foreseeable] harm associated with marketing the product, as designed, to the general public, greatly outweighs any socially acceptable utility, if any.... Therefore, Charter Arms Corporation is "strictly liable" to Plaintiff....

The plaintiffs argue, however, that the consumer expectation test is not the only test of defectiveness under Louisiana law, and that we should apply instead the "risk/utility test" of *Hunt v. City Stores, Inc.*, La. 1980, 387 So.2d 585. In that case the Louisiana Supreme Court stated that, in deciding whether a product is unreasonably dangerous to normal use, "a balancing test is mandated: if the likelihood and gravity of harm outweigh the benefits and utility of the manufactured product, the product is unreasonably dangerous". *Id.* at 589. The plaintiffs assert that this test is more appropriate than a consumer expectation test for cases of this kind, in which the injured party is not the consumer of the product. The plaintiffs conclude that they were entitled to have a jury perform the risk/utility analysis, and that the district court therefore erred in dismissing their products liability claim as a matter of law....

The plaintiffs insisted at oral argument that the small size of the handguns at issue in these cases, which allows them to be readily concealed as weapons by members of the general public to whom they are marketed, is the feature that should be subjected to a risk/utility analysis to decide whether the handguns should be labelled "defective" or "unreasonably dangerous". But the small size of the handgun, rather than being something *wrong* in the design, even when the gun is marketed indiscriminately to the public, is more properly characterized as a central *attribute* of the design. At bottom, then, what the plaintiffs seek is a ruling that it is sufficient to hold a manufacturer strictly liable if the *design* of the product causes injury, rather than a *defect* in the product. The plaintiffs argue that, since the adoption of the risk/utility test in products liability, it is no longer true that a "defect" means that something is "broken" or "designed wrong". Under the plaintiffs' view of the risk/utility test, any product, whether or not it has something wrong with it that allows it to malfunction or cause unintended results, can be subjected to a general balancing test by a jury of the risk of harm resulting when the product is used in a foreseeable manner—either correctly, negligently, or criminally—against the benefits of the product....

Whatever the merits of the *Barker* rule may be, it plainly is not the law in Louisiana. No court in this jurisdiction has ever applied a general risk/utility analysis to a well-made product that functioned precisely as it was designed to do. The plaintiffs have not alleged that the handguns in these cases had something wrong with them—such as a safety mechanism that fails under certain circumstances,

(Continued)

EXHIBIT 10-2 *(Continued)*

> a tendency to misfire, or a trigger structure that can get caught on foreign objects and cause the gun to discharge unexpectedly—that would bring the risk/utility analysis of *Hunt* into play. All they have alleged is that the guns were small and consequently could be concealed, a design attribute that is true of a host of consumer products. We therefore conclude that as a matter of law the plaintiffs cannot recover under Louisiana products liability law, either under the consumer expectation test, or the risk/utility test....

Source: Perkins v. F.I.E. Corporation, 762 F.2d 1250 (5th Cir. 1985).

Similarly, alcoholic beverages are not unreasonably dangerous because a consumer may become intoxicated. Granted, to an alcoholic, alcoholic beverages are dangerous just as the handguns in *Perkins* were dangerous products in the wrong hands. If machine oil somehow entered a bottle of vodka during the manufacturing process, however, there would be an unreasonably dangerous defect if a person became ill after drinking the vodka. It must be kept in mind that the standard is "unreasonably dangerous." The product must be dangerous to the extent beyond that which would be contemplated by the ordinary consumer with ordinary knowledge as to its characteristics.

"To the User or Consumer"

It is not required that the ultimate user or consumer must acquire the product directly from the seller. The person entitled to protection need not have even purchased the product. The person may be a family member of the purchaser or the purchaser's employee or "a guest at his table."[7] Recall from the discussion of the history of products liability that "privity of contract" was a requirement. Under the Restatement, privity of contract is clearly not required. Comment l to this Restatement section also notes that a "user" includes anyone who is passively benefiting from the product such as "passengers in automobiles or airplanes."[8]

BYSTANDERS

The courts have extended products liability based on negligence to bystanders, but the courts are split on extending the protection to bystanders on a strict liability theory. For example, a person may be using a gas-powered hedge trimmer, and one of the parts holding the chain in place comes loose, flies off, and strikes a neighbor who has come over to visit. The neighbor, not a user or a consumer of the product, but a bystander, would likely be able to pursue a negligence claim against the manufacturer because the neighbor is a person "reasonably foreseeable" within the scope of use. The neighbor may or may not be able to pursue a strict liability claim, however, depending upon the jurisdiction. A bystander pedestrian was not able to recover against the manufacturer of a truck with a defective design that obstructed a driver's view.[9] On the other hand, a bystander was allowed to recover when a bottle fell through the bottom of a defective container, which shattered when it hit the floor and injured a bystander's eye.[10]

Workplace Skills Tip

If the paralegal is on the plaintiff or defendant team working for a firm well versed in products liability, typically, these cases will involve a "battle of the experts." You will become familiar with a handful of experts your firm regularly retains in certain types of cases. It will be extremely important to make certain that you obtain from those experts the names of all cases in which they have given previous deposition testimony or trial testimony. Impeachment by prior inconsistent testimony given under oath can be problematic to devastating. Know what your experts have said in the past. Furthermore, the law firm's communications with the experts it has retained are not privileged. An e-mail to the expert could become discoverable so be careful what is said in an e-mail. E-mails are usually fine for routine matters such as confirming a date and time of a deposition. If it is something very important such as obtaining technical information or considering trial strategy, it may be best to talk on the phone with the expert.

"Caused"

The defective/unreasonably dangerous product must have been the cause of the plaintiff's harm or injury. Further, the plaintiff must prove that the personal injury was caused by some defect in the product that existed at the time it was sold by the defendant. If the product was misused or mishandled after it left the seller's control, there is no causation established for strict liability. The same causation principles as were discussed in negligence in Chapter 3 apply to products liability cases based upon a theory of strict liability. For example, Laura is driving a new automobile. As Laura enters an intersection to slow down, she realizes the brakes do not work. She sails through the intersection without incident, but after clearing the intersection, she is struck from behind by another vehicle. While the brakes were clearly defective, in this factual situation, they had nothing to do with causing the collision.

In the same example, assume that the manufacturer of Laura's automobile issued a recall of the defective brakes, which sometimes worked and sometimes did not work. Assume that Laura sold the car to Russ but never brought the car back to have the brakes replaced. Assume also that Laura never told Russ of the defective brakes. Russ is injured because of the defective brakes. Laura's failure to have the brakes replaced and her failure to inform the buyer of the bad brakes would arguably cut off causation for any manufacturer's liability under strict liability. Of course, Russ may have a negligence claim or other type of tort claim, such as fraud or misrepresentation, against Laura.

"The Seller Is Engaged in the Business of Selling Such a Product"

This portion of the Restatement means that strict liability does not apply to a casual sale or an isolated sale of a product by one not regularly engaged in the sale of the product. The seller must actually be in the usual and regular business of selling the product. It applies to the manufacturer and every other supplier, distributor, or retailer involved in moving the product through the stream of commerce. For example, a person's occasional sale of his or her car, boat, or piece of machinery to another will not subject that person to strict liability in tort. A woman who has a hobby of making homemade pies in the summer for a month and selling them would not be subject to strict liability. The basic philosophy behind strict liability is to place special responsibility upon those who undertake the responsibility of operating a regular business to sell products to the general public. This philosophy is lacking for the occasional, isolated sale.

"It Is Expected to and Does Reach the User or Consumer Without Substantial Change in the Condition in Which It Is Sold"

This section of the Restatement makes it clear that strict liability only applies when the product is defective and unreasonably dangerous at the time it leaves the seller's hands/seller's control. There is no liability on the seller if the product has been misused, altered, or mishandled after it leaves the seller's hands. As will be discussed later, a misuse or alteration of the product by the injured party is a defense. The manufacturer, for example, is not liable under strict liability if the product is produced in a safe condition and later mishandling, misuse, or alteration makes it harmful. For example, assume a manufacturer made a product without a defect, which was properly packaged for shipment. Assume the common carrier dropped it during delivery causing an internal part to malfunction and the product to be defective. This element would be lacking, and the manufacturer/seller would not be liable.

COMPONENT PARTS

Unless the product is an isolated product such as a copper plumbing fitting, a certain type of electrical wire, or a hand tool, as examples, many final products are assembled from other manufacturers' component parts. An automobile is a good example. The major car companies will typically purchase numerous component parts from many different manufacturers that make up the end product—the automobile. The manufacturer of the final product can be held strictly liable for any defective component parts supplied by others. The plaintiff may choose to sue the manufacturer only. The manufacturer may then, as a third-party defendant, implead for contribution or indemnity the component part manufacturer. Or the plaintiff may sue both manufacturers in the same action. In a typical products liability case, if any potential manufacturer or other seller is known, they will be joined as defendants. There is a specific Restatement section making a component part manufacturer strictly liable.[11]

Harm or Damage to the User or Consumer

The types of damages discussed in Chapter 4 are recoverable in a products liability case based upon strict liability. In the case of a personal injury, these are compensatory damages consisting of both economic and non-economic damages. In the case of a wrongful death, damages for a wrongful death may be recovered.

PUNITIVE DAMAGES/"DIRTY DOCUMENTS" ASBESTOS CASES

Depending upon the jurisdiction and the conduct of the manufacturer, punitive/ exemplary damages as discussed in Chapter 4 may be recovered. One area of products liability that is still being litigated after many years is the area of exposure to asbestos. Asbestos is a natural mineral of which there are six basic types. Asbestos is mined worldwide, with Russia being the largest producer. Asbestos became particularly popular with the construction industry in the late 19th century because of its favorable characteristics of sound absorption, tensile strength, and good resistance to heat/fire. Its uses were found, among others, in building insulation, cement, concrete, pipes, gaskets, fireproof drywall, flooring, roofs, and even in brake pads.

Various workers in the shipyard industry, the construction industry, and even the automobile brake manufacturing industry were exposed to asbestos dust, particularly in the 1930s through the 1960s. Claims have even been made by spouses who claimed exposure to asbestos from washing the workers' clothes and inhaling the dust from the clothes. Asbestos can cause the disease of asbestosis. It is produced by the inhalation of asbestos-containing dust. It can also cause the more serious mesothelioma and lung cancer. Mesothelioma is a rare form of cancer caused by asbestos, and it typically focuses on the outer lining of the lungs.

The author was extensively involved at one time in his career in the defense of asbestos cases on the part of several manufacturers and suppliers of asbestos products. Part of the asbestos litigation arena involved what are called "The Dirty Documents." Some of those documents refer to various letters written in 1935 between Mr. Sumner Simpson, the president of both Raybestos-Manhattan, Inc. and Johns-Manville Corporation, and corporate in-house counsel, Vandiver Brown. The claim by the plaintiffs is that the purpose of correspondence between Mr. Simpson and Johns-Manville counsel Brown, as well as correspondence between Mr. Simpson and the editor of a trade magazine called "ASBESTOS," was to keep the known dangers of asbestos from the public eye. Mr. Simpson states in his October 1, 1935 letter (Exhibit 10-4): "The less said about asbestos, the better off we are...."

The purpose for mentioning these old letters is that they have come back to haunt asbestos manufacturers in products liability litigation some 50 years after they were written. Plaintiffs have sued asbestos manufacturers and suppliers primarily on the theories of negligence and strict liability for failure to warn, on the conspiracy of acting in concert to conceal asbestos health hazards, and to obtain punitive damages based upon these letters. The letters were originally produced in litigation against Raybestos-Manhattan in the late 1970s. In *Threadgill v. Armstrong World Industries, Inc.*, 928 F.2d 1366 (3rd Cir. 1991), the court reversed the district court for excluding these letters as trial exhibits. The court of appeals for the third circuit held that these documents should have been admitted under Federal Rule 901 (b) (8), the "Ancient Documents" exception to the hearsay rule. For an interesting glimpse back in time, read some old letters from the past in Exhibit 10-3 (A.S. Rossiter letter), Exhibit 10-4 (Sumner Simpson letter), and Exhibit 10-5 (Attorney Vandiver Brown letter). The student can determine for himself or herself whether there is a "smoking gun."

THE ECONOMIC LOSS DOCTRINE

Economic Loss Doctrine
A tort remedy in strict liability (or negligence) is not allowed when the only claim is for damage to the product itself.

In addition to compensatory damages, potential punitive damages for personal injury, and damages for wrongful death, claims may be made for property damage from defective products. However, a line is drawn between a claim made for damage to the product itself and to "other property damage" or personal injury caused by the product. The **economic loss doctrine** draws a line between contract liability and tort liability. The economic loss doctrine means that a tort remedy in strict liability or negligence is not allowed when the only claim is for damage to the product itself. A tort claim in strict liability or negligence can only be made when there is property damage to property other than the product itself or a personal injury results.

EXHIBIT 10-3 Asbestos Litigation A.S. Rossiter Letter

"ASBESTOS"

Published by

SECRETARIAL SERVICE

16th Floor, Inquirer Bldg.
PHILADELPHIA, PA., U. S. A.

September 25, 1935.

Mr. Sumner Simpson, President,
Raybestos-Manhattan, Inc.,
Bridgeport, Conn.

Dear Sir:

You may recall that we have written you on several occasions concerning the publishing of information, or discussion of, asbestosis and the work which has been, and is being done, to eliminate or at least reduce it.

Always you have requested that for certain obvious reasons we publish nothing, and, naturally your wishes have been respected.

Possibly by this time, however, the reasons for your objection to publicity on this subject have been eliminated, and if so, we would like very much to review the whole matter in "ASBESTOS".

Our thought is that we could either prepare from data which we have in our files, or obtain from Mr. W. A. Godfrey of the Cape Asbestos Company, London, who is much interested in the subject, an article on the work done in England and then follow it with an article written by someone in your organization, as to the work done here.

We understand from Mr. Stover that your North Charleston plant, contains very complete dust control equipment and a description of such equipment, if you approve, would make a very interesting part of the article. Possibly even you could supply a photograph or two showing some part of this dust control equipment.

We await with much interest your reply. If there is no serious objection it would seem to be a most interesting subject for the pages of "ASBESTOS", and possibly a discussion of it in "ASBESTOS" along the right lines, would serve to combat some of the rather undesirable publicity given to it in current newspapers.

Very truly yours,
"ASBESTOS"

EXHIBIT 10-4 Asbestos Litigation Sumner Simpson Letter

Bridgeport, Conn.
Oct. 1, 1935

Mr. Vandiver Brown, Attorney,
Johns-Manville Corp.,
22 East 40th St.,
New York City.

My dear Mr. Brown:

      Enclosed is copy of a letter re-
ceived from Miss Rossiter, of "Asbestos."

      As I see it personally, we would
be just as well off to say nothing about
it until our survey is complete. I think
the less said about asbestos, the better off
we are, but at the same time, we cannot
lose track of the fact that there have been
a number of articles on asbestos dust control and asbestosis in the British trade
magazines. The magazine "Asbestos" is in
business to publish articles affecting the
trade and they have been very decent about
not re-printing the English articles.

      I shall be pleased to have your
opinion in the matter.

      Very truly yours,

SS-G.

Enc.   President

Tuesday

EXHIBIT 10-5 Asbestos Litigation Vandiver Brown Letter

Johns-Manville

TWENTY-TWO EAST FORTIETH STREET
NEW YORK, N.Y.

October 3, 1935

Mr. S. Simpson, President,
Raybestos-Manhattan, Inc.,
Bridgeport, Conn.

My dear Mr. Simpson:

I wish to acknowledge receipt of yours of
October 1st enclosing copy of the September 25th letter from
the editor of the magazine "ASBESTOS". I quite agree with
you that our interests are best served by having asbestosis
receive the minimum of publicity. Even if we should eventually decide to raise no objection to the publication of an
article on asbestosis in the magazine in question, I think we
should warn the editors to use American data on the subject
rather than English. Dr. Lanza has frequently remarked, to me
personally and in some of his papers, that the clinical picture presented in North American localities where there is an
asbestos dust hazard is considerably milder than that reported
in England and South Africa.

I believe the question raised by Miss Rossiter
might well be considered at the committee meeting scheduled
for next Tuesday, at which I understand both you and Mr. Judd
will be present.

Very truly yours,

Vandiver Brown
Attorney

VB:T

Workplace Skills Tip

In assisting with a products liability case, whether on the plaintiff team or the defense team, it is important to ascertain whether any national or international standards apply to the product. It will be important to determine whether the manufacturer has or has not met the standards of the various standards organizations whose purpose is to develop uniformity and performance in products. Examples are the American National Standards Institute (ANSI) and American Society for Testing and Materials International (ASTM).

For example, assume that Abraham bought a new state-of-the-art coffee pot to use in his new home. The coffee pot malfunctions in the middle of the night and instead of automatically turning off, it overheats and bursts into flames. Abraham hears the noise, smells the fire, arises, and quickly puts out the small fire. The only damage is to the coffee pot. Abraham would be barred from bringing a products liability action against the dealer or the coffee pot manufacturer on a strict liability theory because of the economic loss rule. This is because the property damage is solely to the product itself—the coffee pot.

Assume that Abraham is not at home, but his girlfriend, Devonne, is staying there. Assume the fire spreads beyond the pot into the cupboards and eventually into the rest of his home causing substantial property damage. Abraham would not be barred from bringing a strict liability claim against the dealer or the coffee pot manufacturer for damages caused to the home. This is because the damage is to "other property," that is, property other than the coffee pot product itself. By the same token, if Devonne suffered burns because of the fire, she could bring a strict liability claim against the dealer and the coffee pot manufacturer because of the personal injury that has occurred from the defective product.

EXHIBIT 10-6 Diagram of Chain of Distribution

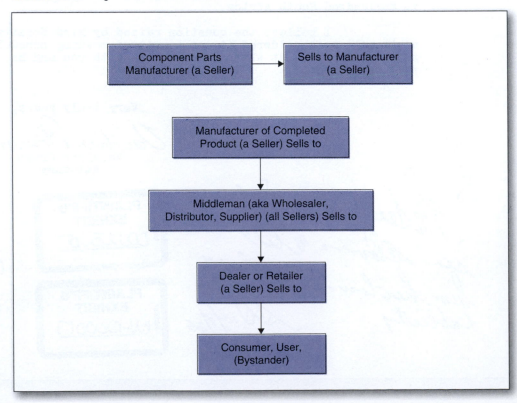

CHAIN OF DISTRIBUTION

For purposes of products liability law based upon strict liability, all those in the chain making a sale before the product reaches the consumer, the user, or possibly, a bystander are considered "sellers." See Exhibit 10-6. Any one or all in the chain of distribution of the product are subject to liability. Any participant in the sale/ marketing of the product may be strictly liable. It may be that under a particular state's law, an entity in the chain such as the dealer or one of the middlemen will be entitled to indemnity from the manufacturer. However, if the manufacturer or other entity in the chain is insolvent, in line with compensating innocent victims, any entity in the chain may then be strictly liable. The manufacturer of the finished product will be liable to a consumer, user, or possibly, a bystander even if the defective portion of the product was the component part manufactured by the component part manufacturer. The manufacturer of the finished product may seek indemnity from the component part manufacturer.

Defenses to Strict Liability in Products Liability Cases

There are various defenses to strict liability in a products liability case. These were discussed in Chapter 6. Misuse of the product is a defense. Other defenses are alteration or modification of the product. Another defense is comparative fault, which has been adopted by most states either judicially or by statute and which was also discussed in Chapter 6. Some statutes simply lump together all defenses under the concept of "fault." The definition of "fault" may then include contributory negligence, failure to warn, reckless conduct, assumption of the risk, misuse of a product and product liability involving negligence, strict liability, or breach of warranty.[12] Assumption of the risk is a defense particularly when the plaintiff knows of the risk involved and proceeds to unreasonably use the product. Some jurisdictions that have adopted comparative fault as cited in the previous paragraph may define comparative fault as including the traditional defenses of contributory negligence and assumption of the risk.

Another defense to strict liability in products cases is a written disclaimer of liability as was also discussed in Chapter 6. In analyzing disclaimers courts analyze the respective bargaining power of the parties. In the typical products case, there is unequal bargaining power between the consumer and the seller. Accordingly, these disclaimers are not likely to be upheld unless the parties are of equal bargaining power such as two businesses. The same principles discussed about disclaimers in Chapter 6 apply to disclaimers in products actions.

Finally, as also mentioned in Chapter 6, there may be a defense of a statute of limitation or a statute of repose. Various jurisdictions will have statutes of limitation and repose governing products liability based upon strict liability.

Products Liability Based on Negligence

MANUFACTURER LIABILITY vs. DEALER LIABILITY

Another theory or basis of liability in products cases is negligence. The history of products liability was traced in the beginning section of this chapter. As discussed there, the landmark products liability case based on negligence was *MacPherson v. Buick Motor Co.*, 217 N.Y. 382 (1916). This is the case that abolished the doctrine of privity and placed a duty of care on a seller to all foreseeable users. Liability extends to a negligent manufacture and design of a product. This liability includes a failure to adequately test and inspect a product. Sometimes, actual proof of exactly how the manufacturer was negligent may be difficult. Proof of the negligence may occur by *res ipsa loquitur*, as studied in Chapter 2.

Products liability based upon negligence may place duties of care on both the manufacturer and other suppliers, such as the retailer. Generally, the dealer—retailer has no duty to test or inspect a manufacturer's products if the dealer has no knowledge that the product would be dangerous in normal use.[13] However, if the dealer actually knows or has reason to know that the product may be dangerous in normal use, there is a duty to inspect and test the product or warn the buyer of the potential harm from the product.

Examples of placing a duty on the dealer to inspect, test, or warn would be when the dealer is buying the product from an unknown or unreliable manufacturer or when the dealer has had complaints from customers about the product. There are other products that, when placed into the stream of commerce, a customer would ordinarily expect a dealer to test and inspect the product before it is sold to the customer. Examples of these are a motor vehicle, a motorcycle, or a speedboat.

Just because a dealer fails to test, inspect, or warn the customer does not, however, relieve the manufacturer of liability. It may depend upon whether or not the dealer had actual knowledge of the defect, knew that the defect made the product dangerous, and sold it without providing a warning. That type of egregious conduct on the part of the dealer may be enough to constitute an intervening independent cause cutting off the chain of liability as discussed in Chapter 4. Various jurisdictions also have statutes governing the liability of manufacturers, suppliers, distributors, and dealers. Just as in strict liability, a manufacturer may be held liable for the negligently manufactured or designed products of component part manufacturers.

DAMAGES

With regard to damages, the plaintiff is entitled to recover those same items of personal injury damages as mentioned in the strict liability section, which are compensatory damages both economic and non-economic, potential punitive damages, and property damage to "other property." The economic loss rule also applies to a claim for damage to the product itself.

Defenses to Negligence Claims in Products Cases

Defenses to negligence are those that were outlined in Chapter 6. These are contributory negligence, assumption of the risk, comparative negligence/fault, and applicable statutes of limitation/repose.

Products Liability Based on Breach of Warranty

This theory or basis of liability is not based upon tort. It is based upon contract. Recall Chapter 1 in which this distinction was first made. Negligence is based upon a breach of a *duty*. Breach of contract is based upon a broken *promise*. An action based on a breach of warranty is a contract action, not a tort action.

EXPRESS WARRANTY

An **express warranty** is a promise or a representation made orally or in writing concerning the product in question. It may be a verbal statement as simple as, "I'm tellin' you, this thing will last you 50 years." It may be contained in a manufacturer's written brochure describing the product as "indestructible" and "our research and development team believes this product will last for at least 100 years." If that express warranty is breached, the buyer has an action against the seller on a contract theory for breach of warranty, which is a breach of a promise.

Express Warranty
A promise or a representation made orally or in writing concerning the product in question.

IMPLIED WARRANTY

There are two implied warranties that tend to arise in products liability actions. These two warranties are also codified in the Uniform Commercial Code (U.C.C.). The first is an **implied warranty of fitness for a particular purpose**. The seller knows that the buyer is buying a product for a particular purpose and is relying on the seller's skill in providing the appropriate product (U.C.C. 2-315). The second is an **implied warranty of merchantability**. This warranty means that the product will be fit for general or ordinary purposes (U.C.C. 2-314). Contract warranty theories are very similar to tort strict liability theories. Due care on the part of the manufacturer is irrelevant in strict liability. Likewise, if a warranty is breached, the manufacturer is liable regardless of how reasonable or how careful the manufacturer was in making or designing the product.

Implied Warranty of Fitness for a Particular Purpose
A warranty in which the seller knows that the buyer is buying a product for a particular purpose and is relying on the seller's skill in providing the appropriate product.

Implied Warranty of Merchantability
This warranty means that the product will be fit for general or ordinary purposes.

Under Section 2-318 of the U.C.C., the states were provided with three alternative versions concerning the doctrine of privity as to a person who is injured. Privity may extend to (1) the family or guests of the immediate buyer when the person is personally injured; (2) any individual who may reasonably be expected to use, consume, or be affected by the goods and who suffers personal injury; or (3) any person who may reasonably be expected to use, consume, or be affected by the goods and who is injured.

Also, the manufacturer may be found to have breached a warranty on a contract theory, even though the product might not necessarily be considered defective under the tort strict liability theory. For example, a simple cooking product such as a turkey fryer that utilizes cooking the turkey in hot oil may not breach a risk/utility test or a consumer expectation test under strict liability, but it may have breached express language of an express warranty, such as "This roaster is guaranteed to be trouble-free!" Yet, a consumer may complain that the fryer may tend to overheat, and if too close to combustible material, it could cause a fire. The reverse

Workplace Skills Tip

The reality is that individual products liability cases are less common. They are extremely expensive for a plaintiff to pursue against a manufacturer. Many manufacturers have seemingly unlimited resources. They will make a plaintiff "jump through the hoops." Discovery is expensive. Extremely knowledgeable experts are typically required and they do not come cheap. It has become a specialty practice. The trend today in products liability is to pursue such cases as a class action or a mass tort action,

if possible. For requirements of a class action, the paralegal should review Rule 23 of the federal rules or the state counterpart in your jurisdiction. A mass tort is a collective injury to a group of people such as an airline crash. Or a mass tort may consist of many victims with several tortfeasors involved but one instrumentality involved such as a drug or asbestos. Incidentally, asbestos litigation has probably been the longest running, largest, and most expensive mass tort litigation in the history of this country.

is also true. It is conceivable that a product might be considered defective under a tort strict liability test for failing to use an alternative design or state-of-the-art design and yet not breach any warranties.

PRIVITY

The concept of privity was discussed at the beginning of this chapter in the context of negligence cases and its abolition under the *MacPherson v. Buick Motor Co.* case. The traditional view is that breach of warranty is a contract action, and so there must be privity of contract between the injured person and the seller. The problem lies with implied warranties more than express warranties. The U.C.C. privity alternatives were discussed earlier under the heading of Implied Warranties. The manufacturer of an automobile, for example, makes express warranties through its advertising upon which the general public may rely.

In the implied warranties scenario, the consumer buys the product from the dealer not the manufacturer. Therefore, in theory, the buyer cannot take advantage of the warranties running from the manufacturer to the dealer. The buyer would have no action against the manufacturer for breach of implied warranty because there was no contract between the buyer and the manufacturer. As the student might expect, the privity rule is disappearing in the implied warranty field because it is a harsh, unrealistic, and impractical rule. The buyer would have to sue the retailer, and the retailer would sue the distributor for indemnity, and then the distributor would sue the manufacturer for indemnity. Multiple lawsuits in the court system are not efficient nor are they preferred. Some jurisdictions still retain privity depending upon the type of case. For the most part, the trend is that privity is being eroded and eliminated as a defense in breach-of-warranty cases. Some states, for example, may eliminate it for only dangerous products. Some, however, such as California, have abolished the requirement of privity for all consumer goods.[14]

CAUSATION

Just as is true for the theories of strict liability and negligence, causation is a required element of proof for the plaintiff.

DAMAGES

Plaintiff must prove all damages proximately caused by the defendant's breach of warranties.

Defenses to Warranty Claims in Products Cases

Contributory negligence is not a defense to breach-of-warranty claims because breach-of-warranty claims are contract claims. Assumption of the risk is a defense. As mentioned earlier in this chapter, some states have incorporated breach-of-warranty claims, whether express or implied, under the concept of comparative fault.

Written disclaimers are a defense to express and implied warranty claims, although it would be difficult for a manufacturer or seller to disclaim language of an express warranty. A disclaimer is typically utilized to attempt to disclaim the implied warranties discussed above. It may be by language as simple as "Buyer takes these products '*as is*.'" The U.C.C. Section 2-316 does provide for disclaimers mentioning a requirement, for example, that the disclaimer must be "conspicuous."

> ### Workplace Skills Tip
>
> In a products liability personal injury case, it is not uncommon to see all three basic theories alleged in the complaint—strict liability, negligence, and breach of warranties. This is the shotgun approach. While the complaint may have been drafted in that fashion initially, the later strategy may change. The plaintiff's team may decide to use a rifle approach. For example, in strict liability, the issue is whether the manufacturer put out a product that was defective and unreasonably dangerous that caused the injury. Bringing a negligence claim alongside of a strict liability claim, however, allows the manufacturer to introduce relevant evidence of how careful and how reasonable it was in making or designing the product. Accordingly, in a particular products case, the plaintiff team may consider dismissing the negligence claims against the manufacturer. Then any evidence produced by the manufacturer to establish how careful the manufacturer was will be inadmissible in the case because it is irrelevant to claims under strict liability. The focus will then be on the defective product, and the jury will not hear any evidence of how careful and how reasonable the manufacturer was concerning its testing, inspecting, designing, and manufacturing of the product.

Under the U.C.C., there is a requirement for the injured purchaser to provide "timely notice of the breach."[15] The applicable statutes of limitation/repose operate as defenses. U.C.C. Section 2-725 provides for a period of four years from delivery of the goods/products. Other statutes of limitation in a particular state may specify other applicable statutes of limitation.

The Consumer Product Safety Act

The Consumer Product Safety Act is a federal statute enacted in 1972. This statute established the Consumer Product Safety Commission. This commission has the authority to develop safety standards and even to effect recalls of products that the commission determines present an unreasonable risk of injury or death. The commission also has the power and authority to ban a product. It has approximately 15,000 products under its wing. Excluded from its authority, however, are certain products that fall under the jurisdiction of another government agency such as the U.S. Food and Drug Administration (food, drugs), the U.S. Department of Transportation (motor vehicles), and the Environmental Protection Agency (pesticides).

The Magnuson-Moss Warranty Act and State Lemon Laws

The Magnuson-Moss Warranty Act is a federal statute enacted in 1975.[16] The statute governs express and implied warranties on certain products. In addition, all 50 states have "lemon laws," which typically apply to new motor vehicles still under warranty. Lemon vehicles are typically ones with a significant manufacturing defect that affects the use, safety, or value of the vehicle. Recovery is typically a replacement or a repurchase of the vehicle less a deduction for mileage and a reimbursement for taxes, title, and fees.

A Final Theory: Products Liability Based on Intention

This chapter has covered the subject of products liability approached from the traditional theories of strict liability, negligence, and breach of warranties. To reiterate a basic principle of tort and personal injury law, it is important to recognize that while one theory of recovery may not be applicable, do not give up. Another theory may apply. Up to this point in this textbook, principles of torts based on negligence, intention, and strict liability have been examined.

It is conceivable that a manufacturer or other seller may be liable on a theory of battery. If the manufacturer or other seller actually knows that its product is defective or otherwise dangerous to the user or consumer and fails to put out a warning concerning the unreasonably dangerous defect, that manufacturer or seller could be liable on a theory of battery. Recall the basic elements of battery outlined in Chapter 7. The intent is proved by the defendant's belief that the harm is *substantially certain* to occur.

Class Actions

As mentioned in the Workplace Skills Tip in this chapter, class actions are a favorite way in which to pursue certain products liability cases. For example, if there is a claim that a certain defective drug was given to treat a certain condition during a certain time period and it caused some type of harm to certain patients, this may be a good candidate for a class action. Rather than trying thousands of individual cases, all of them can be heard together. It can be an efficient process and one that affords judicial economy. For example, instead of having to bring in expensive expert witnesses for each of the thousands of cases, if the case is certified as a class action, the experts involved can testify once concerning all cases. Each plaintiff would, of course, need to prove his or her own particular damages.

Before an action can be certified as a class action to be brought by a representative on behalf of all members of the class, there are certain prerequisites mandated by Rule 23 of the Federal Rules of Civil Procedure or its state counterpart. Depending upon the jurisdictional requirements, a class action may properly be brought in either federal court under this rule or in state court under the Federal Rule 23 counterpart. Under Rule 23 (a), there are four mandated prerequisites of numerosity, commonality, typicality, and that the representative parties will fairly and adequately protect the interests of the class. In addition, there must also be shown one of the three prerequisites outlined in Rule 23 (b). The student is encouraged to read Rule 23 of the Federal Rules of Civil Procedure so as to have some familiarity with this fairly common type of suit utilized in products liability cases.

CASE **10.1** Hypothetical Case: Developing Workplace Skills

You are a paralegal working in a plaintiff's personal injury firm specializing in products liability. You have just received the following memo from the senior partner:

From: Richard L. Pemlaw

To: Suzie Que

Re: RLP 1927-12

The firm has just signed up a new client, Joel Flomberg, a 22-year-old recent college graduate. Joel loves racing cars and bought a brand new sports car from a local dealer. The sports car has a 425-horsepower engine with a speedometer showing 180 mph. The car was marketed by the manufacturer with an intended and recognized appeal to youthful drivers and an appeal that it had a capability of speeds in excess of 100 miles per hour. Joel was out with a buddy, Tom Olsonover, at a local

(Continued)

CASE 10.1 (*Continued*)

bar and had several drinks to the point that Joel became intoxicated. On leaving the bar he remarked to Tom, "Let's see how fast this baby will go!" As he reached approximately 120 miles per hour, Joel suddenly lost control of the vehicle. The tread separated from the body of one of the rear tires. The car went out of control, hit a tree, and Joel was seriously and permanently injured. Suit has been brought on a theory of a defective design and failure of the manufacturer to warn of the danger of tread separation at high speeds. At the time of the accident, there were approximately 1,000 miles on the vehicle. In the course of investigation and discovery of this case, as you know, you discovered that the tires on the vehicle were only rated for a maximum speed of 85 miles per hour. The tire manufacturer's records indicated that it tested these tires for only a maximum safe operating speed of around 85 miles per hour. We have also determined from our experts that the separation of the tread from the left rear tire was not caused by any road hazard or neglected cuts or other abuse in the tread before the accident. We have sued the car manufacturer on a theory of strict liability for failure to warn of the inadequate tires. The manufacturer alleged (1) no duty to warn; (2) the manufacturer should not be liable for the tire manufacturer's component product; and (3) plaintiff's contributory negligence, misuse, and assumption of the risk bars his recovery. None of the advertising or sales materials stated anything about tires except to maintain proper pressure, which is not an issue in this case. Please provide a memo to me discussing the viability of these three defenses. Enter your time on the above file number.

"Put simply, we need our website to tell consumers all about our company without really telling them anything about our company."

CHAPTER **SUMMARY**

Strict liability is a basis for liability concerning the manufacture and sale of products in the stream of commerce. Early product liability cases were analyzed under a contract theory, and there could be no recovery unless the plaintiff was in "privity of contract" with the seller. Eventually, these products cases were analyzed under a tort theory. The landmark case establishing products liability based upon negligence and holding privity is not a defense is *MacPherson v. Buick Motor Co.,* 111 N.E. 1050 (N.Y. 1916).

Early cases based upon a true strict liability theory were those in the area of food consumption. The theory was expanded from food consumption to cosmetics and eventually into other areas. One of the first was cinder building blocks. Shortly after that, strict liability was applied to automobiles in the landmark case of *Henningsen v. Bloomfield Motors,* 161 A.2d 69 (N.J. 1960).

The area of strict liability in torts for products cases is set forth under the Restatement (Second) of Torts § 402A (1965). A seller is considered to be a manufacturer, a wholesaler, a distributor, a supplier, and a retailer/dealer. A "product" is defined in Restatement (Third) of Torts: Products Liability § 19 (1997). A product is considered to be "tangible personal property distributed commercially for use or consumption." "Services" are not considered products. Human blood and human tissue even when distributed commercially are not considered products. Whether or not an item is a "product" is a question of law to be decided by the court.

A defective condition in a product means that the defect causes the product to be unreasonably dangerous. It must be

in that defective condition when it leaves the seller's hands/control. There are three types of unreasonably dangerous defects: (1) manufacturing defects, (2) design defects, and (3) defects in a lack of warning/insufficiency of warning. Tests the courts utilize to determine design defects are: (1) risk/utility, (2) consumer expectation, and (3) state of the art/alternative reasonable design.

An element of strict liability is also that the defective product must be "unreasonably dangerous." There are certain dangerous products, however, such as handguns that are not considered unreasonably dangerous if they are functioning as intended. Another element is that the "user or consumer" be the one who has suffered harm. However, this may include a family member or the purchaser's employee. The strict liability doctrine in products cases has even been extended to bystanders by some courts. The harm must have been proximately caused by the defective product. The seller must be engaged in the business of selling the product. The philosophy behind strict products liability is to place a special responsibility upon those who undertake a regular business regularly placing their products into the stream of commerce.

Damages recoverable are compensatory damages consisting of both economic and non-economic damages. Depending upon the jurisdiction, punitive damages may also be recovered. Defenses to a strict liability claim are misuse, alteration/modification of the product, comparative fault, assumption of the risk, disclaimers of liability, and statutes of limitation/repose. The economic loss rule prevents recovery under this theory for purely economic losses unless there is damage to property other than the product itself, or there is a personal injury.

Products cases may also be based upon a tort theory of negligence. This theory is that established by the *MacPherson* case discussed above. Generally, a dealer/retailer has no duty to test or inspect a manufacturer's product. If the dealer knows or has reason to know the product is dangerous, there is a duty imposed on the dealer to test, inspect, and warn. Causation is required. Damages are the same as those under strict liability. The economic loss rule also applies. The defenses are also the same as those under strict liability except that contributory negligence is also a defense.

Product liability cases are also brought on the theories of breach of express warranty and breach of implied warranties. An express warranty is a promise or representation made orally or in writing concerning the product in question. The two implied warranties are an implied warranty of fitness for a particular purpose and an implied warranty of merchantability. These warranties are also outlined in the U.C.C. Privity has traditionally been required for breach-of-warranty cases, but that doctrine is being eroded by the courts. Causation is required just as it is for negligence and strict liability. Defenses are assumption of the risk, comparative fault, written disclaimers, and statutes of limitation/repose. Under the U.C.C., timely notice must be given of the breach.

A final, potential theory for products liability is that of an intentional tort. If a manufacturer or seller actually knows that its product is defective or dangerous and fails to warn the consumer, the manufacturer or seller could be liable on a theory of battery. Intent is satisfied if the defendant's belief is that the harm is substantially certain to occur.

KEY TERMS

Privity of Contract

Defective Condition

Manufacturing Defects

Design Defects

Risk/Utility Test

Consumer Expectation Text

State of the Art/Alternative
    Reasonable Design Test

Economic Loss Doctrine

Express Warranty

Implied Warranty of Fitness for a
    Particular Purpose

Implied Warranty of Merchantability

REVIEW QUESTIONS

1. Explain the difference between a "manufacturing defect" and a "design defect." Give two examples of each.

2. Assume Clyde buys his favorite can of cherries labeled as "High Quality Washington Cherries." He bites into one that has a pit and breaks a tooth. Clyde sues the manufacturer claiming that the label should have had a warning to be careful because some cherries could contain pits. What is the manufacturer's most likely defense? At the same time, Clyde's girlfriend, Bonnie, buys a new brand of "Down South Peanuts." She eats them and suffers an allergic reaction. Bonnie sues the manufacturer claiming that the label should warn of the possibility of an allergic reaction to peanuts. What is the manufacturer's most likely defense?

3. Vita is using her new carving knife manufactured by Famous Cutlery. As she is slicing a tomato, the handle is wet, the knife slips, and she cuts her index finger almost all the way off. She sues the manufacturer on a theory of strict liability. What arguments might she make? What defenses might Famous Cutlery raise?

4. Terri owns a hobby farm and is an avid hunter. Every fall she hunts elk and deer. Always successful, but not caring for venison herself, she sells the meat for about a month every fall by putting up a sign at the intersection of two township roads where she resides. Russ buys some venison steak. It turns out that it was spoiled, and Russ became deathly ill. When he recovers, Russ sues Terri on a theory of strict liability. What defense will Terri likely raise?

5. Lon was asked by his wife to hang some pictures in their new home. Not being able to find a hammer after the recent move, he spots the new heavy-duty stapler that he just purchased yesterday for his office. The brochure with the stapler contained this language: "Staples up to 120 pages at a time. This stapler is the strongest stapler on the market. It was tested by dropping weights on it and using it to pound in a metal stake. It won't let you down for any of your heavy-duty office projects." The stapler is extra heavy and durable so he decides to use it as a hammer to pound in the nails to hang the pictures. As he does so, a piece of the stapler flies off and hits him in the eye. He sues the manufacturer of the stapler on a theory of negligence, strict liability, and breach of warranty. What arguments might he make? What defenses might the manufacturer raise?

6. Mortimer purchased a brand new garbage truck for his sanitation business directly from Acme Waste Products. In the course of its operation a week later, because of a unique defect in the electrical portion of the engine, the engine caught on fire and seriously damaged the truck almost to the point of a total loss. As a result, Mortimer was without a truck for a substantial length of time and lost $20,000 in profits in addition to the $50,000 damage to the truck. He sues Acme for his damages on a strict liability theory because of the electrical defect. What is Acme's most likely defense? What other theories would be available for Mortimer?

chapter 11

DEFAMATION, INVASION OF PRIVACY, AND OTHER MISCELLANEOUS TORTS

"Never throw mud. You may miss your mark, but you will have dirty hands."

Joseph Parker

LEARNING OBJECTIVES

After studying this chapter, you should be able to:

- Recognize and analyze the tort of defamation and differentiate between libel and slander.

- Recognize and analyze the tort of invasion of privacy and identify the four main theories of that tort.

- Recognize and analyze the tort of misrepresentation.

- Recognize and analyze the tort of malicious prosecution of a criminal action.

- Recognize and analyze the torts of malicious prosecution of a civil action, abuse of process, and spoliation of evidence.

Introduction to Defamation

Defamation is the publication (communication) to a third person of a defamatory (false) statement or material (oral or written) that causes harm to the reputation of the plaintiff with resulting damages. **Libel** is a defamation that is communicated in written form, such as a newspaper, a magazine, a letter, or an e-mail. It tends to be a defamation that can be *read*. **Slander** is a defamation that is communicated orally/verbally. It tends to be a defamation that can be *heard*. Generally, libel tends to be more serious. Something in writing or in printed form tends to be more permanent in nature as opposed to a verbal statement, which is uttered and then disappears. The tort of invasion of the right of privacy will also be discussed in this chapter. The tort of intentional infliction of emotional distress was discussed in Chapter 7. The student should keep in mind that whether or not defamation exists, these two other torts might be established with the particular communicated statement or material.

Publication to a Third Person

Publication is the communication of any defamatory statement or material of any kind, written or oral, to some third person other than to the plaintiff. This is one of the key elements of defamation. The essence of this tort is that there is harm to the *reputation* of the plaintiff. Obviously, any statement made from the defendant only to the plaintiff, no matter how egregious or untrue, does no harm to the reputation of the plaintiff. If the statement was not read or heard by someone else, there can be no claim that the plaintiff's reputation was harmed. Reputation is the evaluation of one's character as held by friends, neighbors,

Defamation
The publication (communication) to a third person of a false statement or material (oral or written) that causes harm to the reputation of the plaintiff with resulting damages.

Libel
A defamation that is communicated in written form, such as a newspaper, a magazine, a letter, or an e-mail. It tends to be a defamation that can be read.

Slander
A defamation that is communicated orally/verbally. It tends to be a defamation that can be heard.

Publication
The communication of any defamatory statement or material of any kind, written or oral, to some third person other than to the plaintiff.

or associates. Depending upon the statement or material involved and its effect on the plaintiff, the plaintiff may have a claim for intentional infliction of emotional distress or a claim for invasion of privacy even if defamation cannot be proved.

The Restatement (Second) of Torts § 577 states: "Publication of defamatory matter is its communication *intentionally or by a negligent act* to one other than the person defamed." (Emphasis added.) Thus, the defamatory communication need not be intentionally done. It may be negligently done. In addition, the publication need not be communicated to a large group of people. The tort is satisfied if the statement is communicated to a single person other than the plaintiff. For example, Larry, Curly, and Moe are out hiking with Moe lagging behind. An argument develops between Larry and Curly. Larry shouts to Curly, "You murderer, I know you killed your wife." Moe has caught up with them and hears the statement. Had Moe not heard the statement, there would be no claimed defamation in the form of slander. Because Moe heard the statement, Curly has a claim for defamation assuming the statement is false.

There are two points to be made in this example. First, it illustrates the requirement of a publication to a third person. Second, publication to a sole third person satisfies the element of publication. Review the decision of *Campbell v. Salazar*, 960 S.W.2d 719 (Tex. App. 1997) in Exhibit 11-1. Note in that case, according to the defendant, she did not make a defamatory statement to a third person about the plaintiff but only asked a question: "Do you think that Barbara took it?" (defendant's cash).

EXHIBIT 11-1 Relevant Case Law

Norma Campbell, Appellant, v. Barbara Salazar, Appellee.

Court of Appeals of Texas, El Paso.

Barajas, Chief Justice.

Teacher brought slander action against woman she had accompanied on trip to Las Vegas, based on claim that woman had accused teacher of stealing money. The 243rd District Court, El Paso County, Javier Alvarez, J., entered judgment on jury verdict for plaintiff, and defendant appealed. The Court of Appeals, Barajas, C.J., held that: (1) findings that defendant had slandered plaintiff, and had acted with actual malice, were supported by evidence; (2) awards of $5,000 in exemplary damages, $15,000 for past mental anguish, and $31,600 in past lost wages were not excessive; (4) plaintiff was properly allowed to amend pleadings during trial; and (5) audio tape recording was properly admitted into evidence.

Affirmed.

OPINION

This is an appeal from a finding by the trial court that Norma Campbell slandered Barbara Salazar. Judgment was rendered for the sum of $58,843.63 that included past mental anguish, past loss of income, exemplary damages, and prejudgment interest. We affirm the judgment of the trial court.

I. SUMMARY OF THE EVIDENCE

Norma Campbell, Appellant, first met Barbara Salazar in the summer of 1992 before leaving on a trip to Las Vegas with Salazar and another friend. While in Las Vegas, Appellant discovered that she was missing $725 when she attempted to make a purchase in a gift shop. Appellant admitted that she did not initially accuse Salazar of taking her money while in Las Vegas, but she admitted that she did make that accusation once she returned home. She testified that no one was present at the time

(Continued)

EXHIBIT 11-1 *(Continued)*

of the accusation. She further testified to telling her friend, Lydi, that she was missing the $725 but denies accusing Salazar of taking the money. Appellant admits that she did tell Lydi, "Do you think that Barbara took it?" She does however deny that she ever told anyone that "Barbara took my money"....

The jury in this case returned a verdict finding that Appellant slandered Salazar and awarded Salazar actual damages for past mental anguish in addition to damages for past loss of income. The jury also found that there was malice and awarded the plaintiff punitive damages. After a final judgment was entered, Appellant filed a motion for judgment n.o.v. and a motion for new trial, which were either denied by the trial judge or overruled by operation of law. Appellant now brings various points of error....

3. ELEMENTS OF SLANDER

In determining whether slander occurred, this Court has provided the following definition. Slander is:

(1) a defamatory statement that is

(2) communicated or published to a third person

(3) without legal excuse....

A statement is defamatory if the words tend to injure a person's reputation, exposing the person to public hatred, contempt, ridicule, or financial injury.... Whether words are capable of the defamatory meaning the plaintiff attributes to them is a question of law for the court.... The court construes the statement as a whole in light of surrounding circumstances based upon how a person of ordinary intelligence would perceive the entire statement. *Id.* Only when the court determines the complained of language to be ambiguous or of doubtful import should a jury be permitted to determine the statement's meaning and the effect the statement has on the ordinary reader or listener.... If a written or oral statement unambiguously and falsely imputes criminal conduct to the plaintiff, it is libelous or slanderous *per se*.... In suits brought by private individuals, truth is an affirmative defense to slander....

Publication of defamatory words means to communicate orally to some third person capable of understanding their defamatory import and in such a way that he did so understand.... If a reasonable person would recognize that his act creates an unreasonable risk that the defamatory statements will be communicated to a third party, his conduct is negligent communication, which amounts to publication as much as an intentional communication.... In addition, although the plaintiff in a libel or slander action must be the particular person about whom the allegedly defamatory statements are made, which normally means the plaintiff must be named, publication does not require that the plaintiff be named, if those who know the plaintiff and are acquainted with him understand that the defamatory publication referred to him.... In reviewing the record and applying the above standards of review and definition of slander, we conclude that the trial court did not err in denying Appellant's motion for new trial or motion for judgment n.o.v. and there was more than a scintilla of evidence for the jury to conclude that Appellant slandered Appellee and this finding is not against the great weight and preponderance of the evidence....

Source: Campbell v. Salazar, 960 S.W. 2d 719 (Ct. App. Tx 1997).

A publication in writing that is libel may not necessarily occur precisely by way of the written word. Assume that Harry and Sally are co-workers in an office, and both are assistant managers. Harry is jealous of Sally because she is extremely competent, and he is concerned that she may obtain the promotion to the position of manager, a position that they both are seeking. Harry is an excellent artist and cartoonist who used to do this type of work professionally for a newspaper. He decides to do a cartoon showing a sexually explicit drawing of Sally and another well-known employee in the office. His artistic abilities are so good that there is no doubt about who the two are as portrayed in the drawing. He posts it on the office bulletin board. This drawing would constitute (1) a communication of (2) defamatory matter to (3) a third person, as Harry would know others would be regularly checking the office bulletin board. Sally and the other employee depicted in the cartoon would have a claim for libel against Harry.

REPUBLICATION OF A DEFAMATORY STATEMENT

Republication
Occurs when the plaintiff is forced or compelled to repeat the defamatory statement.

Publication of a defamatory statement to a third person is a necessary element of the tort of defamation. There is another offshoot to this element of publication, which is called "republication." **Republication** occurs when the plaintiff is forced or compelled to repeat the defamatory statement. This frequently occurs in the employment context when the fired employee, fired for a false, defamatory reason, is seeking other employment. The prospective employer inquires why the employee was terminated at the former job. The employee gives a truthful response that the employee was fired after being told that the employee engaged in some illegal or immoral conduct. The defamatory statement of the former employer is thus republished by the fired employee to the prospective employer just as if the former employer had originally published the defamatory statement directly to the prospective employer. The republication theory in this employment context is controversial, and it has not been adopted as a majority position.

Harm to the Reputation of the Plaintiff

TWO STANDARDS

Besides publication of the statement to a third person, the statement must tend to harm or injure the reputation of the plaintiff. The statement must have a defamatory meaning. There are actually two different standards of reputation injury. One standard is that the statement must tend to lower the plaintiff's reputation in the community where the statement was published or deter others from associating with the plaintiff. The other standard is that the statement must expose the plaintiff to "hatred, contempt or ridicule."[1]

HOW IS THE ALLEGED DEFAMATION UNDERSTOOD BY THE THIRD PERSON?

The issue is how the words of the statement were reasonably understood by the third person, not what the defendant actually meant by making the statement. In the earlier example involving the three hikers, if Larry shouted the accusation of Curly being a murderer to Curly in German and Moe did not understand German, not only would Moe not be able to reasonably determine what Larry meant, Moe would have no idea what Larry even said. There is no room for determining any reasonable interpretation of Larry's statement, even though an accusation of murder would be clear on its face if Moe spoke German. In trying to ascertain the meaning of a statement, the courts look at the fair and natural meaning that will be given to the statement by reasonable people of ordinary intelligence.

Consider the case of an attorney defaming another attorney. The first attorney made statements to the client of the second attorney that the client's lawyer was "stupid" and "he is not going to do anything for you." The court held that these statements were defamatory. This is because they were designed to lower the attorney in the client's estimation and damage the attorney's professional reputation.[2]

STATEMENT MUST REFER TO THE PLAINTIFF

For a statement to be defamatory, a third person must have reasonably interpreted the statement to apply to or refer to the plaintiff. A statement may be clearly defamatory of someone yet not make reference to the particular plaintiff by name. Consider, "A prominent businessman who resides at a rural country estate has been seen with known prostitutes and Mexican drug lords." The evidence to be produced by the plaintiff will need to be that a person or persons reasonably understood the statement to refer to the plaintiff as being the businessman and that the statement tended to lower the plaintiff's reputation in the community.

There can also be defamation by "insinuation." This is defamation that is not *expressed* but rather is *implied*. The statement, on its face, is not defamatory. This occurs when the defamatory meaning of the statement only becomes clear when the defamatory language is combined with some extrinsic facts that are not made a part of the publication. In that case, the plaintiff must prove those extrinsic facts. The plaintiff must also prove that those facts were known to a third person and the innuendo or implication of the statement, when combined with the extrinsic facts, makes the publication defamatory. For example, consider this statement, "Joe Brown was seen walking out of Spencer's Bar and Grille last Monday evening with a gun in his hand." The extrinsic fact that Joe Brown would need to prove for defamation is that there was a murder in Spencer's Bar and Grille last Monday evening in which a patron was shot to death by a man with a pistol.

In 1970, there was a popular movie entitled *A Man Called Horse*. Suit was brought by Jeffrey Dontigney against Paramount Pictures and CBS Broadcasting for defamation. Dontigney, a Native American Mohegan Indian from Connecticut, claimed that the movie was false and non-authentic and that the Native Americans in the movie were falsely portrayed as savages. Defendants argued that Dontigney's complaint failed to allege that any of the statements were "about" or "of and concerning" Mr. Dontigney himself. The court noted that a plaintiff must prove that defendant published false statements about a plaintiff that caused harm. The court, in denying the defamation claim, stated, "Here, Dontigney has alleged no facts from which a reasonable person could infer that any statements or characterizations in 'A Man Called Horse' mentioned or were 'of and concerning plaintiff himself.'"[3]

Facts Must Be False

The essence of a defamation case is that statements said or written about the plaintiff are false. As will be discussed later in this chapter, truth of the statement is a defense. Further, it is defamatory *facts* that create the tort of defamation, not the expression of *opinions*. Obviously, a fact is either true or false. An opinion is a considered judgment. The waters here are often muddied, however. Even if a statement is factual, a court may not find it defamatory if made as a joke or made in anger as verbal abuse. Also, the circumstances and the environment in which the statement was made will be considered. Sometimes it is difficult to tell the difference between a fact and an opinion. Consider some examples:

- "You Goddamn ignorant old son of a bitch…. You are the most ignorant and incompetent county recorder we have ever had; you never do anything."[4] Court held no slander as this was merely verbal abuse at a county office.
- "You are a bleached, blond bastard, a Goddamn son of a bitch and a bum and a tramp!"[5] Court held no slander in an argument between neighbors, as this was merely verbal abuse.
- He is an "iron clad singing member of the Mafia"; "My buddy from the Mafia."[6] Court held no slander as these comments were made in jest—a joke made on a TV show.
- He was a "very poor lawyer."[7] Court held there was no defamation as this was an expression of an opinion not a statement of fact.
- "Motherf_____"[8] Court held no defamation. An untrue statement of fact accusing someone of incest would be defamatory, but a reasonable person would not conclude from this common word of profanity that plaintiff had engaged in sexual intercourse with his mother.
- "You Son of a Bitch."[9] Court held this statement was slanderous. There were rather unique facts in this case. An automobile dealer was in the process of delivering his regular live television commercial when the statement was made by the defendant. A lady in the TV audience thought the defendant was a customer with a grievance concerning the purchase of an automobile. Her testimony was that she came to the conclusion that if one bought a car from plaintiff dealer, one might expect unfavorable treatment from him, thus lowering the plaintiff's reputation.

In trying to reconcile the holdings of some of the above cases, it must be remembered that courts will focus on the totality of the circumstances and the context in which the statement was published. To reiterate a point made earlier, how the alleged defamatory language was reasonably understood by the third person or persons to whom it was published is important. Unless the third person reasonably believes that the publication is uttered in a defamatory sense, such that the plaintiff's reputation was lowered, there is no defamation.

Workplace Skills Tip

A thin-skinned client may believe that he or she was defamed at a public meeting such as a city council meeting, a school board meeting, or some other local meeting. These meetings are typically emotionally charged. Because tempers flare and emotions run high at these events, the people there understand a certain amount of name-calling is to be expected. For that reason, calling someone a "bitch," a "bastard," or a "liar" at a public meeting is probably unlikely to be held to be defamatory.

Damages for Defamation

DAMAGES FOR SLANDER

In a defamation action, how the courts approach the issue of damages depends upon whether the defamatory statement or matter is slander or libel. As discussed earlier, libelous statements or matter, contained in a writing are more permanent in nature than oral statements, which disappear after they are uttered. Accordingly, the libelous statement is treated in a more serious vein. To recover damages for slander, there must be special damages shown. Chapter 4 discussed special damages. These are damages with an economic value that can be determined with a fairly easy mathematical calculation such as lost wages or medical bills. These are actual damages the plaintiff suffers, and they are not presumed by law. If special damages are proved, then the plaintiff may prove general damages also discussed in Chapter 4. Examples of general damages in defamation might be a loss to one's reputation or emotional distress.

However, in the common law, there are four well-recognized exceptions to the requirement of proving special damages in a slander action. These exceptions are called "slander per se" and include:

- A claim that plaintiff committed a "serious crime." ("You raped that girl.")
- A claim that plaintiff has a "loathsome disease." ("No wonder you have AIDS.")
- A claim that plaintiff is "incompetent in his or her trade or profession." ("Doctor Williams is the biggest 'butcher' I've ever seen.")
- A claim that plaintiff is "unchaste." ("She goes to bed with every guy in town.")

DAMAGES FOR LIBEL

If the claim for damages is based on libel, which is a written defamation, and it is clear on its face, the general rule is that general damages will be presumed from the fact of the publication. There is no requirement to first prove special damages as there is in slander. The theory behind this is that libelous statements and material (drawings, cartoons) are more permanent in nature and likely to be seen or read by a larger group of people with a greater potential for damage to the plaintiff's reputation. Consider the example above, "Doctor Williams is the biggest 'butcher' in town." Compare the realistic harm to the plaintiff doctor if the statement was made orally and published to only one person as opposed to the statement being published in a local newspaper or magazine and read by hundreds or thousands of people.

Defenses to Defamation

There are various defenses to the tort of defamation.

TRUTH

Obviously, if the defendant proves that the alleged defamatory statement was true, this is a complete defense. A claims B defamed (slandered) him when B said "A took money from the till yesterday." B proves by independent witnesses and a video surveillance camera from yesterday that, in fact, A did take money from the till. A will not prevail in his defamation action.

CONSENT

The student will recall that consent is a defense to an intentional tort such as battery. Likewise, consent to the publication by the defendant is a defense.

PRIVILEGE

There are various categories of privilege relating to a defense to defamation. The privilege may be absolute or it may be conditional.

Absolute Privilege

This privilege is a complete bar and defense to defamation even if the defendant has engaged in an actual lie or made a false statement intentionally and maliciously. Absolute privilege exists in the process of engaging in any of the three basic governmental functions—legislative, executive, or judicial.

Legislative Privilege

A privilege that operates as an absolute bar to any statement made while on the floor of the governmental body even if it has no relevancy or relationship to the issue under discussion.

Executive Privilege

A privilege that protects high-ranking policymaking officers of the executive branch of government, state or federal, when acting within the scope of their governmental duties.

Judicial Privilege

This privilege provides a defense to any participant in a judicial action or proceeding. The privilege applies to any statements made from the start of the commencement of the action or proceeding until it is concluded.

Conditional Privilege

One that is not absolute, as it is in legislative, executive, and judicial privileges, but requires an element of good faith in making the statement.

Absolute Privilege

An **absolute privilege** is a complete bar and defense to defamation even if the defendant has engaged in an actual lie or made a false statement intentionally and maliciously. Absolute privilege exists in the process of engaging in any of the three basic governmental functions—legislative, executive, or judicial.

- **Legislative privilege.** Legislative privilege is given to, for example, legislators in the various state legislatures or federal legislators in the U.S. Senate or the U.S. House of Representatives. This privilege operates as an absolute bar to any statement made while on the floor of the governmental body even if it has no relevancy or relationship to the issue under discussion.
- **Executive privilege.** Executive privilege protects high-ranking policymaking officers of the executive branch of government, state or federal, when acting within the scope of their governmental duties. Examples at the state level would be a state governor or a state attorney general. At the federal level, examples would be the president, the attorney general, and cabinet members. For the executive privilege to apply, however, there must be some relevancy or reasonable relationship of the claimed defamatory statement to the issue under debate or discussion.
- **Judicial privilege.** Judicial privilege provides a defense to any participant in a judicial action or proceeding. There must be some relevancy or relationship between the claimed defamatory statement and the issues in the judicial action or proceeding. To clarify, the privilege is not available only during a trial or a judicial hearing. The privilege applies to any statements made from the commencement of the action or proceeding until it is concluded. During this time frame, this could include any statements made in a brief, at a deposition, at a discovery hearing, in a letter, in an e-mail, or in written discovery, as examples.

Conditional Privilege

A **conditional privilege** is one that is not absolute, as it is in legislative, executive, and judicial privileges, but requires an element of good faith in making the statement. Some courts do not, for example, afford a full privilege to statements made at a lesser government body such as a city or a township meeting.

A conditional privilege may exist if one is attempting to protect a private interest—either the interest of the defendant or someone else with whom the defendant has a relationship. A relationship may be a family relationship or a business or professional relationship, as examples. In an employment relationship, for example, an employee may volunteer to his or her employer not to hire potential employee X because X is "not to be trusted." The employee would have a conditional privilege in a later defamation suit by X. However, if the employer stated to a friend that he did not hire X because X was not to be trusted, there is no relationship between the employer and the friend except a friendly relationship. The employer would not be able to assert the conditional privilege.

A conditional privilege may also exist if one is attempting to protect a public interest. For example, A tells a state highway trooper that B was intoxicated, struck a pedestrian, and was guilty of a hit and run. The statement, because of the public interest involved, would afford A with a conditional privilege.

As mentioned at the outset, for a conditional privilege to apply, the defendant must make the statement in good faith. If the statement is made knowing it was false with the intent of injuring the plaintiff, the privilege does not apply. For the conditional privilege to apply, the person must have an honest, good faith, sincere belief that the statement was true when made. For an interesting case involving the defense of both an absolute privilege and a conditional privilege, the student must read the case of *Van Eaton v. Fink*, 697 N.E.2d 490 (Ind. Ct. App. 1998) in Exhibit 11-2. This case happens to involve a paralegal.

EXHIBIT 11-2 Relevant Case Law

Mark Van Eaton, Appellant-Plaintiff, v. Donna Fink, Appellee-Defendant.

Court of Appeals of Indiana.

Najam, Judge.

Witness brought defamation action against plaintiff attorney's legal assistant who accused witness of committing perjury in another lawsuit. The Monroe Circuit Court, Kenneth G. Todd, J., granted summary judgment for legal assistant. Witness appealed. The Court of Appeals, Najam, J., held that: (1) absolute privilege applied to legal assistant's statement to defendant attorney, made before trial court entered final judgment for plaintiff, that she had falsified document and that witness had lied about document, and (2) qualified privilege applied to legal assistant's publication of statement via facsimile to plaintiff attorney.

Affirmed.

OPINION

STATEMENT OF THE CASE

Mark Van Eaton ("Van Eaton") filed a Complaint for Damages for Defamation against Donna Fink ("Fink"). Fink filed her Answer and asserted the affirmative defense of privilege....

FACTS

This suit arises from statements made by Fink in connection with another case, *Kirchoff v. Selby*, 686 N.E.2d 121 (Ind. Ct. App. 1997), *reh'g. denied*. Fink worked as a legal assistant for attorney Dean Richards, who represented the Selbys. Attorney Patrick Shoulders represented the Kirchoffs. A jury awarded the Selbys $730,000.00. Before the trial court entered judgment on the verdict, Fink informed Shoulders that she had manufactured an exhibit on behalf of the Selbys, at Richards' request, in order to rehabilitate Van Eaton's testimony. She also stated that Van Eaton had testified falsely when he claimed, on rebuttal, that he had made notes regarding the differences between Exhibit 10 and Exhibit 12 prior to trial. In addition, Fink claimed that she had assisted Richards in the fabrication of Exhibit 61, a Stock Exchange and Subscription Agreement. After her sworn statement was taken before a notary, Fink sent a copy via facsimile to Richards....

DEFAMATION

Next, Van Eaton contends that the trial court erred when it granted summary judgment in favor of Fink because the properly designated portion of Richards' supplemental affidavit creates a genuine issue of material fact as to whether Fink's statements were privileged. We disagree.

EXHIBIT 11-2 *(Continued)*

To maintain an action for defamation, a plaintiff must show a communication with four elements: (1) defamatory imputation; (2) malice; (3) publication; and (4) damages.... A statement is defamatory if it tends to harm the reputation of another so as to lower him in the estimation of the community or to deter third persons from associating or dealing with him.... Publication, in defamation law, can consist of communication to just one individual.... Generally, each individual publication is a separate defamation.... However, not all defamation is actionable.... The law of libel and slander recognizes two classes of privileged communication, absolute and qualified. Id.

Here, the parties do not dispute that Fink's statement, in which she accused Van Eaton of perjury, is defamatory if proven to be false. The parties also do not dispute that Fink published the statement when she gave it to Shoulders and, again, when she sent it via facsimile to Richards. However, Fink contends that her defamatory statements are entitled to either absolute or qualified privilege. We address each claim in turn.

A. ABSOLUTE PRIVILEGE

Indiana law affords absolute privilege to statements made in the course of a judicial proceeding.... Absolute privilege, however, is abrogated when the statements are not relevant and pertinent to the litigation or do not bear some relation thereto. *Id.* Whether a particular communication is relevant and pertinent to the litigation is purely a legal determination for the court. *Id.*

Absolute privilege is based on the idea that:

[P]ublic interest in the freedom of expression by participants in judicial proceedings, uninhibited by the risk of resultant suits for defamation, is so vital and necessary to the integrity of our judicial system that it must be made paramount to the right of the individual to a legal remedy when he has been wronged.

Absolute privilege provides judges, attorneys, parties and witnesses, in connection with a judicial proceeding, immunity from liability even if they publish defamatory material with an improper motive....

A witness is absolutely privileged to publish defamatory matter concerning another in communications preliminary to a proposed judicial proceeding or as part of a judicial proceeding in which he is testifying if it has some relation to the proceeding. RESTATEMENT (SECOND) OF TORTS § 588; ... This rule applies to communications preliminary to a proposed judicial proceeding where the communication has some relation to a proceeding that is reasonably contemplated in good faith and under serious consideration by the witness or a possible party to the proceeding. RESTATEMENT (SECOND) OF TORTS § 588 cmt. e. We hold that the rule also applies to communications subsequent to a judicial proceeding, provided, that the communication is related to the proceeding, made in good faith and in contemplation of further proceedings before the trial court or on appeal.

Here, although the *Kirchoff v. Selby* trial had ended, the trial court's judgment was not yet final. Fink's statement to Shoulders, which contained allegations that she had falsified a document at the direction of Richards during trial and that Van Eaton had lied regarding the falsified document during cross-examination, was made in contemplation that the Kirchoffs would request a new trial based on that information. Thus, Fink's statement to Shoulders is entitled to absolute privilege.

B. QUALIFIED PRIVILEGE

Fink concedes that the separate defamation that occurred when she subsequently published the statement via facsimile to Richards is not entitled to absolute privilege. Instead, she maintains that qualified privilege applies.

The doctrine of qualified privilege protects "communications made in good faith on any subject matter in which the party making the communication has an interest or in reference to which he has a duty, either public or private, either legal, moral, or social, if made to a person having a corresponding interest or duty."... Absent a factual dispute, whether the qualified privilege doctrine protects a statement is a question of law....

(Continued)

EXHIBIT 11-2 *(Continued)*

Here, as Richard's legal assistant, Fink was required to conform to the same standards as a lawyer. *See* Rules of Professional Conduct, Guideline 9.10(j) (legal assistant shall be governed by American Bar Association Model Code of Professional Responsibility and American Bar Association Model Rules of Professional Conduct). A lawyer shall not unlawfully obstruct another party's access to evidence or unlawfully alter, destroy or conceal a document or other material having potential evidentiary value. Ind. Professional Conduct Rule 3.4. A lawyer shall not counsel or assist another person to do any such act. *Id.* A lawyer shall not knowingly make a false statement of material fact to a tribunal or offer evidence the lawyer knows to be false. Ind. Professional Conduct Rule 3.3(a)(1) and (2). Fink's statement contained allegations that she and Richards had falsified evidence presented to the court at the trial. Assuming that Fink and Richards had engaged in the conduct described by Fink, Fink and Richards would have corresponding legal, moral and social duties to correct the injustice that resulted from their behavior.... Rules of Professional Conduct serve as proper standard for legal profession and specifically operate as rules of law in disciplinary proceedings before the Supreme Court). Thus, Fink's publication via facsimile to Richards was entitled to qualified privilege.

Still, Van Eaton contends that Fink abused her qualified privilege because her statement was primarily motivated by ill will and without belief in its truth. In support of his contention, Van Eaton directs us to the one-paragraph supplemental affidavit of Richards and claims that it demonstrates that Fink made her statements in an attempt to extort money from the Selbys. The affidavit states:

> That during the argument [Richards] had with Donna Fink before [he] ordered her from [his] home on September 4, 1995, on Labor Day evening, one of the things that she stated that she was going to do to Dick Gaib and [Richards] was accuse [them] of raping her and further accuse [them] of manufacturing documents. She named numerous documents to [Richards] that she felt could have been manufactured by [Richards]. During the argument, before she left, she did state to [Richards] some of the documents that she was going to state were manufactured, were Exhibit "12" the Confidential Sales Prospectus, and Exhibit "61," the Stock Exchange Agreement. She mentioned numerous other documents that were admitted at the trial. She stated that Mark Van Eaton, Jeff and Diane Selby, [Richards] and Richard Gaib and Jerry Stillwell would be in serious trouble.

Van Eaton mischaracterizes the supplemental affidavit. Although the affidavit shows that Fink was upset with Richards, it does not demonstrate that she attempted to extort money from anyone. Further, we cannot infer from the affidavit that Fink's statement was motivated by "ill will" or that she did not believe in the truth of her statements. Rather the supplemental affidavit indicates that she believed that documents were manufactured. Because Van Eaton has failed to designate material which could establish that Fink abused her qualified privilege, we conclude that the trial court properly granted summary judgment in favor of Fink.

Affirmed.

Source: Van Eaton v. Fink, 697 N.E.2d 490 (Ct. App. Ind. 1998).

Privilege Based upon the Constitution

Protecting a person from defamation is a sound policy objective. However, there may be instances in which the constitutional protections of freedom of speech and freedom of the press may "trump" the interest of protection of one's reputation. The landmark case establishing constitutional privileges is the case of *New York Times Co. v. Sullivan*, 376 U.S. 254 (1964). In that case, Mr. Sullivan, the Commissioner of Public Affairs for the CITY of Montgomery, Alabama, brought suit against several clergymen and the *New York Times* newspaper for running an advertisement falsely accusing Mr. Sullivan and the Montgomery Policy Department of illegal action prompted by racial motives. Some of the statements in the advertisement were not entirely true. The United States Supreme Court held that in order for a public official to recover damages for defamation there must be "actual malice" on the part of the defendant in publishing the defamatory statement or material. The theory and rationale for this decision is that citizens should be able to speak and write about public officials without the fear of a defamation suit.

Closely aligned with the category of public officials are those in the category of "public figures." A public figure is one not necessarily involved in government. However, they are in that group of people who have achieved great publicity, fame, and notoriety such that a person speaking or writing about them will be afforded the same constitutional protection. Examples of prominent people in this category might include in the field of business, Meg Whitman and Donald Trump; in the field of sports, Kobe Bryant and Serena Williams; in the field of entertainment, Lady Gaga and Justin Timberlake; in the field of journalism, Matt Lauer and Megan Kelly.

Actual Malice
Either actual knowledge that the statement or material is false or that defendant acted with reckless disregard for the truth.

In a defamation suit, either a public official or a public figure must prove that the publication was done with **actual malice**. According to *New York Times v. Sullivan*, actual malice is either actual knowledge that the statement or material is false or that defendant acted with reckless disregard for the truth. The U.S. Supreme Court is constantly balancing interests. In this case, the court held that the interests of freedom of speech and freedom of the press were stronger than the interest of protecting one's reputation. However, if one crossed the line and made a statement knowing it was false or with reckless disregard for its truth, the interest of protecting one's reputation is then stronger than protecting a knowing, maliciously made false statement.

Causation in Defamation

As a final note concerning defamation, causation must also be proven. Just as in the tort of negligence, actual cause and proximate cause are elements of the *prima facie* case for this tort.

Invasion of Privacy

Invasion of Privacy
A harmful intrusion into the private life of another person.

Invasion of privacy is a harmful intrusion into the private life of another person. For the tort of invasion of privacy, the Restatement (Second) of Torts § 652A breaks the tort down into four separate categories:

1. An unreasonable intrusion upon the seclusion of another.
2. An appropriation of the other's name or likeness.

Workplace Skills Tip

Be familiar with court fee schedules and rules requiring when a check needs to be written even though the paralegal will not be the person writing the actual check or making any bank transfer. For example, an appellate court rule may state that it will not accept a brief for filing unless the appellate filing fee is paid. Also, many statutes and rules commonly provide that witnesses must be paid a witness fee and mileage, which must be tendered before or at the time of the witness' appearance at the deposition or trial. For court filing fees, check the website of the respective court as it typically contains a list of all the filing fees.

3. An unreasonable publicity given to the other's private life.
4. Publicity that unreasonably places the other in a false light before the public.

As always, it is important to remember that when this tort occurs, some other tort may have occurred, such as defamation, intentional infliction of emotional distress, trespass, or battery. Also, the four categories themselves may overlap in a particular fact pattern. The student should also be aware that this is a tort that has not been recognized by all 50 states.[10]

Unreasonable Intrusion upon the Seclusion of Another

For a *prima facie* case, plaintiff must prove:

- An unreasonable intrusion upon or into the seclusion (private life) of another.
- The intrusion was committed negligently or intentionally.
- Causation.

Note that the first element is an unreasonable intrusion into one's private life or affairs. The intrusion must be only into those avenues of plaintiff's life that plaintiff would reasonably expect would not be invaded by defendant. For example, secretly recording a conversation or bugging the plaintiff's apartment would not be an intrusion or invasion of plaintiff's life that plaintiff would reasonably expect. However, one who had a photograph taken, revealed personal information, and was fingerprinted for a government security position may reasonably expect that the photograph, personal information, and fingerprints will be shared with other agencies within the government.

Employment law is beyond the scope of this textbook but invasion of privacy issues do arise at the workplace. The Internet was in its infancy but rapidly maturing in the 1990s. Today, virtually everyone in an office workplace has a computer with e-mail and Internet access. Generally speaking, employers have the right to monitor e-mail and Internet usage. Some of the theories advanced by employers for this monitoring are to reduce the risk of liability for such claims as sexual harassment, to prevent viruses from infecting their systems, to prevent productivity loss, and to prevent the leaking of confidential trade secrets. If an employee pursues an invasion of privacy claim, it will be necessary to establish that the employee had some reasonable expectation of privacy in the communications. Generally speaking, employers tend to fare better in litigation than employees as this is usually a difficult proof item for the employee to establish.

Many employers will have written policies stating that employers have the right to monitor workplace files (even if marked "personal"), e-mail, Internet usage, and other personal information. "An employer's notice to an employee that workplace files, Internet use, and e-mail may be monitored undermines the reasonableness of an employee's claim that he or she believed such information was private and not subject to search."[11] A written policy gives notice to the employee that monitoring may occur; so therefore, the employee could have had no reasonable expectation of privacy.

The Federal Stored Communications Act (SCA) (18 U.S.C. §§2701-11) prohibits unauthorized access to stored electronic communications. The SCA provides a private cause of action for unauthorized access to stored data located on a computer's hard drive or e-mail server. In addition, the Electronic Privacy

Communications Act (EPCA) (18 U.S.C. §§2510 *et. seq.*) protects most forms of electronic communications from interception, attempted interception, disclosure, and unauthorized access. Questions may arise concerning the monitoring of the employee's use of social media such as Facebook, MySpace, Twitter, LinkedIn, and so forth. There may be a much better argument for the employee that these personal social media sites may not be accessed without authorization based upon the SCA. The issue may arise if a prospective employee refuses to give his or her user name and password to the personal social networking site, and the employer does not hire the person for that reason. Or it may arise when an employee refuses to provide the user name and password to the site while on the job, and the employment is terminated for that reason.

In a recent unpublished federal court decision from New Jersey, *Pietrylo v. Hillstone Restaurant Group,* the court denied the defendant's motion for judgment as a matter of law and for a new trial after a jury verdict in favor of the plaintiffs. Plaintiffs sued the employer for violations of the SCA and for the common law tort of invasion of privacy. The jury, finding violations of the SCA, awarded one plaintiff $2,500 and the other plaintiff $903 in compensatory damages. Each plaintiff was also awarded punitive damages of four times the amount of compensatory damages awarded by the jury. The jury, however, did not find that defendant invaded plaintiffs' common law right of privacy.

In this case, the employer accessed a chat group on MySpace.com, accessed by invitation and then by the member's MySpace account and password. One of the employees, St. Jean, who was a member of the chat group provided her login information to a manager because she felt some pressure to do so. As a result, the manager viewed the site on several different occasions, even though it was clear on the website that it was intended to be private and only accessible to invited members. Because of comments made on the site by the two employee plaintiffs, the two were fired. The co-employee St. Jean was asked during her testimony if she felt something would happen to her if she did not give the manager the password. Her response was "I felt that I probably would have gotten in trouble." Under the SCA, the employer may access this information if authorization is given. In this case, however, the court concluded that the jury could reasonably infer from St. Jean's testimony that the authorization was coerced or provided under pressure. This provided a basis for the jury to infer that the employer's accessing of the site was not, in fact, authorized. Therefore, it can be effectively argued by an employee that if an employer requires employees or prospective employees to provide personal login information as a condition of employment, this may be a violation of the SCA.

Interestingly, as this book goes to print, a new federal act, called the Social Networking Online Protection Act (SNOPA), was just introduced in the U.S. House of Representatives. If it is eventually passed, it would prohibit current and potential employers from requiring a username, password, or other access to online content. Proponents of the bill compare an employer's requesting social networking passwords to requiring current and prospective employees to hand over the keys to their homes.

If a defendant sneaked onto the property of the plaintiff and took pictures of the plaintiff through the window without plaintiff's knowledge, this would be an unreasonable intrusion upon an area of plaintiff's private life. (Note that it would also constitute a trespass.) If defendant took that same picture of the plaintiff while she was walking down a public street rather than secretly through plaintiff's window, there would be no invasion of plaintiff's privacy. It is the invasion itself that makes up the tort even if defendant did not later publish or make use of the information with a third person.

Workplace Skills Tip

As a backup to the attorney, always be considering various theories of liability that may present themselves under a given fact scenario. For example, the text cites the example of a bill collector calling plaintiff repeatedly both at work, knowing that was prohibited, and at home between midnight and one o'clock in the morning. This example was provided to illustrate the tort of invasion of privacy under a particular jurisdiction's state law. However, there may be federal statutes involved in a given fact scenario. Here, conduct of this bill collector would also be subject to an important federal statute— the Federal Fair Debt Collection Practices Act (FDCPA) 15 U.S.C. § 1692. Under that act, there would be a violation for calling the employee at work knowing that practice was prohibited by the employer and also for calling after 9:00 p.m.

The Restatement also notes that the intrusion must be "highly offensive" to a reasonable person.[12] A mere annoyance is not enough. For example, a telemarketer calling occasionally over the dinner hour would probably be considered more of an annoyance or a nuisance. However, the actions of a bill collector who repeatedly called a plaintiff at work knowing that was prohibited would likely be considered highly offensive to a reasonable person. Similarly, calling a plaintiff at plaintiff's home between midnight and one o'clock in the morning would also be considered highly offensive to a reasonable person. The typical damages are emotional distress/mental anguish. The plaintiff does not have to prove special damages or pecuniary loss.

DEFENSES

Consent is a defense. Assume that plaintiff was about to have triplets. Because of her interest in medicine and education, she consents to a local magazine interviewing her at the hospital and taking pictures of her before, during, and after the birth of the triplets. However, if the magazine exceeded the scope of its consent, such as taking pictures of her one seriously disabled child, plaintiff would have a claim for invasion of privacy based upon the taking of those pictures. Consent is a valid defense so long as it was not withdrawn and its scope was not exceeded.

Appropriation of Name or Likeness

The elements of the cause of action for this category of invasion of privacy are:

- An unauthorized use of one's name or likeness for a commercial purpose or for another's own personal use or benefit.
- Causation (note that there is no requirement for it to be "highly offensive").

The privacy interest protected here is that of one's own personal identity. Furthermore, the defendant is expecting some type of personal or financial gain. For example, assume that A checks in to a luxurious resort under the name of B, using B's name and address when registering. Upon checkout, A does not pay the bill. Not only does the resort have a contract action against A for money owed, B has a tort action against A for invasion of privacy based upon A's appropriation of B's name. Assume that A, a local dentist specializing in cosmetic dentistry, utilizes in an advertisement of his dental practice, a photograph of B, a young, attractive local woman with a beautiful smile. B would have a cause of action against A for invasion of privacy under this particular category.

RIGHT OF PUBLICITY

The celebrity may be more likely to prevail on a theory of invasion of the right of publicity rather than on a theory of invasion of the right of privacy. The appropriation of name or likeness protects the celebrity's interest in the commercial exploitation of his or her identity.

That is precisely what occurred in a case involving Johnny Carson, an extremely popular entertainer who hosted "The Tonight Show" for many years beginning in 1962. Mr. Carson was always introduced at the beginning of his show by the words, "Heeeeeere's Johnny!" (a phrase used menacingly by Jack Nicholson in the movie *The Shining*). Carson brought suit against the seller of "Here's Johnny" portable toilets alleging, among other claims, an infringement of the right of privacy and the right of publicity. The court held that Carson could not prevail on any claim for a right of privacy as the facts did not amount to an invasion of any of the interests protected by the right of privacy. However, the court held that he could prevail on a theory of a violation of his right of publicity. See *Carson v. Here's Johnny Portable Toilets, Inc.*, 698 F.2d 831 (6th Cir. 1983) in Exhibit 11-3.

EXHIBIT 11-3 Relevant Case Law

John W. Carson, d/b/a Johnny Carson, an individual, and Johnny Carson Apparel, Inc., a corporation, Plaintiffs-Appellants, v. Here's Johnny Portable Toilets, Inc., a corporation, Defendant-Appellee.

United States Court of Appeals, Sixth Circuit.

Bailey Brown, Senior Circuit Judge.

This case involves claims of unfair competition and invasion of the right of privacy and the right of publicity arising from appellee's adoption of a phrase generally associated with a popular entertainer.

Appellant, John W. Carson (Carson), is the host and star of "The Tonight Show," a well-known television program broadcast five nights a week by the National Broadcasting Company. Carson also appears as an entertainer in night clubs and theaters around the country. From the time he began hosting "The Tonight Show" in 1962, he has been introduced on the show each night with the phrase "Here's Johnny." This method of introduction was first used for Carson in 1957 when he hosted a daily television program for the American Broadcasting Company. The phrase "Here's Johnny" is generally associated with Carson by a substantial segment of the television viewing public. In 1967, Carson first authorized use of this phrase by an outside business venture, permitting it to be used by a chain of restaurants called "Here's Johnny Restaurants."

Appellant Johnny Carson Apparel, Inc. (Apparel), formed in 1970, manufactures and markets men's clothing to retail stores. Carson, the president of Apparel and owner of 20% of its stock, has licensed Apparel to use his name and picture, which appear on virtually all of Apparel's products and promotional material. Apparel has also used, with Carson's consent, the phrase "Here's Johnny" on labels for clothing and in advertising campaigns. In 1977, Apparel granted a license to Marcy Laboratories to use "Here's Johnny" as the name of a line of men's toiletries. The phrase "Here's Johnny" has never been registered by appellants as a trademark or service mark.

Appellee, Here's Johnny Portable Toilets, Inc., is a Michigan corporation engaged in the business of renting and selling "Here's Johnny" portable toilets. Appellee's founder was aware at the time he formed the corporation that "Here's Johnny" was the introductory slogan for Carson on "The Tonight Show." He indicated that he coupled the phrase with a second one, "The World's Foremost Commodian," to make "a good play on a phrase."

(Continued)

EXHIBIT 11-3 *(Continued)*

Shortly after appellee went into business in 1976, appellants brought this action alleging unfair competition, trademark infringement under federal and state law, and invasion of privacy and publicity rights. They sought damages and an injunction prohibiting appellee's further use of the phrase "Here's Johnny" as a corporate name or in connection with the sale or rental of its portable toilets....

We do not believe that Carson's claim that his right of privacy has been invaded is supported by the law or the facts. Apparently, the gist of this claim is that Carson is embarrassed by and considers it odious to be associated with the appellee's product. Clearly, the association does not appeal to Carson's sense of humor. But the facts here presented do not, it appears to us, amount to an invasion of any of the interests protected by the right of privacy. In any event, our disposition of the claim of an invasion of the right of publicity makes it unnecessary for us to accept or reject the claim of an invasion of the right of privacy.

The right of publicity has developed to protect the commercial interest of celebrities in their identities. The theory of the right is that a celebrity's identity can be valuable in the promotion of products, and the celebrity has an interest that may be protected from the unauthorized commercial exploitation of that identity....

The district court dismissed appellants' claim based on the right of publicity because appellee does not use Carson's name or likeness. 498 F.Supp. at 77. It held that it "would not be prudent to allow recovery for a right of publicity claim which does not more specifically identify Johnny Carson." 498 F.Supp. at 78. We believe that, on the contrary, the district court's conception of the right of publicity is too narrow. The right of publicity, as we have stated, is that a celebrity has a protected pecuniary interest in the commercial exploitation of his identity. If the celebrity's identity is commercially exploited, there has been an invasion of his right whether or not his "name or likeness" is used. Carson's identity may be exploited even if his name, John W. Carson, or his picture is not used....

In this case, Earl Braxton, president and owner of Here's Johnny Portable Toilets, Inc., admitted that he knew that the phrase "Here's Johnny" had been used for years to introduce Carson. Moreover, in the opening statement in the district court, appellee's counsel stated:

Now, we've stipulated in this case that the public tends to associate the words "Johnny Carson", the words "Here's Johnny" with plaintiff, John Carson and, Mr. Braxton, in his deposition, admitted that he knew that and probably absent that identification, he would not have chosen it.

App. 68. That the "Here's Johnny" name was selected by Braxton because of its identification with Carson was the clear inference from Braxton's testimony irrespective of such admission in the opening statement.

We therefore conclude that, applying the correct legal standards, appellants are entitled to judgment. The proof showed without question that appellee had appropriated Carson's identity in connection with its corporate name and its product....

It should be obvious from the majority opinion and the dissent that a celebrity's identity may be appropriated in various ways. It is our view that, under the existing authorities, a celebrity's legal right of publicity is invaded whenever his identity is intentionally appropriated for commercial purposes. We simply disagree that the authorities limit the right of publicity as contended by the dissent. It is not fatal to appellant's claim that appellee did not use his "name." Indeed, there would have been no violation of his right of publicity even if appellee had used his name, such as "J. William Carson Portable Toilet" or the "John William Carson Portable Toilet" or the "J.W. Carson Portable Toilet." The reason is that, though literally using appellant's "name," the appellee would not have appropriated Carson's identity as a celebrity. Here there was an appropriation of Carson's identity without using his "name"....

The judgment of the district court is vacated and the case remanded for further proceedings consistent with this opinion.

Source: Carson v. Here's Johnny Portable Toilets, Inc., 698 F.2d 831 (6th cir. 1983).

DEFENSES

Consent is a defense so long as the scope of the consent is not withdrawn or exceeded. As illustrated in the Johnny Carson case, publication of a public figure's name or likeness is not actionable unless the defendant is attempting to use the name or likeness for defendant's own commercial gain.

Unreasonable Publicity Given to the Other's Private Life

The elements of the cause of action for this category of invasion of privacy are:

- The matter or private facts publicized must be highly offensive to a reasonable person.
- The matter or private facts publicized are not of legitimate concern to the public.
- Causation.

PRIVATE FACTS OR MATERIAL

Under this category, the facts disclosed must be true, private facts involving a person's private life. The protection does not apply to facts that may have already been disclosed to the public. For example, there is no protection for certain matters that are a matter of public record, such as a date of birth, the fact and date of a marriage, or the fact that one is a plaintiff or a defendant in a lawsuit. However, disclosing the fact that a woman had an illegitimate child would be a private fact and fall under the protection of this tort category. Similarly, reporting facts that a person stated at a public concert would not contain anything private because they were uttered in public. If a man and a woman routinely sunbathed in the nude in their backyard unprotected by a fence, trees, or shrubs, they could, likewise, hardly complain if a person publicized that fact.

PUBLICITY

The private fact or facts must be publicized by the defendant. There is a distinction between "publicity" and the "publication" required for defamation. As discussed earlier in this chapter on defamation, a publication in the defamation sense is the communicating of a false statement or material to only one person. For this invasion of privacy tort to apply, the communication must truly be to the public or to such a large group that it is likely to become public knowledge. In defamation, the fact is false and it need be communicated to only one person. Here, the fact is true, but it must be communicated to far more than one person; indeed, to the public at large. For example, posting private content on an Internet site such as Twitter would satisfy that requirement.

HIGHLY OFFENSIVE

The publicity generated by the defendant must be "highly offensive." It must be publicity that is unreasonable such that it would be highly offensive to a reasonable person. If a newspaper reported that George, a prominent businessman, had just returned from a business trip in Hong Kong, a reasonable person would likely not take offense at that. However, if the newspaper added an additional true fact that, while there, George became intoxicated, was involved in a fight, and held in jail for several days, a reasonable person would likely take offense at the publicity given to those additional facts.

LEGITIMATE CONCERN TO THE PUBLIC

The public does have a right to learn of many matters that may involve a public interest. If the facts publicized are of a legitimate public interest or concern, there is no invasion of the right to privacy. This requirement involves constitutional issues similar to those in the defamation area as stated in *New York Times Co. v. Sullivan* discussed earlier in this chapter. In *Cox Broadcasting v. Cohn,* 420 U.S. 469 (1975), the United States Supreme Court held that an action for invasion of the right of privacy cannot be maintained when the subject matter of the publicity is a matter of "legitimate concern to the public."

If a newspaper reported that a police officer who arrested a drunk driver had himself been drinking and a half pint of vodka was seen in his squad car, the public has a legitimate interest in the quality, training, and supervision of its law enforcement personnel. The newspaper would likely not be liable in a later suit by the police officer for reporting the additional facts of the arrest involving the police officer himself. Assume a patient reported to a newspaper that during visits to her physician she has noticed marijuana and other drug paraphernalia in the doctor's office. That is likely a matter of the public having an interest in the proper licensing and conduct of physicians treating patients in the community. The doctor's invasion of privacy suit against the newspaper would likely fail.

VOLUNTARY VS. INVOLUNTARY PUBLIC FIGURES

This category of invasion of privacy necessarily brings about the issues of voluntary public figures and involuntary public figures. A **voluntary public figure** is one who is, through his or her status, position, occupation, or profession naturally in the public eye. Such a person generally has no claim for the communication of private facts to the public. For example, a U.S. Cabinet member, a governor, a mayor, a police chief, or a president of a university is voluntarily thrusting himself or herself into the public arena. Consequently, that person's statements and activities can be expected to, and will routinely be, covered in the press.

An **involuntary public figure** is one who has not sought publicity or given consent to it, but because of his or her own actions or conduct, the person has become of legitimate concern to the public. The person has been thrust into the "limelight" and is "news" whether he or she likes it or not. For example, a person accused of a crime may, in the worst way, want to avoid any publicity whatsoever, but he or she naturally becomes "news." A person charged with a sensational crime, a witness to a crime, or a witness to a catastrophic event may be involuntarily thrust into the limelight, thus losing the protection of an invasion of his or her right to privacy. Whether with a voluntary public figure or an involuntary figure, it is certainly conceivable that the reporting of some personal fact could be so private and so over the line that there may be no legitimate public interest to be served by the publicity of that fact. Typically, the tort of invasion of right to privacy, whether based on this category or any of the other three, will be decided by a jury.

Voluntary Public Figure
One who is, through his or her status, position, occupation, or profession naturally in the public eye.

Involuntary Public Figure
One who has not sought publicity or given consent to it, but because of his or her own actions or conduct, the person has become of legitimate concern to the public.

DEFENSES

The student should realize that the essence of this category of invasion of the right to privacy is the communicating of true facts about the plaintiff. Accordingly, truth is not a defense as it would be in defamation, which, by definition, is the publication of a fact that is false. Consent is a defense. That defense is lost if the consent was withdrawn or if the defendant exceeds the scope of the consent given by plaintiff. Further, there is an absolute privilege given to the defendant if the facts or matters communicated were accurately taken from public and official court records. The public has an interest in the reporting of such facts and matters, such as a criminal indictment.

Publicity Unreasonably Placing Plaintiff in False Light before Public

The elements of the cause of action for this category of invasion of privacy are:

- Giving publicity to a matter concerning a person that places the person before the public in a false light.
- Highly offensive.
- Knowledge of falsity or acting in reckless disregard as to its falsity if a public figure.
- Causation.

The element of publicity for this category of invasion of privacy is the same as for unreasonable publicity given to the other's private life. The publicity must be extensive and to the public at large, not to just one individual. This tort is similar to defamation in that the facts or matter published by the defendant are false. The interest protected is the interest of not being made to appear before the public in a false position, in other words, not being made out to be other than he or she really is. Because one of the elements of this category of tort is falsity, if plaintiff can show that plaintiff's reputation was lowered, there may also be a claim for defamation. It is not necessary for this tort action that the plaintiff be defamed, but defamation may also occur. Also, the publicity given must be highly offensive.

Some examples may be of assistance. A local "gentlemen's club" receives some old photos of the plaintiff in skimpy clothing when she was in college. The photos are given to the club by the woman's former boyfriend. Because of her unique red hair and stunning beauty, the club posts them at the entryway with the other photographs of scantily clad women. The implication that she is employed by or associated with this club would likely be highly offensive to a reasonable person. The club's action is a major misrepresentation of her character. A newspaper runs an article on fraud committed by land developers. The newspaper uses an old photograph of Ralph, a local developer in connection with the article. There is an implication that he is one of the land developers who engaged in fraud. This publication by the newspaper clearly gives extensive publicity, it places Ralph in a false light, and it would likely be considered highly offensive. It would also likely satisfy the elements of the tort of defamation—specifically, libel.

For a public figure or public official to prevail on this false light invasion of privacy category, the plaintiff must show that the defendant knew of the false light or acted in reckless disregard of its falsity. Such burden would not be required for a non-public figure or non-public official who could prove negligence on the part of the defendant.

Damages as to All Categories of Invasion of Privacy

Invasion of privacy, irrespective of the four different types or categories just discussed, will allow for money damages to be claimed by the plaintiff. A plaintiff claiming an intrusion upon seclusion/private life may recover damages for the interference with that seclusion or private life. Those damages may be emotional distress and mental anguish. These are sufficient. The plaintiff does not need to prove any special damages or pecuniary loss of any kind. A plaintiff, particularly a celebrity, claiming the appropriation of his or her name or likeness may recover for the reasonable value of the use of that name or likeness. For the non-celebrity, the more common damages would be for emotional distress and mental anguish. A plaintiff claiming publicity was given to his or her private life may recover for the reasonable damages resulting from the adverse publicity, usually emotional distress and mental anguish. A plaintiff who is placed in a false light may recover damages to the harm to his or her reputation because of the false light. Claims for emotional distress, mental anguish, and humiliation are typically made with all or most of these four different theories of invasion of privacy. Depending upon the jurisdiction, punitive/exemplary damages may also be allowed to be claimed by the injured plaintiff.

Misrepresentation and Other Miscellaneous Torts

MISREPRESENTATION

Misrepresentation is a tort that protects a person's economic interest, not the plaintiff's personal interest. As mentioned in the preface to this textbook, some torts are not specifically related to the subject of personal injury and some may not be a frequently encountered tort in the real world of tort/personal injury litigation. However, tort tradition requires that the student have some understanding of this tort and other traditional torts. Misrepresentation may actually be brought on any of the traditional tort theories: negligence, intentional torts, and strict liability. The primary one is the one based on intention, and it will be discussed here.

Misrepresentation
A tort that protects a person's economic interest, not the plaintiff's personal interest.

Intentional (Fraudulent) Misrepresentation

The Restatement (Second) of Torts § 525 (1977) defines the tort and the tort liability of **intentional (fraudulent) misrepresentation** as:

> One who fraudulently makes a misrepresentation of fact, opinion, intention or law for the purpose of inducing another to act or to refrain from action in reliance upon it, is subject to liability to the other in deceit for pecuniary loss caused to him by his justifiable reliance upon the misrepresentation.

Intentional (Fraudulent) Misrepresentation
A fraudulent misrepresentation of fact, opinion, intention, or law for the purpose of inducing another to act or to refrain from action in reliance upon it.

Misrepresentation by Words, Writing, or Conduct

The misrepresentation may be communicated orally, in writing, or by conduct of the defendant. For example, a misrepresentation of fact may occur when defendant, selling a home, represents verbally to the buyer that the home has never had a leaky roof or that the home has never had termites. If those oral statements are untrue, and plaintiff, relying upon those statements, purchases the house, they are oral misrepresentations of fact that have been made by the seller. The same untrue statements about the home may be made by the seller in writing in some type of disclosure form that seller is required to provide to the buyer before a purchase is concluded. Turning back the mileage on a used motor vehicle would be an example of a misrepresentation by conduct.

Misrepresentation by Opinion, Intention, or Law

While the most common misrepresentation may be one of misrepresenting a fact, a misrepresentation can also occur under the Restatement definition with the misrepresentation of an opinion, an intention, or law. Some examples may be helpful:

- Intention—Plaintiff, as part of a decision to buy a parcel of land, may rely on seller's statement that "We're going to buy some more of this land a little farther down the road."
- Opinion—A buyer relies upon the statement of a professional appraiser that "This property is worth at least $2.5 million dollars." A misrepresentation by opinion typically arises when the one making the statement is a professional or has superior knowledge.
- Law—Defendant makes a statement in a prospectus concerning the sale of a security that "The supreme court overruled that decision affecting this stock."

Generally a defendant is not under a duty to disclose facts. Failing to disclose facts is not a misrepresentation.[13] There may be exceptions for those with a duty under a fiduciary relationship such as a trustee/beneficiary relationship or one selling real estate. Many states have a standard sellers' disclosure document in the sale of residential real estate, which may require a seller to disclose information as well as to not make express misrepresentations.

Defendant's Knowledge of False Statements and Intent to Induce Reliance on Them by Plaintiff

The defendant must know that the misrepresentation is false and must intend to induce plaintiff to rely on it. The inducement may be for the plaintiff to take some action or to refrain from taking some action. Because the making of an allegation of fraud is somewhat easy to do but more difficult for defendant to disprove, courts typically require proof by clear and convincing evidence. This is greater than the preponderance of the evidence standard in most civil cases.

Justifiable Reliance

The reliance by the plaintiff must be justifiable. Another way of stating this is that the reliance must have been reasonably foreseeable. For example, if defendant made a representation to one other than the plaintiff but it was reasonably foreseeable that it would be communicated to the plaintiff, the plaintiff can establish justifiable reliance. Assume that a large public corporation made a false statement of some kind to the investment banker putting together its prospectus to sell its stock. While the misrepresentation was not made directly to an individual investor, it is reasonably foreseeable that an investor from the investing public would read and rely on the false statement.

Causation

For this tort, causation is also a requirement. In essence, plaintiff would need to show that plaintiff relied on the false statement. If plaintiff knew the statement was false, then the statement could not have been relied upon and could not have caused the plaintiff's damages.

Defenses

There are various defenses to misrepresentation, depending upon which of the three tort bases is at play. There really are no defenses to the tort of intentional (fraudulent) misrepresentation. The defense strategy is primarily to combat the elements of proof of the tort discussed above.

Contributory negligence is a viable defense to negligent misrepresentation but not to intentional or strict liability misrepresentation. Assumption of the risk is a defense to both negligence and strict liability misrepresentations.

Damages

In misrepresentation cases, most courts hold that the plaintiff is entitled to recover the value of the property as contracted for less the value of the property as actually received. Some courts will allow damages for emotional distress, and in some states, punitive/exemplary damages may be awarded.

Malicious Prosecution of a Criminal Action

Malicious prosecution of a criminal action is a tort in which the claim is that defendant wrongfully instigated a separate criminal action against the plaintiff that caused damage to the plaintiff. The basic elements of the tort are:

1. Defendant instigated a criminal action.
2. The action ended up in a favorable result for plaintiff (acquittal or dismissal).
3. A lack of probable cause.
4. Criminal action was brought for an improper purpose (malice).

Malicious Prosecution of Criminal Action
A tort in which the claim is that defendant wrongfully instituted a separate criminal action against the plaintiff that caused damage to the plaintiff.

INSTIGATION OF CRIMINAL ACTION

The first element is that defendant must have initiated a criminal complaint to law enforcement officials that prompted an arrest.

CRIMINAL ACTION ENDED FAVORABLY FOR PLAINTIFF

This element means that the plaintiff who was the defendant in the criminal case was found not guilty or the prosecution dismissed the case. The defendant must have truly "won" the underlying criminal case. A plea bargain, no matter how favorable to the defendant in the criminal action, will not suffice as satisfying the requirement of the criminal action ending favorably.

LACK OF PROBABLE CAUSE

Plaintiff must show that defendant instigated the criminal action without probable cause, which means that defendant had no honest good faith belief that the criminal charges were true. This is an issue typically decided by the judge. Assume a woman made claims that her former husband had struck her. She decided to bring criminal assault and battery charges. Facts that would tend not to show probable cause would be, for example, the ex-wife's bitterness toward the former husband, a late reporting of the crime, and no evidence of the alleged crime such as cuts or bruises on her body. However, if the plaintiff produced cuts or bruises on her body, a 911 call, a complaint made promptly after the incident, or even a witness to all or part of the incident, these facts would tend to show probable cause for the crime.

ACTION INSTITUTED FOR AN IMPROPER PURPOSE

This element means that defendant in the tort civil action really had no desire to accomplish any criminal justice; rather, defendant just wanted to harm plaintiff. A lack of probable cause may tend to show this element. While the defendant who was responsible for instituting the criminal action is subject to suit, all law enforcement officers, prosecutors, and judges are absolutely privileged against any malicious prosecution claim.

Related Actions—Malicious Prosecution of a Civil Action/Abuse of Process/ Spoliation of Evidence

Malicious Prosecution of a Civil Action
A tort in which the claim is that defendant wrongfully instituted a separate civil action against the plaintiff that caused damage to the plaintiff.

Abuse of Process
This tort centers on the misuse of the criminal or civil judicial process for some ulterior or improper purpose or motive.

Spoliation of Evidence
The act of destroying or hiding evidence adverse to the party.

In addition to malicious prosecution of a criminal action, some jurisdictions recognize a cause of action for **malicious prosecution of a civil action**. This is a tort in which the claim is that defendant wrongfully instituted a separate civil action against the plaintiff that caused damage to the plaintiff. The basic elements are the same as those for the tort of malicious prosecution of a criminal action. This has not been a well-received tort theory, as courts do not want to discourage litigants from resolving their disputes through the judicial process.

There is a tort called **abuse of process**. It centers on the misuse of the criminal or civil judicial process for some ulterior or improper purpose or motive. It must be shown that the defendant intentionally utilized a court process for a purpose other than for which it was intended to accomplish. A further discussion of this tort can be found at Restatement (Second) of Torts § 682 (1977). The tort frequently arises in collection cases in which it is claimed that the defendant is employing certain means of collection such as garnishment or levy for improper purposes, such as to harass the plaintiff. The plaintiff does not need to prove the defendant lacked probable cause and also does not need to prove the previous action/proceeding was resolved in plaintiff's favor.

An emerging tort that the paralegal may encounter is the tort of **spoliation of evidence**. Spoliation of evidence is the act of destroying or hiding evidence adverse to the party. In the course of litigation, it sometimes occurs that a party on the other side will hide or even destroy important evidence in the case. Some courts will handle this by imposing sanctions on the violating party. Others recognize a separate cause of action for this conduct. The typical situation arises when the spoliation is intentional, but it may also occur negligently. In that situation, a court may require the violation of some specific statute, court order, or agreement before there can be liability. At Exhibit 11-4, review the letter from the prudent lawyer to the client concerning the spoliation issue as it relates to e-mails and social media sites.

EXHIBIT 11-4 Spoliation of Evidence Letter

DAVID RICARDO BOSS LAW OFFICE
1220 Central Avenue
Metropolis, Bliss 55413
710-232-4500 Phone   D.R. Boss, Attorney
710-232-4510 Fax   Susan McKinley, Paralegal

October 20, 2012

PRIVILEGED, PERSONAL & CONFIDENTIAL
Ms. Tamara Golddigger
2937 Lakeshore Drive
Metropolis, Bliss 55410

Re: Slip and fall Injury at Discreet Gentlemen Playmate Mansion
    On December 31, 2011

Dear Tammy:

It is imperative you understand that any communications you have by e-mail, text messaging, or any other type of written communication with others relating to your injury and/or legal representation is likely discoverable by the defendant. Please refrain from communicating with anyone regarding the facts of the accident and your injuries. Anything that has already been communicated cannot be altered, destroyed, or changed in any manner. DO NOT delete any postings you have already made, but my office needs to know and see what information is there.

Failure to preserve evidence may negatively impact your case. Some courts have dismissed entire cases with prejudice where the plaintiff lost or destroyed evidence. This is true even in instances in which the failure was not intentional. Other courts have imposed significant monetary penalties for such failures to preserve electronic evidence.

Obviously, we do not want that to happen to you. To preserve the evidence, you need to refrain from doing anything to erase, destroy, delete, alter, or conceal the contents of the evidence. In addition, you must preserve evidence which may be on the computer and to refrain from overwriting or destroying the hard drive on that computer.

Your communication with my office and staff are protected communications, but that is not the case with other people you might communicate with by text messaging, e-mails, Caring Bridge, Facebook, or other social media posts. Please DO NOT post anything regarding your injuries, legal representation, problems you are experiencing, doctor visits, etc. If you have any questions regarding this, please contact me immediately.

Very truly yours,

D.R. Boss, attorney

David Ricardo Boss Law Office

CASE **11.1** Hypothetical Case: Developing Workplace Skills

You are a paralegal in a plaintiff's general personal injury firm. You have received an e-mail from the supervising attorney on your team, which reads as follows:

From: Attorney

To: Paralegal

Re: RNJ 1980-11

I just met with Lola Montini. Lola is a single mother. She was divorced 10 years ago and has custody of two minor children whom she supports. Her husband skipped out, never to be heard from again. She needs to work. Lola was recently fired as a bookkeeper with Marco's Dry Cleaning. Marco's is a chain of dry cleaning shops in this city owned by Marco Stuto. There are 10 of them in our city. Lola has been the head bookkeeper of the entire operation for the past five years. About a month ago, Marco falsely accused her of embezzling money from the company, which Lola adamantly denied. She was able to prove that she did not do so by pulling out some pertinent records. She explained to Marco where he made his mistake and reminded him she needed this job. In spite of that, Marco told her to clean out her desk and leave by the end of the day. Lola said that she believes Marco just wanted to get rid of her because he has a new girlfriend, Maria, who is an accounting major, and he wants to hire her after her college graduation.

Lola interviewed with Angelo's Dry Cleaning, a competitor. Angelo himself interviewed her for the job. In the course of the interview, he asked her point blank why she left Marco's. Lola, even though she knew Marco made a false allegation against her, told the truth that Marco fired her because he accused her of embezzlement. Angelo said that based on what she had told him, he would not be able to hire her.

There is a legal theory in defamation called "republishing" of a defamatory statement. It is also called "compelled self-publication." In this case, the defamatory statement of Marco was "republished" by Lola to Angelo just as if Marco had originally published the statement directly to Angelo. Frankly, I do not know if our state has adopted the theory. Would you please review the law and provide me with a memo outlining the law in this state on this issue? If we have adopted it, are there additional facts we should know? Bill your time to the above referenced file.

"My client is suing to protect his bad name."

CHAPTER **SUMMARY**

Defamation is the publication (communication) to a third person of a defamatory statement or material (oral or written) that causes harm to the reputation of the plaintiff with resulting damage. Libel is defamation in written form. Slander is defamation in oral form. A defamatory statement or material must be published or communicated to some third person other than the plaintiff. The defamation may be done intentionally or negligently. The defamation must tend to harm the plaintiff's reputation. Courts will look to the fair and natural meaning to be given by the defamation by reasonable people of ordinary intelligence. The statement must refer to the plaintiff. Defamation may be implied by insinuation. The facts must be false, as truth is a defense to defamation.

Libelous statements in writing are more serious, as they are more permanent in nature than oral statements. To recover for slander there must be special damages shown.

There are four exceptions to the special damages requirement in slander: (1) a claim that plaintiff committed a serious crime, (2) a claim that plaintiff has a loathsome disease, (3) a claim that plaintiff is incompetent in his or her trade or profession, and (4) a claim that plaintiff is "unchaste."

In libel, there is no requirement to prove special damages. The general rule is that general damages will be presumed from the fact of the written publication.

Some defenses to defamation are truth, consent, and privilege. There are three absolute privileges: (1) legislative privilege, (2) executive privilege, and (3) judicial privilege. These three protect various public interests. A conditional privilege exists if one is attempting to protect a private interest—either the interest of the defendant or someone else with whom the defendant has a relationship. The constitution may grant a privilege in which the interest of freedom of speech and freedom of the press may override the interest of protection of one's reputation. The landmark case in that regard is *New York Times Co. v. Sullivan*, 376 U.S. 254 (1964).

The tort of invasion of privacy recognizes the right to one's privacy in four separate areas: (1) unreasonable intrusion upon the seclusion of another, (2) appropriation of the other's name or likeness, (3) unreasonable publicity given to the other's private life, and (4) publicity that unreasonably places the other in a false light before the public. When these torts occur, some other tort may also have occurred, such as defamation, intentional infliction of emotional distress, battery, or trespass.

Misrepresentation is a tort that protects a person's economic interest. According to the Restatement (Second) of Torts § 525, this tort is defined as: "One who fraudulently makes a misrepresentation of fact, opinion, intention or law for the purpose of inducing another to act or to refrain from action in reliance upon it, is subject to liability to the other in deceit for pecuniary loss caused to him by his justifiable reliance upon the misrepresentation."

There are no defenses to the tort of intentional misrepresentation. The defense strategy is one of trying to combat the plaintiff's elements of proof of the tort. Some courts will allow damages for emotional distress, and some will allow punitive/exemplary damages.

Malicious prosecution of a criminal action is a tort in which defendant wrongfully instituted a separate criminal proceeding against the plaintiff. The action must have ended up favorably for the plaintiff; plaintiff must prove a lack of probable cause and that the criminal action was brought for an improper purpose.

Malicious prosecution of a civil action is a tort in which the claim is that defendant wrongfully instituted a separate civil action against the plaintiff that caused damage to the plaintiff. Abuse of process centers on the misuse of the criminal or civil judicial process for some ulterior or improper purpose or motive. It must be shown that the defendant intentionally utilized a court process for a purpose other than for which it was intended to accomplish. Spoliation of evidence is the act of destroying or hiding evidence adverse to the party. Some courts will handle this by imposing sanctions on the violating party. Other courts recognize a separate cause of action for this conduct.

KEY **TERMS**

Defamation
Libel
Slander
Publication
Republication
Absolute Privilege
Legislative Privilege
Executive Privilege

Judicial Privilege
Conditional Privilege
Actual Malice
Invasion of Privacy
Voluntary Public Figure
Involuntary Public Figure
Misrepresentation

Intentional (Fraudulent)
    Misrepresentation
Malicious Prosecution of a Criminal
    Action
Malicious Prosecution of a Civil Action
Abuse of Process
Spoliation of Evidence

REVIEW **QUESTIONS**

1. What is the difference between libel and slander? From the plaintiff's standpoint, which one has the potential to cause the most damage to the plaintiff? Why?

2. What is meant by "publication" for the tort of defamation?

3. Ronald mails a defamatory letter to Clarence, who is blind. Clarence's roommate Gilbert reads the letter to Clarence. Has there been a publication of the defamatory statements in the letter?

4. Aaron makes this statement to Clifton about Barnabas: "In my opinion, because he stole money from clients, which I personally witnessed, Barnabas should go to prison." For purposes of defamation, is this a statement of fact or one of opinion?

5. What are the four exceptions to the requirement of proving special damages in a slander case?

6. Marion, a paralegal, assists an attorney, R. Hood, in writing a trial brief on the issue of contributory negligence concerning an automobile collision. In the brief, this statement is made about opposing counsel, Mr. Nottingham: "Mr. Nottingham has again confused the law in this case. Perhaps the reason for that is he has been hitting the bottle again after falling off the wagon for the fourth time in the last few years." Attorney Nottingham sues the opposing attorney, Mr. Hood. What is attorney Hood's defense, and what is the likelihood he will prevail?

7. Edgar breaks into the home of John and steals a photograph of John. Edgar publishes it to advertise the brand of whiskey he sells together with false statements about John that would be highly objectionable/offensive to a reasonable person. Considering the four different types of invasion of privacy, which one or ones are present here?

8. Acme Tool and Machine, a large manufacturer of commercial airline engines, has a company policy of having employees submit to urine tests to determine whether an employee is using illegal drugs. Is this an invasion of the employee's privacy?

chapter 12
LOCATING AND OBTAINING MEDICAL RECORDS

LEARNING OBJECTIVES

After studying this chapter, you should be able to:

- Recognize the privileged and confidential nature of medical records, which will reaffirm the paralegal's commitment to the mandate of confidentiality.

- Identify the various methods for locating medical records, whether on plaintiff's or defendant's legal team.

- Identify the various methods for obtaining medical records, whether on plaintiff's or defendant's legal team.

- Recognize that there are different interpretations and perceptions of what are termed "medical records."

- Analyze the impact of both state statutes and the federal HIPAA statute concerning medical records issues.

"God heals and the doctor takes the fee."

Benjamin Franklin

Introduction

Before beginning any discussion on the subject of medical records (sometimes referred to as "the chart"), a crucial point needs to be made: These records are unique, privileged, extremely personal, and absolutely *confidential*. As a personal injury paralegal, whether representing the plaintiff or the defendant, when reviewing those records, the paralegal will become intimately acquainted with the personal life of an individual person. Knowledge gained from a review of medical records, whether on plaintiff's side or defendant's side, is not to be bantered about as though the person is a mere pawn in a legal case. The respect, privacy, and dignity of an individual are at play. Further, as the subject of medical records is examined, it is important to reiterate and reinforce the mandated requirement of confidentiality in the legal profession. If the paralegal breaches the confidentiality of medical records, the attorney will be ultimately responsible with potential ethical and legal malpractice ramifications.

Importance of Medical Records

Whether your role in a personal injury case is representing a plaintiff or a defendant, it can be argued that the plaintiff's medical records are one of the most important aspects of the case. Indeed, many personal injury attorneys, both plaintiff and defense alike, will maintain that it is the most important aspect. The balance between winning and losing a personal injury case before a jury may well depend upon how the scales are tipped by various entries contained in a plaintiff's medical records. It is vitally important, first, to make certain that medical records are obtained from *all available medical facilities* where plaintiff was ever treated, for any reason. Second, those records received from each facility must be *complete*.

Independence and Reliability of Medical Records

The patient's medical records are extremely reliable. Entries in the medical records are entered at the same time as the independent health care providers afford care and treatment to the patient. Those medical personnel are primarily interested in providing to their patient the best medical care and treatment possible. Health care providers have no axe to grind. They could care less which side wins or loses in a personal injury lawsuit. Indeed, some entries in the records will have been made long before a lawsuit was commenced or even contemplated. While it must be realized that a particular physician may tend to be more of an "advocate" for his or her patients, for the most part, the chart entries are honest, accurate entries made by independent, professional health care providers. These providers' sole purpose is to provide the best medical care and treatment to the patient at the time the entries are documented in the chart. All of this is not to say that charting mistakes will not occur from time to time.

Admittedly, reviewing medical records can be tedious and sometimes even downright boring. However, the personal injury paralegal must realize the importance of medical records and understand that it is in this arena that personal injury cases can be won or lost. As in all areas of a personal injury practice, thoroughness is a must. The area of obtaining complete medical records is no exception. Read the *Chacha* case, which demonstrates the vital importance of locating, obtaining, and *disclosing* all medical records, present and past, in Exhibit 12-1.[1]

EXHIBIT 12-1 Relevant Case Law

Ronald Chacha, Appellant, v. Transport USA, Inc. and Juan Carlos Guzman, Appellees.

District Court of Appeal of Florida, Fourth District.

Chacha sued the defendants for personal injuries allegedly arising out of a January 2004 automobile accident. Chacha alleged that as a result of the accident, he sustained permanent injuries, including the "aggravation of a previously existing condition."

In November 2007, Chacha was deposed. During this deposition, Chacha acknowledged that in 1999 he was injured in an accident at work when two glass plates fell on him and landed on his face. He testified that he suffered head, neck, shoulder, arm, and hand injuries from that prior accident. He further testified that he did not injure his back in the 1999 accident, that he never had back pain as a result of the 1999 accident, and that, prior to the 2004 car accident, he had never complained of back pain to any physician who treated him for the earlier accident.

In January 2008, Chacha served answers to interrogatories stating that as a result of the 2004 car accident, he had sustained lower back, neck, head, and right knee injuries. In response to the question of whether he had previously suffered any injury to those parts of the body for which he was claiming damages, Chacha listed only the injuries to his neck and head that he suffered in the 1999 work-related accident. In response to the question of what previous conditions Chacha was claiming were aggravated as a result of the January 2004 car accident, Chacha again listed only head and neck injuries.

Throughout discovery, Chacha continually reported to the defendants that Dr. David B. Ross had treated him for both the 1999 work-related accident and the January 2004 car accident. Chacha also identified Dr. Ross as a treating physician who would testify at trial. In March 2009, defense counsel subpoenaed all of Dr. Ross's medical records relating to Chacha. In May 2009, both parties received those records.

(Continued)

EXHIBIT 12-1 *(Continued)*

Dr. Ross's records revealed that Chacha may have complained to Dr. Ross about back pain prior to the 2004 car accident. The records included notes from seven pre–2004 visits where Dr. Ross noted that Chacha's "lumbosacral spine shows decreased range of motion." After a January 17, 2001 visit, the doctor wrote, "Clinically the patient remains symptomatically the same with headaches, neck pain, low back, and left arm complaints." After a February 18, 2003 visit, Dr. Ross noted, "He still complains of multiple symptoms including headaches, neck pain and low back pain." For the other five pre–2004 visits, however, Dr. Ross made no references to any back pain. In addition, the records included a "Final Report" dated September 18, 2001 in which Dr. Ross never mentioned Chacha having complained of back pain.

On June 23, 2009, two weeks before the scheduled trial date, Dr. Steven Gelbard, Chacha's neuro-surgeon, was deposed. Dr. Gelbard testified that he first treated Chacha in October 2004. Dr. Gelbard further testified that he performed surgery on Chacha for what Dr. Gelbard determined to be a bulg-ing disc. Dr. Gelbard also stated that based on the medical history provided to him by Chacha, it was his professional opinion that Chacha sustained a permanent injury caused by the car accident. This medical history included the fact that Chacha had a work-related accident in 1999 from which he was still suffering residual neck and shoulder pain at the time of the January 2004 car accident. Chacha had never informed Dr. Gelbard, however, of any back injury prior to the January 2004 car accident.

On cross, Dr. Gelbard testified that just prior to the deposition he had been advised by one of Chacha's attorneys that based on medical records obtained from Dr. Ross, Chacha may have com-plained of back pain prior to the 2004 accident. Subsequently, the defendants' attorney presented Dr. Ross's medical records to Dr. Gelbard and had Dr. Gelbard read from sections where Dr. Ross had reported that Chacha was complaining of lower back pain. Dr. Gelbard acknowledged that the information from Dr. Ross's records was something that he was learning for the first time during the deposition. When asked if the records changed his opinion that Chacha's complaints of back pain were caused by or related to the 2004 car accident, Dr. Gelbard replied that he would have to get more information to determine whether the back injury was a pre-existing condition.

On redirect, Dr. Gelbard noted that the reported back complaints prior to 2004 were different from those reported by Chacha after the 2004 accident. Based on this change in lower back complaints, Dr. Gelbard reaffirmed all of the opinions he expressed during direct examination.

On June 30, 2009, seven days before trial, the defendants filed a motion to dismiss for fraud. The defendants contended that Chacha engaged in a scheme of fraud and misrepresentation by deny-ing that he had prior back pain and prior back injuries. The defendants also contended that Chacha sought to manipulate medical testimony bearing on his injuries by concealing his past medical history from his treating physicians.

On July 7, 2009, the morning that the trial was scheduled to begin, the trial court heard arguments on the defendants' motion to dismiss. No witnesses testified and no evidence was introduced at this hearing. After hearing arguments from the attorneys, the trial judge simply stated that the motion to dismiss was "granted."

On July 10, 2009, the trial court entered a written order granting the defendants' motion to dismiss for fraud.

Chacha filed a motion for a rehearing, which the trial court denied by written order. This appeal follows.

A trial court has the inherent authority to dismiss a plaintiff's entire case when there is clear and convincing evidence that the plaintiff has committed "a fraud on the court which permeates the entire proceedings"....

When reviewing a case for fraud, the court should "consider the proper mix of factors" and carefully balance a policy favoring adjudication on the merits with competing policies to maintain the integ-rity of the judicial system....

(Continued)

EXHIBIT 12-1 *(Continued)*

> While we have never explicitly imposed a requirement that a trial court make express written findings of fact supporting its conclusion that a plaintiff perpetrated (or attempted to perpetrate) a fraud on the court, the Florida Supreme Court has recognized such a requirement where a dismissal is based on a violation of a discovery order....
>
> We believe that the same reasoning which makes it an abuse of discretion to dismiss an action based on the violation of a discovery order without express written findings of fact applies equally where dismissal is based on a plaintiff's fraud on the court....
>
> We therefore reverse and remand for the trial court to make express written findings sufficient to assist us in determining that the trial court properly considered "the proper mix of factors" and carefully balanced the policy favoring adjudication on the merits with the competing policy to maintain the integrity of the judicial system. On remand, the trial court is free to reconsider its ultimate ruling.
>
> *Reversed and remanded.*

Source: Chacha v. Transport USA, Inc. 78 So.3d 727 (Fl. Dist. Ct. App. 2012).

Locating Medical Records from Plaintiff's Side

INFORMATION FROM CLIENT

Regardless of the legal theory of the case, or whether the paralegal is on the plaintiff's team or the defendant's team, it is imperative for the personal injury paralegal to locate and then obtain all medical records of the plaintiff. Obviously, in a plaintiff's case, the first and best source for a list of all health care treatment before and after an accident is with the plaintiff client. This is best done by utilizing some form of checklist during the initial interview and with follow-up contacts with the client. It cannot be emphasized enough how critical it is to make certain that *all records* of the plaintiff are obtained.

If requesting records from a clinic in which many different medical specialties are employed, the client may have been rendered medical care and treatment there for various medical issues, some unrelated to the case at hand. For example, a male client who was involved in an automobile accident and received a back injury, which is the subject of the current suit, may have been seen in the past at the clinic by a urologist. The medical problem back then may have been a prostate problem or a urinary tract infection. In the course of taking a history, the client patient may have told his urologist that he has been having back pain because of a car accident, a slip and fall, a twisting, or some other reason. Patients do not always volunteer to a physician historical information that is related precisely to the treatment that brings the patient to the physician.

By requesting all records at the facility, there will no doubt be some records included from the release of information department that may seem totally irrelevant to the injury that is at issue in the case at hand. However, one never knows what piece of information may be there that could have a significant impact on the current case. Assume the plaintiff is a female with a knee injury from a trip and fall, which is the subject of the current suit. Even if the clinic is a specialty clinic, such as an OB/GYN clinic, the paralegal should obtain those records. It is entirely conceivable that the client patient may have said something to her OB/GYN physician about a knee injury in the course of the physician obtaining the history. Do not assume that medical records of a client's treatment for a past unrelated injury or illness might not provide important information concerning the present case.

It is imperative to inform a new plaintiff client at the outset—when the retainer agreement is signed—that once a personal injury lawsuit is commenced, the following will occur: First, both the plaintiff's law firm and the defendant's law firm will have the right to access all of plaintiff's medical records of any kind both before the accident and after the accident. Second, the plaintiff may be required to submit to a medical examination by a physician of the defendant's choosing. This is an independent medical examination (IME) authorized under Rule 35 of the Federal Rules of Civil Procedure and many state counterparts to that federal rule. The subject of IMEs will be discussed in more detail later in this chapter. Also, plaintiff clients need to be told at the outset the importance of not posting anything having to do with their injuries or their physical activities on any social media site. Review the sample initial letter to the client found in Appendix 1 at Exhibit 1-1.

Cases do occur from time to time in which a plaintiff does not mention previous health care providers to the paralegal or the attorney. This may be because a plaintiff has either forgotten about past medical history or is intentionally attempting to conceal it. Such omitted past medical history may include, for example, a past drug problem, alcohol problem, incarceration that was drug or alcohol related, emotional problem, or personal problem. A preexisting, prior injury to the same part of the body as plaintiff is claiming in the present lawsuit is commonly referred to as a **prior**.

Whether omitted intentionally or by an honest lack of memory, previous medical records can result in various repercussions. If the defense attorney learns of any past records with priors, copies will be able to be obtained. This is because the defense attorney may be in possession of blank medical authorizations signed by plaintiff. Defense counsel will then proceed to fill in the name of the facility and proceed to obtain the records. Blank signed medical authorizations should never be given to the defendant's side. This can only serve to provide an opportunity for the nightmarish repercussion of the plaintiff client being set up for an ambush at trial, which is, truly, one of the plaintiff attorney's worst nightmares.

The records obtained secretly by way of the blank medical authorization will surface for the first time at trial, producing surprise and devastation to the plaintiff's case. If there is no blank authorization, but the defense side has come across some potential new health care provider from reviewing existing records, the defense attorney will ask that an authorization be signed for the release of those newly discovered records from the particular medical facility. At that point, the plaintiff's side at least knows of the problem well before trial and has an opportunity to somehow try to overcome it or try to settle the case before trial. Another repercussion is that priors can have the effect of dramatically changing the evaluation of

Prior
A preexisting injury to the same part of the body as plaintiff is claiming in the present lawsuit.

Workplace Skills Tip

On the plaintiff's side, it is crucial to determine whether plaintiff had any "priors." They can destroy a plaintiff's case. People are very mobile today whether because of job transfers, family reasons, economics, or personal reasons. One habit the paralegal should try to incorporate into any medical records system is to request a complete work history and all addresses/cities in which the plaintiff has resided since birth. There may have been important medical treatment provided to the plaintiff at some or all of those locations. It may also have the beneficial effect of jogging a plaintiff's memory of past medical treatment if those past addresses are discussed.

the case. A final repercussion is that if the client is caught in an outright falsehood, it can create a situation in which the plaintiff's attorney may now be placed in the uncomfortable position of considering whether or not to withdraw from the case.

The case may even be one that the court will consider dismissing outright for fraud on the court. This is really the ultimate repercussion. The *Chacha* decision in Exhibit 12-1 involved a failure to disclose previous back injuries, which resulted in the court dismissing the case before it even made its way to the jury for a resolution. The trial court's decision was reversed on appeal. However, from a review of that case, the student must realize the importance of making certain that all medical records are located, obtained, and then forthrightly disclosed under the applicable rules.

INFORMATION FROM EXISTING MEDICAL RECORDS

Another source of additional health care providers consists of those medical records already obtained by the plaintiff's paralegal. The plaintiff's paralegal must be on the alert for any other health care providers documented in the records that are currently in the possession of the paralegal. Any new health care providers disclosed in current and updated medical records must be discussed promptly with the client and those records should be obtained.

INFORMATION FROM OTHER RECORDS

Medical bills, printouts prepared by no-fault carriers, workers' compensation, or health insurance carriers may disclose payment of bills to unknown additional medical facilities. To assist in the task of making certain the paralegal has all medical records from all facilities from the beginning of the case to its conclusion, it is a good practice to do the following:

- In the initial interview, question the client carefully about all current and previous health care providers.
- Prepare an initial list of all health care providers.
- In later conversations with the client as the case progresses, continue to question the client carefully about any new health care providers, particularly as new records are continually gathered.
- Cross-reference known medical care providers with actual medical bills.
- Cross-reference known medical care providers with actual pharmacy bills.
- Cross-reference known medical care providers with any health insurance records.
- Cross-reference known medical care providers with any Social Security records if plaintiff has made a Social Security disability claim.
- Cross-reference known medical care providers with any no-fault records if there is a no-fault system in your jurisdiction.
- Cross-reference known medical care providers with workers' compensation records if the current injury arises out of a work-related incident, such as an auto accident while on the job.
- Review the client's discovery responses and deposition testimony of client, spouse, and family members.
- As records are obtained, note any referrals or consults involving other physicians.
- In a given case, it may be necessary to go to the facility and review the original chart. Sometimes handwritten notes, correspondence, and records from other facilities are not sent in response to the paralegal's request.

- Remember the trait of persistence in the first chapter. Never give up. Constantly update your records. Constantly update your lists. Medical care and treatment are ongoing and continuing. Do not become complacent.
- Remember the trait of good organizational skills in the first chapter. Develop your own system to make certain that medical records are well organized so that a certain document can be retrieved when needed.

PROBLEM RECORDS

If there is something genuinely embarrassing, questionable, or problematic about some newly discovered medical record, the paralegal must disclose it immediately to the supervising attorney. Assume a plaintiff client has a right knee injury, and some old medical record just obtained by the paralegal reveals a previous right knee injury from some years past. If the plaintiff's attorney knows of this prior, he or she may be able to establish that the previous injury completely healed, and plaintiff was having no problem with that knee before the accident in question. Alternatively, the plaintiff's attorney may try to establish that this accident caused an aggravation of the previous injury to that knee. The sooner such prior or other medical problem in the case is known, the better a skillful plaintiff's attorney can effectively deal with it. It is much more difficult to deal with a prior or other medical problem if the attorney learns of it for the first time immediately before trial or worse yet, during trial, or even worse yet, in final argument, after all the evidence is closed.

One of the worst-case scenarios is that the plaintiff has not disclosed a prior, the defendant attorney discovers it, and introduces evidence of it at the last minute at trial. That scenario tends to have an adverse effect on the jury's analysis of the plaintiff's case because it logically raises two significant questions in the jurors' minds: (1) *Causation*: Is this injury being claimed by the plaintiff really caused by this accident or was it caused by the previous trauma or condition that brought about the prior? (2) *Credibility*: Is the plaintiff telling the truth about this injury, and for that matter, how the accident happened and perhaps everything else?

Most people are aware of the national credit reporting agencies. These agencies obtain information upon which lenders decide whether or not to extend credit to a person. There is also a similar reporting agency called the Medical Information Bureau (MIB). This agency compiles medical information to provide to various insurance company members that are considering insuring a particular person for life, health, disability, long-term care, and other health-related insurance. If the law firm is representing a plaintiff, to be prudent, the firm may want to request that the client request a copy of any report that MIB may have on the client.

Locating Medical Records from Defendant's Side

INFORMATION OBTAINED FROM WRITTEN DISCOVERY

The defendant, for obvious ethical reasons, does not have the luxury of being able to simply talk to a plaintiff about his or her medical treatment, present and past. The paralegal for the defense has a few weapons in locating the plaintiff's medical records, however.

For defendant, the primary source for locating all medical facilities where plaintiff has been treated is with discovery, both written and oral. Interrogatories and requests for production of documents should be specially crafted so as to clearly request this medical information. While by no means inclusive, some sample interrogatories concerning medical information are utilized in Exhibit 12-2. A seasoned personal injury defense firm will have developed its own standard set of interrogatories on this issue.

EXHIBIT 12-2 Sample Interrogatories/Medical

1. If you have received or are eligible for any workers' compensation benefits by reason of the loss or injury alleged in the Complaint, give:
   a. Your workers' compensation file number;
   b. The name of your employer;
   c. The name and address of your workers' compensation insurer, if applicable.

2. If you have received or are eligible to receive any money, payments, or benefits from any automobile insurance policy, hospital, dental insurance, health and accident insurance, disability insurance, or any insurance of any kind, by reason of the loss or injury alleged in the Complaint, give:
   a. Your insurance claim file and policy number;
   b. The name and address of the insurance company.

3. To the best of your knowledge, state the injuries that you received in this accident herein.

4. If any injury you had in the accident is claimed to have aggravated any prior condition, then state what conditions were aggravated by what injuries and how such condition was aggravated.

5. List special damages as follows:
   a. Name of doctor, hospital, dentist, chiropractor, drug store, or other   Amount charged

   _____   _____

   _____   _____

   _____   _____

   _____   _____

   b. Loss of income or earnings:
   c. Other special damages:

   _____   _____

   _____   _____

   _____   _____

6. If any person or firm contributed toward the payment of any of your expenses herein, state the name and address of each such firm or person and the amount contributed.

7. If you have any physical or mental infirmities, disabilities, or conditions of any kind (such as diabetes, high blood pressure, heart condition, epilepsy, seizures, neurosis, psychosis, addictions, alcoholism, arthritis, ulcers, bursitis, gout, migraine headaches, or any other of any kind for which you have been treated, examined, or taken medications) prior to the time of the accident, state what they were and from whom treatment was received or by whom medications were prescribed.

8. List all other injuries you may have had, either before the accident in question or after the accident in question, identifying as to whether the injury listed was before or after and give the date of the injury and the place of the injury, the circumstances of the injury, and the names and addresses of any doctors, chiropractors, or hospitals that treated you.

(Continued)

EXHIBIT 12-2 *(Continued)*

9. Give your educational background listing schools attended and the highest grade attained or the degrees that you have.

10. Give your work history for the past 20 years, giving the names and addresses of employers and places of employment along with the type of work you did.

11. State the names and addresses of all physicians, dentists, chiropractors, osteopaths, physical therapists, hospitals, clinics, or any other persons, firms, or entities that provided any kind of care or treatment to you concerning the accident that is the subject matter of your Complaint.

12. State the names and addresses of all physicians, dentists, chiropractors, osteopaths, physical therapists, hospitals, clinics, or any other persons, firms, or entities that provided any kind of care or treatment to you before the accident in question.

13. Have you, by reason of the occurrence alleged in your Complaint, received, claimed, or been advised of the availability of any collateral source benefits, including, but not limited to, any benefits paid or payable under any Workers' Compensation Act, a public or private program, any insurance policy providing medical expenses, disability payments, health or accident benefits, or any other contract or agreement whereby payments, benefits, or services have been received as a result of the occurrence alleged in your Complaint?

14. With respect to each "collateral source," identify by name and address the person or entity by whom payment has been received, state the amount of each payment received, claimed, or available from said source, and state whether the payor of said benefits has asserted any subrogation claim with respect to the benefits paid, claimed, or available.

RULE 35, FEDERAL RULES OF CIVIL PROCEDURE/ MEDICAL AUTHORIZATIONS

Independent Medical Examination (IME)

An examination by a physician of the defendant's choosing when a party places his or her physical or mental condition in controversy.

Rule 35 of the Federal Rules of Civil Procedure and state counterparts of that rule provide for an independent medical examination. An **independent medical examination (IME)** is an examination by a physician of the defendant's choosing when a party places his or her physical or mental condition in controversy. When a plaintiff commences a personal injury action, the plaintiff is placing his or her physical or mental condition in controversy.

The parties will typically stipulate to such an examination but if not, defendant must make a motion to have the plaintiff submit to this examination. On occasion, the independent medical physician retained by the defense may learn about past medical treatment volunteered by the plaintiff to the IME physician. This may be information that plaintiff had not otherwise disclosed to the plaintiff's attorney up to the point of the IME. The IME is, therefore, another potential source of information for the defendant of additional plaintiff's medical records to be obtained.

To reiterate a point made earlier, when on the plaintiff's team, in addition to informing the plaintiff that defendant will have access to all of plaintiff's medical records, plaintiff should also be informed of the possibility of having to submit to an IME. The plaintiff client should also be advised that while the rule has labeled this procedure as an "independent" medical examination, it is really quite far from that. These examinations actually used to be called "adverse medical examinations." In the vast majority of cases, the defense has chosen a physician who has done many of these examinations for that law firm in the past and is someone who tends to minimize a particular injury. The client needs to know that this defense physician is not there to help the plaintiff or to assist in any kind of treatment for the claimed injury. This is not to say that an IME physician, in the vast majority of cases, will not be extremely well qualified. These physicians simply have a philosophy that lends itself to doing these types of examinations. Some of these physicians used regularly by the defense can be effectively cross-examined by the plaintiff on the number of IMEs they perform and the amount of income they generate annually from performing these examinations for the defense.

In the typical personal injury case, the plaintiff's treating physician has made a diagnosis of plaintiff's condition (herniated disc, comminuted fracture of the tibia, muscle sprain/strain of lumbar spine), offered an opinion as to its cause (the motor vehicle accident in question), prescribed a course of treatment (medication, surgery, physical therapy), and offered a prognosis (25% partial permanent impairment of the spine). The **prognosis** is the outlook for the patient's future. This includes such items as whether there is a permanent injury and whether future medical treatment such as prescription medicine or physical therapy will be needed. The defense may be contesting the diagnosis, the cause, the course of treatment, or the prognosis. The defense may be contesting only one of these items, more than one, or all of them. The most prevalent item tends to be whether there is a permanent injury. Obviously, a permanent injury means future damages, and future damages means that the case has far greater monetary value.

Prognosis
The outlook for a patient's future.

The reason for mentioning the IME at this juncture is that some state counterparts to Federal Rule 35 may also provide that the plaintiff must furnish medical reports and signed medical authorizations upon written demand from the defendant. Even without such a provision in this rule, medical authorizations are typically furnished by a plaintiff's attorney upon request by the defendant. Courts generally tend to be liberal in ordering that such signed medical authorizations be provided. Once armed with the signed medical authorizations from the plaintiff, the personal injury paralegal can proceed with the task of locating and obtaining all medical records of the plaintiff.

INFORMATION OBTAINED FROM DEPOSITION OF PLAINTIFF

Another source for the discovery of locations of all of plaintiff's medical treatment for the defendant is at plaintiff's deposition. Written discovery will be served upon the plaintiff, such as interrogatories and request for production of documents. Answers and responses will typically be received before the plaintiff's deposition

Workplace Skills Tip

The personal injury paralegal may participate in making a motion for an IME or defending against a motion of defendant to conduct an IME. While the IME will usually be agreed upon between counsel or typically granted by the court if contested, legitimate disputes may arise. For example, the location of the IME doctor may be some distance from where the plaintiff resides. Plaintiff may argue that the IME is being proposed to harass the plaintiff and incur needless expense when there are many competent physicians available locally. If the IME doctor is one whom the defense routinely uses because that doctor typically finds little to nothing wrong with the plaintiff, the plaintiff may argue that this doctor is not "independent." An issue may arise over whether anyone other than the plaintiff may attend the IME. Another source of controversy may be the qualifications of the IME physician. The rule requires that the defendant's IME doctor must be "suitably licensed or certified."

is taken. Those answers and responses may reveal the locations of some medical facilities in which plaintiff has been treated. However, they may not be complete. At the deposition, other medical treatment facilities can be explored as well as previous addresses where plaintiff resided before the injury in question. This is an area in which the paralegal can provide valuable backup assistance to the lead attorney. The paralegal can assist by providing an outline of areas of inquiry to the attorney before the plaintiff's deposition is taken.

INFORMATION OBTAINED FROM CANVASSING

Another method utilized by the defense to try to ensure that all complete medical records have been obtained is to canvas various medical facilities where plaintiff has resided and possibly surrounding areas. For example, there may be a suspicion or even actual knowledge that plaintiff has received treatment from a podiatrist for a foot injury in a certain city. Simply calling various podiatrists' offices and inquiring if plaintiff has ever been a patient there can sometimes produce results. The inquiry is not to obtain information about care and treatment, which can only be disclosed with a signed medical authorization. The sole inquiry is whether plaintiff is or has ever been a patient there. If the facility will not even disclose the threshold question of whether or not plaintiff has been a patient, then the paralegal can still forward the plaintiff's signed medical authorization to the office. This assumes, of course, that the defense paralegal is in possession of a blank medical authorization in which the podiatrist's name can be entered. The subject of blank medical authorizations will be discussed in a later section in this chapter.

Prudence dictates that the defense should never rely solely on what the plaintiff states as to all locations where he or she has been treated. The same prudence dictates that the defense should never assume all complete medical records have been received from the plaintiff's attorney. For that matter, be skeptical of even the medical records received from the plaintiff's medical facility. They may not send everything. With experience, it will be easier to determine whether or not a complete set of records appears to have been produced. Even an inexperienced paralegal that is alert may spot potentially missing records. For example, in reviewing the records of the plaintiff's treating physician, the paralegal may see a chart entry that "patient has recently seen Dr. Jones in our psychiatry department," and note that no psychiatric records were contained in the records received from the facility. In the end, the defense paralegal will be responsible for ensuring that all complete medical records of the plaintiff have been located and then obtained.

Obtaining Medical Records

UTILIZING PROPER MEDICAL AUTHORIZATION/HIPAA

Health Insurance Portability and Accountability Act (HIPAA)
HIPAA is a federal statute that applies to health care providers and health insurance companies and provides a uniform system for patient privacy protection and patient access to medical records.

Once reasonably satisfied that all health care providers of the plaintiff have been located, the next step is to proceed with the task of obtaining all of those records. Medical facilities today do require that signed medical authorizations be compliant with the **Health Insurance Portability and Accountability Act (HIPAA)**. HIPAA is a federal statute enacted in 1996 (Pub. L. 104-191), which applies to health care providers and health insurance companies and provides a uniform system for patient privacy protection and patient access to medical records. Any such medical authorization will also need to be in compliance with any state statutes in the jurisdiction where the paralegal is working. If there is a conflict between state law and HIPAA, the controlling, determinative law to be applied will depend upon which one affords more protection to the patient. If the federal law affords less privacy protection than the state statute, then the state's law will control—and vice versa.

Medical information concerning the care and treatment by a physician, nurse, psychologist, and others is privileged information. The health care provider cannot disclose this privileged medical information without a proper HIPAA-compliant signed authorization from the patient. The personal injury paralegal may encounter some difficulties in this area. The first difficulty relates to use of the proper medical authorization. Many health care provider facilities will accept a standard universal type of authorization. A sample of that type of medical authorization is contained in Exhibit 12-3. Another medical authorization is also found in Appendix 2, Exhibit 2-1.

However, some health care facilities, such as Mayo Clinic, may have their own special form for a medical authorization that must be utilized before the medical records librarian/custodian/release of information department will release any records. The current Mayo Clinic authorization is contained in Exhibit 12-4. If it is a medical facility with which the paralegal is unfamiliar, the paralegal may need to call a particular facility or simply go online to determine whether a particular facility requires its own special medical authorization. If the authorization is located online, it may be able to be printed and utilized. As mentioned in the Workplace Skills Tip in Chapter 10, use online resources, which contain a wealth of information and can sometimes aid in the area of medical issues.

The basic premise behind HIPAA is to provide more privacy rights to patients and prevent unauthorized disclosures of the patient's records. Make no mistake that health care providers take HIPAA extremely seriously. There are substantial fines, penalties, and even imprisonment for violations. If HIPAA is violated, the right to receive Medicare payments can be lost, and a hospital can lose its accreditation. In 2010, RiteAid, one of the largest drugstore chains, settled a HIPAA privacy case for one million dollars. Employees of healthcare facilities can and have been sentenced to prison for HIPAA violations.

HIPAA has been in existence for enough time that most, if not all, of the wrinkles initially encountered after its passage have been resolved. For example, sometimes a HIPAA release prepared by a law firm was not routinely accepted by the health care provider. The health care provider may have believed that the authorization did not comply with what the health care provider's perception was of a proper HIPAA authorization. It was and is easier to make the change in the firm's authorization or use the health care provider's own authorization even if the provider's authorization is more stringent than HIPAA requires.

Fortunately, today there is much more uniformity and common understanding concerning the language of medical authorizations so the personal injury

Workplace Skills Tip

The immense power of the medical authorization is that the paralegal now has access to some of the most personal, confidential, and revealing information about a person. Whether the paralegal has obtained those medical records for the plaintiff or for the defendant and whether those records are favorable or unfavorable, they must be kept absolutely confidential at all times. While it is natural to become immersed in the busy, day-to-day activities of the legal profession, the ethical requirements must always be kept in the forefront.

EXHIBIT 12-3 Universal Medical Authorization

MEDICAL AUTHORIZATION AND WAIVER OF PRIVILEGE FOR HEALTH CARE PROVIDER

Health Care Provider: _____

Name of Patient: _____ Chart/Patient Number: _____

Date of Birth: _____ Phone Number: _____ Social Security Number: _____

You are hereby authorized to furnish and release to attorneys Bull and Bear, P.A., or their authorized representative, the following:

SPECIFIC DESCRIPTION OF INFORMATION TO BE USED AND DISCLOSED
(Specify dates for each, unless "entire medical record" is selected)

Treatment from: <u>Date of Birth</u> to: <u>Present</u>

☐ Hospital Admission Summary   ☐ Lab Reports
☐ Hospital Discharge Summary   ☐ X-Ray Reports
☐ Operative Report   ☐ X-Ray Films
☐ Progress Notes   ☐ Psychiatric Intake
☐ Entire Medical Record for all dates   ☐ Immunizations
☐ Billing Information   ☐ Pathology Report
☐ Other (please specify):
☐ I authorize verbal and/or written exchange about my medical information

I AUTHORIZE RELEASE OF ALL ALCOHOL AND/OR DRUG ABUSE RECORDS THAT ARE PART OF THE RECORDS I SPECIFIED ABOVE, UNLESS OTHERWISE INDICATED HERE:

☐ Do not release records from alcohol or drug abuse treatment programs that are protected under federal law.

PURPOSE OF THE USE AND DISCLOSURE: LEGAL

I authorize the use and disclosure of my individually identifiable health information as described above. I understand that this authorization is voluntary. I understand that if the person or organization I authorize to receive the information is not a health plan or health care provider, the released information may no longer be protected by federal privacy regulations and could be re-disclosed. I understand that my health care and payment for my health care will not be affected if I do not sign this form. I authorize the release of any and all health information by the above named law firm or their authorized representative to any medical experts consulted or retained by the above named law firm.

I understand that I may revoke this authorization in writing at any time, except to the extent action has already been taken in reliance on it. I understand that this authorization will expire on _____ or, if no date or event is specified, 12 months from the date of signing.

A photocopy or facsimile of this authorization will be treated in the same manner as the original.

_____   _____
Signature of Patient/Guardian/Representative   Date

(If not Patient, state authority/relationship)

EXHIBIT 12-4 Mayo Clinic Medical Authorization

MAYO CLINIC | *Authorization to Release Protected Health Information* | TO BE SCANNED AUTHORIZATION

Mayo Clinic Number	Name *(First, Middle, Last)*	Birth Date *(Month DD, YYYY)*

Instructions: If **any** section is incomplete, this form may be invalid and the request cannot be processed.

Release Information From

☐ Mayo Clinic, 200 First Street SW, Rochester, MN 55905
Attention _____

☐ Other *(Specify facility & address below, including phone/fax if known.)*

_____
_____
_____

Release Information To

☐ Mayo Clinic, 200 First Street SW, Rochester, MN 55905
Attention _____

☐ Other *(Specify facility & address below including phone/fax if known.)*

_____
_____
_____

Purpose of Release

☐ Treatment/Continued Care   ☐ Personal   ☐ Legal Purposes
☐ Application for Insurance   ☐ Disability Determination ☐ Payment of Insurance Claim

☐ Other [_____]

Information to be Released

Service Dates (approximate)	Information Needed By (specify Date)

☐ History and Physical   ☐ EKG's   ☐ Laboratory Reports   ☐ Hospital Notes
☐ Immunization Records   ☐ Pathology Reports ☐ Radiology Reports   ☐ Hospital Discharge Summary
☐ Clinic Notes   ☐ Operative Reports ☐ Radiology Images   ☐ Billing Statements

☐ Other [_____]

I understand the information to be released may include records related to behavioral and/or mental health care, alcohol and drug abuse treatment, HIV/AIDS, and genetics.

This authorization may be revoked at any time except to the extent that action has been taken in reliance upon it. Revocation must be made in writing to the provider/facility releasing the information. I may be charged for copies in accordance with state law. The provider/facility will not condition treatment on whether I sign the authorization. Information used or disclosed pursuant to this authorization may be subject to redisclosure by the recipient and may no longer be protected by federal law.

This authorization will expire one year from the date of signing unless I indicate an earlier date or event here: _____.

ATTENTION: This is a legal document. Please read carefully. By signing, you agree that you understand and accept the terms on this form.

- **If the patient is 18 years of age or older**, the patient must sign and date the form.
- **If the patient is 18 years of age or older and is incapable of signing**, a legally authorized substitute may sign and date the form.

  Please indicate your legal authority and include documentation of your relationship:

  ☐ Legal Guardian or Conservator   ☐ Health Care Agent (Health Care Power of Attorney)

- **If the patient is 17 years of age or younger**, the patient's parent or legal guardian must sign and date the form, unless an exception exists under state or federal law. Please indicate your relationship:

  ☐ Parent   ☐ Legal Guardian

Signature *(Required)*	Date Signed *(Required) (Month DD, YYYY)*
Printed Name of Person Signing *(if Not Patient)*	
Mailing Address of Patient - Street	

City	State	ZIP code	Phone

paralegal should rarely encounter that issue. Even with all of the varying state statutes and the federal HIPAA statute governing this area, most health care providers have adopted or will accept a medical authorization that contains these basic elements:

- The identification of the patient.
- The name of the party to whom the medical information is being released.
- The purpose of the disclosure.
- The nature of the information to be disclosed (dates, condition, specific reports or documents).
- The date signed.
- The time period during which the authorization is effective.
- The signature of the person authorized to give consent to release the medical information.
- A statement that the authorization is subject to revocation by the requesting party, the patient, or the patient's representative.

The paralegal should know that under HIPAA the patient has the right to request a change or correction to the patient's medical records if they contain a mistake. This does not occur frequently. If representing a plaintiff, however, good practice dictates that the paralegal who has scrutinized the records go over those records again with the patient client or have the attorney do so. If the paralegal has noted some questions or inconsistencies in a record, it is best to review the record with the client and attempt to make the change.

"SPECIAL" MEDICAL RECORDS

Issues may arise in the attempt to obtain certain special medical records. These are (1) psychiatric/mental health records (also referred to in HIPAA as "psychotherapy notes"), (2) chemical dependency records, and (3) HIV/AIDS records.

Psychotherapy Notes
Narrowly defined under HIPAA as detailed notes made by a mental health professional documenting conversations during a counseling session, private or group.

Psychotherapy notes are narrowly defined under HIPAA and consist of detailed notes made by a mental health professional documenting conversations during a counseling session, private or group. They are commonly referred to as "mental health records." The practical problem with these types of records is that health care providers may not take the required time to determine which records are technically HIPAA protected and which are not. It is obviously much simpler for the provider to assemble any and all mental health care records of any kind and throw them all together under the category of "psychotherapy notes." Requesting "all medical records" or "all medical records, including mental health records" probably will not cause the health care provider to produce these records. It is prudent practice for the personal injury paralegal to separately request all "psychotherapy notes/mental health care records." Under HIPAA, these records are to be specifically and separately requested anyway. There may also be state statutes governing psychotherapy notes and mental health records.

Chemical Dependency or Drug and Alcohol Records
Records given protection pursuant to 42 CFR Part 2.

Chemical dependency or drug and alcohol records have special federal protection pursuant to 42 CFR Part 2. They are not addressed in HIPAA. These types of records are confidential and may only be released by a proper authorization with conditions specified in Section 2.31 or by court order as specified in Section 2.61. In addition to an order, a subpoena must be issued for these types of records. Health care providers are sensitive to their release because of the federal regulations governing those records. Requesting "all medical records" probably will not bring about a production of these records by the health care provider.

These records should also be specifically and separately requested as required under 42 CFR Part 2, Section 2.61. If the plaintiff refuses to authorize the release of these records, a court order or a subpoena will be necessary.

HIV/AIDS records are not defined or specifically covered under HIPAA. It is possible that a health care provider will release them with a standard HIPAA-compliant general medical authorization. However, state statutes may require a special release for these types of records. To reiterate, state statutes may impose stricter requirements than HIPAA for the release of medical records in general and for these three special categories of medical records in particular. It is prudent practice to specifically and separately request this category of records if they are somehow related to a particular personal injury case.

HIV/AIDS Records
Special records not typically released with a standard medical authorization.

A competent personal injury law firm, whether plaintiff or defendant, should be knowledgeable about HIPAA and its own state's laws about the release of medical information. That firm will likely have its own time-tested forms so that the paralegal should not have to re-invent the wheel as to these three categories of medical records. These three special categories of medical records may end up before the court in a discovery hearing to determine whether plaintiff will be required to disclose such records. This would occur on the assumption that the plaintiff has not authorized the release of such records in one or more of those three categories. Much will depend upon what the plaintiff is claiming in the current personal injury claim.

For example, if there is a claim of depression, anxiety, or mental or emotional distress allegedly caused by the accident, the court may be more inclined to make the plaintiff produce previous mental health records. The same is true of chemical dependency records. If there is a claim that plaintiff turned to using alcohol or drugs because of the accident in question, the court may be more inclined to make the plaintiff produce those records. A case in which a plaintiff claims that defendant negligently or intentionally caused plaintiff to contract HIV/AIDS would likely require a production of those types of records. However, they may be discoverable even in a case in which plaintiff claims he or she could not do a certain type of work following an accident, but defendant claims that the preexisting disease of AIDS would have prevented plaintiff from doing the work regardless.

Note that the sample medical authorization in Appendix 2, Exhibit 2-1, has a separate section for "Sensitive Records," which are described as "HIV or AIDS," "Chemical Dependency," and "Psychotherapy/Mental Health." Note, too, that the authorization form for the release of those records requires the patient to initialize the approval for their release. The Mayo Clinic medical authorization in Exhibit 12-4 contains this statement: "I understand the information to be released may include records related to behavioral and/or mental health care, alcohol and drug abuse treatment, HIV/AIDS, and genetics."

Workplace Skills Tip

As soon as a new health care facility treating the plaintiff has been ascertained, it is a good practice to immediately request those records. There is a certain amount of turnaround time involved, so the sooner the facility receives the request, the better. Medical records are not always received as quickly as the paralegal would like them. Have a diary system for follow-up. More detail on systems for tracking medical records requested is provided later in this chapter. Also, if requesting records for an upcoming deposition or trial, be sure to mention that you must have the records by a definite date.

WHAT ITEMS ARE CONSIDERED MEDICAL RECORDS?

It is important for the paralegal to understand that some health care facilities do not consider certain items to be a part of "medical records." Items such as (1) correspondence, (2) records received from other medical facilities that are in the possession of the health care facility, or (3) physician's written medical reports may not jive with their definition of "medical records." A **certification** may be used in which the medical records librarian/custodian/release of information officer signs a certification as to what is included in the records and what is not. Typically the number of pages being sent is indicated. This practice is not as common as it once was, and it is expensive. A sample certification form is contained in Appendix 2 in Exhibit 2-2. In the author's experience, some physicians such as psychologists and psychiatrists may remove portions of their files. As mentioned earlier in this chapter, with experience, it will become easier to detect when some medical documents appear to be missing. For example, a review of one section in the chart such as nurse's notes may indicate a physician's order for treatment, but no such order is in the orders section of the chart.

If the records received do not appear to be complete, a call to the medical records librarian/custodian/release of information department may be the first step. Both plaintiff and defense firms may utilize the certification form mentioned earlier if certain records are still missing or suspected missing. Other remedies may be used, including a subpoena of the records under Rule 45, a deposition of the medical records librarian/custodian, or a court order upon motion. It may also be necessary for the paralegal to make a personal visit to the medical facility and obtain the entire original chart and review it at the facility.

MEDICAL FACILITIES WITH SIMILAR NAMES

It is important for the paralegal to realize that a medical authorization issued to one medical facility may not necessarily require a production of medical records from its sister entity next door with a similar name. For example, sending a medical authorization to Southwest Regional Medical Clinic may not obtain for you the medical records from the adjoining Southwest Regional Hospital. Issues may also arise when medical facilities are sold, merged, or reorganized. The same is true when names of the facilities are changed, which is usually the case when a facility is sold, merged, or reorganized. For example, sending an authorization to both of these Southwest Regional entities may not produce the medical records from their predecessors, Southwest Medical Clinic and Southwest Hospital. Some clinics and hospitals will not release their predecessor's medical records unless the paralegal specifically requests records from the predecessor facility. It appears picky and technical, but it is up to the paralegal to determine those technicalities and complete the task. If unsure, it is prudent to simply call the administration department or medical records/release of information department to clarify how to obtain records from all current and all predecessor medical facilities.

Certification
A document signed by the medical records custodian/librarian of a health care provider facility stating what medical records are being furnished and what medical records are not being furnished.

Workplace Skills Tip

If a case settles, be certain to immediately cancel any requested records. The client will not want to reimburse a law firm for records received some time after a settlement was reached. The law firm may end up eating that cost.

Medical Authorization Do's and Don'ts

Finally, there are a few additional tips on acquiring medical records. No plaintiff should ever sign and issue to the defense firm a medical authorization that is *blank*—one in which the defense can fill in the name of the medical facility. That is not good practice. This is because it allows the defense to merrily proceed with obtaining medical records on its own without the knowledge of plaintiff. Sometimes a facility will be located by the defense where plaintiff was treated for a prior, but plaintiff has not disclosed that to the plaintiff's attorney. The defense attorney fills in the blank space with the facility's name and proceeds to obtain the medical records without the knowledge of the plaintiff's attorney. It usually ends up with a surprising and devastating result for the plaintiff at trial. The defense may attempt this tactic of using blank medical authorizations. In some cases, with inexperienced or incompetent personal injury counsel, it may succeed.

Similarly, no plaintiff or defendant should ever use a medical authorization requesting medical records *only from the date of the accident*. That is also not good practice. After all, the entire point is to obtain everything—complete medical records of plaintiff from birth, particularly ones that predate the accident in question. A sample letter requesting medical records is contained in Exhibit 12-5. Another similar letter requesting medical records, but setting a deadline for their receipt is found in Appendix 2, Exhibit 2-3. Good personal injury firms, both for plaintiff and for defendant, will have their own individual tried-and-true letters that they will want the paralegal to use.

There will likely be one authorization that the plaintiff's firm uses to obtain records of the firm's own client and another more restrictive authorization that is given to defense counsel to obtain medical records of the client. Such a restrictive authorization may make it clear that any treating physician is not to have any conversations with defense counsel. An example of such an authorization is found in Appendix 2 at Exhibit 2-1A. Such an authorization that is provided by plaintiff to defense counsel may be designated as "defense," "adverse," "restricted," "limited" or other such language to make it clear that the medical records are not being given to the plaintiff patient's attorney but to the adverse attorney. In the case of the authorization shown in the Appendix at Exhibit 2-1A, it is designated as "limited."

Workplace Skills Tip

If you are a paralegal on the defense side in a personal injury case gathering plaintiff's medical records, there may be questions about some entries in the chart from the plaintiff's physician. Ethically, you know that you cannot communicate with the plaintiff who is represented by counsel. However, can you communicate with the plaintiff's physician by e-mail, letter, or phone to attempt to clarify the physician's entries? The answer, of course, depends upon your jurisdiction. It may be absolutely prohibited. It may be allowed. It may be allowed only with the written consent of the plaintiff patient. It may be allowed only in a certain type of case such as a medical malpractice case. Note that the authorization in Exhibit 12-3 addresses this issue with a place for plaintiff to authorize "verbal or written exchange." It is difficult to imagine any scenario under which a plaintiff would allow a member of the defense team to communicate with plaintiff's physician. It is also difficult to imagine the plaintiff's physician communicating with a defendant's representative, even if it were permissible.

EXHIBIT 12-5 Medical Records Request Letter

RANDOLPH L. STEFANS, LPC
111 Main Avenue
P.O. Box 111
Old Town, Bliss 55555

408-232-0000 Phone
408-232-0001 Fax

R.L. Stefans, Attorney
Corinne K. Kool, Paralegal

Date

Medical Records Director/Release of Information
Name of Facility
Street Address/P.O. Box #
City, State Zip

Re: Name of Patient:
         Birth Date:
         Clinic/Hospital # (if known)

Dear Medical Records Director/Release of Information:

Our law firm represents _____ for injuries sustained in an accident that occurred on_____. I would appreciate it if you would send to me photocopies of the following:

1. All medical records on the above-named patient from day one to the present.

Please note that we need all medical records at your facility on this patient both before this accident in question and after this accident in question.

2. Medical bills for care and treatment rendered to this patient arising from the accident in question.

A signed medical authorization is enclosed which will allow for the release of this medical information to our office. We will pay all reasonable costs and charges in connection with this request. I do ask, however, if the cost will exceed the sum of $_____, please contact me first before making copies.

If you have any questions concerning this request, please call my direct line at 408-232-0002.

Thank you.
Very truly yours,
Corinne K. Kool
Paralegal

Tracking and Updating Medical Records

TRACKING

It is recommended that the paralegal use a form documenting when the requests for records were made and when the records were received. A sample "Requested/Received" tracking form that is simple and basic is contained in Exhibit 12-6. Good plaintiff and defense firms will likely have their own forms or systems on the firm's network with which to keep track of and update medical records. A tracking form such as the one in Exhibit 12-6 may also contain e-mail and phone information for the medical facilities and information concerning whether or not the bill for medical records has been paid.

The tracking/follow-up form in Exhibit 12-6 refers to a BATES #. Medical records, when received, will typically be numbered in some fashion. The

EXHIBIT 12-6 Medical Records Tracking Form

John Smith
File No.: 12345.00000
DOB: 03/01/56
DOA: 02/10/10

FACILITY NAME	BATES #__ To #__	REQUESTED	RECEIVED	REVIEWED	INCLUSIVE DATES	NOTES

old-fashioned method was simply to type or handwrite a number at the bottom of each page of all records received from a medical facility. The next progression was with a true handheld Bates stamp. Today, page numbering still referred to as "Bates numbers" can be accomplished with copier machines and computer software programs. For example, a software program as of this writing that will accomplish Bates numbering is Adobe Acrobat 9 Pro Extended.

Numbering the pages of the medical records provides for efficient reference and retrieval. This page numbering is particularly helpful when discussing a page or pages contained in the records with team members, attorneys on the other side, expert witnesses, the client, other witnesses, the court, and in particular, the jury. In final argument, it is very helpful to tell the jury about an entry in the chart, read from it, and then tell them to read the entry, which is located on a particular page of the records.

Each firm will handle the organization of medical records differently, but some firms and legal departments will digitally save separately the different sections in the records. For example, a separate file may be created for hospital records as Progress Notes, Nurses Notes, Operative Reports, Emergency Room Records, Physicians Orders, and even Ambulance Run Reports. The student should examine the sample hospital records in Appendix 2, Exhibit 2-4 beginning with the Come Kwik Ambulance run records and ending with the Nurse's Notes. As the case progresses, an expert witness, an insurance claims representative, or some other person involved in the case may want to review only certain portions of the records. With separate files, more efficiency is created by being able to send only a requested file in the records rather than having to send the entire set of records. It also reduces the size of the e-mail attachment compared with having to send the entire set of records in one large file. A firm may also index records using Bates numbers as a reference.

UPDATING

It is also prudent for the paralegals on both sides of a case to periodically update medical records. Medical care and treatment to a plaintiff patient is ongoing. Oftentimes, new and important information is found in the most recent records.

Workplace Skills Tip

"A picture is worth a thousand words." Particularly when on the plaintiff's side, the paralegal will be involved in assembling good visual aids for the jury. The plaintiff's testimony and the doctors' testimony will have far more impact on the jury if the jury is shown trial exhibits such as x-rays showing the large screw placed into the bone, videotapes of a certain surgery or procedure, photographs of the injury, especially those taken immediately after the accident when plaintiff is still in the hospital, blowups of certain chart entries, and models and charts depicting the various areas of the human anatomy involved in the case.

When the updated medical records are requested, the paralegal may need to supply a new medical authorization to the medical facility. As discussed earlier, a medical authorization may only be valid for a certain length of time, usually one year. There should be some type of diary/docketing system so as to follow up again with the medical facility if the records are not received within a certain time.

If representing a plaintiff, obviously, it will be known with whom the plaintiff is treating and how often. If there is a significant change in health care providers or additional treatment by the same providers for some reason, the plaintiff's paralegal should know of it and update the records accordingly. Defendant is not in that position. Good practice on the part of the defendant paralegal is probably to check every six months to see whether there are additional records, but perhaps more frequently as trial nears. To make certain all updated records are received, it is good practice to request records from the date showing in the law firm file as to the patient's last visit to the facility. As far as frequency of updates of medical records, the paralegal will take the cue from the team member trial attorney that is supervising the file.

Payment for Medical Records/Client Authorization

The paralegal should be familiar with each medical facility's policy for payment of medical records. Some facilities will require payment up front. Some will require a partial payment. Some will bill the entire charge to the law firm. Some state statutes limit the amount health care providers are allowed to charge per page for copies of medical records.

If the paralegal is working in a personal injury defense law firm, under the liability policy, the insurance company has the right to control the defense of the case. A carrier will sometimes request, at the outset of a new case, that only certain records be obtained so that the carrier has just enough minimal information to try to initially evaluate the case. They may instruct the paralegal to not obtain, for example, nurses' notes or lab reports. Usually, however, if it is a case that cannot be settled early on, and it appears to be a case for trial, the insurance company will authorize the eventual obtaining of all medical records.

Spending money to obtain medical records will need to be approved by the client, whether plaintiff, self-insured defendant, or a defendant with an insurance carrier providing the defense. It is good practice to advise the health care facility to first contact the paralegal if the cost of what is being requested will exceed a certain dollar amount. The forms used in this chapter are intended to provide some initial exposure to the paralegal of some basic, sample forms that are used in a personal injury practice. Again, competent plaintiff and defense personal injury firms will likely have their own preferred forms relating to the obtaining of medical records.

Properly locating and obtaining all medical records is a skill that will be enhanced with experience. As the Roman author and politician Cicero observed over 2,000 years ago: "The skill to do comes from the doing."

CASE 12.1 Hypothetical Case: Developing Workplace Skills

You are a paralegal working in a plaintiff's personal injury firm. The firm has just signed up Sarah Williams, a 42-year-old married woman with two children who was rear-ended at a stop sign two years ago. Liability is clear, and she has legitimate injuries well documented by her treating physicians. She is a popular TV personality and quite prominent in the community. She is claiming neck injuries and a low back injury. When you initially interviewed her, she adamantly denied ever having any neck or low back pain in her life and denied ever having made any complaints to any health care provider about neck or low back pain. At her deposition, which you attended, the defense attorney asked her if she had ever had any problems or pain with her neck or low back before this car accident. She emphatically denied that.

In the course of updating medical records, you note in a new record that there is an obscure handwritten entry that is difficult to read but appears to say something to the effect of " cbirth in St. Louis at Smith Gen." You go on the Internet and find that there is a Smith General Hospital in St. Louis, Missouri. They do not require any special authorization. You know her maiden name was Brown and you recall that she was originally from St. Louis. You have several authorizations in your file that Sarah has signed. You forward a signed authorization by her to Smith General Hospital indicating that her maiden name was Brown, and you request all medical records for Sarah Brown/Sarah Williams. When these old records are received, it turns out that when she was 16, she ran away from home, became pregnant, and had a child. During her pregnancy, the chart entries were replete with entries of severe low back pain. You mention it to Sarah. The two of you have become friendly as her case has progressed. She is devastated because she has never told her husband about this child, which she put up for adoption 26 years ago. She tells you it would ruin her marriage and her career, and besides, everyone knows it's common for a woman to have back pain during pregnancy and suggests: "Let's just keep it between the two of us, OK?" What do you do?

"The hospital computer system has a virus. Ironic, isn't it?"

CHAPTER **SUMMARY**

Medical records ("the chart") are privileged records between the physician or other health care provider and the patient. The personal injury paralegal, whether on the plaintiff's side or the defendant's side, will have access to these most personal records. It is important to remember the mandatory requirement of confidentiality when discussing any issues involving medical records.

Entries in medical records are made contemporaneously with the care and treatment afforded to the patient. For the most part, a health care professional is objective and has no interest in the outcome of a personal injury lawsuit. In many

cases, entries are made in a chart before a lawsuit was commenced or even contemplated.

It is important for the paralegal to gather for review all medical records—all of them following the particular accident and all of them before the accident. From the plaintiff's perspective, the first and best source for locating all medical records is the client. There are occasions when plaintiff clients either forget about previous illnesses or injuries, or they outright attempt to conceal them. A prior injury ("a prior") can be devastating to the plaintiff's case if not ascertained early so that the plaintiff's attorney can determine how to deal with it. The prior injury may have completely healed so that the accident caused an entirely new injury. Or the accident may have aggravated a preexisting condition.

The plaintiff's side also has the benefit of the plaintiff's own medical records, which may reveal additional treatment elsewhere by the plaintiff. The plaintiff should be advised that by commencing a lawsuit for personal injuries the plaintiff will need to sign a medical authorization to provide to the defendant. Accordingly, the defendant will have access to all of the plaintiff's records. The plaintiff should also be advised of the possibility of having to submit to an IME. The plaintiff should also be advised to be careful about posting anything concerning the accident or plaintiff's injuries on any social media site. It is also good practice for the paralegal to cross-reference known health care providers with those contained in medical bills, pharmacy bills, no-fault records, or health insurance records, as examples.

The defendant's main source to locate plaintiff's medical records is discovery, both written and oral. A competent and reputable defense firm will have standard interrogatories and requests for production of documents that request all medical records, current and past. Follow-up can occur at the plaintiff's deposition. The defendant will be provided with medical authorizations signed by the plaintiff. This will allow the defendant's side to obtain the same medical records from a medical facility that the plaintiff may also obtain.

The defendant may choose to have the plaintiff submit to an IME, which is allowed under Rule 35 of the Federal Rules of Civil Procedure and many state counterparts.

Information may be learned by the independent medical examiner of other places where plaintiff is currently being treated or was treated in the past. The IME is another source for locating medical records of the plaintiff. Some states' rules similar to Rule 35 also mandate that medical reports and signed medical authorizations of plaintiff be furnished to defendant. Even without a rule or statute, it is common for a plaintiff to provide the defense with medical authorizations without a court order.

Many health care providers will accept a standard, general release. Some providers may require submission of their own unique authorization before they will release a patient's records. All medical authorizations must be in compliance with state statutes and with the Health Insurance Portability and Accountability Act, otherwise known as HIPAA. There are three unique categories of records, which may need to be requested separately. These are (1) psychotherapy notes/mental health records, (2) chemical dependency records, and (3) HIV/AIDS records.

Each medical facility has a different conception of what is meant by "medical records." For example, some facilities do not consider correspondence, medical reports, or records received from other facilities as medical records. If there is a question as to whether or not all complete records have been received, other avenues may need to be pursued. These include a certification by the facility, a subpoena, or a court order. Whether on the plaintiff's side or the defendant's side, a system needs to be in place so that medical records are obtained and periodically updated.

KEY TERMS

Prior
Independent Medical Examination (IME)
Prognosis
Health Insurance Portability and Accountability Act (HIPAA)

Psychotherapy Notes
Chemical Dependency or Drug and Alcohol Records

HIV/AIDS Records
Certification

REVIEW QUESTIONS

1. Why is information found in a plaintiff's medical records more likely to be believed by a jury than conflicting information presented at trial by a plaintiff?
2. What is an independent medical examination, and what is its purpose?
3. What are the three types of medical records that should be specifically and separately requested as opposed to asking for "all medical records"?
4. Why is it not good practice for a plaintiff to sign a blank medical authorization?
5. Why is it not good practice to request records only from the date of the accident going forward?
6. Describe one type of source for locating all health care providers where a plaintiff has been treated that are available to both the plaintiff and the defendant.
7. What are the types of records that a health care facility may not consider to be "medical records"?

chapter 13

REVIEWING AND SUMMARIZING MEDICAL RECORDS

"Nurses are angels in comfortable shoes."

Author unknown

Goals

Before rushing into a discussion of the art of reviewing and summarizing medical records, it may be beneficial to first reflect upon the goals to be accomplished. First and foremost, as mentioned in the last chapter, the personal injury paralegal needs to be familiar with the facts of the accident as well as the facts of the injuries. With that in mind, these are some suggested goals:

- Locate important information regarding the plaintiff's claimed damages (e.g., pain and suffering and permanency of injury).
- Locate important information bearing upon the liability issues in the case (e.g., breach of duty in a negligence case).
- Locate important information regarding causation of the injuries (e.g., was the car accident, slip and fall, or other traumatic event that is the subject matter of the legal action the cause of the plaintiff's personal injuries?).
- Reduce the time that the attorney needs to spend reviewing these records.
- Assemble a summary of the records for the attorney that is efficient and concise.

After locating and obtaining all medical records, the paralegal's ultimate task will be to organize those records, review them, analyze them, and summarize them. The organizational aspect cannot be emphasized enough. If the attorney requests a particular medical document at a meeting, deposition, mediation, arbitration, or at the trial, the paralegal must be able to quickly and efficiently retrieve it. Admittedly, it takes practice, persistence, and hard work to become

LEARNING OBJECTIVES

After studying this chapter, you should be able to:

- Explain the significance of medical records, as they impact not only damages, but also other legal theories of the plaintiff's case.

- Recognize the various medical tools available for assisting in the process of reviewing and analyzing medical records, such as medical abbreviations, medical symbols, and human anatomy charts.

- Discuss the importance and significance of the "history" contained in medical records.

- Discuss the important items of proof contained in various entries in medical records that will impact the outcome of a personal injury case.

- Articulate the various methods of charting.

- State the rationale and techniques for preparing an effective medical records summary.

Workplace Skills Tip

"If it isn't documented in the chart, it didn't happen!" This is an unwritten rule among attorneys concerning medical records. It is sometimes discussed by attorneys involved in a medical malpractice case when a physician claims that the physician did something or told the patient something, but it is not documented in the chart. The inference is that it did not happen. The same is true of the personal injury plaintiff. The plaintiff may testify, for example, that he or she told the physician of a certain complaint or a certain fact. With all of the other detailed information that one finds in a medical chart, it will be hard to convince a jury that the plaintiff made such a statement to the physician if the physician did not document it in the patient's chart.

proficient at organizing, reviewing, analyzing, and summarizing medical records. This is another area where, again referring to the quote of Cicero, the skill to do definitely comes from the doing.

Medical Terminology, Abbreviations, and Symbols

The beginning point for reviewing and analyzing medical records is to become familiar with medical terminology, medical abbreviations, medical symbols, and other pertinent medical information. Appendix 2 is the medical appendix of this textbook. The student may need to review Appendix 2 in understanding some of the medical terminology and abbreviations used in this chapter. For example, a common abbreviation is ROM. This stands for "range of motion." Another one is MVA, which stands for "motor vehicle accident." Some of the following medical documents are contained in Appendix 2, which may need to be referenced as this chapter is studied: Medications (2-5), Medical References (2-6), Physician and Other Medical Specialties (2-7), Common Medical Symbols (2-8), Prefixes and Suffixes (2-9), Medical Abbreviations (2-10), Roots and Combining Forms in Human Anatomy (2-11), Medical Diagrams (2-12), and a sample Medical Records Summary (2-13).

The personal injury paralegal will soon discover that the abbreviations do not necessarily mean what they appear to mean. For example, an abbreviation in the chart of SOB does not refer to what the doctor or nurse thinks of the patient but rather refers to an observation that the patient has "shortness of breath." There are also excellent resources online, which the personal injury paralegal is encouraged to consult for medical information. Examples of such resources are Medline, Medscape, Merck Medicus, NIH, WebMD, and PDR Health. Additional medical resources are outlined in Appendix 2, Exhibit 2-6.

In reviewing medical records, the paralegal will be reading and studying not only typewritten and electronic records, but also handwritten records, which, unfortunately, are not always legible. If you are representing the plaintiff, you have the advantage of simply asking the physician, chiropractor, or nurse, if still available, what it is that they scribbled and scrawled in the chart. The defense may need to retain another such physician, chiropractor, or nurse to assist in deciphering the handwritten language or take the deposition of the person making the entry.

Significance of Medical Records in a Personal Injury Case

MEDICAL RECORDS WILL CONTAIN INFORMATION IN ADDITION TO THE ELEMENT OF DAMAGES

Before there can be any effective review and analysis of medical records, the personal injury paralegal on either side must first have a firm grasp of the facts and the issues of the plaintiff's injury and claimed damages. To be truly effective, however, it is not enough to be familiar with only the plaintiff's injury and claimed damages. For example, if the case involves an automobile accident in which the plaintiff received a serious injury, the paralegal needs to be familiar with the facts of the accident as well as the injury itself. This is because medical records may contain chart entries in which the patient (now a plaintiff) states how the accident occurred. Those statements may support or contradict later testimony at trial.

For example, the tort of negligence was discussed in the earlier chapters. Setting aside the issue of duty, which is for the court to decide, the three remaining issues are breach of duty, causation, and damages. Medical records must and will contain evidence of the fourth element—damages. The effective paralegal, however, must be reviewing those records with a keen eye focused upon any entries that may bear on the elements of breach of duty and causation, in addition to damages.

Damages

The plaintiff has received an injury and has sought some type of medical treatment for that injury. Accordingly, the element of damages will always be reflected in the plaintiff's medical records. Assume the plaintiff is alleging pain and suffering, a type of non-economic or general damages discussed in Chapter 4. One of the personal injury paralegal's focused approaches should then be: Are there any entries in the chart supporting or contradicting the plaintiff's claim of pain and suffering? Consider this physician's chart entry:

> *Pt comes in today with the same persistent dull, aching pain in her right knee … no noticeable improvement in her limp … still off work … continued Percocet.*
>
> J. Hoeffler, M.D.

Now consider this chart entry:

> *This is patient's second visit … no complaints of pain in her right knee … appears to be walking with a normal gait. Pt back to work. Pain meds discontinued.*
>
> G. W. Soule, M.D.

The first chart entry example certainly assists in proving a certain degree of pain and suffering. The doctor notes that the patient has complaints of pain, the limp persists, the patient is still not back to work, and the pain medication Percocet is prescribed.

The second chart entry example does much less in assisting with proof of the element of pain and suffering damages. The plaintiff did continue to seek medical treatment. However, the treating doctor notes there are no longer any complaints of pain, the limp has gone away, the patient is now back to work, and no more pain medication is prescribed.

Continuing with chart entries reflecting upon a damages claim, assume that the plaintiff is claiming an injury that is serious and permanent in nature. Another focused approach of the personal injury paralegal should be: Are there any entries in the chart verifying or contradicting the plaintiff's claim of a serious and permanent injury? Consider this physician's chart entry:

> *It's been almost a year from Pt's MVA. Same persistent complaints. I believe she has a permanent injury to her knee.*
>
> E. Garrity, M.D.

Now consider this physician's chart entry:

> *Pt comes in for re-check of the knee. Almost a year since her MVA. ROM is completely normal. She's back to work and doing all activities. I believe she is completely healed with no residuals.*
>
> Sharon Cook, M.D.

The first entry clearly establishes a permanent injury, which will provide a higher value to the case. The second entry referring to "no residuals" does not establish a permanent injury, thus, giving lower value to the case. These chart entry examples are realistic and representative of what the paralegal may find in a patient's chart. The contrast in the impact of each entry is dramatic as that entry bears upon proof of the element of damages at trial. The paralegal must always keep in mind that the same medical records he or she is reviewing will later become documentary evidence at trial. Those same medical records, good or bad for the client, will also be reviewed by the jury in its deliberations.

Breach of Duty

Entries concerning breach of duty or liability frequently meander into medical records, particularly in an emergency room (ER) record or in the record of a physician's office visit. Continuing with the same MVA and the right knee injury to the female plaintiff, consider entries found in this ER chart from the ER nurse shortly after the automobile collision:

> *Bad Medicine Hospital Emergency Room*
>
> *Date: 4/17/08 Time: 2205*
>
> *37 y/o ♀ arrives at ER ambulatory but with a guarded/limping gait in right leg following MVA approx 2130—happened 3 blocks from hospital. States her cell phone fell out of her hand onto her lap at intersection, she looked down and next thing she knew "this guy's car was right in front of me." Strong odor of alcohol on breath. Pt. alert. Severe laceration to R knee—bleeding profusely—dressing applied. Pt c/o severe pain in right knee with limited ROM. Voices no other complaints.*
>
> Mike Rehder, R.N.

Assume that the patient in this example later brings a personal injury negligence case against the other driver. At trial, plaintiff testified she was, in fact, holding her cell phone in her hand immediately before the collision, but it was the force of the impact that knocked it out of her hand onto her lap. She also testified that she only had two beers at a friend's house approximately two and a half hours before the accident. She testified she was keeping a vigilant lookout and looked both ways before entering the intersection. She testified that as she entered the intersection, the defendant was not there. Plaintiff looked to the right but after looking to the left and then back to the right again, defendant's car was right in front of her, inferring defendant was traveling at a high rate of speed.

At trial, plaintiff will be confronted with the statement she made in the ER. She will potentially be able to be impeached with it as a prior, inconsistent statement, admission, or as a business records document. All of these are exceptions to the hearsay rule in evidence law. Comparing the plaintiff's trial testimony of her drinking two beers two and a half hours before the accident, versus the nurse's note of "strong odor of alcohol on breath" in the ER approximately a half hour after the accident, which version is the jury likely to believe? Comparing the plaintiff's trial testimony of her not dropping her cell phone before the collision and keeping a proper lookout versus the nurse's note of dropping her cell phone before the collision and taking her eyes off the road, which version is the jury likely to believe?

In both instances, the jury is almost certain to believe the independent ER nurse who is making objective observations in the care and treatment of a patient. These are chart entries made only 35 minutes after the accident, which, incidentally, occurred fairly close to the hospital. There is no lawsuit in place and likely the thought of one was not even contemplated at the time the plaintiff came in focused on a painful injury. The ER chart entry is a potent entry bearing on the issue of breach of duty on the plaintiff's part. For a similar situation, review the decision of *Skillern & Sons, Inc. v. Rosen*, 359 S.W.2d 298 (Tex. 1962) in Exhibit 13-1. The plaintiff testified at trial that she had slipped and fallen *inside* defendant's drug store. The ER record, however, noted that she had fallen *outside* the store.

EXHIBIT 13-1 Relevant Case Law

Skillern & Sons, Inc., Petitioner, v. Florence Rosen, Respondent.

Supreme Court of Texas.

Florence Rosen testified that on the afternoon of December 30, 1958, it was snowing, sleeting and raining, and that the streets and sidewalks of downtown Dallas were covered with snow, sleet and slush. She had brought her car into town that day and had promised to pick up her sister, Mrs. Ira Lewis, at the Doctors Building about 5 o'clock. Owing to the bad weather she decided not to drive her car home, but to try to catch a taxicab or bus. This she had been unable to do after waiting some forty-five minutes or an hour. Realizing that she was late, she testified she went into the Skillern drugstore to telephone her sister that she would be late, and to get a cup of coffee. After entering the drugstore she noticed a puddle of water to her left and near the cigar counter and the cash register. She veered around the puddle of water some three or four feet from it. As she did so, her left foot slipped and she fell on her elbow and on her back. As she lay on her back she noticed some droplets of water in the vicinity of where she was lying. Two men came and helped her up. She did not realize that she was hurt, but she was embarrassed and immediately left the drugstore without reporting to any employee of the drugstore that she had fallen. She walked to where her car was parked and drove to the Doctors Building to pick up her sister about 6:30. She parked the car and went in the building to get her sister. At that time her elbow was paining her considerably. She drove her sister to the apartment house, some five miles distant, where they lived together. Her physician, Dr. Bywaters, was called for an appointment and a neighbor in the apartment building, a Mr. Wenger, was called to drive with them to Baylor Hospital. She had difficulty in getting her jacket off on account of the pain in her elbow and on account of a zipper that would not work. Mr. Wenger came in and assisted Florence Rosen in removing her jacket...and respondent received emergency treatment from Dr. Bywaters....

Respondent also complains of the action of the trial court in admitting into evidence records of Gaston Hospital which had to do with her admission into said hospital. We agree with the Court of Civil Appeals that such records were admissible.

(Continued)

EXHIBIT 13-1 *(Continued)*

> The particular part of the record to which objection was made was a page out of the records which purported to be the history given an employee of the hospital by Mrs. Rosen and her sister. In this personal history record was the statement 'The patient slipped yesterday at 5:30 while walking in the slushy snow in front of a local drugstore.' The objections made were that the records were not properly proven up, and that they were hearsay....
>
> We think proper predicate was laid for the introduction of such records by the testimony of the custodian of the records, she having testified that they were made in the regular course of business of Gaston Hospital by an employee of the hospital at or near the time of the entry of the respondent into the hospital, and that it was customary for a record to be kept of the personal history of a patient entering the hospital....
>
> However, some of such statements may be admissible on other grounds: as declarations against interest, spontaneous exclamations, dying declarations, and admissions of a party.... The above statement by Miss Rosen is inconsistent with her testimony at the trial that she fell inside the drugstore, and is therefore an admission.... It appears that the question resolves itself down to this: if the hospital employee to whom Miss Rosen made the admission could have properly testified to the fact that she made such admission, then a proper record thereof would be admissible.... We hold, as the Court of Civil Appeals did, that the trial court was not in error in admitting the part of the hospital record which contained Miss Rosen's statement that she fell in front of the drugstore.

Source: Skillern & Sons, Inc. v. Rosen, 359 S.W.2d 298 (Tx. 1962).

History and Its Importance

Medical History

Any information given by the patient to the health care provider or received by the health care provider from others (relative, ambulance attendant, law enforcement personnel) that relates to current complaints, symptoms, and an explanation of what may be causing it.

Past Medical History

Consists of information received of the patient's illnesses, injuries, and treatment in the past, which may include information about family medical conditions.

Medical history is any information given by the patient to the health care provider or received by the health care provider from others (relative, ambulance attendant, law enforcement personnel) that relates to current complaints, symptoms, and an explanation of what may be causing it. **Past medical history** consists of information received of the patient's illnesses, injuries, and treatment in the past, which may include information about family medical conditions.

A patient's history obtained in the ER can become a critical piece of evidence as shown by the cell phone car accident example and the slip and fall in the *Rosen* decision. It is not uncommon to find in the history portion of the ER record, a fairly detailed description of the accident whether automobile, slip and fall, products liability, dram shop, dog bite, or some other legal theory. In addition to history provided in an ER, the paralegal needs to note the history given by the patient to the nurse and physician in any follow-up visits to the doctor's office following an injury.

History is a vital building block for the physician, nurse, therapist, or other health care provider in providing the proper care and treatment of a patient. If a patient does not relate to the physician, for example, a particular complaint or symptom concerning a part of the body, it makes it extremely difficult, if not impossible, for the physician to render the proper care and treatment for the problem. Obtaining a history of how the accident occurred is arguably relevant, important, and invaluable to the physician in assessing and treating the patient. Certainly, the force of the impact in an MVA is relevant to the nature and severity of the claimed injuries.

These initial statements in the medical records concerning the breach of duty/liability issue may end up aiding the plaintiff's attorney if they are consistent with the other evidence at trial. On the other hand, such statements may end up aiding the defendant if they are inconsistent with plaintiff's other evidence. Prior, inconsistent statements made in the history portion of a medical record may also provide the defense with ammunition for impeachment in cross-examination of the plaintiff.

Workplace Skills Tip

Pay particular attention to the treatment plan as directed by a physician. Assuming it is appropriate for the plaintiff's injuries, is the plaintiff patient following through with the treatment plan? For example, the physician may order physical therapy. If so, review the physical therapy records to determine whether plaintiff is cooperating in the treatment recommended by the physician. Entries such as "no show" or "patient terminated treatment on her own" can be troubling to explain. The plaintiff needs to have it documented with the physician that the treatment was not helping; otherwise, entries such as these can be problematic for the plaintiff's side.

Causation

Just as entries of damages and breach of duty may appear in a chart, so too may entries appear relating to the element of causation. Continuing with the patient who received the right knee injury, assume this chart entry from the treating physician four months after the MVA:

> *Pt in today with new complaints of pain in her neck (started last week) besides her right knee, which was injured in her MVA 4 months ago. She wonders if neck problem was caused by MVA. Told her no because it's been almost 4 months since MVA.*
>
> J.C. Lervick, M.D.

Compare that example of a treating physician's chart entry with this example of the treating physician's chart entry a year after the MVA:

> *It's been a year and pt's persistent rt knee complaints of pain and decreased ROM have been consistent ever since MVA—believe knee problems related to her MVA.*
>
> J. Sooper, M.D.

The first chart entry establishes that a new complaint concerning the neck, which first began four months after the MVA, was not caused by that accident. The plaintiff would be hard-pressed to maintain that position at trial. Also note that the chart entry by the ER nurse noted no neck complaints and specifically noted that the patient voiced "no other complaints" other than the knee. The second chart entry by the treating physician, however, establishes that the knee injury is definitely "related to" (caused by) the accident in question.

These chart entries made by independent health care professionals contemporaneously with the care and treatment of the patient are believable and powerful evidence in a litigant's case. The personal injury paralegal must develop the habit and skill of knowing the legal theories of the case as well as all facts of the case. As has been demonstrated, medical records may contain a wealth of information supporting or contradicting many aspects of the plaintiff's case in addition to the damages aspect.

List and Order of Medical Records

As an aid to the paralegal who may be reviewing medical records for the first time, it may be helpful to have some knowledge beforehand what is actually contained in the records and the typical order in which certain records can be located. Unfortunately, the paralegal will soon realize that what is contained in a physician's office record or in a hospital record is not uniform from physician to physician, hospital to hospital, or state to state. The following would be some of the typical items and the typical order in which they would appear in a history and physical examination:

- CC (chief complaint)
- HPI (history of present illness)
- PMH (past medical history)
  Illnesses
  Surgical history
  Medications
  Allergies
  Social history (married, occupation, habits—drugs, alcohol, smoking)
- Family history
- ROS (review of systems)
- Physical exam
  General
  Head
  Eyes
  Ears
  Nose
  Mouth and throat
  Neck
  Chest
  Lungs
  Heart
  Abdomen
  Extremities
    Breast
    Rectal
    Pelvic
    Vascular
- Neurologic exam
- Psychiatric exam (if done)
- Laboratory tests
  X-ray
  EKG
  Other
- Impression (Or differential diagnosis: The goal of the differential diagnosis process is to consider all possible diagnoses and then to begin the process of ruling out or ruling in until there is a final diagnosis for which treatment can begin. Usually, the most likely diagnosis is listed at the top.)
- Plan

The paralegal will review hospital records as discussed above. So that the paralegal also has some knowledge of these records beforehand, the following would be the typical items and the typical order in which they would appear in a hospital record:

- Face sheet (all I.D. information, insurance, contacts)
- Signature sheet (signature of all providers)
- MAR (Medication administration records: A chronological listing of medications administered with dosages and times of administration.)

- Cardiac monitoring
- Physician orders
- Lab
- Radiology
- Nursing notes
- Discharge planning
- Ancillary services (speech, occupational therapy, social services)
- History and physical/consults
- Physician notes
- Patient consents
- Operative notes
- Discharge summary/other

The student should also review the sample hospital records from "Quality Care Central" contained in Appendix 2, Exhibit 2-4. With regard to ER records, the paralegal should know that each hospital treats these records differently. Some hospitals do not consider an ER admission part of a hospital record.

Medical Proof by Treating Physician

Ultimately, at trial or by trial deposition, the treating physician will be testifying on the following items concerning the plaintiff's personal injury:

- The patient's history.
- The patient's **subjective complaints** on each visit (e.g., complaints of pain, restricted motion, difficulty lifting, problems at work).
- Any **objective findings** verifying those subjective complaints (e.g., tests such as pulmonary function test, X-rays, lab tests, MRI).
- Dates of each examination, test, surgical procedure, and results.
- **Diagnosis**—the condition that is causing the medical complaints.
- Care and treatment (e.g., physical therapy, prosthetics, surgery, medication prescribed).
- Cause of the injury, condition, or symptoms (e.g., the MVA, the dog bite, the explosion of the product).
- Prognosis—how the injury will affect the patient in the future (e.g., future medical care, future medical bills, effect on patient's daily living, permanent impairment, permanent disability).

Subjective Complaints
The patient's own complaints to a health care provider (e.g., complaints of pain, restricted motion, difficulty lifting, and problems at work).

Objective Findings
Any objective findings verifying those subjective complaints (e.g., tests such as pulmonary function test, X-rays, lab tests, MRI).

Diagnosis
The condition that is causing the medical complaints.

Important Items in Medical Records

With the scope of the physician's anticipated testimony in mind as just outlined, there are some important items in the medical records upon which the paralegal should be focused as the case is being prepared for trial. This list is not necessarily exhaustive, but it represents some basic, important items in medical records that bear upon the proof of the plaintiff's personal injury claim at trial:

- Review the history that the patient provides to the health care provider, including the initial visit as well as each visit thereafter. Any physician will tell you that without the element of history it is difficult, if not impossible, to form a proper diagnosis and to properly care for and treat a patient. As discussed earlier in this chapter, history is what the patient (or others, as in ER example above) relates to the health care provider concerning the patient's complaints, symptoms, injuries, and the etiology (cause) of those injuries. As also mentioned earlier, what a patient states in an ER visit, a physician's first office visit, or later visits may also contain statements about how the accident itself occurred, which may or may not support plaintiff's liability theory in a later lawsuit.

- What are the patient's subjective complaints? (pain, limitation of motion, loss of strength, numbness, difficulty walking, lifting, etc.)
- Are the patient's subjective complaints verified by any objective findings? (muscle spasm, abnormal or positive test results, X-ray, lab tests, CT, MRI)
- How soon after the alleged trauma (car accident, slip and fall, product malfunction) did the plaintiff seek medical treatment? Generally, the more time that passes from the traumatic event until symptoms or complaints of an injury first arise, the less likely the traumatic event caused the injury. Did the plaintiff seek medical attention the day of the accident? A week later? A month later? Several months later? Recall the entry earlier in this chapter in which the physician did not believe that neck complaints were related to an MVA that occurred four months earlier.
- In an MVA, in particular, is the injury described as major or minor? What is the force of the impact and amount of damage to vehicles? Were the "jaws of life" needed to remove the plaintiff from the vehicle? Did the plaintiff arrive in the ER by ambulance?
- Are the plaintiff's complaints consistent throughout treatment on different dates with different health care providers?
- Are the plaintiff's complaints consistent with this type of injury? For example, a patient with a low back injury who complains of pain throughout the entire circumference of a leg is not consistent with a pinched sciatic nerve. A pinched sciatic nerve would only produce pain down the back of the leg.
- Pain and suffering is likely to be alleged in the complaint. Are complaints of pain noted in the chart? How frequently? Is pain medication being prescribed? What type(s) of medication and how often? Review the list of medications contained in Appendix 2, Exhibit 2-5.
- Look for priors. This area has already received a great deal of discussion in this chapter and the previous chapter. For example, a plaintiff may claim a severe, disabling low back injury. Plaintiff gives deposition testimony under oath of no previous low back injuries. Past medical records obtained by the defense contradict the testimony of no previous low back injuries. This sets up the plaintiff for a failure in his or her personal injury case. Priors are probably one of the most significant reasons for defense verdicts and reduced verdicts in the trial of a personal injury case.
- Look for any lapses in treatment/overtreatment. A red flag should appear to the paralegal if a substantial amount of time elapses between treatments. Is the plaintiff truly in as severe a condition as alleged? Is the plaintiff truly motivated to become well again? Similarly, it is not uncommon to find evidence of claimed overtreatment, particularly by chiropractors. At some point, why is it that this patient is not showing improvement or cure after all of this treatment? A word of warning—the notes of chiropractors are typically difficult to read and decipher. Chiropractors also use specific codes in describing their treatment on a billing. Some defense teams will use those codes in cross-examination of a chiropractor to try to establish overtreatment of a patient. The subject of medical codes is discussed later in this chapter.

- Be on the alert for any chart entries describing the patient with terms such as **"functional overlay," "psychosomatic,"** or even **"malingerer."** The use of the first two terms by a plaintiff's treating physician can mean that the plaintiff is exaggerating complaints, making complaints because he or she is craving attention, or complaining of pain, but the doctor is finding no physical cause for the pain. A malingerer means that the plaintiff is grossly exaggerating symptoms or just plain pretending or "faking it." Use of any of these terms by a plaintiff's physician generally does not bode well for a plaintiff at a trial before a jury. The use of the first two terms gives the defense the argument that the plaintiff has no real injury—"It's all in his or her head." While extremely rare, the word "malingerer" may show up in a chart. It is a word that can only spell disaster for a plaintiff's personal injury case.

- Physical therapy notes are typically detailed. They tend to show precisely what the patient is capable of doing or not doing. Physical therapists' notes will typically record detail in terms of range of motion, lifting, what the patient has tried to do, cannot do, and is actually capable of performing. Physical therapists as well as lay medical witnesses can be very effective witnesses at trial.

- Do not disregard or overlook handwritten notes in the chart, whether written by a nurse, therapist, or physician. As difficult as these notes may be to decipher, they can be very important. Sometimes even a brief, handwritten note by a nurse documenting a phone call of a patient calling in with certain information can end up being a crucial piece of evidence.

Functional Overlay

The plaintiff may be exaggerating complaints, making complaints because he or she is craving attention, or complaining of pain, but the doctor is finding no physical cause for the pain.

Psychosomatic

The plaintiff may be exaggerating complaints, making complaints because he or she is craving attention, or complaining of pain, but the doctor is finding no physical cause for the pain.

Malingerer

The plaintiff is grossly exaggerating symptoms or just plain pretending or "faking it."

No-Fault Legislation/Motor Vehicle Accidents

Related to the important items in medical records just discussed, the paralegal may be located in a no-fault jurisdiction, which will necessitate focusing on other items in medical records. The subject of no-fault insurance will be discussed in more detail in Chapter 15. It is necessary to have a brief understanding at this point because no-fault statutes impact the subject of medical records.

States with no-fault systems mandate that all motorists carry their own insurance to cover economic losses such as medical bills and wage loss sustained in an MVA. No suit may be maintained against the other driver for those losses. However, if the injured person has received a more serious injury, these statutes will typically allow the injured party to sue the other driver for non-economic losses such as pain and suffering, inconvenience, and permanent impairment/disability if a certain threshold has been met.

For example, the State of Florida's no-fault statute requires that before a tort claim may be maintained for non-economic loss, there must be a "significant and permanent loss of an important bodily function" or a "permanent injury" or a "significant and permanent scarring or disfigurement."[1] The District of Columbia's no-fault statute states that one can maintain a tort civil action from an automobile accident only "if the injury directly results in substantial permanent scarring or disfigurement, substantial and medically demonstrable permanent impairment … or a medically demonstrable impairment that prevents the victim from performing all or substantially all of the material acts and duties that constitute his or her usual and customary daily activities for more than 180 continuous days."[2]

Minnesota's no-fault statute allows a suit for personal injuries if any one of the following threshold requirements is met: (1) a "permanent injury," (2) a "disability for 60 days or more," or (3) reasonable medical expenses that "exceed $4,000."[3]

No-fault statutes only apply to injuries sustained in MVAs. Therefore, a personal injury paralegal who is in a no-fault jurisdiction will need to know what the threshold is for maintaining a personal injury suit in a car accident. The paralegal will need to be focused upon whether or not the medical records are supporting or contradicting the particular jurisdiction's threshold requirements. In reviewing records, entries relating to a permanent injury may be the focus. Entries relating to whether or not a plaintiff is back to work may be the focus if disability is the threshold issue in question.

Assume the paralegal is in a no-fault jurisdiction that has one threshold requirement for a suit for non-economic losses—a permanent injury. Assume that the plaintiff's treating physician has given the opinion that plaintiff has a permanent injury. Assume that plaintiff submits to a physician of defendant's choosing for an IME. Assume the IME physician gives the opinion that the plaintiff has not sustained a permanent injury. What then? Now there is a fact issue created. The jury will be asked in a special verdict form, "Did the plaintiff receive a permanent injury in the MVA in question? If the jury answers "yes," the plaintiff will be able to recover various non-economic damages for items such as pain and suffering, inconvenience, mental anguish, permanent impairment/disability. However, if the jury answers the question "no," the plaintiff will recover no non-economic damages. This is because the statutory threshold requirement to obtain those non-economic damages was not met. Plaintiff's only recovery will be from plaintiff's own no-fault insurance carrier for his or her economic loss—any reasonable medical expenses, lost wages, or other applicable no-fault benefits.

Medical Coding

Medical Coding
A system of classification of medical care and treatment that converts evidence of medical treatment in medical records into universal code numbers.

There is a system of classification of medical care and treatment called **medical coding** that converts evidence of medical treatment in medical records into universal code numbers. Those code numbers are then contained in the medical billing for the particular care and treatment. This coding procedure is used by government health plans, private health insurance companies, workers' compensation carriers, and others. It provides a system for determining, for example, whether a certain procedure such as an appendectomy with its special code is eligible for reimbursement by Medicare. It is used by health insurance carriers, workers' compensation carriers, and no-fault insurance carriers to determine whether the medical diagnosis, procedure, or test is covered under the policy. It is mentioned here because the paralegal, in collecting medical bills of the plaintiff, will likely see these various codes contained within the billing. It is also mentioned here because

Workplace Skills Tip

As the paralegal is reviewing medical records, he or she should be on the alert for chart entries to use as blowups for the jury. Consider some examples: From the patient: "Doc, my leg hurts so much; some days I feel like I could pass out. I can't do my job like I used to, and I know I'll have to quit and do something where I'll make peanuts." From the doctor: "This is absolutely one of the worst fractures I've ever seen." From the nurse: "The patient complains of severe pain."

medical coding/medical classification is a growing field within the health care and insurance industry. Health care facilities and various types of insurance companies hire paralegals to work in the area of reviewing medical records and medical billing. The student should find the case in Exhibit 13-2 interesting, as it relates to the issue of improper billing based upon coding.[4]

EXHIBIT 13-2 Relevant Case Law

State Farm Mutual Automobile Insurance Company, Appellant, v. Twyman E. Bowling and Terry Bowling, Appellees.

District Court of Appeal of Florida, Second District.

Morris, Judge.

State Farm Mutual Automobile Insurance Company appeals a final judgment entered after a jury verdict in favor of its insureds, Twyman Bowling and Terry Bowling, in the amount of their uninsured motorist (UM) policy limits. On appeal, State Farm raises three evidentiary issues. We see no error in the trial court's rulings on two of the issues, but we find merit in the third issue raised by State Farm. Accordingly, we reverse the final judgment and remand for a new trial on damages.

Mr. Bowling filed suit against State Farm seeking coverage under the UM provision of his policy for injuries he received in an automobile accident. Mrs. Bowling filed a claim for loss of consortium. The case proceeded to a jury trial, after which the jury returned a verdict in favor of the Bowlings for $944,154.50. Upon motion by State Farm, the trial court reduced the judgment to the UM policy limits of $100,000.

State Farm's witness list indicated that Debra Pacha had been retained by State Farm as an expert witness to testify to the reasonableness of the charges submitted for the medical treatment provided to Mr. Bowling. Ms. Pacha testified at her deposition that she was asked to testify "concerning the reasonableness of charges for medical treatment rendered to" Mr. Bowling. She testified that she compared the bills to the medical treatment records and found "extreme abuse in regards to the coding, billing[,] and medical record documentation" of four of Mr. Bowling's main medical care providers. She testified that as for those four providers, "there is absolutely nothing within that documentation that is supportive or representative of any of the billed procedures that I have reviewed." Her report also indicated that she reviewed $278,000 in medical bills and found that $111,000 in charges did not have any supporting medical codes....

As in a suit for personal injury, a plaintiff seeking UM coverage must demonstrate that his or her medical expenses are reasonable and necessary.... "Just as she would in a suit against the tortfeasor, the insured [seeking UM recovery] bears the entire burden to prove that her claimed damages were reasonable, necessary, and related to the accident."... "It is well established that the plaintiff in a personal injury suit has the burden to prove the reasonableness and necessity of medical expenses.... To meet this burden, the Bowlings used a one-page summary of Mr. Bowling's medical bills and Mr. Bowling testified that the charges were reasonable. State Farm attempted to refute this evidence with the testimony of Ms. Pacha.

*On appeal, State Farm argues that the trial court erred in excluding the testimony of Ms. Pacha as State Farm's medical billing and coding expert. We agree....

As part of its defense that Mr. Bowling fabricated or exaggerated his injuries, State Farm argued that Mr. Bowling's medical providers fabricated or exaggerated the medical care necessary for his alleged injuries. Ms. Pacha's testimony that the bills did not correlate to the treatment in the medical records was relevant to prove this defense....

As to Ms. Pacha's qualifications, it is clear from her deposition that she has specialized knowledge and training to express an opinion on whether the medical bills were properly coded and whether they correspond to the medical records documenting the purported treatment.... Pacha took

(Continued)

EXHIBIT 13-2 *(Continued)*

multiple education courses in the field of coding, she passed a national board examination, and she is a licensed Registered Medical Coder, which allows "the auditing of the documentation, billing[,] and coding" of physician offices, hospitals, and ambulatory surgical centers. She attained the status of a Diplomate of the American Board of Forensic Examiners after taking an examination and teaching education courses. Moreover, she gained professional experience analyzing and reviewing medical coding for various clients such as the FBI, the State Attorney's Office, Federal Express, Wal–Mart, the insurance industry, and attorneys—both plaintiff and defense. Therefore, Ms. Pacha's training and experience qualify her as an expert in medical billing coding.

In granting the Bowlings' motion to exclude Ms. Pacha's testimony, the trial court found that Ms. Pacha is not qualified to give an expert opinion regarding whether the bills were reasonable. This was error. While Ms. Pacha does not have the necessary medical background to render an opinion on whether the medical care allegedly provided to Mr. Bowling was reasonable, she does have the requisite skill and training to render an opinion on whether the bills submitted by his medical providers accurately reflect the care documented in the medical records of those same providers. This was directly relevant to the amount of damages claimed by the Bowlings....

Ms. Pacha was State Farm's only witness who could testify in support of State Farm's defense that the medical bills submitted for recovery by Mr. Bowling were inaccurate and therefore unreasonable. This testimony was especially important because at least two of Mr. Bowling's medical providers admitted at trial that certain bills included items that should not have been billed.

The trial court abused its discretion in excluding the testimony of Ms. Pacha, and we reverse the final judgment and remand for a new trial on damages consistent with this opinion.

Source: State Farm Mutual Automobile Insurance Company v. Bowling, No. 2D10-1505 (Fla. Dist. Ct. App. 2012).

A sample medical bill that includes medical coding is shown in Exhibit 13-3. Medical coding is done by a person who abstracts and assigns the proper number code into a medical billing. The coder checks the chart to verify that the medical procedure was, in fact, done. The medical coder then assigns the correct code to report the procedure performed and to provide the medical biller with the information necessary to process a claim for reimbursement by the appropriate insurance company or by Medicare. This sample bill is a hospital bill showing treatment for an injury to a foot. The first charge is for lidocaine, a local anesthetic used

Workplace Skills Tip

Though medical coding is an entire profession on its own, you can educate yourself about the basics using online resources. First, however, you need to know what you are looking for. Three important medical coding systems are:

(1) CPT Procedure Codes, which is maintained by the American Medical Association and details medical, surgical, and diagnostic services;

(2) HCPCS Supply/DME Codes Level I, which includes CPT codes, and Level II, which is a system used to identify products, supplies, and services that are absent from the CPT;

(3) ICD-10-CM Diagnosis Codes, which is the new coding system that the Department of Health and Human Services has required the entire medical industry to adopt in an effort to clarify coding as to diagnoses and reasons for seeking medical care.

There are numerous online resources for defining the commonly used codes on medical bills. You can use a search engine such as Google to find the code definition, or you can go to sites such as www.findacode.com and www.icd9data.com.

EXHIBIT 13-3 Medical Bill

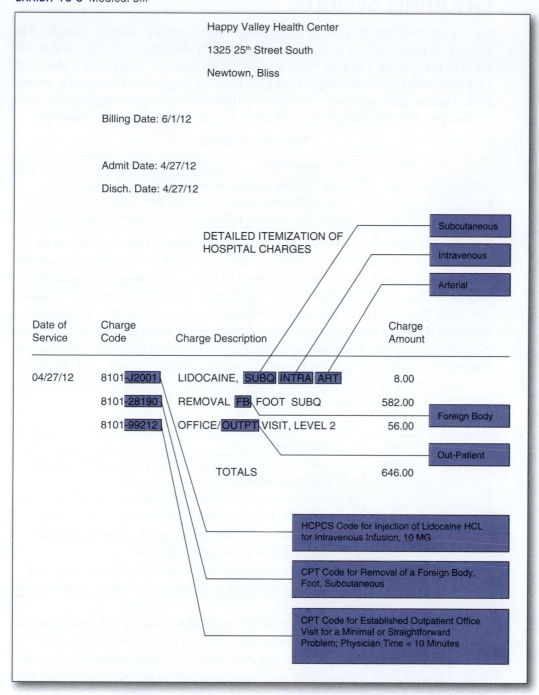

Happy Valley Health Center

1325 25th Street South

Newtown, Bliss

Billing Date: 6/1/12

Admit Date: 4/27/12

Disch. Date: 4/27/12

DETAILED ITEMIZATION OF
HOSPITAL CHARGES

Subcutaneous

Intravenous

Arterial

Date of Service	Charge Code	Charge Description	Charge Amount
04/27/12	8101-J2001	LIDOCAINE, SUBQ INTRA ART	8.00
	8101-28190	REMOVAL FB FOOT SUBQ	582.00
	8101-99212	OFFICE/OUTPT VISIT, LEVEL 2	56.00
		TOTALS	646.00

Foreign Body

Out-Patient

HCPCS Code for Injection of Lidocaine HCL for Intravenous Infusion, 10 MG

CPT Code for Removal of a Foreign Body, Foot, Subcutaneous

CPT Code for Established Outpatient Office Visit for a Minimal or Straightforward Problem; Physician Time = 10 Minutes

for a subcutaneous injection, which is an injection into the fatty part of the skin below the dermis and epidermis. The code for this procedure is 8101-J2001. The prefix 8101 is not actually part of the billing code; it is specific to the Happy Valley Health Center. The code itself is J2001. The next charge is for the removal of "FB." This stands for a "foreign body." This could be anything from a piece of glass to a fishhook. That code is 8101-28190. The final charge is for an office visit, which is a "Level 2." This is a short office visit with a doctor for a minor, straightforward problem. There are four levels of office visits. A "Level 1" is a visit with a nurse. "Level 3" and "Level 4" are reserved for more serious office visits.

Charting Systems

Nurses and physical therapists, in particular, have various charting systems. The goal of all such systems is, of course, to properly document the care and treatment of the patient. The four types of charting systems are (1) **narrative charting**, (2) **problem-oriented charting (SOAP)**, (3) **PIE charting**, and (4) **charting by exception**. The narrative system is simply a narrative diary of each contact by the nurse or therapist with the patient. The following is an example of narrative charting.

Narrative Charting

Date	Time	Progress Notes
10/19/11	0900	c/o weakness and dizziness. Still has sore throat. Temp 102. Leg wound healing well. Eating normally. No change in bowel patterns. No tenderness. No c/o pain.

Problem-oriented charting is the "SOAP" method. This system was developed by Dr. Lawrence Weed in 1969 and revolutionized the charting process. Before its development, it was not uncommon to find in a physician's progress note a comment such as "same as above" or "no change." Under this method, "S" stands for subjective data (what the patient tells the nurse or therapist); "O" stands for objective data (the health care provider's own tests or observations such as blood pressure or weight); "A" stands for assessment or appraisal (what the provider believes is occurring based upon the subjective and objective data); and "P" stands for plan (what is to be done such as "neurologic consult"). The following is an example of "SOAP" charting.

Problem-Oriented Charting (SOAP)

Date	Time	Progress Notes
10/19/11	0900	**S:** Patient reports no change in symptoms since last visit. Scheduled to undergo MRI in 2 wks.
		O: Patient presents with significant guarding with movements. Left straight leg raise limited to 50 degrees. Gait normal.
		A: Patient demonstrating decreased trunk mobility and persisting positive left straight leg raise.
		P: Patient will have progressive pool rehab exercises on a 3x per week basis for 3 weeks as per physician's orders.

PIE charting is similar to the SOAP method because it is focusing on the problem. The initials stand for "problems," "interventions," and "evaluation." In this type of charting, the problem is noted with a "P" plus a number for reference. The following intervention and evaluation entries are also numbered with the same number as the number identifying the problem. The following is an example of PIE charting.

PIE Charting

Date	Time	Progress Notes
10/19/11	0900	P#1: Decreased ROM with left leg.
		IP#1: Instructed patient to do home leg strengthening exercises and ROM exercises.
		EP#1: Patient making progress with home exercises, seems very motivated; wonders if there are any other exercises she could be doing.

Charting by exception was developed to reduce the time required for documentation. The system utilizes a flow sheet with specific abbreviations such as check marks, asterisks, and arrows. A check mark ($\sqrt{}$) signifies that an assessment was made, and there were no abnormal findings. An asterisk symbol (*) signifies that an abnormal finding was noted, and it is described at the bottom of the flow sheet. An arrow symbol ($\rightarrow$) is used to denote that the patient's status is unchanged from the previous entry with the asterisk. The following is an example of exception charting.

Charting by Exception

Upstate Bliss Medical Center
Nursing/Physician Flow Sheet
Date:_____to _____

Cardiovascular assessment	$\sqrt{}$ 1250	* 1630

Significant findings/Initials

1630 Pitting edema R lower extremity

Signature

Summarizing Medical Records

THE SYSTEM

As stated at the outset, ideas are being presented throughout this book about how a certain paralegal task should properly be performed, based on the author's vast experience as a personal injury attorney. However, once the paralegal commences work in a personal injury law firm, corporate legal department, or government agency the paralegal should perform that task in the method and manner required by that firm, legal department, or agency. With regard to many activities of a personal injury paralegal, there is no true right or wrong. Each employer will have a certain method, procedure, or form that it prefers to use concerning an area of its personal injury practice.

Before preparing an effective medical summary for the attorney, the paralegal needs to develop a system for organizing and maintaining all medical records,

Workplace Skills Tip

Just because you joined a firm or organization whose forms and systems were all developed and in place before you arrived does not mean that you cannot improve upon them. However, always ask permission before deviating from the standard form or system and explain politely why your change would be an improvement. The new firm or organization may choose not to take your advice or may be grateful for the suggestion.

which may be voluminous. This was discussed in some detail in Chapter 12. The paralegal may choose to organize working copies in a more logical manner for review and analysis. A complete copy of each set of records should be made. Each page of the copied records should be numbered. Note the date and content of the records received on the "Requested/Received" tracking form, which was mentioned in Exhibit 12-6 in Chapter 12. Keep the original records received from the facility intact—as received—in a separate file folder with the name of the facility on it. These may end up being the medical records from that facility that will be introduced as evidence at trial. As mentioned in Chapter 12, in discussing a particular record in final argument, it makes it easier for the jury if the attorney can simply direct the jury's attention to a page number in a medical record for their review in deliberations.

MEDICAL RECORDS SUMMARY

After medical records have been organized according to office protocol, a medical summary will be completed on a particular facility's records. A separate summary is prepared for each facility. An optional step is to also prepare a complete, chronological summary by date of all records of every facility received. Such a summary is contained in Appendix 2 in Exhibit 2-13. Each personal injury firm, legal department, government agency, or other employer will presumably have its own system.

The individual medical facility summary is a basic summary of an individual health care provider, which is a chronological summarization of the entries in the provider's records. The name of the particular facility is placed at the top. The medical records summary form lists the following in columns: (1) the date of service, (2) the physician and his specialty, (3) the type of record, (4) a *brief* summary of the entry/record, and (5) a "comments," "notes," or "follow-up" section for the paralegal to offer opinions or other comments. An example of the basic medical records summary form just described is as follows:

Happy Valley Clinic

Medical Records Summary of _____

Date of Service	Dr./Facility	Type of Record	Chart Entry	Comments and Follow-Up

If the paralegal maintains the above summary in a spreadsheet such as Microsoft Excel, the paralegal will be able to sort the entries in a variety of ways such as by date, by doctor/facility, and by type of record. This is helpful for spotting patterns or selectively reviewing only certain subsets of data. A paralegal should not place his or her opinions or personal comments in the summary of the entry or record ("Chart Entry"). For example, in the summary of the office visit described above, the paralegal should not add anything in the chart entry to the effect of "She seems to be making a good improvement." That note could be misunderstood by the attorney as coming from the mouth of the physician. Any such opinions or personal comments should be reserved under the column entitled "Comments and Follow-Up" in the summary form so that there is no misunderstanding. This column might be reserved for items such as noting a reference in the chart that patient has been seeing another physician, a reference to a prior, a reference to a consult by another physician, or some other important item perhaps requiring further follow-up or investigation.

As has been stressed throughout this textbook, each attorney, firm, company, or agency will have its own forms for accomplishing certain medical-related tasks such as medical authorizations, letters requesting medical records, and medical summaries. To illustrate this point, review Exhibit 2-13 in Appendix 2 and compare it with a common medical records summary outlined above. The Appendix form is a specialized form in which the attorney wanted all known medical facilities where plaintiff was treated to be integrated together, placed in chronological date order by date of treatment, and for a specific page number to accompany the date of the entry. Note also in that same form, the attorney required the paralegal to note important chart entries in bold or italics.

Memo to Attorney Following Medical Review and Summary

Finally, it can be very beneficial to the attorney if the paralegal provides a memo or e-mail along with the medical summary outlining anything particularly helpful or harmful. It is also beneficial to have the paralegal attach to the memo a copy of the medical document with the helpful or harmful information color highlighted. In addition, as previously mentioned, the paralegal should briefly note in the "Comments" section any particularly noteworthy information from the chart, such as the name of a witness or the fact that plaintiff is now seeing another physician. It is also beneficial to receive from the paralegal his or her observations and any recommended course of action with examples, such as:

- "Plaintiff appears to be over-treating."
- "Plaintiff appears to possibly have a drug addiction."
- "Plaintiff's complaints are not consistent."
- "We should possibly consider an IME."
- "This doctor really goes to bat for us—see comment about permanent injury."

Electronic Medical Record (EMR)

Most of the medical records that the paralegal will be reviewing will be paper-based records. These are records in which the entries are either typed or handwritten. These records do require a significant amount of storage space. Paper records stored in various locations are difficult and time consuming to collate to a single location for review by a health care provider. The process is simplified with electronic records. As might be expected, there is a major shift to EMRs underway in this country. In fact, Congress has adopted the Health Information Technology for Economic and Clinical Health (HITECH) Act. This was enacted as part of the American Recovery and Reinvestment Act. Congress imposed both incentives of $44,000 per physician under Medicare and penalties of decreased Medicare and Medicaid reimbursements for physicians who fail to use EMRs by the year 2015. Thus, EMRs are well on their way to becoming a mainstay in the medical field. The HITECH Act also strengthens HIPAA privacy, security, and enforcement.

A sample EMR is contained in Exhibit 13-4. One definite advantage is that the problem of legibility of handwritten records is eliminated. Another advantage is that they are searchable by keyword, making certain information buried in the voluminous records easier to find. On the other hand, this record is a template that may contain information that is not pertinent to every patient and which contains arguably a myriad of check boxes, diagnostic codes, and irrelevant questions. Criticism has been made that EMRs are more concerned with billing than with patient care. Whether or not electronic record keeping improves efficiency, patient privacy, and the quality of medical health care remains to be seen. For the personal

EXHIBIT 13-4 Electronic Medical Record

Dx of CONGESTIVE HEART FAILURE

Dx of HYPERTENSION

Dx of HYPOTHYROIDISM

Dx of PRESBYOPIA – OU

Dx of PSEUDOPHAKOS – OU

Dx of MACULAR DEGENERATION – DRY – OS

Dx of VERTIGO

Dx of COUMADIN THERAPY

Completed by: _____

Pain Assessment

Pain: has pain; severity level 1; scale utilized: 0–10; duration: >1 week

Reported by: patient

Location: back – lower

Description: aching

Pain increased by: movement

Pain decreased by: rest

Analgesic: no

Completed by: _____

Advance Directive validation

Have you ever been given information about Advance Directives? yes

Do you have a Living Will? no

Do you have a Durable Power of Attorney for heath care? no

Completed by: _____

(Continued)

EXHIBIT 13-4 *(Continued)*

Past Medical History

ATRIAL FIBRILLATION

CONGESTIVE HEART FAILURE – diastolic dysfunction – echocardiogram Dec. 2009 Ef 65%, moderate mitral regurgitation, aortic stenosis (valve area 1.25 cm)

HYPERTENSION

HYPOTHYROIDISM

HYPERLIPIDEMIA

PRESBYOPIA – OU

PSEUDOPHAKOS – OU

MACULAR DEGENERATION – DRY –OS

VERTIGO

COUMADIN THERAPY secondary to atrial fibrillation

Social History: lives with husband, active

Marital Status: married

Occupation: retired

Risk Factors

Alcohol usage

Number of times in the past year >4 drinks: never

---

injury paralegal, as time goes by, EMRs will become more and more prevalent. However, as discussed in this chapter and in Chapter 12, there will always be the need to obtain all records, which include past medical records. Many of those will still remain in a paper form.

Reviewing and Summarizing Medical Records

Reviewing, analyzing, and summarizing medical records is truly an art to be learned and a skill to be honed. There is no magic formula. It requires effort and practice on the part of the paralegal. The key to preparing an effective medical summary is to try to strike a balance between making it too cursory versus simply rehashing everything in the records. Making it too cursory will require the attorney to go back and review the voluminous records. Making it too detailed simply defeats the purpose of a summary. With time, patience, and practice, it will become second nature and the proper balance will be struck. After preparing your first medical summary, hopefully the attorney will provide guidance as to the attorney's expectations for the summary. This is an area of expertise that is invaluable to a personal injury attorney. Believe it or not, the confident and dedicated paralegal will likely reach a point in which his or her knowledge and experience in medical issues will exceed that of the attorney. Many personal injury attorneys come to extensively rely on the knowledge and experience their paralegals have acquired in medical-related issues.

CASE **13.1** Hypothetical Case: Developing Workplace Skills

You are a paralegal in a plaintiff's personal injury firm that handles medical malpractice cases and negligence and abuse cases against nursing homes and retirement homes. The firm represents Margo Young in a case against a local nursing home. Margo's mother, a 80-year-old woman, fell out of bed at the Sunshine Nursing and Retirement Home and was injured. A newer attorney in the firm is handling the case. You receive the following e-mail.

To: CJK

From: Ron Newby

As you know, I have not done this type of work for very long, but I know you are very experienced in medical issues with your nursing background. I'd appreciate it if you'd give me a hand with the Young case. There is a chart entry in this case dated January 14, 2012 that I don't understand. It is attached to this e-mail. Would you please decipher everything for me. Please decipher all medical terms and all abbreviations contained in this chart entry.

Besides deciphering all of the abbreviations, what is "0200," and what is a "Glasgow score"? Also, what is an "Incident Report?" Is that a type of report the defendant nursing home would have to produce in discovery if we asked for it in a RFPD? You can just send me an e-mail back. I would appreciate it if you could provide this to me no later than tomorrow noon. Thanks. Bill your time for this assignment to the Margo Young file-RLN1007.

| 1/14/12
0200 | 80 y/o ♀ found lying on floor moaning–apparently fell out of bed. A&O. MAE but c/o pain LA. LA movement appears WNL Small bruise above LE. PMH: CHF & DJD . Also suffers from EAHF. BP 190/100. Takes Lotrel for HTN. Glasgow score 14. Asked for H2O and helped back into bed. Called Dr. P. E. Grinnell. Incident Report filed. |
| | A. Mickley, R.N. |

"What is your lawyer's diagnosis?"

CHAPTER **SUMMARY**

The personal injury paralegal should determine goals for the tasks of reviewing and summarizing a plaintiff's medical records. Two important goals are (1) to reduce the time that the attorney needs to spend in reviewing those records and (2) to assemble a summary of records for the attorney that is efficient and concise.

While the main thrust of medical records concerns the element of damages, the personal injury paralegal must always be scrutinizing the records for other elements of the particular tort that is being alleged in the case. For example, in a negligence action, in addition to damages, entries in the chart may address the elements of breach of duty and causation.

The history portion of an ER record may contain statements by the patient or others such as ambulance attendants or law enforcement personnel that will describe how the accident occurred. If the plaintiff later testifies at

trial to a different version of how the accident occurred, the plaintiff may be impeached with the ER record under the business records, prior inconsistent statements, and admission exceptions to the hearsay rule. History is information provided to the health care provider, including items such as current complaints, the onset of the symptoms, and family history of illnesses or conditions. History is vital information to the health care provider in providing proper care and treatment to the patient. It is in the history portion of an ER record or in an office visit to a physician that the paralegal may find information concerning other elements of the claim in addition to damages. A personal injury paralegal needs to pay particular attention to the history portion of any medical record.

In becoming efficient and productive in reviewing and analyzing medical records, the personal injury paralegal must learn various medical terminology, medical abbreviations, medical symbols, and other medical information. Other medical information the paralegal will learn are the various types/categories of information contained in medical records and the typical order in which they are found in the records. It is also helpful to study the medical specialties of various physicians (pediatrician, dermatologist), various medications and their use, medical terminology, and charts portraying human anatomy—all of which are contained in Appendix 2.

Some jurisdictions have an automobile no-fault system in place. The significance for the personal injury paralegal is that these statutes typically prescribe a certain threshold that must be reached before a plaintiff may maintain a tort action for non-economic damages. If the threshold is not met, plaintiff makes no tort recovery and is left with having his or her special damages/economic damages (lost wages and medical bills) paid by plaintiff's own no-fault insurance carrier.

The personal injury paralegal may be exposed to medical coding. This is a system for assigning a number code in a medical billing for a particular test, condition, illness, procedure, or surgery mentioned in the medical records. Coding may be important in establishing whether or not proper billing was made by a health care provider when comparing the bill against the medical records themselves.

There are four basic charting systems typically used by nurses and physical therapists: (1) narrative, (2) problem-oriented charting (SOAP), (3) PIE charting, and (4) charting by exception. The paralegal needs to become familiar with the various types in order to become more efficient at reviewing and analyzing medical records.

Each law firm (plaintiff or defense), corporate legal department, or government agency will likely have their own forms to utilize for summarizing medical records. It is an art to be learned. The goal is to not be so brief that the attorney needs to go back and obtain additional information but yet not be so lengthy that it ceases to be a summary. Reviewing and summarizing records are skills that will improve with practice and guidance from the lead attorney. Locating, obtaining, reviewing, and summarizing medical records are skills that can be honed to such a degree that the attorney will come to rely on the paralegal's expertise, which will likely exceed that of the attorney.

KEY TERMS

Medical History
Past Medical History
Subjective Complaints
Objective Findings
Diagnosis

Functional Overlay
Psychosomatic
Malingerer
Medical Coding
Narrative Charting

Problem-Oriented Charting (SOAP)
PIE Charting
Charting by Exception

REVIEW QUESTIONS

1. What are some worthwhile goals for reviewing and summarizing medical records?
2. Explain why it is important to have a good grasp of all issues in the case besides just damages before reviewing the plaintiff's medical records.
3. What is "history" in the medical sense, and why may it play a significant role in a personal injury case?
4. Under what exception(s) to the hearsay rule might an ER record of how an accident occurred come into evidence at trial?
5. In the ER record in the cell phone/knee injury car accident example used in the text, the following words and abbreviations were used:
   a. ambulatory
   b. c/o
   c. pt.
   d. gait
   e. military time of 2130 and 2205

Using both the Internet and the medical abbreviations found in Appendix 2, Exhibit 2-10, look up the meaning of these words and also decipher the time of the accident and the time of arrival at the ER from the military time used in the ER chart entry.

6. What are the four types of charting systems? In the problem-oriented system, what do the initials SOAP stand for?
7. What is the ultimate goal of a good medical summary?

chapter 14

THIRD-PARTY LIABILITY INSURANCE

"There are worse things in life than death. Have you ever spent an evening with an insurance salesman?"

Woody Allen

Introduction

Before considering the subject of insurance in the study of torts and personal injury, one might reasonably ask this question: Why study insurance? The answer lies in a brief review of two previous chapters. Chapter 1 examined the primary purpose of our American tort system, which is to provide reasonable compensation in the form of money damages to an injured victim. The quotation, made tongue in cheek at the beginning of Chapter 6 by the author's senior partner and mentor, observed that: "The best defense in the world is no money."

An injured person's ability to be reasonably compensated by a tortfeasor defendant for a personal injury will depend upon either of the following factors being present:

1. Defendant has adequate personal assets with which to satisfy any judgment.
2. Defendant has sufficient insurance with which to satisfy any judgment.

If both of the two factors are missing, however, all is not lost for the injured party. The injured party's own insurance may afford some relief in the form of money compensation for the injury. That type of insurance is no-fault coverage, uninsured motorist coverage, and underinsured motorist coverage, which will be discussed in the next chapter. The type of insurance and the amount of insurance available in a personal injury case will have the practical effect of influencing the strategy and posturing of the case for trial and settlement. In addition to the all-important facts and law in the case, insurance is sometimes "the elephant in the room."

What Is Insurance?

In today's world, virtually everything can be insured—your house, your car, your furniture, your jewelry, your boat, your motorcycle, your snowmobile, your mortgage, your health, and, of course, your life. The study of insurance can consume an entire book in itself. For our purposes, the important types of insurance for torts and personal injury are third-party liability insurance and certain types of first-party insurance, such as uninsured motorist, underinsured motorist, and no-fault insurance. Before discussing third-party liability insurance, which is the subject matter of this chapter, some general principles of insurance will be discussed.

Quite simply, an **insurance policy** is a contract. One party, the insurer—also referred to by various names, such as "the insurance company," "the company," "the insurance carrier," and "the carrier"—is obligated to pay money upon the occurrence of some specified contingency or loss due to certain causes. In return, the other party to the contract, "the insured" or "policyholder," agrees to pay a certain premium to be protected from the contingency or loss. Insurance policies are governed by the principles of contract law. The rights and obligations of both the insurer and the insured are defined in the insurance contract.

Insurance Policy
A contract between two parties, the insurer and the insured.

The goal of the courts in interpreting an insurance contract is to identify and enforce the intent of the parties. If a contract, such as an insurance contract, contains clear and unambiguous language, there is no need to engage in any rules of construction. Rules of construction are aids to the courts in trying to determine the true meaning and intent of the parties to a contract. These are sometimes also referred to as canons of construction. If a contract is ambiguous, however, the courts may need to resort to those rules or canons of construction. Without trying to provide an exhaustive list, some common examples are:

- Ordinary words are to be given their ordinary meaning unless it is shown that they are mutually understood by the parties to have a special meaning.
- Every part of a contract will be given effect, where possible.
- Written words prevail over printed words.
- The contract will be construed most strongly against the party who drafted it.
- Punctuation will be disregarded when it interferes with the obvious sense or meaning.

A factor favoring an interpretation of an insurance policy against the insurer is that an insurance contract is a contract of adhesion. Contracts of adhesion were discussed in Chapter 6. There is no equal bargaining power between an insured and an insurer. Most students own a motor vehicle, which is, hopefully, insured. Trying to negotiate the premium one pays to the motor vehicle insurer would be as futile as trying to negotiate the price of an airline ticket with an airline company. Some jurisdictions have adopted the **doctrine of reasonable expectations**. This doctrine means that the insurance contract will be interpreted according to the reasonable expectations of the insured, regardless of the insurance policy language.

Doctrine of Reasonable Expectations
The insurance contract will be interpreted according to the reasonable expectations of the insured, regardless of the insurance policy language.

Any type of insurance provided in any insurance policy is governed by each state's insurance laws. Insurance contracts providing insurance against the risk of a loss of any type must meet the minimum requirements of state law. If an insurance policy issued by an insurer fails to meet those requirements, the courts will judicially amend the policy to provide the appropriate coverage consistent with state law. The legal action brought by an insured against an insurer asking the court to reform the policy so that it conforms to state law is called a **reformation action**.

Reformation Action
An action brought to reform an insurance contract to make it conform to applicable state statutes.

Risk Distribution

The basic concept of any insurance is to allocate and distribute risk. Risk is a part of life. If one owns and drives a motor vehicle, there is a risk of becoming involved in a collision with the potential result of property damage, injury, or even death. Assuming one is not a passenger, there are various methods by which one could reduce that risk. Some of those methods are:

- Take a driver's training course.
- Make sure the vehicle is in tip-top mechanical condition.
- Drive infrequently.
- Drive short distances.
- Always wear a seat belt.
- Drive only on roads with minimal traffic.
- Do not drink alcohol or use drugs while driving.
- Do not text or use a cell phone while driving.
- Drive only at certain times of the day.

Another option to reduce the risk of a financial loss from a motor vehicle collision is to purchase insurance to cover that risk. The risk of a financial loss is then being allocated or distributed among many others. For a certain amount of money called the premium, the insured is paying into a general fund into which many others also pay. The insured may suffer a loss and be paid back more than the premium the insured paid in. On the other hand, the insured may suffer no loss and only contribute to the payment of a loss to someone else in the group. However, the insured has traded the risk and the gamble of having a personal, catastrophic, unknown financial loss for a small, known maximum amount, which is the premium paid. The word "gamble" was used. From the insurance company's standpoint, it is making a bet that it will not have to pay out more than it took in from the premiums received from the various insureds. The insurance company determines the amount to be paid for the bet—the premium.

Sharing in the Risk

Insurance companies like it when their insureds share in the risk. The underlying theory is that it encourages less risky behavior on the part of the insureds. Insureds may tend to be more careful if they know that they will share in a loss. How is that risk sharing accomplished? There are different methods. For example, if an insured has collision coverage that covers damage to the insured's own automobile, the insured may have a **deductible** amount of $100, $500, or $1,000. Assume the insured has a deductible of $1,000. This means that if the insured's vehicle is damaged in the sum of $3,000 the insured will pay the first $1,000, and the insurance company will pay the remaining $2,000. If the damage to the vehicle is $1,000 or less, the insured will bear the entire loss.

If the insured has a health insurance policy, there may be a **co-pay** provision for medical or drug expenses. An example is an 80/20 co-pay. The insured will pay 20%, and the insurance company will pay 80% of the expenses up to a certain amount, such as $5,000. After that $5,000 amount is reached, the insurance company will then pay the entire remainder of any incurred medical or drug expenses up to the limit stated in the policy.

Deductible
The out-of-pocket amount that is required to be paid by the insured first after which the insurance company then pays under the policy.

Co-Pay
The amount that is paid by the insured along with the insurer—for example, 80/20 co-pay means insurer pays 80% and insured pays 20%, usually up to a certain amount after which insurer pays all up to the limits of coverage.

Composition of an Insurance Company

All insurance companies are made up of three basic departments or branches:

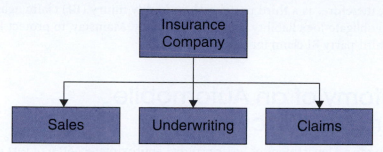

Those in sales are the revered group. By selling the insurance contracts to the insured customers, they bring to the company the premium dollars that make up the company's gross sales or gross income. Those in underwriting determine the amount of the bet, the amount to charge for an insured's premium. That premium is determined by various factors. Continuing with the motor vehicle example, the underwriter will gather facts, including, but not limited to, the age of the driver, the health of the driver, the age and type of the motor vehicle, the insured's past driving record and loss history, whether the vehicle will be driven in an urban or rural area, other people who will be driving the vehicle, and the amount and limits of the insurance coverage. Factors such as these assist the company in determining the company's risk and in providing a basis to set a premium to be charged. If a loss occurs, the claims department is in charge of determining whether coverage is proper, investigating the facts of the claimed loss, and supervising and ultimately denying or paying the claim.

Essentials of Third-Party Liability Insurance

There are two parties to an insurance contract—the insured and the insurer. In a first-party insurance contract, the insurer is indemnifying or protecting the insured for a loss suffered by the insured. Assume that Joe has a health insurance policy with Second Rate Insurance Company. Joe is injured from a trip and fall at home, incurs doctor and hospital bills, and is off work for a year. Second Rate, the health insurance insurer, as Joe's own insurer, will indemnify or pay Joe's doctor and hospital bills. If Joe also has a disability insurance policy with 19th Century Insurance Company, 19th Century, the disability insurance insurer and also as Joe's own insurer, will indemnify or pay a portion of Joe's income loss for the year. In both examples, Joe is making a claim, as a first party, for insurance benefits against his own company, the second party.

A third-party insurance contract or policy insures the insured for a loss sustained by a third party who is not the insured and who is not a party to the insurance contract. That third party is making a claim against the insured. For example, a standard automobile liability insurance policy requires the insurer to pay on behalf of the insured all sums that the insured becomes legally obligated to pay as damages arising out of the ownership, maintenance, or use of a motor vehicle. Assume Joe was operating his motor vehicle with his girlfriend, Mary, sitting next to him as a passenger. Joe falls asleep, and the vehicle goes into a ditch and hits a tree. Mary receives a personal injury. Joe has the standard automobile liability insurance policy with Mainstay Mutual Insurance Company, which protects him from claims for damages made by third parties arising out of an automobile accident. Mary is a third party to the automobile liability insurance policy Joe has with Mainstay Mutual Insurance Company. She was injured by Joe's negligent conduct. She will, therefore, as a third party, make a bodily injury (BI) claim against Joe. This will obligate Joe's liability insurance company, Mainstay, to protect Joe from Mary's third-party BI claim for money damages.

Anatomy of an Automobile Insurance Policy

According to a Department of Justice study,[1] approximately 60% of tort cases are automobile accident related. According to the United States Census Bureau 2012 Statistical Abstract, the National Data Book, in 2009 there were approximately 33,000 people killed in car accidents in the United States and approximately 2.2 million injured. Because of the significant number of automobile accidents, the injuries and deaths caused thereby, and its effect on our tort system, it is important to examine an automobile insurance policy.

    The student's attention is directed to the sample automobile insurance policy issued by the hypothetical AUTOKING Mutual Insurance Company ("AUTOKING") in Appendix 3, Exhibit 3-2. In actuality, it is an automobile insurance policy that will be encountered in the real world. An automobile insurance policy will provide various types of insurance, which will be discussed in this chapter and the next. It will provide third-party insurance. This insurance is also called third-party liability insurance or sometimes just liability insurance. A personal automobile policy such as the AUTOKING policy will also provide first-party insurance. First-party insurance and third-party insurance are two totally different concepts. Both are extremely important to understand, and for that reason, the discussion of the two has been broken into two separate chapters. The focus in this chapter will be on the portion of the automobile policy that relates to BI third-party liability. The focus in the next chapter will be on the portion of the automobile policy that relates to first-party liability protecting the person, specifically, uninsured motorist liability, underinsured motorist liability, and no-fault liability.

Declarations Page

Declarations Sheet
Typically, the first page of an insurance policy, which contains basic information concerning who is covered and what kinds of insurance and limits are included in the policy.

Typically, the first page of an automobile policy is a Declarations Page or a **Declarations Sheet**. It is sometimes referred to as "the Declarations" or "the Dec Sheet." A sample Dec Sheet is shown in Exhibit 14-1, which relates to an AUTOKING automobile insurance policy insuring a motor vehicle owned by hypothetical insureds, Holly and Paul Thompson. Assume that Paul and Holly Thompson are husband and wife who have a daughter named Jessica, who is a student. Jessica lives at home with her parents. Paul and Holly own a 2001 Saturn, which is available for Jessica to drive. Paul and Holly have their own business with a business vehicle insured with another insurance company. The 2001 Saturn is insured with AUTOKING (see Appendix 3, Exhibit 3-2). A Dec Sheet will typically contain various items, such as:

- The name(s) of the insured (the named insured).
- The term of the policy.
- The vehicle(s) insured.

EXHIBIT 14-1 Declarations Sheet

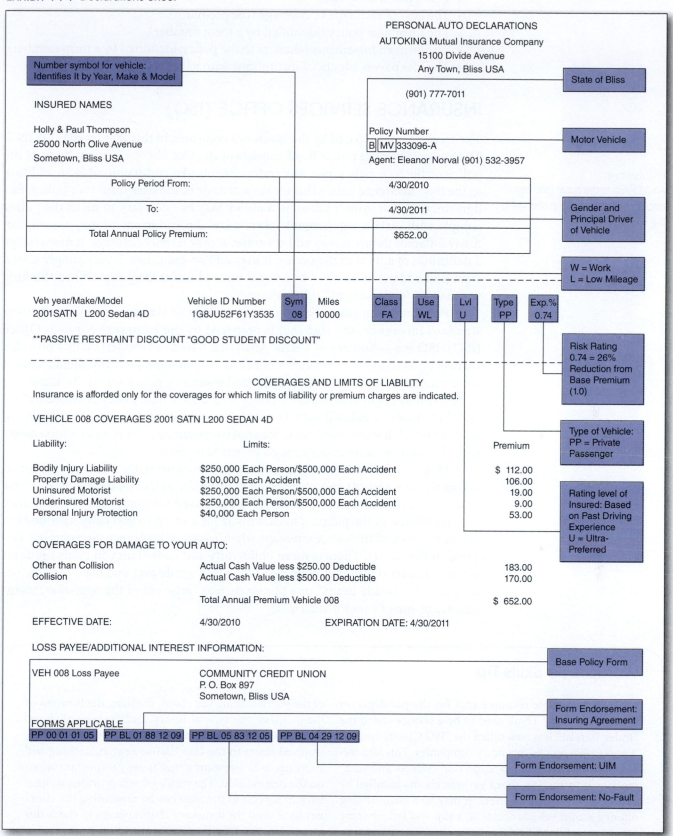

- The types of coverage.
- The cost of each type of coverage (the premium).
- The form base policy (identified by a form number).
- The form endorsements (changes to the policy, identified by a form number).
- The loss payees (financial institutions with a lien on any vehicle).

INSURANCE SERVICES OFFICE (ISO)

Endorsement
An addition to the basic form insurance policy that makes a change in the policy.

The Dec Sheet is prepared by the insurance company, in this case by AUTOKING. The entire insurance policy itself consists of the Dec Sheet, the main body of the policy or the base policy, plus any endorsements. An **endorsement** is an addition to the base insurance policy that makes a change in the base insurance policy. Endorsements of an insurer added to a policy may be necessary to make the policy comply with certain requirements of state law. An endorsement may accomplish many different things. It may add coverage. It may restrict coverage. It may change a definition of a term in the policy. It may add an exclusion. It may simply note a change of address or name an additional insured under the policy. When thinking of the word "endorsement," think "change."

Portions of an insurer's policy may consist of standard forms containing standard insurance language that is prepared by the Insurance Services Office (ISO). ISO is a subsidiary of Verisk Analytics, based in New Jersey. ISO provides various types of information and services to its insurance company clients. One of its services is to provide these standardized insurance policy forms. An insurance company may begin assembling its policy with a form base policy provided by ISO and then continue to build with its own form endorsements unique to the state or states in which it writes insurance. Some of the insurance company's endorsements may also be basic form endorsements prepared by ISO.

One of the advantages of insurance companies using the standard ISO forms is that the same words and phrases are continually and consistently used. These same insurance words and phrases have been used for many years in insurance policies offered to the public. This has made for a uniform and consistent body of law in the area of insurance coverage when issues of insurance coverage are litigated in the courts. There is more uniformity and consistency in court opinions when the court is interpreting some of the same words over and over, such as "occurrence" or "bodily injury" or a phrase such as "arise out of the operation, maintenance or use of a motor vehicle."

Workplace Skills Tip

There is a valuable resource tool for the paralegal on the defense team. There used to be a service called the "Index Bureau." It is now called the "ISO Claims Search." It is available only to insurance companies. This ISO service provides a central location that collects and summarizes information about various claims handled by various member ISO insurers. It may be a claim arising out of a motor vehicle accident, a slip and fall, or some other type of liability claim or workers' compensation claim. The summary will typically disclose the name of the party making the claim, the date, the location of the incident, the type of injury, and the type of claim. Of course, if the particular company did not report the resolved claim to the ISO Claims Search, nothing will show up. It is a resource that is very important when on the defense side. The paralegal will provide excellent backup service to the attorney by reminding the attorney to remind the insurance claims person to check this source on a case that the firm is defending.

BINDER

An insurance term with which the paralegal should be familiar is a **binder**. A binder is a temporary contract for insurance. It is typically issued by the insured's insurance agent immediately following the application for insurance but before receiving official authorization for issuance of the policy from the insurance company. The binder has the legal effect of obligating the insurer to pay the insurance proceeds if a loss happens to occur before the insurer acts upon the application. Otherwise, if the insurer acts upon the application and chooses not to accept coverage, the binder is of no further legal effect.

Binder
A temporary contract for insurance.

A CLOSER LOOK AT THE DEC SHEET

Reviewing the Dec Sheet shown in Exhibit 14-1 from top to bottom will provide valuable insight into many insurance principles with which the personal injury paralegal needs to be familiar. This insurer's Dec Sheet is identified as the "Personal Auto Declarations."

The Insureds

Under the heading of "INSURED NAMES" are listed the names of Holly and Paul Thompson. These two people are named insureds. A named insured is the owner of the policy. A named insured is also the only person with authority to conduct certain important transactions, such as making changes to the policy or canceling the policy. It is not uncommon for an insurance policy to list additional insureds. For example, if the Saturn vehicle was actually used in connection with some separate real estate business owned by the Thompsons, there may be additional language on the form, such as: "ADDITIONAL INSUREDS: P & H Thompson, Real Estate, LLC."

The Policy Number and Insurance Agent

The policy number is listed on the Dec Sheet in the upper right-hand corner as "BMV333096-A." Different insurance companies may use certain letters as code in the policy number to identify the type of policy or the state involved. In this case, AUTOKING includes the letters, "BMV" in the policy number to represent that this is a motor vehicle (MV) policy issued in the state of Bliss (B). Directly below the policy number is the name of the local agent, Eleanor Norval, who sold the policy to the Thompsons and the agent's phone number.

Effective Dates of Policy

The Dec Sheet will also show the exact dates that the policy is in effect. In this case, it is from April 30, 2010 to April 30, 2011. If an automobile accident with this vehicle occurred before April 30, 2010 or after April 30, 2011, there would be no coverage under this insurance contract.

Occurrence Policy
The automobile accident giving rise to the personal injury claim must occur during the policy period.

Occurrence Policies vs. Claims-Made Policies

The AUTOKING policy is an **occurrence policy**. The automobile accident giving rise to the personal injury claim must occur during the policy period. In this case the automobile accident and loss or damage from that accident would need to occur between April 30, 2010 and April 30, 2011. A **claims-made policy**, on the other hand, requires that the claim be made during the policy period, regardless of

Claims-Made Policy
Typically a malpractice insurance policy insuring physicians, attorneys, and other professionals. For coverage, the claim must be made during the policy period.

when the particular occurrence or negligent act occurred. A claims-made policy is typically a malpractice insurance policy insuring physicians, attorneys, and other professionals.

Total Annual Policy Premium Paid for Various Coverages

The next item shown after the policy period is the "Total Annual Policy Premium." It is in the amount of $652. This represents the total premium for all of the various individual premium charges for the different individual coverages under the policy. The individual coverages and their individual premium costs are shown in the middle of the Dec Sheet under "COVERAGES AND LIMITS OF LIABILITY."

Codes/Abbreviations of Underwriting Department

Following the total annual policy premium of $652, there is a display of various columns running horizontally across the page. The columns begin with "Veh year/ Make/Model" and end with "Exp.%." This is a summary of information gathered and analyzed by the underwriting department of AUTOKING to determine the amount of the premium. Some of the information contains codes or abbreviations used by the company's underwriting department. Each insurance company will have its own method of coding. The following is a coding for the hypothetical AUTOKING policy in the hypothetical State of Bliss. Some insurance companies in the real world, however, may use similar or identical types of coding.

For example, beginning with the first heading of "Veh year/Make/Model" at the far left and moving to the right, the vehicle is identified as a 2001 Saturn L200 4-door sedan. The next number is what is frequently referred to as a "VIN" or Vehicle Identification Number. The VIN for this Saturn is the 15-digit number shown there. Continuing to move to the right, there is a "Symbol" heading with a number of "08" underneath. This is a number symbol given to the vehicle that identifies it by year, make, and model. The vehicle has 10,000 miles on it. The "Class" heading of "FA" refers to the gender and principal driver of the vehicle as obtained from the insurance application. The "Use" heading identified as "WL" means that the vehicle will be used to drive to work (W), and it is a low (L) mileage vehicle. The "LvI" heading of "U" is a rating level of the insured based on past driving experience. Insured drivers are classified by AUTOKING as "S" for standard, "B" for below standard, "P" for preferred, and "U" for ultra-preferred. "PP" under the "Type" heading means that the type of vehicle is a private passenger vehicle. Incidentally, AUTOKING would designate a commercial automobile as "CA" and a pickup would be a "PU."

Finally, there is the heading of "Exp.%" and a number of ".74" below that heading. This means that these insureds, the Thompsons, are considered a good risk. AUTOKING starts out by assigning a 1.0 as a basic loss experience rating number to each new insured driver. The insurance company will keep tabs on any moving violations and motor vehicle accidents in which their insureds are involved, particularly as to the frequency of losses and the severity of the losses. As the insured driver continues to remain an insured of AUTOKING each year, a loss experience rating is developed for that insured. For example, if the insured driver continued, year after year, to have no accidents, the 1.0 rating would actually go down a certain amount each year. The Thompsons have apparently been with AUTOKING for some time and have had a good driving record as their experience rating is a .74%. If another insured had frequent accidents with some involving serious injuries or deaths, their experience rating would go up. For example, a driver with those types of accidents may have a 1.25 rating. What this means is that the Thompsons are receiving a 26% reduction from the base premium because of a good driving history. The driver with the 1.25 rating is paying an extra 25% above the base premium because of a poor driving history.

Policy Discounts

The Dec Sheet also indicates other information gathered by the underwriting department. Note there is a "GOOD STUDENT DISCOUNT." This discount is given for any student, high school or college, with a B average. Jessica is apparently a good student as the company is giving a Good Student Discount. There is also a discount for a "Passive Restraint." This means that the vehicle has the appropriate seat belts and airbags.

Liability Coverage

Continuing down the Dec Sheet, the next category is "COVERAGES AND LIMITS OF LIABILITY." Under the heading of "Liability," the first type of liability insurance listed is "Bodily Injury Liability" coverage with limits of $250,000 Each Person and $500,000 Each Accident. **Bodily injury (BI) liability** is third-party liability insurance that covers another person's injury or death caused by the negligence of the insured driver. As discussed in Chapter 4, personal injury damages may include both economic loss such as medical expenses and lost wages and non-economic loss such as pain and suffering and disfigurement. As the name suggests, this type of coverage insures against injury to people, not damage to motor vehicles or any other type of property damage.

Bodily Injury (BI) Liability
Also referred to as BI coverage, which is coverage for claims made by others against the insured for personal injury or death.

Overlapping Coverage

There is an important issue concerning liability insurance that is appropriate to be discussed at this point. If an insured has several vehicles all insured with liability coverage, those coverages may not be added together or "stacked" in order to obtain additional liability coverage. The concept of adding coverages on multiple vehicles owned by an insured by stacking is sometimes permitted in first-party coverage such as uninsured motorist, uninsured motorist, and no-fault, which will be discussed in the next chapter. However, similar to stacking, there may be separate policies that overlap the risk, when an insured is operating another person's vehicle that has liability insurance. This presents the issue of overlapping third-party liability coverages, which is not really stacking. Stacking refers solely to adding coverages of multiple vehicles owned by an insured in the first-party contract.

A policy providing third-party liability protection typically provides coverage for an insured who is driving the vehicle of another person with that person's permission. Assume that one of the three AUTOKING insureds in the Thompson family is operating another insured vehicle owned by another person with that person's permission. For the purpose of the example, assume Holly Thompson is driving an automobile owned by her friend Jill. Assume that Jill is insured with another insurance company, First Rate Mutual, with the same BI coverage limits of $250,000/$500,000. Assume that Holly is negligent and strikes another vehicle causing injury to the other third-party driver, Frank. In a third-party claim made by Frank for his personal injuries, he will likely sue both the owner of the vehicle, Jill, and the driver, Holly. There are overlapping liability coverages with AUTOKING and First Rate Mutual.

Which liability carrier will be primarily responsible for paying the loss—AUTOKING or First Rate? Each state's law will be different. One jurisdiction may follow a "closest to the risk" analysis and make the owner of the vehicle that was involved in the accident the primary policy and the driver's policy the excess policy. Another state may impose primary third-party liability on the driver's liability insurer. As mentioned at the beginning of the insurance discussion, however, an insurance policy is a contract. While it is beyond the scope of this textbook to examine this particular issue in detail, the provisions of each policy will need to be examined to determine the responsibilities of each insurer. This will raise issues of "other insurance" and which policy is "excess." A policy may also provide through an "escape clause" that if other insurance is available to the insured, there will be no coverage under the insured's policy. Another policy may have a "pro rata" clause limiting the liability insurer's responsibility to pay with the other policy on a proportionate or pro rata basis.

Umbrella Policy

Umbrella Policy
Third-party liability coverage that is over and above the regular liability insurance in force; usually issued in increments of $1 million.

The selection of appropriate policy BI limits is important. If they are too low, the insured may be exposing personal assets and income. It is not uncommon for a person to also purchase an **umbrella policy**. An umbrella policy is third-party liability coverage that is over and above the regular liability insurance in force. It is typically reasonable in cost and is sold in increments of $1 million. If the Thompsons had a $1 million umbrella policy they would, in effect, have total third-party BI liability insurance coverage of $1,250,000 for an injury to a person who made a claim against the Thompsons. The umbrella policy may or may not be with AUTOKING. An umbrella policy also covers for losses over and above limits on other policies. For example, if the Thompsons had their home insured with a homeowners policy with liability limits of $500,000, the $1 million umbrella policy would, in effect, provide coverage of $1.5 million for liability claims arising out of their home.

Limits of Liability/Bodily Injury Liability

The limits of BI liability in the AUTOKING automobile policy need to be discussed. In this case there are liability limits of $250,000 for "Each Person" and $500,000 for "Each Accident." Coverage is split up or limited on a per person basis. If there is an automobile accident in which more than one person is injured or killed, the maximum amount that can be paid to any one person is $250,000. This is true even if the nature and extent of the injuries would justify a higher dollar amount. Also, no matter how serious the injuries are to each claimant/plaintiff, the total amount paid to all cannot exceed the sum of $500,000—the maximum aggregate amount of the limits for any one accident.

With regard to limits of liability, each state has its own requirement of minimum liability limits that must be carried on insured motor vehicles. All states except New Hampshire require liability insurance. Alaska has the highest minimum requirement with $50,000/$100,000. Ohio has the lowest with $12,500/$25,000.

Limits of Liability/Property Damage Liability

"Property Damage Liability"(PD) is the next item below "Bodily Injury Liability." This type of third-party liability coverage would be applicable if an insured driver of the Saturn negligently damaged another person's property. The PD limits in the AUTOKING Policy are $100,000. For example, the negligent insured driver may damage another person's garage, house, garden, fence, or motor vehicle. It is common to describe the liability limits in an insurance policy by providing the BI limits followed by the PD limits. For example, a description of 50/100/50 means that the BI limits are $50,000 per person and $100,000 per accident with property damage limits of $50,000. These types of liability limits are referred to as **split liability limits**. The liability limits are broken down by (1) each person, (2) each occurrence, and (3) property damage.

While it may be more common for commercial motor vehicles, it is possible to obtain on a personal vehicle what are called **combined single limits (CSL)**. CSL provide one total limit of liability for all aspects of an accident, including bodily injury and property damage. There is no individual liability limit per person, per accident, or for property damage. If the insured had a $500,000 CSL policy, this is the maximum that could be paid. If one plaintiff received a personal injury award of $300,000, another plaintiff received a personal injury award of $200,000, and there was $75,000 in property damage, the total damage for both injuries and property damage is $575,000. The insured would have $75,000 of personal exposure.

Split Liability Limits
Limits of BI per person, per accident, and property damage, such as $50,000/$100,000/$25,000: $50,000 per person; $100,000 per accident; $25,000 property damage.

Combined Single Limits (CSL)
Limits that include a total for all bodily injury and property damage combined.

Uninsured Motorist, Underinsured Motorist, Personal Injury Protection

The next three types of coverage stated on the Dec Sheet under "COVERAGES AND LIMITS OF LIABILITY" are first-party types of coverage, and they will be discussed in the next chapter. These are uninsured motorist (UM) coverage, underinsured motorist (UIM) coverage, and personal injury protection (no-fault) coverage.

Limits of Liability/Other than Collision (OTC) and Collision

The final two remaining types of coverage listed on the Dec Sheet are under the heading, "COVERAGES FOR DAMAGE TO YOUR AUTO." These are coverages for "Other than Collision" and "Collision." These two types of coverage are also examples of first-party insurance, but they cover the insured motor vehicle, not a person. The term "Other than Collision" (OTC) is a newer term from the older term used for many years called "Comprehensive." **OTC coverage** covers damage to the insured's own automobile in the event that it is stolen or damaged by flood, fire, wind, or hail. If there were a bad windstorm, causing a large tree branch to come down and strike the vehicle and damage it, OTC coverage applies. Note the $250 deductible for this coverage, which is an insurance company's risk-sharing device as discussed earlier in this chapter.

OTC or Comprehensive Coverage
Covers damage to the insured's own automobile in the event that it is stolen or damaged by flood, fire, wind, or hail.

Collision coverage, with the $500 deductible, covers damage to the insured's own automobile if it collides with another vehicle or if another vehicle collides with it. It also covers damage to the insured's automobile for damage received from colliding with another object other than another automobile. In the example above under property damage liability, assume the insured negligently collided with another person's garage damaging both the garage and the insured vehicle. The garage owner would bring a third-party liability claim against the insured for damage to the garage. The insured would be covered under the property damage liability portion of the insured's policy for the garage damage. The insured would bring a first-party claim against the insured's own company for damage to the insured vehicle from colliding with the garage under the collision coverage portion of the insured's policy.

Collision Coverage
Covers damage to the insured's own automobile if it collides with another vehicle or object.

Loss Payee/Additional Interest

The heading "LOSS PAYEE/ADDITIONAL INTEREST INFORMATION" is shown at the bottom of the Dec Sheet. There is a technical difference between the two terms. Note that the Community Credit Union is actually listed as a **loss payee**.

Loss Payee
The person or entity listed in an insurance policy is a lender with some secured interest in the vehicle.

Additional Interest
The person or entity listed in Declarations has an interest in being notified of some change in the policy or cancellation of the policy.

This means that the person or entity listed is a lender with some secured interest in the vehicle. If there were a damage claim, the insurance company would need to place both the named insureds, the Thompsons, and the loss payee, Community Credit Union, on any claim settlement check. An **additional interest** means that the person listed simply has an interest in being notified of some change or cancellation of the policy. A person or entity with an additional interest has no insurance coverage. Their sole right is to be notified of any changes. For example, XYZ Corporation may be a company that is servicing the car loan by receiving payments for Community Credit Union. XYZ Corporation would have an additional interest, but the entity with the actual secured loan on the vehicle would be the loss payee.

Forms Applicable

To complete the top down analysis of the Dec Sheet, the final remaining category at the bottom of the page is "FORMS APPLICABLE." Under that heading, the student will note that there are four sets of numbers each beginning with "PP." Those four sets of numbers are insurance policy forms that have their own unique number. All four of those forms plus the Dec Sheet will make up the entire AUTOKING policy. *All four of those forms referenced at the bottom of the Dec Sheet must be coordinated and read together.*

Form PP 00 01 01 05 (The Base Policy)

The base policy form is the first numbered form, which is PP 00 01 01 05. This portion of the policy will be referred to simply as "the base policy," and the form number will not always be repeated. AUTOKING has its own code for its forms, not unlike other insurance companies. In AUTOKING's case, "PP," as used in all its forms, stands for a private passenger automobile. The numbers "00 01" represent the actual form number used in the AUTOKING private passenger automobile line of insurance business. The numbers, "01 05," the last set of numbers, means that this insurance policy base form was adopted for use in January 2005. This base policy form will contain the insuring agreement, definitions, exclusions, and other important policy information, which will be analyzed in more detail. The base policy form of this automobile insurance policy is made up of several areas that provide a reference to a particular area of insurance identified by "Part." The basic areas or parts are:

- DEFINITIONS
- Part A—LIABILITY COVERAGE
- Part B—MEDICAL PAYMENTS COVERAGE
- Part C—UNINSURED MOTORISTS COVERAGE
- Part D—COVERAGE FOR DAMAGE TO YOUR AUTO
- Part E—DUTIES AFTER AN ACCIDENT OR LOSS
- Part F—GENERAL PROVISIONS

To round out the complete policy, these are the following endorsement forms that are located behind the base policy form PP 00 01 01 05:

- ENDORSEMENT PP BL 04 29 12 09 (UNDERINSURED MOTORIST COVERAGE)
- ENDORSEMENT PP BL 05 83 12 05 (NO-FAULT PERSONAL INJURY PROTECTION)
- ENDORSEMENT PP BL 01 88 12 09 (INSURING AGREEMENT—Same as Exhibit 14-2)

Form Endorsements PP BL 01 88 12 09, PP BL 04 29 12 09, PP BL 05 83 12 05

Under FORMS APPLICABLE, besides the base policy form discussed above, there are three separate additional form endorsements to this policy listed immediately after the designation of the base policy form. These form endorsements must be read as carefully as one would read supplements to a statute. These endorsements change the language of the base policy form. The first form endorsement is PP BL 01 88 12 09. This is an endorsement changing the INSURING AGREEMENT in the base policy form. It is one page, and it is shown in Exhibit 14-2. The abbreviation "PP" AND "BL" have been explained. The number "01 88" refers to the specific form number and "12 09" refers to December 2009. The second form endorsement is PP BL 04 29 12 09. This is an endorsement adding UIM, which will be discussed in the next chapter. The form number for UIM coverage is "04 29" adopted in December 2009. The final form endorsement is PP BL 05 83 12 05. This is an endorsement adding personal injury protection (no-fault) coverage, which will also be discussed in the next chapter. The no-fault form is "05 83" and it was adopted in December 2005. Note that the three endorsements contain the additional letter of BL for the State of Bliss. The base policy does not contain the letters BL. An assumption may be that the base policy form is an ISO form and the three BL form endorsements are unique to the State of Bliss.

EXHIBIT 14-2 Policy Endorsement

THIS ENDORSEMENT CHANGES THE POLICY. PLEASE READ IT CAREFULLY.   PERSONAL AUTO

AMENDMENT OF POLICY PROVISIONS – BLISS   PP BL 01 88 12 09

II. PART A – Liability Coverage

Part A is amended as follows:

A. Paragraph A of the INSURING AGREEMENT is replaced by the following:

INSURING AGREEMENT

We will pay damages for "bodily injury" or "property damage" for which any "insured" becomes legally responsible because of an auto accident. We will settle or defend, as we consider appropriate, any claim or suit asking for these damages. In addition to our limit of liability, we will pay all defense costs we incur. Our duty to settle or defend ends when our limit of liability for this coverage has been exhausted by payment of judgments or settlements. We have the right to investigate, negotiate, and settle any claim with or without your consent. We have no duty to defend any suit or settle any claim for "bodily injury" or "property damage" not covered under this policy.

PP BL 01 88 12 09   Page 1 of 1

A Review of the Policy

In reviewing the AUTOKING Mutual Insurance Company insurance policy in Appendix 3, Exhibit 3-2, the outline of the policy is fairly simple. The policy begins with the base policy containing "Definitions" and proceeds with Parts A through F. Next are the three endorsements. The Dec Sheet is, of course, considered a part of the entire insurance policy. Following a review of the Dec Sheet, it is necessary to examine some important policy provisions in Form PP 00 01 01 05, the base policy. The base policy is the starting point but with the all-important endorsements to be read in conjunction with it. Several key portions of the liability portion of the policy will be examined. These are the INSURING AGREEMENT, the DEFINITIONS, and the EXCLUSIONS.

INSURING AGREEMENT

In the INSURING AGREEMENT under Part A—Liability Coverage of the base policy, the following is stated:

> We will pay damages for "bodily injury" or "property damage" for which any "insured" becomes legally responsible because of an auto accident. Damages include prejudgment interest awarded against the "insured." We will settle or defend, as we consider appropriate, any claim or suit asking for these damages. In addition to our limit of liability, we will pay all defense costs we incur. Our duty to settle or defend ends when our limit of liability for this coverage has been exhausted by payment of judgments or settlements. We have the right to investigate, negotiate, and settle any claim with or without your consent. We have no duty to defend any suit or settle any claim for "bodily injury" or "property damage" not covered under this policy.

However, as has been mentioned, there are endorsements or changes to the policy listed at the bottom of the Dec Sheet, and these are attached behind the base policy, Form PP 00 01 05. One of those endorsements completely replaces the above INSURING AGREEMENT paragraph in the base policy form. The endorsement replacing the INSURING AGREEMENT language is found in endorsement Form PP BL 01 88 12 09. This is the last endorsement found on the last page of the AUTOKING policy in Appendix 3, Exhibit 3-2. It is also reproduced in Exhibit 14-2.

It is crucial to begin a review of any insurance policy with any endorsements referenced in a Declarations Page/Dec Sheet. The language of the INSURING AGREEMENT is an extremely important portion of an automobile liability policy. If the endorsement language in Exhibit 14-2 and the language in the original base policy Form PP 00 01 01 05 are read carefully, it can be seen that the following sentence was eliminated from the language contained in the endorsement Form PP BL 01 88 12 09 in Exhibit 14-2: "*Damages include prejudgment interest awarded against the 'insured.'*"

Any further analysis of the INSURING AGREEMENT in the policy will need to be done from the endorsement Form PP BL 01 88 12 09 and not from the INSURING AGREEMENT language found in the original base policy. If the plaintiff's side were banking on obtaining prejudgment interest in a certain case, they would be disappointed if they did not read the endorsement Form PP BL 01 88 12 09 changing the INSURING AGREEMENT in the base policy form.

DEFINITIONS

Perhaps the law firm has a case in which a plaintiff claims no physical injury but only a psychological or psychiatric injury from the automobile accident. Would that type of injury be covered? The INSURING AGREEMENT speaks of "bodily injury" and that term is in quotes. What does "bodily injury" mean? Would it cover this type of injury? If a word is in quotations, it is likely defined in the Definitions section of the policy. The next step, therefore, is to review the Definitions section of the policy. One needs to determine, of course, if there is any endorsement pertaining to any change in Definitions. With no such endorsement affecting the definition of bodily injury, the definitions in base policy form PP 00 01 01 05 govern. "Bodily Injury" is defined in the Definitions section as: "bodily harm, sickness, or disease, including death that results." Accordingly, such a psychological or psychiatric sickness or disease would be covered. It can be seen that the Definitions portion of an insurance policy is very important. In determining an issue of coverage, courts frequently conduct an analysis of an insurance policy by analyzing the Insuring Agreement and the Definitions portions of the policy.

EXCLUSIONS

Another key portion of the liability policy is the Exclusions section for Part A—LIABILITY COVERAGE. An **exclusion** precludes coverage for certain events or certain actions or conduct engaged in by the insured. Review the main EXCLUSIONS section found in the base policy form PP 00 01 01 05 for Part A. In checking, there are no form endorsements changing the exclusions portion of the base policy. To provide the paralegal student some exposure to exclusions, the first one listed is an important one to examine in the Part A—Liability Coverage section. Under the EXCLUSIONS Section A.1., there is no liability coverage for any insured "who intentionally causes 'bodily injury'...." This is an important exclusion that has been the subject of much litigation. In essence, the policy is covering negligent acts but not intentional, purposeful acts that are in the control of the insured. Note also that exclusion "C." excludes any liability coverage for "*punitive or exemplary damages.*"

Exclusion
An exclusion in an insurance policy precludes coverage for certain events or certain actions or conduct engaged in by the insured.

DUTIES/CONDITIONS

The student should be aware of Part E in the base policy form. That section is entitled "PART E—DUTIES AFTER AN ACCIDENT OR LOSS." These duties are sometimes also referred to as conditions. They place responsibility on the insured for certain actions. If those actions are not accomplished, the insurer has the right to disclaim or void coverage. For example, the first duty under Paragraph A is to promptly notify the insurer of how, when, and where the accident or loss occurred. Furthermore, Paragraph B requires the insured's cooperation in the investigation, settlement, or defense of any claim or suit as well as other conditions. As a practical matter, if there has been a violation of one or more of the insured's duties under this section, the insurer is not necessarily relieved of any further obligation under the policy. Typically, in many jurisdictions, the insurer must show that it was prejudiced or harmed by, for example, a late reporting of a claim. Reporting a claim late may not have made any difference whatsoever in the insurer's ability to properly investigate and defend the claim.

Workplace Skills Tip

As a personal injury paralegal, whether on the plaintiff's team or the defendant's team, you will invariably communicate with various types of insurance companies concerning various types of claims, whether casualty insurance companies, health insurance companies, or workers' compensation insurance companies. Always, always, use the company's claim number when sending a letter or e-mail to the claims representative. If you do not do so, do not be surprised if you never receive a response. Insurance companies live and die by the claim number.

GENERAL PROVISIONS

The student should also note under "Part F—GENERAL PROVISIONS" of the base policy form under "FRAUD" that there is no coverage for any insured "who has made fraudulent statements or engaged in fraudulent conduct in connection with any accident or loss for which coverage is sought under this policy." It can be seen from a review of the AUTOKING insurance policy in Appendix 3, Exhibit 3-2 that there are important provisions that require a coordinating of various sections of the policy. Many cases in litigation will involve issues concerning the Insuring Agreement, the Definitions, and the Exclusions portions of a liability policy.

Duty to Defend vs. Duty to Indemnify

Duty to Defend
The insurer's duty to defend its insured in a third-party liability claim, which will consist of defense attorney fees and other fees and costs of the litigation.

The insurer has a **duty to defend** the insured for any BI or PD claims alleged in a complaint that would be covered under the policy. For example, if the claim alleged in the complaint is that the insured was negligent, there is coverage under a third-party liability policy for negligent acts of an insured. The insurer would retain an attorney to defend the insured for the covered claim of negligence.

There is no duty, however, to defend any claim that is not covered under the policy, such as claims that the insured acted intentionally. For example, assume a claimant made a claim that the insured intentionally struck the claimant and injured the claimant. The plaintiff then brought a suit for damages based on the intentional torts of assault and battery. There would be no coverage because of the intentional acts exclusion discussed above. That very first exclusion excludes coverage for any injuries caused intentionally by the insured. Because assault and battery are clearly intentional torts and not covered under the policy, the insurer has no duty to retain an attorney for the insured to defend the insured against those non-covered claims.

The Insuring Agreement in the AUTOKING endorsement Form PP Bl 01 88 12 09 in Exhibit 14-2 states that "we will pay all defense costs we incur." While the insurer has the duty to defend the insured, it also has the right to control the defense of the case. The insurer will select defense counsel and pay counsel's fees as well as any expert costs and other costs of litigation. In the same form endorsement, the language in the Insuring Agreement is "We will settle or defend, as we consider appropriate, any claim or suit…."

Duty to Indemnify
Insurer has the duty to pay covered claims against the insured.

The **duty to indemnify** means that the insurer has the *duty to pay covered claims* against the insured. It is said that the duty to defend is broader than the duty to indemnify. This just means that if there is any claim alleged in the complaint that is arguably covered, out of several alleged claims that are clearly not covered, the insurer must defend the entire lawsuit and all of the claims. This duty to defend is determined by reviewing the allegations of the complaint. The duty may also be determined by facts obtained by the insurance company in its investigation of the claim that are independent of the complaint.

For example, assume negligence was alleged in one count of the complaint, and the intentional tort of battery was alleged in another count of the complaint. The insurer has the duty to defend both the negligence claim and the intentional tort claim. One claim—negligence—is clearly covered even though the intentional tort claim is clearly not covered because of the intentional acts exclusion. If, for example, the jury determined that the defendant acted intentionally to cause the plaintiff's injury, the insurance company would then have no duty to indemnify or pay the dollar amount awarded against the insured because of the intentional acts exclusion. Up to that point, however, because the one claim of negligence was covered under the policy, the insurer had a duty to defend all claims, including the non-covered claim of battery. If the jury determined that the insured defendant acted negligently, the insurance company would have a duty to indemnify and pay the dollar amount awarded because of the insured's negligence. In short, the insurer must defend the insured against all claims alleged in the complaint even if only one claim is arguably or clearly covered. The insurer has no duty to indemnify the insured, however, for any claim that is not a covered claim under the policy.

Reservation of Rights, Declination, and Declaratory Judgment

In many personal injury cases in which a liability insurer insures a defendant, there may be certain liability insurance coverage issues that affect the handling of the case. There are various methods by which the insurer may choose to handle an insurance coverage issue. If it appears to the insurance company that a particular claim being alleged in the plaintiff's complaint is not covered, but it is not entirely clear, the insurer may send out what is called a **reservation of rights letter**. A sample reservation of rights letter is provided in Exhibit 14-3.

A reservation of rights letter is the insurer's written notice in a letter to the insured that the insurer intends to provide a defense to the insured, but it is retaining the right to withdraw from the defense at any time if it believes there is no coverage. In the defense of an insured under a reservation of rights, the liability insurer has "one foot in and one foot out." There also may be situations in which the amount of the suit is above the policy limits of the insured. In that case, the insurer may advise the insured that its only obligation is to indemnify the insured up to the limits of the policy, and the insured may want to retain personal counsel. In many cases in which the amount of the suit exceeds the policy limits, an insured will retain personal counsel to put pressure on the insurance company to settle the case within the policy limits and protect the insured from personal financial exposure.

Because the insurer is obligated to defend all claims, the issue may arise whether or not the insurer may recover from the insured amounts spent on defense costs in the event it is found that there is no coverage under the policy. This issue could arise in the hypothetical example given earlier in which the complaint had one count of negligence and one count of battery. The insurer is obligated to defend all claims—both covered and non-covered. Negligence is covered; battery is not. If the jury found that a battery occurred, this is not a covered claim. The insurer may bring a claim against its insured to recover defense costs paid in defending the action. The courts are split on this issue. Those that allow recovery

Reservation of Rights Letter
The insurer's written notice in a letter to the insured that the insurer intends to provide a defense to the insured, but it is retaining the right to withdraw from the defense at any time if it believes there is no coverage.

EXHIBIT 14-3 Reservation of Rights Letter

AUTOKING Mutual Insurance Company   March 29, 2012
15100 Divide Avenue
Anytown, Bliss, USA 55515
901-777-7011

Mr. and Mrs. Paul Thompson
25000 North Olive Avenue
Sometown, Bliss, USA 55512

CERTIFIED MAIL   Policy #: BMV 333096-A
RETURN RECEIPT REQUESTED   Date of Loss: 8/8/10
RE: Insureds: Paul & Holly Thompson   Claim #: OFBMVC 112233B

Dear Mr. and Mrs. Thompson:

We are in receipt of a Summons and Complaint that was just filed in Apple County District Court entitled "Susan Jackson v. Jessica Thompson." Please be advised that our company has retained the law firm of Law and Order to represent both of you for the claims arising out of the automobile accident on August 8, 2010. Both of you and your daughter, Jessica Thompson, are insured by AUTOKING Mutual Insurance Company through a personal automobile policy # BMV 333096-A. This policy covers the policy period from April 30, 2010 to April 30, 2011.

Even though our company is affording you a defense of the claims arising out of this accident, our company reserves the right to deny coverage for this loss at any later date. Our company does not wave or forfeit any of the conditions, terms, or provisions of this insurance policy nor does our company waive any past, present, or future rights or defenses under the insurance policy by undertaking the defense of this action.

The allegations in the Complaint are Count 10 Negligence in the operation of the Saturn vehicle by Jessica Thompson while Susan Jackson was a passenger in the vehicle, and Count 20 Jessica was operating the motor vehicle while both Susan Jackson and Jessica Thompson were acting in the course of their employment by a business owned by Jessica's father, Paul Thompson.

Based upon the Complaint referenced above, there are questions concerning insurance coverage under your policy for the claimed personal injury damages of Susan Jackson.

Your attention is directed to the "EXCLUSIONS" portion of the policy. Exclusion A.4 provides:

A. We do not provide Liability Coverage for any "insured": 4. For "bodily injury" to an employee of that "insured" during the course of employment.

It appears that the plaintiff, Susan Jackson, is making a claim that she was an employee and was engaged in the course of employment of a business owned by Paul Thompson at the time of the accident that caused her claimed injuries. A claim made by an employee is not covered if that person is injured during the course of the person's employment as an employee of an insured.

Our company's reservation of rights is not limited to the reasons set forth above, but shall include any additional ground(s) for non-coverage or policy breach that may be revealed subsequently. Our company reserves all of its rights under the law and under the insurance policy. By reserving our right subsequently to deny coverage, our company is not intending to waive any of its rights, including its right to deny coverage or to commence a declaratory judgment action.

Our position set forth on coverage herein is based upon the facts and information currently in our possession. If you have any additional information that could cause us to re-evaluate our position, please contact us. If you have coverage available to you under any other insurance policy, you should report this loss to that company.

Donald Eugene

Claims Adjuster

by the insurer do so on the basis that the insurer was obligated to defend both covered and non-covered claims but received no premium for defending non-covered claims. Other courts take the position that insurers have no right to do this unless expressly referred to in the reservation of rights letter and there is also a policy provision expressly providing for such reimbursement.

An insurer may decide that based upon the allegations in the complaint and the insurer's investigation there is no coverage under the policy for the claims being alleged by the plaintiff. In that case, the insurer may send to the insured what is called a **declination letter**. A declination letter is a letter from the insurer to the insured advising the insured that the insurer declines to extend coverage for the claimed loss. A sample declination letter is provided in Exhibit 14-4. The insurer is walking away from the insured, both feet are definitely out, and the insured is now on his or her own. The insured will then need to retain counsel to defend the case, and the insured's assets will be personally exposed. If the insured has little to no financial resources, as a practical matter, this may affect the handling of the case for the plaintiff's team. It simply may not be worth the time and expense to pursue the case.

Declination Letter
A letter from the insurer to the insured advising the insured that the insurer declines to extend coverage for the claimed loss.

On the other hand, if the insurance company was incorrect in its evaluation of coverage, the insured will likely sue the company for breach of contract and bad faith, which will be discussed in more detail later in this chapter. Also, in a declination of coverage, the plaintiff and the defendant insured may enter into an agreement in which the plaintiff agrees to allow judgment to be taken against the defendant insured for a reasonable amount. However, the plaintiff agrees that it will not attempt to collect the judgment from the defendant insured personally, but only from any insurance proceeds of the liability insurance carrier. The defendant insured assigns all rights under the insurance contract to the plaintiff. The plaintiff may believe that the insurer's position of no coverage is incorrect. The plaintiff will then sue the insurer to collect the money judgment agreed to between plaintiff and the defendant insured, and the insurance coverage issue will be decided in that action.

Another avenue the insurer may take if it believes that there is no coverage under the policy is to bring a **declaratory judgment action**. A declaratory judgment action is an action brought in a civil case asking the court to declare the rights and duties of one or more parties. Typically, in a declaratory judgment action involving coverage under an insurance policy, the facts are not in dispute and one party or both may make a motion for summary judgment. From the insurer's standpoint, defending under a reservation of rights but then simultaneously commencing a declaratory judgment action is probably the most prudent in terms of trying to resolve an insurance coverage issue and also maintain a position of acting in good faith to the insured.

Declaratory Judgment Action
An action brought in a civil case asking the court to declare the rights and duties of one or more parties.

As a practical matter, liability insurance is the usual means by which an injured plaintiff is compensated for a tort injury. The plaintiff's team cannot bring a personal injury action and hope that the defendant has ample liability insurance

Workplace Skills Tip

One of the first items on the list of a paralegal on a plaintiff's personal injury team is to obtain insurance information from the defendant. Rule 26 of the Federal Rules of Civil Procedure makes insurance policies a required disclosure. Know the rules of civil procedure in your jurisdiction, particularly Rule 26 in which insurance policies may specifically be listed as discoverable. It may be that a written production for the policy will need to be made under Rule 34 or an insurance information interrogatory served under Rule 33. Regardless of the method, make this a top priority.

EXHIBIT 14-4 Declination Letter

AUTOKING Mutual Insurance Company   March 29, 2012
15100 Divide Avenue
Anytown, Bliss, USA 55515
901-777-7011

Mr. and Mrs. Paul Thompson
25000 North Olive Avenue
Sometown, Bliss, USA 55512

CERTIFIED MAIL   Policy #: BMV 333096-A
RETURN RECEIPT REQUESTED   Date of Loss: 1/15/11
RE: Insureds: Paul & Holly Thompson   Claim #: OFBMVC 142639B

Dear Mr. and Mrs. Thompson:

We are in receipt of a Summons and Complaint that was just filed in Apple County District Court entitled "Joseph Stewart v. Jessica Thompson." Both you and your daughter, Jessica Thompson, are insured by AUTOKING Mutual Insurance Company through a personal automobile policy #BMV 333096-A. This policy covers the policy period from April 30, 2010 to April 30, 2011. Our company has completed an investigation concerning this claim, and our company has concluded that it must deny coverage to both of you for the loss alleged in the complaint.

A review of the information obtained has disclosed facts that have led our company to conclude that there is no coverage afforded under policy #BMV 333096-A issued to Paul and Holly Thompson. Our company is advising you at this time that we are denying coverage for the loss alleged in the above-mentioned complaint. This means that our company will neither defend you nor indemnify you in connection with the losses and claims alleged in the complaint.

Our company is denying coverage for this loss because our investigation reveals that your daughter, Jessica, intentionally ran down an ex-boyfriend, the plaintiff, Mr. Stewart. The allegations in the Complaint are that on January 15, 2011, in the parking lot of Spencer Richard's Restaurant, Jessica Thompson became extremely angry and intentionally and purposely drove her Saturn automobile into Joseph Stewart causing serious and permanent injuries.

Your attention is directed to the "EXCLUSIONS" portion of the policy. Exclusion A.1 provides

A. We do not provide Liability Coverage for any "insured":

1. Who intentionally causes "bodily injury" or "property damage."

"Bodily injury" is defined in the DEFINITIONS Section of the policy as "bodily harm, sickness, or disease, including death that results."

Our company's right to deny coverage is not limited to the reasons set forth above, but shall include any additional ground(s) for non-coverage or policy breach that may be revealed subsequently. Our company reserves all of its rights under the law and under the insurance policy. By reserving our right subsequently to deny coverage on other grounds, our company is not intending to waive any of its rights, including its right to commence a declaratory judgment action.

Our position set forth on coverage herein is based upon the facts and information currently in our possession. If you have any additional information that could cause us to re-evaluate our position, please contact us. If you have coverage available to you under any other insurance policy, you should report this loss to that company. You are also advised that you should seek legal counsel of your own choosing, at your own expense, to represent you in connection with this matter.

Very truly yours,

Jerry Keller

Claims Adjuster

with no coverage issues. It is not at all uncommon to find insurance coverage issues surfacing in a personal injury case. As has been stressed repeatedly, the main purpose of tort law, as discussed in Chapter 1, is to compensate innocent victims. To try to obtain compensation for a client, the plaintiff's team sometimes needs to be very creative and needs to be familiar with third-party liability and first-party insurance issues. In some personal injury cases for the plaintiff's team, the facts of the accident and the injury to the plaintiff will be subordinated to the important issue of whether or not there is available insurance coverage to compensate the injured plaintiff. It was mentioned in a previous chapter that it is not enough just to make a *recovery*. The ultimate goal is to be able to *collect* the compensation due the plaintiff.

The Tripartite Relationship

In the defense of a third-party insurance liability claim, there is a **tripartite relationship**. This relationship is the triangular one made up of the insurer, the insured, and the defense counsel who is retained by the insurer to represent the insured, but who is paid by the insurer. This relationship can sometimes create both legal and ethical problems for the attorney. The landmark case in this area is the case of *San Diego Navy Federal Credit Union v. Cumis Insurance Society, Inc.*, 208 Cal. Ct. Rptr. 494 (Cal. Ct. App. 1984). In *Cumis*, the insurer defended the insured under a reservation of rights. The insured believed that the counsel selected by Cumis had a conflict and hired its own attorney. *Cumis* held that in instances where the insured and insurer have conflicting interests such as a coverage issue under a reservation of rights, the insurer must pay the reasonable fees and costs of the insured's counsel in addition to the attorney retained by the insurer.

> **Tripartite Relationship**
> The triangular relationship made up of the insurer, the insured, and the defense counsel who is retained to represent the insured, but who is paid by the insurer.

The important issues from the insurance defense counsel's perspective are "Who is the client?" and "To whom do the loyalties lie?" The general consensus among the courts appears to be that there is nothing inherently unethical about this tripartite relationship. The lawyer may represent both the insurer and the insured "in the absence of a disqualifying conflict of interest."[2] The rule is that the attorney may represent both, but when push comes to shove, the real client to whom loyalties lie is the insured even though the insurer is paying the attorney's fees and costs.[3] Further, if the attorney retained by the insurer obtains confidential information from the insured in the course of representing the insured, that information cannot be later used against the insured and in favor of the insurer.[4] As the Arizona Supreme Court stated in *Parsons*: "The attorney who represents an insured owes him 'undeviating and single allegiance' whether the attorney is compensated by the insurer or the insured."[5] The *Parsons* case is shown in Exhibit 14-5. *Parsons* illustrates not only the nature of the tripartite relationship, but also the principle of bad faith, the next section to be discussed.

EXHIBIT 14-5 Relevant Case Law

Ruth Parsons, a single woman, Dawn Parsons and Gail Parsons, minors, by and through their guardian ad litem, Donald S. Robinson, and Michael Smithey, by his guardian ad litem, Appellants, v. Continental National American Group, Appellee.

Supreme Court of Arizona, In Banc.

The Supreme Court, Gordon, J., held that where during course of representing the insured in the personal injury litigation the attorney who had been retained by the insurer to defend said suit obtained information from the insured indicating that the insured acted intentionally, the insurer, which was represented by the same counsel in the garnishment proceedings, was estopped from claiming that the intentional act exclusion applied, notwithstanding that personal injury suit was defended under

(Continued)

EXHIBIT 14-5 *(Continued)*

a reservation of rights agreement, and that since carrier failed to enter into good faith settlement negotiation it was liable for the entire personal injury judgment, notwithstanding that amount of such judgment was twice the policy limits.

Gordon, Justice:

Appellants Ruth, Dawn and Gail Parsons obtained a judgment against appellant and then had issued and served a writ of garnishment on appellee, Continental National American Group (hereinafter referred to as CNA). The Superior Court of Pima County entered judgment in favor of the garnishee, CNA and from this judgment appellants appealed. The Court of Appeals, Division Two, reversed the judgment of the Superior Court, 23 Ariz. App. 597, 535 P.2d 17 (1975). Opinion of the Court of Appeals vacated and judgment of the Superior Court of Pima County reversed, and it is ordered that the judgment be entered in favor of appellants in the sum of $50,000.

We accepted this petition for review because of the importance of the question presented. We are asked to determine whether an insurance carrier in a garnishment action is estopped from denying coverage under its policy when its defense in that action is based upon confidential information obtained by the carrier's attorney from an insured as a result of representing him in the original tort action.

Appellant, Michael Smithey, age 14, brutally assaulted his neighbors, appellants Ruth, Dawn and Gail Parsons, on the night of March 26, 1967.

During April, 1967 Frank Candelaria, CNA claims representative, began an investigation of the incident. On June 6, 1967 he wrote to Howard Watt the private counsel retained by the Smitheys advising him that CNA was 'now in the final stages of our investigation,' and to contact the Parsons' attorney to ascertain what type of settlement they would accept. Watt did contact the Parsons' attorney and requested that a formal demand settlement be tendered and the medical bills be forwarded to Candelaria. On August 11, 1967 Candelaria wrote a detailed letter to his company on his investigation of Michael's background in regards to his school experiences. He concluded the letter with the following:

'In view of this information gathered and in discussion with the boy's father's attorney, Mr. Howard Watts, and with the boy's parents, I am reasonably convinced that the boy was not in control of his senses at the time of this incident.

'It is, therefore, my suggestion that, and unless instructed otherwise, I will proceed to commence settlement negotiations with the claimant's attorney so that this matter may be disposed of as soon as possible.'

Prior to the following dates: August 15, 1967, August 28, 1967, and October 23, 1967, Candelaria tried to settle with the Parsons for the medical expenses and was unsuccessful.

On October 13, 1967 the Parsons filed a complaint alleging that Michael Smithey assaulted the Parsons and that Michael's parents were negligent in their failure to restrain Michael and obtain the necessary medical and psychological attention for him. At the time that the Parsons filed suit they tendered a demand settlement offer of $22,500 which was refused by CNA as 'completely unrealistic.'

CNA's retained counsel undertook the Smithey's defense and also continued to communicate with CNA and advised him on November 10, 1967:

'I have secured a rather complete and confidential file on the minor insured who is now in the Paso Robles School for Boys, a maximum-security institution with facilities for psychiatric treatment, and he will be kept there indefinitely and certainly for at least six months * * *.

'The above referred-to confidential file shows that the boy is fully aware of his acts and that he knew what he was doing was wrong. It follows, therefore, that the assault he committed on claimants can only be a deliberate act on his part.'

(Continued)

EXHIBIT 14-5 *(Continued)*

After CNA had been so advised they sent a reservation of rights letter to the Smitheys stating that the insurance company, as a courtesy to the insureds, would investigate and defend the Parsons' claim, but would do so without waiving any of the rights under the policy. The letter further stated that it was possible the act involved might be found to be an intentional act, and that the policy specifically excludes liability for bodily injury caused by an intentional act. This letter was addressed only to the parents and not to Michael.

In preparing for trial the CNA attorney retained to undertake the defense of the Smitheys interviewed Michael and received a narrative statement from him in regards to the events of March 26, 1967, and then wrote to CNA: 'His own story makes it obvious that his acts were willful and criminal.'

CNA also requested an evaluation of the tort case and the same attorney advised CNA: 'Assuming liability and coverage, the injury is worth the full amount of the policy or $25,000.'

On the issue of liability the trial court directed a verdict for Michael's parents on the grounds that there was no evidence of the parents being negligent. This Court affirmed, Parsons v. Smithey, 109 Ariz. 49, 504 P.2d 1272 (1973). On the question of Michael's liability the trial court granted plaintiff's motion for a directed verdict after the defense presented no evidence and there was no opposition to the motion. Judgment was entered against Michael in the amount of $50,000.

The Parsons then garnished CNA, and moved for a guardian ad litem to be appointed for Michael which was granted by the trial court. On November 23, 1970 appellee Parsons offered to settle with CNA in the amount of its policy limits, $25,000. This offer was not accepted.

CNA successfully defended the garnishment action by claiming that the intentional act exclusion applied. The same law firm and attorney that had previously represented Michael represented the carrier in the garnishment action.

Appellants contend that CNA should be estopped to deny coverage and have waived the intentional act exclusion because the company took advantage of the fiduciary relationship between its agent (the attorney) and Michael Smithey. We agree.

The attorneys, retained by CNA, represented Michael Smithey at the personal liability trial, and, as a result, obtained privileged and confidential information from Michael's confidential file at the Paso Robles School for Boys, during the discovery process and, more importantly, from the attorney-client relationship. Both the A.B.A. Committee on Ethics and Professional Responsibility and the State Bar of Arizona, Committee on Rules of Professional Conduct have held that an attorney that represented the insured at the request of the insurer owes undivided fidelity to the insured, and, therefore, may not reveal any information or conclusions derived therefrom to the insurer that may be detrimental to the insured in any subsequent action....

The attorney who represents an insured owes him 'undeviating and single allegiance' whether the attorney is compensated by the insurer or the insured. Newcomb v. Meiss, 263 Minn. 315, 116 N.W.2d 593 (1962).

The attorney in the instant case should have notified CNA that he could no longer represent them when he obtained any information (as a result of his attorney-client relationship with Michael) that could possibly be detrimental to Michael's interests under the coverage of the policy.

The attorney representing Michael Smithey in the personal injury suit instituted by the Parsons had to be sure at times that the fact he was compensated by the insurance company did not 'adversely affect his judgment on behalf of or dilute his loyalty to (his) client, (Michael Smithey)'. Ethical consideration 5-14. Where an attorney is representing the insured in a personal injury suit, and, at the same time advising the insurer on the question of liability under the policy it is difficult to see how that attorney could give individual loyalty to the insured-client. 'The standards of the legal profession require undeviating fidelity of the lawyer to his client. No exceptions can be tolerated.' Van Dyke v. White, 55 Wash.2d 601, 349 P.2d 430 (1960). This standard is in accord with Ethical Consideration 5-1.

(Continued)

EXHIBIT 14-5 *(Continued)*

> 'EC 5-1. The professional judgment of a lawyer should be exercised, within the bounds of the law, solely for the benefit of his client and free of compromising influences and loyalties. Neither his personal interests, the interests of other clients, nor the desires of third persons should be permitted to dilute his loyalty to his client.'
>
> The attorney in the present case continued to act as Michael's attorney while he was actively working against Michael's interests. When an attorney who is an insurance company's agent uses the confidential relationship between an attorney and a client to gather information so as to deny the insured coverage under the policy in the garnishment proceeding we hold that such conduct constitutes a waiver of any policy defense, and is so contrary to public policy that the insurance company is estopped as a matter of law from disclaiming liability under an exclusionary clause in the policy....
>
> Appellee further urges that if the appellants are entitled to a judgment against the appellee insurance company the only judgment they are entitled to is in the amount of coverage $25,000. We do not agree. The evidence shows that the insurance company was advised by their legal counsel that if they were liable the injury was 'worth the full amount of the policy.' The evidence further shows that CNA could have settled the Parsons' claim against Michael Smithey well within the policy limits and refused to do so on the basis that the settlement was 'completely unrealistic.' It is clear from the record that the carrier failed to enter into good faith settlement negotiations.... In the instant case the further fact that the carrier believed there was no coverage under the policy and so refused to give any consideration to the proposed settlements did not absolve them from liability for the entire judgment entered against the insured.

Source: Parsons v. Continental National American Group, 550 P.2d 94 (Az. 1976).

The Implied Covenant of Good Faith and Fair Dealing (Bad Faith)

Bad Faith

A breach of the implied covenant of good faith and fair dealing on the part of the insurer to the insured.

Most courts hold that in any liability insurance contract, there is an implied covenant of good faith and fair dealing, and if that covenant is breached, this is **bad faith** on the part of the insurer. It provides the basis for a tort action by the insured against the insurer. While the discussion in this chapter is on third-party liability claims, bad faith can also be the basis for a tort action in first-party claims to be discussed in the next chapter. One of the best illustrations of bad faith is the exact fact scenario as presented in the *Parsons* case in Exhibit 14-5. The insured had policy limits of $25,000. The third party apparently had a good case on both liability and damages. The attorney hired to defend the insured even expressed the opinion to the liability insurance company that the case was worth $25,000—the full amount of the policy. The insurer chose to ignore that advice, and the jury verdict ended up being $50,000.

From the insurer's standpoint, it is preferable to decline the offer to settle for the policy limits. From its standpoint, all it owes is the policy limits, which, in the *Parsons* case, was $25,000. The insurer reasons that maybe a jury will award less than that. From the insured's interest, however, to reject the offer to settle for the policy limits and gamble on a jury verdict is gambling with the insured's money since anything over the limits would need to be paid by the insured. The insurer is controlling the defense and what is to be paid or not paid. Thus, courts have taken the position, as the court did in *Parsons,* that if the insurance company wants to gamble, they will gamble with their own money and not the insured's money. The insured could sue the company for bad faith. However, it is fairly common for the insured to assign the insured's bad faith claim rights to the plaintiff, and the plaintiff will then pursue the bad faith claim.

While this scenario in *Parsons* is the classic bad faith scenario, bad faith may consist of other conduct on the part of the insurer, such as attempting to coerce the insured to contribute to a settlement, delaying or failing to properly investigate or defend a claim, rejecting the advice of its own attorney, and failing to keep the insured informed. The insurer may also find a bad faith dilemma even when it is willing to pay its limits. The liability insurance company may be justified in paying out its limits to those who come forward first and make a claim. On the other hand, in another jurisdiction, the insurance company may attempt to place the insurance limits on deposit in court if it would be considered bad faith to make a preferential settlement to those who come forward first.

Commercial General Liability (CGL)

The main focus of this chapter has been on an automobile liability policy. A **commercial general liability policy**, sometimes referred to as a CGL policy, is a common third-party liability policy that businesses utilize to protect themselves from claims of third parties. This might be, for example, a slip and fall in a business or a claim based on a product sold by the business. Just as with automobile insurance policies, many insurance companies will use standard form language from the ISO to assemble their CGL policies. Many of the same or similar provisions discussed in the automobile policy forms are found in the CGL policy forms. In CGL policies, courts will also tend to review the important language contained in the insuring agreement, the definitions, and the exclusions, just as they do in automobile policies.

The concept of risk sharing was discussed at the beginning of this chapter. In a CGL policy, one way for a large business to reduce its premium is to self-insure up to a certain limit. This is called a **self-insured retention (SIR)**. An SIR means that the business assumes the obligation to indemnify and defend itself for claims up to a certain limit. For example, a large business operation may have an SIR of $1 million. The business will assume the obligation to indemnify and defend all claims up to that amount. It is similar to a deductible for a first-party claim such as collision except here the insured is sharing in the risk of a third-party liability claim.

Commercial General Liability Policy (CGL)
A common third-party liability policy that businesses utilize to protect themselves from claims of third parties.

Self-Insured Retention (SIR)
The insured assumes the obligation to indemnify and defend itself for liability claims up to a certain limit.

Direct Action Statutes

In the discussion in this chapter and in all examples used, the injured party sues the defendant who is insured under a third-party liability policy. A small minority of states do have a **direct action statute**. A direct action statute is one that provides for the injured party to commence a direct action against the liability carrier of the insured, thus bypassing the insured completely. Some are limited in their scope such as to automobile accidents only or to cases in which it is shown that the insured tortfeasor is insolvent or bankrupt or to a requirement that judgment must first be obtained against the insured. The direct action statute of Wisconsin is expansive and allows claims against the insurer under all types of liability policies, and no judgment needs to be obtained against the insured. The Wisconsin direct action statute states:

Direct Action Statute
A statute that provides for the injured party to commence an action against the liability carrier of the insured, thus bypassing the insured completely.

> Any bond or policy of insurance covering liability to others for negligence makes the insurer liable, up to the amounts stated in the bond or policy, to the persons entitled to recover against the insured for the death of any person or for injury to persons or property, irrespective of whether the liability is presently established or is contingent and to become fixed or certain by final judgment against the insured.[6]

CASE **14.1** Hypothetical Case: Developing Workplace Skills

You are employed as a personal injury paralegal in a prestigious insurance defense firm. The firm does work for many different liability insurance companies. In exchange for the firm doing excellent litigation work on behalf of the companies' insureds and keeping its fees and expenses in line, the companies tend to be loyal and send many files to the firm. It is also common for the litigation attorneys to call on the various individuals in the claims departments and occasionally take them out for lunch, drinks, or dinner. The best insurance company for whom the firm does work is Improvident Mutual Insurance Company. The firm has done work for this company for nearly 30 years. The claims manager, Bruno Grouchee, has been with Improvident Mutual for the past 30 years and loves this firm. The firm has had very good results for this company and made him look good to his board. He especially enjoys the annual hunting and fishing trips the firm takes him on. This company sends many cases to the firm, and they are usually big cases with complex liability issues and large damages. In terms of revenue, Improvident is the law firm's top insurance company because of the volume of cases and the size of the cases.

The firm just received a large new file from Mr. Grouchee. Improvident Mutual insures Martin Moen. The policy has $5 million in underlying liability limits, and there is an excess/umbrella policy for another $5 million. The plaintiff is Bob Smith. Mr. Smith was exiting a bar called Paul Richard's and was walking across the large bar parking lot to enter his car parked near one of the exits. As he was walking across the lot, he was struck by a vehicle driven by the insured, Mr. Moen. Moen was not driving all that fast. However, after the impact, Smith landed on his head and suffered a catastrophic brain injury. He apparently landed on a wheel stop in the parking lot that had a piece of rebar sticking out of it, and his head hit that. Because of his injuries, he has severe brain damage, and he has no recollection of the accident. There were no eyewitnesses other than Moen. Smith's guardian and personal representative has sued Mr. Moen for negligence in the operation of his vehicle. Moen has turned the summons and complaint over to his liability insurance carrier, Improvident Mutual.

You happened to notice two of the partners give a "high five" when this case came in. You also heard one of them say, "This Moen case is going to take care of our raises and bonuses for the next couple of years! Thank God for Bruno and Improvident Mutual!"

Shortly after the file is received from Improvident Mutual, Mr. Moen comes into the office one day to bring in some photos and other information concerning the accident. The lead attorney is out so you talk with Mr. Moen. In the course of the conversation, he tells you some new information that is not in the insurance file. He tells you that he and Mr. Smith had a heated argument resulting in a shoving match. Moen then left the bar and entered his car to leave. As he was exiting, he noticed Smith had also left and was walking across the lot to his car. Moen informs you that he had been drinking heavily and was still mad at Smith and so he intentionally and purposely struck Smith with his vehicle as he was exiting but he certainly didn't intend such a catastrophic result.

After Mr. Moen leaves, you read the liability insurance policy he has with Improvident Mutual that was included in the file from the company. Fortunately, in the Torts and Personal Injury paralegal course you took in college, you studied insurance. You turn to the Exclusions portion of the policy. Sure enough, the very first exclusion states:

(Continued)

CASE 14.1 *(Continued)*

"A. We do not provide Liability Coverage for any person:

1. Who intentionally causes bodily injury or property damage."

You immediately report this conversation with Mr. Moen to your supervising attorney. A dour expression comes over his face. He says, "I would really like to tell my friend Bruno about this because Bruno would really appreciate knowing about it. He would then deny coverage and we would probably save his company a lot of money. Of course, we would lose one of the most lucrative files this firm has ever had, too. Who's really our client here? Where do our loyalties lie? See if you can find any law on this and draft a brief memo summarizing your findings. Do not bill your time to this file. Bill it to 'miscellaneous.'"

"Can we avoid going through the insurance company?"

CHAPTER SUMMARY

The study of insurance is important because it can affect the ultimate outcome of whether or not a plaintiff will be fully and reasonably compensated for a personal injury. An insurance policy is a contract, and an insurance policy is governed under principles of contract law. The basic concept of any insurance is to allocate and distribute risks. Insurance companies are made up of three separate divisions: sales, underwriting, and claims.

There are two parties to an insurance contract: the insured and the insurer. There is first-party insurance covering a claim of the insured and third-party insurance covering the claim of a third party against the insured. An important document in any insurance policy is the Declarations Page or Dec Sheet. It provides information as to the name(s) of the insured, the term of the policy, vehicles insured, type of coverage, the amount of the premium, form endorsements, and loss payees, among others.

Third-party liability insurance companies have two duties. There is a duty to defend the insured and a duty to indemnify or pay amounts on behalf of the insured. The liability insurance company has the right to control the defense of a case brought against its insured. If an insurance company defends the insured in a case in which there are policy coverage issues, the defense is done under a reservation of rights. If a company determines there is no coverage,

it may issue a declination letter to the insured. The company may also decide to commence a declaratory judgment action to have the court decide any coverage issues.

A tripartite relationship exists among the liability insurer, the insured, and the defense counsel hired by the insurer to defend the insured. The attorney may represent both the insurer and the insured in the defense of a liability claim so long as there is no conflict. The primary duty of the attorney is to the attorney's client who is generally found to be the insured, not the insurer, even though the insurer is paying the fees and costs of the attorney.

Bad faith refers to a breach of the insurer's duty to act in good faith toward its insured. The courts find an implied covenant of good faith and fair dealing in every third-party liability insurance contract. Some courts will find that covenant in first-party insurance contracts as well. Examples of bad faith are not settling a case within the policy limits when there has been a demand for the policy limits by the third party, attempting to coerce the insured to contribute toward a settlement of a claim against the insured, failing to properly investigate or defend a claim, rejecting advice of the insurer's own attorney, and failing to keep the insured informed.

A direct action statute is one that provides for the injured party to commence a direct action against the liability carrier of the insured, thus bypassing the insured completely.

KEY TERMS

Insurance Policy	Bodily Injury (BI) Liability	Duty to Indemnify
Doctrine of Reasonable Expectations	Umbrella Policy	Reservation of Rights Letter
Reformation Action	Split Liability Limits	Declination Letter
Deductible	Combined Single Limits (CSL)	Declaratory Judgment Action
Co-Pay	OTC or Comprehensive Coverage	Tripartite Relationship
Declarations Sheet	Collision Coverage	Bad Faith
Endorsement	Loss Payee	Commercial General Liability Policy
Binder	Additional Interest	(CGL)
Occurrence Policy	Exclusion	Self-Insured Retention (SIR)
Claims Made Policy	Duty to Defend	Direct Action Statute

REVIEW **QUESTIONS**

1. Charlie has a third-party liability insurance policy with Doom Mutual Insurance Company. The Declarations Page states that Charlie is the named insured. Doom's policy defines an insured in the Definitions section of the policy as "the named insured, the named insured's spouse, and any relative living in the same household as the named insured." The insuring agreement portion of the policy refers to the insured as only "the named insured." Charlie's wife, Denise, is driving Charlie's insured vehicle and has a fender bender in which the plaintiff claims a whiplash injury. The plaintiff sues Denise, and she and Charlie turn the claim over to Doom. Doom sends out a declination letter stating that there is no coverage for Denise because she is not the "named insured" under the insuring agreement. Between Denise, the claimed insured, and Doom Mutual Insurance Company, who is likely to prevail in litigation over coverage? Why?

2. Provide the common description/abbreviation for the liability limits of $250,000/$500,000 and a property damage limit of $100,000 based on the Dec Sheet in Exhibit 14-1.

3. Describe what an insurance policy form endorsement is and its importance.

4. Ruth has an automobile insurance policy with Double Deal Mutual Insurance Company with BI limits of 25/50. She also has an umbrella policy of $2 million with the same company. She is in a motor vehicle accident with Fred in which he is severely injured. How much total liability coverage does she have to cover the claim of Fred?

5. A squirrel finds its way into the engine compartment of Ruby's automobile, which has been sitting for three months while she is on a winter vacation. When she returns, she finds that the squirrel has chewed some of the hoses in the engine causing $500 of damage. She also has an insurance policy with AUTOKING Mutual Insurance Company with the same coverages as those in Exhibit 14-1. What type of coverage will cover this loss? Will the entire loss be covered or will she need to pay something out of her own pocket? If so, how much?

6. Explain the difference between a liability insurer's duty to defend and its duty to indemnify its insured for a third-party liability claim.

7. Explain the difference between a reservation of rights letter and a declination letter.

8. Tim has an automobile liability policy with Schlock Mutual Insurance Company. Tim has been sued by Loretta, who sustained serious personal injuries due to the negligence of Tim arising out of an automobile accident. Schlock Mutual is very certain that there will not be any liability coverage for Tim because of a certain clear exclusion in the policy. The company adjuster, Wally, therefore, hires insurance coverage counsel Laye Lowe & Strike to give him a coverage opinion. Wally, in the meantime, hires a different attorney, Rufus, to defend Tim in Loretta's car accident case, but under a reservation of rights. Wally receives a coverage opinion letter from Laye Lowe & Strike giving the opinion that more facts are needed. Wally, however, is so sure there will be no coverage, he sees no reason to incur company expense to gather more facts. He also tells Rufus not to do anything on Loretta's personal injury case except interpose an answer. The case is called for trial. A week before trial Rufus receives a letter from Loretta's counsel offering to settle Loretta's claim for the policy limits. Rufus sends the letter to Wally who laughs and ignores the letter. Rufus has done nothing, pursuant to orders from Wally at Schlock Mutual. Accordingly, he is completely unprepared, and a large verdict comes in well in excess of Tim's liability limits. What potential claims does Tim have against Schlock and Rufus? Discuss.

chapter 15

FIRST-PARTY INSURANCE COVERAGE

"What the insurance companies have done is to reverse the business so that the public at large insures the insurance companies."

Gerry Spence

LEARNING OBJECTIVES

After studying this chapter, you should be able to:

- Recognize and appreciate the differences between third-party insurance and first-party insurance.

- Recognize and analyze important issues in automobile uninsured motorist coverage.

- Recognize and analyze important issues in automobile underinsured motorist coverage.

- Recognize and analyze important issues in automobile no-fault PIP insurance coverage.

First-Party Coverage/General

As discussed in the previous chapter, an insurance policy is a contract in which there are two parties, the insurer and the insured. When a third party, not a party to the contract, makes a claim against the insured, this is third-party coverage. Third-party coverage, or third-party liability, involves a claim for bodily injury (BI) or property damage (PD) by some third person against the insured, which brings into play the BI liability or property damage liability portions of the insured's policy as discussed in the previous chapter. First-party coverage, however, provides coverage for a loss to the insured's own person or property. In the automobile context, examples of first-party coverage insuring the insured's automobile and first discussed in the previous chapter are collision coverage and other than collision (OTC) coverage. First-party coverages insuring the insured's person were also first mentioned in the previous chapter. These coverages are uninsured motorist, underinsured motorist, and no-fault. This chapter will discuss those three first-party coverages in more detail.

First-Party Coverage/Uninsured Motorist (UM) Coverage

INTRODUCTION

In a perfect world, the personal injury case in which the plaintiff's personal injury paralegal is assisting the attorney will involve the at-fault driver having more than adequate third-party liability insurance to reasonably and adequately compensate the client for his or her injuries. Unfortunately, this is not always the case. According to a recent study by the Insurance Research Council, there are approximately one in seven drivers on the road without liability insurance. The downturn in the economy since 2008 and the resulting high unemployment may mean that some people believe they cannot afford the premium for liability insurance.

Uninsured Motorist (UM) Coverage
First-party coverage for the insured in the situation in which the at-fault driver is uninsured.

If on the plaintiff's side, it is essential to obtain the client's own automobile policy to determine whether the client has **uninsured motorist (UM) coverage**. This insurance will provide coverage for the client in the event the third-party at-fault driver is uninsured. UM coverage, in essence, operates as a substitute for the liability insurance that the at-fault motorist failed to procure. Since it operates as a substitute, the insured can present the same economic and non-economic damages against the insured's UM carrier as if the at-fault defendant had liability insurance and had been sued.

The subject matter of this textbook includes personal injury so it is the BI coverage portion of the UM policy that is the focus. However, it is possible to obtain UM property damage (UMPD) insurance for damage to an insured's vehicle caused by an uninsured motorist. Most UM coverage, however, is bodily injury, not property damage. UM bodily injury coverage will be the topic to begin this chapter on first-party coverage.

Some states mandate UM coverage by statute. For example, in Kansas, UM coverage is mandatory, and the UM coverage limits must be equal to the liability coverage limits.[1] In other states, such as Hawaii, UM coverage is optional, but it may need to be offered to the potential policyholder.[2] UM coverage is important coverage for the personal injury paralegal to understand. Unfortunately, if the above statistics are believed, this is a scenario that will arise on a fairly frequent basis. The personal injury paralegal must know and understand the basics of this coverage in order to assist with a personal injury case for a client with UM coverage involved in an accident with a driver who does not have liability insurance.

WHO IS AN UNINSURED MOTORIST?

What is meant by the term "uninsured"? The student's attention is again directed to the AUTOKING automobile insurance policy in Appendix 3. In the AUTOKING policy, refer again to base policy Form PP 00 01 01 05. Refer to "PART C— UNINSURED MOTORISTS COVERAGE" and the heading "Other Additional Definitions for Part C."

Workplace Skills Tip

Organization has been emphasized throughout this book. Each office will presumably have its own various methods of file organization. One helpful method is to utilize different colors to represent different tasks. For example, on an office calendar, a certain color may represent a task such as a deposition, a site inspection, a meeting, a hearing, or a personal matter. If various types of mass mailings are routinely sent out in the course of litigation, various colors of the letters can be used to distinguish the subject matter of the letter involved.

Another good organizational tool is to use the European numbering system when naming computer files or folders. Assume there is a certain task that the paralegal or attorney wants to keep in chronological order, such as a list of cases in an electronic legal research folder. The year is entered first with four digits, followed by the month with two digits and then the day with two digits. For example, 2012-04-27 (April 27, 2012). Using this method will keep all dates in chronological order when you are reviewing a list of the file names.

In reviewing these definitions, it can be seen that there are three basic scenarios under which there can be an uninsured motor vehicle. The policy defines what is considered an uninsured motor vehicle and states:

"Uninsured Motor Vehicle" means a "motor vehicle" for which:

    a. there is no bodily injury liability insurance policy, or bond providing equivalent liability protection, in effect at the time of the accident.

    b. there is an applicable policy or bond but the insurer or issuer thereof refuses to provide coverage, denies coverage, or is or becomes insolvent.

    c. the identity of the owner or operator cannot be ascertained and the "bodily injury" of the "insured" is either caused by actual physical contact of such "motor vehicle" with the "insured," or with a "motor vehicle" occupied by the "insured," or is independently verified by a disinterested witness.

WHAT IS A MOTOR VEHICLE?

Before examining each of the three UM scenarios, the student must again refer to the same PART C—UNINSURED MOTORISTS COVERAGE. Note that under PART C, under the same "Other Additional Definitions for Part C," this definition of "Motor Vehicle":

"Motor Vehicle" means a vehicle, excluding motor vehicles weighing more than twenty thousand pounds, having two or more load-bearing wheels, of a kind required to be registered under the laws of the state of Bliss relating to motor vehicles, designed primarily for operation upon the public streets, roads, and highways, and driven by a power other than muscular power, and includes a trailer drawn by or attached to such a vehicle.

From the definition of the word "motor vehicle," it can be determined that a large vehicle weighing more than twenty thousand pounds does not qualify as a motor vehicle. By the same token, a snowmobile would not qualify, as it does not have wheels. Since there is a requirement of two or more load-bearing wheels, this definition would include a motorcycle. The definition requires that a motor vehicle must be one that is "designed primarily for operation upon the public streets, roads, and highways…." Therefore, a farm tractor and a golf cart are not included, as they are not designed to be driven primarily upon public streets, roads, and highways. How about a road grader? One would also want to determine whether the claimed motor vehicle is one that is "required to be registered under the laws of the state." For example, a particular state may not require government vehicles to be registered, such as city patrol cars, fire engines, an ambulance, or other state-owned or federally owned vehicles. As a practical matter, it would be rare that these types of vehicles would not have liability insurance.

UM/THE FIRST SCENARIO: OTHER DRIVER HAS NO LIABILITY INSURANCE

The first scenario is fairly easy. Unfortunately, not all motor vehicle owners purchase the required liability insurance, for whatever reason. In this scenario, the other driver is clearly ascertained but has no liability insurance that would cover a

Workplace Skills Tip

You may be on the plaintiff's team and represent a plaintiff who has UM coverage and is injured in another state by a driver with lesser mandated liability limits than mandated in your jurisdiction. The paralegal will want to ascertain the liability limits of the out-of-state driver.

Be ready to assist with preparing a UM case in your jurisdiction if the law in your jurisdiction allows it. After all, it is far easier to make a UM claim in your home state than to have to retain another attorney in another state to assist with pursuing an out-of-state liability claim.

third-party BI claim. It is a misdemeanor in most states to be uninsured, but that is no aid and comfort to your client. If that same driver, however, had *some* liability insurance but in an amount less than the liability limits mandated in the state where your client resides, that driver may also be considered uninsured depending upon the language of the policy and the law of the paralegal's jurisdiction.

For example, assume that your client was injured in a motor vehicle collision in another state. The other driver was a resident of that state, which mandated lesser liability limits than the state in which your client is a resident. Recall the discussion in Chapter 14 in which it was pointed out that Alaska required BI limits of 50/100 and Ohio required 12.5/25. If your home state requires mandatory limits of 30/60, but the out-of-state driver had the required mandatory liability limits of 15/30 for his or her state, such driver may still be considered an uninsured motorist. Similarly, if the same accident in the same example happened in the client's home state instead of the other driver's foreign state, the result should be the same.

UM/THE SECOND SCENARIO: INSURER REFUSES COVERAGE OR IS INSOLVENT

The second scenario involves two situations in which BI liability insurance coverage exists on the other vehicle, but either one of two problems will prevent coverage under that policy. First, as discussed previously in Chapter 14 on liability insurance, a liability carrier may decide, under the facts of the case and the language of its policy, that there is no coverage and issue a declination letter to its insured. Or a court, in a declaratory judgment action, may have made a determination of no coverage. Second, a liability carrier may become insolvent/bankrupt and find itself in a situation in which it is unable to honor its duty to indemnify its insured for liability claims. This second scenario will also allow the plaintiff client to assert a UM claim against his or her own company. As an aside to this UM issue, all states have their own version of a state guaranty fund based on a model plan of the National Association of Insurance Commissioners. This fund provides limited protection to those policyholders whose insurance company becomes insolvent.

UM/THE THIRD SCENARIO: HIT-AND-RUN OR PHANTOM VEHICLE

The third scenario is more difficult. This scenario usually presents one of two different fact situations. The first scenario is a hit-and-run in which there may be an actual collision with the other vehicle but the driver flees the scene of the accident. It may also occur in a situation in which there may be a claimed "phantom vehicle" that did not collide with the insured's vehicle but that caused the insured to lose control of his/her vehicle, thus causing personal injury to the insured. Note the requirement under this scenario of being "independently verified by a disinterested witness." This will be a proof at trial issue for the plaintiff insured. For a case describing the proof required for a phantom vehicle, review the case of *Bingenheimer v. State Farm Mutual Automobile Insurance Company,* 100 P.3d 1132 (Or. Ct. App. 2004) in Exhibit 15-1. Note in that case the plaintiff insured attempted to prove that the phantom vehicle was negligent using the doctrine of *res ipsa loquitur,* a concept studied in Chapter 2.

EXHIBIT 15-1 Relevant Case Law

Dolores M. Bingenheimer, Appellant, v. State Farm Mutual Automobile Insurance Company, an Illinois corporation, Respondent and Heidi Thomas and Heather White, Defendants.

Court of Appeals of Oregon.

Background: Driver brought action against her insurer, seeking coverage for injuries under an uninsured motorist (UM) policy on the theory that accident was caused by "phantom vehicle" leaking an oil-like substance. Insurer moved for summary judgment, and the Circuit Court, Multnomah County, Ann L. Fisher, Judge pro tempore, granted the motion. Driver appealed.

Holding: The Court of Appeals, Ortega, J., held that record failed to show that an accident caused by vehicle leaking oil-like substance was of the kind that more probably than not would not have occurred in the absence of negligence.

Affirmed.

Plaintiff was injured in a single-car accident after losing control of her car. She sought coverage for her injuries under her uninsured motorist (UM) policy with defendant State Farm Mutual Automobile Insurance Company (State Farm) on the theory that the accident was caused by a "phantom vehicle" under ORS 742.504(2)(g). She appeals the trial court's grant of summary judgment in favor of State Farm. We affirm.

The facts, stated in the light most favorable to plaintiff as the nonmoving party, are as follows. Plaintiff was driving in the far right lane on Interstate 5 in an area of Portland known as the "Terwilliger curves." It was raining for the first time after a dry spell. As she approached a turn in the road, plaintiff noticed a car in front of her, driven by Heather White, begin to slide and lose control. Plaintiff applied her brakes and attempted to avoid White's sliding car. As plaintiff applied the brakes, her car likewise spun out of control, crossing two lanes of traffic before hitting the median dividing the north-bound and south-bound lanes.

Angela Willis was driving behind both plaintiff and White when she observed both of them lose control of their cars. Following the accident, Willis pulled over and walked back to the area where she had observed the two cars begin to slide. She testified that the area "was very slick with an oil-like substance covering approximately a 10' x 15' portion of the right-hand lane." No evidence was presented as to how the "oil-like substance" came to be on the road surface, and the police report attributes the accident to "extremely wet and curvy conditions."

Plaintiff alleged that the "oil-like substance" described by Willis was deposited on the road by an unknown "phantom vehicle" as a result of negligence of the vehicle's driver. Plaintiff alleged that the substance first caused White to lose control of her car and then caused plaintiff, following behind White, to lose control of her car while attempting to avoid White. Plaintiff originally alleged that she suffered injuries as a result of the negligent actions of both the driver of the "phantom vehicle" and White, but voluntarily dismissed her claims against White before the hearing on summary judgment.

State Farm moved for summary judgment, contending that plaintiff (1) failed to present legally sufficient evidence that a "phantom vehicle" was responsible for the accident and (2) was disqualified from recovering under her UM policy with State Farm because she had settled her claim against

(Continued)

EXHIBIT 15-1 *(Continued)*

White without first obtaining State Farm's consent. The trial court granted State Farm's motion, basing its reasoning on State Farm's first argument without reaching the second argument. . . .

ORS 742.504(1)(a) provides that uninsured motorist coverage must include all sums that the insured is "*legally entitled* to recover as general and special damages from the owner or operator of an uninsured vehicle because of bodily injury sustained by the insured caused by accident and arising out of the ownership, maintenance, or use of such uninsured vehicle." (Emphasis added.) For instances in which the identity of the vehicle alleged to be responsible for the accident cannot be ascertained, ORS 742.504(2)(d)(C) defines "uninsured vehicle" to include a "phantom vehicle." Generally, a phantom vehicle is one that causes an accident resulting in bodily injury to the insured without physically contacting the insured or her vehicle, where the operator or owner cannot be ascertained. ORS 742.504(2)(g).FN3 Accordingly, plaintiff can recover under her uninsured motorist coverage if she can show that she is "legally entitled" to recover damages from the owner or operator of a phantom vehicle.

> FN3. ORS 742.504(2)(g) defines "phantom vehicle," in pertinent part, as follows:
>
> " 'Phantom vehicle' means a vehicle which causes bodily injury to an insured arising out of a motor vehicle accident which is caused by an automobile which has no physical contact with the insured or the vehicle which the insured is occupying at the time of the accident, provided:
>
> "(A) There cannot be ascertained the identity of either the operator or the owner of such phantom vehicle;
>
> "(B) The facts of such accident can be corroborated by competent evidence other than the testimony of the insured or any person having an uninsured motorist claim resulting from the accident * * *."

An insured is "legally entitled" to recover damages under ORS 742.504(1)(a) only if she has a "*viable* tort claim against the responsible party and could have obtained a favorable judgment" in an action against that party. For plaintiff's claim to survive summary judgment here, she must have presented evidence from which an objectively reasonable juror could infer facts necessary to constitute a viable tort claim against the driver of the alleged phantom vehicle. The critical facts to be established to support plaintiff's claim are that (1) plaintiff lost control of her car because of a foreign substance on the road surface (2) deposited there by a phantom vehicle (3) as a result of negligence of the vehicle's driver. Although it may be, as discussed below, that a juror reasonably could infer that plaintiff lost control of her car because of a foreign substance deposited on the road surface by a phantom vehicle, the record here is insufficient to support an inference that such a substance came to be on the road surface as a result of the negligence of the phantom vehicle's owner. Accordingly, plaintiff failed to present facts sufficient to constitute a viable tort claim.

As to the first necessary inference, Willis, who was following behind plaintiff, testified that the area where both plaintiff and White lost control of their cars "was very slick with an oil-like substance covering approximately a 10' x 15' portion of the right-hand lane." A jury reasonably could infer from that testimony that there was a foreign substance on the road that caused plaintiff to lose control of her car.

The second necessary inference presents a closer question. More than one reasonable inference can be drawn from the evidence that there was an "oil-like substance" that covered a 10- by 15-foot area of the right-hand lane where plaintiff lost control of her car. If a jury were to draw the first necessary inference, it may be that the jury then could conclude reasonably that a single vehicle was responsible for the substance on the highway. We need not decide that question, however, because, in all events, plaintiff's case breaks down at the third necessary inference. Even if a jury were to infer that a single phantom vehicle deposited the foreign substance on the roadway, plaintiff has not presented sufficient evidence to support an inference that the driver of that vehicle was negligent.

Although negligence will not be presumed, the lack of evidence of negligence would not necessarily entitle State Farm to summary judgment if plaintiff could provide the necessary basis for application

(Continued)

EXHIBIT 15-1 *(Continued)*

of the doctrine of *res ipsa loquitur, which* allows a plaintiff to establish negligence inferentially even though "the specific negligent conduct may not be identified since there is no proof to establish it." *Kaufman v. Fisher*, 230 Or. 626, 636, 371 P.2d 948 (1962). However, the doctrine applies only where the court first determines that it can be " 'reasonably found by the jury that the accident which oc-curred * * * is of the kind which more probably than not would not have occurred in the absence of negligence on the part of the defendant. If the probability of a non-negligent cause is as great or greater than the probability of a negligent cause, the case should be withdrawn from the jury.

This record does not provide a legally sufficient basis for concluding that an accident caused by a phantom vehicle leaking an "oil-like substance," albeit a substantial amount of that substance, is of the kind that more probably than not would not have occurred in the absence of negligence.

As the Supreme Court recognized in *American Village*, "mechanical objects suffer breakdowns every day without someone being negligent." 269 Or. at 44, 522 P.2d 891. Although an owner or opera-tor's negligence could be responsible for a phantom vehicle leaking an oil-like substance, the record does not establish that such negligence is a more likely cause than other possible causes, such as an unknown defect in the vehicle or recent damage to the vehicle that was beyond the driver's knowledge or control. Without any evidence in the record as to the relative probability of a vehicle leaking an oil-like substance with or without negligence, a jury is without a legally sufficient basis for inferring, based on res ipsa loquitur, that negligence of the driver of an alleged phantom vehicle caused plaintiff's injuries.

Affirmed.

Source: Bingenheimer v. State Farm Mutual Automobile Insurance Company, 196 Or. App. 316, 100 P.3d 1132 (Ct. App. 2004).

Situations may occur, for example, in which the insured driver loses control of the vehicle for whatever reason, it goes off the road and collides with an object, causing injury to that insured driver. Some clever insureds may come up with the idea that if another unknown, phantom vehicle crossed the center line, causing the insured driver to leave the road and collide with a tree with resulting injuries, then the insured driver can recover against the UM portion of the policy. If the true case is that the driver simply fell asleep with the same resulting accident and injuries, this would mean that there is no UM coverage because there is no other unin-sured motorist involved. As a practical matter, an astute personal injury paralegal and the attorney should probably be suspicious of a client who claims an accident with a phantom vehicle but has no real proof substantiating that phantom vehicle with an independent witness, physical evidence, or some other substantial proof. Keep in mind that even if it turns out that there is no UM coverage allowing for

Workplace Skills Tip

When you are on the plaintiff's team, there is nothing wrong with being skeptical of any claims of your client whether related to liability or damages. After all, the plaintiff must go forward with proof at trial. Therefore, the question may be, "How credible is the proof?" The phantom vehicle offers a good example of that principle. The best proof is an independent eyewitness. Even if there are no independent eyewitnesses, however, there may be some good physical evidence that tends to prove the existence of the phantom vehicle. For example, if your client claims that the phantom vehicle struck some other object, either before or after the near miss with the client's vehicle, evidence of damage to that object would be helpful proof. If your client claims the phantom ve-hicle slammed on its brakes, evidence of skid marks on the highway would also be helpful proof.

a recovery of non-economic losses such as pain and suffering because of a lack of proof of the phantom vehicle, the insured will still be able to collect his or her first-party no-fault benefits for economic losses such as lost wages and medical bills in a no-fault jurisdiction.

WHO IS INSURED UNDER THE UM PORTION OF THE POLICY?

Turning again to the AUTOKING policy, under "PART C—UNINSURED MOTORISTS COVERAGE" refer to the section entitled "Who Is An Insured?" There can be numerous insureds, such as the named insured, a spouse, or a family member. Specifically, this would include named insureds in the sample Dec Sheet such as Holly and Paul Thompson, a family member such as the Thompsons' daughter, Jessica, and any other person occupying an insured vehicle. An insured for UM coverage would also be able to assert a UM claim for damages for bodily injury if injured as a pedestrian as well as if injured as an owner, driver, or passenger of an insured vehicle.

IS THE INSURED "LEGALLY ENTITLED" TO RECOVER FROM THE OWNER OR DRIVER OF AN UNINSURED MOTOR VEHICLE?

Students and other lay people may have the misconception that if an injured insured is in a motor vehicle accident with another uninsured driver that the injured insured can then turn the claim in to his or her UM carrier and be paid for the personal injury claim. It does not work quite that way. One of the elements of a UM claim is that the uninsured motorist's negligence or fault must have caused the accident producing the insured's injuries. Note the language of the UM coverage in the same Part C portion at the very beginning of Part C:

> We will pay damages for "bodily injury" an "insured" is legally entitled to collect from the owner or driver of an "uninsured motor vehicle."

Just as the injured client would need to establish negligence, causation, and damages against a third-party tortfeasor, the client must also establish negligence, causation, and damages against the uninsured driver. What is really occurring is that the insured's own insurance company is stepping into the shoes of the uninsured driver. The client's insurance company is saying: "We are now on the side of the uninsured driver. If you want compensation from us, you must now prove that this uninsured driver negligently caused your claimed injuries." Your insurance company is now your adversary, although it can be argued that your own company always is your adversary when making a first-party claim against it. Your insurance company has all the defenses that could be asserted by the uninsured motorist.

Assume an uninsured motorist, Axel, was driving his vehicle reasonably and prudently in his own lane of travel on a public highway. A deer suddenly jumps in front of his vehicle causing an emergency, and he swerves partially into Barbara's lane of travel with a resulting collision between the two vehicles. Barbara receives personal injuries as a result. In a later case Barbara brings against her UM insurance company, a jury or an arbitrator may determine that there was no negligence/fault on the part of the uninsured motorist, Axel. This is because of the sudden emergency created by the deer, which was not of Axel's own making. In this example, there may be no recovery of UM benefits from Barbara's UM insurance coverage because there was no negligence on Axel's part due to the emergency rule.

Assume the same uninsured motorist, Axel, was speeding on a highway at 70 mph with a speed limit of 60 mph, but Barbara, speeding and intoxicated besides, struck the rear of Axel's vehicle causing injuries to herself. While the uninsured motorist Axel may well have been negligent for speeding, it seems clear that his negligence was not the proximate cause of the collision and resulting injuries to Barbara. If that is the case, there will be no recovery of UM benefits from Barbara's UM insurance company because there was no legal liability. The element of negligence was proved but not the element of causation. Also, Barbara's recovery may be barred or reduced depending upon the type of comparative fault system in the jurisdiction.

With regard to the element of damages, assume Barbara was in a no-fault state in which there is a threshold, as was first discussed in Chapter 13. In proving her UM claim, she will need to prove that such threshold was reached. Depending upon the particular state's no-fault threshold, this may mean proving that Barbara has received a serious injury, a permanent injury, a disability for a certain length of time, or incurred medical bills exceeding a certain amount depending upon the particular state's threshold requirement.

IS THE BODILY INJURY CAUSED BY ACCIDENT ARISING OUT OF THE "OPERATION, MAINTENANCE, OR USE" OF AN UNINSURED MOTOR VEHICLE?

The UM coverage in PART C in the AUTOKING policy, on the first page, states a requirement that "the bodily injury must be caused by accident arising out of the operation, maintenance, or use of an 'uninsured motor vehicle.'" In fact, that is a typical requirement in an automobile insurance policy whether for UM coverage, third-party liability coverage discussed in the previous chapter, or underinsured motorist coverage and no-fault coverage to be discussed later in this chapter. In *Collier v. Employers National Insurance Company*, 861 S.W.2d 286 (Tex. App. 1993), plaintiff received injuries when a passing car fired a shotgun into his vehicle. No UM coverage was allowed. The court noted that there was no actual collision between the two vehicles and the injury did not arise out of the inherent nature of a motor vehicle. In analyzing whether or not an injury or death arises out of the use of the motor vehicle, courts weigh the argument that "use" means any act that occurs in, on, or around a motor vehicle against the argument that "use" means use of a motor vehicle as a motor vehicle. In that analysis, the courts consider whether the accident arose out of the inherent nature of the motor vehicle. The courts also consider whether the motor vehicle merely contributed to causing the accident or actually caused the accident.

STACKING

Some states allow what is called "stacking" UM coverage and some do not. **Stacking** means that an insured is allowed to recover from more than one of the insured's UM automobile insurance policies. Assume, for example, an insured owns three vehicles with $30,000/$60,000 in UM limits. If stacking is allowed, the insured now has $90,000/$180,000 in maximum limits. Obviously if the insured has only one vehicle, there is no other coverage with which to stack. Some states do allow stacking, and there may be no limit on the amount of vehicles that could have UM

Stacking
An insured is allowed to recover insurance proceeds from more than one automobile insurance policy.

Workplace Skills Tip

When on the plaintiff's team, in making a claim for UM benefits, it is crucial to know the law in your jurisdiction on stacking. If stacking of numerous vehicles is allowed, it is important to obtain a listing of all the client insured's motor vehicles and to obtain all insurance policies covering those vehicles. If stacking is allowed, it will make your job easier if the same insurer insures all of the vehicles, as the language in all of the policies is likely to be identical.

insurance and be stacked. However, there are some states that absolutely prohibit such stacking of UM coverage. Recall that any insurance policy must conform to applicable state statutes. An insurance company could not prohibit stacking in its policy if a state statute required that stacking of multiple vehicles be allowed. The statute always trumps the insurance policy. Of course, any insurance agent should advise that, with stacking allowed, the premium is higher than with no stacking. The UM coverage in the AUTOKING policy specifically prohibits stacking of both UM coverage and UIM coverage under "Limits of Liability," item 5, which states:

5. Regardless of the number of "motor vehicles" involved, the number of persons covered or claims made, vehicles or premiums shown in the policy or premiums paid, the limit of liability for uninsured motorists or underinsured motorists coverage may not be added to or stacked upon limits for such coverage applying to other "motor vehicles" to determine the amount of coverage available to an "insured" in any one accident.

Along the same lines of stacking, additional UM coverage can also be obtained in an umbrella policy.

Other UM Issues

EXCLUSIONS

There are exclusions for UM coverage. Refer to Part C of the AUTOKING policy under "When Uninsured Motorists Coverage Does Not Apply." The following are some examples of exclusions for this type of coverage:

1. If the insured "without our written consent, settles with any person or organization who may be liable for the bodily injury" (Exclusion 2). The purpose of this exclusion is that if the insured did make such a settlement, it would have the effect of destroying the UM insurer's right of subrogation against the negligent uninsured motorist.
2. If the insured "has failed to report the accident to the proper law enforcement authorities as soon as practicable" (Exclusion 4).

DEDUCTIONS FOR OTHER BENEFITS AND SUBROGATION

There may be certain deductions or offsets from UM coverage for other payments such as no-fault benefits or workers' compensation benefits that have been paid to the insured as a result of the accident. That is the case in the AUTOKING policy in PART C, "Limits of Liability," item 3. The UM carrier will also have a right of subrogation. The insurance concept of subrogation was first discussed in the study of damages in Chapter 4. Subrogation allows a party who has paid money to a claimant or a plaintiff to recover that amount from the negligent tortfeasor. Subrogation is not unique to UM coverage. In fact, the insurance company will have a right of subrogation for any amounts paid to an insured under any type of coverage in the automobile policy if there is the potential of a third-party tortfeasor being involved in causing the loss, damage, or injury. This right is found in the base policy Form PP 00 01 01 05 under "PART F—GENERAL PROVISIONS." Specifically, it is found under "OUR RIGHT TO RECOVER PAYMENT." The UM carrier may attempt to recover from the negligent uninsured motorist the money it has paid to the insured under the UM coverage by way of settlement or judgment.

TRIAL OR ALTERNATIVE DISPUTE RESOLUTION/ARBITRATION

Finally, a review of the policy is necessary to determine the important issue of whether the insured may bring a lawsuit in the appropriate court against the UM carrier or whether arbitration is required. In the AUTOKING policy, not unlike many automobile policies, arbitration is required. Note under Part C, "Deciding Fault and Amount," the discussion of resolving the UM dispute by binding arbitration with three arbitrators. The alternative dispute resolution (ADR) technique of arbitration and binding arbitration was first discussed in Chapter 1. Its application is resurfacing in the very last chapter of this textbook. As this torts and personal journey has progressed, hopefully, the student has recognized the building block process of torts and personal injury.

DUTIES AFTER AN ACCIDENT OR LOSS

Review Part E of the AUTOKING base policy in Appendix 3. It is entitled "PART E—DUTIES AFTER AN ACCIDENT OR LOSS." These duties, which are sometimes referred to as conditions, place responsibilities upon the insured. As was pointed out in Chapter 14, if the insured does not do what is required, the insurer has the right to void or disclaim coverage. Note Section C, in PART E: "A person seeking Uninsured Motorists Coverage must also promptly notify the police if a hit-and-run driver is involved." This duty has the effect of showing that the claim is legitimate plus it allows for a prompt and full investigation so that the ultimate responsibility can, hopefully, be placed on the hit-and-run driver.

Underinsured Motorist Coverage (UIM)

INTRODUCTION

Underinsured motorist coverage, also referred to as UIM coverage, is another form of first-party coverage that may be found in an automobile policy along with the other coverages discussed up to this point. While UM and UIM tend to be grouped together and they sound alike, they are two totally different types of coverages. UIM and UM are typically sold together, although UM may be required in one state, but UIM coverage may be optional. Some states may make neither UM nor UIM mandatory. Some states may make both coverages mandatory. UIM insurance provides another layer of protection.

Underinsured Motorist (UIM) Coverage
First-party coverage for the insured in the situation in which the other negligent driver actually has liability insurance, but it is not adequate to cover the injured person's loss.

Underinsured motorist (UIM) coverage is first-party coverage for the insured in the situation in which the other negligent driver actually has liability insurance, but it is not adequate to cover the injured person's loss. It is supplemental insurance coverage. After collecting from the at-fault motorist's liability insurance, the injured insured may then claim the additional amount of the insured's damages, up to the UIM limits, from the insured's own UIM insurer.

There is one basic difference between this type of insurance and UM insurance. An uninsured motorist has no liability insurance whatsoever, whereas the underinsured motorist has liability insurance, but it is less than the insured's UIM limits. It may be a requirement in a jurisdiction that before a UIM claim is made, the UIM insured who is injured must first make an effort to recover from the at-fault motorist's liability insurance. If the plaintiff has a motor vehicle accident with a person whose liability coverage cannot cover the plaintiff's damages, the plaintiff's UIM coverage will then make up the difference up to the limit of the plaintiff's own UIM BI coverage. The various states differ in their approach of the amount of UIM coverage available when the damages exceed the at-fault driver's liability limits.

THE MEANING OF "UNDERINSURED" AND DIFFERENT APPROACHES TO UIM RECOVERY

Assume this factual scenario. The insured, Sam Johnson (Sam), is driving his motor vehicle and comes to a stop at a stoplight. As he is stopped waiting for the light to change, a drunk driver, Amos, rear-ends Sam. Amos has liability insurance with limits of $50,000 per person. Sam has underinsured motorist coverage of $100,000 per person. Assume the liability carrier for Amos wants to settle the case with Sam for $40,000. Depending upon the UIM approach utilized by a particular jurisdiction, a different result will be reached. These are the two basic approaches to a UIM recovery, but a particular state may modify either approach somewhat.

UIM Add-On

Some states allow the insured's UIM coverage to be an add-on to the at-fault underinsured driver's BI liability limits. With this approach, the **UIM add-on** benefits are added to the amount of the BI liability insurance proceeds received from the underinsured at-fault driver. In our example above, assume Sam settled with Amos's liability insurance company for $40,000. There would be an additional $100,000 in UIM benefits available. With this add-on type of coverage, the UIM coverage is supplemental and is added to the underinsured at-fault driver's BI liability limits.

UIM Add-On
UIM benefits are added to the amount of the BI liability insurance proceeds received from the underinsured at-fault driver.

The UIM case may then be settled between Sam and his UIM carrier, or it will be litigated. If a jury or arbitrator, depending on how the policy states the case is to be resolved, determines that Sam's damages are $150,000, his UIM carrier will pay the full UIM limits of $100,000. In this case, the plaintiff will have collected a *maximum sum of $140,000* for his damages—$40,000 from the settlement with Amos's liability carrier and $100,000 from Sam's UIM carrier. If his damages were determined to be $100,000, Sam would receive the full $100,000 award—$40,000 from the liability carrier and $60,000 from Sam's UIM carrier.

UIM Difference in Limits

Some states' approach to UIM is to use the difference between the third-party liability limits of the other driver and the UIM first-party limits of the injured insured. **UIM difference in limits** means that the insured has UIM coverage available only if the amount of the insured's UIM coverage limits exceed the at-fault driver's third-party liability policy limits. Using the same hypothetical example, if Sam's UIM limits were $50,000 (instead of $100,000)—the same as Amos's $50,000 third-party liability limits—Sam would have no UIM coverage. That is because there is no difference in the two limits. The two limits of UIM and liability are equal in the amount of $50,000. Sam's only avenue of recovery would be from the $50,000 limits of Amos's liability insurance policy. With this approach, the injured party's UIM limits need to exceed the at-fault party's BI liability limits to trigger the use of UIM benefits.

Returning to the hypothetical example, assume Sam has the $100,000 of UIM limits. If Sam settled with Amos's liability carrier for the sum of $40,000, there would be an additional $50,000 in UIM benefits available from Sam's carrier ($100,000 UIM limits less $50,000 liability limits). With the same jury or arbitrator award of $150,000 in damages for Sam, he will collect a *maximum sum of $90,000*—$40,000 from the settlement with Amos's third-party liability carrier and $50,000 from his UIM carrier. With an award of $100,000, his recovery is still the maximum amount of $90,000.

UIM Difference in Limits
The insured has UIM coverage available only if the amount of the insured's UIM coverage limits exceed the at-fault driver's third-party liability policy limits.

DO LIABILITY LIMITS NEED TO BE EXHAUSTED BEFORE THE INSURED MAY MAKE A UIM CLAIM?

The above example with Sam and Amos assumes a settlement can be achieved with the other driver's liability carrier for less than the liability limits. In some states, there can be no UIM coverage available until and unless the full BI liability limits of the underinsured motorist have been paid by way of a settlement or a judgment. In that type of jurisdiction, Sam would not want to accept the $40,000 settlement from Amos's liability carrier because he would not be able to pursue a further UIM claim against his own company. In other states, the full limits of liability do not have to be exhausted. In those states, Sam could settle his liability case against Amos for the $40,000 and still pursue his UIM claim against his own company. Further, in many states, before a UIM claim can even be pursued, the insured must have the liability claim fully resolved either by way of judgment or settlement.

NOTICE TO THE UIM CARRIER

With UIM coverage, another common feature is that the injured insured must provide notice to the UIM insurer when commencing a lawsuit against the underinsured tortfeasor or before concluding any settlement with the tortfeasor. The reason for this is that if a UIM insurer pays underinsured motorist benefits to its insured who is injured, the insurer has a right of subrogation against the underinsured tortfeasor driver. If the insured has already settled a claim with the tortfeasor's liability carrier, releases need to be signed releasing the tortfeasor. Such release would extinguish the subrogation claim of the UIM carrier.

Providing notice to the UIM carrier preserves the carrier's option of pursuing a potential subrogation claim against the tortfeasor and preserves the insured's right to bring a UIM claim. The UIM carrier can then request the injured insured to reject the tortfeasor's settlement offer. One method of accomplishing a protection of the interests of both the UIM carrier and the injured insured is to have the UIM carrier substitute its check for the amount the tortfeasor's insurer has offered. This method is used in some jurisdictions. With that type of procedure, the

Workplace Skills Tip

If the paralegal is on the plaintiff's team, in handling a UIM claim, it is an area in which some excellent backup can be provided to the attorney by making sure proper notice is given to the UIM insurance company. While the attorney should know the insurance policy and the law in the jurisdiction, be sure to check any notice requirement in the policy and under the applicable state law. If notice is not given to the UIM carrier, it will preclude making a UIM claim for additional compensation for your client. It would be a shame as well as malpractice to settle a personal injury claim with the tortfeasor's liability insurance carrier without first giving any required and proper notice to the UIM carrier.

insured's right to obtain what the insured believes is a good settlement from the tortfeasor is preserved and the UIM carrier's right to bring a subrogation action against the tortfeasor is preserved. Various jurisdictions may provide for other and different methods of balancing the two interests of the UIM carrier and its insured.

WHO IS AN INSURED UNDER THE UIM PORTION OF THE POLICY?

Refer to the same sample AUTOKING policy in Appendix 3 and note the UIM policy form PP BL 04 29 12 09 entitled "UNDERINSURED MOTORISTS COVERAGE—STATE OF BLISS." Refer to the same language as discussed under UM coverage, namely, "Who Is an Insured?" Again, there are numerous insureds. In fact, the definition of an "insured" in the UIM portion of the policy is identical to the UM portion.

IS THE INSURED "LEGALLY ENTITLED" TO RECOVER FROM THE OWNER OR DRIVER OF AN UNDERINSURED MOTOR VEHICLE?

This discussion was had under the identical heading above for UM coverage. The language in the UIM endorsement portion of the AUTOKING policy under "INSURING AGREEMENT" has the same requirement of "legally entitled." For the injured party to prevail under UIM coverage, he or she must prove causal negligence or fault on the underinsured driver.

IS THE BODILY INJURY CAUSED BY ACCIDENT ARISING OUT OF THE "OPERATION, MAINTENANCE, OR USE" OF AN UNDERINSURED MOTOR VEHICLE?

This requirement is also contained in the "INSURING AGREEMENT" in the UIM endorsement. The language is a bit different, but it provides that the damages must be caused by accident and "arising out of the maintenance or use of" an underinsured motor vehicle.

STACKING

The issue of stacking was addressed in the discussion of UM coverage. Stacking is, likewise, not allowed under this AUTOKING policy's UIM coverage under "Limits of Liability." Just as with UM coverage, depending upon each jurisdiction's insurance statutes, stacking may or may not be allowed for UIM coverage. Also, just as with UM coverage, additional UIM coverage may be obtained in an umbrella policy.

Other UIM Issues

EXCLUSIONS

Exclusions in UIM coverage may be identical to those for UM coverage. In reviewing the exclusions in the UM and UIM coverages in the AUTOKING policy, the exclusions are identical.

DEDUCTIONS FOR OTHER BENEFITS AND SUBROGATION

Under the "Limits of Liability" section in the UIM coverage, the deductions are identical as those in the UM coverage. Also, as pointed out previously in the UM portion, the same right of subrogation for UIM benefits paid is found in "PART F—GENERAL PROVISIONS" of the base policy, Form PP 00 01 01 05 under "OUR RIGHT TO RECOVER PAYMENT."

TRIAL OR ADR/ARBITRATION

Typically, the procedure for resolving a UIM dispute is the same for resolving a UM dispute. Note in reviewing the UIM portion of the AUTOKING policy form PP BL 04 29 12 09 under "Deciding Fault and Amount" that the identical arbitration procedure is used to resolve UIM claims as it is to resolve UM claims. The procedure for presenting a BI claim, whether UM or UIM, and whether in arbitration or before a jury, is the same. The arbitration procedure is more informal as originally discussed in Chapter 1. Even in this informal setting, the plaintiff will be presenting evidence of breach of duty, causation, and damages and asking the arbitrators to award a certain dollar amount for compensatory damages, just as in a jury trial. UM damages and UIM damages in an arbitration are presented exactly as if the injured party had sued the at-fault motorist in court.

Checklist for UM/UIM Coverage

Based on the discussion of both UM and UIM coverages, a brief suggested checklist might consist of the following:

✓ What is the applicable statute of limitation?
✓ Is the injured person an insured?

Workplace Skills Tip

If the plaintiff client of the firm is injured in his or her own vehicle at a time when some other person is driving, and the client's injuries are worth more than the liability insurance the client had on the vehicle, the client likely cannot make a UIM claim. UIM coverage is intended to protect the client insured from others who fail to have sufficient liability insurance. UIM insurance is not a substitute for the client's failure to have adequate liability insurance on the client's own vehicle.

✓ Was the personal injury caused by a motor vehicle?

✓ Was the personal injury caused by an uninsured motor vehicle/underinsured motor vehicle?

✓ Was the personal injury caused by a motor vehicle accident that arose out of the operation, maintenance, or use of an uninsured motor vehicle/underinsured motor vehicle?

✓ Can the injured person prove liability—breach of duty, causation, and damages against the uninsured motorist/underinsured motorist?

✓ Has any required notice been properly provided to the UM/UIM carrier?

✓ If more than one vehicle is owned and insured, is stacking allowed?

✓ Are there any applicable exclusions so that there would be no UM/UIM coverage?

✓ Are there any deductions from the UM/UIM benefits?

✓ How is the case to be resolved—in court or by some ADR method?

Personal Injury (No-Fault) Protection

INTRODUCTION TO NO-FAULT INSURANCE AND ITS PURPOSE

No-fault insurance was first briefly discussed in Chapter 14. It surfaced initially by legal scholars in the late 1960s. The basic premise of no-fault insurance was that the tort system, when it came to motor vehicles, was not working all that well. High settlements and high jury verdicts meant increased costs to all in the form of higher liability insurance premiums. Similarly, there were instances of under-compensation for injuries because of comparative fault or contributory negligence as discussed in Chapter 6. Another basic complaint was the time and expense incurred in pursuing litigation, with many cases dragging on for years and years. The theory advanced by no-fault supporters was that insurance premiums would be reduced.

No-Fault Insurance
Provides certain economic benefits such as medical bills and lost wages from one's own insurance company rather than having to sue the at-fault driver.

The basic concept of **no-fault insurance** is to provide certain economic benefits such as known medical bills and lost wages from one's own insurance company rather than having to sue the at-fault driver. These benefits are obtained quickly rather than having to engage in time-consuming and costly litigation. The concept of no-fault insurance is to pay economic losses such as medical bills, lost wages, and other out-of-pocket costs but retain the right to sue the other driver if a certain threshold is met. The injured person may bring a third-party tort claim against the other driver only if there is a more serious injury involved. To reiterate, even if an insured is not able to prevail with a UM or a UIM claim for whatever reason, the insured will be able to obtain his or her first-party no-fault benefits for economic loss in a jurisdiction that has no-fault statutes.

No-fault insurance has the effect of restricting the ability of the injured person from bringing a tort action against the third party for non-economic losses such as pain and suffering or disability and disfigurement arising out of the motor vehicle collision (see Exhibit 15-2). Florida's no-fault statute, for example, discussed in Chapter 14, pointed out that the threshold is a "significant and permanent loss of an important bodily function." The threshold may relate to describing the injury in terms of "permanent" or "serious." Alternative threshold limits may relate to reaching a certain threshold for medical bills, such as $2,500, or a certain number of days an injured person must be disabled, such as 60 days or more.

Reaching any one of the established thresholds allows the injured insured to bring suit against the other driver. If the injured insured does not reach any one of a particular state's alternative enumerated thresholds, the insured will simply recover his or her economic losses from his or her own insurer up to the no-fault limits for each particular loss. As of this writing, there are currently 21 states and the District of Columbia that have some form of no-fault system. See the table below for a listing of states and their corresponding statutes.

STATE	STATUTE
Arkansas	AR ST § 23-89-201
Connecticut	CT ST § 38a-363
District of Columbia	DC CODE § 31-2401
Florida	FL ST § 627.730
Georgia	GA ST § 33-34-1
Hawaii	HI ST § 431:10C-103
Kansas	KS ST § 40-3101
Kentucky	KY ST § 304.39-010
Maryland	MD INSURANCE § 19-505
Massachusetts	MA ST 90 § 34A
Michigan	MI ST § 500.3101
Minnesota	MN ST § 65B.41
New Jersey	NJ ST § 17:28-1.4
New York	NY INS § 2328
North Dakota	ND ST § 26.1-41-01
Oregon	OR ST § 742.518
Pennsylvania	PA ST § 1705
Rhode Island	RI ST § 27-7-2.5
South Carolina	SC ST § 38-77-10
Texas	TX INS § 1952.151
Utah	UT ST § 31A-22-302
Washington	WA ST § 48.22.085

SCHEDULE OF BENEFITS

The benefits afforded under a no-fault policy are typically called **personal injury protection (PIP)**. The student's attention is again directed to the AUTOKING automobile policy. The no-fault coverage is contained in a separate form. This is the same form as referenced at the bottom of the Dec Sheet previously discussed. Personal Auto Policy Form PP BL 05 83 12 05 of the AUTOKING policy provides for personal injury protection coverage. The *SCHEDULE* on the first page of this form enumerates various benefits, such as medical expenses, rehabilitation expenses,

Personal Injury Protection (PIP)
The first-party benefits afforded under an automobile no-fault policy.

EXHIBIT 15-2 No-Fault System

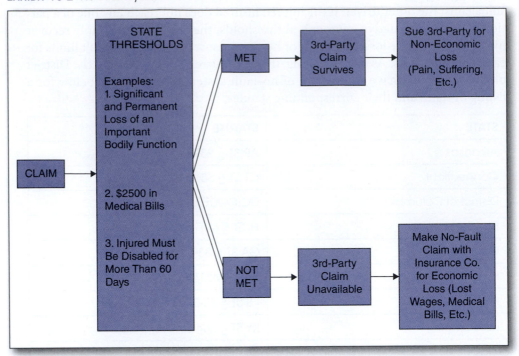

and work loss. The typical benefits for which an injured insured may make a claim following a motor vehicle accident are medical expenses and work loss. These two items will be examined in more detail. By doing so, this will shed some light on other benefits under this type of coverage. For easy reference, this schedule, which is on the very first page of the no-fault coverage portion of the policy, is shown in Exhibit 15-3.

MEDICAL EXPENSES

The AUTOKING PIP coverage provides for the payment of medical expenses. Under "Part II. PERSONAL INJURY PROTECTION COVERAGE INSURING AGREEMENT," some covered medical expenses are defined as "medical, surgical, diagnostic, x-ray, dental, prosthetic, ambulance, hospital, or professional nursing services." Other such medical expenses are not covered, such as "charges for drugs sold without a prescription" and "charges for experimental treatments" or "charges for medically unproven treatments." Although not all types of medical expenses are covered under this no-fault PIP policy, the vast majority will be covered under the basic definition.

WORK LOSS

Under the same Part II of the PIP insuring agreement, benefits are paid for work loss. "Work loss" is defined under item 3 as "85% of loss of income from work an 'insured,' who would normally be employed in gainful activity during the disability period, would have performed had such 'insured' not been injured." Assume the injured insured is off work for three weeks and earns $500 a week from his or her job. In this case, 85% of $500 is $425 a week. Multiplied by three is $1,275. But the injured insured will not receive that much in PIP work loss benefits. Review the schedule for PIP protection benefits. There are two columns—one for Benefits and

EXHIBIT 15-3 Schedule of No-Fault Benefits

THIS ENDORSEMENT CHANGES THE POLICY. PLEASE READ IT CAREFULLY.

PERSONAL INJURY PROTECTION COVERAGE—STATE OF BLISS

With respect to coverage provided by this endorsement, the provisions of the policy apply unless modified by the endorsement.

SCHEDULE

Benefits	Limit of Liability
Medical Expenses	No specific dollar amount
Rehabilitation Expenses	No specific dollar amount
Work Loss	$200 per week
Survivors' Income Loss	$200 per week
Replacement Services Loss	$25 per day
Survivors' Replacement Services Loss	$25 per day
Funeral Expenses	$5,000
Maximum Limit for the Total of All Personal Injury Protection Benefits	$40,000

one for Limit of Liability. Under the benefit of work loss is the limit of liability of "$200 per week." Therefore, if the 85% calculation produces a number in excess of $200, the maximum amount payable per week is $200. The amount of work loss to be paid for the three-week loss in this example is $600 ($200 × 3).

MAXIMUM LIMIT

In the schedule in Exhibit 15-3 at the bottom, it states "Maximum Limit for the Total of All Personal Injury Protection Benefits $40,000." Limits of no-fault PIP are just as important to know as limits for third-party BI liability, first-party UM coverage, and first-party UIM coverage. Assume the insured is in a serious automobile accident and incurs $30,000 of medical bills and is off work for approximately 10 months or 40 actual weeks. The insured earns $1,000 a week so his actual income loss is $40,000 ($1,000 × 40 weeks). However, for no-fault benefits under the insured's AUTOKING policy, there is the limit on work loss of $200 per week. Accordingly, the maximum amount to be recovered is $8,000 ($200 × 40 weeks).

At this point, the insured has been paid $30,000 of medical expenses benefits and $8,000 of work loss benefits or a total of $38,000. The balance of the $2,000 may be used for any other benefits. For example, the insured may incur further medical bills or some further wage loss or even some rehabilitation expense or replacement services. However, once the company has paid the sum of $40,000 for any benefits, the total limits of PIP benefits have been exhausted. In theory, if a plaintiff had $40,000 of medical bills and no lost wages or other losses, the full $40,000 would be paid for medical expenses benefits. Similarly, if an insured had some type of injury with smaller medical bills of $2,000, but the type of injury caused a severe wage loss, the entire remaining $38,000 could be used for work loss benefits.

It is not uncommon for states' insurance statutes to require insurance companies to place different types of limits on PIP benefits. For example, there may be the same maximum limit of $40,000, but the policy may have a work loss limit of $20,000 and a medical expense limit of $20,000. In our example above, this company would only pay $20,000 of the $30,000 of medical expenses incurred. Finally, also note there are limits for some of the other benefits in the policy. These other policy limits are:

- Survivors' Income Loss ($200 per week)
- Replacement Services Loss ($25 per day)
- Survivors' Replacement Services Loss ($25 per day)
- Funeral Expenses ($5,000)

WHO IS AN INSURED? DOES COVERAGE FOLLOW THE PERSON OR THE VEHICLE?

Immediately following the SCHEDULE on the first part of the no-fault endorsement portion of the AUTOKING policy are found the DEFINITIONS. An "Insured" for no-fault benefits is defined, which is similar to the definition of an insured in UM and UIM coverages. The definition of "insured" for no-fault benefits contains the similar language of "named insured," "spouse," and "family member." "Insured" also means the named insured or any family member who sustains bodily injury while occupying any motor vehicle. Some states' no-fault insurance statutes and policies issued in conformity with those statutes provide that no-fault coverage "follows the person," and some no-fault coverage "follows the vehicle."

For example, assume an accident involving no-fault coverage in a jurisdiction that follows the vehicle. Assume one of the AUTOKING insureds, such as Jessica Thompson, is the driver of the insured Saturn. Her friend Blair is a passenger, and there is an accident in which both are injured. Both Jessica and Blair would receive their no-fault benefits from AUTOKING, the insurer of Jessica's vehicle, even if Blair had her own no-fault insurance covering her own vehicle. Similarly, if Jessica were a passenger in Blair's vehicle and there was an accident with the same injuries, Jessica would receive her no-fault benefits from Blair's no-fault insurer. Now, assume the same accident and injuries involving coverage in a jurisdiction that "follows the person." In that scenario, Jessica would process her no-fault claim with her own automobile no-fault carrier, AUTOKING, and Blair would process her no-fault claim with her own automobile no-fault carrier.

Workplace Skills Tip

If the paralegal is representing a plaintiff in a no-fault state, it will be critical to obtain all of the client's no-fault records from the client's no-fault insurer. This can be accomplished with a form authorization that will produce everything in the no-fault carrier's file. Sometimes this file is a wealth of information. There may be photographs of the accident scene, written witness' statements including even a statement from the firm's own client, medical records, and medical reports. There will also likely be a spreadsheet or log showing any work loss and medical bills paid as well as any other PIP benefits paid. Obtaining this information will eliminate any surprise at your client's deposition or at trial and will be an opportunity to double check the client's economic damages of wage loss and medical bills.

Other No-Fault Issues

In the no-fault portion of the AUTOKING policy, a motor vehicle is defined as a vehicle that "has more than three load-bearing wheels." In the UM and UIM portion the definition is broader, using the language "two or more load-bearing wheels." This no-fault policy, presumably written in accordance with the State of Bliss's insurance laws, is limiting coverage primarily to various motor vehicles, the main subject of no-fault insurance. A motorcycle would not be covered.

There may be offsets to no-fault payments in a no-fault policy. For example, in the AUTOKING policy, if the injured insured is injured in an automobile accident while on the job, there is a specific deduction for all sums paid by workers' compensation (see AUTOKING Policy Part II PIP "Limit of Liability B"). Similar to the UM and UM coverages, the bodily injury must be caused by "an accident" and must arise out of "the operation, maintenance, or use of a 'motor vehicle' as a vehicle" (see AUTOKING Policy Part II "PERSONAL INJURY PROTECTION COVERAGE INSURING AGREEMENT A.1.2").

As with any other type of insurance policy, no-fault coverage will have exclusions. Under the same insuring agreement just mentioned, there is a section on "EXCLUSIONS." The same type of intentional act exclusion as found in the liability coverage and the UM and UIM coverages is contained in exclusion 4. Exclusion 5 excludes coverage for racing.

Just as with a UM claim and a UIM claim, it must be determined whether the claim is one that can be resolved in court or whether arbitration is required. In the AUTOKING policy, arbitration is the proper forum for this dispute just as it was for a UM and a UIM dispute. The arbitration procedure is set forth under the section on "ARBITRATION." The student should note that the arbitration procedure is a bit different for the resolution of a dispute concerning a no-fault claim compared with the procedure for resolving a UM and UIM dispute. Only one arbitrator will decide the issues, not three.

Bad Faith

The concept of bad faith was discussed in Chapter 14 on third-party liability. It was mentioned there that bad faith can also occur in first-party insurance contracts. This can include, for example, those involving life, disability, health, fire, UM, UIM, and no-fault insurance. The landmark case that established bad faith in a first-party insurance policy involving a fire loss is *Gruenberg v. Aetna Ins. Co.*, 510 P.2d 1032 (Cal. 1973) (see Exhibit 15-4).

Some courts follow the *Gruenberg* decision rationale and hold that it is bad faith for an insurer to fail to pay its insured for a first-party loss. For courts that do not follow the California approach, the courts recognize that in third-party insurance, the insurer owes a fiduciary duty to defend and indemnify the insured while also having the right to control the defense. In a first-party coverage situation, however, the insurer and the insured are outright adverse to each other.

The State of Minnesota recently passed a novel statute dealing with bad faith in first-party contracts. It is called the Minnesota Good Faith Law.[3] This statute applies to first-party claims, including claims discussed in this chapter relating to UM, UIM, and no-fault. The court is entitled to award significant taxable costs to an insured against an insurer. The insured must show the insurer had no reasonable basis for denying benefits, and the insurer knew of the lack of a reasonable

EXHIBIT 15-4 Relevant Case Law

Jerome Gruenberg, Plaintiff and Appellant, v. Aetna Insurance Company et al., Defendants and Respondents.

Supreme Court of California.

Insured brought action against insurers and others seeking damages resulting from alleged bad faith and outrageous conduct in denying payment of three fire policies. The Superior Court, Los Angeles County, John L. Cole, J., dismissed the complaint, and insured appealed. The Supreme Court, Sullivan, J., held that complaint of insured against several insurers and others sufficiently alleged a breach on part of insurers of their duty of good faith and fair dealing which they owed insured, where insured alleged in essence that insurers willfully and maliciously entered into a scheme to deprive insured of the benefits of fire policies in that they encouraged the bringing of criminal charges against insured by falsely implying that insured had a motive to commit arson, and in that, knowing that insured would not appear for an examination by insurers during pendency of criminal charges against him, insurers used his failure to appear as a pretense for denying liability on the policies, and that damages may be awarded for mental distress, without a showing that plaintiff has suffered severe emotional distress or substantial damages therefrom, where plaintiff has sustained substantial property damage. . . .

Sulivan, Justice.

Plaintiff's complaint, containing only one count, alleged in substance the following: On and after April 7, 1969, plaintiff was the owner of a cocktail lounge and restaurant business in Los Angeles known as the Brass Rail. The business premises were insured against fire loss in the aggregate sum of $35,000 by the three defendant insurers, Aetna Insurance Company (Aetna), Yosemite Insurance Company (Yosemite), and American Home Assurance Company (American).

In the early hours of the morning of November 9, 1969, a fire occurred at the Brass Rail. Plaintiff was notified and immediately went to the scene. While there, he became involved in an argument with a member of the arson detail of the Los Angeles Fire Department and was placed under arrest.

On November 10, 1969, defendant insurers, upon being informed of the fire, engaged the services of defendant P. E. Brown and Company (Brown). Carl Busching, a claims adjuster employed by Brown, went to the Brass Rail to investigate the fire and inspect the premises. While he was there, he stated to an arson investigator of the Los Angeles Fire Department that plaintiff had excessive coverage under his fire insurance policies. Eventually the premises were locked and nothing was removed until November 14, 1969, when Busching authorized the removal of the rubble and debris.

About November 13, 1969, plaintiff was charged in a felony complaint with the crimes of arson (Pen.Code, s 448a) and defrauding an insurer (Pen.Code, s 548). A preliminary hearing was set for January 12, 1970.

Defendant insurance companies also retained defendant law firm Cummins, White, Briedenbach & Alphson (Cummins) to represent them in the matter of plaintiff's claim of fire loss. On November 25, 1969, defendant Donald Ricketts, an attorney-employee of Cummins, demanded in writing that plaintiff appear at the offices of said firm on December 12, 1969, to submit to an examination under oath and to produce certain documents. On November 26, 1969, plaintiff's attorney responded by letter to Ricketts explaining that he had advised plaintiff not to make any statements concerning the fire loss while criminal charges were pending. The letter also requested that the insurers waive the requirement of an examination until the criminal charges lodged against plaintiff were concluded. Ricketts refused the request and warned that failure to appear for the examination would void coverage under the policies. On December 16, 1969, Ricketts, on behalf of the Cummins law firm, advised plaintiff's attorney in writing that defendant insurers were denying liability under the policies because of plaintiff's failure to submit to an examination under oath and to produce documents. . . .

On January 12, 1970, a preliminary hearing was held on the complaint charging plaintiff with arson and defrauding an insurer. Busching appeared as a witness for the prosecution and restated his

(Continued)

EXHIBIT 15-4 *(Continued)*

belief that plaintiff had excessive fire insurance coverage for his business. The charges were dismissed by the magistrate for lack of probable cause.

On January 26, 1970, plaintiff's attorney advised defendant insurers that plaintiff was now prepared to submit himself for an examination. However, the insurers reaffirmed their position that they were denying liability because of plaintiff's failure to appear.

According to the allegations of the complaint, all defendants other than the insurance company defendants were the agents and employees of the three defendant companies and were acting within the scope of such agency and employment when the acts attributed to them were committed. It was further alleged that 'the defendants and each of them joined together and acted in concert to falsely imply that the plaintiff had a motive to deliberately set fire to and burn down his place of business (and that) (t)he purpose of the defendants in creating such false implication was to establish a grounds (sic) upon which the defendant Insurers could avoid paying the amounts due to plaintiff under the policies of insurance issued by the defendant Insurers.' To carry out their purpose, defendants 'conducted themselves in the following manner': (a) defendant Busching stated to an arson investigator that plaintiff had acquired excessive fire insurance coverage; (b) defendant insurers demanded that plaintiff submit to an examination under oath and to produce certain documents 'in order to enable them to secure further evidence to support the false implication that plaintiff was guilty of arson'; and (c) defendant Busching, appearing as a witness for the People at the preliminary hearing on the felony complaint, reaffirmed his statement made to the arson investigator.

As a 'direct and proximate result of the outrageous conduct and bad faith of the defendants,' plaintiff suffered 'severe economic damage,' 'severe emotional upset and distress,' loss of earnings and various special damages. Plaintiff sought both compensatory and punitive damages. . . .

It is manifest that a common legal principle underlies all of the foregoing decisions; namely, that in every insurance contract there is an implied covenant of good faith and fair dealing. The duty to so act is imminent in the contract whether the company is attending to the claims of third persons against the insured or the claims of the insured itself. Accordingly, when the insurer unreasonably and in bad faith withholds payment of the claim of its insured, it is subject to liability in tort. . . .

We conclude, therefore, that the duty of good faith and fair dealing on the part of defendant insurance companies is an absolute one. At the same time, we do not say that the parties cannot define, by the terms of the contract, their respective obligations and duties. We say merely that no matter how those duties are stated, the non-performance by one party of its contractual duties cannot excuse a breach of the duty of good faith and fair dealing by the other party while the contract between them is in effect and not rescinded. . . .

In summary, we conclude that plaintiff has stated facts sufficient to constitute a cause of action in tort against defendant insurance companies for breach of their implied duty of good faith and fair dealing; that plaintiff's failure to appear at the office of the insurers' counsel in order to submit to an examination under oath and to produce certain documents, as appearing from the allegations of the complaint, is not fatal to the statement of such cause of action; and that plaintiff has stated facts sufficient for the recovery of damages for mental distress whether or not these facts constitute 'extreme' or 'outrageous' conduct.

Source: Gruenberg v. Aetna Ins. Co., 9 Cal.3d 566, 510 P.2d 1032 (1973).

basis for denying the benefits of the insurance policy or acted in reckless disregard of the lack of a reasonable basis for denying the benefits of the policy. The court may award pre-judgment interest, post-judgment interest, and costs and disbursements. In addition, the court may also award an amount equal to one-half of the proceeds awarded that are in excess of an amount offered by the insurer at least 10 days before the trial begins or $250,000, whichever is less, plus reasonable attorneys' fees. For example, assume the insurance company offered $30,000 on a policy with $100,000 limits, but the jury awarded the insured the sum of $250,000. Assuming the bad faith was proven, in addition to the policy limits of $100,000, the plaintiff would receive an additional $110,000, which is half of the difference between what was offered and what the jury awarded.

The student needs to carefully review and study the sample automobile policy of the fictitious AUTOKING Mutual Insurance Company. It contains many standard policy forms and standard ISO language that will be found in any jurisdiction. Further, for the student's assistance, Appendix 3 also includes an AUTOMOBILE INSURANCE POLICY CHECKLIST (First-Party Coverage), which is a checklist of items to be aware of in the handling of any UM claim, UIM claim, no-fault claim, or other first-party insurance claim.

CASE **15.1** Hypothetical Case: Developing Workplace Skills

You are a paralegal in a law firm specializing in plaintiff's personal injury. You have received this e-mail from the lead attorney on the team handling a case:

You are somewhat new to this case, but I need you to do something for me in the next week. We represent Sheila Williams and her husband, John Williams. By way of background, Sheila was seriously injured in a motor vehicle accident on October 10, 2010. She received serious injuries consisting of a broken leg, which has left her with a 40% partial permanent impairment of her right lower extremity according to Dr. Howard, a local orthopedic surgeon. She also received some serious scarring/disfigurement to her face and has had several plastic surgeries with the prominent local plastic surgeon, Dr. Mary Shea. She is a physically attractive, well-dressed, articulate, 35-year-old woman who will make a very good witness in front of a jury. She has been married for 10 years, and she and her husband have two small children. I have the case evaluated at around $500,000. Sheila was broadsided by another vehicle at a rural intersection outside of town when the other driver ran a stop sign. The other driver is Melvin Duff. Duff has liability insurance with Payless Mutual Insurance Company with bodily injury limits of $50,000/$100,000. This is the minimum liability limits required in our state.

I have just entered into a tentative settlement with Payless for a settlement of the Williamses' liability claim for the full $50,000 of limits. To their credit, they agreed to pay their limits because of the clear liability and the damages obviously exceeding that amount. Our clients have an automobile policy with Righteous Mutual Automobile Liability Company. Fortunately, they have UIM coverage with limits of $500,000.00. By letter, a month or so ago, I put Righteous on notice of a potential UIM claim on behalf of the Williams after a settlement with the liability carrier. I also informed the local claims adjuster, Fred Barnes, that as soon as we settle the liability claim with the underinsured driver's carrier, Payless, we will be pursuing a UIM claim with Righteous. Barnes's title is "Senior Claims Supervisor." His claim number is RMPA459876-002. The address of this company is 400 South 3rd Street, Suite 2100, Largetown, Bliss 00000.

Our Supreme Court, in the case of *Schmidt v. Olson*, decided in 2003, held that before an injured party can pursue a UIM claim with his or her own UIM carrier, written notice must be given to the UIM carrier of the proposed settlement with the underinsured driver's liability carrier. I need you to prepare a draft letter to the UIM carrier. Even though I have previously advised Righteous of the potential UIM claim, to be safe, we need to write the

(Continued)

CASE 15.1 *(Continued)*

"Schmidt letter." Under, *Schmidt*, the UIM carrier *must* be informed of the following information:

- The name of the injured party, the name of the underinsured driver, and the name of the driver's liability carrier.
- The date of the loss.
- The liability limits of the liability carrier of the other driver.
- The amount of the proposed settlement with the liability carrier.
- A liability settlement will be concluded with the liability carrier unless the UIM carrier wishes to preserve its subrogation rights, which can be done by the UIM carrier substituting its check for the amount of the settlement within forty-five (45) days.
- If such substituted check is not received within forty-five (45) days, the liability carrier's check for the agreed settlement will be accepted and releases will be executed by the injured party client in favor of the underinsured driver.
- A UIM claim will now be pursued against the UIM carrier.

We'll send it certified mail/return receipt requested. Make sure the 45 days is clear by providing a definite date by which the substituted check must be received in our office. This letter can be short and sweet and can be covered in one page, if possible. You do not need to elaborate on the injuries to our client. I just provided that to you as background information. Concentrate only on the basic information required by *Schmidt* so that we can pursue our UIM claim. You may want to review the *Schmidt* decision, also. As a practical matter, I will be talking with Barnes who will likely tell me, at some point, if his company is planning to substitute their check. Regardless, we must give this notice before we can proceed with this UIM claim. See me if you have any questions. Bill time to above file.

"I specialize in home and auto insurance."

CHAPTER **SUMMARY**

Common first-party coverages in an automobile insurance policy are uninsured motorist (UM) coverage and underinsured motorist (UIM) coverage. Also, many states still have no-fault insurance, which provides personal injury protection (PIP). For UM coverage, it is important to determine the definition of an uninsured motor vehicle. Standard language definitions are that it is a vehicle that has no liability insurance, or there is liability insurance, but the insurer has denied coverage or is or has become insolvent, or the identity of the other driver cannot be ascertained (hit-and-run or "phantom vehicle").

In UM, the injured insured is making a claim against his or her own insurance company. However, the insured must prove that he or she is "legally entitled" to recover from the owner or driver of an uninsured motor vehicle. In other words, the insured needs to prove the other driver was causally negligent for the collision.

The bodily injury must arise out of the "operation, maintenance, or use" of the uninsured motor vehicle. Stacking means that an insured may be allowed to recover from

more than one UM policy if different vehicles are owned with UM coverage. Stacking may or may not be allowed depending upon the policy and the jurisdiction. Other issues in UM to determine are who is an insured, exclusions, deductions from UM benefits for other benefits, and subrogation. An important issue to determine is whether a dispute can be handled in court or whether it must be handled in arbitration.

Underinsured motorist coverage (UIM) protects the first-party insured for the situation in which the other driver has liability insurance, but it is not enough to cover the insured's loss. There are two basic approaches to UIM recoveries. The first is "add-on" coverage, which is UIM coverage that is added on top of the other driver's liability limits. The other is a "difference in limits" approach. This means that the UIM amount available is the difference between the liability limits of the other driver and the insured's UIM limits. Individual states may modify either of these two basic approaches.

In some states the liability limits need to be exhausted before the insured may make a UIM claim. In UIM coverage cases, typically, the UIM carrier must be given notice of the settlement with the other driver's liability carrier. This is so that the UIM carrier can protect its subrogation interest against the other driver. Important provisions to review in the UIM portion of the policy are the meaning of "underinsured," who is an "insured," the "legally entitled" requirement, the "operation, maintenance, or use" requirement, exclusions, deductions from UIM benefits for other benefits, and whether the dispute may be resolved in court or by arbitration.

No-fault insurance is a product of the late 1960s when there was a movement brought on by the number of automobile accidents and rising premium costs. The concept of no-fault is to provide economic benefits (wage loss, medical bills) from the insured's own company rather than having to sue the other driver in a time-consuming and costly process. The benefits provided under no-fault are typically entitled "personal injury protection." These benefits are for such items as medical expenses, rehabilitation expenses, work loss, replacement services, and in the case of death, survivors' replacement services loss and funeral expenses. It is important to determine the limits of each benefit and the total limits for all combined benefits.

In no-fault coverage, it is important to determine who is an insured and whether the no-fault coverage follows the vehicle or the person. States and policies vary as to that issue. Many of the same issues as discussed in UM and UIM apply to no-fault coverage such as definitions, exclusions, and trial or arbitration.

An important aspect of first-party coverage is to determine whether the jurisdiction recognizes the tort of bad faith in the first-party context. It is more prevalent in the third-party context, but many states recognize bad faith even in the first-party context, which would include UM, UIM, and no-fault.

KEY **TERMS**

Uninsured Motorist (UM) Coverage
Stacking
Underinsured Motorist (UIM)
 Coverage

UIM Add-On
UIM Difference in Limits

No-Fault Insurance
Personal Injury Protection (PIP)

REVIEW **QUESTIONS**

1. Maggie had just been to the grocery store. She was preoccupied and put a sack of groceries on top of her car while unloading them from the cart. Times are tough and she just couldn't afford to put any insurance on her car. She forgot about the grocery sack on top of her car. As she was exiting the parking lot, she made a turn and the sack of groceries fell off the car. Stephanie had just parked her car and was walking into the store. Some of the items from the grocery sack struck Stephanie in the face, causing a personal injury. Stephanie makes a UM claim. What will Stephanie's UM carrier likely argue for its position that there is no coverage for this loss?

2. Bill is on a freeway doing the speed of 70 miles per hour. He changes lanes without looking to see whether the other lane is clear. It is not, and he collides with a vehicle being driven by Sarah. Sarah has no liability insurance on her vehicle, but Bill does have UM coverage. He makes a claim for UM benefits to his insurance company. What is the difficulty with Bill's UM claim?

3. What is the difference between UM coverage and UIM coverage?

4. Connie owns a motor vehicle with $50,000 of UIM coverage. She is in a collision with another driver, Jim, who has the state's minimum liability limits of $30,000 on his vehicle. Connie is injured and settles her case with Jim's liability carrier for $25,000 after providing proper notice to her UIM carrier. Assuming the statutory approach in this state is "add-on" UIM coverage, how much UIM coverage will be available for her UIM claim?

5. Assume the same facts of the accident as in question 4. However, assume the jurisdiction is a UIM "difference in limits" state. How much UIM coverage is available for Connie concerning her collision with Jim?

6. Connie's attorney sues her UIM carrier in court for her UIM claim and asks for a jury trial. The UIM carrier interposes an answer to the complaint and raises a lack of jurisdiction defense related to a court trial being improper for resolving the UIM case. What does the UIM policy likely contain in it for a resolution of a UIM claim?

7. Walt is a passenger in a motor vehicle driven by his friend, Thomas. Thomas misses a turn and goes into the ditch, and Walt is seriously injured. Walt has no-fault PIP protection on his vehicle with $20,000 of medical coverage and $20,000 of work loss coverage with a maximum limit of $40,000 for all PIP benefits. Thomas has a no-fault PIP policy on his vehicle with no dollar limit on medical expenses or work loss but a maximum limit of $30,000 for all PIP benefits. Walt has $25,000 in medical bills and $2,000 in lost wages. Walt lives in another state, and the accident happened in the state where Thomas lives. Because of that, there is a quirk in the law that allows the injured party to choose which no-fault policy to make a claim for benefits. In this case, Walt can choose either his own policy or Thomas' policy. Which one should he choose? Why?

Endnotes

Chapter 1

1. *Hearing Before the Committee on the Judiciary United States Senate,* June 28–30 and July 1, 2010 Serial No. J-111-98 2010.
2. *Hearing Before the Committee on the Judiciary United States Senate,* January 9–13, 2006 Serial No. J-109-56 2006.
3. *Handbook of the Law of Torts,* Prosser (4th ed. 1971).

Chapter 2

1. *Holsten v. Massey,* 490 S.E.2d 864 (W. Va. 1997).
2. *Bjorndahl v. Weitman,* 184 P.3d 1115 (Or. 2008).
3. *Yarborough v. Berner,* 467 S.W.2d 188 (Tex. 1971) (below the age of 5); *Swindell v. Hellkamp,* 242 So.2d 708 (Fla. 1970) (below the age of 6); *Pino v. Szuch,* 408 S.E.2d 55 (W. Va. 1991) (below the age of 7).
4. *Lester v. Sayles,* 850 S.W.2d 858 (Mo. 1993); *Toetschinger v. Ihnot,* 250 N.W.2d 204 (Minn. 1977).
5. *Holzhauer v. Saks & Co.,* 697 A.2d 89 (Md. 1997).

Chapter 3

1. *Summers v. Tice,* 33 Cal.2d 80, 199 P.2d 1.
2. *Benn v. Thomas,* 512 N.W.2d 537 (Iowa 1994).
3. *Kush,* by *Marszalek v. City of Buffalo,* 449 N.E.2d 725 (N.Y. 1983).
4. § 768.81 (3), Florida Statutes Supp. 1988; upheld in FN 2 *Fabre v. Marin,* 623 So.2d 1182 (Fla. 1993).

Chapter 4

1. *AMA Guides to Evaluation of Permanent Impairment,* 6th ed. (2007).
2. *Edwards v. Atchison,* 684 N.E.2d 919 (Ill. App. Ct. 1997).
3. *Jones & Laughlin Steel Corp. v. Pfeiffer,* 462 U.S. 523 (1983).

Chapter 5

1. *Barclay v. Ports America Baltimore, Inc.,* 47 A.3d 560 (Md. Ct. Spec. App. 2011).
2. *Newman v. White Water Whirlpool,* 197 P.3d 654 (Utah 2008).
3. *Pontillo v. The Warehouse Bar & Grill, L.L.C.,* 19 So.3d 797, 799 (Miss. Ct. App. 2009).
4. *Id.* at 799.
5. *Karangelen v. Snyder,* 391 A.2d 474 (Md. Ct. Spec. App. 1978).
6. *Id.* at 476–77.
7. *Hutchings v. Bourdages,* 189 N.W.2d 706 (Minn. 1971); *Kerns v. Lewis,* 224 N.W. 647 (Mich. 1929).
8. *Stover v. Critchfield,* 510 N.W.2d 681 (S.D. 1994).
9. *Fredrickson v. Kluever,* 152 N.W.2d 346 (S.D. 1967).
10. *Varela v. Fisher Roofing Co., Inc.,* 567 N.W.2d 569 (Neb. 1997).
11. *Torres v. Parkhouse Tire Service, Inc.,* 30 P.3d 57 (Cal. 2001).

Chapter 7

1. *United States v. Watson,* 423 U. S. 411 (1976).
2. *Bennett v. Krakowski,* 671 F.3d 553 (6th Cir. 2011) (applying Michigan law).

Chapter 8

1. *United States v. Causby,* 378 U.S. 256 (1946).
2. 14 C.F.R. § 91.119.
3. Restatement (Second) of Torts §163 (1965).

4. Restatement (Second) of Torts § 221 (1965).
5. Restatement (Second) of Torts § 260 (1965).
6. *Steele v. City of Houston,* 603 S.W.2d 786 (Tex. 1980).

Chapter 9

1. Restatement (Third) of Torts § 22 (2010).
2. *Gallick v. Barto,* 828 F. Supp. 1168 (M.D. Pa. 1993).
3. *Id.* at 1174.
4. *Burton v. Moorhead,* 8 Sess. Cas., 4th Ser., 892 (Scotland 1881).
5. *Young v. Proctor,* 495 A.2d 828 (Me. 1985).
6. Restatement (Third) of Torts-PEH § 20 (2010).

Chapter 10

1. Restatement (Second) of Torts § 402A (1965), Comment.
2. Restatement (Second) of Torts § 402A (1965), Comment d.
3. Restatement (Third) of Torts § 19 (1998), Comment b.
4. Restatement (Third) of Torts § 19 (1998), Comment d.
5. *Turcotte v. Ford Motor Company,* 494 F.2d 173 (2d. Cir. 1974).
6. *Perkins v. F.I.E. Corporation,* 762 F.2d 1250 (5th Cir. 1985).
7. Restatement (Second) of Torts § 402A (1965), Comment l.
8. Restatement (Second) of Torts § 402A (1965), Comment l.
9. *Ewen v. McLean Trucking Co.,* 706 P.2d 929 (Or. 1985).
10. *Coca Cola Bottling Co. v. Reeves,* 486 So.2d 374 (Miss. 1986).
11. Restatement (Third) of Torts § 5 (2000).
12. Section 32-03.2-02 N.D.C.C., Chapter 6.
13. Restatement (Second) of Torts § 402A (1965).
14. Cal. Civ. Code Section 1790 *et. seq.*
15. U.C.C. Section 2-607 (3) (a).
16. 15 U.S.C. § 2310 *et. seq.*

Chapter 11

1. Restatement (Second) of Torts § 559 (1977).
2. *Lemeshewsky v. Dumaine,* 464 So.2d 973 (La. 1985).
3. *Dontigney v. Paramount Pictures Corp.,* 411 F.Supp.2d 89 (D. Conn. 2006).
4. *Vinson v. O'Malley,* 220 P. 393 (Ariz. 1923).
5. *Notarmuzzi v. Shevack,* 108 N.Y.S.2d 172 (N.Y. App. Div. 1951).
6. *Arno v. Stewart,* 54 Cal. Rptr. 392 (Cal. Ct. App. 1966).
7. *Sullivan v. Conway,* 157 F.3d 1092 (7th Cir. 1998).
8. *Bullock v. Jeon,* 487 S.E.2d 692 (Ga. 1997).
9. *White v. Valenta,* 44 Cal. Rptr. 241 (Cal. Ct. App. 1965).
10. Restatement (Second) of Torts § 652A (1977) REPORTER'S NOTE.
11. *U.S. v. Bailey,* 272 F. Supp.2d 822, 835 (D. Neb. 2003).
12. Restatement (Second) of Torts § 652B (1977).
13. Restatement (Second) of Torts § 551 (1977).

Chapter 12

1. *Chacha v. Transport USA, Inc.* 78 So.3d 727 (Fl. Dist. Ct. App. 2012).

Chapter 13

1. FSA § 627.737.
2. DC ST § 31-2405.
3. M.S.A. § 65B.
4. *State Farm Mutual Automobile Insurance Company v. Bowling,* No. 2D10-1505 (Fla. Dist. Ct. App. 2012).

Chapter 14

1. Bureau of Justice Statistical Bulletin, November 2009, NCJ 228129, Thomas H. Cohen, J.D. PhD. *http://bjs.ojp.usdoj.gov/content/pub/pdf /tbjtsc05.pdf*.
2. *U.S. Specialty Insurance Company v. Burd*, No. 6:09-CV-231 (M.D. Fla 2012).
3. *Pine Island Farmers Coop v. Erstad & Riemer, P.A.*, 649 N.W.2d 444 (Minn. 2002).
4. *Parsons v. Continental National American Group*, 550 P.2d 94 (Ariz. 1976).
5. *Id.* at 98.
6. Wis. Stat. § 632.24.

Chapter 15

1. K.S.A. § 40-284(a).
2. HRS. § 431:10c-301.
3. M.S.A. § 604.18 (2008).

appendix **1-General**

exhibit **1-1**

INITIAL LETTER TO CLIENT

RANDOLPH L. STEFANS, LPC
111 Main Avenue
P.O. Box 111
Old Town, Bliss 55555

408-232-0000 Phone   R. L. Stefans, Attorney
408-232-0001 Fax   Corinne K. Kool, Paralegal

Date:

Name & Address

Re:

Dear (name of client):

Our law firm is pleased that you have chosen us to represent you for damages for personal injuries that you sustained in the accident that occurred on _____. Our firm has a long and successful history of representing clients in personal injury actions.

As we begin, we do have some important items to bring to your attention because, for most people, this is a new and sometimes frustrating experience. Some of these items we discussed in our office conference and some items are new.

1. We believe that your case has considerable merit and we will pursue it diligently. However, there are no guarantees in any lawsuit. Asking a jury for money can somewhat be compared tongue in cheek to asking people to donate to a church or charitable drive. They don't have to give you anything, and if they do, sometimes it is not as much as was expected.

2. Do not talk to anyone but the people in our law firm concerning your case. It is highly unlikely that the insurance adjuster will have any further contact with you now that she knows you are represented by counsel. If she does attempt to communicate with you, however, simply refer her to me. The same is true for anyone who attempts to talk to you concerning this case.

3. In line with number 2, above, be extremely careful what you express concerning your case and your injuries to other people, even good friends. All of the communications between you and me are privileged and subject to the attorney–client privilege and the work product doctrine. The same is not true as to other individuals.

4. I would also admonish you to be cautious concerning any of your communication on social media sites such as Facebook, Twitter, and the like. Even if you innocently post an item having to do with your participating in a physical activity, it could fall into the wrong hands, be misconstrued, and detrimentally affect your case. Along the same lines be aware that insurance companies sometimes will place you under surveillance and may also attempt to talk to friends, neighbors, and co-workers.

5. We previously talked about "special" or "economic" damages, which are your medical expenses and your wage loss. You have provided to us the days you have lost

Exhibit 1-1   **383**

from work as a result of this accident, and I understand you are back to work. If you should happen to miss other work in the future, please document it and advise us of any further work loss. I understand you have a health insurance policy that is covering all of your medical bills, and it appears that the coverage should be sufficient to cover all of your medical bills in this case. We will contact your health insurance carrier directly, but please provide us with any documents you receive from them by U.S. mail or by e-mail.

6. Please keep us advised of any change in your address, phone number, e-mail address, employment, family, other illnesses or accidents as well as any change in physicians from whom you are receiving medical care and treatment.

7. When you were in the office we had you sign some "medical authorizations" so that we could obtain all of your medical records both before this accident in question and after. You will also be required by the defendant to sign medical authorizations so that the defendant and his attorney can, likewise, have access to those same records. In addition, as I mentioned in the office, it is likely that the defense will have you submit to an independent medical examination by a physician of their choosing. We will discuss that issue in more detail if and when it arises.

8. We also discussed that in the course of this litigation, the defense will take your oral deposition. This is an informal proceeding that will take place in my office in which the defense attorney will ask you questions under oath with a court reporter taking down the questions and your answers. The questions will primarily concern the accident and your injuries. I will be there to defend your interests, and we will have plenty of time to go over your anticipated testimony when that event arrives.

9. You are under the care of some very capable physicians and hopefully you will improve under their care. Please follow their treatment orders faithfully and be sure to keep your appointments. Sometimes the defense will try to make a big deal out of missed appointments or a "gap" in treatment for some length of time. If there is any question concerning any issue of your medical care and treatment as it affects your case, don't hesitate to contact me.

10. You brought to my office some photographs taken by your best friend of your motor vehicle and of you in the hospital shortly after the accident. If there are any photographs that your friend or you come across that you have not provided to me, please make certain that I receive them.

11. I will keep you informed of the progress of the case as well as any possible settlement offers. If we receive any offers of settlement, which is likely in this case, I will discuss them with you. I will offer my input but the decision to settle or not is totally your decision, of course.

Keep in communication with us, and if there are any questions about your case, do not hesitate to contact me or my legal assistant, Corinne.

Very truly yours,

R. L. Stefans

exhibit **1-2**

WRITTEN CLIENT SETTLEMENT AUTHORIZATION

SETTLEMENT AUTHORIZATION

The undersigned hereby acknowledge that with regard to settlement of our claims for the death of _____ in a motor vehicle accident on ___(date)___ the following has been explained to us by our attorney, ___(name)___ .

1. By accepting the sum of $_____ in full and complete settlement of this claim, we will not be receiving any additional compensation from ___(defendant and insurance company)___ , or anyone else, for any damages sustained as a result of the death of ___(name)___ on ___(date)___ .

2. Out of the settlement proceeds of $ ___(amount)___ , attorney's fees and costs in the amount of $ ___(total fees & costs)___ will be deducted.

3. We further understand that we have the right to a jury trial and our attorney has explained to us that he was more than willing to try this case to a jury, if that were our wish. We further understand that if this matter were submitted to a jury, it could award an amount greater than the $ ___(settlement amount)___ we have accepted. ___(attorney name)___ has also explained to us that a jury verdict could result in an amount less than the sum of $ ___(settlement amount)___ . Bearing all of this in mind, it is our decision and we have instructed ___(attorney name)___ and authorized him to accept the sum of $ ___(settlement amount)___ in full, complete, and final settlement of all claims arising from the death of ___(name)___ on ___(date)___ .

4. We acknowledge that we have considered this matter and are satisfied that taking all factors into consideration, it is in our best interest to settle the case for the sum of $ ___(settlement amount)___ , less attorney's fees and expenses, and have instructed our attorney accordingly.

5. We also understand that the ultimate decision to settle has been our decision, with the advice and counsel of our attorney.

6. We also understand that the settlement amount is confidential and we are not to disclose the settlement figure to anyone.

Dated this _____ day of _____, 20___. _____ (Name)

_____ (Name)

exhibit **1-3**

CLIENT REJECTION LETTER

RANDOLPH L. STEFANS, LPC
111 Main Avenue
P.O. Box 111
Old Town, Bliss 55555

408-232-0000 Phone   R. L. Stefans, Attorney
408-232-0001 Fax   Corinne K. Kool, Paralegal

Date:

CERTIFIED MAIL
RETURN RECEIPT REQUESTED
And E-mail _____
Client name and address and e-mail address

Re:

Dear _____:

This letter follows the office meeting I had with you on _____ and the later telephone conversation I had with you on _____. We discussed this law firm's representation of you concerning the injury you sustained in the motor vehicle collision on _____.

After reviewing the information you provided to me and the results of my own investigation, I have decided that I will not be able to represent you in this matter. That decision is not indicative of the relative merits of your case, because another attorney may have a different opinion. Frankly, I would urge you to contact another attorney and to do so quickly. This is because there are certain deadlines imposed by law as to the timely commencement of a lawsuit called statutes of limitation.

Accordingly, you should take prompt action to meet with another attorney so as not to jeopardize any claim you may have because of the passage of time. I am enclosing with this letter the packet of photographs and records that you delivered to me at our office conference on _____.

Please accept our best to you with regard to this matter.

Very truly yours,

Randolph L. Stefans

RLS:lrj

exhibit **1-3A**

CLIENT REJECTION LETTER (MEDICAL MALPRACTICE CASE)

Date:

Name & Address

Re:

Dear _____:

Thank you for contacting us concerning a potential medical negligence claim. We appreciate the opportunity to discuss this with you. As I told you (by telephone last night), I have concluded that this is not a case that I am interested in investigating further.

To be successful in a medical negligence case, you must prove that (1) the health care provider acted negligently, (2) an injury occurred, and (3) the negligent act directly caused the injury. In addition, the injury must be serious enough to justify the significant expenditure of time and expense associated with a medical negligence case. In declining your case, we are not telling you that you do not have a case or that there is no merit to it. We are simply saying that we are not willing to represent you in your potential claim.

The statute of limitation in our state regarding a medical malpractice action is generally _____ (#) years. That is, you must start your medical malpractice action within _____ years of the date when you knew, or with reasonable diligence should have known of your injury, its cause, and the defendant's possible negligence. There are some limited exceptions that may allow an action to be brought later than _____ years. Exactly which statute of limitations applies to your case required far more information than we have available to us about your case. *It is, therefore, important that you consult with counsel willing to thoroughly evaluate all aspects of your case as soon as possible so that your rights are protected.*

We appreciate having the opportunity to talk with you, but please understand that we do not represent you on any potential claim regarding the above matter and we will not be doing anything further on your behalf. I am returning the medical records you sent to me. Good luck.

Sincerely yours,

(Attorney Name)

exhibit **1-4**

CONTINGENCY FEE AGREEMENT (SHORT FORM)

RETAINER CONTRACT

The undersigned does hereby retain the law firm of Randolph L. Stefans, LPC, to represent the undersigned in asserting claim against any and all who may be claimed to be responsible for any injury, loss, or damage sustained by the aforesaid persons, arising out of an act or occurrence that took place at or near _____ on or about _____, 201___.

Payment to RANDOLPH L. STEFANS, LPC, shall be contingent upon a recovery of money being made, and if there is no recovery of money, then no fee will be paid or charged.

In the event there is a recovery of money, then the undersigned agree that RANDOLPH L. STEFANS, LPC, shall receive for their services one-third (1/3) of all monies paid or monies in the future payable by way of settlement or judgment. Expenses incurred or advanced on behalf of the aforesaid persons will be repaid to RANDOLPH L. STEFANS, LPC, by the undersigned, from the undersigned's share of any recovery and will be deducted from the contingency fee owing to the law firm. In the event there is no money recovery, the undersigned shall remain liable to RANDOLPH L. STEFANS for such expenses. Further, in the event that an appeal is necessary, then RANDOLPH L. STEFANS, LPC, shall receive for their services forty percent (40%) of all monies thereafter paid or monies in the future payable by way of settlement or judgment.

If I agree to accept a structured settlement that calls for periodic payments in the future, I agree that RANDOLPH L. STEFANS, LPC, at its option, may either be paid its fee based upon the present value of the total structured settlement from any cash sum paid at the time of settlement, or it may be paid the percentage referred to above of the cash sum paid at the time of settlement, plus the percentage referred to above, of all periodic payments.

I have read this agreement, voluntarily signed it, and received a copy of it.

Dated: _____ 20_____. _____ Client(s)

_____ for Randolph L. Stefans, LPC

exhibit **1-4A**

CONTINGENCY FEE AGREEMENT (LONG FORM–MEDICAL MALPRACTICE CASE

RETAINER AGREEMENT

We, _____, hereby retain _____ Law Firm to make an investigation of and represent us in a medical malpractice claim for damages against Dr. _____ and _____ Clinic, (address), resulting from an incident that occurred on or about ___(date)___, and we agree to pay them for their services as follows:

(1) Forty (40) percent of any amount recovered;
(2) Forty-five (45) percent of any amount recovered if an appeal is taken, either by us or any other party.

No settlement of this claim may be made without our express authorization. If the case is resolved on a structured basis (a lump sum cash payment plus periodic cash payments), we further agree that the fee payable to _____ Law Firm shall be payable in full on the date of the first cash payment and shall be based on the then present value of the whole structured settlement. We also understand that other attorneys in addition to the _____ Law Firm may be involved in representing us. In the event other attorneys become involved, we understand that we will be advised accordingly and there will be no additional legal fees charged and the law firms are jointly responsible for this claim and that they will share the attorneys' fees paid by us for their services.

In addition, we will reimburse _____ Law Firm for any out-of-pocket expenses advanced by them for investigation or litigation on our behalf. In the event a recovery is made by settlement, trial, or appeal, the expenses shall be deducted from our share of the recovery after the attorneys' fees have been calculated and deducted from the recovery. These expenses shall include services rendered by medical consultants who are retained to examine my medical records. We understand that a recovery cannot be guaranteed. We will not remain responsible for expenses if there is no recovery.

We understand _____ Law Firm may need to obtain medical records in the investigation and prosecution of this case, and we hereby authorize them to do so. We also authorize our lawyers to re-release copies of any medical records they receive if, in their discretion, it would be appropriate to do so in the investigation and prosecution of this case.

Exhibit 1-4A   **389**

We have been advised that we must cooperate with our attorneys in the handling of our case. We realize that our cooperation is a key element in the successful conclusion of our case.

We understand that this type of investigation is extremely time consuming and highly problematical with regard to the chances of success. We further understand that these cases take many months to analyze, gather information, and study. For these reasons, we recognize the right of _____ Law Firm to withdraw from the case and return the file to us at the firm's discretion, whenever the firm is of the opinion that the chances for success do not economically justify going forward.

We understand that _____ Law Firm has implemented a file retention program under which they will keep our file for a certain number of years after termination of our representation. When this case is completed, _____ Law Firm will notify us that they are closing the file and that they will keep the file in storage for a stated number of years after the file's closure. After the stated number of years has passed, we will be contacted and the file either will be returned to us or will be destroyed in a manner that ensures confidentiality of the information contained therein.

We have been advised that our case will take a great deal of time to bring to a conclusion and our patience will be required.

We have read this agreement, it has also been explained to us, we agree to its terms, and we voluntarily sign it.

Dated: _____

_____
(Client name)

Dated: _____

_____
(Client name)

I hereby accept the above retainer.

_____ LAW FIRM

Dated: _____

_____
(Attorney)

exhibit 1-5

PLAINTIFF'S SETTLEMENT DEMAND LETTER

RANDOLPH L. STEFANS, LPC
111 Main Avenue
P.O. Box 111
Old Town, Bliss 55555

408-232-0000 Phone   R. L. Stefans, Attorney
408-232-0001 Fax   Corinne K. Kool, Paralegal

September 6, 2012

Mr. Dorian Gray
NoPay Mutual Insurance Company
P.O. Box 2502
Wrongturn, Harmony 05221

Re: Our Client: Paul Browning
    Your Insured: David Kotes
    Your Claim No: 02-PA-2222
    Date of Loss: 10-10-2009

Dear Mr. Gray:

Our law firm represents Paul Browning in making claim for his personal injuries, losses, and damages against your insured, David Kotes, arising out of the motor vehicle/motorcycle collision that occurred on October 10, 2009. Paul is a single, 23-year-old young man who lives with his parents. He is a 2007 high school graduate from Old Town High School here in Old Town. He had been doing carpentry and general construction work for his uncle, Delbert, who owns Delbert Webber Construction, Inc. Paul had worked there since his high school graduation and up to the time of this unfortunate incident.

FACTS

On October 10, 2009, at approximately 6:00 p.m., our client Paul Browning was proceeding south on First Avenue in the City of Old Town, state of Bliss. The speed limit in this area is 30 m.p.h. City Policeman Grover Honest's motor vehicle accident report indicates that the weather was clear, and the road surface was dry and free of defects. There were no traffic control signals at the intersection of First Avenue and Black Street, where this collision occurred.

Your insured, David Kotes, who was 65 years old at the time of the accident, had been proceeding north on First Avenue alone in his 2008 Cadillac Seville. As Mr. Kotes approached the intersection, he started to make a left-hand turn onto Black Street. The

Exhibit 1-5   **391**

left front portion of his vehicle struck the left side of Mr. Browning's motorcycle squarely striking his left leg. Paul was then hurled headfirst over the handlebars of his motorcycle into the tailgate of a pickup truck parked at the southwest corner of the intersection. Witnesses will testify that at the time of this severe impact, Paul flew over the handlebars of his motorcycle in a somersault fashion. While still airborne, he hit his head on the tailgate of a pickup truck parked at the curb in front of the drug store on the southwest corner of the intersection. His body fell to the street at a spot approximately 25 feet from the point of impact. Witnesses noticed a considerable amount of blood on Paul's head, face, and helmet.

You will note Officer Honest's report indicates that Mr. Kotes failed to yield the right-of-way to Paul and also made an improper left-hand turn by not utilizing a turn signal. Officer Honest's report is enclosed.

LIABILITY

There is no dispute that your insured, Mr. Kotes, failed to yield the right-of-way. Our client was in the intersection first. Your client made an improper turn in front of and directly into Paul and his motorcycle. Mr. Kotes also failed to have his left turn signal operating at the time of the collision, a fact that could have mitigated or avoided this unfortunate accident. Officer's Honest's report also indicates that Mr. Kotes stated to Officer Honest, "I'm sorry I forgot to turn on my turn signal. I was thinking about what I needed to buy at the drug store and I was looking down toward the store and I just didn't see the motorcycle." Mr. Kotes had a duty to keep a proper lookout, to yield to Mr. Browning who was already in the intersection, and to use his left turn signal. As a result of the negligence of your insured, Paul Browning suffered serious and permanent injuries, which will be described.

INJURIES

Paul was taken by ambulance to the Old Town Community Hospital. After a brief examination, he was immediately transported by ambulance to the University of Bliss Hospital where he arrived at approximately 7:45 p.m. Paul received the following injuries:

1. Compound skull fracture of the left frontal region with lacerations of the dura and laceration of the frontal lobe of the brain.
2. Compound fracture of the left tibia.
3. Compound fracture of the left fibula.
4. Nasal fracture.
5. Teeth injuries.
6. Multiple facial lacerations and abrasions (with resulting facial scarring today).
7. Likely emotional distress and instability.

At the University of Bliss Hospital, Paul was taken to the operating room since the examining doctors noted brain tissue extruding through the site of the compound frontal skull fracture. The first operation involved a debridement of the scalp wound, elevation of depressed bone fragments in the left frontal area of the skull, and repair of the lacerated dura and left frontal lobe of the brain. At the same time, the orthopedic surgeons performed a closed reduction of Paul's leg fractures and debrided and irrigated the leg wounds. On October 17, 2009, Paul underwent another operation in which the otolaryngologists repaired the nasal fracture with open and closed reductions. Subsequently, the orthopedic surgeons removed Paul's initial long-leg cast after intravenous Demerol and valium. The fractured leg bones were again reduced and aligned to correct the deformity and a new long-leg cast was applied. Paul was released from his initial confinement at the University of Bliss Hospital on December 7, 2009. He was confined to a bed and to his parent's home until February 15, 2010, after which he was on crutches until approximately June 2010.

Paul has been treated periodically in the Out-Patient Clinic of the University of Bliss Hospital by Dr. Marvin Bones, his orthopedic surgeon, and Dr. Ronald Ego, his neurosurgeon. Paul has indicated that his physicians have cautioned him to refrain from any activities that would cause strain to the slow-healing leg fractures or would cause risk of further injury to the weakened frontal portion of his skull. On November 5, 2010, Paul was again admitted to the University of Bliss Hospital. Dr. Bones operated to remove the compression plate and screws from his left leg. He was again put in a leg cast and instructed to only gradually increase his weight-bearing activities. He had extensive dental work performed for the front upper and lower teeth by his local dentist, Dr. Melvin Belli, DDS.

At the present time he has been discharged from the neurosurgery and orthopedic departments of the University of Bliss Hospital. He actually has a "hole" in his head, which is located between the top of his nose and his left eyebrow. Dr. Ego may, in the future, attempt to remove this defect. He also has very noticeable and permanent scarring around his left eye and eyebrow.

As mentioned, Paul was employed locally here in Old Town as a carpenter by his uncle, Mr. Webber, who is primarily a single-family home contractor. I am enclosing the report of Dr. Bones dated June 1, 2012, and the report of Dr. Ego dated July 8, 2012. Dr. Bones indicates that he has a permanent and serious injury to his leg, and he should not continue with employment in the carpentry or construction trades or in any job involving heavy physical labor. Dr. Ego has the same opinion because of the possibility of re-injuring the site of the skull fracture in the event of a fall or if he is struck in the head.

Finally, Paul's mother and father state that their son is a "changed person." Because of the head and brain injury, for the first several months, Paul did nothing but sleep and complain of head and leg pain. He was and is constantly depressed. Before the collision in question, Paul was very outgoing and happy-go-lucky. Now he is nervous, irritable, and depressed. Sometimes his parents catch him sitting alone and crying out loud like a baby. The parents believe that he is depressed because he cannot do construction work and the other activities he loved to do such as softball, waterskiing, jogging, and hiking.

Paul has been totally disabled since this collision. He has been referred to both a state and a federal Job Corps retraining and rehabilitation program. He was recently certified as handicapped by the Bliss Division of Vocational Rehabilitation. Dr. Ruby O. Stronsky, medical consultant for the department, believes that Paul suffered a disability and an employment limitation. He has only a high school diploma and has done nothing but carpentry and construction work since graduating from high school two years ago. He will receive re-training in an occupation requiring light work. Dr. Stronsky's report of August 27, 2012, is enclosed. In addition, Paul has seen Dr. I. M. Freudian, a nationally prominent psychiatrist. Dr. Freudian believes that Paul has suffered severe, permanent, and disabling emotional and psychiatric problems caused by this collision on October 10, 2009. His report of August 6, 2012, is enclosed. Finally, we have retained a CPA/economist, Dr. Hiram "Hi" Dollarz from the University of Bliss, to evaluate Paul's economic loss, particularly his loss of future earning capacity. Dr. Dollarz has reviewed Paul's loss of earnings as a carpenter, factored in lower earnings from different employment as per Dr. Stronsky's report, and calculated the present value of his future loss of earning capacity based on a future earning life to age 60 as a carpenter. That future loss of earning capacity reduced to present value is $427,000. Dr. Dollarz' report of August 15, 2012, is enclosed.

SPECIAL DAMAGES

Paul's special/economic damages are as follows and supporting bills are enclosed:

Tri-City Ambulance Service	$530.00
Old Town Community Hospital	$1,243.78
University of Bliss Hospital	$98,765.34
University Orthopedic	$38,231.21

Exhibit 1-5   **393**

University Neurosurgery	$23,067.96
University Otolaryngology	$3,212.62
Bliss Vocational Rehab	$5,678.98
Old Town Home Healthcare	$2,341.09
Dr. I. M. Freudian	$7,634.78
M. L. Belli, DDS	$1,722.43

Paul was earning approximately $32,000 a year as a carpenter for two years before this tragic collision. With almost three years since the collision, his wage loss is now approximately $96,000 ($32,000 X 3).

CONCLUSION

Paul will be unable to do most of his physical activities mentioned above as well as engage in carpentry/construction work. This collision has greatly impacted his ability to earn a living. He faces living a life with a permanently scarred and deformed forehead, eye, and face. He will always live in fear that he may at any time fall on his head or strike the soft spot on his forehead, which will cause irreparable injury and brain damage. He must also now learn to live as a "changed person" as described by his parents, a person who is constantly nervous, irritable, and depressed. We believe a jury will conclude that Paul has suffered extensive damages for pain and suffering, past and future, and for a loss of future earning capacity.

It is our understanding that Mr. Kotes has an automobile liability insurance policy with your company in the amount of $500,000 per person and $1 million per accident. If this is correct, this is to notify you that we are willing to accept at this time, the full amount of that policy or $500,000 in full settlement of this case. If this offer to settle is not accepted and it is necessary to go to trial, it is likely that the verdict will far exceed the coverage that exists. If we receive a verdict in excess of the limits of the policy, we will have to pursue the defendant personally. It seems rather obvious that this extremely serious case should be settled now. We would urge you to accept this amount in order to protect your insured and to eliminate any potential bad faith exposure on the part of your company.

Very truly yours,

Randolph L. Stefans

Enclosures

exhibit **1-6**

STANDARD TIME ENTRIES

- Prepare _____.

  (e.g., summons & complaint; answer; interrogatories; demand for medical records; request for production of documents; third-party summons and complaint; request for admissions; answers to interrogatories; notice to take deposition of _____ ; subpoena for _____ served upon _____; notice of motion and motion with supporting papers; other)

- Report to company or client representative _____ (list name) regarding _____.

  (e.g., change in trial date; recent conference with witness Martin Jones—be specific and give a good description)

- Prepare correspondence to _____ regarding _____.

  (e.g., correspondence to Attorney Miller regarding past due answers to our interrogatories)

- Telephone conference with _____ regarding _____.

  (Be specific as to substance of conversation.)

- Prepare memo regarding _____.

  (e.g., conference with eyewitness Jones)

- Review correspondence from _____ regarding _____.

  (Be specific and descriptive as to substance of correspondence.)

- Review correspondence from _____ with enclosures.

- Review and study _____.

  (e.g., medical records from Hart Medical Clinic, plaintiff's answers to our interrogatories)

- Conference with _____ regarding _____.

- Prepare rough draft of _____ for _____.

  (proposed areas of questioning)   (upcoming deposition of Dr. P. Brown)

- Review _____ to help _____ (attorney initials) prepare for deposition of _____.

  (Describe specifically what was reviewed.)

- Attend deposition of _____ (local) to assist _____ (attorney initials).

Exhibit 1-6   **395**

- Attend deposition of _____ in city, state (out of town) to assist _____ (attorney initials).

  (May need to break out travel time—some insurance companies and other clients will require it to be broken out and will pay only a percentage of "windshield time." If on defense, know each company's guidelines.)

- Prepare deposition summary of _____.

- Review and summarize _____ of plaintiff from _____

  for _____ (e.g., What? Medical records from Hart Medical Clinic; workers' compensation records from State of Bliss. Why? Use at trial; upcoming conference; etc.)

- Review applicable law regarding _____.

  (Some insurance companies will require pre-approval if exceeds certain number of hours. If on defense, know guidelines.)

- Prepare memorandum of law (brief) regarding _____ in support of (opposition to) _____

- Prepare notice of motion and motion (to) _____ (for) _____.

- Review _____ and assist _____ (attorney initials) with preparation for hearing on motion (to) _____ (for) _____.

  (Describe specifically what was reviewed.)

- Obtain jury list from Court Administrator (Clerk of Court) and conduct jury investigation thereon.

  (If on defense side, may need approval from company to conduct jury investigation.)

- Review _____ and assist _____ (attorney initials) with preparation of trial of case.

  (May need more detail—describe what was reviewed.)

- Attend and assist _____ (attorney initials) with trial of case.

exhibit **1-7**

DAILY TIME SHEET

TIMEKEEPER: _____   DATE: _____

Time	File No. File Name	Description/Summary of Activity

Enter time on all files based on 1/10 of an hour. EXAMPLES: 0.1 = 6 Minutes (Minimum);
0.3 = 18 Minutes

appendix **2-Medical**

exhibit 2-1

MEDICAL AUTHORIZATION

AUTHORIZATION FOR DISCLOSURE OF
HEALTH INFORMATION

Patient Name: _____ Maiden/Other Name: _____

Chart Number: _____ Birthdate: _____

I hereby authorize: _____
NAME OF HEALTHCARE PROVIDER

_____

to release my records to: _____
NAME

_____
ADDRESS

The disclosure is being made for the following purpose(s):
☐ Diagnosis & Treatment ☐ Legal
☐ Insurance/Billing ☐ Other: _____
☐ Personal

I understand that if the person or entity that receives the information is not a healthcare provider or health plan covered by federal privacy regulations, the information described above may be redisclosed and no longer protected by these regulations.

Information to Be Released:	Date of Service:	Information to Be Released:	Date of Service:
☐ Pertinent Records for Continuing Care	_____	☐ Radiology Films	_____
☐ Discharge Summaries	_____	☐ OB/GYN	_____
☐ History & Physical	_____	☐ Pediatric	_____
☐ Report of Operations	_____	☐ Immunizations	_____
☐ Consultations	_____	☐ Oncology	_____
☐ Pathology Reports	_____	☐ Physical Medicine	_____
☐ Laboratory Reports	_____	☐ Cardiology	_____
☐ Radiology Reports	_____	☐ Other: _____	_____

Authorization of Release of the Indicated Sensitive Records (*requires patient's initials*):

	Patient's Initials:		Patient's Initials:
☐ HIV or AIDS	_____	☐ Psychotherapy/Mental Health	_____
☐ Chemical Dependency	_____	☐ Other: _____	_____

I release the above-named healthcare provider from all legal responsibility and/or liability that may arise from the release of the records I have specified.

I understand that I may refuse to sign this authorization and that my refusal to sign will not affect my ability to obtain treatment or payment or my eligibility for benefits except as permitted by law.

I understand that I may revoke this authorization in writing at any time to the hospital Privacy Officer except to the extent that action has been taken in reliance on this authorization or if the authorization was obtained as a condition of obtaining insurance coverage. Other law provides the insurer with the right to contest a claim under the policy or the policy itself.

This authorization will remain in effect until: _____ (date). If no date is indicated, authorization will remain in effect for one year from the signature date, and will automatically expire without my revocation.

_____   _____
Signature of Patient or Representative   Date

_____   _____
Name of Personal Representative (if applicable)   Relationship to the patient and representative's authority to act for the patient

_____
Printed Name of Innovis Representative Taking Request

exhibit **2-1A**

LIMITED MEDICAL AUTHORIZATION

AUTHORIZATION TO RELEASE PROTECTED HEALTH CARE INFORMATION

TO _____ (Health Care Provider)
_____ (Address)
_____ (City, State, Zip)
The patient giving this release is (Patient's Name)_____
Patient's Social Security No.:_____ Date of Birth: _____
_____ are NOT my attorneys and they are
referred to in this authorization as "ADVERSE ATTORNEYS."
The above-named health care provider is hereby authorized to release to ADVERSE ATTORNEYS, or their representative, the following records.

Except for the communications necessary to obtain the records authorized by this authorization, **ADVERSE ATTORNEYS** are **NOT** authorized to speak about my health care, physical condition, or mental condition to you or to any of my health care professionals privately without myself or my attorney being present.

The cost of furnishing records pursuant to this request is to be paid by **ADVERSE ATTORNEYS**.

You may release to **ADVERSE ATTORNEYS** all medical records, including but not limited to: office notes, history, physical, consultation notes, discharge summaries, order and progress notes, laboratory results, nurses notes, emergency room records, operative record, inpatient records and films or x-rays, MRIs, CT scans, PET scans, pharmacy and drug records, and medical bills concerning any medical treatment that I have received from you or your institution.

A photostatic copy of this authorization shall be as valid as the original authorization.

The purpose of this authorization and request is to obtain medical records pertaining to my physical condition, which may be relevant to certain personal injury litigation.

I have the right to revoke this authorization in writing by providing a signed, written notice of revocation to the health care provider listed above and to **ADVERSE ATTORNEYS**, except to the extent that the provider listed above has taken action in reliance on this authorization. Medical providers may not condition treatment or payment on whether the above-listed patient executes this authorization. I understand that the information disclosed pursuant to this authorization may be subject to re-disclosure and no longer protected by the privacy regulations promulgated pursuant to the Health Insurance Portability and Accountability Act (HIPAA).

_____This authorization expires two years from the date of my signature below.
OR
_____This authorization expires _____ (date of expiration).
(PATIENT)
If patient is under the age of 18 or otherwise unable to sign, signature should be by parent or legally authorized representative, and relationship to patient should be stated.)
Date of Signature: _____

399

exhibit **2-2**

MEDICAL RECORDS CERTIFICATION

I, _____, certify that the attached records are true
(Print or Type Name)

and complete copies of all medical records relating to:

PATIENT:

D.O.B.:

OUR FILE NO.:

FACILITY:

DATE: _____

SIGNATURE: _____

MEDICAL RECORDS CUSTODIAN

exhibit **2-3**

LETTER REQUESTING MEDICAL RECORDS

RANDOLPH L. STEFANS, LPC
111 Main Avenue
P.O. Box 111
Old Town, Bliss 55555

408-232-0000 Phone   R. L. Stefans, Attorney
408-232-0001 Fax   Corinne K. Kool, Paralegal

Date:

Medical Records Director/Release of Information
Name of Facility
Street Address/P.O. Box #
City, State Zip

Re: Name of Patient:
     Birth Date:
     Clinic/Hospital No. (if known):

Dear Medical Records Director/Release of Information:

Our law firm represents _____ for injuries sustained in an accident that occurred
on _____. I would appreciate it if you would send to me photocopies of the following:

1. All medical records on the above-named patient from day one to the present. *Please
   note that we need all medical records at your facility on this patient both before this accident in question and after this accident in question.*
2. Medical bills for care and treatment rendered to this patient arising from the accident in question.

A signed medical authorization is enclosed, which will allow for the release of this medical
information to our office. We will pay all reasonable costs and charges in connection with
this request. I do ask, however, if the cost will exceed the sum of $_____, please contact
me first before making copies.

Please be advised that the trial of this matter is set to commence on _____.
Accordingly, it is imperative that I receive these medical records no later than _____.*

If you have any questions concerning this request, please call my direct line at 408-232-0002.

Thank you.

Very truly yours,

Corinne K. Kool

Paralegal

*This paragraph may need to be added for the final request of medical records when the
case is approaching trial. A follow-up by phone within a few days is considered prudent.

exhibit **2-4**

HOSPITAL RECORDS— QUALITY CARE CENTRAL

⧗ Come Kwik Ambulance Service

Reason for Call: MVA	**Name:** John Q Doe
Date / Time of Call: 12/28/99 — 1345	**Address:** 123 Main St
Attendant: T.J.	**City, Zip:** Anywhere USA
Attendant: D.V.	**Telephone:** 555 1234
First Responder: PD	**Birthdate:** 1-8-55 **Age:** 44 **Weight:** 185#
Receiving Facility: Quality Care	**Primary Physician:** Welby

Time Called	1	3	4	5
Enroute	1	3	4	6
Arrive @Scene	1	3	5	0
Leave Scene	1	4	0	0
Arrive @ Hospital	1	4	0	5

VS-
1400 - 112 - 18 - 124/44

Presenting Problem: MVA - CHEST TRAUMA

History of Current Problem: PATIENT - BELTED DRIVER of PICKUP INVOLVED IN T-BONE MVA AIRBAG FAILED TO DEPLOY. STEERING WHEEL BROKE. DENIES L.O.C. C/O PAIN WITH INSPIRATION NO MUSCLE SKELETAL TRAUMA NOTED. WINDSHIELD BROKE GLASS FRAGMENTS EMBEDDED IN FACIAL ABRASIONS.

Allergies: P.C.N.
Current Meds: INSULIN HCTZ

Past History: DIABETES HYPERTENSION

Time	Medication and Treatment Record
	C-COLLAR LONG BOARD Ⓡ ANTECUBETAL 16 G
	Ⓛ ANTECUBETAL IV - N.S., O₂@2L/NC

RECEIVING RN OR MD: _Nurse RN_

(Come Kwik Ambulance Service etc.)

Exhibit 2-4 **403**

tient: _Do_   **Quality Care Central** ✦

DRUG ALLERGIES: PCN		
Date	Time	
01/02/00	9A	Admit ICU
		S/P Cardiac Arrest
		IV NS @ KVO
		Lasix 10mg IV Now and q̄ 12°
		Dopamine gtt – titrate to keep SBP < 100
		Get baseline CBC, GS, Cardiac Enzymes, PT/
		and order CBC q̄ AM
		EKG q̄ AM
		EEG - NOW
		CxR q̄ AM & PRN
		NG to LIS
		Vent Settings TV-800 RR-18 PEEP-5
		FiO₂ - 80%. √ ABG q̄ 1 hr
		Decadron 10mg IV Now and q̄ 12 hr
		Welby MD

PHYSICIAN'S ORDERS

tient: _Doe_   **Quality Care Central**

DRUG ALLERGIES: PCN		
Date	Time	
01/02/xx	1600	Cardiology Consult
		Neurology Consult
		Valium gtt @ 2mg/hr p̄ EEG
		WELBY MD
4/02/10	0730	Pt. is DNR per family request
		WELBY MD

PHYSICIAN'S ORDERS

Exhibit 2-4   **405**

 # Come Kwik Ambulance Service

Reason for Call: CODE BLUE	Name: John Q Doe
Date / Time of Call: 1-2-00 0808	Address: 123 Main St
Attendant: T.J.	City, Zip: Anywhere USA
Attendant: D.V.	Telephone: 555 1234
First Responder: PD	Birthdate: 1-8-55 Age: 44 Weight: #185
Receiving Facility: Quality Care	Primary Physician: Welby

Time Called	0	8	0	8
Enroute	0	8	0	8
Arrive @Scene	0	8	1	2
Leave Scene	0	8	1	4
Arrive @ Hospital	0	8	2	0

Presenting Problem: Full Arrest

History of Current Problem: PT WITH C/O C.P. THROUGHOUT THE NIGHT WIFE FOUND PATIENT WITHOUT PULSE OR RESPIRATIONS. APPROX. 10 MINUTES AGO. CPR INITIATED. UNKNOWN DOWN TIME. UPON OUR ARRIV CPR IN PROGRESS PT IN V-FIB → DEFIB X3. CONVERTED TO SINUS TACH PULSES PRESENT X4EXT. INTUBATED BAGGED c̄ 100% O2. TRANSPORTED CODE THREE

Allergies: PCN
Current Meds: INSULIN, HCTZ, IBUPROFEN, VICODIN

Past History: DIABETES, HYPERTENSION, MVA WITH CHEST TRAUMA 5 DAYS AGO

Time	Medication and Treatment Record
	DEFIB X3 INTUBATED IV O2 @ 100%

RECEIVING RN OR MD: _____

Quality Care Central

Medical Record No: 12345	Account No: 678	Admit Date 12/28/98	Time 1405	◯MVA - Trauma Room #3

Patient Name: John Q. Doe

Patient Address: 123 Main

Primary Physician: M. Welby, MD.	Discharge Date/Time 12/28/98-2310	Date of Birth: 1-8-55	Home Phone: 555-1234	Prehospital Treatment: O₂@2L/ long board, collar, IV's x2 INC #1. LR @TKO #2. NS @TKO

Allergies: PCN
Medications: Insulin, HCTZ

Past Medical History: IDDM, hypertension

Last Meal: McDonald's @ 1230
Nursing Assessment: 44 YO ♂ arrived by ambulance following MVA @ approx. 1335. T-b. encounter with pt's vehicle striking passenger side of other auto. Seat belted, air bag did not discharge. Approx. rate of speed 30 mph. No LOC. Pt alert 0x3 appropriate. PERRL, lungs clear bilaterally. Seat belt injury noted with ecchymosis strip from (L) shoulder to (R) hip. Inverted "FORD" emblem noted midsternum. MAE, peripheral pulses present x4. Pt. c/o generalized chest pain and lower back pain. No numbness or tingling. Multiple small cuts and abrasions noted on face and upper chest. Shards of glass imbedding above (L) eyebrow. N.Norman RN.

Temp: 37°	P: 110	R: 28	B.P. 120/60	Wt: 185#	Ht: 6'0"	Mode of Arrival: Ambulance

Physical Exam: As above. Lungs clean, heart RRR s̄ murmur. Chest tender to palpation - midsternal to (L) MCL radiating to mid axillary. BS active MILD TENDER LLQ. EXTREMITIES-∅ deformities Dorsal PEDis 2+, BABINSKI: NEG CN II-XII GROSSLY INTACT Full ROM x4 extremities. X-rays: C spine, T spine, L-spine negative. CBC: plt → 350, WBC - 8.7, Hbg 14.6, Glu - 302, LDH - 330, AST - 31 Amylase 92

Diagnosis: Musculo-skeletal trauma 2° MVA.

Treatment and Orders: Ibuprofen 600mg. PO q̄ 6-8° c̄ Food (#30) Ice x II days then heat. Off work x 2 days. RTC if no improvement in 5-7 days

J.Smith PA

Medications:		Diagnosis Codes:
Time	Type/Dose	
1455 - Toradol 60mg	NN-RN	Disposition: Home Time: 2310

Exhibit 2-4   **407**

Quality Care Central

12/28/99	1445
Sodium	140
Potassium	3.8
Chloride	100
CO2 Total	29
BUN	17
Creatinine	0.9
Glucose	302

12/28/99	1445
WBC	8.7
RBC	3.8
HGB	14.6
HCT	40
MCV	98.7
~CHC	34.5
~lt	350

12/28/99	1445
LDH	330
AST	31
Amylase	92

LABORATORY RESULTS

Quality Care Central

CHART COPY

Date/ Time	Description	Requisition Number
12/28/99- 1425	CXR- AP	1023456
12/28/99- 1425	C-spines	1023457
12/28/99- 1425	T-spines	1023458
12/28/99- 1425	L-spines	1023459

AP PORTABLE CHEST: 12/28/99 1445

Unable to obtain acceptable quality view with portable film. Need to repeat in x-ray department when patient stabilized.

C-SPINE FILM: 12/28/99 1445

No prior films for comparison. The lower cervical spine is visualized during the lateral phase of examination only on swimmer's views. No gross evidence of trauma to this region is identified. Vertebral alignment appears intact. A small anterior osteophyte is present at the anteroinferior margin at C5. The examination of the cervical spine is otherwise unremarkable.

T-SPINE FILM: 12/28/99 1445

The upper thoracic spine is somewhat indistinctly visualized during the lateral phase of the examination. No gross abnormalities of this area, however, are identified. No evidence of acute bony trauma to the thoracic spine is identified.

L-SPINE FILM: 12/28/99 1445

Examination of the lumbar spine is unremarkable.

Radiologist: Dr. Kylie
Released on: 12/30/99 1345

D: 12/28/99 16:10
T: 12/29/99 08:30

Electronically Signed by: Dr. S. Kylie, MD

RADIOLOGY REPORT

Exhibit 2-4   **409**

Quality Care Central

PATIENT NAME: John Q. Doe
MEDICAL RECORDS NUMBER: 12345
DOB: 1/8/55
ADMISSION DATE: 12/28/99
DISCHARGE DATE: 12/28/99
ATTENDING: M. Welby, MD
DICTATING PHYSICIAN: Smith, MD

HISTORY OF PRESENT ILLNESS:

Patient is a 44 year old male involved in an MVA. Pt was the belted driver of a
pick-up truck that was traveling at approximately 30 mph when it struck another
vehicle that reportedly ran a stop sign. Mechanism of injury was 90 degree T-bone
type impact. Air bag reportedly failed to discharge. Patient denied loss of
consciousness at the scene and was transported to Quality Care Central ER for
evaluation.

Upon arrival in the ER, pt was immobilized with long board and C-collar. Two IV's
were infusing and oxygen was applied at 2 liters per nasal cannula. Patient
complained of chest and lower back pain. Ecchymosis was noted over seat belt injury.

CXR, C, T, and L spine films were all normal. Trauma labs were within normal limits
except for elevated glucose.

Patient was discharged to home with Ibuprofen 600 mg prescription and instructions
to return if no improvement was noted.

FINAL DIAGNOSIS:

1. Status post Motor Vehicle Accident
2. Musculoskeletal injury secondary to MVA
3. Diabetes Mellitus

Dictated: 12/28/99
Transcribed: 1/29/99

DISCHARGE SUMMARY

Quality Care Central

Medical Record No: 12345	Account No: 678	Admit Date 1/1/00	Time 1205	CC: chest pain following MVA
Patient Name: John Q. Doe				
Patient Address: 123 Main				
Primary Physician: M. Welby, M.D.	Discharge Date/Time 1/1/00 -1310	Date of Birth: 1-8-55	Home Phone: 555-1234	Prehospital Treatment: NONE

Allergies: PCN
Medications: Insulin, HCTZ Ibuprofen 600mg

Past Medical History: IDDM, HTN, MVA on 12/28/99

Last Meal: 1000
Nursing Assessment: 44 YOM involved in MVA 4 days ago. Seen here and discharged with Ibuprofen Rx. Continues to have midsternal chest pain but now accompanied by SOB and pain with inspiration. Denies other pain. Ecchymosis present on chest.
N Bokke RN

Temp: 37³ P: 110 R: 28 B.P. 162/90 Wt: 183# Ht: 6'0" Mode of Arrival: Ambulatory

Physical Exam: Pt returned to ER with $\bar{c}$ chest pain that worsens with deep breath. Lungs clear to auscultation. RSS

Diagnosis: Inadequate pain control for musculoskeletal pain 2° MVA last week.

Treatment and Orders: Vicodin, $\bar{i}$-$\bar{i}\bar{i}$ q 4° prn (#30)

Jones MD

Medications:		Diagnosis Codes:
Time	Type/Dose	Disposition: ____ Time: 1310

Exhibit 2-4   **411**

Quality Care Central

PATIENT NAME: John Q. Doe
MEDICAL RECORDS NUMBER: 12345
DOB: 1/8/55
ADMISSION DATE: 1/01/00
DISCHARGE DATE: 1/01/00
ATTENDING: M. Welby, MD
DICTATING PHYSICIAN: Jones, MD

HISTORY OF PRESENT ILLNESS:

Patient is a 44 year old male involved in an MVA last week. Trauma work-up at that time negative except for musculoskeletal pain from seat belt injury.

Presented to Emergency Room with continued complaint of chest pain associated with inspiration. Denied other complaints.

Patient was discharged to home with Vicodin prescription and instructions to return if no improvement was noted.

FINAL DIAGNOSIS:

1. Inadequate pain control of musculoskeletal injury
2. Status post Motor Vehicle Accident
3. Musculoskeletal injury secondary to MVA
4. Diabetes Melitis

Dictated: 12/28/99
Transcribed: 1/29/99

DISCHARGE SUMMARY

Quality Care Central

Medical Record No: 12345	Account No: 678	Admit Date 1/2/00	Time 0820	*Code Blue*
Patient Name: John Q. Doe				
Patient Address: 123 Main				

Primary Physician: M. Welby	Discharge Date/Time Admitted	Date of Birth: 1-8-55	Home Phone: 555-1234	Prehospital Treatment: CPR, intubation, I.V., Epi, Lido, Defibrilated x tir

Allergies: Unknown
Medications: Unknown   } Chart unavailable

Past Medical History: Unknown – } MVA last week.

Last Meal: Unknown.

Nursing Assessment: Pt found down on livingroom floor by wife this AM. Had been awake most of the night with c/o CP. CPR initiated. Ambulance called. Defibrilated x 3. Original rhythm was V-fib. Upon arrival to ETC, pt. unresponsive, pupils fixed and dilated, no gag reflex noted. Lungs with coarse crackles throughout. Orally intubated with froathy pink tinged secretions noted in ETT. O₂ administered per ambu at 100% NG inserted with scant returns. No bowl sounds noted x 4 quads. Peripheral pulses weak x 4 ext but easily palpated. 0830-12 LEAB 0835 to x-ray dept for CXR. 0845 Report called to ICU. 0855-Transported to ICU per cart in critical condition. Thrum RN Foley to SD inserted

Temp: 96 ²º⁸ P: 136 R: per ambu B.P. 90/40	Wt: — Ht: —	Mode of Arrival: Ambulance

Physical Exam: As above. Found apneic and pulseless. Unknown time period of arrest prior to initiation of CPR. First responders arrived. Initial rhythm – V.fib. def. x? → sinus tach. Continues in sinus tach. 12-Lead shows anterior MI. CXR - Perfuse pulm edema. Remains unresponsive. Pupils fixed and dilated. Ø response to noxious stimuli. Discussed gravity of situation with patients family

Diagnosis: S/p Cardiac Arrest, S/p MVA last week.

Treatment and Orders: Admit ICU

JSmith

Medications:	Lasix 20mg IV- 0830	Diagnosis Codes:
Time	Type/Dose	
0840-Decadron 10mg IV		Disposition: ICU Time: 0855

EMERGENCY TREATMENT CENTER

Exhibit 2-4 **413**

Quality Care Central ✦

PATIENT NAME: John Q. Doe
MEDICAL RECORDS NUMBER: 12345
DOB: 1/8/55
ADMISSION DATE: 01/02/00
ATTENDING: M. Welby, MD

cc: s/p Cardiac Arrest – Coma

HPI: 44 year old gentleman who was involved in an MVA five days ago. He experienced trauma to the chest secondary to seat belt injury and air bag failure. He was seen in the ER and discharged with pain medications. He returned to the ER on 1/1/00 with continued chest pain on inspiration. Vicodin was then prescribed. This AM patient was found on the floor in his living room. He was apneic and pulseless. CPR was not started until first responders arrived. At that time, he was found to be in V-fib and was defibrillated three times and converted to an agonal rhythm that was converted with atropine and epinephrine.

PMH: IDDM X 15 years, HTN, MVA on 12/28/99

MEDS: Humulin Insulin
        HCTZ
        Ibuprofen
        Vicodin

Allergies: PCN (rash)

SOC: Lives with wife and 4 children- 2 sons and 2-daughters
       Dairy Farmer
       Quit smoking 5 years ago – prior to that 1 pack /day
       θ drugs
       occasional EtoH

VS: 36.2 R   116   18   102/72

P.E.: General: Unresponsive to voice, light, noxious stimuli
        HEENT: Pupils fixed/ dilated, negative occulocephalic reflex,
                    EOM's not intact, TM's clear, abrasions as
                    noted above,
        Lungs: Coarse crackles noted throughout on ant. / lateral auscultation
                    Left greater than right
        Heart: RRR, tachycardic, S3 no murmur, θ JVD
        ABD: (-) bowel sounds, soft, flat
        Neuro: As above
        Ext: slight lower ext. edema. DP and PT pulses weakly palpable bilat.

Quality Care Central

01/02/00   1°MD: M. Welby, MD

CC: Cardiac Arrest → Coma

HPI: 44 YoM who was involved in MVA 5 days ago. Trauma to chest 2° seatbelt injury and air bag failure. Returned to ER yesterday c̄ c/o continued CP. - Vicodin prescribed. This AM pt was found pulseless and apneic by his wife. ~~Defib~~ error defib x iii. Original rhythm V-fib. converted to sinus tach.

Currently unresponsive to all stimuli. Pupils fixed and dilated 8/8. Intermittent myoclonic type jerking noted bilaterally in upper extremities. Fading ecchymotic areas noted over anterior chest wall. Facial and upper chest abrasions present & healing.

PMH: IDDM x 15 years
       HTN

MEDS: Humulin Insulin
       HCTZ
       Ibuprofen
       Vicodin

Allergies: PCN (rash)

SOC: Lives with wife and 4 children   2 sons   2 daughters
     Dairy Farmer
     Quit smoking 5 years ago - prior to that 1 pack/day
     Ø drugs
     occassional EtOH

VS - 36³ ® - 116 - 18 - ¹⁰²/₇₂

P.E.   gen = Unresponsive to voice, light, noxious stimuli
       HEENT = Pupils fixed/dilated, Negative occulocephalic reflex
          EOM I, TMs - clear, abrasions as noted above.
       Lungs = Coarse Crackles (rhonchi) noted throughout on ant/lat
          auscultation. L > R

       Heart = RRR, tachycardic, S₃ no murmur, Ø JVD

PROGRESS NOTES (continued)

Exhibit 2-4   **415**

Quality Care Central ✦

01/02/00 Admission Note - continued

Abd= ⊖ BS, Soft, flat
Neuro= As above
extremities= slight lower ext edema
      DP & PT pulses weakly palpable blbd

LABS= UA neg - Sp Gr = 1.020

10.2 / 11.0 / 38.2 \ 272		135	102	16 / 130
		4.8	22	0.9

CXR= Infitrates throughout - Pulm Edema

A/P: 44 year old male
      S/P code - coma
① R/o anoxic injury
   Decadron IV
   EEG - ASAP — Neurology Consult
   Discuss c̄ family

② Pulm. Edema
   ? Cardiac Contusions - Cardiology Consult
   EKG - Now & q Am
   Lasix
   monitor electrolytes
   Consider ECHO
   Consider Nipride gtt

③. Hypotension
   Dopamine
   IV - NS @ TKO for now
   consider pulm. art. Catheter

WELBY MD.

Quality Care Central

Patient _John Q Doe_

Date/ Time	Temp	Pulse	Resp	B/P	Nurse's Narrative
					by Welby MD. Family
					present Wife requests
					autopsy Chaplain Morgue
					notified _M.Sm_
1230					Transported to morgue
					belongings sent with
					wife _M.Sm RN_

NURSE'S NOTES

Exhibit 2-4   **417**

Quality Care Central ✸

Patient   John Q Doe

Date/ Time	Temp	Pulse	Resp	B/P	Nurse's Narrative
1/2/00 0910 continued					(Neuro:) Unresponsive to noxious, Pupils fixed & dilated 7/7 Doll's eyes negative, EEG ordered (IV's): ® antecub @ TKO ℒ antecubetal @ TKO ⁓⁓⁓ RN
0930		110	18	108/60	Wife / Children here Questions answered.
0945		104	18	90/54	Welby MD here. Labs drawn. Remains in Sinus tach. No Δ in neuro status. ⁓⁓⁓ RN⁓
1000		98	18	88/50	EEG done. ⁓⁓⁓ RN.
1015		98	18	108/56	Cardiology consult. No change in assessment. ⁓⁓⁓ RN ⁓⁓⁓
1030		110	18	80/50	No U/O in last hour. Dr. Welby notified. ⁓⁓⁓
1105		118	18	104/62	IV lasix given - Minimal response. ⁓⁓⁓ RN. Experience paroxysmal V-fib. Pt. did not spontaneously convert. Asystole-Pronounced.

NURSE'S NOTES

Quality Care Central

Patient __John Q Doe__

Date/ Time	Temp	Pulse	Resp	B/P	Nurse's Narrative
0910	36²⁷	124	18	96/42	Pt. arrived per cart from ER
					following a cardiopulmonary arrest
					this am.
					⊂CV⊃ Sinus tach c̄ frequent PVC's. S₁ S₂
					c̄ murmur noted on anterior/lateral
					auscultation. Skin cool, dry, pale.
					Nail beds blue and mottling noted
					in feet bilaterally. PT/DP doppled
					bilaterally. Arterial line in right
					radial artery c good waveform.
					⊂Pulm.⊃ orally intubated on BEAR.
					vent T.V.= 1000 RR-18 PEEP=5
					FiO₂=80%. O₂ Sats= 98%. Lungs with
					crackles throughout. Not over breathing
					the vent.
					⊂G.I.⊃ Abd. flat soft. NG to LIS
					placement confirmed with air.
					pH=5 Guaiac (−) returns. Bowel
					Sounds hypoactive.
					⊂GU⊃ Foley to SD. Clear yellow
					urine in scant amounts.
					⊂M/S:⊃ No abnormalities noted.
					⊂Int:⊃ Abrasions to face and upper
					body. Bruising noted over chest.

NURSE'S NOTES

Exhibit 2-4   **419**

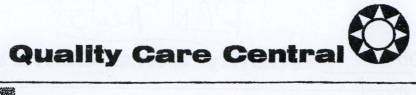

Quality Care Central

01/02/00   0845

Sodium	145
Potassium	4.8
Chloride	105
CO2 Total	29
BUN	14
Creatinine	0.7
Glucose	278

01/02/00   0845

WBC	10.7
RBC	4.8
HGB	13.6
HCT	38
MCV	96.7
MCHC	29.5
Plt	400

01/02/00   0845

CPK	345
CKMB	4.5
CKMB-Index	3.0
Troponin- I	2.87

LABORATORY RESULTS

PRN meds

Quality Care Central

`ME: ___Doe___

ALLERGIES: PCN					
	Date:	01/02/00	01/03	01/04	01/05
Date/ Initial	Medication				
1/21	Lasix 10mg IV	RB	/	/	/
1/2/00	Decadron 10mg IV	RB	/	/	/

MEDICATION ADMINISTRATION

Exhibit 2-4   **421**

NAME: _Doe_   **Quality Care Central** ✦

ALLERGIES: PCN					
	Date:	01/02	01/03	01/04	01/05
Date/ Initial	Medication				
01/02/00 NP	Lasix 10mg IV 08-20				
01/02/00	Decadron 10mg IV 08-20				

MEDICATION ADMINISTRATION

**MEDICATION/
TREATMENT**

Quality Care Central

PATIENT NAME: John Q. Doe
MEDICAL RECORDS NUMBER: 12345
DOB: 1/8/55
ADMISSION DATE: 01/02/00
ATTENDING: M. Welby, MD

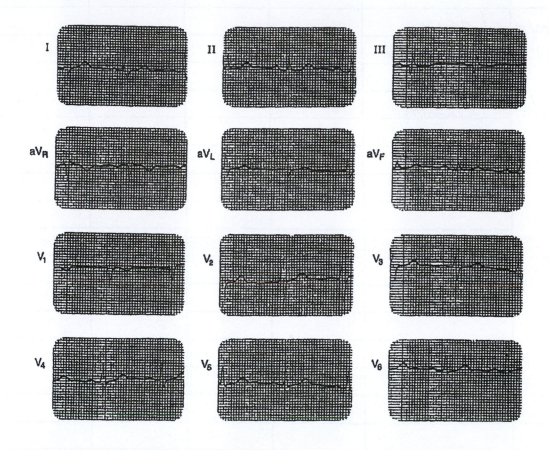

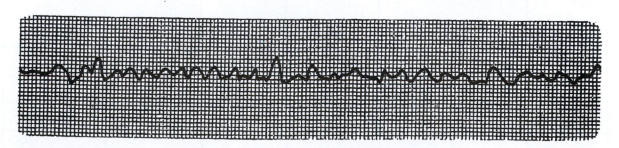

EKG REPORTS

Exhibit 2-4   **423**

Quality Care Central

PATIENT NAME: John Q. Doe
MEDICAL RECORDS NUMBER: 12345
DOB: 1/8/55
ADMISSION DATE: 01/02/00
ATTENDING: M. Welby, MD

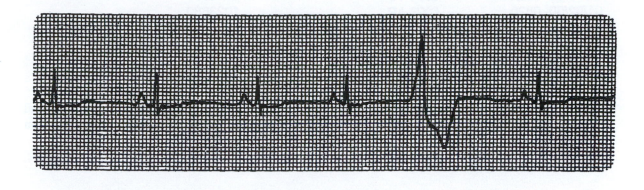

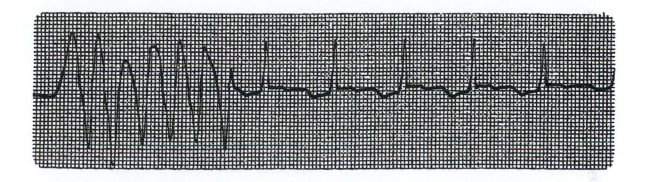

EKG REPORTS

Quality Care Central

CHART COPY

Date/ Time	Description	Requisition Number
01/02/00- 0820	CXR- AP	1023678
01/02/00- 0820	CXR-AP	1023680

AP PORTABLE CHEST: 01/02/00   0840

Extensive pulmonary edema noted with obvious engorgement of pulmonary vasculature. An endotracheal tube is noted in the right main bronchial. ETT should be pulled back 2 cm. A nasogastric tube has been placed and the tip is noted below the hemidiaphragm. No cardiomegaly noted.

AP PORTABLE CHEST: 01/02/00   0845

No significant changes noted in pulmonary vasculature and alveolar edema. ETT now in the main stem of the bronchus. Pulmonary artery catheter now present with the distal tip positioned appropriately in the pulmonary artery.

Radiologist: Dr. Kylie
Released on: 01/02/00 1345

D: 01/03/00 00:05
T: 01/03/00 13:50

Electronically Signed by: Dr. M. Kylie, MD

RADIOLOGY REPORT

Exhibit 2-4   **425**

Quality Care Central

01/0?/00 (1030)	S/p Arrest - Anoxic Encephalopathy. EEG - Diffuse Cerebral Dysfunction Discussed gravity of situation with wife and children. DNR Now. Myoclonic Seizures throughout Night - treated successfully c̄ Valium WELBY MD
01/0?/00 (1105)	Pt experienced episode of V-fib followed by asystole. Family notified. Counseling/support offered. Wife requests autopsy. WELBY MD.

Progress Notes

J.Q Doe

Quality Care Central

Consultation Requested: Neurology	Requesting Physician: WELBY
Date / Time of Request: 01/02/00 9:00 AM	Date / Time of Consultation: _____

Reason for Consultation: S/P Arrest, Unknown Down-time
R/O Anoxic Encephalopathy

REPORT OF FINDINGS:

1/02/00 9AM Mr. Doe is a 44 year old man who was seen for a neurological evaluation following a cardiopulmonary arrest. He is currently unresponsive to noxious stimuli. He was involved in an MVA on 12/28/99, taken by ambulance to the E.R. and later discharged with pain meds. He continued to have CP and was found pulseless and apneic by his wife this AM.
Allergies: PCN   MEDICATIONS: Insulin, HCTZ, Ibuprofen, Vicodin.
PMH- DIABETES, HTN   SH-Married, 3 children
ROS- not possible.   Examination: Unresponsive to pain, light, noise
No posturing noted. Occulocephalic reflex negative. No spontaneous respirations. Pupils fixed and dilated. Abnormal EEG.
No spontaneous extremity movements

Impression: Coma 2° anoxic encephalopathy post arrest

Plan: Will discuss gravity of situation with attending
and pt's family.

Consulting Service: Neurology	Consulting Physician Neuron MD.

CONSULTATION

Exhibit 2-4   **427**

Quality Care Central

Consultation Requested: Cardiology	Requesting Physician: WELBY

Date / Time of Request: 1/2/00 10AM	Date / Time of Consultation:

Reason for Consultation:

S/p Arrest - Unknown Down Time
Assess Cardiac Status.

REPORT OF FINDINGS:

1/2/00 - 1030 History of present illness: Found by wife this morning in full arrest. Unknown period of time between arrest and initiation of CPR. Pt. was found by paramedics to be in V-fib. He was then defibrillate x 3 into an agonal rhythm which converted to a sinus tach with atropine and epinephrine. Upon arrival in the ER, the 12 lead showed 3mm ST depression with T-wave inversion. An echocardiogram was performed in the ER which showed anterior wall hypokenesis. Pt had been in MVA last week.

Allergies: PCN

PMH: Diabetes, hypertension

Medication: Insulin, HCTZ, Ibuprofen, Vicodin.

F/S H: Nonsmoker. Married with 3 children

P.E: VSS: 92-24 (vent) - 110/70

Neck: Supple, with healing abrasions

Cardiac: RRR, Normal S₁S₂. There is a 4/6 systolic murmur radiating from the apex to the axilla consistent with mitral regurg.

Abd: Hypoactive bowel sounds x 4 quads. NG in place

Extremities: edema x 4 extremities.

Neuro- Unresponsive to noxious. Pupils unresponsive.

Pulm- Orally intubated on ventilator. CXR- shows pulm. edema.

EKG- Sinus tach with posterior ST depression in III and aVR.

Echo- anterior wall hypokinesis with evidence of localized effusion.

Impression: S/P Code, Cardiac Contusion - 2° Chest Compressions or MVA.

Plan: Stabilize neurologically, Treat with Lasix, IV, and beta blocker

Consulting Service: Cardiology	Consulting Physician Corry-Narry, MD

CONSULTATION

exhibit **2-5**

MEDICATIONS

1. Narcotics/pain control/analgesic

Morphine	
Codeine	(Tylenol w/Codeine, Robitussin)
Hydrocodone	(Vicodin, Hycodan, Lorcet)
Hydromorphone	(Dilaudid)
Oxycodone	(Percodan, Percocet)
Other narcotics:	alwin, Demerol

   These drugs have the most stringent classification for controlled substances, with a very high abuse potential. Inventory and distribution are tightly controlled.

2. Anti-inflammatory (nonsteroidal anti-inflammatory drug—NSAID)

Anabolic steroids:	Testosterone, Nandrolone, Oxymetholone
Aspirin	
Naproxen	(Aleve, Naprosyn, Anaprox DS)
Relafen	(NSAID)
Cataflam	(NSAID)
Indomethacin	(Indocin)
Celebrex	(NSAID)
Ansaid	(NSAID)
Orudis	(NSAID)
Clinoril	(NSAID)
Tolectin	(NSAID)
Voltaren	(NSAID)
Acetaminophen	(Tylenol various brand names)

3. Muscle relaxants

Diazepam	(Valium)
Cyclobenzaprine	HCL (Flexeril)
Carisoprodol	(Soma)
Methocarbamol	(Robaxin)
Chlorzoxazone	(Parafon Forte)
Orphenadrine citrate	(Norflex)

4. Antidepressants

Amitriptyline	(Elavil)
Venlafaxine	(Effexor)
Bupropion	(Wellbutrin)

Exhibit 2-5   **429**

Fluoxetine	(Prozac)
Sertraline	(Zoloft)
Paroxetine	(Paxil)
Imipramine	(Tofranil)
Nortriptyline	(Pamelor)
Lorazepam	(Ativan)

5. Reflux and peptic ulcer disease

Ranitidine	(Zantac)
Cimetidine	(Tagamet)
Famotidine	(Pepcid)
Omeprazole	(Prilosec)
Compazine	(treatment of nausea and non-psychotic anxiety)
Vistaril	(treatment of nausea and anxiety and tension)

6. Antipsychotics (used to help patients organize chaotic and disorganized thinking)

Haloperidol	(Haldol)
Risperidone	(Risperdal)
Chlorpromazine	(Thorazine)
Thioridazine	(Mellaril)
Fluphenazine	(Prolixin)
Trifluoperazine	(Stelazine)
Thiothixene	(Navane)
Lithium	(Carbolith)
Aripiprazole	(Abilify)
Quetiapine	(Seroquel)

7. Antibiotics

Ampicillin	Ancef
Oxacillin	Cephalexin (Keflex)
Augmentin	Rocephin
Cipro	Cefixime (Suprax)

8. Headache medications

Cafergot

Imitrex

Midrin

Sansert

9. Seizure medications

Dilantin	Neurontin
Clonopin	Phenobarbital
Tegretol	Sertan
Depakene	

10. Antihypertensive medications

Lotensin	Vasotec
Lotrel	Atenolol (Tenormin)
Nifedipine (Procardia)	Cardizem
Lisinopril (Zestril)	Verapamil (Calan SR)

According to WebMD, IMS Institute for Healthcare Informatics states that the following are the most prescribed drugs in the United States:

Hydrocodone	Pain Reliever (Narcotic)
Acetaminophen	Pain Reliever/Analgesic (Non-narcotic)
Zocor	Cholesterol
Lisinopril	High blood pressure
Synthroid	Thyroid hormone
Norvasc	High blood pressure
Prilosec	Antacid
Azithromycin	Z-pak antibiotic
Amoxicillin	Antibiotic
Glucophage	Diabetes
Hydrochlorothiazide	High blood pressure

If there is a question concerning any drug, a good reference to check is the *Physicians Desk Reference*, referred to as the *PDR*.

exhibit **2-6**

MEDICAL REFERENCES

Diagnostic & Statistical Manual of Mental Disorders

Dorland's Illustrated Medical Dictionary

Grant's Atlas of Anatomy

Gray's Anatomy

Guides to the Evaluation of Permanent Impairment.

Medical Abbreviations, Neil M. Davis

Medline

Merck Manual

Physician's Desk Reference (PDR)

Stedman's

Taber's Medical Dictionary

WebMD

exhibit **2-7**

PHYSICIAN AND OTHER MEDICAL SPECIALTIES

This list of specialties is not exhaustive by any means. Some of the more common physician specialties and sub-specialties as well as other non-physician specialties and fields are listed.

Allergist	A physician specializing in the diagnosis and treatment of patient reactions to irritating agents or allergens, such as food, medicine, and pollens.
Anesthesiologist	A physician specializing in delivering anesthesia during surgical, obstetric, or diagnostic procedures.
Audiologist	One who specializes in identifying, diagnosing, and treating hearing disorders.
Bariatrician	One who is focused on the care of obese patients.
Cardiologist	A physician specializing in the diagnosis and treatment of heart, lungs, and blood vessels.
Cardiovascular Surgeon	A physician primarily specializing in performing surgery of the heart and blood vessels.
Chiropractor	One who is not a medical doctor but who focuses on a therapeutic method of treatment based on interaction of the spine and nervous system.
Critical Care Physician	A physician based in ICU or CCU with broad knowledge of care and treatment of a critically ill patient.
Dermatologist	A physician specializing in the skin and its diseases.
Emergency Medicine	A physician specializing in emergency room medicine.
Endocrinologist	A physician specializing in the diagnosis and treatment of the glands of internal secretion and hormonal disorders and diseases.
Family Practice	A general practitioner who is generally considered the primary care physician. This physician is concerned with the health care of a patient and patient's family, including all ages.
Gastroenterologist	A physician specializing in diseases of the digestive tract and organs, including stomach, bowels, liver, and gall bladder.
General Practice	A physician concerned with diagnosis and treatment of disease by both medical and surgical methods, regardless of the particular organ system, location in body, or patient's age.
Gerontologist	A physician specializing in the aging process with special skills in treating the elderly.

Exhibit 2-7   **433**

Gynecologist	A physician specializing in health care for women with focus on the female reproductive system, menstrual disorders, contraceptives, fertility, and determining pregnancy. (See Obstetrician.)
Hematologist	A physician specializing in diseases of the blood, blood clotting mechanisms, bone marrow, spleen, and lymph glands.
Holistic Medicine	A type of medicine that focuses on the whole person, examining the physical, mental, spiritual, and emotional well-being of a patient prior to determining treatment.
Immunologist	A physician specializing in the body's ability to fight infectious or irritating substances that threaten the body with disease; treating disorders involving the immune system.
Infectious Disease	A physician specializing in diseases caused by infections, whether bacterial infections, viral infections, and/or fungal infections. The concern is with all types of infectious diseases in all organs of the human body.
Internal Medicine/ Internist	A physician focused on long-term comprehensive care who manages common illnesses and complex medical issues, primarily in adults.
Neurologist	A physician specializing in the treatment of disorders of the nervous system, brain, spinal cord, and peripheral nerves.
Neurosurgeon	A physician specializing in operative and non-operative management of the central, peripheral, and autonomic nervous system.
Nephrologist	A physician specializing in diseases and disorders of the kidney, high blood pressure, fluid and mineral balance, and dialysis.
Neonatologist	A physician specializing in the diagnosis and treatment of disorders of the newborn infant. This physician may serve as a consultant to pediatricians.
Obstetrician	A physician specializing in women's reproductive organs as well as care during pregnancy (prenatal), childbirth, and postnatal care. A physician with this specialty and gynecology is sometimes referred to as an "OB/GYN doctor."
Oncologist	A physician specializing in the diagnosis and treatment of all types of cancer along with other benign and malignant tumors.
Ophthalmologist	A physician specializing in the diagnosis and medical and surgical treatment of diseases of the eye, eyelid, and orbital problems.
Orthopedist/Orthopedic Surgeon	A physician specializing in preservation or restoration of function of extremities, spine, and other bone and joint structures by medical, surgical, and physical means.

Otolaryngologist/ENT	A physician specializing in the medical and surgical treatment of the ears, nose, throat, and respiratory and upper alimentary systems. This specialist is also referred to as an otorhinolaryngologist.
Otorhinolaryngologist	See column above.
Pathologist	A physician specializing in the study of diseases and the structural and functional changes they cause. They may examine abnormal changes in tissues removed during operations and postmortem examinations.
Pediatrician	A physician specializing in the care and treatment of children.
Physiatrist/Physical Medicine	A physician specializing in rehabilitation and physical medicine who is concerned with maximal restoration of physical, psychological, social, vocational function, and alleviation of pain.
Plastic Surgeon	A physician specializing in the repair and reconstruction of defects of the skin with emphasis on the face, head, limbs, breast, and external genitalia.
Proctologist	A physician specializing in the disorders of the rectum and the anus.
Psychiatrist	A physician specializing in the branch of medicine that deals with the study, treatment, and prevention of mental, addictive, and emotional disorders.
Psychologist	A specialist focused on the treatment of mental functions and behaviors.
Pulmonologist	A physician specializing in disorders and diseases of the lungs and airways.
Radiologist	A physician specializing in the use and diagnostic and therapeutic applications of radiant energy.
Rheumatologist	A physician specializing in the treatment of disorders and diseases of the joints, muscles, bones, and tendons, typically arthritis, back pain, and muscle sprains and strains.
Surgeon	A physician specializing in performing surgery. The physician treats diseases, injuries, and deformities by manual or operative methods. This type of physician may have many subspecialties such as general surgeon, orthopedic surgeon, thoracic surgeon, or neurosurgeon.
Toxicologist	One concerned with treating patients who have been exposed to poisons such as medications, drug reactions, and environmental toxins.
Urgent Care	One specially trained in providing treatment of non-emergency illnesses and injuries, such as minor abrasions, sore throats, and ear infections.
Urologist	A physician specializing in the disorders and diseases of the urinary tract and male reproductive tract.

exhibit **2-8**

COMMON MEDICAL SYMBOLS

QUANTIFYING AND COMPARING SYMBOLS

- < less than
- > greater than
- ≤ less than or equal to
- ≥ greater than or equal to
- ↑ increase or elevated
- ↓ decrease or lowered
- : ratio or "is to"
- *i* one
- *ii* two
- *iii* three

GENDER AND OTHER SYMBOLS

- ♂ or male
- ♀ or female
- ♦ sex unknown
- # number, fracture, or pound
- − absent, minus, negative
- + present, plus, positive
- Δ change

PHYSICAL ASSESSMENT

Glasgow Coma Scale (three categories are rated)

Eye Opening
- Spontaneous   4
- To sound   3
- To pain   2
- None   1

Motor Response
- Obeys commands   6
- Localizes pain   5
- Normal flexion   4
- Abnormal flexion   3
- Extension   2
- None   1

Verbal Response
- Oriented   5
- Confused conversation   4
- Inappropriate words   3
- Incomprehensible sounds 2
- None   1

OBSTETRIC SYMBOLS AND DEFINITIONS

Gynecology is the branch of medicine dealing with health care for women, such as diagnosis, care, and treatment of diseases and disorders affecting female reproductive organs, menstrual disorders, menopause, prescription of contraceptives, and ordering tests to determine pregnancy. Obstetrics is the branch of medicine dealing with the diagnosis, care, and treatment of women's reproductive organs/tracts and care during pregnancy (prenatal care), childbirth, and postnatal care. Sometimes a physician will have both specialties and will be referred to as an "OB/GYN" doctor.

NEWBORN APGAR SCORES

A newborn child is scored 1 minute and 5 minutes after birth. Five signs are evaluated: heart rate, respiratory effort, muscle tone, reflex irritability (soft rubber catheter inserted), and color, as follows:

Clinical Sign	Score		
	0	**1**	**2**
Heart rate	Absent	<100	>100
Respiratory effort	Absent	Slow and irregular	Good and crying
Muscle tone	Flaccid	Some flexion arms/legs	Active movement
Reflex irritability	No responses	Crying	Crying vigorously
Color	Blue or pale	Pink body, blue extremities	Pink entire body

- **Primagravida** refers to a woman who is pregnant for the first time; also sometimes called *gravida.*
- **Gravida** refers to a woman who is or has been pregnant, irrespective of the pregnancy outcome. With the first pregnancy, she becomes a primagravida, and with additional pregnancies, she is referred to as *multigravida.*
- **Nulligravida** refers to a woman who is not pregnant and who has never been pregnant.
- **Primapara** refers to a woman who has been delivered only once of a fetus or fetuses who reached viability. Completion of any pregnancy beyond the stage of abortion bestows parity ("para") upon the mother.
- **Parturient** refers to a woman in labor.
- **Puerpera** refers to a woman who has just given birth.

Gravida is usually followed by a number, which refers to the number of prior deliveries a woman has had. For example, "gravida 3 para 2" is describing a woman who is experiencing her third pregnancy and she has had two prior deliveries.

exhibit **2-9**

PREFIXES AND SUFFIXES

Prefix	Meaning
a-, an-	Without, not lack of
ab-	Away from
ad-	To, toward, near
amphi-	On both sides, double
ana-	Up, toward, apart
ante-	Before, in front of, forward
anti-	Against, opposing
aut-, auto-	Self
bi-	Two, double, twice
cata-	Down, under, lower, against
circum-	Around
contra-	Opposed, against
de-	Down, from
di-	Two, twice
dia-	Between, through, apart, across, completely
dis-	Apart or free from
dys-	Difficult, bad, painful
e-, ec-, ex-	Out of, from, away from
ext-, ecto-, exo-	Outer, outside, situated on
em-, en-	In
end-, endo-, ent-, ento-	Within, inner
ep-, epi-	Upon, on, over
extra-, extro-	Outside of, beyond, outward
hemi-	Half
hyper-	Excessive, above, beyond
hyp-, hypo-	Under, deficient, beneath
im-, in-	In, into, within
infra-	Below, beneath
inter-	Between
intra-	Within
intro-	Into, within
mes-, meso-	Middle
micr-, micro-	Small
mult-, multi-	Many
neo-	New, recent
pan-	All, entire

para-	Beside, beyond, after
peri-	Around
poly-	Many, much excessive
post-	After, behind
pre-, pro-	Before, in front of
pseud-, pseudo-	False
re-	Again, backward
semi-	Half
sub-	Under, beneath
super-, supra-	Above, superior, excess
trans-	Across, through

Suffix	Meaning
-ac, -al, -ic, -ous, -tic	Pertaining to, relating to
-algia, -dynia	Pain
-ate, -ize	Use, subject to
-cele	Protrusion (hernia)
-centesis	Surgical puncture to remove fluid
-cle, -cule, -ole, -ola, -ule, -ulum, -ulus	Small
-cyte	Cell
-ectomy	Cutting out
-emesis	Vomit
-emia	Blood condition
-esis, -ia, -iasis, -ism, -ity, -osis, -sis, -tion, -y	State or condition
-genesis	Beginning process, origin
-gram, -graphy	Recording, written record
-graph	Instrument that records
-istible, -ile	Capable, able
-ites, -itis	Inflammation
-ology	Science, study of
-oma	Tumor
-penia	Deficiency of, lack of
-phobia	Abnormal fear or intolerance
-plasty	Surgical shaping or formation
-pnea	Breathing
-ptosis	Prolapse, downward displacement
-rrhage, -rrhagia	Excessive flow
-rrhaphy	Suturing in place
-rrea	Flow or discharge
-rrhexis	Rupture
-scope	Instrument for examining
-scopy	Act of examining
-stomy	Surgical opening
-tome	Instrument for
-tomy	Cutting, incision

exhibit **2-10**

MEDICAL ABBREVIATIONS

Abbreviation	Meaning
A	Accommodation; acetum; angstrom unit; anode; anterior
a	Accommodation; ampere; anterior; area
ā	Before
A_2	Aortic second sound
AAA	Abdominal aortic aneurysm
Ab	Antibody
ABD	Abdominal/abdomen
abd	Abdomen
ABG	Arterial blood gas
ABO	Three basic blood groups
Abx	Antibiotic
AC	Adrenal cortex
Ac	Before a meal
acc	Accommodation
ACE	Adrenocortical hormone
ACh	Acetylcholine
ACLS	Advanced Cardiac Life Support
ACTH	Adrenocorticotropic hormone
AD	Right ear (*auris dextra*); advance directive
ADH	Antidiuretic hormone
ADHD	Attention-deficit hyperactivity disorder
ADL	Activities of daily living
Ad lib	Freely; as desired
ADS	Antidiuretic substance
Adv	Advance
AED	Automatic external defibrillator
AF	Atrial fibrillation
AFB	Acid-fast bacillus
A/G; A-G ratio	Albumin-globulin ratio
AHF	Antihemophilic factor
AICD	Automatic implantable cardiac defibrillator
AIDS	Acquired immunodeficiency syndrome
aj	Ankle jerk

AKA	Above the knee amputation
Al	Aluminum
Alb	Albumin
ALS	Amyotrophic lateral sclerosis
ALT	Alanine aminotransferase
Am	Mixed astigmatism
AM	Morning
a.m.a.	Against medical advice
AMI	Acute myocardial infarction
amp.	Ampere
ana	So much of each, or aa
anat	Anatomy or anatomic
ANS	Autonomic nervous system
ANT	Anterior
AO	Anodal opening; atrioventricular valve openings
A&O	Alert and oriented
AOP	Anodal opening picture
AOS	Anodal opening sound
A-P; AP; A/P	Anterior-posterior; apical pulse
A.P.	Anterior pituitary gland
APA	Antipernicious anemia
APAP	Acetaminophen
APE	Acute pulmonary edema
APTT	Activated partial thromboplastin time
ARC	Anomalous retinal correspondence; AIDS-related complex
ARD	Acute respiratory disease
ARDS	Acute respiratory disease syndrome
Ag	Silver
ARMD	Age-related macular degeneration
AS	Left ear (*auris sinistra*)
As	Arsenic
As.	Astigmatism
ASA	Acetylsalicylic acid (aspirin)
ASAP	As soon as possible
ASD	Atrial septal defect
AsH	Hypermetropic astigmatism
ASHD	Arteriosclerotic heart disease
AsM	Myopic astigmatism
ASS	Anterior superior spine
AST	Asparate aminotransferase (formerly SGOT)
Ast	Astigmatism
ASU	Ambulatory surgical unit
ATS	Anxiety tension state; antitetanic serum
AU	Angstrom unit
Au	Gold

Exhibit 2-10   **441**

A-V; AV; A/V	Arteriovenous; atrioventricular
Av	Average or avoirdupois
AVR	Aortic valve repair
ax	Axis; axillary
B	Boron; bacillus; Beta
Ba	Barium
BAC	Blood alcohol concentration
Bact	Bacterium
BBB	Blood-brain barrier
BBT	Basal body temperature
BC	Birth control
BCC	Basal cell carcinoma
BCLS	Basic cardiac life support
BE	Barium enema
Be	Beryllium
BFP	Biologically false positivity (in syphilis tests)
Bi	Bismuth
bid; b.i.d.	Twice a day (*bis in die*)
BIPAP	Bilevel positive airway pressure
BIVAD	Biventricular assist device
BK	Below the knee
BKA	Below the knee amputation
BM	Bowel movement
BMR	Basal metabolic rate
BP; B/P	Blood pressure; buccopulpal
bp	Boiling point
BPH	Benign prostatic hypertrophy
bpm	Beats per minute
BRP	Bathroom privileges
BS	Breath sounds; bowel sounds; blood sugar
BSA	Body surface area
BSE	Breast self-examination
BSO	Bilateral salpingo-oophorectomy
BSP	Bromsulphalein
BUN	Blood urea nitrogen
BVM	Bag-value mask (Ambu-bag)
BW	Birth weight
Bx	Biopsy
$\bar{C}$	Carbon; centigrade; Celsius
°C	Degrees Celsius
c or $\bar{c}$	With
C_{alb}	Albumin clearance
C_{cr}	Creatinine clearance
C_{in}	Inulin clearance
CA	Chronological age; cervicoaxial; cancer; carcinoma

Ca	Calcium; cancer; carcinoma
CABG	Coronary artery bypass graft
CABS	Coronary artery bypass surgery
$CaCo_3$	Calcium carbonate
CAD	Coronary artery disease
Cal	Calorie
CA&O	Conscious, alert and oriented
C&S	Culture and sensitivity
CAPD	Continuous abdominal peritoneal dialysis; complete blood count
CAT	Computerized (axial) tomography scan
CBC or cbc	Complete blood count
CBG	Complete blood glucose
CBI	Continuous bladder irrigation
CC	Chief complaint
cc	Cubic centimeter
CCl_4	Carbon tetrachloride
CCU	Coronary care unit, critical care unit
CDC	Centers for disease control and prevention
CF	Cystic fibrosis
cf	Compare or bring together
Cg; Cgm	Centigram
CH	Crown-heel (length of fetus)
$CHCL_3$	Chloroform
CH_3COOH	Acetic acid
CHD	Coronary heart disease
ChE	Cholinesterase
CHF	Congestive heart failure
$C_5H_4N_4O_3$	Uric acid
CHO	Carbohydrate
CH_2OH	Ethyl alcohol
Cl	Chlorine; cardiac index
CICU	Cardiac intensive care unit
CK	Creatine kinase
cm	Centimeter
CMR	Cerebral metabolic rate
CMS	Circulation motion sensation
CMV	Cytomegalovirus
CNS	Central nervous system
c/o	Complains of
CO	Carbon monoxide; cardiac output
CO_2	Carbon dioxide
Co	Cobalt
COLD	Chronic obstructive lung disorder
COPD	Chronic obstructive pulmonary disease

Exhibit 2-10   **443**

CP	Chest pain, cerebral palsy; care plan
CPAC	Continuous positive airway pressure
CPC	Clinicopathologic conference
CPD	Cephalopelvic disproportion
CPR	Cardiopulmonary resuscitation
CR	Crown-rump length (length of a fetus)
CRNA	Certified registered nurse anesthetist
CS	Culture and sensitivity; c-section
cs	Chem-stick (blood sugar)
CSF	Cerebrospinal fluid
CSM	Cerebrospinal meningitis; circulation, sensory and motor
CT	Computed tomography
Cu	Copper
$CuSo_4$	Copper sulfate
CV	Cardiovascular
CVA	Cerebrovascular accident; costovertebral angle
CVP	Central venous pressure
CW	Chest wall
Cx	Culture; circumflex (coronary artery)
CXR	Chest x-ray
D	Dose; vitamin D; right (*dexter*)
DAH	Disordered action of the heart
DAT	Diet as tolerated
D&C	Dilation (dilatation) and curretage
DC	Direct current
dc	Discontinue; discharge
DCA	Deoxycorticosterone acetate
Dcg	Degeneration; degree
dg	Decigram
D.H.S.	Department of Human Services
DIC	Disseminated intravascular coagulation
diff	Differential blood count
DJD	Degenerative joint disease
DKA	Diabetic ketoacidosis
dl	Deciliter
DM	Diabetes mellitus
DNA	Deoxyribonucleic acid
DNAR	Do not attempt resuscitation
DNR	Do not resuscitate
DOA	Dead on arrival
DOB	Date of birth
DOE	Dyspnea on exertion
dr	Dram
DTs	Delirium tremens
DTR	Deep tendon reflex

Dx	Diagnosis
D5W	Dextrose 5% in water
E	Eye
EAHF	Eczema, asthma, and hay fever
EBL	Estimated blood loss
ECF	Extended care facility; extra cellular fluid
ECG	Electrocardiogram; electrocardiograph
ECHO	Echocardiography
ECT	Electroconvulsive therapy
ED	Erythema dose; effective dose; erectile dysfunction
ED$_{50}$	Median effective dose
EDC	Estimated date of confinement
EDD	Estimated date of delivery
EEG	Electroencephalogram, electroencephalograph
EENT	Eye, ear, nose, and throat
EGD	Esophageal gastric duodenoscopy
EKG	Electrocardiogram, electrocardiograph
Em	Emmetropia
EMB	Eosin-methylene blue
EMC	Encephalomyocarditis
EMF	Erythrocyte maturation factor
EMG	Electromyogram
EMS	Emergency medical service
ENT	Ear, nose, and throat
EOM	Extraocular movement
EPR	Electrophrenic respiration
EPS	Extrapyramidal symptoms
ER	Emergency room (hospital); external resistance
ERCP	Endoscopic retrograde cholanglopancreatography
ERG	Electroretinogram
ERS	Emergency response system
ESR	Erythrocyte sedimentation rate
EST	Electroshock therapy
ET	Endotracheal tube
Et	Ethyl
ETOH	Alcohol or alcoholic
exc	Excision
ext	Extract
°F	Degrees Fahrenheit
F	Fahrenheit; field of vision; formula; female
f	Female
FA	Fatty acid
FANA	Fluorescent antinuclear antibody test
F&R	Force and rhythm (pulse)
FBS	Fasting blood sugar

Exhibit 2-10   **445**

FD	Fatal dose; focal distance
Fe	Iron
FeCl$_3$	Ferric Chloride
FHR	Fetal heart rate
FHT	Fetal heart tone
fld	Fluid
fl dr	Fluid dram
fl oz	Fluid ounce
FR	Flocculation reaction
FS	Finger stick (blood sugar)
FSH	Follicle-stimulating hormone
FT	Feeding tube
ft	Foot
FUO	Fever of unknown origin
Fx	Fracture
Gm; g; gm	Gram
GA	Gingivoaxial
Galv	Galvanic
GB	Gallbladder
GBS	Gallbladder series
GC	Gonococcus or gonorrheal
GCS	Glasgow Coma Scale
GDM	Gestational diabetes mellitus
GERD	Gastroesophageal reflux disease
GFR	Glomerular filtration rate
GH	Growth hormone
GI	Gastrointestinal
GLA	Gingivolinguoaxial
GP	General practitioner; general paresis
gr	Grain
Grad	By degrees (*gradatim*)
Grav I, II, III, etc.	Pregnancy one, two, three, etc. (*gravida*)
GSW	Gunshot wound
GT	Gastric tube
gt	Drop (*gutta*)
GTT	Glucose tolerance test
gtt	Drops (*guttae*); drip
GU	Genitourinary
Gyn/GYN	Gynecology
H	Hydrogen
H$^+$	Hydrogen ion
h; hr	Hour
H&E	Hematoxylin and eosin stain
HA	Headache
HAV	Hepatitis A virus

Hb; Hgb	Hemoglobin
H_3BO_3	Boric acid
HBV	Hepatitis B virus
HC	Hospital corps
HCO_3	Bicarbonate
HCG	Human chorionic gonadotropin
HCHO	Formaldehyde
HCl	Hydrochloric acid
HCN	Hydrocyanic acid
H_2CO_3	Carbonic acid
HCT	Hematocrit
HCTZ	Hydrochlorothiazide
HCV	Hepatitis C virus
HD	Hearing distance
HDL	High density lipoprotein
He	Helium
HEENT	Head, eye, ear, nose, and throat
Hg	Mercury
Hgb	Hemoglobin
Hib	*Haemophilus influenza* type B
HIV	Human immunodeficiency (AIDS) virus
HNO_3	Nitric acid
H_2O	Water
H_2O_2	Hydrogen peroxide
HOH	Hard of hearing
HOP	High oxygen pressure
H&P	History and physical
H_2SO_4	Sulfuric acid
HR	Heart rate
HS	Hour of sleep, bedtime
HSV	Herpes simplex virus
HTN	Hypertension
Hy	Hyperopia
Hx	History
I	Iodine
^{131}I	Radioactive isotope of iodine (atomic weight 131)
^{132}I	Radioactive isotope of iodine (atomic weight 132)
I&O	Intake and output
IABP	Intra-aortic balloon pump
IB	Inclusion body
IBW	Ideal body weight
IC	Intracardiac
ICP	Intracranial pressure
ICS	Intercostal space
ICSH	Interstitial cell-stimulating hormone

Exhibit 2-10   **447**

ICU	Intensive care unit
ID	Intradermal
Id.	The same (*idem*)
IDDM	Insulin-dependent diabetes mellitus
IFMC	Iowa Foundation for Medical Care
Ig	Immunoglobulin
IH	Infectious hepatitis
IM	Intramuscular; infectious mononucleosis
I&O	Intake and output
In or "	Inch
IO	Interosseous
IOP	Intraocular pressure
IQ	Intelligence quotient
IS	Intercostal space
IU	Immunizing unit; international units
IUCD	Intrauterine contraceptive device
IUD	Intrauterine device
IUFD	Intrauterine fetal death
IV	Intravenous
IVBS	IV piggyback
IVP	Intravenous pyelogram; intravenous push
IVU	Intravenous urogram/urography
J	Joule
JP (JP drain)	Jackson-Pratt
JVD	Jugular vein distention
K/K+	Potassium
k	Constant
KBr	Potassium bromide
kc	Kilocycle
KCl	Potassium chloride
kev	Kilo electron volts
kg	Kilogram
KI	Potassium iodide
kj	Knee jerk
km	Kilometer
KOH	Potassium hydroxide
KUB	Kidney, ureter, and bladder
kv	Kilovolt
KVO	Keep vein open
kw	Kilowatt
L	Left; liter; length; lumbar; lethal; pound
LA	Left arm
L&A	Light and accommodation
LAD	Left anterior descending
lb	Pound (*libra*)

LB	Large bowel (x-ray film)
LBW	Low birth weight
LCM	Left costal margin
L&D	Labor and delivery
LD	Lethal dose; perception of light difference
LDL	Low density lipoprotein
LDH	Lactate dehydrogenase
LE	Lupus erythematosus; lower extremity
LEEP	Loop electrical excision procedure
LFD	Least fatal dose of a toxin
LFT	Liver function test
LGA	Large for gestational age
LH	Luteinizing hormone
Li	Lithium
LIF	Left iliac fossa
lig	Ligament
LIH	Left inguinal hernia
Liq	Liquor
LLL	Left lower lobe
LLL or LLE	Left lower leg/left lower extremity
LLQ	Left lower quadrant
LMP	Last menstrual period
LNMP	Last normal menstrual period
LOC	Level of consciousness
LP	Lumbar puncture
LPF	Leukocytosis-promoting factor
LR	Lactated Ringer's
LTC	Left to count; (AR term) long term care
LTH	Luteotropic hormone
LUE	Left upper extremity
LUL	Left upper lobe
LUQ	Left upper quadrant
LV	Left ventricle
LVAD	Left ventricular assist device
L&W	Living and well
M	Myopia; meter; muscle; male; thousand
m	Meter
MA	Mental age
MAC	Monitored anesthesia care
MAE	Moves all extremities
MAO	Monoamine oxidase
MAP	Mean arterial pressure
MAT	Multifocal atrial tachycardia
MBD	Minimal brain dysfunction
mc, mCi	Millicurie

Exhibit 2-10   **449**

mcg	Microgram
MCH	Mean corpuscular hemoglobin
MCHC	Mean corpuscular hemoglobin concentration
MCL	Modified chest level
MCV	Mean corpuscular volume
MD	Muscular dystrophy
MDI	Metered-dose inhaler
Me	Methyl
MED	Minimal erythema dose; minimal effective dose
mEq	Milliequivalent
mEq/L	Milliequivalent per liter
ME ratio	Myeloid-erythroid ratio
Mg	Magnesium
mg	Milligram
M Hg	Millimeters of mercury
MI	Myocardial infarction
MID	Midline
ml	Milliliter
MLD	Median or minimum lethal dose
MM	Mucous membrane
mm	Millimeter; muscles
mmHg	Millimeters of mercury
mmm	Millimicron
MMR	Mumps, measles, rubella
Mn	Manganese
mN	Millinormal
MRI	Magnetic resonance imaging
MS	Multiple sclerosis
MSL	Midsternal line
MT	Medical technologist; membrane tympani
MW	Molecular weight
My	Myopia
N	Nitrogen
n	Normal
Na	Sodium
NaBr	Sodium bromide
NACl	Sodium chloride
$Na_2C_2O_4$	Sodium oxalate
Na_2CO_3	Sodium carbonate
NAD	No appreciable disease; no acute distress/no apparent distress
NaF	Sodium fluoride
$NaHCO_3$	Sodium bicarbonate
Na_2HPO_4	Sodium phosphate
NAI	Sodium iodide

$NaNO_3$	Sodium nitrate
Na_2O_2	Sodium peroxide
NaOH	Sodium hydroxide
Na_2SO_4	Sodium sulfate
Ne	Neon
NG	Nasogastric
NH_3	Ammonia
Ni	Nickel
NIH	National Institutes of Health
Nl	Normal
NMR	Nuclear magnetic resonance
NPN	Nonprotein nitrogen
NPO; n.p.o.	Nothing by mouth (*non per os*)
NRC	Normal retinal correspondence
NS	Normal saline
NSAID	Nonsteroidal anti-inflammatory drug
NTG	Nitroglycerine
NTP	Normal temperature and pressure
NYD	Not yet diagnosed
N&V	Nausea and vomiting
O	Oxygen; oculus; pint
O_2	Oxygen; both eyes
O_3	Oxone
OB	Obstetrics
OBS	Organic brain syndrome
OD	Right eye (*oculus dexter*)
OPD	Outpatient department
OR	Operating room
ORIF	Open reduction and internal fixation
OS	Left eye (*oculus sinister*)
Os	Osmium
OT	Occupational therapy
OU	Each eye (*oculus uterque*); both eyes
oz; $\bar{3}$	Ounce
P or $\bar{p}$	After
P	Phosphorus; pulse; pupil
P_2	Pulmonic second sound
P-A; P/A; PA	Posterior-anterior
P&A	Percussion and auscultation
PAB; PABA	Para-aminobenzoic acid
Pap Test	Papanicolaou smear
PAS; PASA	Para-aminosalicylic acid
Pb	Lead
PBI	Protein-bound iodine
PCV	Packed cell volume

Exhibit 2-10   **451**

PD	Interpupillary distance
pd	Prism diopter; pupillary distance
PDA	Patent ductus arteriosus
PDR	*Physician's Desk Reference*
PE	Physical examination; pulmonary embolism; pulmonary edema
PEARLA or PERRLA	Pupils equal and react to light accommodation
PEG	Pneumoencephalography
PET	Positron emission tomography
PGA	Pteroylglutamic acid (folic acid)
PH	Past history
pH	Hydrogen ion concentration (alkalinity and acidity in urine and blood analysis)
Pharm; Phar.	Pharmacy
PI	Previous illness; protamine insulin
PID	Pelvic inflammatory disease
PK	Psychokinesis
PKU	Phenylketonuria
PL	Light perception
PM	Postmortem; evening
PMB	Polymorphonuclear basophil leukocytes (polys)
PMH	Past medical history
PMS	Premenstrual syndrome
PN	Percussion note
PNH	Paroxysmal nocturnal hemoglobinuria
PO; p.o.	Orally (*peros*)
po	By mouth
PPD	Purified protein derivative (TB test)
PR	Per rectum
Pr	Presbyopia; prism
PRN; p.r.n.	As required (*pro re nata*); as needed
pro time	Prothrombin time
PSP	Phenolsulfonphthalein
pt	Pint
Pt	Platinum; patient
PT	Prothrombin time; physical therapy
PTA	Plasma thromboplastin antecedent
PTC	Plasma thromboplastin component
PTT	Partial thromboplastin time
Pu	Plutonium
PUO	Pyrexia of unknown origin
Px	Pneumothorax
PZI	Protamine zinc insulin
Q	Electric quantity
qns	Quantity not sufficient

qt	Quart
Quat	Fourt (*quattuor*)
R	Respiration; right; *Rickettsia*; roentgen
R$_x$	Take; prescribed for, used for; prescription
RA	Rheumatoid arthritis; right arm
Ra	Radium
rad	Unit of measurement of the absorbed dose of ionizing radiation; root
RAI	Radioactive iodine
RAIU	Radioactive iodine uptake
RBC; rbc	Red blood cell; red blood count
RCM	Relative cardiac dullness
RCM	Right costal margin
RE	Right eye
Re	Rhenium
Rect	Rectified
Reg umb	Umbilical region
RES	Reticuloendothelial system
Rh	Symbol of rhesus factor; symbol for rhodium
RhA	Rheumatoid arthritis
RHD	Relative hepatic dullness; rheumatic heart disease
RL	Ringer's lactate
RLE	Right lower extremity
RLL	Right lower lobe; right lower leg
RLQ	Right lower quadrant
RM	Respiratory movement
RML	Right middle lobe of lung
Rn	Radon
RNA	Ribonucleic acid
ROM	Range of motion
R/O	Rule out
RPF	Renal plasma flow
RPM; rpm	Revolutions per minute
RQ	Respiratory quotient
RT	Reading test; respiratory therapy or respiratory therapist
RU	Rat unit
RUL	Right upper lobe
RUQ	Right upper quadrant
S	Sulfur
S.	Sacral
s or s̄	Without
S-A; S/A; SA	Sinoatrial
SAS	Sodium acetate solution
SB	Small bowel (x-ray film); sternal border
SBFT	Small bowel follow through

Exhibit 2-10   **453**

Sb	Antimony
SC	Closure of semilunar valves
Se	Selenium
SD	Skin dose
Sed rate	Sedimentation rate
SGOT	Serum glutamic oxaloacetic transaminase
SGPT	Serum glutamic pyruvic transaminase
SH	Serum hepatitis
S.I.	Soluble insulin
SIDS	Sudden infant death syndrome
SL	Sublingual
Sn	Tin
SOB	Shortness of breath
Sol	Solution, dissolved
SP	Spirit
s/p	Status post
sp. gr.; SG; s.g.	Specific gravity
Sph	Spherical
SPI	Serum precipitable iodine
spir	Spirit
SQ	Subcutaneous
SR	Sedimentation rate
Sr	Strontium
ss or s/s	Signs and symptoms
SSS	Specific soluble substance; sick sinus syndrome
sss	Layer upon layer (*stratum super stratum*)
ST	Speech therapy; speech therapist
st	Let it stand (*stet; stent*)
Staph	*Staphylococcus*
stat	Immediate (*statim*)
STD	Sexually transmitted disease; skin test dose
STH	Somatotropic hormone
Strep	*Streptococcus*
STS	Serologic test for syphilis
STU	Skin test unit
sv	Alcoholic spirit (*spiritus vini*)
Sym	Symmetrical
Sx	Seizure
T	Temperature; thoracic
t	Temporal
T_3	Triiodothyronine
T_4	Thyroxine
TA	Toxin-antitoxin
Ta	Tantalum
T&A	Tonsillectomy and adenoidectomy

TAH	Total abdominal hysterectomy
TAM	Toxoid-antitoxoid mixture
TAT	Toxin-antitoxin; tetanus antitoxin
TB	Tuberculin; Tuberculosis; tubercle bacillus
Tb	Terbium
TCA	Trichloroacetic acid
Te	Tellurium; tetanus
TEM	Triethylenemelamine
Th	Thorium
TIA	Transient ischemic attack
TIBC	Total iron-binding capacity
Tl	Thallium
Tm	Thulium; symbol for maximal tubular excretory capacity (kidneys)
TNT	Trinitrotoluene
TNTC	Too numerous to mention
TO	Telephone order
TP	Tuberculin precipitation
TPI	*Treponema pallidum* immobilization test for syphilis
TRP	Temperature, pulse, and respiration
tr	Tincture
TRU	Turbidity reducing unit
TS	Test solution
TSH	Thyroid-stimulating hormone
TSP	Trisodium phosphate
TST	Triple sugar iron test
TUR; TURP	Transurethral resection
U	Uranium; unit
UA	Urinalysis
UBI	Ultraviolet blood irradiation
UC	Urine culture
UGI	Upper gastrointestinal series
UIBC	Unsaturated iron-binding capacity
Umb; umb	Umbilicus
URI	Upper respiratory infection
US	Ultrasonic; ultrasound
USP	*U.S. Pharmacopeia*
UTI	Urinary tract infection
V	Vanadium; vision; visual acuity
v	Volt
VA	Visual acuity
V&T	Volume and tension
VC	Vital capacity
VD	Venereal disease
VDA	Visual discriminatory acuity

Exhibit 2-10   **455**

VDG	Venereal disease—gonorrhea
VDM	Vasodepressor material
VDRL	Venereal Disease Research Laboratories (sometimes used to mean venereal disease report)
VDS	Venereal disease—syphilis
VEM	Vasoexciter material
Vf	Field of vision
VHD	Valvular heart disease
VIA	Virus inactivating agent
VLDL	Very low density lipoprotein
VMA	Vanillylmandelic acid
VO	Verbal order
VR	Vocal resonance
VS	Volumetric solution; vital signs
VSS	Vital signs stable
Vs	Venesection
VSD	Ventricular septal defect
VW	Vessel wall
W	Tungsten
w	Watt
WBC; wbc	White blood cell; white blood count
WD	Well developed
WL	Wavelength
WN	Well nourished
WNL	Within normal limits
WR	Wassermann reaction
wt	Weight
X-ray/XR	Roentgen ray
YO	Year old
Z	Symbol for atomic number
Zn	Zinc

exhibit **2-11**

ROOTS AND COMBINING FORMS IN HUMAN ANATOMY

Word or Combining Form	Meaning
adeno-	Gland
adreno-	Adrenal gland
angio-, angi-	Vessel, usually a blood vessel
arterio-	Artery
arteriolo-	Arteriole
arthro-	Joint
articulus (pl. articuli)	Latin for joint
atrio-	Atrium, upper chamber of the heart
auriculo-	Ear-shaped appendage of either atrium of the heart; the pinna or flap of the ear
axilla (pl. axillae)	Latin for armpit
blepharo-, blephar-	Eyelid or eyelash
brachium	Latin for arm, mainly the arm above the elbow
bronchio-, broncho-	Bronchus
bucca	Latin for cheek
calx	Latin for heel
canthus (pl. canthi), cantho-	The angle at either end of the slit between the eyelids
caput (pl. capita)	Latin for head
cardio-	Heart
carpus, carpo-	Latin for wrist, also the eight bones of the wrist collectively
cephalo-	Relating to the head
cerebello-	Cerebellum, a part of the brain
cerebro-	Cerebrum, a part of the brain
cervix (pl. cervices), cervico-	Latin for neck or neck-like part
cheilo-, cheil-	Greek for lip
cheiro-, chiro-, cheir-, chir-	Hand
cholangio-	Bile duct or bile duct capillaries
chole-, chol-, cholo-	Bile
cholecyst, cholecysto-	Greek for gallbladder

Exhibit 2-11   **457**

choledocho-	Common bile duct
chondro-, chonr-, chrondri-, chondrio-	Cartilage
chordo-	Cord; may be a vocal cord or the spermatic cord
cilium (pl. cilia)	Latin for eyelid or eyelash or any minute hairlike process attached to the free surface of a tissue or cell
cleido-, cleid-	Collar bone or clavicle
colpo-	Vagina
condyle	Latin for a rounded projection (knuckle) on a bone
cor	Heart
core-, coro-	Pupil of eye
corpus	Latin for body or main part of any organ, or a mass of specialized tissue
costo-	Rib
coxa	Latin for hip or hip joint
cubitus	Latin for elbow, but used mainly to refer to the forearm
cutis	Latin for skin
cysto-	Bladder or sac, most often used in reference to the urinary bladder, but also refers to the gallbladder
-cyte	Suffix denoting a cell; the root to which it is attached designates the type of cell such as a leukocyte (white cell)
cyto-	Cell
dacryo-	Tear
dactylo-	Digit, usually a finger but sometimes a toe
dento-, dent-, denta, denti, dentia	Tooth or teeth
derm-, derma-, dermato-, dermo-	Skin
digit	Finger or toe
dorsum (pl. dorsa), dorso-	Latin for back
duodeno-	Duodenum, a section of the intestinal track about 12 inches long
encephalo-	Brain, or sometimes the head
entero-	Intestine
episio	Vulva
facio-	Face
fibrio-	Fiber
frons, fronto-	Latin for forehead
gastro-, gastr-, gaster-	Stomach
genu	Latin for knee
gingiva	Gum
Glio-	Glue or gluey substance, or more specifically the neuroglia, the supporting substance of the nervous system

glosso-, gloss	Tongue
gnatho-, gnath-	Jaw
hallus (pl. halluces)	Latin for great toe
hepato-, hepat-, hepatico-	Liver
histo-	Tissue
hystero-	Womb or uterus
ileo-	Ileum, a part of the intestinal tract
ilio-	Ilium, or flank
inguen	Latin for groin
Irido-	Iris of eye
jejuno-	Jejunum, a section of the intestinal tract
kerato-	Cornea, or horny tissue
labio	Lip, especially of the mouth
laparo-	Loin or flank, sometimes used to refer to the abdomen
laryngo-	Larynx or voice box
latus, latero-	Latin for side
lieno-	Spleen
lingua	Latin for tongue
lumbus	Latin for loin
lumen	Latin for light, cavity or channel within a vessel or tubular organ
lympho-	Lymph; used to refer to lymphatic vessel or to lymphocytes
mamma (pl. mammae)	Latin for breast or mammary gland
manus	Latin for hand
masto-, mast-	Breast
melia	Latin for limbs (melos)
Meningo	Meninges, coverings of the brain and spinal cord
mentum	Latin for chin
metra-, metro-	Uterus
myelo-	Bone marrow or spinal cord
myo-, my-	Combining form for muscle
naris (pl. nares)	Latin for one of the openings into the nasal cavity
naso-	Nose
nephro-	Kidney
neuro-	Nerve
nodus	Latin for knot or node
nucha	Latin for back, or nape, of neck
occiput	Latin for back part of the head
oculo-	Eye
odonto-	Tooth or teeth
omo-	Shoulder
omphalo-	Navel (umbilicus)

Exhibit 2-11   **459**

oophoro-	Ovary
ophthalmo-, ophthalm-	Eye
ora	Latin for mouth
orb	Latin for sphere or eyeball
orbit	Bony socket containing the eye
orchio-, orchi-, orchido-	Testicle or testis
os	Latin for bone; also a term for mouth or any orifice of the body
oscheo-	Scrotum
osteo-	Bone
oto-	Ear
palato-	Palate or roof of mouth
palpebra (pl. palpebrea)	Latin for eyelid
papilla (pl. papillae)	Latin for nipple or nipple-shaped projection
pectus	Latin for chest, thorax, or breast
pes, ped-, pod-	Foot
phalanx (pl. phalanges)	Greek for a line or array of soldiers; used in connection with fingers or toes
Phallo	Latin for penis
pharyngo-	Relating to the pharynx
phleb-, phlebo-	Vein
phren-	Greek for diaphragm and the mind
pilo-	Hair
plantar	Latin for sole of foot
pleuro-	Pleura, side or rib
pneumo-, pneumato-, pneumono-	Air, gas, or respiration and lungs
poples	Latin for posterior surface of the knee
proct-, procto-	Anus or rectum
pulmo-	Lung
pyel-, pyelo-	Pelvis of the kidney
rachi-, rachio-	Spine
recto-	Rectum
ren	Latin for kidney
rhino-, rhin-	Nose
sacro-	Sacrum (the Latin *sacrum* means sacred)
salpingo-	Fallopian tube or Eustachian tube
sarco-	Flesh or fleshy
soma, somato-	Greek for body
splanchno-	Viscera or organs of any one of the great cavities of the body
spleno-	Spleen
spondylo-	Spinal column or a vertebra
sterno-	Sternum, or breastbone
steth-, stetho-	Chest
stomato-, stomo	Mouth

talus	Latin for ankle, also refers to an ankle bone
tarso-	Instep of the foot, also edge of eyelid
tendo, teno-, tenonto-	Tendon
thele	Greek for nipple
thoraco-	Chest or thorax
thymo-	Thymus gland
thyro-	Thyroid gland
trachelo	Neck of neckline suture, such as the cervix
tracheo-	Trachea
tricho-	Hair
unguis	Latin for nail of finger or toe
uretero-	Ureter, the vessel that conveys urine from the kidney to the bladder
urethro-	Urethra, a tube discharging urine from the bladder
vas (pl. vasa), vaso-	Latin for vessel (Vas may also be used as vas deferens, part of the genital organ in the male.)
vena (pl. venae), veno-	Latin for vein
venter	Latin for stomach or belly, belly-shaped or hollowed part
ventri-, ventro-	Front (anterior aspect) of a body
ventro-	Belly, front or anterior aspect of the body
vesico-	Bladder; also pertains to a blister

GREEK AND LATIN DERIVATIVES

Root or Combining Form	Meaning
-algia	Pain
ankylo-	Bent or crooked
audi-, audio-	Hear, hearing
auto-	Self
bio-	Life, biology
brachy-	Short
brady-	Slow
brevi-	Short
caus-, caut-	Burn
cav-	Hollow
-centesis-	Puncture, perforate
cryo-	Cold
crypto-	Hidden
dextro-	Right, right side
diplo-	Double, twice
-duct-	Lead
-dynia	Pain
dys-	Difficult, bad, disordered, painful

Exhibit 2-11   **461**

-ectas-	Dilate
-edem-	Swelling
eso-	Within, inward
-esthes-	Sensation
eu-	Well, good
eury-	Broad, wide
-fiss-	Split, cleft
-flect-, -flex-	Bend
flu-, flux-	Flow
gen/o-	Producing
glyc/o-	Sugar, sweet
gravis	Heavy
haplo-	Single, simple
hetero-, heter-	Other, different
homo-, homeo-	Same, alike
hydro-	Wet, water
-iatr/o-	Treatment
iso-	Equal, alike
-kin/e-, -kin/o-, -kineto-	Movement, motion
latus, lat-	Broad, wide
leio-	Smooth
levo-	Left, to the left
-liga-	Bind
-logy	Study
longus, long-	Long
ly/o-, lys/o-	Dissolve
macro-	Large
magna-	Large, great
mal-	Ill, bad
malac/o-	Soft, softening
medi-	Middle
mega-, meg/alo-, meg/aly-	Large, oversized
meso-	Middle, mid
micro-	Small
minimus	Smallest
mio-	Less, decrease
-morph-, -morpho-	Form, structure, shape
multi-	Many, much
necro-	Death
neo-	New
olfact-	Smell
oligo-	Few, little
-op/ia	Vision
opt/ico-, opt/o	Seeing
ortho-	Straight, normal, correct

oxy-	Sharp, quick
pachy-	Thick
paleo-	Old, primitive
palpit-	Flutter
-par-, -partus	Labor
-pep-	Digest
-pexy	Fix
-phag-, -phago-	Eating
-phas-	Speak
-phil-	Affinity, love for
-phobia	Fear
-plas-	Form, grow
platy-	Flat, wide
-plegia	Paralysis
pleo-	More
-pne-, -pneo-	Breathe
-poiesis	Formation, production
poly-	Many, much
pronus	Face down
pseudo-	False, spurious
-ptosis	Fall
-rrhagia	Burst forth
-rrhaphy	Suture
-rrhea	Flow, discharge
-rrhexis	Rupture
schist/o, -schiz/o	Split, cleft, division
sclero-	Hardness
scolio-	Twisted, crooked
-scope	Examine
spasm/o-	Spasm
-stasis	Standing still, stoppage
-staxis	Drop
steno-	Narrow
stereo-	Solid, three dimensions
supinus	Face up
tachy-	Rapid, fast
-teg, -tect-	Cover
tele-, telo-	Distant, end
-therap-	Treat, cure
thermo-	Heat
-tomy	Cut, incise
trachy-	Rough
-troph-, -tropho-	Nourishment, food
volv-	Turn
xero-	Dry

exhibit **2-12**

MEDICAL DIAGRAMS

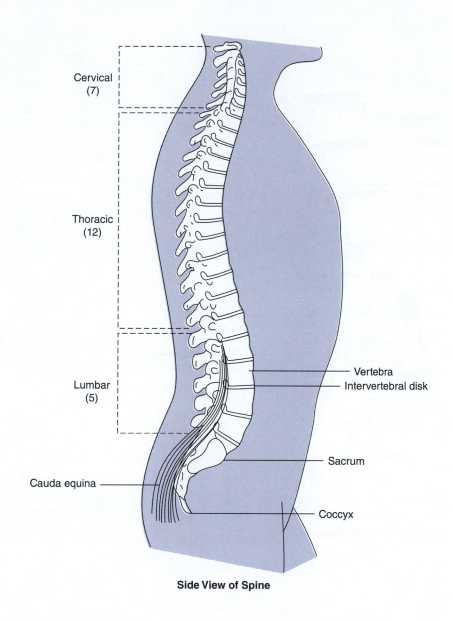

Cervical (7)

Thoracic (12)

Lumbar (5)

Cauda equina

Vertebra
Intervertebral disk

Sacrum

Coccyx

Side View of Spine

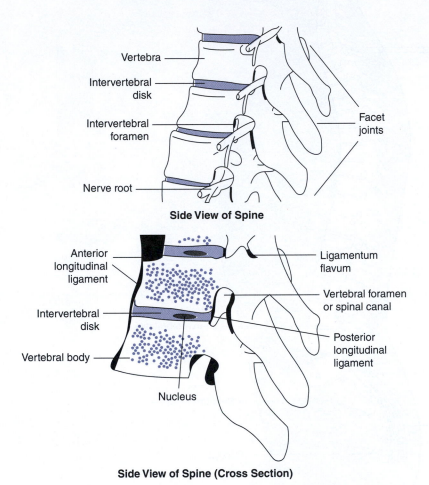

Vertebra

Intervertebral disk

Intervertebral foramen

Nerve root

Facet joints

Side View of Spine

Anterior longitudinal ligament

Intervertebral disk

Vertebral body

Nucleus

Ligamentum flavum

Vertebral foramen or spinal canal

Posterior longitudinal ligament

Side View of Spine (Cross Section)

Exhibit 2-12   **465**

Normal Spine

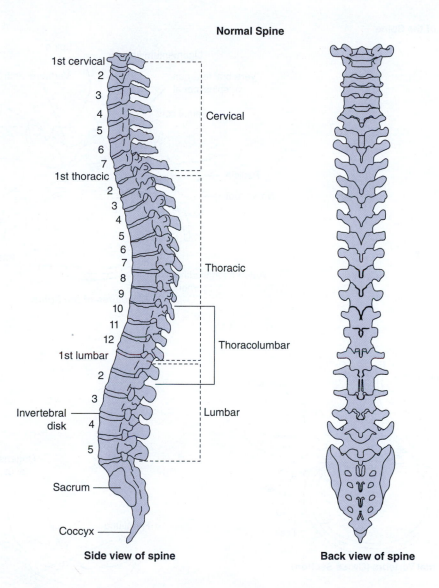

1st cervical
2
3
4
5
6
7
1st thoracic
2
3
4
5
6
7
8
9
10
11
12
1st lumbar
2
3
Invertebral disk
4
5
Sacrum
Coccyx

Cervical

Thoracic

Thoracolumbar

Lumbar

Side view of spine

Back view of spine

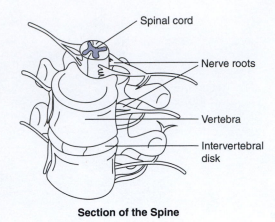

Spinal cord

Nerve roots

Vertebra

Intervertebral disk

Section of the Spine

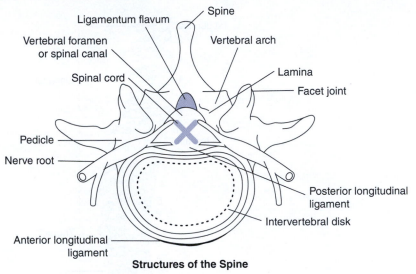

Ligamentum flavum

Spine

Vertebral foramen or spinal canal

Vertebral arch

Spinal cord

Lamina

Facet joint

Pedicle

Nerve root

Posterior longitudinal ligament

Intervertebral disk

Anterior longitudinal ligament

Structures of the Spine

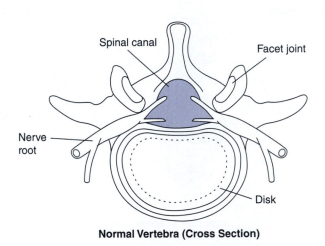

Spinal canal

Facet joint

Nerve root

Disk

Normal Vertebra (Cross Section)

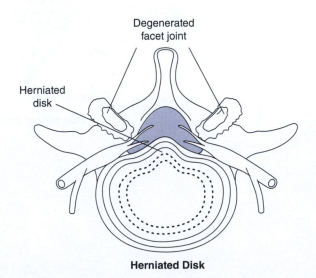

Degenerated facet joint

Herniated disk

Herniated Disk

exhibit **2-13**

MEDICAL RECORDS SUMMARY

MEDICAL RECORDS SUMMARY

OF

ELAINE "MA" BARKER

Date of Accident: 04/28/09

File No: RLS-1158

Updated: September 8, 2010

Facilities reviewed and placed in chronological date order:

Johnstown Hospital

Mercy Hospital

Modern Care Clinic

DATE	FACILITY/PAGE	SUMMARY OF TREATMENT
12/4/06	Modern 1079	Office visit, physical-cold-cough. Pain of severity 5 described as aching in ribs. History of recent rib fracture on right side and osteoporosis. Diagnosis: pneumonia.
6/11/07	Johnstown 127	Podiatry. Painful toes.
6/28/07	Modern 1060	Office visit to discuss episode on 5/24/07 where her vision was blurred and she slept all afternoon. Denies pain. Had eye exam in Valleydale, no abnormalities found. Plan: echocardiogram and baby aspirin daily.
7/24/07	Modern 1049	Transthoracic echocardiogram.
8/24/07	Johnstown 126	Podiatry. Painful nails, calluses, hammertoe.
10/29/07	Johnstown 125	Podiatry. Painful nails and calluses.
11/29/07	Modern 1041	Office visit for cold and congestion. Assessment upper respiratory infection.
12/2/07	Johnstown 85 Modern 1031-1040	Hospitalized for pneumonia. Discharged home 12/6/07.
12/31/07	Johnstown 124	Podiatry. Painful nails, calluses, hammertoe.
1/14/08	Modern 1018	Chest x-ray report. Diffuse osteopenia with mild wedging of thoracic vertebral bodies, unchanged. Prominent anterior osteophytes of the mid thoracic spine.
1/14/08	Modern 1023	Office visit recheck pneumonia. Denies pain.
3/21/08	Johnstown 123	Podiatry. Painful nails, calluses, and bunion.

3/31/08	Johnstown 82 Modern 1016	ER right rib pain. Leaning over washing machine 2-3 days ago and felt something pop. No pain until this evening. Assessment: rib fracture. Given rib belt to use. Discharged home.
3/31/08	Modern 1015 Johnstown	X-ray report, right ribs. Bones are demineralized. Slightly displaced fracture anterolateral segment of 7th or 8th rib. *Dorsal spine has multiple compression fractures vertebral bodies and degenerative spondylosis. Fracture dorsal vertebral bodies could be chronic.*
4/14/08	Modern 1009	Office visit 3 month recheck. Also pulled muscle in right flank two weeks ago and seen in ER. Has pain in right flank, severity 0-4, intermittent pain. Physician note p 1009 no mention of pneumonia—follow-up of cracked ribs after leaning over washer-dryer, right upper anterolateral chest area. Seems in ER and x-rays done. Also previous spine compression fracture, history of osteoporosis. Assessment: (1) significant osteoporosis with recent rib fractures and (2) urinary incontinence.
5/30/08	Johnstown 122	Podiatry. Painful nails and calluses.
7/24/08	Modern 1001	Office visit 3 month recheck of broken ribs. Denies pain. Assessment: (1) bilateral hearing loss (2) mild urinary incontinence (3) Osteoporosis with broken ribs in most recent past, tolerating Boniva well. Follow up this fall with general health physical.
8/4/08	Johnstown 121	Podiatry. Painful nails.
10/6/08	Johnstown 120	Podiatry. Painful hammertoes right foot, corns, and calluses on feet.
10/23/08	Modern 987	Office visit physical. Denies pain. States hands going to sleep at night, ankle swelling. Assessment: (1) hypothyroidism (2) mild congestive heart failure with mild fluid retention (3) history of hypertension (3) hyperlipidemia (4) osteoporosis (5) postherpetic neuralgia (&) bilateral carpal tunnel syndrome symptoms
12/8/08	Johnstown 119	Podiatry. Painful hammertoes, corns, calluses, and nails.
2/12/09	Johnstown 118	Podiatry. Painful nails and calluses on both feet. Bunion on left foot.
2/17/09	Modern 971-974	Office visit dizziness, joint stiffness. Vertigo, meclizine 25 mg every 6 hours as needed.
4/17/09	Johnstown 117	Podiatry. Painful nails and calluses on both feet.
4/28/09	*ACCIDENT*	FELL AT VALLEYDALE LEGION

Exhibit 2-13   **469**

5/11/09	Johnstown 75-77 Modern 948	*Brought to ER via private vehicle with low back pain. No specific time of onset but spent part of morning picking up her house. No specific event but general low back soreness throughout day.* Was seen earlier today by Dr. Mohs, urinalysis completed. *Patient reports she fell two weeks ago at VALLEYDALE LEGION when she tripped over a cord. Fell on left knee. Left leg had some bruises but those symptoms have essentially resolved.* CT lumbosacral spine, no acute fracture. Osteoarthritis with degenerative disk disease. Patient to continue usual medications. Advised to stop Tylenol or alternate with Darvocet. Follow up with Dr. Wellsley on as needed basis. CT report (p. 77, 950) loose bony fragment identified, maybe old or new.
5/11/09	Modern 962-963 Modern 968-969	Office visit, back pain, starting in low back and radiating upward and to sides, severity 9. Started yesterday. Health concerns: Fell 2 weeks ago (p. 962). *"has had some back pain that started yesterday. She did not have any injury, fall, or anything else that seem to bring this on. She just woke up and had a significant pain. She will get spasms of pain with this." (p. 968)* Assessment: Muscle strain of low back. Use Tylenol Arthritis strength 2x every 8 hours as needed. Follow up as needed.
5/13/09	Johnstown 51-73	ER and admitted to hospital, low back pain. Admitted and treated for pain control and dehydration. Fell couple of weeks ago at VALLEYDALE LEGION, onto her knees, then her back and going out for a couple of seconds. Bilateral low back pain secondary to muscle spasms. Treated with IV morphine, then Duragesic patch.
5/16/09	Mercy 244-350 Modern 951 (Mercy discharge summary)	Transferred to swing bed in Valleydale from Johnstown after a fall and pain in her back. Progressed slowly with PT-able to walk independently with walker at time of discharge. Pain med requirements decreased to one Ultram at end of day at discharge. Also had episode of heart failure when transferred from Johnstown Hospital and found to have low Vitamin D. Treated with Lasix. Dx: (1) Back pain secondary to fall; (2) Osteoporosis (3) Vitamin D deficiency (4) Congestive heart failure secondary to fluid overload (5) hypothyroidism
5/16/09	Johnstown 51-73	Discharged to Valleydale swing bed unit. Family taking her by car.
5/28/09	Mercy 244-250	Discharge.

6/3/09	Modern 947	Phone note. Home health wondering if dizziness is caused by tramadol? Will not take anymore. Wondering if they can give her meclizine 25 mg for dizziness? Intervention: no, let tramadol wear off.
6/4/09	Modern 946	Phone note, call from home health nurse. Dizziness and nausea yesterday, thought to be due to tramadol. Medication has been withheld, took two Tylenol Arthritis this morning and hasn't helped with back pain. Continued nausea and dizziness. Has order for Darvocet for back pain, try this? Intervention: Meclizine 25 mg every 6 hrs for vertigo.
6/8/09	Modern 942	Office visit, recently discharged from hospital, back pain secondary to fall. Pain in lower and middle back, severity 5-6, aching, constant, pressure, sharp, soreness. No mention of fracture in CT, was identification of loose bony fragment involving the fact joint but there would be no indication for surgical repair of that anyway. Continue with Advil if needed. Try Tylenol Arthritis again. Advised to continue calcium 1500 mg daily. Chest congestion likely related to congestive heart failure—increased her furosemide. Return for follow up on this next week as well as on her back pain.
6/15/09	Modern 938	Office visit recheck medications. Follow up on back pain secondary to fall. Pain in low, mid and upper back, aching pain. Seen last week after discharge from nursing home. Advised to stop Advil since she is not seeing any increased benefit from them. Tolerating Tylenol Arthritis well so encouraged to take that every 8 hours for pain, continue exercises and working on posture. Ambulating well with cane and has walker at home, which she should continue to use as needed. Strongly encouraged to use cane at all times. Continue furosemide to help with fluid retention.
6/22/09	Mercy 351-352	Physical Therapy Dept. Has been receiving PT since 6/1/09. Patient now believes she is strong enough to begin PT as outpatient. Low back pain secondary to fall. History: fell 4/28/09 tripping over a cord under a rug at VALLEYDALE LEGION and injuring low back. Low back pain symptoms since fall in April. Symptoms today are more TS, possible she could have compression issues in TS as well.
6/22/09	Johnstown 116	Podiatry. Painful nails on both feet and calluses on left foot.

Exhibit 2-13   **471**

6/22/09	Modern 934	Office visit. Fell in April and continues with back pain (lower). Pain assessment: low back severity 8, increased with movement. Increase Tylenol Arthritis dosage and Try Flexeril. Follow up if needed.
6/24/09	Mercy 354	PT note. LBP and mid back pain decreased some.
6/29/09	Mercy 354	PT note. Feeling a little better. Still some c/o right side right mid-LBP.
7/1/09	Mercy 354	PT note. c/o right rib pain, otherwise better.
7/8/09	Mercy 354	PT note. Pt states she is having a lot of pain today.
7/10/09	Mercy 354	PT note. Less pain but hurts into right side esp with exercise with resistance.
7/15/09	Mercy 355	PT note. Still c/o pain under right ribs and across right mid back.
7/23/09	Modern 929, 932	Office visit recheck. Fell 4/28/09 at ABC LEGION and was in hospital 4 days and swing bed in Valleydale. Having right side pain. Was having PT in Valleydale, continue? Pain assessment: denies pain. Pain worse with activity, better with rest. Feels she has improved significantly with PT. Order CT scan of abdomen and pelvis to be sure not missing anything.
7/27/09	Johnstown 50 Modern 924	Report CT scan of abdomen. Right flank pain, s/p fall 4/28/09.
8/24/09	Johnstown 115	Podiatry. Painful nails and calluses both feet.
9/8/09	Modern 918	Office visit rash. Denies pain.
10/2/09	Johnstown 46-47	Decreased hearing—audiology evaluation.
10/21/09	Modern 913	Audiology report.
10/26/09	Johnstown 114	Podiatry. Painful nails and calluses both feet.
11/25/09	Modern 877	Office visit. SOB and wheezy. No pain.
11/30/09	Modern 869	Office visit. SOB with increased wheezing this past weekend. Denies pain.
12/28/09	Johnstown 113	Podiatry. Painful nails and calluses both feet.
12/31/09	Modern 850	Transthoracic echocardiogram.
1/4/10	Modern 844	Office visit for rash and sinus fullness. Denies pain. Antibiotic therapy.
1/11/10	Modern 836	Office visit echo results. *Denies pain, but notes low back pain which she thinks is due to osteoporosis.*
1/26/10	Modern 825	Recheck. No pain. Cardiolite stress test recommended.
2/26/10	Johnstown 40	Cardiolite stress test.
2/26/10	Modern 820	Cardiolite stress test report. Results abnormal, some impaired blood supply to inferolateral wall of heart muscle. Cardiology consult recommended.
3/1/10	*Johnstown 112*	Podiatry. Painful nails and calluses both feet, hammertoe of lesser digits of both feet.

4/1/10	Modern 806-811	Office visit. Discuss test results from cardiology. Denies pain.
4/21/10	Modern 792	Follow up on medication/atrial fibrillation. Dizziness/vertigo. Pain severity level 1, low back aching. Increased with movement, decreased with rest. PT recommended for vertigo.
4/22/10	Modern 787	Physical therapy for vertigo (6 year duration). Good strength and ROM.
5/3/10	Johnstown 111	Podiatry. Painful nails on toes of both feet and corn on 2nd toe of right foot and great toe of left foot. Hammertoe deformities of lesser toe both feet.
5/5/10	Modern 779	Check x-ray report.
5/5/10	Modern 780	Recheck mediation. No pain. Dizziness and short of breath.
5/20/10	Modern 774	Recheck atrial fibrillation. No pain.
7/6/10	Johnstown 110	Podiatry. Painful nails and calluses on both feet, bunion on great left toe.
7/13/10	Modern 740	Chest x-ray report.
7/13/10	Modern 742	Recheck lungs. No pain reported.
7/15/10	Johnstown 33	CT of chest.
7/15/10	Modern 735	CT of chest/left lung mass. Left subclavian artery aneurysm.
7/22/10	Modern 726	Recheck subclavian/thoracic aneurism. Pain assessment: mid back pain, aching, soreness. Increased with movement, decreased by heat. Severity level 3-4.
8/11/10	Modern 716	Office visit for CT results. Aneurysm, left subclavian artery. Recheck in 3 months. No pain.
8/18/10	Modern 809	Imaging report of thoracic spine, back pain, fall. Osteoporotic compressions noted of indeterminate ago. Nuclear bone imaging recommended for further evaluation for acute fracture sites.
8/18/10	Modern 710	*Back pain after falling last night. Tipped over backward with walker, fell back into chair and tipped chair over backward. Impression: back and rib pain secondary to fall and muscle contusion.* Darvocet for pain.
8/20/10	Johnstown 23	X-ray report. (1) Obstipation with nonspecific ileus. (2) Status post abdominal surgery. (3) Osteoporosis of the bones with degenerative disk disease of lumbosacral spine. (4) There is calcified arteriosclerotic disease of the aorta with mild aneurismal dilatation distal abdominal aorta measuring about 3.2 cm in its wide. CT correlation would be beneficial.

Exhibit 2-13   **473**

8/20/10	Johnstown 25	ER evaluation. Nausea and abdominal pain. States she fell last Tuesday and injured her left upper arm and back. No LOC. Evaluated in clinic 8/19/10 and told no fracture. Dx: UTI, constitution possibly secondary to pain medicine. RX given. Return to ER or follow up with physician if needed.
8/20/10	Modern 707 Johnstown 3	ER for nausea and abdominal pain. Impression: urinary tract infection and constipation secondary to pain medicines. Given Phenergan gel and Zofran. Follow up as needed.
8/22/10	Johnstown 4	Discharge summary. Abdominal pain. Family requested transfer to Biltmore.
8/27/10	Mercy 358	Swing bed admission following ER and transferred to Modern for abdominal pain, weakness and PE. Transferred to Biltmore.
8/27/10	Mercy 370	Transfer sheet from Mercy Hospital to Biltmore Hospital. Chief complaint abdominal pain.
8/27/10	Mercy 373	Interagency discharge form. *Patient fell at home on 8/17.* Went to Johnstown ER and started on Fentanyl patch for pain. Did not eat or drink much since then. Went back into Johnstown ER, thought had ileus/bowel obstruction. Refused NG tube and wanted to be sent to Mayberry. Admitted.
8/27/10	Modern 704 Johnstown 6	ER for abdominal pain, chest wall pain and nausea. Was seen earlier in ER with UTI. Impression: abdominal pain with intractable nausea. Admitted to hospital for IV fluids and antibiotic therapy.

appendix **3-Insurance**

exhibit 3-1

INSURANCE POLICY CHECKLIST

All insurance policies (obtain all from client)

Health and accident

Disability

Automobile (If more than one vehicle, obtain all polices)

Commercial general liability

Umbrella

Other

Automobile

Uninsured Motorist (UM) Coverage

Determine proper endorsement in policy

Limits

Who is an uninsured motorist? (Definitions)

1. Other driver no liability insurance (what if other driver has liability insurance but less than mandatory limit in home state)
2. Other driver's carrier denied coverage/insolvent
3. Hit and run/Phantom vehicle

What is a "motor vehicle"? (Definitions)

Who is an "insured"? (Definitions)

What is "bodily injury"? (Definitions)

"Legally entitled" requirement

Arise out of "operation, maintenance, or use" of uninsured M/V?

Stacking allowed

Exclusions

Deductions/offsets

Subrogation

Other insurance/priority of payment

Conditions/duties after accident or loss

Definitions

Arbitration or court

Bad faith available for first-party coverage?

Statute of limitation/notices to be given

Other

Underinsured Motorist (UIM) Coverage

Determine proper endorsement in policy

Limits

Who is an underinsured motorist?
1. Add-on
2. Modified add-on
3. Difference in limits

What is a "motor vehicle"? (Definitions)

Who is an "insured"? (Definitions)

What is "bodily injury"? (Definitions)

"Legally entitled" requirement

Arise out of "operation, maintenance, or use" of underinsured M/V?

Settlement of liability claim need to be for full limits?

Notice required to other driver's liability carrier?

Stacking allowed

Exclusions

Deductions/offsets

Subrogation

Other insurance/priority of payment

Conditions/duties after accident or loss

Definitions

Arbitration or court

Bad faith available for first-party coverage?

Statute of limitation/notices to be given

Other

No Fault

Basic limits medical and non-medical

Threshold—medical, disability, permanency, other limit

What is a "motor vehicle"? (Definitions)

Who is an "insured"? coverage follow vehicle or person? (Definitions)

What is "bodily injury"? (Definitions)

Arise out of "operation, maintenance, or use" of M/V?

Stacking allowed

Exclusions

Deductions/offsets

Subrogation

Other insurance/priority of payment

Conditions/duties after accident or loss

Definitions

Coordination of benefits

Arbitration or court

Bad faith available for first-party coverage?

Statute of limitation/notices to be given

Other

exhibit **3-2**

AUTOKING AUTOMOBILE INSURANCE POLICY

AUTOKING MUTUAL INSURANCE COMPANY

**PERSONAL AUTO
PP 00 01 01 05**

PERSONAL AUTO POLICY

AGREEMENT

In return for payment of the premium and subject to all the terms of this policy, we agree with you as follows:

DEFINITIONS

  A. Throughout this policy, "you" and "your" refer to:
      1. The "named insured" shown in the Declarations; and
      2. The spouse, if a resident of the same household.

      If the spouse ceases to be a resident of the same household during the policy period or prior to the inception of this policy, the spouse will be considered "you" and "your" under this policy but only until the earlier of:

      1. The end of 90 days following the spouse's change of residence;
      2. The effective date of another policy listing the spouse as named insured; or
      3. The end of the policy period.
  B. "We," "us," and "our" refer to the company providing this insurance.
      For purposes of this policy, a private passenger-type auto, pickup, or van shall be deemed to be owned by a person if leased:
      1. Under a written agreement to that person; and
      2. For a continuous period of at least 6 months.
  D. "Bodily injury" means bodily harm, sickness, or disease, including death that results.
  E. "Business" includes trade, profession, or occupation.
  F. "Family member" means a person related to you by blood, marriage, or adoption, including a ward or foster child, who is a resident of your household.
  G. "Occupying" means in, upon, getting in, on, out, or off.
  H. "Property damage" means physical injury to, destruction of, or loss of use of tangible property.
  I. "Trailer" means a vehicle designed to be pulled by a:
      1. Private passenger auto; or
      2. Pickup or van.
      It also means a farm wagon or farm implement while towed by a vehicle listed in 1. or 2. above.

J. "Your covered auto" means:
 1. Any vehicle shown in the Declarations.
 2. A "newly acquired auto."
 3. Any "trailer" you own.
 4. Any auto or "trailer" you do not own while used as a temporary substitute for any other vehicle described in this definition which is out of normal use because of its:
    a. Breakdown;
    b. Repair;
    c. Servicing;
    d. Loss; or
    e. Destruction.

 This Provision (J.4.) does not apply to Coverage for Damage to Your Auto.

K. "Newly acquired auto":
 1. "Newly acquired auto" means any of the following types of vehicles you become the owner of during the policy period.
    a. A private passenger auto; or
    b. A pickup or van, for which no other insurance policy provides coverage, that:
       (1) Has a gross vehicle weight of less than 10,000 lbs.; and
       (2) Is not used for the delivery or transportation of goods and materials unless such use is:
           (a) Incidental to your "business" of installing, maintaining, or repairing furnishings or equipment; or
           (b) For farming or ranching.
 2. Coverage for a "newly acquired auto" is provided as described below only if you pay us any added premium due. If you ask us to insure a "newly acquired auto" after a specified time period described below has elapsed, any coverage we provide for a "newly acquired auto" will begin at the time you request the coverage.
    a. For any coverage provided in this policy except Coverage for Damage to Your Auto, a "newly acquired auto" will have the broadest coverage we now provide for any vehicle shown in the Declarations. Coverage begins on the date you become the owner. However, for this coverage to apply a "newly acquired auto" which is an addition to any vehicle shown in the Declarations, you must ask us to insure it within 30 days after you become the owner. If a "newly acquired auto" replaces a vehicle shown in the Declarations, coverage is provided for this vehicle without your having to ask us to insure it.
    b. Collision Coverage for a "newly acquired auto" begins on the date you become the owner. However, for this coverage to apply, you must ask us to insure it within:
       1. 30 days after you become the owner if the Declarations indicate that Collision Coverage applies to at least one auto. In this case, the "newly acquired auto" will have the broadest coverage we now provide for any auto shown in the Declarations.
       2. Four days after you become the owner if the Declarations do not indicate that Collision Coverage applies to at least one auto. If you comply with the 4-day requirement and a loss occurred before you asked us to insure the "newly acquired auto," a Collision deductible of $500 will apply.
    c. Other Than Collision Coverage for a "newly acquired auto" begins on the date you become the owner. However, for this coverage to apply, you must ask us to insure it within:
       1. 30 days after you become the owner if the Declarations indicate that Other Than Collision Coverage applies to at least one auto. In this case, the "newly acquired auto" will have the broadest coverage we now provide for any auto shown in the Declarations.

Exhibit 3-2   **479**

    2. Four days after you become the owner if the Declarations do not indicate that Other Than Collision Coverage applies to at least one auto. If you comply with the 4-day requirement and a loss occurred before you asked us to insure the "newly acquired auto," an Other Than Collision deductible of $500 will apply.

L. "Diminution in value" means the actual or perceived loss in market or resale value that results from a direct and accidental loss.

PART A—LIABILITY COVERAGE

Insuring Agreement

A. We will pay damages for "bodily injury" or "property damage" for which any "insured" becomes legally responsible because of an auto accident. Damages include prejudgment interest awarded against the "insured." We will settle or defend, as we consider appropriate, any claim or suit asking for these damages. In addition to our limit of liability, we will pay all defense costs we incur. Our duty to settle or defend ends when our limit of liability for this coverage has been exhausted by payment of judgments or settlements. We have the right to investigate, negotiate, and settle any claim with or without your consent. We have no duty to defend any suit or settle any claim for "bodily injury" or "property damage" not covered under this policy.

B. "Insured" as used in this Part means:

    1. You or any "family member" for the ownership, maintenance, or use of any auto or "trailer."

    2. Any person using "your covered auto."

    3. For "your covered auto," any person or organization but only with respect to legal responsibility for acts or omissions of a person for whom coverage is afforded under this Part.

    4. For any auto or "trailer," other than "your covered auto," any other person or organization but only with respect to legal responsibility for acts or omissions of you or any "family member" for whom coverage is afforded under this Part. This Provision (B.4.) applies only if the person or organization does not own or hire the auto or "trailer."

SUPPLEMENTARY PAYMENTS

In addition to our limit of liability, we will pay on behalf of an "insured":

    1. Up to $250 for the cost of bail bonds required because of an accident, including related traffic law violations. The accident must result in "bodily injury" or "property damage" covered under this policy.

    2. Premiums on appeal bonds and bonds to release attachments in any suit we defend.

    3. Interest accruing after a judgment is entered in any suit we defend. Our duty to pay interest ends when we offer to pay that part of the judgment that does not exceed our limit of liability for this coverage.

    4. Up to $200 a day for loss of earnings, but not other income, because of attendance at hearings or trials at our request.

    5. Other reasonable expenses incurred at our request.

EXCLUSIONS

A. We do not provide Liability Coverage for any "insured":

    1. Who intentionally causes "bodily injury" or "property damage."

    2. For "property damage" to property owned or being transported by that "insured."

3. For "property damage" to property:
   a. Rented to;
   b. Used by; or
   c. In the care of;

that "insured."

This Exclusion (A.3.) does not apply to "property damage" to a residence or private garage.

4. For "bodily Injury" to an employee of that "insured" during the course of employment. This Exclusion (A.4.) does not apply to "bodily injury" to a domestic employee unless workers' compensation benefits are required or available for that domestic employee.

5. For that "insured's" liability arising out of the ownership or operation of a vehicle while it is being used as a public or livery conveyance. This Exclusion (A.5.) does not apply to a share-the-expense car pool.

6. While employed or otherwise engaged in the "business" of:
   a. Selling;
   b. Repairing;
   c. Servicing;
   d. Storing; or
   e. Parking;

vehicles designed for use mainly on public highways. This includes road testing and delivery. This Exclusion (A.6.) does not apply to the ownership, maintenance, or use of "your covered auto" by:
   a. You;
   b. Any "family member"; or
   c. Any partner, agent, or employee of you or any "family member."

7. Maintaining or using any vehicle while that "insured" is employed or otherwise engaged in any "business" (other than farming or ranching) not described in Exclusion A.6.

This Exclusion (A.7.) does not apply to the maintenance or use of a:
   a. Private passenger auto;
   b. Pickup or van; or
   c. "Trailer" used with a vehicle described in a. or b. above.

8. Using a vehicle without a reasonable belief that that "insured" is entitled to do so. This Exclusion (A.8.) does not apply to a "family member" using "your covered auto" that is owned by you.

9. For "bodily injury" or "property damage" for which that "insured":
   a. Is an insured under a nuclear energy liability policy; or
   b. Would be an insured under a nuclear energy liability policy but for its termination upon exhaustion of its limit of liability.

A. nuclear energy liability policy is a policy issued by any of the following or their successors:
   a. Nuclear Energy Liability Insurance Association;
   b. Mutual Atomic Energy Liability Underwriters; or
   c. Nuclear Insurance Association of Canada.

10. For any "bodily injury" or "property damage":
    a. For which the United States might be liable for the "insured's" use of any vehicle; or
    b. Arising out of the ownership, maintenance, use, or operation of farm machinery.

B. We do not provide Liability Coverage for the ownership, maintenance, or use of:

1. Any vehicle which:
   a. Has fewer than four wheels; or
   b. Is designed mainly for use off public roads.

Exhibit 3-2   **481**

This Exclusion (B.1.) does not apply:

    a. While such vehicle is being used by an "insured" in a medical emergency;

    b. To any "trailer"; or

    c. To any non-owned golf cart.

2. Any vehicle, other than "your covered auto," which is:

    a. Owned by you; or

    b. Furnished or available for your regular use.

3. Any vehicle, other than "your covered auto," which is:

    a. Owned by any "family member"; or

    b. Furnished or available for the regular use of any "family member."

However, this Exclusion (B.3.) does not apply to you while you are maintaining or "occupying" any vehicle that is:

    a. Owned by a "family member"; or

    b. Furnished or available for the regular use of a "family member."

4. Any vehicle, located inside a facility designed for racing, for the purpose of:

    a. Competing in; or

    b. Practicing or preparing for; any prearranged or organized racing or speed contest.

C. We do not provide Liability Coverage for any punitive or exemplary damages.

D. We do not provide Liability Coverage for "bodily injury" arising out of the passage of a communicable disease from any "insured" to another person.

E. We do not provide Liability Coverage for "bodily injury" or "property damage" arising out of sexual molestation, corporal punishment, or physical or mental abuse inflicted upon any person by or at the direction of an "insured" or an "insured's" employee.

LIMIT OF LIABILITY

A. The limit of liability shown in the Declarations for each person for Bodily Injury Liability is our maximum limit of liability for all damages, including damages for care, loss of services, or death, arising out of "bodily injury" sustained by any one person in any one auto accident. Subject to this limit for each person, the limit of liability shown in the Declarations for each accident for Bodily Injury Liability is our maximum limit of liability for all damages for "bodily injury" resulting from any one auto accident. The limit of liability shown in the Declarations for each accident for Property Damage Liability is our maximum limit of liability for all "property damage" resulting from any one auto accident.

This is the most we will pay regardless of the number of:

1. "Insureds";

2. Claims made;

3. Vehicles or premiums shown in the Declarations; or

4. Vehicles involved in the auto accident.

B. No one will be entitled to receive duplicate payments for the same elements of loss under this coverage and:

1. Part B or Part C of this policy; or

2. Any Underinsured Motorists Coverage provided by this policy.

OUT OF STATE COVERAGE

If an auto accident to which this policy applies occurs in any state or province other than the one in which "your covered auto" is principally garaged, we will interpret your policy for that accident as follows:

A. If the state or province has:

1. A financial responsibility or similar law specifying limits of liability for "bodily injury" or "property damage" higher than the limit shown in the Declarations, your policy will provide the higher specified limit.

2. A compulsory insurance or similar law requiring a nonresident to maintain insurance whenever the nonresident uses a vehicle in that state or province, your policy will provide at least the required minimum amounts and types of coverage.

B. No one will be entitled to duplicate payments for the same elements of loss.

FINANCIAL RESPONSIBILITY

When this policy is certified as future proof of financial responsibility, this policy shall comply with the law to the extent required.

OTHER INSURANCE

If there is other applicable liability insurance we will pay only our share of the loss. Our share is the proportion that our limit of liability bears to the total of all applicable limits. However, any insurance we provide for a vehicle you do not own shall be excess over any other collectible insurance.

PART B—MEDICAL PAYMENTS COVERAGE

Insuring Agreement

A. We will pay reasonable expenses incurred for necessary medical and funeral services because of "bodily injury":
  1. Caused by accident; and
  2. Sustained by an "insured."

We will pay only those expenses incurred for services rendered within 3 years from the date of the accident.

B. "Insured" as used in this Part means:
  1. You or any "family member":
    a. While "occupying"; or
    b. As a pedestrian when struck by; a motor vehicle designed for use mainly on public roads or a trailer of any type.
  2. Any other person while "occupying" "your covered auto."

EXCLUSIONS

We do not provide Medical Payments Coverage for any "insured" for "bodily Injury":
  1. Sustained while "occupying" any motorized vehicle having fewer than four wheels.
  2. Sustained while "occupying" "your covered auto" when it is being used as a public or livery conveyance. This Exclusion (2.) does not apply to a share-the-expense car pool.
  3. Sustained while "occupying" any vehicle located for use as a residence or premises.
  4. Occurring during the course of employment if workers' compensation benefits are required or available for the "bodily injury."
  5. Sustained while "occupying," or when struck by, any vehicle (other than "your covered auto") that is:
    a. Owned by you; or
    b. Furnished or available for your regular use.
  6. Sustained while "occupying," or when struck by, any vehicle (other than "your covered auto") that is:
    a. Owned by any "family member"; or
    b. Furnished or available for the regular use of any "family member."

However, this Exclusion (6.) does not apply to you.

Exhibit 3-2   **483**

7. Sustained while "occupying" a vehicle without a reasonable belief that that "insured" is entitled to do so. This Exclusion (7.) does not apply to a "family member" using "your covered auto" that is owned by you.
8. Sustained while "occupying" a vehicle when it is being used in the "business" of an "insured." This Exclusion (8.) does not apply to "bodily injury" sustained while "occupying" a:
   a. Private passenger auto;
   b. Pickup or van that you own; or
   c. "Trailer" used with a vehicle described in a. or b. above.
9. Caused by or as a consequence of:
   a. Discharge of a nuclear weapon (even if accidental);
   b. War (declared or undeclared);
   c. Civil war;
   d. Insurrection; or
   e. Rebellion or revolution.
10. From or as a consequence of the following, whether controlled or uncontrolled or however caused:
    a. Nuclear reaction;
    b. Radiation; or
    c. Radioactive contamination.
11. Sustained while "occupying" any vehicle located inside a facility designed for racing for the purpose of:
    a. Competing in; or
    b. Practicing or preparing for; any prearranged or organized racing or speed contest.

LIMIT OF LIABILITY

A. The limit of liability shown in the Declarations for this coverage is our maximum limit of liability for each person injured in anyone accident. This is the most we will pay regardless of the number of:
   1. "Insureds";
   2. Claims made;
   3. Vehicles or premiums shown in the Declarations; or
   4. Vehicles involved in the accident.
B. No one will be entitled to receive duplicate payments for the same elements of loss under this coverage and:
   1. Part A or Part C of this policy; or
   2. Any Underinsured Motorists Coverage provided by this policy.

OTHER INSURANCE

If there is other applicable auto medical payments insurance, we will pay only our share of the loss. Our share is the proportion that our limit of liability bears to the total of all applicable limits. However, any insurance we provide with respect to a vehicle you do not own shall be excess over any other collectible auto insurance providing payments for medical or funeral expenses.

PART C—UNINSURED MOTORISTS COVERAGE

We will pay damages for "bodily injury" an "insured" is legally entitled to collect from the owner or driver of an "uninsured motor vehicle." The "bodily injury" must be caused by accident arising out of the operation, maintenance, of use of an "uninsured motor vehicle."

WHO IS AN INSURED?

"Insured" means the person or persons covered by uninsured motorists coverage. This is:

1. any person named In the Declarations;
2. his or her spouse if living with that person;
3. any "family member"; and
4. any other person while "occupying":
    a. "your covered auto." Its use has to be within the scope of your consent.
    b. an auto not owned by you or any person living in your household. It has to be driven by one of the persons in 1., 2., or 3. above. Its use has to be within the scope of the owner's consent.

Such other person "occupying" an auto used to carry persons for a charge other than on a share expense basis is not an "insured."

5. any person entitled to recover damages because of "bodily injury" to an "insured" under 1. through 4. above.

OTHER ADDITIONAL DEFINITIONS FOR PART C

1. "Motor Vehicle" means a vehicle, excluding motor vehicles weighing more than twenty thousand pounds, having two or more load-bearing wheels, of a kind required to be registered under the laws of the state of Bliss relating to motor vehicles, designed primarily for operation upon the public streets, roads, and highways, and driven by power other than muscular power, and includes a trailer drawn by or attached to such a vehicle.
2. "Uninsured Motor Vehicle" means a "motor vehicle" for which:

    a. there is no bodily injury liability insurance policy, or bond providing equivalent liability protection, in effect at the time of the accident.
    b. there is an applicable policy or bond but the insurer or issuer thereof refuses to provide coverage, denies coverage, or is or becomes insolvent.
    c. the identity of the owner or operator cannot be ascertained and the "bodily injury" of the "insured" is either caused by actual physical contact of such "motor vehicle" with the "insured," or with a "motor vehicle" occupied by the "insured," or is independently verified by a disinterested witness.
3. The term "uninsured motor vehicle" does not mean a "motor vehicle":
    a. insured under the liability coverage of this policy.
    b. owned by any governmental unit, political subdivision, or agency thereof.
    c. located for use as a residence or premises.
    d. with respect to uninsured motorists coverage, a self-insured motor vehicle within the meaning of the financial or safety responsibility law of the state in which the motor vehicle is registered, or any similar state or federal law.
    e. operated by any person who is specifically excluded from coverage in the policy.
4. The term "underinsured motor vehicle" may not be construed to include an uninsured motor vehicle.

WHEN UNINSURED MOTORISTS COVERAGE DOES NOT APPLY

THERE IS NO COVERAGE UNDER UNINSURED MOTORISTS COVERAGE:

1. For the recovery of punitive, exemplary, or other noncompensatory damages.
2. FOR ANY "INSURED" WHO, WITHOUT OUR WRITTEN CONSENT, SETTLES WITH ANY PERSON OR ORGANIZATION WHO MAY BE LIABLE FOR THE "BODILY INJURY."

Exhibit 3-2   **485**

3. TO THE EXTENT IT BENEFITS:
    a. ANY WORKERS' COMPENSATION OR DISABILITY BENEFITS INSURANCE COMPANY.
    b. A SELF-INSURER UNDER ANY WORKERS' COMPENSATION, OR DISABILITY BENEFITS OR SIMILAR LAW.
    c. ANY GOVERNMENTAL BODY OR AGENCY.
4. If the "insured" has failed to report the accident to the proper law enforcement authorities as soon as practicable.
5. For any "insured" who is injured while operating or "occupying" a "motor vehicle" without the specific permission of the owner of the vehicle or without reasonable belief that they are entitled to do so.
6. For damages for pain, suffering, mental anguish, inconvenience, or other noneconomic loss that could not have been recovered had the owner or operator of the "motor vehicle" responsible for such loss maintained the security required under any applicable state no-fault law.
7. With respect to which the applicable statute of limitations has expired on the "insured's" claim against the uninsured or underinsured motorist.
8. There is no coverage until the limits of liability of all bodily injury liability bonds and policies that apply have been used up by payments of judgments or settlements or such limits or the remaining part of them have been offered to the "insured" in writing.

THERE IS NO UNINSURED MOTORISTS COVERAGE:

FOR "BODILY INJURY" TO AN "INSURED" WHILE "OCCUPYING" A "MOTOR VEHICLE" OWNED BY YOU OR ANY PERSON LIVING IN YOUR HOUSEHOLD IF IT IS NOT INSURED FOR THIS COVERAGE UNDER THIS POLICY.

LIMITS OF LIABILITY

1. The amount of coverage is shown on the front of the Declarations under Each Person-Each Occurrence.

    Under Each Person is the amount of coverage for all damages due to "bodily injury" to one person.

    Under Each Occurrence is the total amount of coverage for all damages due to "bodily injury" to two or more persons in the same accident.
2. The maximum liability of the uninsured motorists coverage is the lower of:
    a. The amount of compensatory damages, established but not recovered by any agreement, settlement, or judgment with or for the person or organization legally liable for the "bodily injury" resulting therefrom; or
    b. The limits of liability of the uninsured motorists coverage.
3. Any amount payable under this coverage shall be reduced by any amount paid or payable to or for the "insured":
    a. under any workers' compensation, disability benefits, or similar law; or
    b. by or for any person or organization who is or who may be held legally liable for the "bodily injury" to the "insured"; or
    c. for "bodily Injury" under the liability coverage; or
    d. amounts paid or payable under any valid and collectible motor vehicle medical payments, personal injury protection insurance, or similar motor vehicle coverages.
4. Any benefits paid or payable under the no-fault coverages, or which would be payable except for a deductible, will not be paid again as damages under this coverage.
5. Regardless of the number of "motor vehicles" involved, the number of persons covered, or claims made, vehicles or premiums shown in the policy or premiums paid, the limit of liability for uninsured motorists or underinsured motorists coverage may not be

added to or stacked upon limits for such coverage applying to other "motor vehicles" to determine the amount of coverage available to an "insured" in any one accident.

6. Any payment made to a person under this coverage shall reduce any amount payable to that person under the bodily injury liability coverage of this policy.

7. Any payment made to a person under this coverage shall reduce any amount payable to that person under the Underinsured Motorist Coverage of this policy.

BLISS LAW GOVERNS

The rights and obligations of the company with respect to Uninsured Motorist Coverage shall be governed by the laws of the State of Bliss without regard to its principles of conflict of laws.

DECIDING FAULT AND AMOUNT

Two questions must be decided by agreement between the "insured" and us:

1. Does the owner or driver of the "uninsured motor vehicle" legally owe the "insured" damages; and

2. If so, in what amount?

If there is no agreement, the "insured" and we may agree that issues of liability and damages be determined by binding arbitration. Each party shall select a competent and impartial arbitrator. These two shall select a third one. If unable to agree on the third one within 30 days either party may request a judge of a court of record in the county in which the arbitration is pending to select a third one. The written decision of any two arbitrators shall be binding on each party.

The cost of the arbitrator and any expert witness shall be paid by the party who hired them. The cost of the third arbitrator and other expenses of arbitration shall be shared equally by both parties. The arbitration shall take place in the county in which the "named insured" resides unless the parties agree to another place. State court rules governing procedure and admission of evidence shall be used.

We are not bound by any judgment against any person or organization obtained without our WRITTEN CONSENT.

PAYMENT OF ANY AMOUNT DUE

We will pay any amount due under this part:

1. to the "insured";
2. to a parent or guardian if the "insured" is a minor or an incompetent person;
3. to the surviving spouse; or
4. at our option, to a person authorized by law to receive such payment.

IF THERE IS OTHER COVERAGE

1. If the "insured" is injured as a pedestrian or while "occupying" "your covered auto" and "your covered auto" is described on the Declarations page of another policy, providing uninsured motorists coverage, we are liable only for our share. Our share is that percent of the damages that the limit of liability of this policy bears to the total of all uninsured motorists coverage that applies to the accident.

2. If the "insured" is injured while "occupying" a vehicle that is not "your covered auto" or a "newly acquired auto," this coverage applies as excess to any other uninsured motorists coverage.

Exhibit 3-2   **487**

3. If the "insured" is injured as a pedestrian or while "occupying" "your covered auto" and other underinsured motorists coverage applies:
   a. the total limit of liability shall not exceed the highest limit of liability of anyone policy; and
   b. we are liable only for our share. Our share is that percent of the damages that the limit of liability of this policy bears to the total of all underinsured motorists coverage that applies to the accident.

4. If more than one policy applies, the following order of priority applies:

   FIRST
   a policy covering a "motor vehicle" occupied by the injured person at the time of the accident.

   SECOND
   a policy covering a "motor vehicle" not involved in the accident under which the injured person is a "named insured."

   THIRD
   a policy covering a "motor vehicle" not involved in the accident under which the injured person is an "insured" other than a "named insured."

However, if the vehicle the "insured" is operating at the time of the accident is not owned by the "insured" and has been borrowed, rented, or leased from anyone who is engaged in the "business" of selling, repairing, servicing, storing, leasing, or parking "motor vehicles" and that vehicle is insured under a policy affording Uninsured or Underinsured Motorists coverage to that owner the following order of priority shall apply:

   FIRST
   a policy covering a "motor vehicle" not involved in the accident under which the injured person is a "named insured."

   SECOND
   a policy covering a motor vehicle not involved in the accident under which the injured person is an "insured" other than a "named insured."

   THIRD
   a policy covering a motor vehicle occupied by the injured person at the time of the accident.

   Coverage available under a lower priority policy applies only to the extent it exceeds the coverage of a higher priority policy.
   THESE COVERAGES DO NOT APPLY IF THERE IS OTHER UNINSURED MOTORISTS COVERAGE ON A "NEWLY ACQUIRED AUTO."

PART D—COVERAGE FOR DAMAGE TO YOUR AUTO

INSURING AGREEMENT

A. We will pay for direct and accidental loss to "your covered auto" or any "non-owned auto," including their equipment, minus any applicable deductible shown in the Declarations. If loss to more than one "your covered auto" or "non-owned auto" results from the same "collision," only the highest applicable deductible will apply. We will pay for loss to "your covered auto" caused by:

1. Other than "collision" only if the Declarations indicate that Other Than Collision Coverage is provided for that auto.
2. "Collision" only if the Declarations indicate that Collision Coverage is provided for that auto.

If there is a loss to a "non-owned auto," we will provide the broadest coverage applicable to any "your covered auto" shown in the Declarations.

B. "Collision" means the upset of "your covered auto" or a "non-owned auto" or their impact with another vehicle or object.
Loss caused by the following is considered other than "collision":

1. Missiles or falling objects;
2. Fire;
3. Theft or larceny;
4. Explosion or earthquake;
5. Windstorm;
6. Hail, water, or flood;
7. Malicious mischief or vandalism;
8. Riot or civil commotion;
9. Contact with bird or animal; or
10. Breakage of glass.

If breakage of glass is caused by a "collision," you may elect to have it considered a loss caused by "collision."

C. "Non-owned auto" means:

1. Any private passenger auto, pickup, van, or "trailer" not owned by or furnished or available for the regular use of you or any "family member" while in the custody of or being operated by you or any "family member"; or
2. Any auto or "trailer" you do not own while used as a temporary substitute for "your covered auto" that is out of normal use because of its:

   a. Breakdown;
   b. Repair;
   c. Servicing;
   d. Loss; or
   e. Destruction.

TRANSPORTATION EXPENSES

A. In addition, we will pay, without application of a deductible, up to a maximum of $600 for:

1. Temporary transportation expenses not exceeding $20 per day incurred by you in the event of a loss to "your covered auto." We will pay for such expenses if the loss is caused by:

   a. Other than "collision" only if the Declarations indicate that Other Than Collision Coverage is provided for that auto.
   b. "Collision" only if the Declarations indicate that Collision Coverage is provided for that auto.

Exhibit 3-2   **489**

2. Expenses for which you become legally responsible in the event of loss to a "non-owned auto." We will pay for such expenses if the loss is caused by:

    a. Other than "collision" only if the Declarations indicate that Other Than Collision Coverage is provided for any "your covered auto."

    b. "Collision" only if the Declarations indicate that Collision Coverage is provided for any "your covered auto."

However, the most we will pay for any expenses for loss of use is $20 per day.

B. If the loss is caused by:

1. A total theft of "your covered auto" or a "non-owned auto," we will pay only expenses incurred during the period:

    a. Beginning 48 hours after the theft; and

    b. Ending when "your covered auto" or the "non-owned auto" is returned to use or we pay for its loss.

2. Other than theft of a "your covered auto" or a "non-owned auto," we will pay only expenses beginning when the auto is withdrawn from use for more than 24 hours.

C. Our payment will be limited to that period of time reasonably required to repair or replace the "your covered auto" or the "non-owned auto."

CLOTHES AND LUGGAGE

In addition, we will pay, without application of a deductible, up to a maximum of $200 per occurrence for clothes and luggage owned by you or any "family member." These items have to be in or on an auto covered by this part. "Your covered auto" has to be covered under this policy for:

1. Other Than Collision Coverage and the loss caused by fire, lightning, flood, falling objects, explosion, earthquake, or theft. If the loss is due to theft, the entire auto must have been stolen; or

2. Collision Coverage and the loss caused by "collision."

$200 is the most we will pay in any one occurrence even though more than one person has a loss. This coverage is excess over any other coverage.

EXCLUSIONS

We will not pay for:

1. Loss to "your covered auto" or any "non-owned auto" that occurs while it is being used as a public or livery conveyance. This Exclusion (1.) does not apply to a share-the-expense car pool.

2. Damage due and confined to:

    a. Wear and tear;

    b. Freezing;

    c. Mechanical or electrical breakdown or failure; or

    d. Road damage to tires.

This Exclusion (2.) does not apply if the damage results from the total theft of "your covered auto" or any "non-owned auto."

3. Loss due to or as a consequence of:

    a. Radioactive contamination;

    b. Discharge of any nuclear weapon (even if accidental);

    c. War (declared or undeclared);

    d. Civil war;

    e. Insurrection; or

    f. Rebellion or revolution.

4. Loss to any electronic equipment designed for the reproduction of sound and any accessories used with such equipment. This includes but is not limited to:
   a. Radios and stereos;
   b. Tape decks; or
   c. Compact disc players.

   This Exclusion (4.) does not apply to equipment designed solely for the reproduction of sound and accessories used with such equipment, provided:
   a. The equipment is permanently installed in "your covered auto" or any "non-owned auto"; or
   b. The equipment is:
      (1) Removable from a housing unit that is permanently installed in the auto;
      (2) Designed to be solely operated by use of the power from the auto's electrical system; and
      (3) In or upon "your covered auto" or any "non-owned auto" at the time of loss.

5. Loss to any electronic equipment that receives or transmits audio, visual, or data signals and any accessories used with such equipment. This includes but is not limited to:
   a. Citizens band radios;
   b. Telephones;
   c. Two-way mobile radios;
   d. Scanning monitor receivers;
   e. Television monitor receivers;
   f. Video cassette recorders;
   g. Audio cassette recorders; or
   h. Personal computers.

This Exclusion (5.) does not apply to:
   a. Any electronic equipment that is necessary for the normal operation of the auto or the monitoring of the auto's operating systems; or
   b. A permanently installed telephone designed to be operated by use of the power from the auto's electrical system and any accessories used with the telephone.

6. Loss to tapes, records, discs, or other media used with equipment described In Exclusions 4. and 5.

7. A total loss to "your covered auto" or any "non-owned auto" due to destruction or confiscation by governmental or civil authorities.

This Exclusion (7.) does not apply to the interests of Loss Payees in "your covered auto."

8. Loss to:
   a. A "trailer," camper body, or motor home that is not shown in the Declarations; or
   b. Facilities or equipment used with such "trailer," camper body, or motor home. Facilities or equipment include but are not limited to:
      (1) Cooking, dining, plumbing, or refrigeration facilities;
      (2) Awnings or cabanas; or
      (3) Any other facilities or equipment used with a "trailer," camper body, or motor home.

This Exclusion (8.) does not apply to a:
   a. "Trailer," and its facilities or equipment that you do not own; or
   b. "Trailer," camper body, or the facilities or equipment in or attached to the "trailer" or camper body that you:
      (1) Acquire during the policy period; and
      (2) Ask us to insure within 30 days after you become the owner.

9. Loss to any "non-owned auto" when used by you or any "family member" without a reasonable belief that you or that "family member" are entitled to do so.

10. Loss to equipment designed or used for the detection or location of radar or laser.

Exhibit 3-2   **491**

11. Loss to any custom furnishings or equipment in or upon any pickup or van. Custom furnishings or equipment include but are not limited to:
    a. Special carpeting or insulation;
    b. Furniture or bars;
    c. Height-extending roofs; or
    d. Custom murals, paintings, or other decals or graphics.

This Exclusion (11.) does not apply to a cap, cover, or bed liner in or upon any "your covered auto" that is a pickup.

12. Loss to any "non-owned auto" being maintained or used by any person while employed or otherwise engaged in the "business" of:
    a. Selling;
    b. Repairing;
    c. Servicing;
    d. Storing; or
    d. Parking;

vehicles designed for use on public highways. This includes road testing and delivery.

13. Loss to "your covered auto" or any "non-owned auto," located inside a facility designed for racing, for the purpose of:
    a. Competing in; or
    b. Practicing or preparing for;

any prearranged or organized racing or speed contest.

14. Loss to, or loss of use of, a "non-owned auto" rented by:
    a. You; or
    b. Any "family member";

if a rental vehicle company is precluded from recovering such loss or loss of use, from you or that "family member," pursuant to the provisions of any applicable rental agreement or state law.

15. Loss to "your covered auto" or any "non-owned auto" due to diminution of value."

LIMIT OF LIABILITY

A. Our limit of liability for loss will be the lesser of the:
   1. Actual cash value of the stolen or damaged property; or
   2. Amount necessary to repair or replace the property with other property of like kind and quality.

However, the most we will pay for loss to:
   1. Any "non-owned auto" that is a trailer is $500.
   2. Equipment designed solely for the reproduction of sound, including any accessories used with such equipment, which is installed in locations not used by the auto manufacturer for installation of such equipment or accessories, is $1,000.

B. An adjustment for depreciation and physical condition will be made in determining actual cash value in the event of a total loss.

C. If a repair or replacement results in better than like kind or quality, we will not pay for the amount of the betterment.

PAYMENT OF LOSS

We may pay for loss in money or repair or replace the damaged or stolen property. We may, at our expense, return any stolen property to:

1. You; or
2. The address shown in this policy.

   If we return stolen property we will pay for any damage resulting from the theft. We may keep all or part of the property at an agreed or appraised value.

   If we pay for loss in money, our payment will include the applicable sales tax for the damaged or stolen property.

NO BENEFIT TO BAILEE

This insurance shall not directly or indirectly benefit any carrier or other bailee for hire.

OTHER SOURCES OF RECOVERY

If other sources of recovery also cover the loss, we will pay only our share of the loss. Our share is the proportion that our limit of liability bears to the total of all applicable limits. However, any insurance we provide with respect to a "non-owned auto" shall be excess over any other collectible source of recovery including, but not limited to:

1. Any coverage provided by the owner of the "non-owned auto";
2. Any other applicable physical damage insurance;
3. Any other source of recovery applicable to the loss.

APPRAISAL

A. If we and you do not agree on the amount of loss, either may demand an appraisal of the loss. In this event, each party will select a competent appraiser. The two appraisers will select an umpire. The appraisers will state separately the actual cash value and the amount of loss. If they fail to agree, they will submit their differences to the umpire. A decision agreed to by any two will be binding. Each party will:

   1. Pay its chosen appraiser; and
   2. Bear the expenses of the appraisal and umpire equally.

B. We do not waive any of our rights under this policy by agreeing to an appraisal.

PART E—DUTIES AFTER AN ACCIDENT OR LOSS

We have no duty to provide coverage under this policy unless there has been full compliance with the following duties:

A. We must be notified promptly of how, when, and where the accident or loss happened. Notice should also include the names and addresses of any injured persons and of any witnesses.

B. A person seeking any coverage must:
   1. Cooperate with us in the investigation, settlement, or defense of any claim or suit.
   2. Promptly send us copies of any notices or legal papers received in connection with the accident or loss.
   3. Submit, as often as we reasonably require:
      a. To physical exams by physicians we select. We will pay for these exams.
      b. To examination under oath and subscribe the same.
   4. Authorize us to obtain:
      a. Medical reports; and
      b. Other pertinent records.
   5. Submit a proof of loss when required by us.

C. A person seeking Uninsured Motorists Coverage must also:
   1. Promptly notify the police if a hit-and-run driver is involved;
   2. Promptly send us copies of the legal papers if a suit is brought.

D. A person seeking Coverage for Damage to Your Auto must also:
   1. Take reasonable steps after loss to protect "your covered auto" or any "non-owned auto" and their equipment from further loss. We will pay reasonable expenses incurred to do this.
   2. Promptly notify the police if "your covered auto" or any "non-owned auto" is stolen.
   3. Permit us to inspect and appraise the damaged property before its repair or disposal.

Exhibit 3-2   **493**

PART F—GENERAL PROVISIONS

BANKRUPTCY

Bankruptcy or insolvency of the "insured" shall not relieve us of any obligations under this policy.

CHANGES

A. This policy contains all the agreements between you and us. Its terms may not be changed or waived except by endorsement issued by us.
B. If there is a change to the information used to develop the policy premium, we may adjust your premium. Changes during the policy term that may result in a premium increase or decrease include, but are not limited to, changes in:
   1. The number, type, or use classification of insured vehicles;
   2. Operators using insured vehicles;
   3. The place of principal garaging of insured vehicles;
   4. Coverage, deductible, or limits.
   If a change resulting from A. or B. requires a premium adjustment, we will make the premium adjustment in accordance with our manual rules.
C. If we make a change that broadens coverage under this edition of your policy without additional premium charge, that change will automatically apply to your policy as of the date we implement the change in your state. This Paragraph (C.) does not apply to changes implemented with a general program revision that includes both broadenings and restrictions in coverage, whether that general program revision is implemented through introduction of:
   1. A subsequent edition of your policy; or
   2. An Amendatory Endorsement.

FRAUD

We do not provide coverage for any "insured" who has made fraudulent statements or engaged in fraudulent conduct in connection with any accident or loss for which coverage is sought under this policy.

LEGAL ACTION AGAINST US

A. No legal action may be brought against us until there has been full compliance with all the terms of this policy. In addition, under Part A, no legal action maybe brought against us until:
   1. We agree in writing that the "insured" has an obligation to pay; or
   2. The amount of that obligation has been finally determined by judgment after trial.
B. No person or organization has any right under this policy to bring us into any action to determine the liability of "insured."

OUR RIGHT TO RECOVER PAYMENT

A. If we make a payment under this policy and the person to or for whom payment was made has right to recover damages from another we shall be subrogated to that right. That person shall do:
   1. Whatever is necessary to enable us to exercise our rights; and
   2. Nothing after loss to prejudice them.
However, our rights in this Paragraph (A.) do not apply under Part D against any person using "your covered auto" with a reasonable belief that that person is entitled to do so.
B. If we make a payment under this policy and the person to or for whom payment is made recovers damages from another, that person shall:
   1. Hold in trust for us the proceeds of the recovery; and
   2. Reimburse us to the extent of our payment.

POLICY PERIOD AND TERRITORY

A. This policy applies only to accidents and losses that occur:
   1. During the policy period as shown in the Declarations; and
   2. Within the policy territory.
B. The policy territory is:
   1. The United States of America, its territories, or possessions;
   2. Puerto Rico; or
   3. Canada.

This policy also applies to loss to, or accidents involving, "your covered auto" while being transported between their ports.

TERMINATION

A. Cancellation

This policy may be cancelled during the policy period as follows:

1. The named insured shown in the Declarations may cancel by:
   a. Returning this policy to us; or
   b. Giving us advance written notice of the date cancellation is to take effect.

2. We may cancel by mailing to the named insured shown in the Declarations at the address shown in this policy:
   a. At least 10 days notice:
      1. If cancellation is for nonpayment of premium; or
      2. If notice is mailed during the first 60 days this policy is in effect and this is not a renewal or continuation policy; or
   b. At least 20 days notice in all other cases.
3. After this policy is in effect for 60 days, or if this is a renewal or continuation policy, we will cancel only:
   a. For nonpayment of premium; or
   b. If your driver's license or that of:
      1. Any driver who lives with you; or
      2. Any driver who customarily uses "your covered auto"; has been suspended or revoked. This must have occurred:
         (1) During the policy period; or
         (2) Since the last anniversary of the original effective date if the policy period is other than 1 year; or
   c. If the policy was obtained through material misrepresentation.

B. Nonrenewal

If we decide not to renew or continue this policy, we will mail notice to the named insured shown in the Declarations at the address shown in this policy. Notice will be mailed at least 20 days before the end of the policy period. Subject to this notice requirement, if the policy period is:

1. Less than 6 months, we will have the right not to renew or continue this policy every 6 months, beginning 6 months after its original effective date.
2. 6 months or longer, but less than one year, we will have the right not to renew or continue this policy at the end of the policy period.
3. 1 year or longer, we will have the right not to renew or continue this policy at each anniversary of its original effective date.

C. Automatic Termination

If we offer to renew or continue and you or your representative do not accept, this policy will automatically terminate at the end of the current policy period. Failure to pay the required renewal or continuation premium when due shall mean that you have not accepted our offer.

Exhibit 3-2   **495**

If you obtain other insurance on "your covered auto," any similar insurance provided by this policy will terminate as to that auto on the effective date of the other insurance.

D. Other Termination Provisions

1. We may deliver any notice instead of mailing it. Proof of mailing of any notice shall be sufficient proof of notice.
2. If this policy is cancelled, you may be entitled to a premium refund. If so, we will send you the refund. The premium refund, if any, will be computed according to our manuals. However, making or offering to make the refund is not a condition of cancellation.
3. The effective date of cancellation stated in the notice shall become the end of the policy period.

TRANSFER OF YOUR INTEREST IN THIS POLICY

A. Your rights and duties under this policy may not be assigned without our written consent. However, if a named insured shown in the Declarations dies, coverage will be provided for:

1. The surviving spouse if resident in the same household at the time of death. Coverage applies to the spouse as if a named insured shown in the Declarations; and
2. The legal representative of the deceased person as if a named insured shown in the Declarations. This applies only with respect to the representative's legal responsibility to maintain or use "your covered auto."

B. Coverage will only be provided until the end of the policy period.

TWO OR MORE AUTO POLICIES

If this policy and any other auto insurance policy issued to you by us apply to the same accident, the maximum limit of our liability under all the policies shall not exceed the highest applicable limit of liability under anyone policy.

MEMBERSHIP

1. Membership
The first insured named in the Declarations, by accepting this policy, becomes a member of this Company with all the rights and privileges of a member as provided in the Articles of Incorporation and the Bylaws of the Company in force at the time this policy takes effect or that may become in force during the continuation of this policy, and is entitled to vote at all meetings of members. Upon cancellation or other termination of the policy, such insured shall cease to be a member of this Company and his or her rights and interests in the Company shall terminate. This policy is on the mutual or participating plan and such insured, during the continuation of the policy, shall be entitled to participate in such savings and earnings of the Company as the Board of Directors may determine to distribute to policyholders of his or her class or division.

2. Non-Assessable
The policy is non-assessable.

IN WITNESS WHEREOF, THE AUTOKING MUTUAL INSURANCE COMPANY has caused this policy to be signed by its President and its Secretary.

Jon Benson
President

Sally Wright
Secretary

THIS ENDORSEMENT CHANGES THE POLICY. PLEASE READ IT CAREFULLY.
UNDERINSURED MOTORISTS COVERAGE—STATE OF BLISS
With respect to the coverage provided by this endorsement, the provisions of the policy apply unless modified by the endorsement.

INSURING AGREEMENT

We will pay damages for "bodily injury":

1. caused by accident; and
2. arising out of the maintenance or use of an "underinsured motor vehicle."

These must be damages an "insured":

1. has not been compensated for; and
2. is legally entitled to recover from the owner or driver of an "underinsured motor vehicle."

Who Is an Insured?

"Insured" means the person or persons covered by underinsured motorists coverage.
This is:

1. any person named in the Declarations;
2. his or her spouse if living with that person;
3. any "family member"; and
4. any other person while "occupying":
   a. "your covered auto." Its use has to be within the scope of your consent.
   b. an auto not owned by you or any person living in your household. It has to be driven by one of the persons in 1., 2. or 3. above. Its use has to be within the scope of the owner's consent.

Such other person "occupying" an auto used to carry persons for a charge other than on a share expense basis is not an "insured."

5. any person entitled to recover damages because of "bodily injury" to an "insured" under 1. through 4. above.

Other Additional Definitions

"Motor Vehicle" means a vehicle, excluding motor vehicles weighing more than twenty thousand pounds, having two or more load-bearing wheels, of a kind required to be registered under the laws of the State of Bliss relating to motor vehicles, designed primarily for operation upon the public streets, roads, and highways, and driven by power other than muscular power, and includes a trailer drawn by or attached to such a vehicle.

"Underinsured Motor Vehicle" means a "motor vehicle" for which there is bodily injury liability insurance policy, or bond providing equivalent liability protection, in effect at the time of the accident, but the applicable limit of bodily injury liability of such policy or bond:
   a. is less than the applicable limit for underinsured motorists coverage under this policy; or
   b. has been reduced by payments to other persons who sustained "bodily injury" in the accident to an amount less than the limit for underinsured motorists coverage under this policy.

The term "underinsured motor vehicle" does not mean a "motor vehicle":
   a. insured under the liability coverage of this policy.
   b. owned by any governmental unit, political subdivision, or agency thereof.
   c. located for use as a residence or premises.
   d. with respect to uninsured motorists coverage, a self-insured motor vehicle within the meaning of the financial or safety responsibility law of the state in which the motor vehicle is registered, or any similar state or federal law.

Exhibit 3-2   **497**

e. operated by any person who is specifically excluded from coverage in the policy.

The term "underinsured motor vehicle" may not be construed to include an "uninsured motor vehicle."

When Underinsured Motorists Coverage Does Not Apply

THERE IS NO COVERAGE UNDER UNDERINSURED MOTORISTS COVERAGE:

1. For the recovery of punitive, exemplary, or other noncompensatory damages.
2. FOR ANY "INSURED" WHO, WITHOUT OUR WRITTEN CONSENT, SETTLES WITH ANY PERSON OR ORGANIZATION WHO MAY BE LIABLE FOR THE "BODILY INJURY."
3. TO THE EXTENT IT BENEFITS:
    a. ANY WORKERS' COMPENSATION OR DISABILITY BENEFITS INSURANCE COMPANY.
    b. A SELF-INSURER UNDER ANY WORKERS' COMPENSATION, OR DISABILITY BENEFITS OR SIMILAR LAW.
    c. ANY GOVERNMENTAL BODY OR AGENCY.
4. If the "insured" has failed to report the accident to the proper law enforcement authorities as soon as practicable.
5. For any "insured" who is injured while operating or occupying a "motor vehicle" without the specific permission of the owner of the vehicle or without reasonable belief that they are entitled to do so.
6. For damages for pain, suffering, mental anguish, inconvenience, or other noneconomic loss that could not have been recovered had the owner or operator of the "motor vehicle" responsible for such loss maintained the security required under any applicable state no-fault law.
7. With respect to which the applicable statute of limitations has expired on the "insured's" claim against the uninsured or underinsured motorist.
8. There is no coverage until the limits of liability of all bodily injury liability bonds and policies that apply have been used up by payments of judgments or settlements or such limits or the remaining part of them have been offered to the "insured" in writing.

THERE IS NO UNDERINSURED MOTORISTS COVERAGE:

FOR "BODILY INJURY" TO AN "INSURED" WHILE "OCCUPYING" A "MOTOR VEHICLE" OWNED BY YOU OR ANY PERSON LIVING IN YOUR HOUSEHOLD IF IT IS NOT INSURED FOR THIS COVERAGE UNDER THIS POLICY.

Limits of Liability

1. The amount of coverage is shown on the front of the Declarations under Each Person-Each Occurrence.

Under Each Person is the amount of coverage for all damages due to bodily injury to one person.

Under Each Occurrence is the total amount of coverage for all damages due to "bodily injury" to two or more persons in the same accident.

2. The maximum liability of the underinsured motorists coverage is the lower of:
    a. The amount of compensatory damages, established but not recovered by any agreement, settlement, or judgment with or for the person or organization legally liable for the "bodily injury" resulting therefrom; or
    b. The limits of liability of the underinsured motorists coverage.

3. Any amount payable under this coverage shall be reduced by any amount paid or payable to or for the insured:
    a. under any workers' compensation, disability benefits, or similar law; or
    b. by or for any person or organization who is or who may be held legally liable for the "bodily injury" to the "insured"; or
    c. for "bodily injury" under the liability coverage; or
    d. amounts paid or payable under any valid and collectible motor vehicle medical payments, personal injury protection insurance, or similar motor vehicle coverages.
4. Any payment made to a person under this coverage shall reduce any amount payable to that person under the bodily injury liability coverage of this policy.
5. Any benefits paid or payable under the no-fault coverages, or that would be payable except for a deductible, will not be paid again as damages under this coverage.
6. Regardless of the number of "motor vehicles" involved, the number of persons covered or claims made, vehicles or premiums shown in the policy or premiums paid, the limit of liability for uninsured motorists or underinsured motorists coverage may not be added to or stacked upon limits for such coverage applying to other "motor vehicles" to determine the amount of coverage available to an "insured" in any one accident.
7. Any payment made to a person under this coverage shall reduce any amount payable to that person under the Uninsured Motorist Coverage of this policy.

State of Bliss law Governs

The rights and obligations of the Company with respect to Underinsured Motorist Coverage shall be governed by the laws of the State of Bliss without regard to its principles of conflict of laws.

Deciding Fault and Amount

Two questions must be decided by agreement between the "insured" and us:

1. Does the owner or driver of the "underinsured motor vehicle" legally owe the "insured" damages; and
2. If so, in what amount?

If there is no agreement, the "insured" and we may agree that issues of liability and damages be determined by binding arbitration: Each party shall select a competent and impartial arbitrator. These two shall select a third one. If unable to agree on the third one within 30 days, either party may request a judge of a court of record in the county in which the arbitration is pending to select a third one. The written decision of any two arbitrators shall be binding on each party.

The cost of the arbitrator and any expert witness shall be paid by the party who hired them. The cost of the third arbitrator and other expenses of arbitration shall be shared equally by both parties. The arbitration shall take place in the county in which the "named insured" resides unless the parties agree to another place. State court rules governing procedure and admission of evidence shall be used.

We are not bound by any judgment against any person or organization obtained without our WRITTEN CONSENT.

Payment of Any Amount Due

We will pay any amount due under this part:

1. to the "insured";
2. to a parent or guardian if the "insured" is a minor or an incompetent person;
3. to the surviving spouse; or
4. at our option, to a person authorized by law to receive such payment.

Exhibit 3-2   **499**

If There Is Other Coverage

1. If the "insured" is injured as a pedestrian or while "occupying" "your covered auto" and "your covered auto" is described on the Declarations page of another policy providing uninsured motorists coverage, we are liable only for our share. Our share is that percent of the damages that the limit of liability of this policy bears to the total of all uninsured motorists coverage that applies to the accident.
2. If the "insured" is injured while "occupying" a vehicle that is not "your covered auto," this coverage applies as excess to any other uninsured or underinsured motorists coverage.
3. If the "insured" is injured as a pedestrian or while "occupying" "your covered auto" and other underinsured motorists coverage applies:
   a. the total limit of liability shall not exceed the highest limit of liability of any one policy; and
   b. we are liable only for our share. Our share is that percent of the damages that the limit of liability of this policy bears to the total of all underinsured motorists coverage that applies to the accident.
4. If more than one policy applies, the following order of priority applies:

   FIRST
   a policy covering a "motor vehicle" occupied by the injured person at the time of the accident.

   SECOND
   a policy covering a "motor vehicle" not involved in the accident under which the injured person is a "named insured."

   THIRD
   a policy covering a "motor vehicle" not involved in the accident under which the injured person is an insured other than a "named insured."

However, if the vehicle the "insured" is operating at the time of the accident is not owned by the "insured" and has been borrowed, rented, or leased from anyone who is engaged in the "business" of selling, repairing, servicing, storing, leasing, or parking "motor vehicles" and that vehicle is insured under a policy affording Uninsured or Underinsured Motorists coverage to that owner, the following order of priority shall apply:

   FIRST
   a policy covering a "motor vehicle" not involved in the accident under which the injured person is a "named insured."

   SECOND
   a policy covering a motor vehicle not involved in the accident under which the injured person is an "insured" other than a "named insured."

THIRD
a policy covering a motor
vehicle occupied by the
injured person at the time
of the accident.

Coverage available under a lower priority policy applies only to the extent it exceeds the coverage of a higher priority policy.

THESE COVERAGES DO NOT APPLY IF THERE IS OTHER UNDERINSURED MOTORISTS COVERAGE ON A "NEWLY ACQUIRED AUTO."

PERSONAL AUTO
PP BL 05 83 12 05

THIS ENDORSEMENT CHANGES THE POLICY. PLEASE READ IT CAREFULLY.
PERSONAL INJURY PROTECTION COVERAGE—STATE OF BLISS
With respect to coverage provided by this endorsement, the provisions of the policy apply unless modified by the endorsement.

SCHEDULE

Benefits	Limit of Liability
Medical Expenses	No specific dollar amount
Rehabilitation Expenses	No specific dollar amount
Work Loss	$200 per week
Survivors' Income Loss	$200 per week
Replacement Services Loss	$25 per day
Survivors' Replacement Services Loss	$25 per day
Funeral Expenses	$5,000
Maximum Limit for the Total of All Personal Injury Protection Benefits	$40,000

DEFINITIONS

The Definitions section is amended as follows:
  A. The following definitions are replaced:
    1. "Family member" means:
      a. A spouse;
      b. Any other person related to the "named insured" by blood, marriage, or adoption; or
      c. A ward or foster child; who is a resident of the "named insured's" household or who usually makes his or her home in the same household but temporarily lives elsewhere.
    2. "Occupying" means to be in or upon.
    3. "Your covered auto" means a "motor vehicle" with respect to which:
      a. Security is required under the provisions of the State of Bliss Auto Accident Reparations Act; and
      b. The bodily injury liability coverage of this policy applies and for which a specific premium is charged.
  B. The following definitions are added:
    1. "Motor vehicle" means a vehicle that:
      a. Has more than three load-bearing wheels;
      b. Is required to be registered under State of Bliss law;
      c. Is designed primarily for operation upon the public streets, roads, and highways; and
      d. Is driven by power other than muscular power.

Exhibit 3-2   **501**

This includes a trailer designed for use with such vehicle.

    2. "Pedestrian" means any person not "occupying":

        a. A "motor vehicle"; or

        b. Any other vehicle designed to be driven or drawn by power other than muscular power.

    3. "Ride-sharing arrangement" means the transportation of persons in a "motor vehicle" if the transportation:

        a. Is incidental to another purpose of the driver or owner; and

        b. Is not provided for a fee. This includes such arrangements known as carpools and vanpools as defined under State of Bliss law.

    4. "Survivor" means a dependent survivor of a deceased "insured" and includes only:

        a. The surviving spouse if residing in the deceased's household at the time of death. Such spouse's dependency shall end upon remarriage.

        b. Other persons receiving support from the deceased at the time of death that would qualify them as dependents of the deceased for federal income tax purposes under the Federal Internal Revenue Code.

C. As used in this endorsement:

    1. "Insured" means:

        a. The "named insured" or any "family member" who sustains "bodily injury" while:

            (1) "Occupying" any "motor vehicle"; or

            (2) A "pedestrian," struck by any "motor vehicle" or motorcycle.

        b. Any other person who sustains "bodily injury" while:

            (1) "Occupying" or while a "pedestrian" struck by "your covered auto"; or

            (2) "Occupying" a "motor vehicle" not owned by the "named insured" or any "family member," if the "bodily injury" results from the operation of such "motor vehicle" by that "named insured" or "family member."

    2. "Named insured" means the person named in the Declarations.

II. PERSONAL INJURY PROTECTION COVERAGE INSURING AGREEMENT

A. We will pay, in accordance with the State of Bliss Auto Accident Reparations Act, personal injury protection benefits to or for an "insured" who sustains "bodily injury." The "bodily injury" must:

    1. Be caused by an accident; and

    2. Arise out of the operation, maintenance, or use of a "motor vehicle" as a vehicle.

B. Subject to the limits shown in the Schedule or Declarations, these benefits consist of the following:

    1. Medical expenses. Usual and customary charges incurred for reasonable and necessary:

        a. Medical, surgical, diagnostic, x-ray, dental, prosthetic, ambulance, hospital, or professional nursing services; or

        b. Services for remedial treatment and care.

Usual and Customary charges do not include:

        a. The portion of the charge for a room in any:

            (1) Hospital, clinic, convalescent, or nursing home; or

            (2) Extended care facility or any other similar facility;

in excess of the reasonable and customary charge for semiprivate accommodations unless intensive care is medically needed.

        b. Charges for drugs sold without a prescription;

        c. Charges for experimental treatments, or

        d. Charges for medically unproven treatments.

    2. Rehabilitation expenses. The cost of a procedure or treatment for rehabilitation or a course of rehabilitative occupational training if:

        a. The procedure, treatment, or training is:

            (1) Reasonable and appropriate for the particular case;

            (2) Likely to contribute substantially to medical or occupational rehabilitation; and

        b. The cost is reasonable in relation to its probable rehabilitative effects.

3. Work loss. 85% of loss of income from work an "insured," who would normally be employed in gainful activity during the disability period, would have performed had such "insured" not been injured. Work loss shall be reduced by income:
   a. From substitute work actually performed by the "insured"; or
   b. The "insured" would have earned from available, appropriate substitute work that such "insured" was capable of performing but unreasonably failed to undertake.

4. Replacement services loss. Expenses incurred in obtaining ordinary and necessary services instead of those that an "insured" would have performed for the benefit of the "insured" or the "insured's" household had such "insured" not been injured. Replacement services loss does not include:
   a. Expenses for services the "insured" would have performed for income;
   b. Expenses for services obtained from any family member"; or
   c. Any loss after the death of the "insured."

5. Survivors' income loss. Loss sustained after an "insured's" death by the "insured's" "survivors" during their dependency. Such loss consists of the loss of contributions the "survivors" would have received for their support from such "insured," out of income from work the "insured" would normally have performed, had such "insured" not died.

6. Survivors' replacement loss. Expenses incurred after an "insured's" death by the "insured's" "survivors," in obtaining ordinary and necessary services instead of those such "insured" would have performed for the benefit of the "insured's" household. Survivors' replacement services loss does not include expenses for services:
   a. The "insured" would have performed for income; or
   b. Obtained from any "family member."

7. Funeral expenses. Reasonable expenses incurred for professional funeral, cremation, and burial.

EXCLUSIONS

A. We do not provide Personal Injury Protection Coverage for "bodily injury" sustained by any "insured":
   1. If such injury arises out of conduct within the course of a business of:
      a. Repairing;
      b. Servicing; or
      c. Otherwise maintaining;
   a "motor vehicle." This exclusion (A.1.) does not apply to such conduct that:
      a. involves the actual operation of a "motor vehicle" on the business premises; or
      b. occurs off the business premises.
   2. Arising out of conduct in the course of loading or unloading any "motor vehicle" unless such injury occurs while "occupying" such "motor vehicle."
   3. While "occupying" any "motor vehicle" without the express or implied consent of the owner or while not in lawful possession of any "motor vehicle."
   4. If such injury was intentionally caused by that "insured" or resulted from that "insured" intentionally attempting to cause "bodily injury" to himself or herself or another person. If any "insured" dies as a result of intentionally causing or attempting to cause "bodily injury" to oneself, we will not provide coverage for survivors' income loss or survivors' replacement services loss.
   5. While in the course of, or in practice or preparation for, racing or speed contest.
   6. Arising out of the operation, maintenance, or use of any "motor vehicle" while located for use as a residence or premises.
   7. If such injury arises out of the "insured's" entering or alighting from a stopped "motor vehicle" and such injury was not caused by another "motor vehicle."

Exhibit 3-2   **503**

B. We do not provide Personal Injury Protection Coverage for "bodily injury" sustained by:

1. The "named insured" while "occupying" any "motor vehicle," other than "your covered auto," which is owned by the "named insured";

2. Any "family member" while "occupying" any "motor vehicle" that is owned by that "family member" and for which the security required by the State of Bliss Auto Accident Reparations Act is not in effect.

3. The "named insured" or any "family member" while occupying," or while a "pedestrian" struck by, any motor vehicle other than:

   a. "Your covered auto"; or

   b. A "motor vehicle" being used in a "ride-sharing arrangement":

for which the security required by the State of Bliss Auto Accident Reparations Act is in effect.

4. Any "pedestrian," other than the "named insured" or any "family member," if the accident occurs outside of the State of Bliss.

C. We do not provide Personal Injury Protection Coverage for "bodily injury":

1. Due to:

   a. War (declared or undeclared);

   b. Civil war;

   c. Insurrection;

   d. Rebellion or revolution; or

   e. Any act or condition incident to any of the above.

2. Resulting from the radioactive, toxic, explosive, or other hazardous properties of nuclear material.

COORDINATION OF MEDICAL EXPENSES

We will not provide Personal Injury Protection Coverage for medical expenses exceeding $10,000, to the extent that such expenses are paid or payable under any other insurance, service, benefit, or reimbursement plan.

This provision does not apply to medical expenses that are paid or payable under:

1. Medicare benefits provided by the federal government; or

2. Other personal injury protection benefits.

LIMIT OF LIABILITY

A. The limits of liability shown in the Schedule or Declarations for Personal Injury Protection Coverage are the most we will pay to or for an "insured" as the result of any one "motor vehicle" accident, regardless of the number of:

1. "Insureds";

2. Policies or approved plans of self-insurance applicable;

3. "Your covered autos"; or

4. Claims made.

B. Any amount payable for Personal Injury Protection Coverage shall be reduced by all sums paid or payable to an "insured" for the same elements of loss under any workers' compensation law.

OTHER INSURANCE

A. If there is other applicable personal injury protection coverage, any coverage we provide under this endorsement with respect to "bodily injury" sustained by an "insured":

1. Will apply on a primary basis, if the accident arises out of the use or operation of "your covered auto."

2. Will apply on an excess basis, if:

   a. The accident involves the operation of "your covered auto" in a "ride-sharing arrangement"; and

    b. The "insured" is a "named insured" or "family member" under another policy affording personal injury protection coverage required by the State of Bliss Auto Accident Reparations Act.

   3. As defined in Section b.2. of the definition of "insured," will apply on a primary basis, if the accident arises out of the use or operation of a "motor vehicle" that is insured under a policy affording coverage to someone engaged in the business of:

    a. Selling;

    b. Repairing;

    c. Servicing;

    d. Storing;

    e. Leasing; or

    f. Parking

"motor vehicles." This provision (A.3.) applies only if the "named insured" or any "family member" is neither the person engaged in such business nor that person's employee or agent.

 B. If there is other applicable personal injury protection coverage, including approved plans of self-insurance:

   1. The maximum recovery for the total of all personal injury protection benefits under all such insurance shall not exceed the amount that would have been payable under the coverage providing the highest limit of liability.

   2. We will pay only our share. Our share is the proportion that our limit of liability bears to the total of all applicable limits of liability.

 C. No one will be entitled to duplicate payments for the same elements of loss under this or any other similar insurance, including approved plans of self-insurance.

 D. In consideration of coverage provided by this endorsement and the adjustment of applicable premiums:

   1. Any amount payable under Uninsured Motorists Coverage shall be reduced by any amount paid or payable for personal injury protection benefits under this or any other automobile insurance policy.

   2. Any Medical Payments Coverage afforded under this policy shall be excess over any personal injury protection benefits paid or payable under this or any other automobile insurance policy.

III. PART E—Duties After an Accident or Loss

Part E is amended as follows:

 A. Duty B.5. is replaced by the following:

An "insured" or someone on the "insured's" behalf must promptly give us written proof of claim, under oath if required. Such proof of claim shall include:

   1. Full details of the nature and extent of the "bodily injury";

   2. Treatment and rehabilitation received and contemplated; and

   3. Any other information that may assist us in determining the amount due and payable.

 B. Duty B.3. is replaced by the following:

An "insured" seeking Personal Injury Protection Coverage must:

   3. Submit, as often as we reasonably require:

    a. To mental or physical exams by physicians we select. We will pay for these exams.

    b. To examination under oath and subscribe the same.

 C. The following duty is added:

If an "insured," the "insured's" legal representative or the "insured's" "survivors" take legal action, against a person or organization who may be legally responsible, to recover damages for "bodily injury," that person must promptly forward to us a copy of the summons and complaint or other process served in connection with such action.

IV. PART F—General Provisions

Part F is amended as follows:

 A. The Our Right to Recover Payment provision is replaced by the following:

Exhibit 3-2   **505**

SUBROGATION

Subject to any applicable limitation set forth in the State of Bliss Auto Accident Reparations Act, if we make a payment under this coverage we shall be subrogated, to the extent of such payment, to the rights of the person to or for whom the payment was made. That person shall:

1. Execute and deliver the instruments and papers and do whatever else is necessary to secure such rights; and
2. Do nothing after loss to prejudice such rights.

REIMBURSEMENT AND TRUST

If we make a payment under coverage to any person:

1. And the person to or for whom payment is made recovers damages from any person or organization legally responsible for the "bodily injury," we shall be entitled to the proceeds of the recovery, to the extent of our payment.
2. We shall have a lien to the extent of our payment. Notice of the lien may be given to:
   a. The person or organization causing such "bodily injury";
   b. The person or organization's agent or insurer; or
   c. A court having jurisdiction.
3. That person shall:
   a. Hold in trust for us, all rights of recovery that person has against another person or organization because of the "bodily injury";
   b. Do whatever is proper to secure such rights;
   c. Do nothing after loss to prejudice them; and
   d. Execute and deliver to us, instruments and papers as may be appropriate to secure that person's and our rights and obligations.

ARBITRATION

If there is no agreement, either the "insured" or we may demand that issues of fact relating to claims for Personal Injury Protection benefits be determined by binding arbitration. If unable to agree on an arbitrator within 30 days, either party may request a judge of a court of record in the county in which the arbitration is pending to select one. The written decision of the arbitrator shall be binding on each party.

The cost of the arbitrator and any expert witness shall be shared equally by both parties. The arbitration shall take place in the county in which the named insured resides unless the parties agree to another place. State court rules governing procedure and admission of evidence shall be used.

B. Paragraph B. of the Policy Period and Territory provision is replaced by the following:

POLICY PERIOD AND TERRITORY

A. The policy territory is:

1. The United States of America, its territories, or possessions; or
2. Canada.

B. The following condition is added:

CONSTITUTIONALITY CLAUSE

The premium for and coverages of the policy have been established in reliance upon the State of Bliss Auto Accident Reparations Act. If a court of competent jurisdiction:

1. Declares; or
2. Enters a judgment that renders;

the provisions of the State of Bliss Auto Accident Reparations Act invalid or unenforceable in whole or in part, we shall have the right to:

1. Recompute the premium payable for the policy; and
2. At our option, void or amend the provisions of this endorsement.

PERSONAL AUTO
PP BL 01 88 12 09

THIS ENDORSEMENT CHANGES THE POLICY. PLEASE READ IT CAREFULLY.

AMENDMENT OF POLICY PROVISIONS—BLISS

II.PART A—Liability Coverage

Part A is amended as follows:

A. Paragraph A of the Insuring Agreement is replaced by the following:

INSURING AGREEMENT

We will pay damages for "bodily injury" or "property damage" for which any "insured" becomes legally responsible because of an auto accident. We will settle or defend, as we consider appropriate, any claim or suit asking for these damages. In addition to our limit of liability, we will pay all defense costs we incur. Our duty to settle or defend ends when our limit of liability for this coverage has been exhausted by payment of judgments or settlements. We have the right to investigate, negotiate, and settle any claim with or without your consent. We have no duty to defend any suit or settle any claim for "bodily injury" or "property damage" not covered under this policy.

PP BL 01 88 12 09   Page 1 of 1

GLOSSARY

Absolute Privilege   This privilege is a complete bar and defense to defamation even if the defendant has engaged in an actual lie or made a false statement intentionally and maliciously. Absolute privilege exists in the process of engaging in any of the three basic governmental functions—legislative, executive, or judicial.

Abuse of Process   This tort centers on the misuse of the criminal or civil judicial process for some ulterior or improper purpose or motive.

Accrues   A claim accrues when a plaintiff had reason to know of harm or injury caused by defendant's wrongful act or omission or should have reasonably known.

Act of Commission   An affirmative negligent act. See "misfeasance."

Act of Omission   A negligent failure to act. See "nonfeasance."

Actual Cause   The third element of negligence; defendant's negligent conduct must have been the cause in fact of the plaintiff's injury. If plaintiff would not have been injured but for the defendant's negligent conduct, the negligent conduct is an actual cause of plaintiff's injury.

Actual Malice   Either actual knowledge that the statement or material is false or that defendant acted with reckless disregard for the truth.

Additional Interest   The person or entity listed in Declarations has an interest in being notified of some change in the policy or cancellation of the policy.

Administrative Law   Law that is developed from rules established by various public agencies, both state and federal. Examples of federal agencies are the Federal Trade Commission, the National Labor Relations Board, and the Equal Employment Opportunity Commission (EEOC).

Adverse Possession   A method of acquiring title to real property by the actual, open, adverse, and continuous possession of it to the exclusion of the owner for the prescribed period of time prescribed by state law.

Affirmative Defense   A defense interposed in the defendant's answer that will have the legal effect of defeating a plaintiff's claim even if the facts supporting the plaintiff's claim are true.

Agent   One receiving the power and authority from the principal to accomplish actions on behalf of the principal.

Alternative Dispute Resolution (ADR)   A term that encompasses numerous means for resolving a litigant's case without involvement of the judicial process in which a judge or jury traditionally decides the case.

Alternative Liability   Plaintiff is injured by the negligent conduct of only one of two or more defendants but it is unknown which defendant actually caused the injury.

American Law Institute (ALI)   An independent organization formed in 1923 that is made up of various attorneys, judges, and law professors who have compiled various Restatements of the Law over the years in several areas of the law, including torts.

American Rule   A rule that each party pays for his or her own attorneys' fees unless a statute or contract provides otherwise.

Arbitration   A form of ADR in which the dispute is submitted to either one arbitrator or a panel of arbitrators who will actually decide the case just as a judge or a jury would do.

Assault   An intentional tort consisting of an act by the defendant intending to cause apprehension in the plaintiff.

Assumption of the Risk   The plaintiff's giving consent, expressly or impliedly, to confronting the harm or danger from a risk caused by the defendant.

Attractive Nuisance Doctrine   This doctrine imposes on a land occupier a higher duty of care with respect to conditions and activities on the land that involve a risk of harm to children who are unable to recognize the danger.

Bad Faith   A breach of the implied covenant of good faith and fair dealing on the part of the insurer to the insured.

Baseball Arbitration   A form of ADR in which each side provides the arbitrator with a final number. The arbitrator picks one or the other.

Battery   An intentional tort consisting of an act by the defendant who intends and accomplishes a harmful or offensive touching on the plaintiff.

Binder   A temporary contract for insurance.

Binding Arbitration   ADR arbitration in which the decision of the arbitrator is final and neither party may appeal except upon very limited grounds.

Bodily Injury (BI) Liability   Also referred to as BI coverage, which is coverage for claims made by others against the insured for personal injury or death.

Breach of Duty   The second element of negligence. Defendant's act or omission exposed the plaintiff to an unreasonable risk of injury or harm.

Business Invitee   One who enters upon the land occupier's premises for a purpose that is related to the business conducted on the premises.

"But for" Test   A test to determine actual cause. "But for" the defendant's negligent act or omission, plaintiff would not have been injured.

Case of First Impression   A case that arises for the first time and there is no precedent to guide the judge.

Certification   A document signed by the medical records custodian/librarian of a health care provider facility stating what medical records are being furnished and what medical records are not being furnished.

Charitable Immunity   At common law, under the doctrine of charitable immunity, tort immunity was granted for non-governmental charitable organizations. The theory is that the money on hand in these organizations came from donated funds that were to be used for the common good.

Charting by Exception   Charting developed to reduce the time required for documentation. The system utilizes a flow sheet with specific abbreviations such as check marks, asterisks, and arrows.

Chattels   Another word for personal property as opposed to real property.

Chemical Dependency or Drug and Alcohol Records   Medical records given protection pursuant to 42 CFR Part 2.

Claims-Made Policy   Typically a malpractice insurance policy insuring physicians, attorneys, and other professionals. For coverage, the claim must be made during the policy period.

Co-Pay   The amount that is paid by the insured along with the insurer—for example, 80/20 co-pay means insurer pays 80% and insured pays 20%, usually up to a certain amount after which insurer pays all up to the limits of coverage.

Collateral Source Rule   The plaintiff may recover all of plaintiff's damages and the damages do not need to be reduced by any payments plaintiff received from another source.

Collision Coverage   Covers damage to the insured's own automobile if it collides with another vehicle or object.

Colossus   Software program utilized by some insurance companies to evaluate a personal injury case.

Combined Single Limits (CSL)   Limits that include a total for all bodily injury and property damage combined.

Coming and Going Rule   A legal principle in employment law that means that an employer is not vicariously liable for the negligence of an employee who is either coming to work or going from work.

Commercial General Liability Policy (CGL)   A common third-party liability policy that businesses utilize to protect themselves from claims of third parties.

Common Law   "Judge-made" law as established from the English system of law, originating sometime in the 1150s.

Comparative Negligence   The trier of fact determines the percentage of negligence of each party and the plaintiff's recovery will then be reduced or barred—depending upon the percentage assessed against the plaintiff.

Compensation   The primary public policy purpose for tort law. A tortfeasor should be responsible for payment of reasonable money damages to the plaintiff the tortfeasor has injured.

Compensatory Damages   Those monetary/money damages that are awarded to compensate the plaintiff and make the plaintiff whole.

Complicity   A defense to a dram shop action that is the act of affirmatively assisting with an illegal sale of alcoholic beverages.

Concurrent Liability   Separate negligent acts of two or more defendants concur or combine to cause a single personal injury to the plaintiff.

Conditional Privilege   One that is not absolute, as it is in legislative, executive, and judicial privileges, but requires an element of good faith in making the statement.

Consent   A recognized defense to certain intentional torts to the person.

Constitution   A written document embodying a set of fundamental principles by which a state or federal government is governed. It constitutes a source of law.

Consumer Expectation Test   A test to determine whether a design defect exists. Plaintiff must prove the product did not perform up to the standard of safety that an ordinary consumer would have expected.

Contingency Fee   A fee paid only if there is a favorable result, whether by litigation or by settlement; typically a percentage of the amount recovered such as one-third of the recovery.

Contract of Adhesion   A contract in which one party, in superior bargaining position, sets the terms of the agreement and the other party has no negotiating power.

Contract   A legally enforceable oral or written agreement between at least two parties with mutual obligations.

Contribution   The right of one tortfeasor to recover from the other joint tortfeasor(s) when that tortfeasor has paid or may be liable to pay more than his or her proportionate share to the injured party.

Contributory Negligence   Conduct that falls below the standard to which the plaintiff must conform for the plaintiff's own safety or protection and that contributes to the causing of the plaintiff's own personal injury.

Conversion   An intentional tort consisting of a substantial invasion of another's chattel interest.

CTULA   This literally means a constant trespasser upon a limited area.

Dangerous Propensity   A trait or characteristic of a domestic animal that is abnormal to its class that presents a danger such that strict liability will be imposed.

Declarations Sheet   Typically, the first page of an insurance policy, which contains basic information concerning who is covered and what kinds of insurance and limits are included in the policy.

Declaratory Judgment Action   An action brought in a civil case asking the court to declare the rights and duties of one or more parties.

Declination Letter   A letter from the insurer to the insured advising the insured that the insurer declines to extend coverage for the claimed loss.

Deductible   The out-of-pocket amount that is required to be paid by the insured first after which the insurance company then pays under the policy.

Defamation   The publication (communication) to a third person of a false statement or material (oral or written) that causes harm to the reputation of the plaintiff with resulting damages.

Defective Condition   The defect renders the product "unreasonably dangerous" for its use or consumption.

Dependent Intervening Force   An act of a third person or an animal that is a natural, normal, or usual response to the occurrence caused by defendant's negligent conduct.

Design Defects   Those defects in which the product was manufactured properly, but its design created an undue risk of harm to the user or consumer in a normal use of the product.

Deterrence   A public policy of tort law based upon the threat of knowing that if a tort is committed, the tortfeasor may be subject to a civil lawsuit and the imposition of money damages.

Diagnosis   The condition that is causing the medical complaints.

Direct Action Statute   A statute that provides for the injured party to commence an action against the liability carrier of the insured, thus bypassing the insured completely.

Disability   "An alteration of an individual's capacity to meet personal, social, or occupational demands because of an impairment." *AMA Guides to the Evaluation of Permanent Impairment*

Discipline Privilege   A privilege granted to teachers and parents to use reasonable force for the proper discipline, control, and education of minor children.

Discovery Rule   Statute of limitation does not begin to run until the plaintiff discovers the injury and the defendant's likely connection to the injury.

Discretionary Function   A function in which the governmental employee has some discretion or choice in his or her decision.

Dispossession   Conduct in which the defendant attempts to assert dominion, control, or even ownership rights over those of the lawful owner.

Distribution of Risk   A public policy of tort law based upon the principle of which party should bear the risk of loss as between a plaintiff and a defendant.

Doctrine of Reasonable Expectations   The insurance contract will be interpreted according to the reasonable expectations of the insured, regardless of the insurance policy language.

Dog Bite Statute   Imposes strict liability on the owner for injuries caused by the dog, even though the owner knew of no previous dangerous propensities.

Domitae Naturae   Common law reference to domestic animals; literally "domesticated nature."

Dram Shop Liability   Statutory liability imposed on those business establishments (and in some cases, those "social hosts") who sell or furnish alcoholic beverages to minors and to those who have noticeably had too much to drink.

Duty to Defend   The insurer's duty to defend its insured in a third-party liability claim, which will consist of defense attorney fees and other fees and costs of the litigation.

Duty to Indemnify   Insurer has the duty to pay covered claims against the insured.

Duty   An obligation; in tort law, a legal obligation not a moral obligation. It is the first element of negligence, meaning that a person has a duty to act reasonably or to reasonably refrain from acting in such a way so as to not cause harm or injury to another person.

Economic Damages   These damages are synonymous with "special damages," which include losses such as medical expenses, lost wages, or the cost of hiring household help, all of which do have a specific itemized value and can be more easily determined or calculated on a simple mathematical basis.

Economic Loss Doctrine   A tort remedy in strict liability or negligence is not allowed when the only claim is for damage to the product itself.

"Eggshell Plaintiff" Rule   The causation principle that makes the negligent defendant liable for an unforeseeable result because of a preexisting condition of the plaintiff.

Emergency Rule   A rule of negligence law in which a person is excused from liability if the person is confronted with an emergency not of his or her own making even if the person does not choose the safest or best course of action.

Endorsement   An addition to the basic form insurance policy that makes a change in the policy.

English Rule   A rule that the loser pays the other side's attorneys' fees. It applies to both the plaintiff and the defendant.

Entrant   A person who enters or stays upon the land of another.

Exclusion   An exclusion in an insurance policy precludes coverage for certain events or certain actions or conduct engaged in by the insured.

Exculpatory Provisions   A provision placed in writing by the defendant to try to limit or exclude liability in advance.

Executive Privilege   A privilege that protects high-ranking policymaking officers of the executive branch of government, state or federal, when acting within the scope of their governmental duties.

Exemplary Damages   A type of civil damages, the purpose of which is not to compensate the plaintiff but "to make an example of" the defendant.

Express Warranty   A promise or a representation made orally or in writing concerning the product in question.

False Imprisonment   An intentional act of the defendant that results in the confinement of the plaintiff.

Family Immunity   Tort immunity given to husband-wife and parent-child relationships.

Family Purpose Doctrine   A legal doctrine rendering the owner of a motor vehicle legally responsible for damages caused by the driver's negligent operation of the vehicle if the driver is a member of the owner's immediate family or household and is driving the vehicle with the express or implied permission of the owner.

Ferae Naturae   Common law reference to wild animals; literally "wild nature.".

Firefighter's Rule   A rule expressing the defense of assumption of the risk as to first responders necessarily involved in clearly recognized risks—law enforcement, ambulance, and firefighters.

Foreseeability Test   A test of proximate cause that limits the scope of defendant's liability. Foreseeability requires that in order to impose liability on a defendant his or her negligent conduct must not have produced a remote, unusual, or bizarre result.

Frolic and Detour Rule   A legal principle in employment law that means an employer is not vicariously liable for the negligence of an employee who deviates or departs from the business of the employer to serve the employee's own personal purpose.

Functional Overlay   The plaintiff may be exaggerating complaints, making complaints because he or she is craving attention, or complaining of pain, but the doctor is finding no physical cause for the pain.

Future Damages   Those damages that are reasonably certain to occur from the date of the trial until a reasonable time into the future.

General Damages   These damages are synonymous with "non-economic damages," which include losses such as pain and suffering, disfigurement, or mental anguish, all of which have no specific, itemized value.

General Verdict   A decision by the jury briefly stating which party won or lost.

Good Samaritan Law   Statutes enacted to provide immunity from suit to those who voluntarily choose, on a moral basis, to tend to others who are ill or injured.

Governmental Function   A function performed solely by the government such as police, fire, and the court system.

Gross Negligence   Severe or extreme carelessness bordering on reckless conduct.

Harmful Touching   A touching in the tort of battery that causes, for example, pain, suffering, anguish, impairment, disfigurement, or disability to the plaintiff.

Health Insurance Portability and Accountability Act (HIPAA)   HIPAA is a federal statute that applies to health care providers and health insurance companies and provides a uniform system for patient privacy protection and patient access to medical records.

Hedonic Damages   Damages awarded for the loss of the enjoyment of life or the quality of life.

HIV/AIDS Records   Special medical records not typically released with a standard medical authorization.

Impairment   "An alteration of an individual's health status; a deviation from normal in a body part or organ system and its functioning." *AMA Guides to the Evaluation of Permanent Impairment*

Implied Warranty of Fitness for a Particular Purpose   A warranty in which the seller knows that the buyer is buying a product for a particular purpose and is relying on the seller's skill in providing the appropriate product.

Implied Warranty of Merchantability   This warranty means that the product will be fit for general or ordinary purposes.

Indemnity   An equitable remedy allowing one party to recover the entire amount from the other party.

Independent Contractor   A person who contracts with a principal to perform a task according to that person's own methods and who is not under the principal's control regarding the method and the manner of the work.

Independent Intervening Force   A force that is an unnatural, abnormal, or unusual response to the occurrence caused by the defendant's negligent conduct.

Independent Medical Examination (IME)   An examination by a physician of the defendant's choosing when a party places his or her physical or mental condition in controversy.

Indirect Causation   Some force intervenes between the defendant's negligent conduct and the occurrence of plaintiff's harm or injury; typically an act of God, an animal, or the act of a third person, not the plaintiff.

Inference   Evidence in a case that creates a conclusion that the trier of fact may or may not choose to accept.

Injunction   A form of equitable relief in which the court is asked to put a halt to the defendant's wrongful act.

Insurance Policy   A contract between two parties, the insurer and the insured.

Intentional (Fraudulent) Misrepresentation   A fraudulent misrepresentation of fact, opinion, intention, or law for the purpose of inducing another to act or to refrain from action in reliance upon it.

Intentional Infliction of Emotional Distress   An intentional tort consisting of extreme or outrageous conduct (or words) by the defendant who intends to cause severe emotional distress to the plaintiff.

Intentional Torts   A basis of tort law consisting of a tortfeasor's intentional or purposeful action intending and causing loss, damage, harm, or injury to the injured party's person or property.

Intermeddling   Intentionally interfering with the chattel in some manner but without the intent to challenge the plaintiff's ownership interest in the chattel.

Invasion of Privacy   A harmful intrusion into the private life of another person.

Invitee   One who comes onto the land with the land occupier's permission—express or implied—for a purpose related to an interest of the land occupier.

Involuntary Public Figure   One who has not sought publicity or given consent to it, but because of his or her own actions or conduct, the person has become of legitimate concern to the public.

Joint and Several Liability   In a situation in which two or more defendants are found liable for damages, the plaintiff may collect the entire award either proportionately if each is able to pay his or her proportionate share or from any one of the defendants or from any and all of the defendants in various amounts until the legal obligation is fully satisfied.

Joint Enterprise An arrangement in which each person has authority, express or implied, to act for all in the group concerning the control or means employed to execute the common purpose the group intends to carry out.

Joint Liability Two or more defendants are legally responsible for the monetary award.

Judicial Privilege This privilege provides a defense to any participant in a judicial action or proceeding. The privilege applies to any statements made from the start of the commencement of the action or proceeding until it is concluded.

Jury Instruction Guide (JIG) A compilation of jury instructions that state the applicable law in a particular jurisdiction; it may be called by other names such as a pattern jury instruction.

Justice A public policy purpose of tort law based upon a basic concept of fairness by a judge or jury.

Last Clear Chance This doctrine states that plaintiff's contributory negligence does not bar plaintiff's recovery if the defendant, immediately before the accident, had the "last clear chance" to avoid the accident but did not do so.

Legislative Privilege A privilege that operates as an absolute bar to any statement made while on the floor of the governmental body even if it has no relevancy or relationship to the issue under discussion.

Libel A defamation that is communicated in written form, such as a newspaper, a magazine, a letter, or an e-mail. It tends to be a defamation that can be read.

Licensee One who comes onto the land with the land occupier's permission—express or implied—for the primary purpose or benefit of the licensee.

Loss of Consortium A loss of the services between one spouse and another or between a parent and child.

Loss of Earning Capacity Those money damages that will result in the future from the plaintiff not being able to earn the same amount of money that he or she earned before the incident in question.

Loss of Earnings Past damages for an actual loss of income from the date of the incident caused by defendant's negligent conduct and continuing up to the date of trial.

Loss Payee The person or entity listed in an insurance policy is a lender with some secured interest in the vehicle.

Malicious Prosecution of Civil Action A tort in which the claim is that defendant wrongfully instituted a separate civil action against the plaintiff that caused damage to the plaintiff.

Malicious Prosecution of Criminal Action A tort in which the claim is that defendant wrongfully instituted a separate criminal action against the plaintiff that caused damage to the plaintiff.

Malingerer The plaintiff is grossly exaggerating symptoms or just plain pretending or "faking it."

Manufacturing Defects Those defects that do not meet the manufacturer's own manufacturing standards or guidelines.

Mediation A form of ADR that is non-binding—the mediator has no power or authority to decide the case and the mediator acts as a "facilitator" to try to help resolve the case.

Medical Coding A system of classification of medical care and treatment that converts evidence of medical treatment in medical records into universal code numbers.

Medical History Any information given by the patient to the health care provider or received by the health care provider from others (relative, ambulance attendant, law enforcement personnel) that relates to current complaints, symptoms, and an explanation of what may be causing it.

Ministerial Function A function in which the governmental employee has no discretion or choice; the employee is carrying out orders or complying with certain established duties.

Misfeasance An affirmative negligent act as opposed to a failure to act.

Misrepresentation A tort that protects a person's economic interest, not the plaintiff's personal interest.

Mitigation of Damages A plaintiff has a duty to take steps to avoid further injury; sometimes referred to as the "avoidable consequences rule."

Narrative Charting A narrative diary of each contact by the nurse or therapist with the patient.

Negligence *Per Se* An act is considered negligent (breach of duty) because of the violation of a statute.

Negligence An act or omission by the tortfeasor that is a failure to use due care under the circumstances and that causes loss, damage, or injury to the injured party.

Negligent Infliction of Emotional Distress   A type of non-economic/general damages caused by negligence.

Neutral Evaluation   Non-binding ADR procedure in which the parties agree that they will each submit their side of the case to a neutral person who will provide a written evaluation concerning the issues in the case.

No-Fault Insurance   Provides certain economic benefits such as medical bills and lost wages from one's own insurance company rather than having to sue the at-fault driver.

Nominal Damages   Those damages awarded to a plaintiff that validate a plaintiff's claim but by their small amount, establish plaintiff has suffered no significant loss.

Non-Economic Damages   These damages are synonymous with "general damages," which include losses such as pain and suffering, disfigurement, or mental anguish, all of which have no specific, itemized value.

Nonfeasance   A negligent failure to act. See "act of omission."

Objective Findings   Any objective findings verifying those subjective complaints (e.g., tests such as pulmonary function test, x-rays, lab tests, MRI).

Occurrence Policy   The automobile accident giving rise to the personal injury claim must occur during the policy period.

Offensive Touching   A touching in the tort of battery that would offend the sense of personal dignity of a reasonable person.

OTC or Comprehensive Coverage   Covers damage to the insured's own automobile in the event that it is stolen or damaged by flood, fire, wind, or hail.

Past Damages   Those damages that have been suffered or incurred from the date of the loss caused by defendant's negligent conduct to the date of the trial.

Past Medical History   Consists of information received of the patient's illnesses, injuries, and treatment in the past, which may include information about family medical conditions.

Pecuniary Loss   In a death action, the money loss of the value of the companionship, support, services, and contributions a survivor(s) would have received from the decedent had he or she lived.

Permissive Use Statute   A statute that makes the owner of a motor vehicle liable for damages caused by one to whom the owner has given permission, express or implied, to drive the motor vehicle.

Personal Injury Protection (PIP)   The first-party benefits afforded under an automobile no-fault policy.

Personal Injury   An injury to a person's body, mind, or emotions.

PIE Charting   Medical charting using problems, interventions, and evaluation.

Precedent   Also known as "*stare decisis*," it is a concept of a judge following decisions of earlier judges, which provides uniformity and stability to the law.

Preponderance of Evidence   The greater weight of the evidence so that proof of a fact is "more likely than not" true.

Prescription   A way of acquiring an easement by the adverse, open, obvious, and continuous use of another's property for a prescribed period of time after which it ripens into a permanent right to use the property.

Presumption   An evidentiary principle providing that once plaintiff offers some evidence or proof of a fact, the burden of proof shifts to the defendant.

***Prima Facie* Case**   This term is derived from Latin and one meaning is "at first sight." Because a tort is defined by certain elements, it means that the plaintiff has the burden of proof of establishing facts as to each element.

Principal   In agency law the party for whom another person acts and from whom that person obtains authority to act.

Prior   A preexisting injury to the same part of the body as plaintiff is claiming in the present lawsuit.

Private Nuisance   An interference with the plaintiff's interest in the use or enjoyment of plaintiff's property and the interference is not one of trespass.

Privity of Contract   Legal rights and obligations are created by parties to a contract; a defense in products liability cases.

Problem-Oriented Charting (SOAP)   Medical charting using four criteria: subjective, objective, assessment, plan.

Prognosis   The outlook for a patient's future.

Proprietary Function   A function that the government entity may perform but that could also be performed just as well by private entities. Examples are the providing of utilities such as water, electricity, gas, and ambulance services.

Proximate Cause   The primary cause of an injury; the natural, direct, and uninterrupted consequence of negligent conduct without which the injury would not have occurred.

Psychosomatic   The plaintiff may be exaggerating complaints, making complaints because he or she is craving attention, or complaining of pain, but the doctor is finding no physical cause for the pain.

Psychotherapy Notes   Narrowly defined under HIPAA as detailed notes made by a mental health professional documenting conversations during a counseling session, private or group.

Publication   The communication of any defamatory statement or material of any kind, written or oral, to some third person other than to the plaintiff.

Public Duty Doctrine   For a public officer to be liable, a separate duty must be owed to an individual and not a duty owed to the public as a whole.

Public Invitee   A person coming onto the land who is invited as a member of the public for a purpose that is open to the public.

Public Nuisance   An act by the defendant that causes inconvenience or damage to the public.

Punitive Damages   A type of civil damages, the purpose of which is not to compensate the plaintiff but "to punish" the defendant.

Reasonable Person Standard   The test for determining duty in a negligence action. To avoid civil tort liability, a person must act as a reasonable person of ordinary prudence would act under the same or similar circumstances. It is an objective test.

Reasonably Foreseeable Injury   A plaintiff who is owed a duty of care that is owed to anyone whose personal injury was caused by a negligent tortfeasor (Justice Andrews view in *Palsgraf*).

Reasonably Foreseeable Plaintiff   A plaintiff who is owed a duty of care because the plaintiff is in the foreseeable "zone of danger" (Justice Cardozo view in *Palsgraf*).

Reception Statutes   Statutes utilized by British colonies in America after independence was achieved from England that gave full legal effect to the existing body of English common law.

Recreational Use Statute   Statutes that protect and provide immunity to owners of land from personal injury suits commenced by a person who was using the land for "recreational purposes."

Reformation Action   An action brought to reform an insurance contract to make it conform with applicable state statutes.

Republication   Occurs when the plaintiff is forced or compelled to repeat the defamatory statement.

Reservation of Rights Letter   The insurer's written notice in a letter to the insured that the insurer intends to provide a defense to the insured, but it is retaining the right to withdraw from the defense at any time if it believes there is no coverage.

Respondeat Superior   The Latin phrase means literally, "Let the master answer." The employer is liable or responsible for a tort that is committed by the employee while the employee is acting within the scope of the employment relationship.

Res Ipsa Loquitur   Literally, "the thing speaks for itself." A legal doctrine aiding the plaintiff's proof. It applies in those instances in which defendant is in a better position than plaintiff to prove what occurred. The evidentiary burden is placed on defendant if certain requirements are met.

Restatements of the Law   A source of secondary law in the nature of a treatise prepared by ALI, which provides analysis of law in several areas, including torts.

Risk/Utility Test   A test to determine whether a design defect exists that considers whether the product's risks outweigh its benefits or utility. Plaintiff must prove the defendant could have removed the danger caused by the defect without otherwise seriously affecting its utility and price.

Section 1983 Action   Refers to an action brought under 42 U.S.C. 1983 imposing liability for damages if one acts under "color of state law" to deprive another of a federal constitutional right.

Self-Defense   A privileged defense in which the defendant may use means of self-defense that are reasonably necessary to prevent or defend against the plaintiff's threatened harm to the defendant.

Self-Insured Retention (SIR)   The insured assumes the obligation to indemnify and defend itself for liability claims up to a certain limit.

Several Liability   A defendant is liable only for his or her separate, proportionate part of a monetary award.

Shopkeepers' Privilege   A limited privilege belonging to business owners who are allowed to temporarily stop and detain people whom they reasonably suspect of shoplifting.

Slander   A defamation that is communicated orally/verbally. It tends to be a defamation that can be heard.

Sovereign Immunity   Beginning with the old English common law, government entities could not be sued for any torts that were committed by the King and his official court. "The King can do no wrong." Official government individuals were completely immune from any tort liability.

Special Damages   These damages are synonymous with "economic damages," which include losses such as medical expenses, lost wages, or the cost of hiring household help, all of which do have a specific itemized value and can be more easily determined or calculated on a simple mathematical basis.

Special Verdict   A written form verdict in which several specific questions formulated by the court are answered by the jury, which will determine the outcome of the case.

Split Liability Limits   Limits of BI per person, per accident, and property damage, such as $50,000/100,000/25,000: $50,000 per person; $100,000 per accident; $25,000 property damage.

Spoliation of Evidence   The act of destroying or hiding evidence adverse to the party.

Stacking   An insured is allowed to recover insurance proceeds from more than one automobile insurance policy.

Standards of Conduct   A public policy purpose of tort law in which a person is expected to meet certain minimum standards of conduct.

Stare Decisis   Also known as precedent; a concept of judges respecting previous judicial decisions.

State of the Art/Alternative Reasonable Design Test   This test means that a product is defective if the risk of harm could have been reduced by a reasonably different design that is state of the art.

Statute of Limitation   In civil law and procedure, a statute that prescribes the maximum period of time in which a civil lawsuit must be commenced or it is forever barred.

Statute of Repose   A statute that determines the maximum period of time that an action may be brought, regardless of when the claim may have accrued.

Statutory Law   A source of law that is based upon a statute enacted by a legislative body, whether state or federal.

Strict Liability   Liability imposed upon a defendant based upon defendant's ownership or possession of animals, wild or domestic, or by engaging in abnormally dangerous activities; liability without fault.

Subjective Complaints   The patient's own complaints to a health care provider (e.g., complaints of pain, restricted motion, difficulty lifting, and problems at work).

Subrogation   A legal principle meaning that if one party, typically an insurer, has paid money and benefits to a plaintiff, that party may recover the amount paid from the negligent defendant.

"Substantial Factor" Rule   A test of causation involving multiple tortfeasors; a tortfeasor is liable to the plaintiff if the tortfeasor's negligent act or omission was a "substantial factor" in producing the injury.

Summary Jury Trial   A non-binding ADR technique in which a select number of people are assembled to hear a mock trial and a jury will render a mock verdict.

Survival Statute   Allows the decedent's claim to survive and damages can be awarded to the decedent's estate for those damages the decedent could have pursued.

Tolled (Statute of Limitation)   The time period for a statute of limitation is suspended until a certain circumstance or condition occurs or while a certain circumstance or condition is occurring.

Tolling Agreement   An agreement between the parties that alter the statute of limitation for an agreed upon period of time so that it does not continue to run for that period of time.

Tortfeasor   The person responsible for committing the tort.

Tort Reform   A movement to change the American tort system with a view toward curbing the number of civil lawsuits and reducing certain tort damages.

Tort   A wrongful act other than a breach of contract that injures another and for which the law imposes civil liability.

Transferred Intent   An intentional tort doctrine meaning that if the defendant does an act intending to cause harm to a person, the defendant will be liable if the harm occurs to some other unintended and unexpected person.

Treble Damages   A form of damages in the nature of punitive/exemplary damages imposed by statute; purpose is to punish or make an example of a wrongdoer who commits an intentional, willful, or reckless act.

Trespasser   A person who comes upon the land without the permission of the land occupier.

Trespass to Chattels An intentional tort consisting of an intrusion upon the chattels (personal property) of another without consent or privilege to do so. The intrusion may be a dispossession or an intermeddling.

Trespass to Land An intentional tort consisting of an intrusion upon the land of another without consent or privilege to do so.

Trier of Fact The person who decides all of the contested issues in a case, including a personal injury case. The trier of fact may be a jury, a judge, or an arbitrator.

Tripartite Relationship The triangular relationship made up of the insurer, the insured, and the defense counsel who is retained to represent the insured, but who is paid by the insurer.

UIM Add-On UIM benefits are added to the amount of the BI liability insurance proceeds received from the underinsured at-fault driver.

UIM Difference in Limits The insured has UIM coverage available only if the amount of the insured's UIM coverage limits exceed the at-fault driver's third-party liability policy limits.

Umbrella Policy Third-party liability coverage that is over and above the regular liability insurance in force; usually issued in increments of $1 million.

Unavoidable Accident An occurrence or happening without any fault or negligence on a person; typically a cause is an "act of God."

Underinsured Motorist (UIM) Coverage First-party coverage for the insured in the situation in which the other negligent driver actually has liability insurance, but it is not adequate to cover the injured person's loss.

Uninsured Motorist (UM) Coverage First-party coverage for the insured in the situation in which the at-fault driver is uninsured.

Vicarious Liability A fundamental rule of agency law that means that the principal is liable for the actions of the agent who was acting on the principal's behalf.

Voluntary Public Figure One who is, through his or her status, position, occupation, or profession naturally in the public eye.

Workers' Compensation A type of insurance or special fund that provides an employee with certain wage loss benefits, medical benefits, and other statutory benefits for an injury (or death) that arises out of and in the course of employment.

Wrongful Death Statute Creates a new cause of action for the surviving next of kin in which they may recover their pecuniary loss from the death of the decedent.

Zone of Danger A test formulated by Justice Cardozo in the *Palsgraf* case that states a defendant owes a duty only to a plaintiff who is in an area the defendant might expect that a plaintiff would be injured.

INDEX